SUCCESSFUL PUBLIC POLICY

LESSONS FROM AUSTRALIA AND NEW ZEALAND

SUCCESSFUL PUBLIC POLICY

LESSONS FROM AUSTRALIA AND NEW ZEALAND

Edited by Joannah Luetjens, Michael Mintrom and Paul 't Hart

PRESS

Published by ANU Press
The Australian National University
Acton ACT 2601, Australia
Email: anupress@anu.edu.au

Available to download for free at press.anu.edu.au

ISBN (print): 9781760462789
ISBN (online): 9781760462796

WorldCat (print): 1099185215
WorldCat (online): 1099185362

DOI: 10.22459/SPP.2019

Cover design and layout by ANU Press

Contents

Part II: Policy successes in New Zealand

Acknowledgements

This book swims against the currents of scepticism, negativism and disillusionment with politics and government that beset many nations today. It looks purposefully at the 'bright side' of public policy in Australia and New Zealand, and provides detailed case studies of instances in which governments by and large got it right and made positive differences to the lives and wellbeing of countless citizens, to the strength of their economies and, sometimes, to their country's standing in the world.

In selecting the public policies to study as success cases, we sought advice from two panels—one in Australia and one in New Zealand. These panels comprised senior academics with deep knowledge of public policy and practitioners with many years of experience in and around government at the highest levels. We wish to thank Guy Beatson, Jonathan Boston, Jennifer Curtin, John Daley, Michael Di Francesco, Grant Duncan, Meredith Edwards, Derek Gill, Arthur Grimes, Brian Head, Ken Henry, Girol Karacaoglu, Terry Moran, Mark Prebble, Graham Scott, Peter Shergold, Gary Sturgess, Anne Tiernan and Sally Washington for generously sharing their thoughts. As well as providing initial nominations of success cases, many also offered further comments on our shortlists of cases and helped in the identification of potential chapter authors.

We could not have produced this book without the expertise, hard work and enthusiasm of our contributing authors. When we invited them to participate, many confessed to feeling a sense of joy to be given the opportunity to grapple with a story of positive accomplishment. We thank them for their exemplary work.

This book is one product of the Successful Public Governance (SPG) research program at Utrecht University. The program has been made possible by the European Research Council (ERC) under the European Union's Horizon 2020 research and innovation program (Grant Agreement

No. 694266). The ERC's support is gratefully acknowledged. In addition to the present study, readers interested in case studies of policy successes are advised to consult this project's 'twin'—also available in open-access form online—containing 15 similar case studies of policy success from around the world (Mallory Compton and Paul 't Hart, eds, *Great Policy Successes*, Oxford University Press, 2019). Other activities and outputs from this program can be found at www.successfulpublicgovernance.com. Joannah Luetjens and Paul 't Hart would like to thank their SPG team colleagues for their support and feedback throughout the making of this book.

Professor Ken Smith, Dean and Chief Executive Officer of the Australia and New Zealand School of Government (ANZSOG), has been a staunch supporter of this book project. We gratefully acknowledge ANZSOG's financial and logistical assistance for the authors' workshop held in Melbourne in June 2018. As the premier provider of public sector executive education in Australia and New Zealand, ANZSOG will be a key ally in ensuring that the case studies in this book play their part as intended. For one, several of the case studies will be abridged and adapted into very concise teaching tools and will be published in ANZSOG's John L. Alford's case library (www.anzsog.edu.au/resource-library/case-library/the-case-program)—aptly named in acknowledgement of our former colleague Professor John Alford, whose leadership on case teaching has inspired us.

Special thanks go to Madeline Thomas, Research and Administrative Officer at ANZSOG, who cheerfully and effectively contributed at every stage to the logistics and editing activities associated with the project. We also wish to thank John Wanna and Sam Vincent, who provided extensive support in getting the book from manuscript to publication with ANU Press. Any omissions or errors of course remain entirely our responsibility.

Utrecht/Melbourne
November 2018

Contributors

Philip Alpers, Adjunct Associate Professor, University of Sydney

Stephen Bell, Professor of Political Economy, University of Queensland

Emma Blomkamp, Honorary Research Fellow, University of Melbourne

Amohia Boulton, Research Centre Director, Whakauae Research Services

Anne-marie Boxall, Adjunct Associate Professor, University of Sydney

David Capie, Associate Professor of International Relations, Victoria University of Wellington

Jacqueline Cumming, Professor of Health Policy and Management, Victoria University of Wellington

Grant Duncan, Associate Professor, School of People, Environment and Planning, Massey University

Meredith Edwards, Emeritus Professor, University of Canberra

Sandy Farquhar, Senior lecturer, University of Auckland

Alan Fenna, Professor of Politics, Curtin University

Lisa Fitzgerald, Senior lecturer, University of Queensland

Becky Freeman, Senior lecturer, University of Sydney

Zareh Ghazarian, Senior lecturer, Monash University

Andrew Gibbons, Associate Professor at the School of Education, Auckland University of Technology

Derek Gill, Research Associate at the Institute for Governance and Policy Studies, Victoria University of Wellington, and Principal Economist, New Zealand Institute of Economic Research

R. Quentin Grafton, Professor of Economics, The Australian National University

Ross Guest, Professor of Economics, Griffith University

Janine Hayward, Professor of Political Science, University of Otago

Lisa Herron, Postgraduate student, University of Queensland

Timothy Higgins, Associate Professor in Actuarial Studies, The Australian National University

Andrew Hindmoor, Professor of Politics, University of Sheffield

James Horne, Visiting Fellow, The Australian National University

Jenny M. Lewis, Professor of Public Policy, University of Melbourne

Joannah Luetjens, Doctoral candidate, Utrecht University

Kirsten MacDonald, Senior lecturer, Griffith University

Michael Mintrom, Professor of Public Sector Management, Monash University

Charlotte Moore, Doctoral candidate, University of Auckland

Allyson Mutch, Senior lecturer, University of Queensland

Verna Smith, Senior lecturer, Victoria University of Wellington

Paul 't Hart, Professor of Public Administration, Utrecht University

Madeline Thomas, Research and Administrative Officer, the Australia and New Zealand School of Government

Binh Tran-Nam, Professor of Taxation, University of New South Wales

Abbreviations

AAR	Alliance of Australian Retailers
ABS	Australian Bureau of Statistics
ACC	Accident Compensation Corporation (New Zealand)
ACCC	Australian Competition and Consumer Commission
ACOSS	Australian Council of Social Service
ACT	Australian Capital Territory
ACTU	Australian Council of Trade Unions
AFAO	Australian Federation of AIDS Organisations
AIDS	acquired immune deficiency syndrome
ALP	Australian Labor Party
AMA	Australian Medical Association
ANAO	Australian National Audit Office
ANU	The Australian National University
ANZ	Australia and New Zealand Bank
ANZSOG	Australia and New Zealand School of Government
ANZUS	Australia, New Zealand, United States Security
APMC	Australasian Police Ministers Council
APRA	Australian Prudential Regulation Authority
ART	antiretroviral treatment
ASIC	Australian Securities and Investments Commission
ATO	Australian Taxation Office
AWB	Australian Wheat Board
BBCT	broad-based consumption tax
BER	Building the Education Revolution

BOM	Bureau of Meteorology
BPS	budget policy statement
CBD	central business district
CDC	Centers for Disease Control and Prevention (US)
CEO	chief executive officer
CND	Campaign for Nuclear Disarmament
COAG	Council of Australian Governments
CSA	Child Support Agency
CSCG	Child Support Consultative Group
CSEAG	Child Support Evaluation Advisory Group
CSS	Child Support Scheme
DEET	Department of Employment, Education and Training
DSS	Department of Social Security
ECE	early childhood education
ERC	European Research Council
EU	European Union
FEC	Finance and Expenditure Select Committee
FLC	Family Law Council
FPP	first-past-the-post
FRA	*Fiscal Responsibility Act* (New Zealand)
GAAP	generally accepted accounting principles
GDP	gross domestic product
GFC	Global Financial Crisis
GP	general practitioner
GRID	gay-related immune deficiency
GST	goods and services tax
HAART	highly active antiretroviral therapy
HEAC	Higher Education Administration Charge
HECS	Higher Education Contribution Scheme
HELP	Higher Education Loans Program
HIP	Homeowners Insulation Program
HIV	human immunodeficiency virus

HMO	health maintenance organisation
ICL	income-contingent loan
IDC	interdepartmental committee
IIO	irrigation infrastructure operator
IMF	International Monetary Fund
IT	information technology
LGBTI	lesbian, gay, bisexual, transgender and/or intersex
MCC	Melbourne City Council
MDB	Murray–Darling Basin
MDBA	Murray–Darling Basin Authority
MDBC	Murray–Darling Basin Commission
MDBMC	Murray–Darling Basin Ministerial Council
MMBW	Melbourne Metropolitan Board of Works
MMP	mixed-member proportional
MP	Member of Parliament
MTCS	Ministerial Taskforce on Child Support
MVA	Melbourne Voters' Action
NAB	National Australia Bank
NACAIDS	National Advisory Committee on AIDS
NAPWHA	National Association of People with HIV Australia
NCC	National Competition Council
NCP	National Competition Policy
NCV	National Committee on Violence
NFA	National Firearms Agreement
NGO	non-governmental organisation
NPM	New Public Management
NSW	New South Wales
NWI	National Water Initiative
NZBRT	New Zealand Business Roundtable
NZEI	New Zealand Educational Institute
NZS	New Zealand Superannuation

OECD	Organisation for Economic Co-operation and Development
OTS	Office of Treaty Settlements
PAYG	pay-as-you-go
PBS	Pharmaceutical Benefits Scheme
PLHIV	people living with HIV
PM&C	Department of the Prime Minister and Cabinet
PrEP	pre-exposure prophylaxis
PSGE	post-settlement governance entity
RBA	Reserve Bank of Australia
Scarlet Alliance	Australian Sex Workers Association
SDL	sustainable diversion limit
SOE	state-owned enterprise
SPG	Successful Public Governance
SSAA	Sporting Shooters' Association of Australia
UN	United Nations
UNAIDS	Joint United Nations Programme on HIV/AIDS
US	United States
VAT	value-added tax
VET	vocational education and training
WA	Western Australia
WHO	World Health Organization
WHO FCTC	World Health Organization Framework Convention on Tobacco Control
WIIE	*whānau* innovation, integration and engagement
WINZ	Work and Income New Zealand
WST	wholesale sales tax

List of illustrations

Boxes

Figures, map and plate

Tables

Foreword

Professor Ken Smith

How is it that some public policies come to be viewed as highly successful? This important question motivates the analysis in this book. In the context of the very significant resources allocated to analysis of policy and regulatory failure, professors Michael Mintrom and Paul 't Hart came up with the concept of bringing interdisciplinary authors together to workshop important recent public policy successes in Australia and New Zealand. I was keen for ANZSOG to support the project to rebalance the analysis from what at times seems to be an obsession with critiquing and cataloguing failure. Understanding the reasons for failure is clearly important, but it is also important in these times of diminishing trust to recognise why and how successful policy outcomes can be achieved. Until recently, few efforts have been made to think hard about these questions, let alone in a systematic fashion. While much effort has gone into the scholarship and practice of policy analysis and design, far less has gone into exploring the intersection between the workings of a policy, the process by which it was developed and implemented, and the politics surrounding it. This volume offers a systematic way of considering the factors impacting on policy success.

Reading this book, I have been struck by the compelling narratives and positive messages found throughout the case chapters. There will no doubt be ongoing debate about whether the policies analysed were all resoundingly successful, but few will doubt the impact on the people of our two nations of the initiatives outlined in these chapters. As the editors outline in Chapter 1: 'Policy successes, like policy failures, are in the eye of the beholder'.

The volume presents many policies that have received global recognition for their effectiveness. For example, Australia's response to the public health challenges of HIV/AIDS and Aotearoa New Zealand's Treaty of Waitangi settlement and reparation policy for settlement of historical injustices suffered by Māori are just two very different but powerful examples of major reform strategies initially led by political leaders, which garnered largely bipartisan support and drove new forms of public administration.

In quite a few instances, the policy reforms challenged powerful vested interests, such as the leadership of New Zealand's economic turn-around in the mid-1980s and Australia's gun control legislation implemented after the Port Arthur massacre in 1996. In both cases, the political leaders of the time—prime ministers David Lange of New Zealand and John Howard of Australia—led policy responses that Sir Humphrey would only describe as courageous and that were often opposed by large sections of their own support base. But both relied heavily on independent and expert advice from their public services and kept a keen eye on the broader public interest, rather than simply responding to narrower sectional interests.

I cannot do justice here to all the excellent case examples covered in this book. However, the bottom line is that there is much to be learned from the trajectories of successful policy reforms from one jurisdiction to another, even with the major differences in the nature of our governmental arrangements. What struck me in nearly all the case studies is the importance of the reinforcing interrelationships between the political, policy advisory and implementation systems, and the importance of preparation, persistence and timing in seizing opportunities for reforms.

This volume represents a terrific example of how ANZSOG serves as a catalyst for improvements in the design and effective implementation of government policies and programs. It sets forth a strong analytical framework that is then rigorously applied across diverse areas of public policy. The result is a highly readable—and highly instructive—collection of in-depth cases. In their various ways, these cases contribute insights that together form compelling patterns suggestive of what makes public policy successful. Clearly, this volume will prove a vital teaching resource in public policy courses in the future. I can also see in this collection many starting points for additional research. It is my sincere hope that this work will ultimately lead to many more successful public policies emerging in Australia and New Zealand and elsewhere in the decades ahead.

Beyond these contributions on the nature of policy development and program management, this book is also reflective of the ANZSOG enterprise in how it came together as a project. The intellectual framework for the book was developed by Professor 't Hart and colleagues at Utrecht University. That framework was then systematically applied in the Australian and New Zealand contexts through an effort that brought on Joannah Luetjens and Professor Michael Mintrom as co-leaders. Together, they made effective use of ANZSOG networks to identify the cases for inclusion and the chapter authors. It is important to acknowledge that Joannah began her career with ANZSOG as a research and administrative officer working directly with Michael Mintrom. Having acquired a graduate degree and amassed a strong publication record, she moved to Utrecht to pursue her doctoral studies with Paul 't Hart. Anyone who has been involved with ANZSOG knows that professors Mintrom and 't Hart, in their various ways as program directors, have each contributed to ANZSOG consistently over many years. The editors of this book have been joined here by many other academics and senior practitioners who have made—and will no doubt continue to make—important contributions to ANZSOG's teaching and research efforts since we were established in 2002.

Let me end by congratulating Joannah, Michael and Paul on the completion of this important book. I also offer my sincere thanks to all the authors of the case chapters. Ultimately, this is a book for optimists, for those who recognise the powerful, positive role that governments can play in making the world a better place for their citizens. I commend this work to all who have an interest in advising or implementing successful public policy and who aspire to leadership roles in and around government.

Professor Ken Smith
Dean and Chief Executive Officer
ANZSOG
November 2018

1

On studying policy successes in Australia and New Zealand

Joannah Luetjens, Michael Mintrom and Paul 't Hart[1]

Through public policies, governments have enormous potential to shape the lives of their citizens. Actions taken at any given time can affect both present conditions and future trajectories. Much is at stake when new public policies are forged or when established ones are reformed. Since the development of Australia and New Zealand in the nineteenth century as outposts of the British Empire, successive governments in both countries have progressively shaped independent identities for these nations and their populations. Australia and New Zealand have emerged as nations willing to engage in much public policy experimentation. As a result, both countries have together amassed a rich body of experience in public policy development that resonates with policy developments in Europe, Scandinavia and North America. Along the way, members of the policymaking communities in both countries have kept up a lively, mutually beneficial trade in policy ideas, policy emulation and lesson-drawing.

1 The authors wish to acknowledge the considerable overlap between this introductory chapter and the introduction in the companion volume (Mallory Compton and Paul 't Hart, eds, *Great Policy Successes*, Oxford University Press, 2019).

Why this book, why now?

For those wanting to know how public policy is made and how it evolves from aspirations and ideas expressed in speeches and documents to tangible social outcomes (or lack thereof), the 1970s produced some classic accounts, which are now established in academic curriculums and the canon of academic research worldwide. The two best-known works from this foundational set of policy studies are Jeffrey Pressman and Aaron Wildavsky's *Implementation* (1973) and Peter Hall's *Great Planning Disasters* (1982). The former is an intensive, book-length case study of how a federal employment promotion policy launched in the United States with a great sense of urgency and momentum played out on the ground with very limited success in Oakland, California. The latter volume presents a collection of public policy failures from around the Anglosphere: 'positive' planning disasters (adopted planning projects that ran into cost escalation, underperformance, withdrawal of political support or unintended consequences so big they completely dwarfed the intended aims) and 'negative' planning disasters (instances in which pressing public problems were not addressed because of political stalemate).

Taken together, these studies were emblematic of an era in which the alleged 'ungovernability' of Western societies and their welfare states was a dominant theme (Crozier et al. 1975; Rose 1979; Offe 1984). Having seized a much more prominent role in public life after World War II, Western governments were ambitious to achieve planned change, but internal complexities and the vagaries of democratic political decision-making often thwarted those ambitions. Generations of public policy and public administration students were steeped in pessimistic diagnoses from these classic studies. Waves of similar studies followed in the 1990s (Butler et al. 1994; Bovens and 't Hart 1996; Gray and 't Hart 1998) and more recently (Allern and Pollack 2012; Crewe and King 2013; Light 2014; Schuck 2014; Oppermann and Spencer 2016). These works imply that much of the time governments are up to no good, incompetent, politically paralysed and prone to overreach (e.g. Scott 1998; Schuck 2014).

And yet, in many parts of the world, including Australia and New Zealand, across many public policy domains, the bulk of public projects, programs and services perform not so badly at all, and sometimes even highly successfully (Goderis 2015). These cases are chronically underexposed and understudied. Major policy accomplishments, striking performance in difficult circumstances and thousands of taken-for-granted everyday forms of effective public value creation by and through governments are not deemed newsworthy. They cannot be exploited for political gain by oppositions and critics of incumbent officeholders. Curiously, academic students of public policy have had almost nothing to say about them (cf. Bovens et al. 2001; McConnell 2010; Moore 2013). This is despite vigorous calls to recognise the major and often hidden and unacknowledged contributions of governments to successes claimed by and widely attributed to now revered companies such as Google (Mazzucato 2013).

We cannot properly 'see', let alone recognise and explain, variations in government performance when media, political and academic discourses alike are saturated with accounts of their shortcomings and failures but are next to silent on contributions and successes. The dominance of the language of disappointment, incompetence, failure, unintended consequences, alienation, corruption, disenchantment and crisis in public and academic discourse about government, politics and public policy is not inconsequential (Hay 2007). It risks creating self-fulfilling prophecies in the way we look at, talk about, think of, evaluate and emotionally relate to public institutions. The current ascent of 'anti-system' populist politicians speaks volumes, and the message is hardly reassuring. The 'declinist' discourse of the current age has permeated our thinking about government and public policy. It prevents us from seeing, acknowledging and learning from past and present instances of highly effective and highly valued public policymaking.

This book is intended to help turn that tide. It aims to reset the agenda for teaching, research and dialogue on public policy performance in Australia and New Zealand. This is done through a set of in-depth case studies of the genesis and evolution of standout public policy accomplishments, across a range of sectors and challenges. Through these accounts, we engage with the conceptual, methodological and theoretical challenges that have plagued extant research, seeking to evaluate, explain and design successful public policy.

There are many ways to 'get at' questions of public policy success. Existing conceptual and comparative studies of public policy success (Bovens et al. 2001; Patashnik 2008; McConnell 2010) suggest that achieving it involves two major tasks: *craft work*, which is devising, adopting and implementing programs and reforms that have a meaningful impact on the public issues giving rise to their existence; and *political work*—forming and maintaining coalitions of stakeholders to persuasively propagate these programs. This political work extends to nurturing and protecting elite and public perceptions of the policy's or program's ideology, intent, instruments, implementation and impact during the often long and arduous road from ideas to outcomes. Success must be experienced and actively communicated or it will go unnoticed and underappreciated. The present volume aims to shed light on how these two fundamental tasks—program and process design, and coalition-building and reputation management—are being taken up and carried out to effect highly successful public policymaking.

This collection of cases of successful public policy follows in the footsteps of the studies of failure developed by Peter Hall and, before him, Jeffrey Pressman and Aaron Wildavsky. Descriptively, these cases are important in their own right; rich narratives of instances of policy success in a variety of contexts can help to increase awareness of the fact that government and public policy actually work remarkably well at least some of the time. Analytically, we have encouraged the authors of these cases to emulate powerful exemplars in the study of successful, high-performing, highly reputed public organisations (Selznick 1949; Kaufman 1960; Carpenter 2001; Goodsell 2011). This has allowed us to employ 'soft induction' to identify commonalities and mechanisms at play and present these as a foundation for future policy designers and researchers.

How do we know a 'successful public policy' when we see one?

Policy successes, like policy failures, are in the eye of the beholder. They are not mere facts but stories. Undoubtedly, 'events'—real impacts on real people—are a necessary condition for their occurrence. But, in the end, policy successes do not so much occur; they are made. To claim that X—a public policy, program or project—is a 'success' is effectively an act of interpretation, indeed of framing. To say this in a public capacity and in a public forum makes it an inherently political act. It amounts to giving a strong vote of confidence to certain acts and practices of governance. In effect, it singles them out, elevates them and validates them. For such an act to be consequential it needs to stick; others need to become convinced of its truth and need to emulate it. The claim 'X is a success' needs to become a more widely accepted and shared narrative. When it does, it becomes performative: X looks better and better because so many say so, so often. When the narrative endures, X becomes enshrined in collective memory through repeated retelling and other rituals. Examples of the latter include the conferral of awards on people or organisations associated with X, who then subsequently receive invitations to come before captive audiences to spread the word; the high place that X occupies in rankings; and the favourable judgements of X by official arbiters of public value in a society, such as audit agencies or watchdog bodies, not to mention the court of public opinion. Once they have achieved iconic status, success tales—no matter how selective and biased certain critics and soft voices may claim them to be (see, for example, Schram and Soss 2001)—serve as important artefacts in the construction of the self-images and reputational claims of the policymakers, governments, agencies and societal stakeholders that credibly claim authorship of their making and preservation (Van Assche et al. 2011).

We must tread carefully in this treacherous terrain. We needed to arrive at a transparent and widely applicable conceptualisation of 'policy success' to be deployed throughout the cases in this volume and a basic set of descriptive research tools allowing us to spot and characterise the 'successes' presented here. To get to that point, we surmise that *policy assessment is necessarily a multidimensional, multiperspective and political process*. At the most basic level, we distinguish between the programmatic *performance* of a policy and its political legitimacy. Successful programmatic performance is essentially about designing smart programs that will really have an impact on the issues they are supposed to tackle and delivering those programs in such a manner that they produce valuable social outcomes. Successful attainment of political *legitimacy* for a policy involves the extent to which *both* the social outcomes of policy interventions *and* the manner in which they are achieved are seen as appropriate by relevant stakeholders and accountability forums in view of the systemic values in which they are embedded (Fischer 1995; Hough et al. 2010).

The relationship between these two dimensions of policy evaluation is not straightforward. There can be (and often are) asymmetries: politically popular policies are not necessarily programmatically effective or efficient, and vice versa. Moreover, there is not necessarily a shared normative and informational basis on which different actors in governance processes assess their performance, legitimacy and endurance (Bovens et al. 2001). Many factors influence the beliefs and practices through which people form judgements about governance. Different stakeholders have different vantage points, values and interests with regard to a policy, and thus may experience and assess it differently. An appeal to 'the facts' does not necessarily help to settle these differences. Indeed, like policymaking, policy evaluation occurs in a context of multiple, often competing, cultural and political frames and narratives, each of which privileges some facts and considerations over others (Hajer and Wagenaar 2003). Policy evaluation is inherently political in its approach and implications, no matter how deep the espoused commitment to scientific rigour of many of its practitioners. This is not something we can get around; it is something we have to acknowledge and be mindful of without sliding into thinking that it is all and only political—and that, therefore, 'anything goes' when it comes to assessing the success or otherwise of a policy (Bovens et al. 2006).

Allan McConnell (2010) added a third dimension to Mark Bovens and Paul 't Hart's programmatic–political dichotomy, and produced a three-dimensional assessment map that we have adapted for our purposes (cf. Newman 2014):

- *Programmatic assessment:* This is 'classic' evaluation research focus on a policy's goals, the theory of change underpinning it and the selection of the policy instruments it deploys—all culminating in judgements about the degree to which a policy achieves valuable impacts.
- *Process assessment:* The focus here is on how the processes of policy design, decision-making and delivery are organised and managed, and whether these processes contribute to not only the policy's technical problem-solving capacity (effectiveness and efficiency), but also its social appropriateness and in particular the sense of procedural justice among key stakeholders and the wider public (Van den Bos et al. 2014).
- *Political assessment:* This dimension assesses the degree to which the policymakers and agencies involved in driving and delivering the policy are able to build and maintain fungible political coalitions supporting it, and the degree to which their association with it enhances their reputations. In other words, it examines both the political requirements for policy success and the distribution of political costs and benefits among the actors associated with it.

Table 1.1 A policy success assessment map

I. Programmatic assessment: Purposeful and valued action	II. Process assessment: Thoughtful and fair policymaking practices	III. Political assessment: Stakeholder and public legitimacy for the policy
A well-developed and empirically feasible *public value proposition* and theory of change (ends–means relationships) underpins the policy *Achievement* of (or considerable momentum towards) the policy's intended and/or other *beneficial social outcomes* Costs/benefits associated with the policy are distributed equitably in society	The policy process allows for *robust deliberation* about and *thoughtful consideration* of: the relevant values and interests; the hierarchy of goals and objectives; contextual constraints; the (mix of) policy instruments; and the institutional arrangements and capacities necessary for effective policy implementation Stakeholders overwhelmingly experience the making and/or delivery of policy as *just and fair*	A relatively broad and deep political *coalition* supports the policy's value proposition, instruments and current results Association with the policy *enhances the political capital* of the responsible policymakers *Association with the policy enhances the organisational reputation* of the relevant public agencies
IV. Temporal assessment		
Endurance of the *policy's value proposition* (i.e. the proposed 'high-level' intent and commitment underpinning its rationale and design, combined with the flexible adaptation of its 'on-the-ground' and 'programmatic' features to changing circumstances and in relation to performance feedback) Degree to which the policy's programmatic, process and political *performance is maintained* over time Degree to which the policy confers *legitimacy on the broader political system*		

Table 1.1 presents our map for assessing policy success. As the table demonstrates, we have added a fourth dimension to McConnell's three-dimensional assessment framework: success over time. This follows from the third assumption underpinning this volume—namely, that *the success or otherwise of a public policy, program or project should be studied not as a snapshot but as a film*. A policy's success is therefore also to be assessed in terms of how performance and legitimacy *develop over time* as a policy advances from proposal, design and delivery to impact. It is also important to interpret the extent to which elements of the assessment of the policy—that is, its process, impact and political legitimacy—evolve over time. Contexts change, unintended consequences emerge and surprises are thrown at history. Successful policies are those that adapt to these developments through 'dynamic conservatism' in program (re)design and learning-based program delivery. Success can also be a function of political astuteness in the safeguarding of supporting coalitions and the maintenance of a policy's public reputation and legitimacy.

Building on both these assumptions, we propose the following definition of a successful public policy:

> A policy is a complete success to the extent that: a) it demonstrably creates widely valued social outcomes; through b) design, decision-making and delivery processes that enhance both its problem-solving capacity and its political legitimacy; and it c) sustains this performance for a considerable period even in the face of changing circumstances.

This conceptualisation formed the basis of an assessment framework that has given the authors contributing to this volume a consistent set of perspectives and criteria to consider in analysing their cases. By articulating specific elements of each dimension of success—programmatic, process and political—in unambiguous and conceptually distinct terms, this framework lends a structure to case study authors in both contemporaneous evaluation and dynamic consideration of policy developments over time.

Studying policy success: Methodological considerations

Having established a working method for 'seeing' policy success in operational terms, we next review the broader methodological challenges faced by anyone interested in understanding policy success. Before we do so, it is important to point out that researchers have approached this task in a wide range of ways. Broadly, three types of approaches can be discerned.

At the *macro level*, there are studies of overall government performance. These usually take the form of cross-national and cross-regional datasets. Some researchers focus on the input and throughput side of government—for example, the quality of government dataset that captures cross-national differences in the trustworthiness, reliability, impartiality, incorruptibility and competence of public institutions (Rothstein 2011). Of more direct relevance from a policy success point of view are datasets and balanced scorecard exercises focusing on aggregate governance outputs, outcomes and productivity in specific domains of government activity, performed and propagated by, for example, the World Bank, the Organisation for Economic Co-operation and Development (OECD) and many national audit offices and government think tanks (Goderis 2015). At the *meso level*, social problem, policy domain and program evaluation specialists regularly examine populations of cases to identify areas of high performance. Examples include crime prevention, adult literacy, refugee settlement and early childhood education programs. Drawing on this evidence, these analysts then examine 'what works' and assess whether these programs or key features of them can be replicated and transferred to other contexts (e.g. Isaacs 2008; Blunch 2017; Weisburd et al. 2017; see also Lundin et al. 2015). Finally, at the *micro level*, researchers probe deeply into the context, design, decision-making, implementation, reception, assessment and evolution of single or a limited number of policies or programs, as Peter Hall in his study and Jeffrey Pressman and Aaron Wildavsky in theirs, for instance.

Each of these three approaches comes with a distinctive set of potential strengths and weaknesses. The macro studies offer the big-picture, helicopter perspective of linkages between governance activities and social outcomes. They offer good insight into the social and economic consequences of the design of public institutions and the effect of public spending patterns. They generally offer no or limited insight into what occurs in the 'black box' in which these linkages take shape.

The meso studies drill down to the level of programs and come closer to establishing the nature of the links between their inputs, throughputs, outputs and outcomes. Structured, focused comparative designs that at the same time control for institutional and contextual factors can yield richer pictures of 'what works'. A key limitation of these population comparisons is that considerations of parsimony limit the depth of attention that is given to the nuances of context, chance, choice, communication, cooperation and conflict within each of the units of analysis. As a result, it often proves difficult for meso studies to convincingly explain *why* things work well or not so well.

That is precisely the main potential strength of case study designs. These micro-level qualitative studies have the biggest potential of opening the black box and examining the actor constellations, institutional arrangements, power relationships, leadership and decision-making processes and the realities of frontline service delivery involved. Analysts working in this tradition have a better shot at reconstructing the constellations of factors and social mechanisms that converge to produce policy successes. This hypothesis-generating potential of micro studies is significantly enhanced when they are conducted in a fashion that allows for systematic comparison across cases. Yet, efforts to empirically generalise their findings must be done cautiously as there always remains the possibility that a similar convergence of factors and social mechanisms in other, unexamined contexts might have yielded different outcomes.

This volume is set in the micro tradition. We have sought to deliver on its potential strengths in hypothesis generation and identification of emerging patterns across cases, while navigating the inherent limitations of the micro tradition and its methodological challenges. Some of these are generic and also challenge macro and meso approaches, while some are specific to the micro genre of success studies. We will now briefly discuss those methodological challenges.

A constructed, political concept

Success is not an event, but a label people use to express a value judgement about events. A policy success does not come prelabelled in the world; it is constructed in the stories we tell and the stories we come to hold true *about* a policy. These stories are seldom self-evident, consistent or uniformly shared. Public policies themselves are the product of 'pulling and hauling', 'puzzling and powering' between multiple parties inside and outside government. The words we use to make meaning of policy matter. Meaning-making is inherently political in that—intentionally or not—meanings ascribed to policies can have a bearing on 'who gets what, when and how' (Lasswell 1936; Stone 2001). The processes of arguing, bargaining and influencing that occur in the agenda-setting and design stages of a policy in fact permeate the entire policy cycle. They do not stop when policymakers, legislatures, auditors or even independent researchers pause to take stock and pass a verdict on a policy or program.

Persuasive though we hope it has been, the conceptual points we have made in the preceding pages are not about to be universally embraced any time soon. All the authors of the case studies presented in this volume have been asked to work with these conceptual tools, following a template for inquiry. However, not only do they come to the project with their own preconceptions, but also they in turn have to rely on textual and human sources in their research that are part of the political fray of the case at hand. We advise readers therefore not to take any of the labels and interpretations concerning a policy's alleged 'success' for granted, but to constantly question what frames—and whose frames—are at work here and examine by what evidence they are underpinned.

Case selection

Conceptual definition of the outcome of interest—policy success—is just the start of the battle for valid inference. With defined concepts in hand, a researcher must next choose an appropriate sample from which to draw conclusions. If the first lesson in any undergraduate research methods course is that 'correlation is not causation', the second is sure to be in the spirit of 'thou shalt not select on the dependent variable'. Although criteria for sample selection vary across the quantitative–qualitative divide (Mahoney and Goertz 2006), it is agreed that the cases you choose affect the answers you get (Geddes 2003). The message is hammered into the minds of young scholars that—for reasons that are well understood—selecting cases based on the value of the dependent variable can profoundly bias statistical findings, fouling generalisation and average effect estimation (e.g. Heckman 1976). And yet, how a researcher selects their cases should be driven principally by the research question. Case selection should be a deliberate and well-considered procedure tailored to the specific research question at hand and the type of explanation sought (King et al. 1994; Brady and Collier 2010). There are defensible reasons to violate the dependent variable rule and select only or mostly 'positive' cases (Brady and Collier 2010). In this multiple-case project, we are *not* seeking causal explanation or formal comparison. Nor do we endeavour to arrive at universal generalisability of our findings. We are, instead, interested in documenting, understanding and problematising the actors, contexts, ideas and institutions that interact to produce the outcome of value: successful public policy. We believe that exploratory work of this kind is a fundamental precursor to quantitative studies that could usefully identify and test the strength of empirical regularities contributing to policy successes. Our case study selection decisions were made with these considerations in mind.

Our detailed case studies of highly successful public policies in Australia and New Zealand have been carefully chosen after intensive consultation with panels of public policy experts in both countries. The expert panels included professors of public policy, heads of think tanks, senior public policy practitioners and former secretaries of the Treasury, the Department of the Prime Minister and Cabinet and other central agencies. Experts were asked to list up to five cases from their country that they considered to be exemplary examples of successful policies and were provided with the operational definition of a successful policy (see above). Experts were also asked to provide the names of two other people they believed should be approached. This was to triangulate suggestions across expert respondents.

In total, 23 experts participated in the process. Once the initial lists of successful policies were created, they were returned to the country expert panels for confirmation and comment.

The selection method was designed to be both replicable and reliable—that is, we selected our cases using a process of consultation that other researchers could easily replicate. Further, we are confident that if others did replicate our process—even if they began with a different initial set of experts to consult—they would end up with a list of cases that correlated highly with the list we developed. We believe we have chosen the most salient examples of successful public policy from both countries over the past few decades.

Following our consultation process and the collation of the list of successful public policies, we invited potential authors to write on the selected cases. Authors were chosen based on their senior work experience or their academic research expertise. Most of the authors in this volume were matched to cases on which they already held extensive knowledge. Many have previously published work relating to these public policies, although the treatment of them specifically as cases of successful public policy was a unique experience in every case.

Moving pictures: Time and policy assessment

In assessing policy outcomes, where one stands often depends on when one looks, and with what kind of temporal perspective in mind. With the passing of time, public and political perceptions of the processes and outcomes of a public policy can shift. A case in point is the construction of the Sydney Opera House (1954–73). During the conflict-ridden and traumatic implementation phase of this highly adventurous architectural project, it was considered a major fiasco. Construction took 10 years longer than initially planned, and the costs exploded from the 1954 tender of A$7 million to well over A$100 million on completion in 1973. Significantly, the architect walked out midcourse following a series of confrontations with an increasingly sceptical Minister of Public Works whose party had won the NSW election that year promising to rein in the 'out of control' Opera House project. Not surprisingly, Peter Hall (1982) dutifully included the Opera House project in his *Great Planning Disasters*, researched in the mid-1970s and first published in 1979.

Yet this failure frame did not last. During the late 1970s and the 1980s, the Opera House became a major tourist attraction, and it has since evolved into a globally recognised architectural icon. The original budget overruns thus came to be viewed in a different light. The fact that most of the building costs had not come from the public purse but from a series of designated public lotteries—long wilfully overlooked in the political debate—made a comeback. More importantly, later generations hardly cared about the original costs, as the benefits—both monetary and cultural—had so clearly outstripped them. Over time, the weight accorded to 'project management' criteria—where success is defined as delivering according to specifications, on time and within budget—receded. The dominant evaluative lenses became strategic, macroeconomic and symbolic.

A prime source of analytical biases therefore involves the variety of possible time horizons and the registration of the various effects policies have over time. The objectives of policies may vary in terms of their temporal scope (in economic policy planning, a differentiation between short-term, medium-term and long-term policies is quite common) and temporal quality (unique/nonrecurrent versus permanent/iterative policies). This affects the timing and nature of assessments about their effects when implemented. Policymakers are in fact continuously vacillating between different time horizons in setting priorities, allocating budgets and making decisions. At the same time, many elected officials and others subject to the vagaries of the electoral cycle are predisposed to judge policy proposals or feedback about past policies first and foremost in terms of their short-term political implications.

Short-term effects are also more easily registered than long-term effects, which are likely to become intertwined with other phenomena in complex and often unintended ways. Moreover, short-term and long-term effects may in some cases be at odds with one another, the latter reversing or neutralising the former. In general, the longer the time frame used for the assessment of policy outcomes, the bigger is the scope for controversy about their meaning and evaluation. Similarly, the processes and outcomes of policies aimed at nonrecurrent outcomes (such as development of specific infrastructural assets, successful hosting of sporting events or global summits or responses to a natural disaster) tend to be more easily grasped than those of policies with iterative objectives that are constantly being renegotiated and adapted by different participants and in the face of changing circumstances. In evaluating efforts to significantly change the behaviour of large numbers of people in particular, a limited time frame is inappropriate because it neglects both the severity of the initial administrative problems and the possibility of learning by doing.

An overview of the volume

Having discussed our rationale for studying policy successes and how we identified cases for inclusion in this volume, we now review the topics of the selected cases, the common set of analytical questions we asked authors to work through in their chapters and some emerging patterns we have observed across the cases.

The cases

This volume contains 20 chapter-length studies of specific cases of successful public policy from Australia and New Zealand. Of these, 12 come from Australia and eight from New Zealand. The cases come from a broad range of policy areas. Economic policy is represented by six chapters—four from Australia and two from New Zealand. Two of the Australian cases relate to the Global Financial Crisis (GFC) of 2008–09 and responses to it. Promoting greater market efficiency is treated in one case each from Australia and New Zealand. The goods and services tax (GST) was proposed as a policy success in both Australia and New Zealand. We chose to have this success case portrayed using the Australian experience, although the New Zealand experience with the GST is mentioned in the chapter on the economic reforms of the 1980s. Health policy is represented by three chapters. There is a chapter on Medicare in Australia and another on the Accident Compensation Corporation in New Zealand. There is also a chapter on Australia's responses to the human immunodeficiency virus/acquired immune deficiency syndrome (HIV/AIDS) epidemic. Education policy is treated in two chapters—one devoted to the funding of higher education in Australia through student loans and the other to New Zealand's policy approaches to promoting early childhood education. In other social policy areas, a chapter is included on child support in Australia and another on national superannuation in New Zealand. Two chapters relate to policies in New Zealand addressing issues of high importance to Māori and the pursuit of biculturalism. The first considers the processes to address historical injustices through Treaty of Waitangi settlements, while the second considers how Whānau Ora has been pursued to improve the wellbeing of Māori families in New Zealand.

Beyond these chapters, we have several that cover a range of other policy topics. There is one on urban public policy that explores efforts to make Melbourne more liveable. Another chapter explores the success of gun control efforts in Australia. Continuing the theme of addressing social problems, a further chapter explores efforts to reduce the appeal of smoking to young Australians. Infrastructure policy is represented in the cases by a chapter on the creation of water markets in Australia. In the realm of foreign policy, we include a chapter on New Zealand's nuclear-free stance.

Analytical questions

The narratives presented in each of the following chapters provide insights into how success occurred in each case. Each chapter has been designed to answer the guiding questions set out in Box 1.1. While we did not require chapter authors to answer all of these questions exactly as they have been posed, we did ask that the general line of inquiry be closely followed. This has resulted in chapters that tell their own stories in an accessible fashion, while also relating in clear thematic ways to the other chapters in the volume.

Box 1.1 Guiding questions for case analysis

1. What is this case about and why is it included in this volume? What, in other words, is its fundamental 'claim to success' in terms of the definition and the assessment dimensions contained in Table 1.1?
2. What were the social, political and institutional contexts in which the policy (program, project, initiative) was developed?
3. What specific challenges was it seeking to tackle; what, if any, specific aims did it seek to achieve?
4. Who were the policy's main drivers and stewards, and how did they raise and maintain support for the policy?
5. How did the policy design process—the progression from ambitions and ideas to plans and instruments—unfold, and what factors shaped it most?
6. How did the political decision-making process leading up to its adoption—the progression from proposals (bills, proposals) to commitments (laws, budgets)—unfold, and what factors shaped it most?
7. How did the implementation process—'what happens after a bill becomes a law' (Bardach 1977)—unfold, and what factors shaped it most?

8. How did the legitimacy of the policy—the political and public support garnered—unfold, and what factors shaped it most?
9. How did changes over time in the operating or political context (such as government turnover, fiscal positions, critical incidents) affect:
   a. the policy's central features
   b. levels of popular support or perceived legitimacy?
10. What, overall, can policy analysts and policy actors learn from this instance of policy success:
    a. How have the lessons learned evolved over time? Has this case always been a 'success' and, if not, what changed?
    b. How likely is this case to remain a 'success' in the future? What are potential future problems with this policy case or a similar class of cases?
11. What unique factors might limit how broadly the lessons from this case can be applied (in terms of political, social or economic contexts or policy domain, etc.)?

The result is a diverse set of cases explored with a common set of reference points. This approach offers many opportunities for comparisons to be drawn between various groups of chapters and for themes to be drawn out from across the whole set. Next, we offer one way of reading these chapters thematically, by noting some of the emerging patterns that have struck us as we have worked closely with these chapters.

How success happens: Emerging patterns

Across the diverse set of cases included in this volume, a variety of emerging patterns can be detected and highlighted. Here, we note six, each of which appears across four or more of the cases.

Pattern one: Targeting and framing

Successful public policies tend to address a problem that was well defined and broadly acknowledged at the outset of the policy development process. Take, for example, the introduction of the Higher Education Contribution Scheme (HECS) in Australia. There was a strong desire to expand the number of school-leavers attending university. However, there was a concern that government subsidisation of university attendance served too much as a benefit to the middle class. The student loan scheme was devised in such a way that access to university was expanded while ensuring that the flow of benefits was not skewed towards more privileged groups in society. Likewise, Australia's National Competition Policy was devised to acknowledge costs to the Australian economy created by regulations that protected certain industries, exclusive government ownership or some combination of the two. The industries that were targeted managed major network utilities providing Australia's gas and electricity infrastructure as well as water and transport. The policy enjoyed support from the Commonwealth Government and governments in the states and territories. Many other examples are found throughout this volume of policies responding to problems that were broadly acknowledged and well defined.

Pattern two: Ripening, not running

The proposed policy solution had been carefully developed, debated and refined over a reasonable period. There is no particular pattern as to how this careful policy development takes place. In the case of New Zealand's Accident Compensation Corporation, the policy that gave form to this entity had its genesis in the report of a royal commission of inquiry. There was nothing remarkable about the royal commission itself; however, the report was presented in a fashion that placed unwavering focus on the wellbeing of the affected population while also giving appropriate consideration to concerns about efficiency. The report was exceptionally clear in presenting the case for policy change. This theme is reinforced in the chapter on the economic reforms in New Zealand in the 1980s, when Treasury advice was devised over a lengthy period and in a way that placed significant weight on intellectual coherence. Across the Australian cases in this volume, multiple examples are provided of successful public policies having their origins in conceptually coherent, evidence-informed advice, the best of which also paid careful attention to issues of effective implementation. This theme is strongly on display in the cases on HECS and child support. It is echoed in the cases on Medicare and gun control, among others.

Pattern three: Champions and stewards

As we might expect from the literature on policy entrepreneurship, often strong support from policy champions came when the policies were first being introduced. This dynamic is seen, for example, in the cases of HECS and gun control in Australia. In New Zealand, the actions of policy champions were very clearly on display during the period of economic reform in the 1980s. It is also interesting to observe that sometimes these policy champions might emerge after the policy has been adopted. In this sense, the work of these champions—and the supportive coalition—becomes most crucial during the implementation phase. A powerful example of this is provided by the New Zealand case of Treaty of Waitangi settlements. Here, a policy position asserted by a Labour Party government was maintained by the incoming National Party government. But, most significantly, the actions of the responsible minister in that government, who led treaty settlements for many years, made the whole process a success. All of those actions were concerned with implementing and embedding the treaty settlement institutions and processes, which would manage the reconciliation efforts. This support for the policy is remarkable, given that it frequently was the focus of public disquiet about the cost to taxpayers of settling treaty grievances.

Pattern four: Strike while the iron is hot

The policy was viewed as an appropriate response from the government, given the circumstances. In other words, it was the right thing at the right time. This theme is strongly apparent in the case of gun control in Australia. The policy approach had been in development; however, a horrendous mass shooting in Tasmania provided the impetus for rapid moves to bring about policy change in keeping with the development work that had already been done. The policy response in Australia to the HIV/AIDS epidemic represents another case of a policy being implemented to address a well-documented crisis. The two chapters that discuss aspects of Australia's response to the GFC further illustrate this pattern—a pattern that is also found in several of the New Zealand cases. For example, the *Fiscal Responsibility Act* was adopted at a time when the government was facing serious debt problems. Evidence of an emerging crisis was clear and the proposed policy was judged to be a broadly appropriate response.

Pattern five: Engineering support

Many of the policies discussed here enjoyed bipartisan and broad stakeholder support. It is rare for policies to enjoy such support from the outset. We counted the survival of a policy over time as a key indicator of its success, so all of the policies included in this volume have survived changes of government from leadership by the party that gave it initial support to a party that may well have once opposed it. Particularly interesting to observe are cases where support eventually came from quarters where opposition to the policy had at one time been fierce. New Zealand's nuclear-free policy is a good example. It was introduced in 1987 by the

Labour Government. National Party–led governments subsequently left the policy in place, sensing this was what the public wanted. Even so, in 2005, the leader of the National Party claimed that, if his party was elected to government, the policy would be 'gone by lunchtime'. That caused a lot of controversy. In 2007, on the twentieth anniversary of the law, the National Party's spokesperson for foreign affairs conceded that 'the retention of this legislation that is called iconic, and that is symbolic of our independence of thought and judgment in international affairs, is not in question' (New Zealand Parliament 2007: 9759). This statement makes explicit a common response to successful public policies: with time, they come to be treated as part of the broader fabric of a jurisdiction. The same could be said of the introduction of the GST and of child support and gun control in Australia. Bipartisan support that was often lacking when successful policies were initially adopted came to develop as the policy itself attained a degree of maturity.

Pattern six: Implementation, implementation, implementation

In a well-received report on why some large government policy initiatives have gone badly wrong in Australia's recent past, Peter Shergold (2015: 4) emphasised that 'policy is only as good as the manner in which it is implemented'. In most of the cases discussed in the present volume, despite their sensible design and the broad support they tended to enjoy, implementation was not at all straightforward. We think this is a surprising finding because past scholarly discussions of policy failure have frequently focused on problems during implementation (Pressman and Wildavsky 1973). In the case of the drive to make Melbourne a more liveable city, there were various challenges that meant implementation occurred in a slow, incremental fashion. Yet, that tough work on a variety of policy fronts finally paid off. When people started to see the benefits of the implementation efforts, assessments of the overall initiative became far more positive. Likewise, the introduction of water markets in Australia had its fair share of frustrations. Indeed, some of those frustrations remain. However, overall, this effort is now viewed as a major policy success. In New Zealand, evidence of success emerging from implementation problems is provided by the case of Whānau Ora. Initially, problems arose because the approach required actors in government to work across silos and to challenge some of their business-as-usual approaches to service delivery. And, even while many now view the policy as a success in terms of assisting Māori families under stress, it still attracts criticism from those in society who dislike governments treating different groups differently.

This brief highlighting of patterns across the cases suggests that the presence of certain key factors can increase the likelihood that a public policy will be viewed as a success. Much more could be said. We are aware, too, that the evidence is messy and patterns that are carried strongly across some cases are more muted in others. Nonetheless, it is our contention that drawing out and discussing patterns in this manner can be incredibly useful in supporting the development of critical insights regarding the development, delivery, maintenance and reform of public policies.

Conclusion

All people involved in the development and implementation of public policy can draw lessons from the past. Those lessons hold the potential to guide practice in highly productive ways. Until recently, efforts to draw lessons from the past have tended to focus on cases of failure. While it is certainly true that important lessons can be drawn from failure, similarly important lessons can be drawn from success. This volume contributes to an emerging body of work that emphasises the value of studying successful public policy. The cases presented here, drawn from Australia and New Zealand, offer a wealth of insights into the factors that appear to support the attainment of expected policy outcomes and that contribute to widely shared views that a policy has been a success.

We have developed this volume with the intention of encouraging further study of successful public policy. The chapter cases included here offer a good representation of well-regarded public policies that have been adopted in Australia and New Zealand over the past few decades. The set of cases is by no means exhaustive. We are aware of other cases that could have been included in this volume. We also anticipate that others will be inspired by the cases here to look for and identify evidence of success in other public policies adopted in Australia, New Zealand and elsewhere. As we noted earlier, several of the authors who contributed to this volume have previously written at length on the public policy cases covered here. However, the approach of exploring these cases as instances of policy success is unique to this volume. We are confident that the cases here—and others not represented—could be explored in even greater depth in future works, all with the purpose of identifying mechanisms and practices conducive to policy success.

In sum, we are delighted to introduce this terrific set of cases exploring examples of successful public policy. We are also excited by the agenda-setting nature of this volume. We hope it helps to change the frame of professional, public and political debates about government that are so often geared towards its problems and shortcomings. We hope that others will soon take insights emerging from this collective effort as starting points for the development and testing of hypotheses about the conditions that seem to support the emergence of public policies as broadly acknowledged successes. Finally, we hope the studies included here will inspire many emerging and established policy advocates, analysts, designers and implementers to do all they can to ensure the policies on which they work will one day be considered significant successes.

References

Allern, S. and Pollack, E. (eds) 2012. *Scandalous! The mediated construction of political scandals in four Nordic countries*. Gothenburg: Nordicom.

Bardach, E. 1977. *The Implementation Game*. Cambridge, MA: MIT Press.

Blunch, N. H. 2017. 'Adult literacy programs in developing countries.' *IZA World of Labor* 2017: 374. doi.org/10.15185/izawol.374.

Bovens, M. and 't Hart, P. 1996. *Understanding Policy Fiascos*. New Brunswick, NJ: Transaction.

Bovens, M., 't Hart, P. and Kuipers, S. 2006. 'The politics of policy evaluation.' In M. Moran and R. E. Goodin (eds), *Oxford Handbook of Public Policy*. Oxford: Oxford University Press.

Bovens, M., 't Hart, P. and Peters, B. G. (eds) 2001. *Success and Failure in Public Governance: A comparative analysis*. Cheltenham, UK: Edward Elgar. doi.org/10.4337/9781843762850.

Brady, H. E. and Collier, D. 2010. *Rethinking Social Inquiry: Diverse tools, shared standards*. 2nd edn. Plymouth: Rowman & Littlefield.

Butler, D., Adonis, A. and Travers, T. 1994. *Failure in British Government: The politics of the poll tax*. Oxford: Oxford University Press.

Carpenter, D. 2001. *The Forging of Bureaucratic Autonomy: Reputations, networks, and policy innovation in executive agencies, 1862–1928*. Princeton, NJ: Princeton University Press.

Crewe, I. and King, A. 2013. *The Blunders of Our Governments*. London: Oneworld.

Crozier, M. J., Huntington, S. P. and Watanuki, J. 1975. *The Crisis of Democracy*. New York: NYU Press.

Fischer, F. 1995. *Evaluating Public Policy*. Chicago: Nelson Hall.

Geddes, B. 2003. *Paradigms and Sandcastles: Theory building and research design in comparative politics*. Ann Arbor: University of Michigan Press.

Goderis, B. (ed.) 2015. *Public Sector Achievement in 36 Countries: A comparative assessment of inputs, outputs and outcomes*. The Hague: The Netherlands Institute for Social Research.

Goodsell, C. T. 2011. *Mission Mystique: Belief systems in public agencies*. Washington, DC: CQ Press.

Gray, P. and 't Hart, P. (eds) 1998. *Public Policy Disasters*. London: Routledge.

Hajer, M. and Wagenaar, H. (eds) 2003. *Deliberative Policy Analysis: Understanding governance in the network society*. Cambridge: Cambridge University Press.

Hall, P. 1982. *Great Planning Disasters*. Berkeley, CA: University of California Press.

Hall, P. 1993. 'Policy paradigms, social learning, and the state: The case of economic policymaking in Britain.' *Comparative Politics* 25(3): 275–310. doi.org/10.2307/422246.

Hay, C. 2007. *Why We Hate Politics*. Cambridge: Polity Press.

Heckman, J. A. 1976. 'The common structure of statistical models of truncation, sample selection and limited dependent variables and a simple estimator for such models.' *Annals of Economic and Social Measurement* 5(4): 475–92.

Hough, M., Jackson, J., Bradford, B., Myhill, A. and Quinton, P. 2010. 'Procedural justice, trust, and institutional legitimacy.' *Policing* 4(3): 203–10. doi.org/10.1093/police/paq027.

Isaacs, J. 2008. *Impacts of Early Childhood Programs*. Washington, DC: The Brookings Institution.

Kaufman, H. 1960. *The Forest Ranger: A study in administrative behavior*. Baltimore: Johns Hopkins University Press.

Kim, J. Y. 2014. 'Brazil's contribution to a world free of poverty.' *The World Bank Opinion*, 24 March. Accessed from: www.worldbank.org/en/news/opinion/2014/03/24/brazil-contribution-world-without-poverty.

King, G., Keohane, R. O. and Verba, S. 1994. *Designing Social Inquiry: Scientific inference in qualitative research*. Princeton, NJ: Princeton University Press.

Lasswell, H. D. 1936. *Politics: Who gets what, when and how*. New York: Whittlesey House.

Light, P. C. 2014. *A Cascade of Failures: Why government fails, and how to stop it*. Washington, DC: Brookings Institution.

Lundin, B., Öberg, P. and Josefsson, C. 2015. 'Learning from success: Are successful governments role models?' *Public Administration* 3(3): 733–52. doi.org/10.1111/padm.12162.

McConnell, A. 2010. *Understanding Policy Success: Rethinking public policy*. Basingstoke, UK: Palgrave Macmillan. doi.org/10.1007/978-1-137-08228-2.

Mahoney, J. and Goertz, G. 2006. 'A tale of two cultures: Contrasting quantitative and qualitative research.' *Political Analysis* 14(3): 227–49. doi.org/10.1093/pan/mpj017.

Mazzucato, M. 2013. *The Entrepreneurial State: Debunking public vs. private sector myths*. London: Anthem Press.

Mettler, S. 2002. 'Bringing the state back into civic engagement: Policy feedback effects of the G. I. Bill for World War II veterans.' *American Political Science Review* 96(2): 351–65. doi.org/10.1017/S0003055402000217.

Moore, M. H. 2013. *Recognizing Public Value*. Harvard, MA: Harvard University Press.

Newman, J. 2014. 'Measuring policy success: Case studies from Australia and Canada.' *Australian Journal of Public Administration* 73(2): 192–205. doi.org/10.1111/1467-8500.12076.

New Zealand Parliament 2007. *New Zealand Parliamentary Debates* (12 June) 639, 9759. Available from: www.parliament.nz/en/pb/hansard-debates/rhr/document/48HansD_20070612_00001019/motions-nuclear-free-legislation-20th-anniversary.

Offe, C. 1984. 'Ungovernability: On the renaissance of conservative theories of crisis.' In J. Habermas (ed.), *Observation on 'The Spiritual Situation of the Age.'* Cambridge, MA: MIT Press.

Oppermann, K. and Spencer, A. 2016. 'Telling stories of failure: Narrative constructions of foreign policy fiascos.' *Journal of European Public Policy* 23(5): 685–701. doi.org/10.1080/13501763.2015.1127272.

Patashnik, E. 2008. *Reform at Risk*. Princeton, NJ: Princeton University Press.

Pressman, J. L. and Wildavsky, A. 1973. *Implementation*. Berkeley, CA: University of California Press.

Rose, R. 1979. 'Ungovernability: Is there fire behind the smoke?' *Political Studies* 27(3): 351–70. doi.org/10.1111/j.1467-9248.1979.tb01209.x.

Rothstein, B. 2011. *The Quality of Government: Corruption, social trust and inequality in international perspective*. Chicago: University of Chicago Press. doi.org/10.7208/chicago/9780226729589.001.0001.

Schram, S. and Soss, J. 2001. 'Success stories: Welfare reform, policy discourse, and the politics of research.' *The ANNALS of the American Academy of Political and Social Science* 577(September): 49–65. doi.org/10.1177/000271620157700105.

Schuck, P. H. 2014. *Why Government Fails So Often*. Princeton, NJ: Princeton University Press.

Scott, J. C. 1998. *Seeing Like A State: How certain schemes to improve the human condition have failed*. New Haven, CT: Yale University Press.

Selznick, P. 1949. *TVA and the Grass Roots*. Berkeley, CA: University of California Press.

Shergold, P. 2015. *Learning from Failure: Why large government policy initiatives have gone so badly wrong in the past and how the chances of success in the future can be improved*. Canberra: Australian Public Service Commission.

Stone, D. 2001. *Policy Paradox: The art of political decision making*. Rev. edn. New York: Norton.

Van Assche, K., Beunen, R. and Duineveld, M. 2011. 'Performing success and failure in governance: Dutch planning experiences.' *Public Administration* 90(3): 567–81. doi.org/10.1111/j.1467-9299.2011.01972.x.

Van den Bos, K., Van der Velden, L. and Lind, E. A. 2014. 'On the role of perceived procedural justice in citizens' reactions to government decisions and the handling of conflicts.' *Utrecht Law Review* 10(4): 1–26. doi.org/10.18352/ulr.287.

Weisburd, D., Farrington, D. P. and Gill, C. with Ajzenstadt, M., Bennett, T., Bowers, K., Caudy, M. S., Holloway, K., Johnson, S., Lösel, F., Mallender, J., Perry, A., Tang, L. L., Taxman, F., Telep, C., Tierney, R., Ttofi, M. M., Watson, C., Wilson, D. B. and Wooditch, A. 2017. 'What works in crime prevention and rehabilitation: An assessment of systematic reviews.' *Criminology and Public Policy* 16(2): 415–49. doi.org/10.1111/1745-9133.12298.

Wildavsky, A. 1987. *Speaking Truth to Power: The art and craft of policy analysis*. New Brunswick, NJ: Transaction Books.

Part I: Policy successes in Australia

2

Responding to HIV/AIDS: Mobilisation through partnerships in a public health crisis

Lisa Fitzgerald and Allyson Mutch, with Lisa Herron[1]

Australia's response to HIV/AIDS

> As incoming Minister for Health, I was presented with a ministerial briefing, a fat folder with health issues roughly organised in order of priority. Well down the list, at 34 or 35, there was a reference to a phenomenon entitled GRID—gay-related immune deficiency. I was informed that this was a fatal immune disorder affecting homosexuals in the conditions or 'life styles' of American gays. It was not, I was assured, likely to be of any immediate priority for an Australian minister. Within two years, we had close to 1000 cases of human immunodeficiency virus [HIV] infection in Australia. AIDS, as it was by then called, had moved near the top of the national agenda. (Blewett 1996: 343)

When Neal Blewett, the newly elected Commonwealth Minister for Health, took office in 1983, AIDS was a new, unidentifiable, infectious and lethal disease affecting some of the most stigmatised communities

1 We would like to acknowledge and thank our colleagues Chris Howard, Bernard Gardner and Kate van Dooren. We would particularly like to thank Chris and Bernard for drawing on their extensive knowledge and experience of the HIV field to provide insight and critique. We also acknowledge people living with HIV who so generously share their lived experiences to improve the lives of all people living with HIV.

in Australia. There were no medical explanations, little understanding of the communities affected and no overseas policy models to guide action. Australia's response to HIV/AIDS required a new approach (Blewett 1997). What followed was groundbreaking policy embedded in three key principles: partnership, community engagement and bipartisan support. This framework has ensured Australia's national policy response to HIV/AIDS has been lauded as one of the best in the world (Gupta et al. 2008; Brown et al. 2014; Holt 2017).

Evaluating policy success

What were the foundations of Australia's HIV policy success? At the programmatic level, a strong values base of human rights and collaborative partnership between government, affected communities, clinicians and researchers has underpinned national policy (Bowtell 1997; Drielsma 1997; Brown et al. 2014). Social public health, centred on social and collective experiences of HIV, has been fundamental to policy design, with the focus on facilitating and enabling the social and legal environments for affected communities (Aggleton and Kippax 2014). The first Australian National HIV/AIDS Strategy, in 1989, closely adhered to these values as it sought to define policy goals: restrict the spread of HIV/AIDS transmission, care for those infected and educate and support healthcare professionals (Commonwealth of Australia 1989). Subsequent national strategies have maintained this strong values base, but policy goals have evolved.

The outcomes of Australia's national HIV/AIDS policy clearly illustrate its success. Australia's sustained low prevalence of HIV is comparable with other resource-rich countries (Holt 2017). Since 1984, 37,225 people have been diagnosed with HIV, and 27,545 people were living with HIV in 2017 (0.13 per cent of the population) (Kirby Institute 2018). This compares with 0.16 per cent of the population in the United Kingdom and 3.9 per cent (392.4 per 100,000) in the United States (Kirwan et al. 2016; CDC 2018). Within Australia, the epidemic has been contained in the groups initially impacted (Bowtell 2005): men who have sex with men (70 per cent of new cases in the past decade); a few cases in people who inject drugs; and no recorded cases between sex workers and clients (Holt 2017). But success should not be measured only epidemiologically. The collaborative nature of policy design and the empowerment of affected communities have seen increased awareness of the human rights of marginalised groups, including people living with HIV (PLHIV); lesbian, gay, bisexual, transgender and/or intersex (LGBTI) people; sex workers; and people who inject drugs. Radical changes in community behaviour, including a revolution in safe sex and drug-using practices, have occurred (Brown et al. 2014). Outcomes of the policy process have included policy partnerships, innovative public health programs and healthcare services, linkages between primary care, specialists and community organisation services and research engaging the community, health providers and policymakers (Department of Health 2014).

HIV emerged in Australia at the time that Medicare—the nationally coordinated universal health insurance system—was introduced, in 1984 (Chapter 11, this volume), which was fundamental to providing care for those who developed AIDS and for funding ongoing support and treatment of PLHIV (Bowtell 1997). The Pharmaceutical Benefits Scheme (PBS), Australia's subsidised medication scheme, provided copayments for HIV-related medications including biomedical prevention medication such as pre-exposure prophylaxis (PrEP). Federal and state governments also cofunded community-supported education and prevention. Modelling demonstrates that significant investment in prevention and care has saved billions of dollars through averted infection and expenditure on treatment and care (Applied Economics 2003; Kwon et al. 2012).

At the process level, the design and choice of policy instruments have been contextual, innovative and at times remarkably courageous. At the beginning of the Australian epidemic, well before policy formulation, affected communities harnessed the momentum achieved through their rights-based movements to lead the response (Power 2011). Government drew on this action, resourcing communities to 'own' their epidemic and work with peers (Mindel and Kippax 2013). Under the strong leadership of Blewett, the Hawke Labor Government worked within a model that valued the inclusion of affected communities in policy decision-making processes, community-led education and prevention strategies and resource allocation (Bowtell 1997; Brown et al. 2014). HIV/AIDS policy development was an example of 'grassroots-up' policy design (Bowtell 2005: 5). Well-resourced, empowered affected communities provided rapid feedback loops to mobilise the community and identify solutions that fed into policy (Nous Group 2015). This participatory strategy was an essential contributor to policy success (Misztal 1991; Kippax and Race 2003; O'Donnell and Perche 2016).

The policy process effectively and adaptively deployed a mix of policy instruments. Social policy dimensions were prioritised across multiple social, political, behavioural and health service levels, operating within supportive environments and national and state policy development and reform, with reorientation of health services and research investment (Brown et al. 2014). Innovative harm-reduction prevention programs and peer education were developed around the sensitivities of (stigmatised) health-related practices (AFAO 2012). The multipronged mix of policy instruments has been flexible, adapted to evidence and changing epidemics, and has supported the diversity of priority populations and contexts. A pragmatic, evidence-based approach that values different types of evidence, including the knowledge and understandings of affected communities, makes this policy so innovative. National centres in social, epidemiological and medical research have conducted groundbreaking research that has enabled policy design to be shaped by evidence (Bernard et al. 2008; Brown et al. 2014). The collaborative process undertaken in the development of policy—including the establishment of innovative policy instruments—has been an essential element of success (AFAO 2012).

At the political level, policy was established through a broad and deep political coalition and continues through commitment to bipartisanship. A multisectoral approach—across federal and state/territory governments and opposition parties, community groups, clinicians and researchers—has been a feature (Bowtell 2005). The mobilisation of goodwill and public support has seen early political players—particularly Blewett and his opposition counterpart, Dr Peter Baume—praised for their action and success. Australia has been a key player driving international HIV policy over the history of the epidemic, including through the 'Melbourne Declaration' in 2014 (Whittaker 2014). Many best-practice policy approaches developed in Australia have been taken up internationally (AFAO 2012). Leading community organisations—including the Australian Federation of AIDS Organisations (AFAO), Scarlett Alliance and the National Association of People with HIV Australia (NAPWHA)—are internationally recognised and work globally. In terms of public legitimacy, enduring national HIV policies have been supported by the majority of Australians and the response has been cited as a successful demonstration of leadership and willingness to make decisions (Bowtell 1997).

It is at the temporal level that the success of Australia's national HIV policy has been challenged due to complex and shifting epidemiological, biomedical, social and political contexts. Policy success has waxed and waned through temporal and contextual complexity, yet the underlying value proposition of human rights, partnership and social public health has endured and adapted to changing circumstances. Bipartisan commitment has continued across national strategies and through successive federal and state governments (Brown et al. 2014). However, the degree to which the policy's programmatic, process and political performance has been maintained over time is a more complex story and 'not without periods of disharmony or different levels of participation and/or commitment' (Brown et al. 2014: 38).

This chapter outlines nearly 40 years of policy development in HIV/AIDS. The story is not a snapshot but a long film with a complicated script, and many characters and scenes. We, as public health academics, are the directors, and consequently the focus of this chapter is on the story of Australia's national HIV policy, not those of the states and territories (each state/territory has its own story to tell—some successful, others with mixed results). We outline the history of national policy processes, teasing out key successes, and highlight how performance and legitimacy have been maintained and challenged. We discuss the strong foundational, programmatic and values base of Australia's policy response, and the tensions/challenges in this story of success, particularly in temporal policy and political processes. These tensions and challenges occur through shifting contexts—most notably: 1) the changing context of HIV (biomedical advancements in treatment and prevention, the movement of HIV as a manageable chronic condition and the increasing diversity of affected communities); and 2) changing governments and neoliberal policy agendas (shifts in and reductions of funding and increasing focus on biomedicalisation). This complex historical narrative comprises three acts: 1982–95, the early response of partnerships and prevention; 1996–2009, 'new hope, disinvestment and political neglect' (Brown et al. 2014: 37); and 2010 to the present, a time of targets and biomedicine (Newman et al. 2010; Brown et al. 2014; Cameron and Goodwin 2014).

Australia's HIV/AIDS policy in context

To consider the success of Australia's immediate and enduring approach to HIV, the first part of our 'film' examines the social, historical and political contexts that shaped early policy and provided the foundations for action. In 1981, the first official report of what would become the start of the AIDS epidemic was published by the US Centers for Disease Control and Prevention (CDC 2006). The CDC (2006) identified a rare illness, pneumocystis, that had infected five gay men in Los Angeles; within days, doctors from across the country were registering similar cases. By the end of 1981, 270 cases and 121 deaths from what was then known as gay-related immune deficiency (GRID) had been reported in the United States (CDC 2006). Mainstream and gay media in the United States reported the 'gay pneumonia', often using stigmatising terms including 'gay cancer' and 'gay plague' (Power 2011). In 1982, acquired immune deficiency syndrome (AIDS) became the official name for the mystery disease with no known cause or cure (Robinson and Wilson 2012).

Australia's first case of AIDS, diagnosed in an American tourist, was identified in October 1982 in Sydney. Six months later, the first Australian citizen, who had been living overseas, was diagnosed, in Melbourne, and, on 8 July 1983, the first Australian died from AIDS (Brown et al. 2014). The epidemic grew rapidly from there: between 1983 and 1985, an estimated 4,500 Australians—predominately gay men living in Sydney and Melbourne—were infected with HIV (Brown et al. 2014). As the disease spread, media reporting followed. In 1982, six months after Australia's gay press began reporting on AIDS, mainstream media picked up the story (Mindel and Kippax 2013). Coverage increased dramatically as time went on, escalating when four Queensland babies died in November 1983 after receiving blood transfusions containing HIV (Plummer and Irwin 2006). As media reports increased, so too did public concern that AIDS would spread to heterosexual communities (Brown et al. 2014). Public outcry, along with the increasing incidence of AIDS and growing numbers of people dying, was a catalyst for activism and support within the gay community.

Brandt (1986: 231) observes that the 'way a society responds to problems of disease reveals its deepest cultural, social and moral values'. HIV was associated with social and sexual practices considered by many at the time to be deviant and immoral (Power 2011). HIV/AIDS predominantly affected marginalised groups in Australian society: gay men, sex workers and drug users. The historical context of stigma and discrimination experienced by these populations, along with restrictive laws associated with socially prescribed 'deviant practices', was the key context in which the policy response was situated. Homosexual behaviour between men remained illegal in many Australian states until the mid-1980s, and into the 1990s in Queensland and Tasmania. Punitive legislation related to sex work and people who injected drugs was also a key barrier to HIV prevention (Feachem 1995).

Mobilisation of the gay community

Mobilisation of the gay community from the outset of the epidemic was as much about the threat of AIDS as it was about the threat to fledgling civil liberties and emerging public acceptance of gay men and lesbian women in Australia (Power 2011). The gay and lesbian rights movement was a feature of Australia's political landscape well before the emergence of AIDS and became vital to policy formation (Power 2011). Homophobia was historically entrenched within Australian society, with legal, religious and medical efforts to punish and control homosexuality (Power 2011). The emergence of new political movements from the 1960s—for example, for the rights of women, Aboriginal and Torres Strait Islander peoples, people living with disabilities, gay men and lesbian women—advanced new social agendas. Gay and lesbian activism demanded civil rights, legal protection and the decriminalisation of homosexuality. This activism provided increasing visibility through the emergence of gay communities, particularly in Sydney and Melbourne, and new frames of understanding for LGBTI communities (Power 2011).

This history of organised activism meant gay men were in a strong position to respond to the arrival of AIDS in Australia (Drielsma 1997; Bowtell 2005; Power 2011; Mindel and Kippax 2013). The gay liberation movement prompted the formation of geographically dense social and sexual networks, connections to left-wing politics and close relationships between communities. The Australian movement was linked to international gay liberation movements, particularly in the United States (Mindel and Kippax 2013). Communication between gay communities internationally meant Australia received up to date information about HIV/AIDS and was able to respond rapidly. Gay men active in the liberation movement were highly educated and articulate, with skills in advocacy and political lobbying; they also quickly became experts in scientific and medical information about the virus (Mindel and Kippax 2013). Existing organisational structures and political frameworks, as well as gay and lesbian media, were reoriented immediately to focus on the epidemic (Power 2011). Gay communities in Sydney, Melbourne and Brisbane drew on their resources to organise socially and politically (Altman 1994). Urban gay communities became the battlegrounds in the war on AIDS (Altman 1994). The gay community was passionate about effective prevention and care of those affected. Community volunteerism was a feature of the early response, with people taking on formal caring roles when healthcare providers would not. New partnerships were formed between PLHIV, carers and healthcare providers, based on holistic models of health. This mobilisation occurred across the developed world, where existing gay organisations, communities and networks produced the early prevention, education and care responses—well before action from AIDS organisations or governments (Kippax and Race 2003).

The first community-based organisations established in Australia, in 1984, included the AIDS Action Committees in New South Wales, Victoria, Western Australia and the Australian Capital Territory (ACT) (Mindel and Kippax 2013). Their purpose was to lobby government and educate the community (Plummer and Irwin 2006). The action committees became AIDS councils—established in all states and territories by 1985. The AIDS councils produced early HIV prevention material, which was recognised as highly successful in raising awareness of HIV and safe sex (Mindel and Kippax 2013). These organisations also continued the fight for structural policy changes, including the decriminalisation of homosexuality.

Activism and PLHIV

As the epidemic took hold, PLHIV also began to play an active role in advocacy and the politicisation of their rights. PLHIV participated in organisations such as the AIDS Coalition to Unleash Power (ACT UP), which were involved in treatment activism (Whittaker 1992). Internationally, the Denver Principles 1983 and 'The Greater Involvement of People Living with HIV (GIPA) Declaration' of 1994, signed by the Australian Government, were guiding principles for the meaningful participation of PLHIV in all stages of policy and program development and implementation. The NAPWHA was formed in 1989, representing community-based organisations of PLHIV. NAPWHA has been a key organisation working with government, providing advocacy, policy, health promotion and presentation on a national level and making sure the voices of HIV-positive people are heard (NAPWHA 2017).

Advocacy within the sex worker community

Advocacy within the sex worker community also occurred in the early stages of Australia's epidemic. Sex work organisations were established in Australia in the late 1970s, with a focus on advocating for sex workers' health and industry and legal concerns. In response to HIV/AIDS, sex work groups formalised and new groups were established in all states and territories (Bates and Berg 2014). From 1986, sex work organisations received government funding for work related to HIV/AIDS, enabling them to formalise organisational structures, employ staff and develop peer education programs (Bates and Berg 2014). Scarlet Alliance (the Australian Sex Workers Association) was formed in 1989. The enabling environment established for sex workers to provide effective preventive education to peers and clients was immensely successful. Peer education programs improved working conditions, educated clients and promoted safe sex practices. These actions were instrumental in lowering rates of sexually transmitted infections and prevented the spread of HIV within Australia's sex work population (Donovan et al. 2012).

Mobilisation of people who inject drugs

People who inject drugs were also a key group during the early phase of the epidemic; however, due to the high stigmatisation of drug use, mobilisation of this group occurred slightly later than action within the gay and sex work communities. Community mobilisation developed alongside the adoption of harm minimisation as the official national drug policy in 1985 (Madden and Wodak 2014). Gay organisations provided models to drug-user groups around advocacy and mobilisation to fight HIV/AIDS, enabling them to make a significant contribution to Australia's response to HIV (Madden and Wodak 2014). They advocated for harm-reduction drug policies and education, established peer education and needle exchange programs and fought for free and non-judgemental access to sterile injecting equipment and accurate information about HIV. In 1989, the Australian IV League formed, representing the interests of injecting drug users (Hulse 1997).

Mobilisation of Aboriginal and Torres Strait Islander communities

From the outset of the epidemic, Aboriginal and Torres Strait Islander peoples mobilised, recognising the potential threat from the epidemic to their people and communities. Aboriginal and Torres Strait Islander peoples' issues were included from the beginning of the response, with partnerships forged between Indigenous peoples, government and affected communities in national and jurisdictional HIV policy development. Focus was placed on workforce development, surveillance and the establishment of Aboriginal and Torres Strait Islander–specific HIV-related organisations and projects (Ward et al. 2014). The Aboriginal Community Controlled Service movement, developed in the 1970s, designed and delivered locally relevant HIV promotion messages, including the successful 'Condoman' and 'Lubelicious' campaigns (Ward et al. 2014).

Political context and leadership

The political context of the time also had a significant impact on Australia's policy response. As the epidemic emerged, the newly elected Hawke Labor Government took power, in March 1983. The Labor Government was philosophically predisposed to federalism and centralisation of political initiatives and had a strong belief in preventive and community health programs. One of its earliest policy initiatives was the implementation of Medicare (Chapter 11, this volume). Having a national healthcare system funded and driven federally enabled the government to develop a nationally structured and coordinated approach to HIV/AIDS that could be implemented by state and territory governments in accordance with local contexts and needs (Misztal 1993).

Dr Neal Blewett, the Commonwealth Minister for Health (1983–90), is praised as a key actor and architect of Australia's policy response to HIV/AIDS (Ballard 1989). Blewett (1997), a former professor of political science, believed in the socialisation of health, moving away from the monopolisation of health policy by medical professionals and health bureaucrats. He drove the implementation of Medicare, which saw the government and the union movement pitted against a medical establishment opposed to the socialisation of health care (Misztal 1991; Drielsma 1997).

When Blewett took office, AIDS was a new and incurable communicable disease, which politicians, clinicians and bureaucrats knew little about and were unready to manage. Blewett (1996: 343) recognised that being unprepared had its advantages; there was 'no bureaucratic elite to struggle against' and 'no group of medical specialists with a vested interest in the field', providing a 'rare opportunity for creative policy making'. Blewett focused on what he has called a 'rational approach' to policymaking:

> [W]e are for the first time in history in a position to address rationally a major new disease, and we must let the logic of the epidemic impose itself on planning decisions. (Blewett 1996: S237)

Debate about the early direction of AIDS policy in Australia occurred within a sociocultural context in which the traditionally dominant medical profession's claim to ownership was challenged, and conflict arose between medical professionals and affected communities over control and self-determination (Drielsma 1997). This conflict reflected two distinct positions: medicine's traditional 'public health medical model', which focused on diagnosis, treatment, isolation and quarantine; and the 'new public health', enshrined in the Ottawa Charter for Health Promotion, which focused on the social determinants of health, equity, social justice, advocacy, intersectoral community-based responses, prevention and health promotion (Drielsma 1997; Madden and Wodak 2014).

AIDS was a 'public health crisis' affecting marginalised communities (Wodak and Lurie 1997: 129). Blewett (1988) recognised the need for a creative and rapid response, but he also acknowledged the need to address public fear about AIDS and provide reassurance that rational government action could stop it. In late 1984, Blewett toured the United States—a trip he described as the most influential experience directing his early views of AIDS (Blewett 1988). The tour highlighted US president Ronald Reagan's slow, partisan and limited national policy approach, as well as the work being done in California, which was characterised by partnerships between medical professionals and affected communities, in both public health campaigns and service delivery (Perrow and Guillen 1990). This prompted Blewett to strive for a national nonpartisan approach and the active engagement of affected communities (Mindel and Kippax 2013).

Designing, implementing and delivering a national response to HIV

As the social and political contexts of the 1970s and 1980s shaped Australia's early community response to HIV/AIDS, so, too, policy has adapted and evolved in line with social, epidemiological, political, medical and generational changes over the past four decades. Reflecting these changes, we identify three distinct policy periods: 1982–95, which saw the early response of partnerships and prevention; 1996–2009, a period of 'new hope, disinvestment and political neglect' (Brown et al. 2014: 37); and 2010 to the present, a time of targets and biomedicine (Newman et al. 2010; Brown et al. 2014; Cameron and Godwin 2014). The objectives and policy measures adopted during these eras demonstrate the temporal success of Australia's HIV policy and its ability to reflect the changing nature of the epidemic and evolve with emerging evidence and evaluation of national strategies and interventions. The following acts of our film traverse these three policy periods, considering design, development, implementation and delivery processes, particularly in relation to Australia's seven national HIV/AIDS strategies.

1982–1995: The early response—Partnership and prevention

The AIDS issue was not a value-neutral political space. To contain the virus, the government needed to negotiate tensions between encouraging safe sex and drug-using practices and the moral discourses that stigmatised affected communities. Acknowledging this, Blewett (1988: S236) saw an urgent need to confront public fear with clear and concise political leadership and strong policy that engaged affected communities in the development of effective strategies to address socially 'taboo practices'. Working in partnership with affected communities, clinicians, researchers, senior health bureaucrats and the states and territories, Blewett actively led the nation's response, establishing the legitimacy needed to support the first National HIV/AIDS Strategy in 1989.

The federal government, largely supported by the states and territories, played multiple roles in the establishment of a multifaceted AIDS policy. Early on, it established its position as consultant and negotiator, bringing together key stakeholders (Moodie et al. 2003; Mindel and Kippax 2013). Through partnerships, the federal government was also positioned as an enabler, facilitating and funding innovative and effective education strategies, safe sex campaigns, needle exchange programs and community-based care programs developed and implemented by affected communities (Plummer and Irwin 2006). Stepping through this discussion of policy design, development and implementation, we reflect on these key roles and consider their contribution to the legitimacy and success of the national strategy in the first policy era.

Consultation and negotiation

Policy development relies on good-quality information and evidence; however, beyond information and evidence generated by and disseminated through affected communities, traditional sources of health information were notably absent in the early 1980s. Acknowledging this, Blewett (1988) established channels of communication and advisory structures that included representatives of affected communities and medical professionals to inform the nation's health ministers. These advisory structures did not follow the traditional health policymaking processes frequently monopolised by senior bureaucrats and medical professionals, but instead demonstrated the government's commitment to consultation and the engagement of all interested groups (Bowtell 1997, 2005).

The first advisory group began as a working party established by the National Health and Medical Research Council in June 1983 (Ballard 1989). This group was reconstituted in late 1984 as the AIDS Task Force to provide scientific and medical advice (Mindel and Kippax 2013). The National Advisory Committee on AIDS (NACAIDS) followed in November 1984 and provided advice on education and prevention. NACAIDS included state and federal government representatives (early on, Queensland refused to participate as its government did not support the inclusion of representatives from the gay community), representatives of the AIDS councils, the Australian Federation of Haemophilia and other key non-governmental organisations (Hulse 1997). The two advisory groups were designed to ensure information from affected communities, along with emerging clinical and research evidence, was reported directly to the health minister and his department (Mindel and Kippax 2013).

The two committees did not act in harmony. Early on, the AIDS Task Force sought to use its medical authority to dominate the agenda, suggesting government establish compulsory testing and notification, enact stronger legislative controls in relation to homosexuality, prostitution and injecting drug use and close gay entertainment venues

(Drielsma 1997). Blewett sought advice from NACAIDS, which argued that compulsory testing would drive people away and instead proposed the establishment of voluntary testing with counselling, peer-based support and nondiscriminatory care for people with AIDS (Drielsma 1997; Hulse 1997).

In November 1986, a third committee was established to manage the political response and ensure AIDS was not used as a political football (Blewett 1988). The Parliamentary Liaison Group, a nonpartisan committee of concerned federal Members of Parliament (MPs), was established to keep MPs abreast of the epidemic and the achievements of community-based education and prevention campaigns (Sendziuk 2003). Dr Peter Baume, opposition spokesman for health, played a critical role supporting Blewett through the management of divisive views within his own political party. Through the Parliamentary Liaison Group, the government was able to present a united political front on AIDS, which in turn enhanced the legitimacy of the response (Blewett 1988).

As the federal government confirmed its skill as consultant and negotiator, it also demonstrated clear leadership for the states and territories, which had initially considered AIDS too challenging and 'politically unattractive' (Misztal 1993: 125). Yet despite their general support, each jurisdiction had its own distinct legislative challenges—for example, disease monitoring, testing and data collection and service delivery procedures—to navigate (Misztal 1993). To implement the federal government's programs, the states and territories needed to engage with legislative frameworks to ensure the policy's overarching philosophical position of harm minimisation could be enacted (Madden and Wodak 2014). Not all state and territory governments embraced the principles of harm minimisation, community empowerment or the explicit education materials developed by the community. Queensland's conservative government, led by premier Joh Bjelke-Petersen, maintained homosexuality as a criminal act and refused to work with the local AIDS council or endorse its prevention efforts (Sendziuk 2003; Bowtell 2007).

Through concerted action, Blewett negotiated support at the 1985 Australian health ministers conference for the first National Health Strategy for the Control of AIDS—a precursor to the 1989 strategy (Department of Health 1986; Sendziuk 2003). As the federal government worked with the community to roll out its comprehensive and innovative package of prevention strategies—including the infamous 'Grim Reaper' advertising campaign in 1987—it worked with the states and territories to establish matched funding to support this effort. In establishing funding agreements, the Commonwealth stipulated that at least half the funds were to be spent on peer-led education and community programs, and one-quarter of the prevention budget was to be administered by local AIDS councils (Hulse 1997; Sendziuk 2003; Mindel and Kippax 2013). Queensland again opposed this, but not to be blindsided, Blewett set about identifying novel ways to transfer funds to support education in that state, including using the Sisters of Mercy as 'holy money launderers' (Blewett 1997: 177).

Overall, through the establishment of the three central advisory committees, along with intensive engagement with the states and territories, the government built national consensus on HIV/AIDS in a participatory, collaborative manner (Ballard 1989).

Enabling governance

Acknowledging the feasibility and effectiveness of the community-led response, government became an enabler of community action, actively supporting and funding campaigns (Ballard 1989; Misztal 1991; Plummer and Irwin 2006; Power 2011; Mindel and Kippax 2013). Kippax and Race (2003: 2) argued that 'prevention was all that there was and whatever the misgivings and lack of faith, as well as moral and ideological posturing, there was a sense of urgency', which empowered government to pursue community activism. Describing the adoption of contextual, innovative and courageous strategies, Blewett (1996: 343) acknowledged this 'heroic period' as a time when 'we were explorers in an unknown land with monsters lurking in every covert. It had all the exhilaration and the danger of making policy where there was none' (Blewett 1997: 178).

During this 'heroic period', the potential for community outrage at the production of explicit preventive education material was ever present, but this was greatly reduced by distribution and dissemination through locations where only affected communities would see them (such as the gay press, sex-on-premise venues and social venues) (Hulse 1997; Willett 2014). Some adverse media attention did emerge, but governments (state and federal) continued to support and fund these materials, particularly in light of growing evidence of their effectiveness in raising awareness of HIV and increasing rates of safe sex (Mindel and Kippax 2013).

Needle exchange programs were another example of an innovative, community-led harm-minimisation strategy that, coupled with the expansion of methadone maintenance treatment, became central to Australia's success in containing the spread of HIV, particularly through the community of injecting drug users (Madden and Wodak 2014). In 1985, following revelations that prime minister Bob Hawke's daughter was an injecting drug user, the federal government held a special premiers' conference, at which harm minimisation was officially adopted as part of the national drug policy—although how it was to be implemented in practice was not immediately apparent (Madden and Wodak 2014). The first needle exchange was established in 1986 in Sydney. This pilot was an illegal act of civil disobedience by local drug and alcohol workers, but the police did not prosecute and the NSW Government quickly responded by amending legislation and establishing a legal exchange program (Wodak and Lurie 1997; Madden and Wodak 2014). At the time, needle exchange was conceived as a 'plausible idea' rather than an intervention based on demonstrated effectiveness, but subsequent evaluation and research have demonstrated its effectiveness (Wodak and Lurie 1997). By 1993, all states had needle exchange programs (Wodak and Lurie 1997).

Another key intervention that saw the government lead the way in preventing the spread of HIV was in relation to protecting the blood supply (Plummer and Irwin 2005). Universal screening of the blood supply, adopted in April 1985, is attributed with reducing the transmission of HIV via medical procedures, from about 14 per cent in 1985 to less than 1 per cent in 1991–92 (Misztal 1991; Plummer and Irwin 2005; Mindel and Kippax 2013).

Overall, the first era of HIV/AIDS policy in Australia was characterised by strong leadership, effective partnerships, bipartisan political support and the active engagement of affected communities in the design, development and delivery of a multilevel strategy. In essence, this 'social public health' approach moved beyond traditional models of public health to recognise 'the collective nature of epidemics and work with affected communities and social networks to transform social relations' (Mindel and Kippax 2013: 350). The adoption by government of a social public health approach was groundbreaking for the time. Brown and colleagues (2014: 40) argue it demonstrates

> that an adaptive and politically active response working across multiple social, political, economic, behavioural and health-service levels, operating within supportive environments, are [sic] the most likely to reduce the transmission and impact of HIV.

Finally, as our narrative of the first era of policy draws to a close, we must acknowledge the affirmative evaluation of the first strategy and the sharp and continued decline in new HIV diagnoses following their peak in 1987 (Plummer and Irwin 2006). These outcomes provided government with confidence to continue to draw on the foundational principles of social public health in subsequent strategies, including the second national strategy, released in 1993 (Commonwealth of Australia 1993; Mindel and Kippax 2013). In essence, the foundations for policy success were laid early, but as we move to the next era, and the second act of our film, we see new challenges begin to emerge.

1996–2009: 'New hope, disinvestment and political neglect'

The third national strategy was released in 1996 at the start of a new era of HIV in Australia—a period Brown et al. (2014: 37) label a time of 'new hope, disinvestment and political neglect'. Many changes were taking place at social, biomedical, political and epidemiological levels. Medical advances and the arrival of highly active antiretroviral therapy (HAART) in 1996 heralded 'new hope'; HIV could now be seen as a long-term, manageable chronic condition rather than an incurable disease (Newman et al. 2010).

In the same year, Australia elected a new conservative Commonwealth Government, led by John Howard. Howard's self-described 'socially conservative' government stood in stark contrast to the Hawke/Keating Labor governments. Yet despite early concerns that the government's 'tough on drugs' response would impact on HIV policy, it maintained a bipartisan approach and health minister Michael Wooldridge quietly continued to support and fund HIV-targeted harm-minimisation strategies, including needle and syringe programs (Madden and Wodak 2014).

The third national strategy maintained the principles and goals of previous strategies, but was extended to include sexual health, hepatitis C and other communicable diseases (Department of Health and Family Services 1996; Mindel and Kippax 2013). This broadened policy framework led to the 'mainstreaming' of HIV funding, services and administrative processes within communicable disease structures (AFAO 2012). This was the first of many changes during this era that saw HIV policy shift from an innovative community-engaged space to 'a more "traditional" and "institutionalised" response' (Brown et al. 2014: 37). Advisory structures returned to the remit of elite experts (that is, doctors and bureaucrats), moving away from independent advice provided by affected communities (Bowtell 2007).

During this period, funding arrangements began to shift, in line with the neoliberalist agenda that was gaining momentum nationally and globally. The National Public Health Partnership established between the Commonwealth and states and territories developed outcome-based funding agreements, resulting in changes to service agreements and funding arrangements for community-based organisations (Bernard et al. 2008). In Victoria, this resulted in a 50 per cent decrease in funding for HIV programs as the conservative Victorian Government ceased the matched funding arrangement that had been in place for HIV prevention and services, and compulsory tendering was introduced (Bernard et al. 2008; Griew 2008). The result was a fracturing of partnerships and a significant loss of trust between the government and the community (Bernard et al. 2008).

On the eve of the fourth national strategy (1999–2004), there was a decreasing sense of urgency and an increasing level of political complacency in relation to HIV. For some, HIV had been controlled and significant investment was no longer needed (Moodie et al. 2003; Altman 2006). During this period, Tony Abbott assumed the role of federal health minister, resulting in further reductions in investment in programs that conflicted 'with the minister's support for "traditional values"' (Altman 2006: 52). Paradoxically, as funding began to decline, government interference increased, particularly in relation to the censorship of prevention materials (Altman 2006).

The loss of momentum that occurred during this era was also seen in some sections of the gay community, as media coverage, public support and awareness and community engagement began to decline (Whittaker 2011). However, after a period of relative stability, new HIV diagnoses began to rise between 1999 and 2006, particularly among gay men in Victoria and Queensland (Mindel and Kippax 2013). As a consequence, the need for renewed effort received some attention in the fifth national strategy (2005–08), which reemphasised prevention, education, early diagnosis and treatment (Mindel and Kippax 2013).

In 2007, a bolder analysis of the increasing incidence in HIV was driven by New South Wales, which established a national taskforce of leading social and epidemiological researchers, clinicians, state-based bureaucrats, HIV community members and an observer from the Commonwealth Government (Mindel and Kippax 2013). The taskforce debated explanations for the increased incidence, particularly in relation to changing sexual practices; however, New South Wales was able to demonstrate how—through ongoing commitment to partnerships with the community and continued investment in community-led education and prevention programs—it had managed to contain incidence rates (O'Donnell et al. 2010). In contrast, Victoria's decreased investment and fracturing relationships appeared to be associated with an increasing incidence of HIV diagnoses (Bernard et al. 2008; Fairley et al. 2008).

As we draw an end to the second act, we illustrate that, despite the establishment of strong foundations in the first era, temporal and contextual elements in the second era challenged the policy success. Biomedical advancements in HIV were groundbreaking, but these fed into neoliberal discourses of individual responsibility for health. The role of government as consultant, negotiator and enabler changed to a new role as controller of (shifting) funding arrangements and service agreements. Increasing tensions emerged between policy partners and fatigue rose in the gay community—battle weary after years on the front line of the response. Incidence rates started to rise, particularly in states that had disinvested. The focus on social public health began to wane and biomedicalisation took hold. However, although tensions emerged, the core underlying values base of human rights and partnerships continued to drive a multifaceted, collaborative national policy response.

2010 – present: Biomedicine and a time of targets

Since the introduction of HAART in 1996, biomedical advances in HIV prevention and treatment have gained considerable pace. In the third policy era, biomedicine has assumed centre-stage and now dominates the HIV landscape. During this time, the Sixth National HIV Strategy 2010–2013 was implemented and the Seventh National HIV Strategy 2014–2017 was released (an eighth strategy is in development). Drawing on the 2011 United Nations Political Declaration on HIV and AIDs (UNAIDS 2011), the seventh strategy was the first national strategy to set key targets guiding Australia 'towards the elimination of HIV transmission by 2020' (Department of Health 2014: 1; O'Donnell and Perche 2016).

During this era, clinical trials have played a central role in the increasing predominance of biomedicine. In particular, the results of the 2011 HIV Prevention Trials Network 052 trial were instrumental in demonstrating the efficacy of antiretroviral treatment (ART) in reducing HIV transmission among serodiscordant couples, when the HIV-positive partner had an undetectable viral load (Cohen et al. 2011). From this, the Joint United Nations Programme on HIV/AIDS (UNAIDS) moved to establish treatment as prevention as a core policy agenda. Treatment as prevention is founded on the principles that regular HIV testing, early initiation of treatment and achievement of an undetectable viral load are central to achieving reductions in the transmission of HIV and the elimination of the disease (Montaner et al. 2014; UNAIDS 2014a, 2014b).

To promote regular testing, Australia has adopted key testing technologies, including rapid point-of-care testing for HIV—a quick and reliable alternative to conventional testing that provides results within 30 minutes, without the need for clinical supervision or laboratory analysis (Arora et al. 2013). Australia approved point-of-care testing in 2011 as part of its National HIV Testing Policy and has supported its rollout across nonclinical and community settings including sex-on-premise venues (Mutch et al. 2017).

PrEP, a third key element of biomedicine's HIV prevention armoury, has been adopted in Australia. The 2010 iPrEx trial demonstrated the efficacy of Truvada (an ART) for PrEP to prevent the acquisition of HIV (Grant et al. 2014; Brown et al. 2015). In 2018, the Australian Pharmaceutical Benefits Advisory Committee approved its inclusion on the PBS.

This third era of 'targets and biomedicine' is a time of hope and anticipation as we potentially near the 'end of AIDS' and set targets to end new cases of HIV by 2020 (Holt 2017). We now have the biotechnology to prevent the transmission of HIV with treatment as prevention and PrEP, but as a consequence we see an increasing dominance and influence of biomedicalisation on policy formation (Aggleton and Kippax 2014). Policy attention has shifted to the 'front end' of the response, diverted from the social and legislative factors that were the cornerstone of our early response and fundamental to a social public health approach. Tensions have emerged between partnerships—particularly affected communities and policymakers—over the focus on the biomedical at the expense of the social, particularly the psychosocial needs of PLHIV (Cameron and Godwin 2014). Policy and associated funding are increasingly attached to the number of people tested on treatment and with undetectable viral loads. But through these changes the core values and program base of the Australian national HIV policy continues, although tensions remain between partners due to funding uncertainty and tender processes that pit partners against each other (O'Keefe and Forbes 2015).

Despite these challenges, target setting has brought partners together with renewed energy as HIV becomes an item on the policy agenda for politicians keen to 'end HIV' on their watch. Policymakers, clinicians, researchers and communities are again working collaboratively to drive programmatic and policy development and maintain the core values of Australia's HIV response (AFAO 2012; Muchamore 2015).

Analysis and conclusions

Australia's policy response to HIV/AIDS provides key lessons for understanding policy success. First, context matters. The early phases of the epidemic occurred within a unique social and political context—a 'perfect storm' in which new ways of doing public health policy based on human rights and community partnerships was emerging. Advocacy, the mobilisation of affected communities and a government unafraid to make bold policy decisions and take on the role of consultant, negotiator and enabler were central to the collective development of a pragmatic, multifaceted policy response. Core values, programmatic design, multifaceted policy instruments and bipartisan political support central to the first era have carried through three subsequent eras and seven national strategies. However, while there is a tendency to bask in this success, critical analysis using a temporal lens demonstrates that some key features have waned over time as the context of HIV has changed, particularly in relation to biomedical advancements, neoliberal policy agendas and the corresponding impact on relationships between governments and community organisations.

What were key foundations of policy success? Australia's response to HIV/AIDS was bipartisan, collaborative and well funded (Holt 2017). Early success is attributed to immediate action by affected communities (particularly gay men, people who inject drugs and sex workers and Aboriginal and Torres Strait Islander peoples), who drove education and prevention messages, resulting in changes in community practices around safe sex and safe injecting (Plummer and Irwin 2006; Aggleton and Kippax 2014; Holt 2017). Success at the policy level is embedded in the government's role as an enabler, harnessing community mobilisation (Brown et al. 2014). Collaborative partnerships between affected communities, community organisations, clinicians, researchers and governments were fundamental.

A 'social public health approach' was foundational in directing the development and delivery of policy (Aggleton and Kippax 2014). This broader social focus facilitated and enabled the social and legal environments for priority populations and sustained government funding of multipronged interventions across national, state, community and health services (Brown et al. 2014). Multiple forms of evidence drawn from the community and research informed 'an effective yet malleable response' (Aggleton and Kippax 2014: 189; Brown et al. 2014).

Sustained leadership was a key feature. The role of Blewett and his pragmatic, bipartisan approach—which actively engaged the community and allowed the states and territories to drive and develop interventions and strategies particular to their localised epidemics—was central to Australia's success (Brown et al. 2014).

Advocacy and investment were also critical to policy success (Brown et al. 2014). Yet, despite international recognition of Australia's effort, fatigue, complacency, political drift and some fractured partnerships have impeded recent progress and sustained low incidence rates, and the success of new biomedical treatment and prevention has also contributed to HIV slipping from the centre of the policy agenda (Moodie et al. 2003;

Cameron and Godwin 2014; O'Donnell and Perche 2016). This slip began in the 1990s with the 'mainstreaming' of HIV funding and services (Bowtell 2005). Complacency and 'HIV fatigue' occurred in the policy arena, in health departments and the broader community as the 'threat' subsided in Australia (Moodie et al. 2003). However, differences across the states and territories in the types of prevention strategies used and financial investments made are inextricably connected to the effectiveness of the ongoing response to HIV (Bernard et al. 2008). State and territory governments that reduced investment and capacity, particularly in the second era, were 'less successful in responding to the complexities of changing epidemics, social practices and cultural engagement' (Brown et al. 2014: 37).

Future challenges

Australia is at a crossroads in HIV; it is a time of both 'unprecedented opportunity and ongoing challenge' (Department of Health 2014: iii). The biomedicalisation of prevention and treatment has given us the knowledge to substantially reduce new HIV infections and perhaps herald the 'end of AIDS', but after nearly four decades of the epidemic, along with restrictions on national budgets and health spending, there is some sense of weariness and complacency (Whittaker 2014). Continuing policy success requires regeneration of partnerships, with the agility to respond to changing epidemiological and medical developments. Organisations representing PLHIV emphasise future challenges of better recognising and meeting the needs of marginalised communities not currently benefiting equally from Australia's HIV response (Kirby Institute 2018). These challenges include the meaningful involvement of and expert contributions from PLHIV (NAPWHA 2017); we cannot risk leaving behind those communities most affected.

Future challenges also include an ageing population of PLHIV with increasing comorbidities, the increasing diversity of affected communities, rising rates of HIV in particular communities, including Aboriginal and Torres Strait Island peoples, and a complexity of interactions between biomedical, social, behavioural and structural responses (Aggleton et al. 2011; Brown et al. 2014; Holt 2017; Ward et al. 2018). These are complex and crosscutting issues that need careful policy development and analysis.

From the beginning of the epidemic in Australia, community groups highlighted the need to address structural barriers and enablers to reduce the epidemic. Criminal sanctions relating to HIV transmission, the lack of drug law reform and the continued criminalisation of sex work still hamper evidence-based health promotion (ACT Human Rights and Discrimination Commission 2013). A human rights agenda requires decriminalisation of drug use to provide an enabling environment for health promotion and decriminalisation of peer distribution of syringes (Cameron and Godwin 2014). Decriminalisation of adult sex work is needed to ensure continuing safety and effective HIV prevention in the sex industry (Bates and Berg 2014). Law reform to enhance enabling environments requires political leadership and commitment beyond the health sector, with the support of champions and advocacy from multiple sectors. Long-established structures and agencies in the health and community sectors need to innovate and evolve (Muchamore 2015).

The values base of human rights, partnership and collaboration has underpinned the HIV policy response with great success, but we still have a way to go. Social public health alongside biomedical advances must drive policy success into the fifth decade of the national HIV/AIDS policy if we are to see real policy success and the elimination of new cases of HIV and ensure no one is left behind (Kippax et al. 2013). Having now looked through our historical film of Australia's response to HIV/AIDS and considered the intersections between the social, political and generational contexts that drove policy and action during those early years, we leave our cinema goers with an important point of reflection: would such a successful policy response be possible today?

References

ACT Human Rights and Discrimination Commission 2013. *Legal issues in Australian public health: A series of 7 papers on the impacts of discrimination and criminalisation on public health approaches to blood borne viruses and sexually transmissible infections*. Prepared for the Commonwealth Ministerial Advisory Committee on Blood-Borne Viruses and STIs. Canberra.

Aggleton, P. and Kippax, S. 2014. 'Australia's HIV prevention response: Introduction to the special issue.' *AIDS Education and Prevention* 26: 187–90. doi.org/10.1521/aeap.2014.26.3.187.

Aggleton, P., Yankah, E. and Crewe, M. 2011. 'Education and HIV/AIDS: 30 years on.' *AIDS Education and Prevention* 23(6): 495–507. doi.org/10.1521/aeap.2011.23.6.495.

Altman, D. 1994. *Power and Community: Organizational and cultural responses to AIDS*. London: Taylor & Francis.

Altman, D. 2006. 'The margins of our attention: 25 years of HIV and AIDS.' *The Monthly* 58(Dec–Jan): 52–6.

Applied Economics 2003. *Returns on Investment in Public Health: An epidemiological and economic analysis prepared for the Department of Health and Ageing*. Canberra: Department of Health and Ageing.

Arora, D. R., Maheshwari, M. and Arora, B. 2013. 'Rapid point-of-care testing for detection of HIV and clinical monitoring.' *ISRN AIDS* 2013. doi.org/10.1155/2013/287269.

Australian Federation of AIDS Organisations (AFAO) 2012. *Implementing the United Nations Political Declaration on HIV/AIDS in Australia's Domestic HIV Response: Turning political will into action*. Sydney: AFAO.

Ballard, J. 1989. 'The politics of AIDS.' In H. Gardner (ed.), *The Politics of Health: The Australian experience*. Melbourne: Churchill Livingstone.

Bates, J. and Berg, R. 2014. 'Sex workers as safe sex advocates: Sex workers protect both themselves and the wider community from HIV.' *AIDS Education and Prevention* 26: 191–201. doi.org/10.1521/aeap.2014.26.3.191.

Bernard, D., Kippax, S. and Baxter, D. 2008. 'Effective partnership and adequate investment underpin a successful response: Key factors in dealing with HIV increases.' *Sexual Health* 5: 193–201. doi.org/10.1071/SH07078.

Blewett, N. 1988. 'Political dimensions of AIDS.' *AIDS* 2: S235–S238. doi.org/10.1097/00002030-198800001-00036.

Blewett, N. 1996. 'Valuing the past … investing in the future.' *Australian and New Zealand Journal of Public Health* 20(4): 343–5. doi.org/10.1111/j.1467-842X.1996.tb01042.x.

Blewett, N. 1997. 'An inside view: Comments on Hulse's "Australia's public health response to HIV and HCV: A role for 'affected' communities".' *Drug and Alcohol Review* 16: 177–8. doi.org/10.1080/09595239700186471.

Bowtell, W. 1997. 'A successful model of public health management: Comments on Hulse's "Australia's public health response to HIV and HCV: A role for 'affected' communities".' *Drug and Alcohol Review* 16: 180–1.

Bowtell, W. 2005. *Australia's Response to HIV/AIDS 1982–2005*. Sydney: Lowy Institute for International Policy.

Bowtell, W. 2007. 'Applying the paradox of prevention: Eradicate HIV.' *Griffith Review* 17(Spring): 11–42.

Brandt, A. 1986. 'AIDS: from social history to social policy.' *Law, Medicine & Health Care: A publication of the American Society of Law & Medicine* 14: 231. doi.org/10.1111/j.1748-720X.1986.tb00990.x.

Brown, G., O'Donnell, D., Crooks, L. and Lake, R. 2014. 'Mobilisation, politics, investment and constant adaptation: Lessons from the Australian health-promotion response to HIV.' *Health Promotion Journal of Australia* 25: 35–41. doi.org/10.1071/HE13078.

Brown, G., Reeders, D., Dowsett, G. W., Ellard, J., Carman, M., Hendry, N. and Wallace, J. 2015. 'Investigating combination HIV prevention: Isolated interventions or complex system.' *Journal of the International AIDS Society* 18(1). doi.org/10.7448/IAS.18.1.20499.

Cameron, S. and Godwin, J. 2014. 'Barriers to legal and human rights in Australia in the era of HIV treatment as prevention.' *AIDS Education and Prevention* 26: 202–13. doi.org/10.1521/aeap.2014.26.3.202.

Centers for Disease Control and Prevention (CDC) 2006. Evolution of HIV/AIDS prevention programs: United States, 1981–2006.' *MMWR: Morbidity and Mortality Weekly Report* 55(21): 597.

Centers for Disease Control and Prevention (CDC) 2018. *Estimated HIV incidence and prevalence in the United States, 2010–2015*. HIV Surveillance Supplemental Report 23 (No. 1). Atlanta, GA: CDC.

Cohen, M. S., Chen, Y. Q., McCauley, M., Gamble, T., Hosseinipour, M. C., Kumarasamy, N., Hakim, J. G., Kumwenda, J., Grinsztejn, B., Pilotto, J. H. S., Godbole, S. V., Mehendale, S., Chariyalertsak, S., Santos, B. R., Mayer, K. H., Hoffman, I. F., Eshleman, S. H., Piwowar-Manning, E., Wang, L., Makhema, J., Mills, L. A., De Bruyn, G., Sanne, I., Eron, J., Gallant, J., Havlir, D., Swindells, S., Ribaudo, H., Elharrar, V., Burns, D., Taha, T. E., Nielsen-Saines, K., Celentano, D., Essex, M. and Fleming, T. R. 2011. 'Prevention of HIV-1 infection with early antiretroviral therapy.' *The New England Journal of Medicine* 365: 493–505. doi.org/10.1056/NEJMoa1105243.

Commonwealth of Australia 1989. *National HIV/AIDS strategy: A policy information paper*. Canberra: AGPS.

Commonwealth of Australia 1993. *National HIV/AIDS Strategy 1993–94 to 1995–96: Valuing the past … investing in the future*. Canberra: AGPS.

Department of Health 1986. *Australia's Response to AIDS*. Canberra: Commonwealth of Australia.

Department of Health 2014. *Seventh National HIV Strategy 2014–2017*. Canberra: Commonwealth of Australia.

Department of Health and Family Services 1996. *Partnerships in Practice: National HIV/AIDS strategy 1996–97 to 1998–99*. Canberra: AGPS.

Donovan, B., Harcourt, C., Egger, S., Watchirs Smith, L., Schneider, K., Kaldor, J., Chen, M., Fairley, C. and Tabrizi, S. 2012. *The sex industry in New South Wales: A report to the NSW Ministry of Health*. Sydney: Kirby Institute.

Drielsma, P. 1997. 'AIDS policy and public health models: An Australian analysis.' *Australian Journal of Social Issues* 32: 87–99. doi.org/10.1002/j.1839-4655.1997.tb01293.x.

Fairley, C. K., Grulich, A. E., Imrie, J. C. and Pitts, M. 2008. 'Investment in HIV prevention works: A natural experiment.' *Sexual Health* 5: 207–10. doi.org/10.1071/SH08017.

Feachem, R. 1995. *Valuing the Past … Investing in the Future: Evaluation of the National HIV/AIDS Strategy 1993–94 to 1995–96*. Canberra: AGPS.

Grant, R. M., Anderson, P. L., McMahan, V., Liu, A., Amico, K. R., Mehrotra, M. and Buchbinder, S. 2014. 'Uptake of pre-exposure prophylaxis, sexual practices, and HIV incidence in men and transgender women who have sex with men: A cohort study.' *The Lancet Infectious Diseases* 14: 820–9. doi.org/10.1016/S1473-3099(14)70847-3.

Griew, R. 2008. 'Policy and strategic implications of Australia's divergent HIV epidemic among gay men.' *Sexual Health* 2: 203–5. doi.org/10.1.1.553.977.

Gupta, G. R., Parkhurst, J. O., Ogden, J. A., Aggleton, P. and Mahal, A. 2008. 'Structural approaches to HIV prevention.' *The Lancet* 372: 764–75. doi.org/10.1016/S0140-6736(08)60887-9.

Holt, M. 2017. 'Progress and challenges in ending HIV and AIDS in Australia.' *AIDS and Behavior* 21(2): 331–4. doi.org/10.1007/s10461-016-1642-0.

Hulse, G. K. 1997. 'Australia's public health response to HIV and HCV: A role for "affected" communities.' *Drug and Alcohol Review* 16(2): 171–6. doi.org/10.1080/09595239700186461.

Joint United Nations Programme on HIV/AIDS (UNAIDS) 2011. *Political Declaration on HIV and AIDS: Intensifying our efforts to eliminate HIV and AIDS*. Geneva: UNAIDS.

Joint United Nations Programme on HIV/AIDS (UNAIDS) 2014a. *90–90–90: An ambitious treatment target to help end the AIDS epidemic*. Geneva: UNAIDS.

Joint United Nations Programme on HIV/AIDS (UNAIDS) 2014b. *Fast-Track: Ending the AIDS epidemic by 2030*. Geneva: UNAIDS.

Kippax, S. and Race, K. 2003. 'Sustaining safe practice: Twenty years on.' *Social Science and Medicine* 57: 1–12. doi.org/10.1016/S0277-9536(02)00303-9.

Kippax, S., Stephenson, N., Parker, R. G. and Aggleton, P. 2013. 'Between individual agency and structure in HIV prevention: Understanding the middle ground of social practice.' *American Journal of Public Health* 103: 1367. doi.org/10.2105/AJPH.2013.301301.

Kirby Institute 2018. *HIV in Australia: Annual surveillance short report 2018*. Sydney: Kirby Institute.

Kirwan, P., Chau, C., Brown, A., Gill, O., Delpech, V. and Contributors 2016. *HIV in the UK: 2016 Report*. London: Public Health England.

Kwon, A. J., Anderson, C. J., Kerr, J. C., Thein, M. H.-H., Zhang, G. L., Iversen, P. J., Dore, P. G., Kaldor, P. J., Law, P. M., Maher, P. L. and Wilson, P. D. 2012. 'Estimating the cost-effectiveness of needle-syringe programs in Australia.' *AIDS* 26: 2201–10. doi.org/10.1097/QAD.0b013e3283578b5d.

Madden, A. and Wodak, A. 2014. 'Australia's response to HIV among people who inject drugs.' *AIDS Education and Prevention* 26: 234–44. doi.org/10.1521/aeap.2014.26.3.234.

Mindel, A. and Kippax, S. 2013. 'A national strategic approach to improving the health of gay and bisexual men: Experience in Australia.' In S. Aral, K. Fenton and J. Lipshutz (eds), *The New Public Health and STD/HIV Prevention: Personal, public and health system approaches*. New York: Springer. doi.org/10.1007/978-1-4614-4526-5_17.

Misztal, B. A. 1991. 'HIV/AIDS policies in Australia: Bureaucracy and collective action.' *International Journal of Sociology and Social Policy* 11(4): 62–82. doi.org/10.1108/eb013137.

Misztal, B. 1993. 'Management of HIV/AIDS in the Australian federal system.' *Social Policy & Administration* 27(2): 124–40. doi.org/10.1111/j.1467-9515.1993.tb00396.x.

Montaner, J., Lima, V., Harrigan, P., Lourenço, L., Yip, B., Nosyk, B., Wood, E., Kerr, T., Shannon, K., Moore, D. and Hogg, R. S. 2014. 'Expansion of HAART coverage is associated with sustained decreases in HIV/AIDS morbidity, mortality and HIV transmission: The "HIV treatment as prevention" experience in a Canadian setting.' *PLOS One* 9(2): e87872. doi.org/10.1371/journal.pone.0087872.

Moodie, R., Edwards, A. and Payne, M. 2003. 'Review of the national HIV/AIDS strategy 1999–2000 to 2003–04: Getting back on track … revitalising Australia's response to HIV/AIDS.' In A. Wilson, N. Partridge and L. Calzavara (eds), *2002 Reviews of the National HIV/AIDS and Hepatitis C Strategies and Strategic Research*. Canberra: Commonwealth of Australia.

Muchamore, I. 2015. 'Communities, policies and the enabling environment.' *HIV Australia* 13: 5–6.

Mutch, A., Lui, C. W., Dean, J., Mao, L., Lemoire, J., Debattista, J., Howard, C., Whittaker, A. and Fitzgerald, L. 2017. 'Increasing HIV testing among hard-to-reach groups: Examination of RAPID, a community-based testing service in Queensland, Australia.' *BMC Health Services Research* 17. doi.org/10.1186/s12913-017-2249-5.

National Association of People with HIV Australia (NAPWHA) 2017. *Annual Report 2016–2017*. Sydney: NAPWHA.

Newman, C., Mao, L., Canavan, P., Kidd, M., Saltman, D. and Kippax, S. 2010. 'HIV generations? Generational discourse in interviews with Australian general practitioners and their HIV positive gay male patients.' *Social Science and Medicine* 70: 1721–7. doi.org/10.1016/j.socscimed.2010.02.006.

Nous Group 2015. 'The Nous Project: Exploring the value of the community-based organisations in Australia's HIV response.' *HIV Australia* 14(2): 12–14.

O'Donnell, D. and Perche, D. 2016. 'Resetting the agenda: The makings of "a new era".' *Sexual Health* 13: 328–34. doi.org/10.1071/SH16010.

O'Donnell, D., Grulich, A., Garsia, R., Parkhill, N. and Browne, K. 2010. 'HIV in NSW in 2010: Sustaining success in an evolving epidemic.' *NSW Public Health Bulletin* 21: 49–53. doi.org/10.1071/NB10022.

O'Keefe, F. and Forbes, L. 2015. 'Target-setting: Australia and the global context.' *HIV Australia* 13(1): 4.

Perrow, C. and Guillen, M. F. 1990. *The AIDS Disaster: The failure of organizations in New York and the nation*. New Haven, CT: Yale University Press.

Plummer, D. and Irwin, L. 2006. 'Grassroots activities, national initiatives and HIV prevention: Clues to explain Australia's dramatic early success in controlling the HIV epidemic.' *International Journal of STD & AIDS* 17(12): 787–93.

Power, J. 2011. *Movement, Knowledge, Emotion: Gay activism and HIV/AIDS in Australia*. Canberra: ANU E Press.

Robinson, S. and Wilson, E. 2012. 'Working together? Medical professionals, gay community organisations and the response to HIV/AIDS in Australia, 1983–1985.' *Social History of Medicine* 25(3): 701–18. doi.org/10.1093/shm/hkr172.

Sendziuk, P. 2003. *Learning to Trust: Australian responses to AIDS*. Sydney: UNSW Press.

Ward, J., Costello-Czok, M., Willis, J., Saunders, M. and Shannon, C. 2014. 'So far, so good: Maintenance of prevention is required to stem HIV incidence in Aboriginal and Torres Strait Islander communities in Australia.' *AIDS Education and Prevention* 26: 267–79. doi.org/10.1521/aeap.2014.26.3.267.

Ward, J., McManus, H., McGregor, S., Hawke, K., Giele, C., Su, J. Y., McDonald, A., Guy, R., Donovan, B. and Kaldor, J. M. 2018. 'HIV incidence in Indigenous and non-Indigenous populations in Australia: A population-level observational study.' *The Lancet HIV* 5(9): e506–e514. doi.org/10.1016/S2352-3018(18)30135-8.

Whittaker, A. M. 1992. 'Living with HIV: Resistance by positive people.' *Medical Anthropology Quarterly* 6: 385–90. doi.org/10.1525/maq.1992.6.4.02a00050.

Whittaker, B. 2011. 'Australia should lead a global HIV prevention revolution.' *HIV Australia* 9: 7–8.

Whittaker, B. 2014. 'Transforming Australia's HIV prevention and treatment efforts to achieve an AIDS-free generation: The United Nations political declaration on HIV/AIDS and the Melbourne declaration "Action on HIV".' *Sexual Health* 11: 101–6. doi.org/10.1071/SH13056.

Willett, G. 2014. 'How we saved our lives: The gay community and the Australian response to AIDS.' *HIV Australia* 12(3): 4.

Wodak, A. and Lurie, P. 1997. 'A tale of two countries: Attempts to control HIV among injecting drug users in Australia and the United States.' *Journal of Drug Issues* 27: 117–34. doi.org/10.1177/002204269702700108.

3

The Higher Education Contribution Scheme: Keeping tertiary education affordable and accessible

Timothy Higgins[1]

A policy success?

The Higher Education Contribution Scheme (HECS)[2] was a key part of the 1988 Dawkins reforms to the Australian higher education landscape.[3] In 1987, there was an urgent economic case for expansion of the higher education sector, which led then education minister John Dawkins to embark on a path of ambitious and radical policy reform. The organisational process was efficient and rapid and the capable individuals assisting Dawkins were deliberately chosen, setting out persuasive arguments

1 I would like to acknowledge and thank Bruce Chapman and Meredith Edwards for their helpful comments on an earlier version of this chapter, and John Dawkins for directing me to a number of useful resources as I researched the early history of HECS.

2 HECS was renamed HECS-HELP after being incorporated into the umbrella Higher Education Loan Program (HELP) introduced in the 2003–04 Budget. We refer to HECS and HECS-HELP interchangeably in this chapter.

3 The focus of this chapter is on HECS, rather than the broader Dawkins higher education reforms, of which HECS was just one, albeit central, part. For a detailed insider's account of the development of HECS, see Edwards et al. (2001). For comprehensive accounts of the history, development and assessment of the consequences of the Dawkins reforms more broadly, see Macintyre et al. (2017) and Croucher et al. (2013).

for student contributions and carefully designed policy features and parameters that were critical to the acceptance of HECS. HECS has successfully facilitated the growth in higher education participation and graduate outcomes that motivated its development. The policy has broad public and political support and endures 30 years after implementation. It is also a policy export success, with many countries adopting income-contingent loan (ICL) schemes following Australia's pioneering lead. Its endurance, broad public and political acceptance and international adoption are testament to the operational efficiency and economic and social fairness of HECS.

A summary of why HECS is considered a policy success follows. The remaining sections of this chapter set out in greater detail the context, motivation, people involved, development and delivery processes, policy changes since implementation and the challenges and risks HECS faces today.

Programmatic assessment

The political and economic environment of the 1980s set the scene for the development of HECS. As the 1980s progressed, it was clear that, for the sake of productivity and prosperity, a larger skilled workforce was needed, and there was increasing unmet demand by school completers for university places. Fiscal pressures meant it was neither politically nor economically attractive for government to fund expansion of the higher education sector predominantly through public funds.

It was also apparent that those attending university were predominantly from the middle and upper classes and, moreover, the private benefits for those with university degrees were substantial. It was therefore unfair that taxpayers should be footing the bill for privileged students to attend university. This amounted to 'middle-class welfare'. These arguments were used to justify the public value proposition that students should contribute to the costs of their education.

Abolition of fees under the Whitlam Government in 1974 was considered to be a central element of Australian Labor Party (ALP) ideology, with so-called free education on the ALP platform; thus, the reintroduction of fees appeared politically implausible. Nor, it was argued, did fee reintroduction make sense on equity grounds, since upfront fees would harm access for poorer students. The challenge facing Dawkins and the Labor Government in 1987 was to finance expansion of the higher education sector through contributions from the students who directly benefited, but in a way that did not involve reintroduction of upfront tuition fees.

The attraction of HECS was that it provided students with a deferred loan to cover tuition fees, ensuring that those without upfront funds could still participate. Unlike conventional loans, HECS was an ICL, such that repayments would be a proportion of income, repaid only if and when income exceeded average earnings, thereby reducing to zero a debtor's risk of default and minimising financial hardship. Thus, only relatively well-off debtors would repay, and the scheme was 'fair' because repayments would be made only by those with above-average earnings.

The evidence is compelling that HECS achieved its intended social outcomes by successfully facilitating expansion of the higher education system and graduate population without compromising access. Although the introduction of HECS meant that students were faced with fees—albeit deferred—the revenue HECS provided to universities created places for many who were previously turned away. Following implementation, much of the unmet demand by school completers was met and growth in the number of domestic students outpaced population growth, increasing from 2.3 per cent of the estimated resident population in 1985 to 3.3 per cent by 1995 (James et al. 2013). By 2016, the higher education sector's domestic student load (in equivalent full-time student load) had reached 740,223—more than double the 1987 level—and more than 2.5 million individuals have now benefited from the scheme (Ey 2018). The increased participation rates have translated into a more educated and employable workforce, with the proportion of the working-age population with a degree rising from 8 per cent in 1988 to 31 per cent in 2018 (ABS 2017).

Research undertaken soon after its implementation found HECS had little effect on deterring enrolments. While absolute increases in participation numbers were higher among more advantaged students, there was little change in the proportions of applicants from different socioeconomic groups: 'The tide of expanded participation lifted all boats' (James et al. 2013: 141). Changes to HECS parameters over the intervening years have pushed a greater share of costs on to students, but despite these and other changes, research has shown that, on balance, neither the introduction of HECS nor subsequent policy change has significantly affected participation or the socioeconomic mix of students attending university (Chapman and Nicholls 2013; James et al. 2013).

As intended, HECS shifted the costs of higher education from the public to the students who benefited directly. Following the introduction of HECS, the public share of expenditure on higher education declined sharply while the private share increased. In 1987, Commonwealth funding made up more than 80 per cent of university income, whereas in 2017 it covered close to 40 per cent of spending on universities (excluding outlays and subsidies from unpaid Higher Education Loans Program, or HELP, loans) (Norton et al. 2018). That the majority of Australian tertiary education expenditure is derived from private sources contrasts with the Organisation for Economic Co-operation and Development (OECD) average split of 70 per cent public and 30 per cent private (OECD 2017). Nevertheless, overall funding remains internationally competitive; total investment in tertiary education in Australia in 2014 was 1.8 per cent of gross domestic product (GDP), exceeding the OECD average of 1.6 per cent (OECD 2017: Table B2.3). It can be argued that, by reducing government spending while ensuring a healthy higher education sector, HECS has succeeded in facilitating the affordable expansion of the sector.

However, quantifying the private and public returns to higher education is problematic, and what constitutes affordability is subjective. The debate about the 'correct' level of student charges versus public funding continues, yet the arguments put forward in 1988 for student contributions still hold today; graduates continue to receive very high private benefits from university (Daly et al. 2015) and the socioeconomic mix of participants is still weighted towards the middle and upper classes.

Process assessment

The policy process moved quickly following the appointment in July 1987 of Dawkins as minister for the Department of Employment, Education and Training (DEET), with HECS becoming law only 18 months later, on 1 January 1989. Key to the success were the drive and focus of Dawkins and the rigour involved in the policy design and decision-making process. Dawkins selected skilled advisors to review the higher education sector and gather information that supported the case for change. The team included ANU economist Bruce Chapman, whom Dawkins tasked with setting out options for student contributions. Despite the speed of delivery, the policy idea of HECS was not conceived or proposed from the outset. There was no published research paper setting out the idea to which the government could refer. Instead, the Wran committee, established by Dawkins to review the different funding options set out by Chapman, objectively assessed options before settling on HECS, which seemed to meet the needs for expansion via user pays while not harming access. Edwards et al. (2001: 134) remark on the importance of the 'intellectual depth and substance' of the analytical stage of the policy design process.

Edwards also recalls that, while the consultation process was brief, it was particularly well focused (personal correspondence). The objectivity and rigour of the analysis of the problems with existing funding arrangements and options for reform, and the clear articulation of the economic arguments, helped Dawkins and his supporters deliver the policy.

Political assessment

The endurance of HECS is a testament to its success, as both major political parties view it as an essential component of the Australian higher education system. HECS is regarded by the media and policy commentators as a key example of Australia's policy export success stories. Following Australia's demonstration of the feasibility of an ICL for higher education tuition, ICL schemes were adopted in eight other countries, including New Zealand (in 1992), the United Kingdom (1997), Ethiopia (2001), Hungary (2003) and South Korea (2011), with other countries currently seriously investigating implementation, including Colombia, Brazil and Malaysia (Chapman 2018).

Public, industry and academic acceptance and acknowledgement of the success of HECS are also apparent through the accolades lauded on Chapman—widely regarded as the 'architect' of HECS. Most recently, this has included the *Australian Financial Review*'s Higher Education Lifetime Achievement Award (Dodd 2017), for which the judges noted that, because of HECS, 'Australia has been able to expand access to higher education in an equitable and cost-effective way'. The Australian HECS system has also been lauded in the international media (see, for example, Chingos and Dynarksi 2018).

While the success of HECS has led to domestic expansion into other education sectors, this has also revealed limitations and risks. Expansion into the vocational education sector through the introduction of vocational education and training (VET) FEE-HELP in 2008 exposed an imbalance in the risk-sharing arrangements between educational institutions and government. The current arrangement of capped and uniform HECS charges has also limited incentives for the higher education sector to innovate and diversify. HECS has been resilient and endured for the past 30 years, but the rising stock and cost of debt and calls to reform the higher education sector pose challenges. The pressures and challenges facing HECS are discussed in the final section of this chapter.

Setting the scene

Before 1973, students paid tuition fees to attend university in Australia, although the majority of students were on scholarships and fees covered only 15 per cent of the costs of tuition. The full abolition of fees in 1973 by the Whitlam Government became a key feature of the ALP's platform and ideology. Unsurprisingly, this was particularly popular among students and, as demand and enrolments increased throughout the 1970s, public funding for the university sector became strained. Subsequent attempts to reintroduce fees for first degrees under the Fraser Government failed, due in part to strong student protests. The Fraser Government introduced fees for second and higher degree students (Edwards et al. 2001), but pressure on education funding continued to grow. Despite recognition of the need to expand the supply of higher education places to increase skills and reduce youth unemployment, public funding as a proportion of GDP fell from 1.36 per cent in 1975 to 1.08 per cent by 1982 (Dawkins 1987a).

In 1983, the new Hawke Labor Government came to power, inheriting a dire budgetary position (Dawkins 2018). A slowing economy and global recession in the early 1980s had put considerable pressure on government, and Labor responded by embarking on significant policy reforms, including financial deregulation to improve competition and economic efficiency. A surging trade deficit led to a decline in the Australian dollar and expansion of the financial sector drove up inflation. Deteriorating conditions in the economy led to treasurer Paul Keating's provocative warning in 1986 that Australia risked becoming 'a banana republic'. In 1987, Labor announced plans for microeconomic reform, but it was clear that fiscal constraints meant the university sector could not expect an increase in public spending (Macintyre et al. 2017). By 1987, the university sector was reliant for 85 per cent of its revenue on the federal government, while public funding had dropped to 1 per cent of GDP (Dawkins 1987a).

Despite the moves towards deregulation and market-based competition in other parts of the economy, Labor's ideology of 'free' education and fears that fees would limit equality of access inhibited plans to open up domestic higher education enrolments to market forces (Norton 2013). While the domestic market remained constrained, in 1986, the government opened the higher education sector to full-fee-paying international students, removing caps on numbers and allowing universities to retain the majority of tuition fees (Macintyre et al. 2017). However, in contrast with the present situation, where full-fee international students make up over 17 per cent of university revenue (Universities Australia 2015), in 1987, international student enrolments numbered only approximately 1,000—providing very little towards university revenue.

Rising unmet demand for domestic university places from qualified year 12 students made clear the deficiencies in the system. This demand was brought on to a large extent by changing skill requirements during the 1980s, as low-skilled jobs declined, leading to high levels of youth unemployment and a push for greater school retention rates. The percentage of students staying on to year 12 rose from 36 per cent in 1982 to 53 per in 1987, and it was estimated that more than 10,000 qualified school-leavers were unable to secure a university place (Macintyre et al. 2017). The excess demand in turn pushed up the tertiary entrance scores needed to secure a university offer (James et al. 2013). It was also clear from demographic trends that the projected population of 17–22-year-olds was rapidly increasing and would continue to do so for some years (Dawkins 1987a).

The case for expansion and improved performance of the higher education sector was argued by government agencies and independent organisations, including the Committee for Economic Development of Australia, which released a report in 1985 on education for development, and the Economic Planning Advisory Council, which produced a 1986 paper on human capital and productivity growth (Macintyre et al. 2017). Encouragement for change also came from abroad. In the late 1980s, the OECD released reports on the Australian economy calling for the education system to address skill needs and comparatively low participation rates.

An attempt to address the funding needs for expansion by partly shifting costs to students was taken up by finance minister Peter Walsh in his proposal of an annual fee of $1,500 in 1985. A smaller amount, of $250 per year, known as the Higher Education Administration Charge (HEAC), was instead introduced by the government in 1986 (Chapman and Nicholls 2013), but this covered only a small proportion of the costs of higher education. Furthermore, its introduction led to vocal student protests and there were concerns within the ALP that this fee could deter attendance by students with low financial means (Edwards et al. 2001). Nevertheless, HEAC was the first chink in the armour of free tuition that had been ALP ideology since Whitlam and provided impetus for the reforms to come.

Defining the challenges

In 1986, when HEAC was introduced, Dawkins was the Minister for Trade and the Minister Assisting the Prime Minister on Youth Affairs in the second Hawke Government, where he gained some knowledge of issues facing students. Dawkins was shadow education minister from 1980 to the start of 1983, and his experience in the education portfolio also gave him awareness of its importance to the economy and the need for reform. In July 1987, he became minister of the newly created DEET, which merged the Department of Employment with the Department of Education and Training. The ability to manage these portfolios holistically was timely and important given the skills shortages in the labour market and the need for the education system to address these shortages.

Dawkins quickly set about driving policy change. Within a week of taking charge of DEET, he initiated a review of higher education administration. There were no terms of reference and no calls for submissions. By mid-October, he announced that the Commonwealth Tertiary Education Commission—the independent body that administered Commonwealth grants—would be abolished and replaced with a new body, the National Board of Employment, Education and Training, with more restricted functions, which would advise the minister and whose staff would be appointed by DEET (Macintyre et al. 2017). By moving administration into DEET, Dawkins gained control of the higher education financing and policy processes with less risk of interference as the government embarked on reform.

Dawkins set out the challenges and rationale for reform in September 1987 in a paper titled *The Challenge for Higher Education in Australia* (Dawkins 1987b). The paper provided an overview of the shortcomings in the higher education system and made clear that the expansion should not be funded exclusively by taxpayers. But, unlike Walsh in 1985, Dawkins did not put forward tuition fees as an option, instead remarking that private sources should be considered.

The challenges were reiterated in a green paper released in December 1987 (Dawkins 1987a). As noted by Edwards et al. (2001), although this was a policy discussion paper, the style of the green paper was decisive, clearly outlining the government's ambitions for major reform. The first part of the paper proposed an indicative goal of 125,000 graduates by 2001, compared with 88,000 in 1986, with this number chosen with reference to Australia's relatively poor participation rate and graduate outputs compared with other OECD countries. To achieve this expansion, higher education enrolments would need to increase by up to 200,000, or over 40 per cent, by 2001.

The second part set out plans to achieve the needed reforms and establish a unified national higher education system. Changes would include closure of the binary system that had separated universities from Colleges of Advanced Education. This, and minimum student load requirements, would facilitate consolidation, resulting in fewer and larger institutions and administrative efficiencies. Other changes included course rationalisation and changes to Commonwealth and state responsibilities, institutional management processes and staffing arrangements.

The third part of the paper was titled 'Funding the System', but was intentionally kept brief, with Dawkins instead choosing to cover funding options in a separate report. Nevertheless, the green paper estimated that funding would need to increase by 30 to 40 per cent over existing Commonwealth levels to meet the needs for expansion. It was made clear that public funding for this increase was unlikely and, moreover, traditional sources of non-Commonwealth revenue (such as endowments, benefits and donations and commercial activities) would not be sufficient. Funding expansion of the sector from the public purse by raising taxes or debt was not seen as a viable option. Increases in student load had already put pressure on the funding levels per student. The macroeconomic and fiscal pressures in the broader economy were substantial and, moreover, as noted by Chapman and Hicks (2018), the Hawke Government would have had a strong incentive to develop an image of competent economic management to distinguish itself from the previous Labor Government of 1972–75.

While the green paper did not spell out the proposal for what later became HECS, it indicated that students, former students and/or their parents may need to be called on to contribute. The paper concluded by announcing that a committee would be established to 'consider sources of funding involving the direct beneficiaries of higher education' (Dawkins 1987a: 87), with recommendations to be reported in early 1988.

Agents of change

The daunting challenge was to develop policy so that students would pay a fair share for their education, but in a way that would not harm access for those with limited financial means. The political barriers appeared intractable given the ALP platform of no fees, but, as noted by those at the coalface of the development of HECS (Edwards et al. 2001; Chapman 2018), Dawkins had the right mix of determination, energy, political savvy and stubbornness.

Critical to the acceptance of HECS were the people appointed to formulate the arguments and assist in the development of the reforms. Edwards et al. (2001: 103) recollects that Dawkins deliberately chose staff for the taskforce for the green paper from the employment and training division of DEET 'who appreciated the needs of the labour market and whose thinking was unlikely to be restricted by existing policy practices'. To ensure continual feedback and engagement with the university sector, Dawkins also appointed a group of vice-chancellors to provide feedback, which became known as the 'purple circle'.

In what turned out to be a crucial decision, in mid-1987, Dawkins also appointed Chapman to the team. Dawkins asked Chapman to prepare a report for inclusion in the green paper, outlining the costs and benefits of different user-pays higher education options. Chapman's paper included upfront fees with scholarships for the 'deserving poor' and government-subsidised bank loans, as well as the novel idea of an income-contingent charge to be repaid through the tax system following graduation—something no other country had implemented. Because of the novelty of the policy, and the expected negative reaction from the ALP once fees were put on the table for serious discussion, Dawkins omitted Chapman's report from the green paper and instead established a committee to critically assess the options raised.

The committee was chaired by Neville Wran, an ALP icon and former premier of New South Wales. Also joining were Meredith Edwards, first assistant secretary from the Department of Social Security, and Bob Gregory, a professor of economics from The Australian National University with expertise in labour economics. Secretary of the committee was Mike Gallagher, first assistant secretary in the Department of Immigration, Local Government and Ethnic Affairs. Chapman served as a consultant and the committee was supported by an able secretariat, many of whose members were part of the green paper taskforce. The terms of reference for the Wran committee implicitly indicated the government's intention to reintroduce tuition fees.

The Wran Report and the origin of HECS

Prior to setting out options for financing, the Wran Report set out arguments for user pays, supported by data collected by Chapman and the committee secretariat. University students came predominantly from middle and upper-class families and, moreover, they benefited from attending university through higher employment rates and higher lifetime earnings. An inequity existed between those who participated and benefited and those who paid; the current system of no fees amounted to middle-class welfare. The argument for reintroduction of some level of fees was also strengthened by references to research that appeared to indicate little evidence of change in the socioeconomic mix of students following fee abolition in 1974 (Wran 1988).[4]

Options set out for raising contributions from individual beneficiaries included vouchers, fee schemes with and without exemptions, fee schemes with commercial or government-financed loans, graduate taxes and income-contingent debt arrangements. The Wran committee assessed these options on their impact on student demand and on equity by considering whether and how access and capacity to pay would be

4 Macintyre et al. (2013) note, however, that Don Anderson, the author of this early research, protested that his research findings were misrepresented.

affected for students with different levels of disadvantage. Important also were the consequences to size and timing of revenue and administrative simplicity and costs.

The last two options considered were a graduate tax and ICLs, both of which involved repayments calculated as a proportion of taxable income. Arrangements by which graduates could use their human capital as equity to fund education were well known, having been first suggested by Friedman (1955).[5] Unlike commercial or conventional loans, which would require repayment regardless of the capacity to repay, a graduate tax would eliminate repayment hardship and the risk of default. A graduate tax in its standard form, however, involves graduates repaying a proportion of their income *for the duration of their working lives*, with the consequence that the amount repaid would be unrelated to the fees charged. Furthermore, if only graduates were required to pay the tax, this could provide a disincentive to graduate. Chapman's paper also proposed a closely related option for an ICL, although in the report this was referred to as a tax debit scheme (Wran 1988). Unlike a graduate tax, the size of the liability would be fixed and directly linked to the costs of an individual's education and years of study. Repayments would therefore be not open-ended but limited to tuition fees. By linking repayments to a proportion of income, and by requiring repayment only once earnings reached a relatively high level, there would be low impact on equity and access. Furthermore, by requiring all students who incurred a debt to repay through an ICL, regardless of whether or not they graduated, all users would contribute.

Edwards et al. (2001) recall that discussions of the relative merits of the different options continued over several meetings. The compelling features of an ICL ultimately convinced the committee that this scheme was superior to the others considered:

> [T]he user tax debt linked to cost of provision and the number of years of study is the only scheme that collects contributions from users and beneficiaries without compromising the Government's growth and equity objectives for higher education. (Wran 1988: 29)

5 Closely related ideas for funding higher education in Australia were put forward during the 1980s by various economists. See Macintyre et al. (2017) for details of some of these proposals.

The committee then turned to the task of setting scheme parameters that would be politically acceptable. A student contribution equal to 20 per cent of Commonwealth outlays on higher education was proposed—equivalent to $1,800 per annum in 1988 prices for a full-time student—as this was comparable both with average student charges prior to fee abolition in 1974 and with fees charged overseas at publicly funded higher education institutions (Wran 1988). Rather than a single fee level, however, the committee recommended three levels to reflect broad differences in the costs of course provision. Debtors should repay only if and when their income exceeded the annual average earnings of all employees, or $21,500 in 1988 terms. Thus, most students would start repaying only once they entered the workforce, and the equity advantages were intentionally highlighted; those with little or no capacity to pay would not be required to do so, including those from disadvantaged backgrounds with low incomes and parents taking time off work for childrearing. For individuals whose income exceeded the threshold, the committee recommended a repayment rate of 2 per cent of income (Wran 1988).

After settling on the ICL as the preferred option, the problem remained that large initial outlays of public funds would be required, yet revenue from repayments would emerge only gradually over many years. This revenue lag could delay implementation of the reforms. A contentious issue was whether to raise revenue by requiring upfront contributions from students from wealthy families. The line of argument was that affluent families could afford tuition fees and so should be required to pay for their child to attend university. Another perspective—strongly advocated by Edwards et al. (2001) and supported by policy analysis—was that some students were unable to share in family income for a variety of reasons, so means-tested upfront contributions would harm access. Ultimately, rather than compulsory upfront payments, a decision was made to implement a 15 per cent loan discount to encourage upfront payments (Wran 1988; Edwards et al. 2001).

The core recommendation of the Wran committee was introduction of this new higher education contribution scheme, to be implemented from 1 January 1989 to new and existing students studying after that date.

Administration would involve higher education institutions notifying DEET of each student's debt, which would in turn pass this information to the Australian Taxation Office (ATO).[6]

Release of the report was delayed to late April 1988, in part because acceptance of collection by the ATO was not initially forthcoming. Chapman was tasked with initial discussions with the ATO and recalls that, as an academic with little experience in policy implementation, he was naive about the expected response. At first, the ATO resisted collection, arguing that, on principle, it collected taxes and was not a debt collection agency, but its opposition waned on learning of Edwards's presence on the Wran committee. Edwards had been a ministerial consultant during development of the child support policy and the ATO had agreed to collect payments from noncustodial parents for child maintenance despite these payments not being a 'tax'. This precedent, as well as pressure from Keating (Chapman, personal correspondence), paved the way for the ATO to accept collection of HECS debts. The efficiencies of collecting through the ATO were also recognised. Edwards et al. (2001) and Chapman reflect that the initial caution by the ATO was rational and appropriate given its predominant role as a tax rather than a debt collection agency and the uncertainty regarding ATO resourcing needs once HECS was implemented.

Prior to release of the Wran Report, the name chosen for the loan scheme was the Australian Contribution to the Cost of Education Students Scheme (ACCESS). The provocative acronym faced criticism from higher education and student unions in a pre-release briefing (Chapman and Nicholls 2013), as well as from ALP elder Gough Whitlam (Macintyre et al. 2013). The name was soon changed to the Higher Education Contribution Scheme.

6 In addition to HECS, the committee made recommendations to abolish HEAC, increase income support coverage and rates, establish a tripartite body to develop arrangements for industry contributions and establish a trust fund to ensure HECS revenue was earmarked for improving student places and financial support (Wran 1988).

The path to legislation

How HECS progressed so quickly from proposal to commitment to legislation is testament to the strength of the underlying economic arguments and the determination of Dawkins and his supporters.

Following the release of the Wran Report, the government was faced with the task of consulting with and convincing stakeholders and the public of the merits of the proposal. The report highlighted the selling points of HECS: 'free' higher education funding amounted to middle-class welfare and was regressive, so students should contribute to the costs of their education; and the scheme was fair because repayments would be required only from those with income above average taxpayer earnings. Dawkins and Walsh emphasised these points to gain political and public support for the scheme (Chapman and Hicks 2018).

Nevertheless, once the Wran Report was released, there were various levels of opposition from different quarters. This is no surprise. The ALP's platform at the time was opposed to fees, and the proposed ICL scheme had no international precedent—it was untested and there was no empirical evidence that it would succeed. Student rallies and demonstrations against HECS followed (Macintyre et al. 2013). The complexity and novelty of the policy led to difficulties in conveying the idea and to a misunderstanding among some opponents and the media. Many incorrectly referred to the scheme as a 'graduate tax' or simply as a 'tuition fee' (see, for example, Reid 1988). But when reliably worded polls were conducted, it was clear that a majority of the community was supportive of students paying at least part of the cost of their courses (Commonwealth of Australia 1988). Print media opinion pieces and editorials were also mostly supportive, acknowledging that deferred contingent repayments would not harm access (Chapman and Nicholls 2013).

Nevertheless, national student and staff unions lobbied the ALP Caucus, many members of which shared their strong views on keeping fees out of university (Macintyre et al. 2013). It was critical for Dawkins to secure support from the various Labor factions if there was to be hope for the policy. A cross-factional caucus consultative group was established to consider the Wran Report in May 1988, making recommendations to the Cabinet in July on the preferred scheme parameters, including the income threshold and repayment rates (Commonwealth of Australia

1988). Importantly, Dawkins had the full confidence and support of Hawke and Keating (Dawkins 2018), and Keating helped to bring some of the factions into line.

The critical turning point came at the ALP National Conference in June 1988, with a close vote supporting a change to the policy platform of 'free tertiary education' to one that was instead free at the point of entry, thereby ensuring that qualified Australians would retain access to a tertiary education regardless of their means (Chapman and Nicholls 2013). This motion was seconded by the Australian Council of Trade Unions (ACTU) president Simon Crean. Bringing the ACTU on board was crucial for success. While the union's position prior to the national conference had been rejection of schemes requiring direct student or graduate contributions, blue-collar unions dominated the membership of the ACTU, and its members were paying taxes to fund the higher education costs of privileged students. The ACTU acknowledged that the Wran proposal was clearly preferable to other mechanisms for collection of student contributions (Commonwealth of Australia 1988). The heads of the universities were easier to persuade. The Australian Vice-Chancellors' Committee desired expansion of the sector but accepted that additional public funding might not be forthcoming and recognised that the Wran proposals were 'both feasible and the least inequitable of proposals for supplementary sources of funds' (Commonwealth of Australia 1988: 33).

When the Higher Education Funding Bill 1988 was introduced into parliament, Dawkins cautioned the opposition that HECS was 'a pre-condition for implementation of the other aspects of its higher education package' (Reid 1988). Nevertheless, the opposition ultimately voted against the Bill in the upper house. Dawkins recalls that the Bill drafted was 'basically Senate-proof'; it specified how much additional revenue each university would get if HECS was accepted, compared with a much lower amount if HECS was not passed (Dawkins 2018). Thanks in part to the wording of the Bill, and negotiation with the Australian Democrats, who had initially expressed strong opposition to HECS, the Higher Education Funding Bill was passed in December 1988, less than five months after the Cabinet's decision to adopt HECS as policy.

Once the dust settled, the scheme ultimately adopted looked very similar to that proposed by the Wran committee, but with a number of modifications: rather than three levels of charges, a flat contribution level of $1,800 was chosen; the initial income threshold was increased slightly, to $22,000; graduated rates of repayment of 1, 2 and 3 per cent that varied by income were introduced;[7] and students in certain courses (such as nursing) were exempted (Commonwealth of Australia 1988; Edwards et al. 2001).

Delivery, legitimacy and endurance

In the years following implementation, the success of HECS in facilitating expansion was apparent. Funded student places increased by 23 per cent between 1988 and 1993 (Williams 2013), which came on the back of growth in private student contributions. It was perhaps not surprising, then, that by 1993 the Liberal Party had changed its opinion, despite opposing the original reforms and in 1989 promising to abolish HECS if elected (Parliament of Australia 1989: 4361), to be replaced with upfront fees accompanied by fee-exempt scholarships. When John Hewson released the Liberal Party's 'Fightback!' economic policy package in the leadup to the 1993 election, this included a promise to keep HECS (Norton 2013). The Liberal Party had long been in favour of market-oriented fee flexibility and a voucher mechanism to distribute government subsidies and recognised that the income-contingent mechanism of HECS could be used to collect loan repayments.[8]

The legitimacy of HECS was reinforced in 1996 when the Coalition took power and the Howard Government chose its retention. They did, however, put their own mark on the policy, announcing the most wide-reaching changes to HECS since its introduction. That changes were announced in 1996 was not unexpected. In 1990, within one year of becoming legislation, repayment rates had risen by 1 percentage point and had then been increased by a further percentage point in 1994, despite the Wran committee recommending that a rate greater than 2 per cent would 'represent an unacceptably high annual additional tax impost' (Wran 1988: 58; Ey 2018). But, in 1996, the changes shifted

7 The Wran committee expressed concern that a threshold of $21,500 would imply a high tax rate when individuals crossed the threshold, and instead recommended that DEET and the ATO develop phasing arrangements to reduce this effect (Wran 1988: 62). A feature of the Australian HECS system is that the repayment rates are applied to total income and not the marginal income that exceeds the income threshold. This has been subject to criticism (Highfield and Warren 2015) and differs from the repayment systems in the United Kingdom and New Zealand, which are based on marginal income.

8 See Norton (2013) for comprehensive coverage of Coalition education policies and reactions in the leadup to and following the Dawkins reforms.

considerably more costs on to students. The most controversial change at the time was the lowering of the first repayment threshold to $20,701. This was more than $10,000 less than average earnings,[9] breaking the link between repayment thresholds and average earnings that had been a key selling point of HECS.

The other notable changes were an almost doubling of average tuition charges per full-time year and introduction of differential HECS whereby three charge bands replaced the single flat rate. The bands broadly reflected the cost of course delivery, as was originally proposed in the Wran committee report and supported by the departments of Treasury and finance in 1988 (Commonwealth of Australia 1988); however, private returns also figured in the decision, with law courses placed in the highest charge band despite low costs of delivery (*Higher Education Legislation Amendment Act 1996* [Cwlth]).

The increased HECS charges and reductions in repayment thresholds were introduced partly in response to a large budget deficit (Norton 2013). For better or worse, government funding was reduced and universities became more reliant directly on students for revenue. Between 1996 and 2001, the Commonwealth contribution to university income (excluding HECS) fell from 56.7 per cent to 43.8 per cent, while HECS income increased from 11.6 per cent to 17.4 per cent (Jackson 2003).[10]

The break in the link between the first repayment threshold and average earnings was partly restored in 2005 when the first threshold was increased. This was coupled with new repayment rates ranging from 4 per cent to 8 per cent. But the significant change in 2005 was to the organisational structure and funding arrangements. By 2005, the role of ICLs had expanded beyond HECS into a growing number of satellite programs, including the Postgraduate Education Loan Scheme, which provided HECS-style loans for full-fee postgraduate coursework students. In the interests of administrative and structural efficiency, an overarching umbrella scheme was introduced, the HELP (Ey 2018). HELP subsumed

9 Author's calculations.

10 It was also the case that universities became increasingly reliant on student fee income from international students during this period.

HECS (thereafter known as HECS-HELP) and introduced FEE-HELP, which targeted full-fee-paying domestic students in nonsubsidised courses.[11]

Introduction of FEE-HELP was a particularly significant expansion of the original policy, because it extended HECS-style loans beyond the capped Commonwealth-subsidised places covered through HECS, including expansion into approved private institutions, and in so doing improved access to and diversity of opportunity for postgraduate students across the country: 'It gave students choices they would not otherwise have had between public and private education, between universities and smaller colleges, and between postgraduate courses in public universities' (Norton 2013: 297). Like HECS, FEE-HELP has endured since its inception.

The 2005 policy reforms also included significant changes to the funding arrangement between government and public universities. In 2005, a per-student funding model based on the concept of Commonwealth-supported places was introduced. Under this arrangement, the level of funding paid through the Commonwealth Grant Scheme to each higher education institution was calculated according to the number of Commonwealth-supported places and the corresponding funding rate for each place, which was set by the government and varied by field of study. This method of distributing government funding for higher education is still used today.

Significantly for HECS, universities were given permission to set their own student contribution levels—albeit up to a maximum set by the Commonwealth—and to retain the fees charged. Although the intention of this change was to promote competition in fees, in practice, universities raised their student contribution level to the maximum permitted—approximately 25 per cent above previous HECS charge amounts. As noted by Norton and Cherastidtham (2016), this was not surprising given demand for student places greatly exceeded supply. Moreover, as discussed in the final section of this chapter, because price sensitivity is low under an ICL, increasing fees would be expected to have very little effect on deterring enrolments.

11 FEE-HELP replaced the previous Open Learning Deferred Payment Scheme, the Postgraduate Education Loan Scheme and the Bridging for Overseas-Trained Professionals Loan Scheme. To mitigate the costs to taxpayers of unpaid debt and forgone interest, a 20 per cent loan fee was applied to FEE-HELP loans. OS-HELP was also introduced for students studying overseas for short durations.

In the almost 15 years since the 2005 reforms to HECS, changes have been relatively minor—testament to the efficiency and fairness of the original design. Some of the more notable changes have included the removal of discounts on upfront and voluntary repayments and introduction of arrangements to collect debt from borrowers who move overseas, in response to recognition of an oversight in the original design.

In contrast to the relatively incidental modifications to HECS parameters, changes to higher education funding in the past decade have been significant, with consequences to the growth of outstanding HECS debt. In 2012, the 'demand-driven' funding system was introduced and caps on the majority of Commonwealth-supported bachelor degree places at public universities were lifted (Norton and Cherastidtham 2016). This increased competition, but also the growth of student numbers, taxpayer outlays and the potential costs associated with HECS.

It was estimated that uncapping of places would add an additional $7.6 billion to taxpayer costs over five years, and these rising costs were part of the reasoning behind a radical proposal for change to the sector announced in 2014 by then education minster Christopher Pyne. The major piece of the proposed reforms was fee deregulation, coupled with a 20 per cent reduction to the Commonwealth's contribution (Commonwealth of Australia 2014). The proposed reforms were motivated in part by the belief that the existing uniformity of tuition fees was a constraint on innovation and that providing universities with the freedom to set their own fees would foster competition and efficiency and drive improvements in the quality of courses and programs. The proposals were met with concerns that deregulation could lead to a doubling—or worse—of fees and debt (DEET 2015). The government was unable to make a convincing case that the proposed reforms would produce the desired improvements to the sector, and the proposals were abandoned.

The clearest warning about the potential risks of market-driven fees in the presence of ICLs emerged following introduction of VET FEE-HELP for students in higher-level VET courses in 2008 and the subsequent closure of this scheme in 2016. Discussion of these and other risks and challenges facing HECS, and the key lessons from this policy case, is given in the next section.

Current pressures and future challenges

The demand-driven system and expansion of HECS have led to a significant rise in the stock of outstanding debt. As of June 2017, outstanding HELP debts totalled $55 billion—the majority of which derives from HECS (DEET 2017). Approximately 30 per cent of this is expected to not be repaid, but long-run taxpayer costs are dependent on future graduate earnings and the government cost of borrowing, so are highly uncertain. These costs arise because some borrowers will not earn enough to repay their loans in full (outstanding debt is forgiven when the debtor dies) and because loans are indexed against inflation, which is lower than the yield on the government securities issued to finance the loans. The rising costs of HELP have led to policy proposals that would further shift costs from taxpayers to students or would better target existing subsidies to those most in need. Proposals have included reducing the income thresholds, applying a real interest rate on outstanding debt, charging loan surcharges to new HECS debtors, recovering outstanding debt from deceased estates and tying HECS repayment to family income rather than individual income (Norton and Cherastidtham 2014, 2016).

Perhaps the most contentious debate concerns the disparities in HECS charges between different fields of study, the size of HECS charges and, specifically, what the overall split between public and private funding should be, noting that HELP costs are just one component of public expenditure on higher education. Determining how the costs should be distributed is problematic, partly because of the difficulty in quantifying the size of public benefits and because the debate tends to be driven more by political and ideological differences than by economic analysis.

Despite the gradual shift to greater user pays over the past 30 years, participation rates have remained strong under HECS. Why? First, HELP removes financial barriers to entry and repayments are required only if income exceeds the minimum threshold. Second, the private returns to higher education over secondary and vocational education are considerable (e.g. Norton 2012; Daly et al. 2015). Third, because HECS repayments are a proportion of income, a higher debt means additional repayments 10–15 years from now—far in the future from the perspective of an 18-year-old student.

For these reasons, price sensitivity is very low under HECS. While this can be seen as a positive because it encourages participation, it also means that education providers have strong economic incentives to charge high fees, potentially in excess of the costs of the provision of education. This is because education providers face no direct financial consequences if students do not repay; when a student takes out a HELP loan, the government pays the tuition fees directly to the education provider and the student then repays the loan to the government if they earn enough in the future.

HECS tuition fees are capped and regulated, so excessive fees are not present. However, when VET-FEE HELP was introduced, providers could set their own fees in many parts of the sector. Some education providers engaged in price gouging and predatory lending to secure enrolments with little care for students' suitability or the prospects of course completion. Completion rates were consequently very poor and the number of loans and estimates of unpaid HELP debt ballooned (DEET 2017: 43). This led to closure of the scheme and replacement with the VET Student Loans scheme in January 2017, which has much tighter lending restrictions and loan amounts.

To hold universities more accountable for the prices charged and the quality of education, some have proposed linking the provision of government subsidies to HELP debt recovery or requiring universities to take on some of the risk of nonrepayment (Ergas 2014; Leaver 2015). One risk of proposals in which behaviour, funding or price is linked to debt recovery is that universities may favour disciplines that yield greater financial returns at the expense of socially important, but traditionally lower-paying disciplines. How to ensure that universities have 'skin in the game' is an unresolved challenge for ICL systems and government-subsidised student loan schemes more broadly.

Key lessons

The successful development, implementation and endurance of HECS was thanks to the fortuitous combination of the right fiscal and political environment, a determined and decisive minister and a supportive Cabinet, a capable group of individuals to conceive and develop the policy, a compelling argument for change grounded in fairness and an efficient design with administratively simple collection.

Perhaps most critically, the political will and authority for change were strong (Dawkins 2018). The development and introduction of HECS occurred in an environment in which there was a university funding crisis and a compelling argument for student contributions on the grounds of equity. Dawkins led from the front and, while he faced challenges convincing ALP factions of the need for and merits of HECS, he had the support of the Cabinet, including the prime minister and the treasurer.

The policy design process that led to HECS was set and controlled by Dawkins and occurred quickly, providing limited time or opportunity for opponents to disagree (Edwards et al. 2001). Critical was the choice of Wran committee members and secretariat staff and selection of Chapman as advisor. Dawkins handpicked committee members with diverse policy and economic experience and secretariat staff with knowledge of the higher education environment and with the skills to produce objective and rigorous analysis (Edwards et al. 2001). The strength of arguments and comprehensiveness of the analysis helped convince the ALP and key interest groups of the inequity of the existing system and the merits of the deferred loan scheme. The analysis also stymied the influence of critics, who struggled to come up with superior policy alternatives.

Framing and language were critical to selling the policy proposal. Bob Gregory (2009: 239), a member of the Wran committee, noted that the advocates of HECS never described it as 'a fee regime with an optional and innovative loan system attached'. Rather, it was first and foremost a loan scheme. Gregory (2009) also notes that because the number of policy parameters for HECS was relatively small, this enabled decision-making to proceed quickly and did not distract from the task of selling the policy idea. Furthermore, since HECS was introduced on a greenfield policy site, policy constraints and conflicts did not exist to divert the development process.

Administrative efficiency and simplicity were crucial to the success and endurance of HECS. The serendipitous precedent of the collection of childcare maintenance payments by the ATO ensured the feasibility of its collection of HECS repayments. Efficiency of collection has since become recognised as a fundamental requirement and benefit of ICL schemes (Chapman et al. 2014).

While Australia's two main political parties have embraced HECS as an essential feature of higher education policy, the scheme has been subject to incremental change, often driven by the political attraction of budgetary savings. Both parties have been responsible for reductions in Commonwealth spending on higher education, pushing greater costs on to students through increases in tuition fees and modifications to repayment thresholds and rates.[12] This is not surprising. Demanding a greater share of costs from 'privileged' students rather than all taxpayers attracts less political and public resistance. It is also the case that changes to HECS are often not based on economic theory or evidence-based analysis, but are driven by compromise to achieve specific political objectives.

A final lesson is that the endurance of HECS has been dependent on the regulatory environment in which it operates. As discussed above, the imbalance in the risk-sharing arrangements between educational institutions and government and the very low price sensitivity of students due in part to the design of HECS have meant that caps on tuition fees have been necessary to guard against price gouging and blowouts in public costs. But, while government regulation can prevent exploitation of the system, the current arrangements of uniform HECS charges and uneven risk-sharing arguably restrict the incentives and opportunities for the higher education sector to innovate and diversify in teaching and course offerings. Dawkins believes the 1987 reforms are now out of date and has called for increased competition and a gradual transition to fee flexibility, albeit subject to strict provisions and controls (Dodd 2016).

The legitimacy and endurance of HECS have been due in large part to the fairness of the policy. It is considered fair because students, who benefit directly, contribute to the costs of their education. It is also seen as fair because it enables access to those without upfront funds and the risk of financial hardship is mitigated because repayments are based on income. A challenge when designing future reform is to do so without jeopardising the continued role of HECS as an affordable and equitable means of funding higher education.

12 In August 2018, legislation was passed that will reduce the first threshold to $45,000 (*Higher Education Support Legislation Amendment (Student Loan Sustainability) Act 2018* [Cwlth]).

References

Australian Bureau of Statistics (ABS) 2017. *Education and Work, Australia*. Cat. No. 6227.0. Canberra: ABS.

Chapman, B. 2018. 'HECS: A hybrid model for higher-education financing.' In M. Fabian and R. Breunig (eds), *Hybrid Public Policy Innovations: Contemporary policy beyond ideology*. London: Taylor & Francis.

Chapman, B. and Hicks, T. 2018. 'The political economy of the Higher Education Contribution Scheme.' In B. Cantwell, H. Coates and R. King (eds), *Handbook on the Politics of Higher Education*. Cheltenham, UK: Edward Elgar.

Chapman, B. and Nicholls, J. 2013. 'HECS.' In G. Croucher, S. Marginson, A. Norton and J. Wells (eds), *The Dawkins Revolution: 25 years on*. Melbourne: Melbourne University Publishing.

Chapman, B., Higgins, T. and Stiglitz, J. 2014. *Income Contingent Loans: Theory, practice and prospects*. London: Palgrave Macmillan.

Chingos, M. and Dynarksi, S. 2018. 'An international final four: Which country handles student debt best?' *The New York Times*, 2 April.

Commonwealth of Australia 1988. *Establishing a Higher Education Contribution Scheme*. Cabinet Submission No. 5922, 4 August. Canberra: Commonwealth of Australia.

Commonwealth of Australia 2014. *Budget 2014–15: Higher education*. Canberra: Commonwealth of Australia.

Croucher, G., Marginson, S., Norton, A. and Wells, J. (eds) 2013. *The Dawkins Revolution: 25 years on*. Melbourne: Melbourne University Publishing.

Daly, A., Lewis, P., Corliss, M. and Heaslip, T. 2015. 'The private rate of return to a university degree in Australia.' *Australian Journal of Education* 59(1): 97–112. doi.org/10.1177/0004944114565117.

Dawkins, J. 1987a. *Higher education: A policy discussion paper*. Green Paper, December. Canberra: AGPS.

Dawkins, J. 1987b. *The Challenge for Higher Education in Australia*. Canberra: AGPS.

Dawkins, J. 2018. The 2018 Wilson Dialogue: Removing reform roadblocks. National Gallery of Australia, Canberra, 30 May.

Department of Employment, Education and Training (DEET) 2015. *Higher Education in Australia: A review of reviews from Dawkins to today*. Canberra: Commonwealth of Australia.

Department of Employment, Education and Training (DEET) 2017. *Department of Education and Training Annual Report 2016–17*. Canberra: Commonwealth of Australia.

Dodd, T. 2016. 'John Dawkins says his university reforms are "completely out of date".' *Australian Financial Review*, 26 September.

Dodd, T. 2017. 'ANU economist Bruce Chapman honoured with the AFR Higher Education Lifetime Achievement Award.' *Australian Financial Review*, 30 August.

Edwards, M., with Howard, C. and Miller, R. 2001. *Social Policy, Public Policy: From problem to practice*. Sydney: Allen & Unwin.

Ergas, H. 2014. 'Creating mayhem more fun, but revolting radicals miss serious issue.' *The Australian*, 19 May.

Ey, C. 2018. *The Higher Education Loan Program (HELP) and related loans: A chronology*. Research Paper Series 2017–18. Canberra: Parliamentary Library.

Friedman, M. 1955. *Capitalism and Freedom*. Chicago: University of Chicago Press.

Gregory, B. 2009. 'Musing and memories on the introduction of HECS and where to next on income contingent loans.' *Australian Journal of Labour Economics* 12(2): 237–43.

Highfield, R. and Warren, N. 2015. 'Does the Australian Higher Education Loan Program (HELP) undermine personal income tax integrity?' *eJournal of Tax Research* 13(1): 202–61.

Jackson, K. 2003. *Higher education funding policy*. Parliamentary Library E-Brief. Canberra: Parliamentary Library. Available from: www.aph.gov.au/About_Parliament/Parliamentary_Departments/Parliamentary_Library/Publications_Archive/archive/hefunding.

James, R., Karmel, T. and Bexley, E. 2013. 'Participation.' In G. Croucher, S. Marginson, A. Norton and J. Wells (eds), *The Dawkins Revolution: 25 years on*. Melbourne: Melbourne University Publishing.

Leaver, S. 2015. *An incentive compatible model for higher education deregulation*. Submission No. 35, The Principles of the Higher Education and Research Reform Bill 2014, and Related Matters. Canberra.

Macintyre, S., Brett, A. and Croucher, G. 2017. *No End of a Lesson: Australia's unified national system of higher education*. Melbourne: Melbourne University Publishing.

Macintyre, S., Croucher, G., Davis, G. and Marginson, S. 2013. 'Making the unified national system.' In G. Croucher, S. Marginson, A. Norton and J. Wells (eds), *The Dawkins Revolution: 25 years on*. Melbourne: Melbourne University Publishing.

Norton, A. 2012. *Graduate Winners: Assessing the public and private benefits of higher education*. Melbourne: Grattan Institute.

Norton, A. 2013. 'The coalition.' In G. Croucher, S. Marginson, A. Norton and J. Wells (eds), *The Dawkins Revolution: 25 years on*. Melbourne: Melbourne University Publishing.

Norton, A. and Cherastidtham, I. 2014. *Doubtful Debt: The rising cost of student loans*. Melbourne: Grattan Institute.

Norton, A. and Cherastidtham, I. 2016. *HELP for the Future*. Melbourne: Grattan Institute.

Norton, A., Cherastidtham, I. and Mackey, W. 2018. *Mapping Australian Higher Education 2018*. Melbourne: Grattan Institute.

Organisation for Economic Co-operation and Development (OECD) 2017. *Education at a Glance 2017: OECD indicators*. Paris: OECD Publishing. doi.org/10.1787/eag-2017-en.

Parliament of Australia 1989. Senate, *Debates*, No. 138, 12 December, p. 4361. Canberra: Parliament of Australia.

Reid, R. 1988. 'Opposition stance the final hurdle for graduate tax.' *Australian Financial Review*, 8 November.

Universities Australia 2015. *Higher Education and Research Facts and Figures*. November. Canberra: Universities Australia.

Williams, R. 2013. 'System funding and institutional allocation.' In G. Croucher, S. Marginson, A. Norton and J. Wells (eds), *The Dawkins Revolution: 25 years on*. Melbourne: Melbourne University Publishing.

Wran, N. 1988. *Report of the Committee on Higher Education Funding*. 27 April. Canberra: AGPS.

4

The 53-billion-dollar question: Was Australia's 2009–2010 fiscal stimulus a good thing?

Alan Fenna and Paul 't Hart

> Mum: Ken, should I take my money out of the bank?
>
> Ken: There's no need for that, Mum. Australia's banks are among the best of the best in the world. They are firmly regulated and have not taken any inappropriate risks.
>
> Mum: Well, that is as may be, but all my neighbours and friends are taking their money out all the same.

When Ken Henry, the secretary of Australia's federal Department of the Treasury, had this phone conversation with his mother shortly after the collapse of US financial giant Lehman Brothers in September 2008, it quaintly confirmed what he and his colleagues had begun to fear for some time.[1] Despite the solidity of its own economic fundamentals, Australia was going to be significantly affected by the meltdown of the US financial system. When Lehman came to the brink in late 2008, US authorities

1 Portions of this chapter and the quotations from the Treasury officials stem from Paul 't Hart and John Wanna, *The Treasury and the financial crisis. Parts A and B* (2011-119.1, ANZSOG Case Library, Canberra, available from www.anzsog.edu.au/resource-library/case-library/treasury-and-the-global-financial-crisis-the-a-2011-119-1). A few paragraphs were adapted from Fenna (2010).

could not find a buyer and were forced to let it go under, sending major shock waves through global financial markets that quickly produced a global credit squeeze and subsequent bank failures and recession.

Around the world, alarms were being sounded about the financial system. Ordinary citizens like Ken's mother were becoming increasingly concerned and beginning to act—as data on ATM withdrawals and other major money movements were indicating—even in Australia. And yet, during the Global Financial Crisis (GFC) that followed, Australia would become one of a handful of OECD economies that did not experience a major breakdown in its financial institutions and the only one to avoid an economic recession during the crisis.

Here, we focus on the Australian Government's macroeconomic policy response to the turbulence in world financial markets, which took the form of two stimulus packages of unprecedented size. They were framed by prime minister Kevin Rudd (2009) as the right response to a 'seismic event' that was heralding a 'turning point between one epoch and the next where one orthodoxy is overthrown and another takes its place'. Rudd presented the measures as a repudiation of neoliberalism and a (re)embracing of a social-democratic policy philosophy.

Although avoidance of an economic recession was the primary objective of the crisis response measures that were taken between October 2008 and April 2009, it was not the only one. The specific Keynesian economic stimulus spending programs put in place had substantive objectives of their own in areas such as education, energy efficiency, housing and infrastructure.

The 'euphoria moment' (Kelly 2014: 173) for Rudd, treasurer Wayne Swan and the other key policymakers came on 3 June 2009, when the March quarter figure of 0.4 per cent growth was revealed. To their immense relief and pride, it confirmed that they had pulled off the improbable: avoiding two consecutive quarters of negative growth (the technical definition of recession) in the midst of global economic mayhem. The government's vigorous action was looking like a policymaking triumph. But the euphoria would not last, and the question of how the fiscal policy response of the Rudd Government should be assessed became ever more vexed. Had the A$53 billion spend been worth it? Or did it contribute less than thought or realised at the time to solving the problem and more to creating subsequent problems and thus be more aptly characterised as a 'policy overreaction' (Maor 2012)?

This question was hotly debated, first and foremost in the media and political arenas, but also among economists and within key policy institutions such as the Department of the Treasury. In this chapter, we shall not attempt to settle this debate; instead, we use the controversy surrounding assessment of the fiscal stimulus policy to illustrate the challenges of evaluating public policy (and, in particular, major one-off public policy interventions).

Preparing for the looming crisis

Australia had 'form' when it came to major economic downturns. The stock market crash of 1929 and ensuing depression hit Australia hard and destroyed the newly elected Scullin Labor Government. The depth and duration of the Great Depression left deep scars. The 1970s crisis of stagflation (high inflation plus recession) also saw an initially muddled macroeconomic policy response with a pattern of stop/go economic growth and two recessions—one in the mid-1970s and another in the early 1980s (Bell and Keating 2018). Financial deregulation during the 1980s and the entry of foreign banks encouraged Australian banks to defend their market share through aggressive credit practices that led to a credit-fuelled asset price boom. That eventually ended with high interest rates as a control mechanism and a 'hard landing' in the form of a deep recession in the early 1990s. Economic policymakers assumed at the time that the automatic stabilisers (government expenditure, which increases automatically in a recession) would kick in, but that proved overly optimistic and a deep and costly recession in the early 1990s resulted (Kelly 1992; Pitchford 1993).

While recovery from that infamous 'recession we had to have' was initially slow, uninterrupted growth followed. By the mid-2000s, only a few veteran policymakers had experienced an economic recession and it was a very different concern that preoccupied them in the later years of the Howard Government. The Treasury and the Reserve Bank of Australia (RBA) were worried about the threat of inflation in the boom period given the procyclical effect of increased government spending and tax cuts. The RBA responded by raising interest rates to put a brake on economic activity.

War-gaming

Yet even a decade and a half after it had missed the onset of the previous recession, the Treasury was still concerned about the fear of another 'hard landing'. To avoid being caught out when a downturn did come along, Treasury officials decided in the early 2000s to undertake some 'war-gaming' of economic shocks. These anticipatory and preparatory exercises were undertaken discreetly. For the most part, they involved the senior echelons of the Treasury and, in some cases, their counterparts in the financial regulators and at the International Monetary Fund (IMF). Several mock economic crisis scenarios were run, challenging officials to spot and react to a sudden economic deterioration and the massive uncertainty it would generate in and beyond the markets.

It is interesting to note the range of scenarios considered in these exercises. Most modelled a sudden severe recession that increased unemployment dramatically. Other tests were then run on the effects on various sectors and the profitability of the banks and on the medium-term fiscal position of the Commonwealth Budget. The main worries emerging from the exercises were sudden layoffs, a surge in unemployment, the cost to the Budget and the long-term effects of getting (or not getting) those thrown out of work back into the workforce. However, a banking crisis, let alone a global financial system shock, was not among the contingencies considered.

And yet that was the scenario beginning to unfold when the Rudd Government took office in November 2007. There had been early signs that all was not well in the world's financial systems and, notwithstanding it publicly talking up the underlying strength of the Australian economy and its banking system, behind the scenes, the government and the new prime minister in particular were anxious to gauge the depth and magnitude of the risks Australia faced.

On 29 February 2008, Rudd invited Ken Henry at short notice to accompany him on a flight to Gladstone, Queensland, specifically to discuss 'what might go wrong'. He wanted to know how a global financial crisis might affect Australia. At the time, Henry said he was not entirely sure since the dimensions of any looming crisis were unknown. There was a chance a serious financial meltdown might occur but that seemed unlikely. The Treasury would need to undertake specific research and modelling to investigate the strength of the financial markets.

He nevertheless took Rudd through a range of possible responses to a number of bad weather scenarios. The options included using the current strong fiscal balance sheet to provide economic stimulus, ways to ensure wholesale lending in financial markets and the use of a planned financial claims scheme that could help mop up after the collapse of particular financial institutions.

Eve of the crisis

As the financial crisis loomed, Australia's four financial regulators coordinated their actions and utterances. The Australian Prudential Regulation Authority (APRA), the Australian Securities and Investments Commission (ASIC), the RBA and the Treasury were already talking to each other regularly through the Council of Financial Regulators platform and elsewhere. Nevertheless, during 2007 and early 2008, monetary and fiscal policy were still working against each other, reflecting the 'countervailing forces'—as the government described the events that were increasingly affecting the Australian economy.

In its later years, the Howard Government had been making almost annual tax cuts, while also running regular budgetary surpluses (Fenna 2007). Then treasurer Peter Costello had announced at the outset of the hard-fought 2007 election campaign that, if reelected, the Coalition would deliver $43 billion in tax cuts over the next three years. In keeping with his 'small target' strategy during the election campaign, Rudd had pledged to adopt the bulk of these cuts once elected. A substantial tranche of these commitments was to be implemented in the 2008–09 Budget. The RBA was still raising interest rates in March 2008 to counter these inflationary fiscal policies.

The federal Budget, brought down in May 2008, was mildly contractionary. Then, in early September, the RBA brought to an end its long series of interest rate rises, with a cut of 25 basis points (0.25 per cent). Later that month, the four regulators signed a memorandum of understanding on financial distress management. It established the principles for decision-making, the various responsibilities for each of the four regulators, strategies for detection of financial stress and a commitment to a 'coordination of responses' including communication. Was the system ready for the shock that was about to hit?

Post-Lehman: Australian responses

The ripple effect of the Lehman crash was instant and global. Neither the Australian share market nor the value of the Australian dollar was spared. Broadly speaking, there were three sets of instruments available for responding to the crisis: monetary, fiscal and regulatory. With the RBA independently setting interest rates and regulatory policy concerned primarily with the integrity of the financial system, the government's sole discretionary tool for staving off recession was fiscal.

Monetary responses

The Treasury knew the RBA was going to make a substantial cut as the crisis deepened but thought it would be of the order of 50 basis points (0.5 per cent). However, given the rapidly deteriorating global situation, the bank's board adopted a cut twice this size to underscore the point. The dramatic rate cut indicated that the RBA, too, had now shifted its frame towards managing a prospective economic downturn and sent a clear message to local and global markets. It had the scope to do so, with domestic interest rates sitting at nearly 7 per cent—high by world standards at the time. Central banks in other countries followed suit in cutting interest rates—a concerted effort to provide a circuit-breaker—although they had considerably less room to manoeuvre.

During the long weekend in October that followed the rate cut, Australia's economic policymakers had to face a stark reality. Panic was a real possibility unless the government, the banks, businesses, consumers and depositors held their nerve and reaffirmed confidence in the system. Henry's mother asking her son for advice on whether she also should withdraw her savings helped him realise the fragile psychology of community confidence in the market system. Cash withdrawals were at unprecedented levels: $5 billion was withdrawn in a few weeks.

These signals underscored to policymakers the turbulence of the times. Suddenly, not a single bank or other financial institution could be allowed to collapse because of the knock-on effect to systemic confidence. In effect, each institution had now become 'too important to fail'. Like the RBA, the government had to act to ease growing market nervousness. As one official observed when interviewed by one of the authors:

> Any financial system works on confidence. And confidence is fragile. It all works on confidence. So, this place [the Treasury] is a place where you give confidence back to the minister.

In the more prosaic words of another Treasury executive: 'Everyone knew time was of the essence. You had to whack before the market would open on the Monday.'

Key decisions were made quickly. First, the government curbed speculative behaviour by announcing that 'short-selling' (selling stocks you do not own until the price drops and then buying them back at the lower price) would not be permitted on local money markets as this was exacerbating the crisis. Second, the government issued a guarantee on savings deposits up to a total of $1 million. Third, the government applied a similar guarantee to wholesale funds for the banking and nonbanking sectors.

The first stimulus

Boosting confidence in the financial system was only part of the equation. The other big part of the October long weekend discussions was to do what had been unthinkable just three months before: boost aggregate demand in an economy that was at severe risk of sliding straight from potential inflation into recession. The Treasury's executive board was interested in getting the biggest bang for the buck—or, more technically, 'assessing the efficacy of the various fiscal multipliers to keep domestic demand buoyant'. The Treasury had been quietly assessing various domestic fiscal stimulus options, comparing the economic benefits of tax cuts, direct payments and infrastructure spending—estimating which would work best and quickest.

There had been much discussion in academic and policy circles about the relative merits of tax cuts versus cash injections. The United States had long favoured tax breaks, but the Treasury—primed as it was to prevent the fiasco of its 1990–92 recession experience—was coming to the view that a cash stimulus would maximise consumer spending in the short term. Less importance was attached to the substance on which the money was spent, so long as dollars got into people's pockets quickly:

> We knew we would be distributing funds to dead people and people living overseas. But we also know that their number was negligible, and that cash transfers could be delivered so much quicker than any tax cut could. We were happy to make that trade-off.

The first stimulus package—titled the Economic Security Strategy by a prime minister who saw the meltdown as the economic equivalent of a national security crisis—entailed government spending of some $10.4 billion (0.9 per cent of GDP). It was hastily put together over a weekend of intense deliberation, for implementation in November 2008, in a couple of days of fluctuating proposals and counterproposals, during which the Cabinet's Strategic Priorities and Budget Committee—comprising the prime minister, deputy prime minister, treasurer and finance minister—bunkered down with their key advisors and closest senior officials.

In Henry's much-cited phrase, the Treasury's advice to the government was to 'go hard, go early, go households'. The idea was to get money into the hands of consumers with a high propensity to spend who might be facing a household liquidity problem if credit dried up or banks threatened to foreclose on their mortgages. As early as November, the Treasury started advising that more needed to be done. This led to another set of measures being announced just before Christmas 2008. The government committed $4.7 billion (or 0.4 per cent of GDP) to 'shovel-ready' state government infrastructure projects that could start immediately and help to maintain employment levels in the construction and supply industries. Long gone was any concern about inflationary pressures the stimulus measures might fuel. The common assumption was that recession was unavoidable; the stimulus would hopefully soften the landing the national economy was likely to experience. The approach was one of trial and error: provide some stimulus, step back to see how it worked and then decide if another dose was needed.

The second stimulus

Around Christmas, the prime minister became concerned that the government was not doing enough to avert increased unemployment. The Treasury's estimates that unemployment might jump to 10 per cent became a real driver of decisive action. The aim was straightforward, as one official stated: 'Keep people out of Centrelink … We did not want to lose yet another generation to long-term unemployment as we had done in the early 1990s.'

The $43 billion Nation Building and Jobs Plan (3.5 per cent of GDP), which emerged from these discussions and was announced on 3 February 2009, included another $12 billion wave of cash injections to households:

cheques of up to $950 per person for the unemployed, employees earning less than $100,000, students, self-funded superannuants and farmers meeting certain criteria. In addition, $23 billion in major capital works programs were launched, targeting school buildings (situated on Crown land, which enabled quick movement from plans to shovels), social and defence housing and road and rail infrastructure. In addition, there were 'green' programs subsidising the uptake of renewable energy technology and the installation of household roof insulation ($4 billion). In other words, a wide range of government programs was now going to be used to pump money into the domestic economy. Rudd wanted things that were not a transient part of the landscape—as cash splashes and tax credits by their very nature are—but would be signature achievements of his Labor Government.

During the drafting of the second stimulus package, Rudd and Swan were acutely aware of the risks to the country's fiscal position and reputation this entailed. This led to an ironic situation, as one Treasury official recalled when interviewed by the authors:

> The impact on the surplus was a major concern of Rudd's during the stimulus II discussions. Now it was us at Treasury having to push the politicians to spend rather than the reverse. Rudd was concerned about his reputation for fiscal prudence. We took him through various components of aggregate demand and showed him what would happen if we did not intervene in a big way. Essentially, we had to turn him into a Keynesian over the summer of 2009.

The government's concern for its economic reputation had already been on public display following the announcement of the first stimulus package. It was clear to informed observers of economic policy that the combination of unprecedented public stimulus spending, higher levels of unemployment and decreased tax revenues would push the Budget into deficit. However, the prime minister and the treasurer were initially most reluctant to be caught saying so in public. They first tried to avoid speaking the 'D-word' at all. When that became clearly untenable, they used softening language ('temporary deficit') to counter opposition claims that the government was throwing all caution to the wind and was using the economic conditions to embark on a spending spree.

At the same time, Rudd did not hesitate to use his new convictions as a political weapon against the Liberal opposition (Taylor and Uren 2010). He found time in his summer schedule to write an essay in which he denounced the neoliberalism that had failed to civilise global capital and extolled the 'social democracy' the world now required to clean up the mess (Rudd 2009). In sharp contrast with the great crisis of the 1930s, when responses were tragically hamstrung by the then prevailing ideology of sound money and balanced budgets (Eichengreen and Temin 2000), responses to the crisis of 2008–09 were going to be informed by an ideology of social-democratic Keynesianism—at least in Australia.

Auspicious conditions

The government delivered an upfront stimulus that was designed to minimise lags and maximise impact. The Treasury saw the need for a timely response as the lesson of the 1990–92 recession. When the full seriousness of the recession became evident, this was followed by the deficit budget and infrastructure spending program of May 2009. From a projected surplus of 1.8 per cent of GDP, the government's first budget moved into a 2.7 per cent deficit by the end of the year—a $53 billion reversal. A yet larger deficit, of 5.7 per cent of GDP, was projected for 2009–10, with substantial deficits continuing into the forward years. Reinforcing this countercyclical fiscal policy was aggressive interest rate–cutting by the RBA. Such a willing embrace of traditional Keynesianism was made possible by a highly unusual confluence of conducive conditions at the level of theory, in the economy and the fiscal position of the government, the nature of the crisis and the international response.

It was the first time since the postwar boom that there was consensus support for deficit spending. Domestically, this was most evident in the unusual degree of business support. Both the Business Council of Australia (BCA 2009) and the Australian Industry Group (Ridout 2009) endorsed a Keynesian approach. It was also consistent with the urgent recommendations of authoritative bodies such as the OECD and the IMF (Spilimbergo et al. 2008). Contributing to this consensus was the rehabilitation of Keynesianism within mainstream economics. For a number of leading macroeconomists, greater specification of Keynesianism's microeconomic logic had given the approach a firmer theoretical basis (Blinder 1988; Chari and Kehoe 2006; Mankiw 2006; Akerlof 2007a, 2007b).

Economic and financial circumstances

The 2008 downturn was the first of its kind since a low-inflation environment was restored in the early 1990s. For the first time in decades, it became possible to reflate without reigniting inflation. In addition, having inflation under control allowed fiscal policy to function in concert with monetary policy, with very low interest rates around the world supporting expansionary fiscal policy (OECD 2009: 44). The economy also was maximally obliging as far as timing was concerned—with advance signals coming from the growing crisis in the financial sector overseas, the IMF (2008) announcing as early as April an impending global downturn, the collapse of Lehman Brothers in mid-September confirming the seriousness of events and the low risk of an immediate recovery and with the IMF (2009: xv) warning over a year later against 'premature exit from accommodative monetary and fiscal policies'. Fiscal conditions were equally auspicious, as the greatly improved budgetary position of governments across the OECD had helped reinstate Keynesian fiscal policy—not least in Australia (Fenna 2007, 2010).

Calls to reverse the trend towards procyclical rather than countercyclical public works spending by reviving the notion of an ongoing 'ready shelf' of capital works proposals (see, for example, Hughes 2001) reflected a broad sense that Australia's capital stock had been neglected through years of fiscal tightening. The incoming Rudd Government had already made large-scale infrastructure investment a priority; funds had been set aside, the government was working through its revived model of cooperative federalism to inject substantial investment through the states into major transportation projects and an infrastructure advisory body had been established (Albanese 2008).

The external economy

Finally, the stimulus packages were launched amid the most benign external environment ever faced by the Australian economy in a recession. The coordinated and comprehensive response of the world's major economies meant that Australia stood to benefit from a 'global Keynesianism'. The contrast between that coordinated international response and the beggar-thy-neighbour policies of the 1930s could not be starker. And it was not just the advanced economies. China responded to decline in demand for its manufactured exports by implementing an enormous Keynesian program of basic infrastructure investment that ensured continued demand for Australia's two leading exports, coal and iron ore. Australia benefited thus not just from the global Keynesianism, but also, most particularly, from the fact that the usual collapse in demand for its resource exports did not occur. Although the advanced economies in general experienced an 11.7 per cent fall in exports in 2009, Australia's exports actually grew by 0.6 per cent (Department of the Treasury 2010). The extraordinary rise in Australia's terms of trade of the previous few years was arrested, but only briefly; within months, the minerals boom was back on and the talk was again of skill shortages. The much-feared and much-used analogy with the 1930s simply did not apply.

Assessing the stimulus: Challenges of evaluation

Regardless of how uniquely conducive the circumstances were, Australia's response to the global financial turbulence was a remarkable episode in economic policy history. The sheer scale of the crisis response cannot fail to impress: the RBA's dramatic series of interest rate cuts in the early months of the crisis (adding up to 4.75 per cent overall), the government's sweeping deposit guarantee, two stimulus programs comprising dozens of billions of dollars and a total stimulus of 4.5 per cent of GDP in about 18 months. These were audacious moves under conditions of radical uncertainty.

The key question is, however, was it all worth it? This is where the story becomes complex and contested, and where more generally applicable insights might be gained about the intricacies of evaluation that determine the reputation of public policies—'success', 'failure' or 'somewhere in between' (see McConnell 2011)—and thus how they will end up being framed in the political process, in popular and institutional memory and in public policy textbooks. Let us demonstrate these complexities by discussing what happens when we apply the 'three-P' approach of this volume to the case of the stimulus packages.

Programmatic assessment

Did the fiscal stimulus achieve its stated goals; was it good economic policy that averted recession? This ought to be a reasonably easy question to answer. However, it is complicated by two things. One is the difficulty of determining cause and effect. The other is the fact that ideological presuppositions play a powerful role in any such analysis, with those who favour Keynesian interventionism persuaded of one view and those who oppose it persuaded of another. In Eichengreen's (2015: 9) words, 'George Bernard Shaw's aphorism that you can lay all the economists end to end and they still can't reach a conclusion' is entirely apposite when it comes to these questions.

The success of active Keynesianism?

Fiscal stimulus must obviously be assessed, in the first instance, in terms of its impact on the three main economic indicators: GDP, unemployment and inflation. At first blush, Australia's born-again Keynesianism was a great success by these criteria. Australia's macroeconomic performance was outstanding, looking at key macroeconomic indicators such as rates of GDP growth (–0.5 per cent in Q4/2008, 1.1 per cent in Q1/2009 and 0.6 per cent in Q2/2009); household consumption (–0.2 per cent in Q4/2008, 0.5 per cent and 0.8 per cent in Q1 and Q2/2009, respectively); and unemployment levels (which peaked at 5.9 per cent in Q2/2009 and were back to 4.9 per cent in Q4/2010). Most importantly, there was only one quarter of economic contraction. In the government's view, this was the result of its stimulus spending, which had been 'contributing around 2 percentage points to annual GDP growth' (Department of the Treasury 2010).

Taking even a slightly closer look, however, things soon become more complex and ambiguous. Concerning the size and effect of the stimulus, for example, the budget papers from the previous year—when the emphasis was on justifying the budget blowout rather than celebrating its success—noted that a good part of the stimulatory deficit was entirely involuntary. It followed automatically from the downturn's widening scissors effect of a declining tax take and rising transfer payments. Indeed, the 2009 budget papers estimated that fully two-thirds to three-quarters of the 'deterioration in the budget position' was to be accounted for this way (Department of the Treasury 2009). Thanks to the 'automatic stabilisers', any modern budget has Keynesian qualities under these circumstances unless governments take deliberate action to neutralise or moderate their effects (Van den Noord 2000; Darby and Melitz 2008). The key question is therefore not whether in an economic downturn government spending proportionately increases, stimulating the economy, but how much, when, where and for how long there should be additional discretionary stimulatory spending. Do the automatic stabilisers 'need help' or not, when providing such help in a big way entails substantial expense and is likely to leave a long tail of indebtedness?

This leads to the vexed question of the counterfactual: What if no stimulus had been provided? Would a combination of the automatic stabilisers, permissive monetary policy and robust Chinese demand have been able to save the Australian economy from recession? And what if they had not? What would have been the impact on GDP and the fiscal position? More importantly, what would have been the human and societal impacts of, say, a two-year recession taking hold in early 2009? Even relatively shallow recessions come at considerable social costs—in terms of unemployment, homelessness, anxiety and depression, ill health and domestic violence—and leave long shadows on other parts of government policy, notably, the welfare system.

The different components

Even if we focus on the stimulus in its own right, it is not self-evident what specific criteria should be applied and how they should be weighted. Clearly, we have to set separate criteria for the income support and capital works components of the stimulus packages but there are no set criteria for each that meet with a broad consensus among economists.

We might propose that the income support components of the stimulus can be said to have been fully successful to the extent that: 1) the money reached people's pockets as quickly as intended; 2) the proportion of money lost or distributed to people not entitled to it was (very) low; 3) a significant proportion of the money was actually spent, and spent quickly, by consumers so as to give a clear boost to domestic demand to make up for anticipated and actual reductions in foreign demand; and 4) the experience of this rapid and massive handout and the spending it elicited contributed significantly to business and consumer confidence in the economy so as to preserve the psychological foundation underpinning future business and consumer behaviour necessary for continued economic growth.

Likewise, the programmatic success of the capital works components might be assessed in terms of: 1) the scale and timing of actual expenditure; 2) their primary effects on business continuity and employment in the various construction industries involved and the broader flow-on effect in associated sectors; 3) their secondary effects—for example, the extent to which the construction works undertaken contributed to the government's non-economic goals for the various programs, such as enhancing the performance of the education system, reducing Australia's carbon emissions and bringing down household energy bills, to name a few; 4) the absence or minimal size of unintended consequences, including rorting and misappropriation of funds, price hikes in the construction sector and other implementation mishaps; and 5) the extent to which the government's strategy for recouping the significant additional outlays and bringing the Budget back into the black in the medium term worked as planned.

Debating the response's success

Not surprisingly, key members of the Rudd Government, but also senior Treasury officials, have argued that the stimulus did what it was supposed to do, that many of its secondary objectives (in education and energy efficiency) were also achieved and that some spillage was to be expected but it was relatively minimal. In their reading of the evidence, the all-important Keynesian multiplier effect of government expenditure was robust. Henry's successor as treasury secretary, Martin Parkinson, asserted that Australia's fiscal multiplier was about 0.7 for the cash handouts (such as the $950 cheques; but see the more cautious assessment of Leigh 2012) and up to 1.3 for public investment (such as the building of school halls). Deputy secretary David Gruen hailed the speed of the operation, describing it as 'an extraordinarily rapid fiscal policy response'—an assessment later echoed by the OECD (Gruen and Clark 2010). Treasurer Swan's chief of staff put forward figures vindicating the initiative (Barrett 2011).

Influential contemporary observers George Megalogenis (2012: 330–44), John Quiggin (2013) and Paul Kelly (2014) supported that view, with the last claiming:

> Australia survived the financial crisis without a recession because of two factors—the pre-crisis strength of its financial position and soundness of its banks; and the speed with which monetary and fiscal action was taken when the crisis hit. (p. 160)

International commentary such as that from economist Joseph Stiglitz (2010) roundly claimed that 'Rudd's stimulus worked: Australia had the shortest and shallowest of recessions of the advanced industrial countries' (see also Ahlens 2009). These interpretations have been supported by more systematic evaluation through economic modelling (Li and Spencer 2016). They are also consistent with the lessons that mainstream economics drew from the crisis (Romer 2012): that countercyclical fiscal policy is a key tool in short-run stabilisation, particularly when monetary policy has reached the 'zero lower bound' (which was not the case in Australia, however).

In contrast, economist Tony Makin (2016: 12), who conducted an evaluation of the episode in a 2016 report for the Treasury, after the Coalition had been returned to office, concluded:

> [F]iscal stimulus was not primarily responsible for saving the Australian economy from a narrowly defined recession in the March quarter of 2009, but a combination of lower interest rates, a major exchange rate depreciation, strong foreign demand for mining exports, especially from China, and a then more flexible labour market.

Other, earlier research suggested that, without the increased Chinese demand for resources, 'Australia distinguished itself from other advanced economies by escaping a technical recession, defined as two quarters of negative growth in real GDP' (Day 2011: 23). Moreover, Makin (2016: 13) argued:

> [T]he nature of Australia's fiscal stimulus was misconceived because it emphasised transfers, unproductive expenditure such as school halls and pink batts [insulation], rather than tax relief and/or supply side reform, as occurred for instance in New Zealand where marginal income tax rates were reduced, infrastructure was improved and the regulatory burden on business was lowered. The scale of spending was unnecessarily large and subsequently proved counterproductive by working against keeping interest rates and the exchange rate lower for considerably longer, as occurred during the Asian crisis.

Li and Spencer (2016: 109) likewise note:

> [T]he macroeconomic effects of such a large-scale fiscal stimulus are far-reaching; the short-run benefits may be ultimately undone as a result of a necessary budgetary contraction in the medium to long run. Indeed, the fiscal stimulus package has largely contributed to the rapidly rising public debt of the Australian Federal government since 2008.

The assessment put forward by Makin echoed what the opposition and the Murdoch press had asserted at the time. In addition to emphasising the alleged ineffectiveness of spending and the many errors of process in its delivery (see further below), many of these disparaging assessments of the stimulus policy reflect their authors' commitment to balanced budgets and scepticism about active fiscal policy (e.g. Makin 2018). If deficit and debt are taken to be overriding considerations, one cannot avoid concluding that Australia's GFC response was anything other than a policy overreaction.

Process assessment

When it comes to process evaluation, critics attacked the mismanagement that allegedly beset the capital works programs funded by the second stimulus. Media stories started to appear about misuse of funds and outright rorting of the school building program in some places. Subsequent investigations came up with mixed conclusions (ANAO 2010; Lewis et al. 2014). Although proportionately small in dollar terms, the Energy Efficient Homes Package—and particularly the component of it concerned with ceiling insulation (then named the Homeowners Insulation Program, or HIP)—generated a disproportionate amount of critical comment and publicity, both during the 12 months or so it ran and subsequently (RCHIP 2014: 1).

The HIP turned into a political nightmare for environment minister Peter Garrett after the deaths of four apprentices in unrelated incidents in quick succession, followed by a spate of fires and other incidents in houses that had recently been insulated. Industry stakeholders came forward saying they had warned the department that the program would distort the market, outstrip the production capacity of bona fide suppliers and installers, and had insufficient quality controls and financial checks and balances in place, but their views had been ignored. The so-called 'pink batts fiasco' was born, triggering inquiries, Garrett's apologies and subsequent demotion, early suspension and then termination of the program and a hugely costly remedial home inspection and repair effort to be paid for from the program budget (Hinterleitner and Sager 2015). The investigations that ensued left no doubt that the pressure to put money out the door fast had become the driving force in the design and management of the program. A royal commission found the program management capacity of the administering department was not up to the task of meeting the politically imposed commencement deadline of 1 July 2009 and that the implementation of the HIP was 'unduly rushed' (RCHIP 2014: 25; Lewis 2012).

In sum, the implementation of key programs within the second stimulus package was compromised by the urgency imposed on those administering it, exposing a woeful lack of administrative capacity, resulting in a plethora of deviations from standards of good process (cf. Althaus 2011). From a macroeconomic perspective, the great sense of urgency was understandable, as the perennial problem of countercyclical stimulus has been mistiming. Rudd, Swan and the other policymakers were well aware of that. The prime minister himself, his office and his department cracked the whip accordingly, exposing the limits of the Commonwealth Government's implementation capacity and generating significant unintended consequences in its capstone programs, such as Building the Education Revolution (BER), the HIP and green loans (e.g. Dollery and Hovey 2010; Kortt and Dollery 2012a, 2012b).

Moreover, despite the Herculean efforts of Commonwealth and state bureaucrats, who were hamstrung by institutional arrangements that were never geared to deliver with due diligence at the extreme speed required, the greatest part of the BER construction projects simply failed to get under way until the threat of recession had already blown over (ANAO 2010: 15–16). In other words, the sheer size and complexity of programs making up the second stimulus package elicited implementation processes that put the bulk of the fiscal injection into the national economy at a time when monetary policy had already started to tighten.

Political assessment

At the time of their announcement, the stimulus packages were broadly supported by the policy community and business. The packages initially boosted the government's popularity and in particular that of its irrepressible and highly visible prime minister. Rudd's strategy to reframe the terms of the economic policy debate—exploiting the GFC to push neoliberalism to the political margins, thus discrediting the Liberal Party's ongoing commitment to it—was much less successful, and he quickly abandoned the effort.

But this popularity was fleeting. As the Australian economy's buoyancy returned, it soon became apparent that the Australian public had barely noticed the economic 'non-event' of the recession that did not happen. It is unlikely the public knew or cared about the praise heaped on Australian policymakers in international powerhouses of economic policy analysis such as the OECD and the IMF. Moreover, the Labor Government's subsequent policy woes in unrelated areas (its painful U-turn on carbon pricing) and leadership struggles eclipsed any attempts to remind the public of its economic competence. The Liberal Opposition successfully played the deficit card as the government, now led by Julia Gillard, failed to make good on its promise of a speedy return to surplus. It also kept up its allegations about politically induced bureaucratic failures that had marred the implementation of flagship stimulus programs such as the HIP and BER. Ongoing media reports and review findings provided it with plenty of ammunition, which it used with aplomb in the 2010 and 2013 federal elections.

And so, the political assessment of the fiscal stimulus depends strongly on whose perspective is being adopted. Internationally, Australia gained reputational capital from its GFC response. International economic experts and forums lauded Australian policymakers, looking as they did only at the short-term and macroeconomic indicators such as GDP and employment. Some pointed to the G20 mechanism's crucial role—heavily lobbied for by Rudd—in providing the platform through which the leading economies adopted a more concerted and forceful approach than had been the case during the Great Depression of the 1930s (Ikenberry and Mo 2013; Drezner 2014).

There was less universal support among domestic economic policy observers. Had Australia really saved itself from recession through the stimulus effort or had it simply been 'the lucky country' all over again by experiencing this crisis under the most favourable set of circumstances imaginable (see, for example, Fenna 2010)? Domestic critics of the stimulus also made much more of its adverse impact on the government's fiscal position than foreign observers, who were more open to acknowledging how modest were Australian post-GFC debt levels compared with those of most other Western governments. Gradually, the domestic political momentum of the policy dissipated. Once the focus of assessment shifted from the stimulus and its immediate impact in the early quarters of 2009 towards the implementation and effects of its constituent programs, what had been a fleeting political asset initially turned into a political liability of major proportions (Walter 2017). Although the verdict on the BER is mixed and contested, the HIP in particular will go down in history as a textbook case of how not to roll out a (stimulus) program. Ministerial as well as Senior Executive Service heads rolled as a result of it, and the Energy Efficiency Group within the Department of the Environment was conspicuously transferred out of its home department into the new Department of Climate Change.

Conclusions

In their review of the Rudd Government's economic policy, Garnett and Lewis (2011: 196) conclude:

> The evaluation of the impact of the stimulus package on jobs and growth is unlikely to be settled empirically and, as with many debates in economics, views will, to a large extent, depend on the politics and the economic doctrine adhered to.

So, can one responsibly stick highly suggestive labels such as 'success' (and 'failure') on complex public policy episodes such as the Australian Government's response to the GFC (or indeed major public construction or information technology projects)? This case study provides cause for reflection on a number of points.

First, it amply demonstrates that programmatic, process and political modes of evaluation do not necessarily simply 'add up' to a coherent summative judgement, but instead point in different directions. Different stakeholders and observers come to different summative assessments of a policy episode because they focus on different modes of assessment and accord weight to different criteria within each mode. A typical policy technocrat will be most keen to assess whether a policy 'works' programmatically and less focused on its political ramifications, while the opposite will be the case for a political analyst, for example. Even within the realm of programmatic evaluation, the design choices to be made lead to different judgements: does one operationalise programmatic success in terms of goal achievement (have governments delivered what they said they would do at the outset) or 'goal-free' evaluation, by constructing a social welfare function, utilising intersubjective indicators of user experience and satisfaction or some other composite measure of the 'public value' produced (Moore 2013; Youker et al. 2014)? Likewise, 'good process' criteria can be 'technocratic'—systematic, structured, vigilant and 'debiased' in the use of information, advice and evidence in the policymaking process (Janis 1989)—or 'democratic', combining transparency, consultation and the participation of stakeholders, or based on procedural justice and perceived fairness of treatment (Fung 2006).

Second, although for heuristic purposes programmatic, process and political evaluation have been presented as distinct modes of assessment, this case study shows that, in practice, there are all sorts of connections between policy processes and their programmatic or political outcomes. This is clear in looking at the programmatic need for speed in the delivery of stimulus ('go early') and the way in which the prime minister, the Office of the Prime Minister and the Department of the Prime Minister and Cabinet then imposed a breakneck pace on departments and state governments in the process of designing and delivering the main stimulus programs—which, in turn, had programmatic and eventually also political consequences. Any attempt to make a holistic assessment and learn from complex policy experiences such as the stimulus program would have to be attuned to these types of interactive effects.

Third, the case study shows the difference of perspective and thus assessment associated with taking a holistic and a bird's-eye view of the policy (as international organisations tended to do) versus drilling down to its constituent programs and projects (as local media, political actors and evaluators tended to do).

Fourth, it brings out the challenges of causal attribution: to what extent was Australia's economic fate in 2009–10 shaped by the policy in question (the fiscal stimulus) and to what extent by larger structural, contextual and temporal factors? In relatively rare, one-shot policy episodes such as Keynesian stimulus packages, comparisons across time and space to find referent cases against which to benchmark the case under study are tricky. The analyst is forced to rely (implicitly or explicitly) on counterfactual judgements about what outcomes would have resulted from differently designed and administered forms of stimulus or, indeed, in the absence of any stimulus at all.

Fifth, we see how judgements about policy success and failure evolve over time. Within Australia, the programmatic assessment of the stimulus was initially very favourable but started to be painted in more guarded and critical strokes in the second half of 2009. Likewise, as time went on, the political momentum of the policy shifted from initially strong/positive to weak/indifferent (the 'non-event' that had not registered with the public) to actively critical and bruising (the HIP, BER and green loans sagas). Clearly, what one assesses also determines what will be seen, and what lenses and criteria tend to be used. The temporal progression of a policy or project's political reputation can also move from critical to favourable; in many large-scale public projects, the construction period is a political nightmare, but once the facility is open and more and more people develop firsthand experience of its benefits and—intended or unintended—beneficial side-effects start to develop, the frame starts to improve (Schulman 1980).

Finally, we see how the assessment of high-profile and high-risk policy interventions such as the Rudd Government's GFC response becomes entangled with political processes of impression management—credit-claiming, blame avoidance and crisis exploitation—as well as institutional processes of investigation, accountability and learning. A multitude of actors and bodies weaves stories about what happened, why it happened, how it should be judged and what consequences it should have. These stories are part of the 'framing contests' in which the reputation of the policy and the political capital of those associated with its adoption and implementation are at stake, and the lessons from its purported success or failure are to be learned.

Evaluators of cases such as the stimulus packages have to come to terms with these realities. They pose methodological challenges of scoping and design, criteria choice, data collection, causality and attribution. And they pose additional political challenges of situating oneself in the inevitably political (and often politicised) process by which we collectively seek to make sense of and learn from major public policy interventions.

References

Ahlens, S. 2009. *Fiscal responses to the financial crisis*. Kiel Policy Brief, 11 October. Kiel, Germany: Kiel Institute for the World Economy.

Akerlof, G. A. 2007a. 'The missing motivation in macroeconomics.' *American Economic Review* 97(1): 5–36. doi.org/10.1257/aer.97.1.5.

Akerlof, G. A. 2007b. 'The new case for Keynesianism.' *Challenge* 50(4): 5–16. doi.org/10.2753/0577-5132500401.

Albanese, A. 2008. A new era in 'nation building' begins today. Transcript. Commonwealth Government, Canberra.

Althaus, C. 2011. 'Assessing the capacity to deliver: The BER experience.' *Australian Journal of Public Administration* 70(4): 421–36. doi.org/10.1111/j.1467-8500.2011.00748.x.

Australian National Audit Office (ANAO) 2010. *Building the Education Revolution: Primary schools for the 21st century*. Canberra: ANAO.

Barrett, C. 2011. *Australia and the Great Recession*. Sydney: Per Capita.

Bell, S. and Keating, M. 2018. *Fair Share: Competing claims and Australia's economic future*. Melbourne: Melbourne University Publishing.

Blinder, A. S. 1988. 'The fall and rise of Keynesian economics.' *Economic Record* 64(187): 278–94. doi.org/10.1111/j.1475-4932.1988.tb02067.x.

Business Council of Australia (BCA) 2009. *BCA Budget Submission 2009–10: How can we foster and support economic resilience?* Melbourne: BCA.

Chari, V. V. and Kehoe, P. J. 2006. 'Modern macroeconomics in practice: How theory is shaping policy.' *Journal of Economic Perspectives* 20(4): 3–28. doi.org/10.1257/jep.20.4.3.

Darby, J. and Melitz, J. 2008. 'Social spending and automatic stabilizers in the OECD.' *Economic Policy* 23(56): 715–56. doi.org/10.1111/j.1468-0327.2008.00210.x.

Day, C. 2011. 'China's fiscal stimulus and the recession Australia never had: Is a growth slowdown now inevitable?' *Agenda* 18(1): 23–34. doi.org/10.22459/AG.18.01.2011.03.

Department of the Treasury 2009. *Budget Paper No. 1: Budget strategy and outlook 2009–10*. Canberra: Commonwealth of Australia.

Department of the Treasury 2010. *Budget Paper No. 1: Budget strategy and outlook 2010–11*. Canberra: Commonwealth of Australia.

Dollery, B. and Hovey, M. 2010. 'Australian federal government failure: The rise and fall of the home insulation program.' *Economic Papers* 29(3): 342–52. doi.org/10.1111/j.1759-3441.2010.00079.x.

Drezner, D. W. 2014. 'The system worked: Global economic governance during the great recession.' *World Politics* 66(1): 123–64. doi.org/10.1017/S0043887113000348.

Eichengreen, B. 2015. *Hall of Mirrors: The Great Depression, the great recession, and the uses—and misuses—of history*. New York: Oxford University Press.

Eichengreen, B. and Temin, P. 2000. 'The gold standard and the great depression.' *Contemporary European History* 9(2): 183–207.

Fenna, A. 2007. 'Governing in good times: Fiscal policy and tax reform in Australia 1996–2006.' *Australian Journal of Political Science* 42(2): 329–50. doi.org/10.1080/10361140701320059.

Fenna, A. 2010. 'The return of Keynesianism in Australia: The Rudd Government and the lessons of recessions past.' *Australian Journal of Political Science* 45(3): 353–69. doi.org/10.1080/10361146.2010.499863.

Fung, A. 2006. 'Democratizing the policy process.' In M. Moran, M. Rein and R. E. Goodin (eds), *The Oxford Handbook of Public Policy*. New York: Oxford University Press.

Garnett, A. and Lewis, P. 2011. 'The economy.' In C. Aulich and M. Evans (eds), *The Rudd Government: Australian Commonwealth administration 2007–2010*. Canberra: ANU E Press.

Gruen, D. and Clark, C. 2010. 'What have we learnt? The Great Depression in Australia from the perspective of today.' *Economic Analysis and Policy* 40(1): 3–20. doi.org/10.1016/S0313-5926(10)50001-8.

Hinterleitner, M. and Sager, F. 2015. 'Avoiding blame: A comprehensive framework and the Australian home insulation program fiasco.' *Policy Studies Journal* 43(1): 139–61. doi.org/10.1111/psj.12088.

Hughes, B. 2001. 'Can the "ready shelf" be restored to the shelf?' In Australian Council of Social Service (ed.), *Riding the Roller-Coaster: The role of fiscal policy in avoiding and easing recessions*. Sydney: Australian Council of Social Service.

Ikenberry, G. J. and Mo, J. 2013. *The Rise of Korean Leadership: Emerging powers and the liberal international order*. New York: Springer. doi.org/10.1057/9781137351128.

International Monetary Fund (IMF) 2008. *World Economic Outlook: Housing and the business cycle*. Washington, DC: IMF.

International Monetary Fund (IMF) 2009. *World Economic Outlook: Sustaining the recovery*. Washington, DC: IMF.

Janis, I. L. 1989. *Crucial Decisions: Leadership in policymaking and crisis management*. New York: Free Press.

Kelly, P. 1992. *The End of Certainty: Power, politics and business in Australia*. Sydney: Allen & Unwin.

Kelly, P. 2014. *Triumph and Demise: The broken promise of a Labor generation*. Melbourne: Melbourne University Publishing.

Kortt, M. A. and Dollery, B. 2012a. 'Australian government failure and the green loans program.' *International Journal of Public Administration* 35(2): 150–8. doi.org/10.1080/01900692.2011.635464.

Kortt, M. A. and Dollery, B. 2012b. 'The home insulation program: An example of Australian government failure.' *Australian Journal of Public Administration* 71(1): 65–75. doi.org/10.1111/j.1467-8500.2012.00754.x.

Leigh, A. 2012. 'How much did the 2009 Australian fiscal stimulus boost demand? Evidence from household-reported spending effects.' *B. E. Journal of Macroeconomics* 12(1): Art. 4. doi.org/10.1515/1935-1690.2035.

Lewis, C. 2012. 'A recent scandal: The home insulation program.' In K. M. Dowding and C. Lewis (eds), *Ministerial Careers and Accountability in the Australian Commonwealth Government.* Canberra: ANU E Press. doi.org/10.22459/MCAACG.09.2012.08.

Lewis, C., Dollery, B. and Kortt, M. A. 2014. 'Building the education revolution: Another case of Australian government failure?' *International Journal of Public Administration* 37(3): 299–307. doi.org/10.1080/01900692.2013.836660.

Li, S. M. and Spencer, A. H. 2016. 'Effectiveness of the Australian fiscal stimulus package: A DSGE analysis.' *Economic Record* 92(296): 94–120. doi.org/10.1111/1475-4932.12224.

McConnell, A. 2011. 'Success? Failure? Something in between? A framework for evaluating crisis management.' *Policy and Society* 30(2): 63–76. doi.org/10.1016/j.polsoc.2011.03.002.

Makin, A. J. 2016. *The effectiveness of fiscal policy: A review.* External Paper No. 2016-01. Canberra: Department of the Treasury.

Makin, A. J. 2018. *The Limits of Fiscal Policy.* London: Palgrave Macmillan. doi.org/10.1007/978-3-319-90158-9.

Mankiw, N. G. 2006. 'The macroeconomist as scientist and engineer.' *Journal of Economic Perspectives* 20(4): 29–46. doi.org/10.1257/jep.20.4.29.

Maor, M. 2012. 'Policy overreaction.' *Journal of Public Policy* 32(3): 231–59. doi.org/10.1017/S0143814X1200013X.

Megalogenis, G. 2012. *The Australian Moment.* Sydney: Penguin.

Moore, M. 2013. *Recognizing Public Value.* Cambridge, MA: Harvard University Press.

Organisation for Economic Co-operation and Development (OECD) 2009. *Economic Policy Reforms: Going for growth.* Paris: OECD Publishing.

Pitchford, J. 1993. 'Macroeconomic policy and recession in Australia, 1982–1992.' *Australian Economic History Review* 33(2): 96–111. doi.org/10.1111/aehr.332006.

Quiggin, J. 2013. *Macroeconomic policy after the Global Financial Crisis.* Risk and Sustainable Management Group Working Paper No. P13_3. Brisbane: University of Queensland.

Ridout, H. 2009. *Federal Budget 'A Matter of Give and Take'.* Canberra: Australian Industry Group.

Romer, D. 2012. 'What have we learned about fiscal policy from the crisis?' In O. J. Blanchard, D. Rober, A. M. Spence and J. Stiglitz (eds), *In the Wake of the Crisis: Leading economists reassess economic policy.* Cambridge, MA: MIT Press.

Royal Commission into the Home Insulation Program (RCHIP) 2014. *Report of the Royal Commission into the Home Insulation Program.* Canberra: Commonwealth of Australia.

Rudd, K. 2009. 'The great financial crisis.' *The Monthly,* February.

Schulman, P. 1980. *Large-Scale Policymaking.* New York: Elsevier.

Spilimbergo, A., Symansky, S., Blanchard, O. and Cottarelli, C. 2008. *Fiscal policy for the crisis.* IMF Staff Position Notes. Washington, DC: International Monetary Fund.

Stiglitz, J. 2010. 'The crisis Down Under.' *Project Syndicate,* 5 May. Available from: www.project-syndicate.org/commentary/the-crisis-down-under?barrier=accessreg.

Taylor, L. and Uren, D. 2010. *Shitstorm: Inside Labor's darkest days.* Melbourne: Melbourne University Publishing.

't Hart, P. and Wanna, J. 2011. *The Treasury and the financial crisis: Parts A and B.* ANZSOG Case Library, 2011-119.1. Melbourne: Australia and New Zealand School of Government. Available from: www.anzsog.edu.au/resource-library/case-library/treasury-and-the-global-financial-crisis-the-a-2011-119-1.

Van den Noord, P. 2000. *The size and role of automatic stabilisers in the 1990s and beyond.* Economics Department Working Papers. Paris: Organisation for Economic Co-operation and Development.

Walter, A. 2017. 'Australia and the aftermath of the GFC.' In M. Beeson and S. Hameiri (eds), *Navigating the New International Disorder: Australia in world affairs 2011–2015.* Oxford: Oxford University Press.

Youker, B., Ingraham, A. and Bayer, N. 2014. 'An assessment of goal-free evaluation.' *Evaluation and Program Planning* 46(2): 10–16. doi.org/10.1016/j.evalprogplan.2014.05.002.

5

'Marvellous Melbourne': Making the world's most liveable city

Emma Blomkamp and Jenny M. Lewis

Background: The rise, fall and return of Marvellous Melbourne

During the 1880s, the term 'Marvellous Melbourne' was coined to capture a booming city, of which its inhabitants (known as Melburnians) were extremely proud.[1] With about half a million people, it was larger than many European cities at the time, despite its location on the other side of the world, in the south-east of Australia. Money was poured into building lavishly decorated banks, hotels and coffee palaces (temperance hotels that refused to serve alcohol). The Royal Exhibition Building was built for the 1880 Melbourne International Exhibition. This was—and happily remains—a building on a grand scale, epitomising the wealth, opulence, excitement, energy and spirit of Marvellous Melbourne (Museums Victoria 2018).

Of course, the good times did not last; the early 1890s saw the inevitable bust that followed the boom of speculation. While Melbourne developers had built some stunning and multilevel buildings in the city for nonresidential purposes, housing was built outside the centre, laying the

1 Our heartfelt thanks to Benjamin Maltby for his excellent and thorough historical research assistance on this chapter.

footprints for an expansive set of suburbs. The City of Melbourne as it exists today had earlier and much less salubrious beginnings. The settlement was illegal in the eyes of the British-backed governor based in Sydney and, as was the case across the landmass being colonised by Britain, it notoriously involved the dispossession of the Indigenous inhabitants of the area through deception and worse (Campbell 1987; Presland 1994). The gold rush of the mid-nineteenth century laid the foundations for many landmark buildings and streetscapes that remain today. But the 1880s, more than any other period, continue to define Melbourne's shape and mentality. It bequeathed the city a set of 'good bones', but also created a raft of future planning challenges that came to a head a century later in the 1980s. A determined set of changes introduced over a long period was required to address these.

These policy changes—amounting to a tale of governance rather than a single dramatic policy—are mapped out in this chapter as a success story. By the 1980s, Melbourne was in decline, with major industrial difficulties and economic stagnation. Yet, in 1990, it was named alongside Seattle and Montreal as one of the world's most liveable cities (Department of Planning and Development et al. 1994: 23). This position has been maintained in various rankings until the present day. Such rankings are fraught with definitional and simplification issues, but Melbourne has appeared at or close to the top of several of these—seven years at the top of *The Economist*'s Global Liveability Ranking (EIU 2017) and, in 2018, top of *Time Out*'s 'Happiest Cities' and fourth on its list of 'Most Exciting Cities' (Manning 2018)—indicating it is a desirable place for many to live in and visit.

The transformation of Melbourne back to a city that can be considered marvellous in terms of its desirability as a place to live, work and play has been underpinned by a set of interacting state and city government policy moves. Hence, the success explored in this chapter is not of a single policy, but of governance change, involving two governments at different levels whose choices and their effects on each other produced benefits. In summary, as elaborated more fully below, there has been a high degree of programmatic, process and political success, which has been maintained over time. There are, not surprisingly, winners and losers in this tale of urban revitalisation. Melbourne's transformation has benefited property developers and those who can afford to visit and live in the city, at the expense of the less wealthy, including some of the artists and activists who actually helped to change it. There has nonetheless been a substantial level of convergence in perceptions of the value proposition of the new governance arrangements and a conferring of legitimacy on the political system because of the success of Melbourne as a liveable city.

Marvellous Melbourne as a governance success

Making Melbourne one of the world's most liveable cities meets this book's criteria of policy success, as it created widely valued social outcomes through policy design, decision-making and delivery that have enhanced problem-solving capacity and political legitimacy. This programmatic, political and process success has been sustained for a considerable period, with a broad coalition of actors and initiatives uniting to make Melbourne more liveable. The city and state governments continue to focus their urban policies on 'liveability', indicating the ongoing strength of this policy frame and the powerful influence of international indicators.

First, in terms of *programmatic* success, the state government in the 1980s undertook a set of purposeful and valued actions to fundamentally remove planning and development powers from the municipal level and the Melbourne Metropolitan Board of Works (MMBW, a statutory planning authority) and move them to the state level. Both levels of government were interested in transforming the central business district (CBD) from a place that was only for working into a more inviting place outside business hours. Hugely important to this was the reform of liquor licensing laws—which enabled many new cafés and restaurants to open and serve alcohol—and a focus on retail development and revitalisation projects. These important first steps were foreshadowed and followed by a consistent approach to urban planning by the city government, tilted towards liveability and a people-centric approach.

The relationship with the incumbent state government throughout this period has experienced several vicissitudes that make the overall consistency remarkable. The achievement of liveability as a major goal can be measured by Melbourne's place in global rankings, but also by the ongoing growth of the city and continuing demand for inner city housing as the centre has become a desirable place to live. Clearly, these changes have brought benefits to many—but not to everyone, with poorer inhabitants being squeezed out of previously cheap accommodation and those who cannot afford to live in the city or the inner suburbs facing long commutes from dormitory suburbs on the fringes of the urban sprawl. Critics also claim that developers rather than citizens are the ones who have benefited most from Melbourne's apartment-building bonanza.

Second, in regard to the *process*, a careful choice of policy instruments was made and wielded by the state government in terms of 'hard' instruments. These included transferring planning powers to the state government and reforming laws (John Cain's Labor Government) and major amalgamations of municipalities and the replacement of elected councillors with state government–appointed commissioners (Jeff Kennett's conservative government), while elections were held for the new, much larger municipal governments. In the case of the city government—and, given its reduced planning powers, limited resources and political turmoil due to amalgamation, this was probably not surprising—the reliance was on 'soft' instruments, such as strategy documents, long-term plans for the city and 'Postcode 3000' (described below) and a series of 'Places for People' strategies. Through the development of these policy instruments emerged a new shared understanding of the role and responsibility of the city government—as guardian and architect of public spaces—and a consistent emphasis on good urban design.

There was serious public disgruntlement over the state government's increased powers, but it yielded the opportunity for major projects (Docklands, Southbank, the tennis centre, Crown Casino) and many new apartment buildings to be approved more easily. The decision-making process was firm but initially unpopular; only once the benefits of the revitalised city became apparent were the changes seen as correct and beneficial. The delivery process achieved the intended outcomes. The combination of instruments used by the different levels of government meant there was broader planning being directed from above, which removed this more politically contentious aspect from the city government (and the MMBW), leading them to focus on liveability. The importance of having the same public servant leading urban design for the city since 1983—Rob Adams, who as at 2019 was still in his post—and his experience and sustained vision over such a long time appear to have been crucial. He clearly is an adept political strategist who has mastered the craft of policy navigation. There is likely a bigger story here about how the administrative side of the city government has achieved substantial continuity, while the political side has twice been removed and replaced, and the city boundaries and governance changed substantially with council amalgamations in the 1990s.

Third, this is a fascinating case in regard to *politics and public legitimacy*. The reformist Cain (Labor) Government (1982–90) made some bold policy moves throughout the 1980s. It was prepared to weather short-term unhappiness in the hope that the longer-term gains from city development and revitalisation, and the attraction of major events to Melbourne, would eventually win people over. Similarly, the Kennett (Liberal) Government (1992–99) was willing to suffer short-term unhappiness from the electorate over municipal government amalgamations in 1993, changes to Melbourne's boundaries in 1995, a reduction in the number of city government politicians and the introduction of a longer mayoral term. The state government has the more contentious role in relation to planning, and doubts about the wisdom of continuing to build so many high-rise apartments in the city centre continue to this day. But the major events and many of the revitalisation projects that began in the 1980s have provided the state government with revenue, as well as political capital and organisational reputation.

While these state government moves were in train, the city government—and, in particular, its administrative arm—was establishing its vision of a liveable city. The new planning arrangements and community activists (some of whom were later elected as local politicians) encouraged them to focus on the social and cultural dimensions of the city. While the changes to municipal government initially created conflicts with a range of community and business groups (Gardner and Clark 1998: 137), these tensions were reduced by a strategy in 1985 that clearly delineated state and city government responsibilities for different domains. Throughout the development of the 1985 strategy plan, the City of Melbourne brought different stakeholders together to work on revitalising the city (Ord 2018). Local individuals and groups, and the city itself, however, were not always included in state government–led initiatives. Initially unpopular developments, such as Docklands, demonstrate the consequences of top-down planning that fails to recognise existing community assets and aspirations (Gehl 2018). The political capital and organisational reputation of the city government have been enhanced by the obvious changes and vibrancy of the city, backed up by its high rankings on liveability scales.

In summary, we argue that this is a success story first and foremost because of its 'programmatic' outcomes. Melbourne has been transformed into a world-class liveable city and has become marvellous again. This success has been achieved through an interacting set of state and city government policy choices. The state adopted a set of 'hard' instruments that limited the city's capacities. The city adopted 'soft' strategies within its more limited scope, but also decided to do things differently. The persistence of a committed and astute urban designer in the city government, whose 'people-centric' vision for Melbourne has not wavered in more than 30 years, has been important. The early pain of change has now given way to broad support for the directions taken. But some are concerned that planning laws have allowed too many new skyscrapers to be built and that the city's population is growing too rapidly for the infrastructure to cope. There are also losers among the less wealthy who cannot afford to live in the world's most liveable city.

Contexts, challenges and agents of urban transformation

Paradoxically, the factors that have made Melbourne so liveable are both how 'unliveable' it used to be and the state's removal of the municipal government's and the MMBW's planning powers. The industrial decline of the 1980s and established preferences for suburban living and car-centric city design, along with the weak financial position of the city government, led to dramatic changes at many levels, against a backdrop of broader sociocultural and governmental shifts. The main challenge for both state and local governments over this period was in facilitating economic and cultural revitalisation to transform Melbourne into a city where people wanted to live, work and play. Playing a key role in the new governance arrangements were the Cain and Kennett state governments. Although they were from opposite ends of the political spectrum, both took a bold, reformist approach to urban planning. This was supported and enacted by the City of Melbourne, where Adams has had an enduring influence as the Director of Urban Design (and similar roles), extending from 1983 until the present.

Table 5.1 Key changes and elections in Melbourne city and Victorian state governments, 1981–2001

Victorian state government	Year	Melbourne City Council
Rupert Hamer's Liberal Government in power since 1972. Lindsay Thompson becomes premier after Hamer's resignation	1981	Council sacked by Hamer Government and replaced with commissioners
John Cain's Labor Government elected. Removes city government's planning powers and delegates authority for city planning to planning minister Evan Walker	1982	Council reinstated with reduced number (21) of councillors, majority of whom are Labor Party members/supporters
Amendment 150 to the Melbourne Metropolitan Planning Scheme introduces 'new zones and controls'	1983	Council begins its review of the 1974 MCC Strategy Plan Rob Adams employed as consultant
'Central Melbourne, Framework for the Future' released	1984	
John Cain reelected. Centralisation of planning power in the Cain Labor Government	1985–86	'City of Melbourne Strategy Plan' released
Cain Government releases 'Shaping Melbourne's Future'	1987	First female Lord Mayor (Alexis Ord)
John Cain reelected. Nieuwenhuysen reforms liberalise liquor licensing laws	1988–89	
Joan Kirner replaces John Cain as premier	1990–91	Elizabeth Proust takes over as council CEO
Jeff Kennett's Liberal Government elected. Planning policy at state level reduced dramatically	1992	'Directions: 1992–1995' reviews the 1985 strategy plan. 'Postcode 3000' policy introduced
Local Government (General Amendment) Act 1993 reduces the number of city governments in Victoria from 210 to 78, and *City of Melbourne Act* removes local politicians and restructures Melbourne City Council boundaries	1993–95	Council sacked by the Kennett Government and replaced with four commissioners (as part of the *City of Melbourne Act*). Large electoral reforms implemented within the council
Jeff Kennett reelected	1996–98	Council fully reinstated
Steve Bracks' Labor Government elected. New *City of Melbourne Act* reforms council structure and voting	1999–2001	Council dismissed, to prepare for the Bracks Government's new *City of Melbourne Act* (to be introduced in 2001)

= Liberal (conservative)

= Labor

= Commissioners (appointed)

In stark contrast to the opulence and vibrancy of 'Marvellous Melbourne' a century earlier, by the 1980s, the city was widely considered an urban backwater. Residential and retail activity had largely shifted to the suburbs, city streets were dominated by cars and noisy trams and many heritage buildings were threatened with demolition or had already been replaced with modernist high-rises (Dovey and Jones 2018: 9). In 1983, there were fewer than 800 houses and no supermarkets in the CBD (Neilson 2013). Danish architect Jan Gehl (2018: 21) writes of his first impressions of Melbourne in the late 1970s:

> The city was indeed boring and suffered quite a bit from the double impact of Modernist planning and automobile invasion. Going to the city centre in the evening was not a great experience at all. It was deserted. A few service people attended to the many high-rise office buildings, but otherwise it was a quiet scene. It was even worse on the weekend—the city centre was as if neutron-bombed.

By the early 2000s, however, the city had been brought back to life. Gehl, who returned to Melbourne in 2004 to document the changes that had occurred in the centre of the city since his first 'Places for People' study was conducted there in 1994, summarised the improvements:

> [A] much larger residential community in the city centre; an increasing student population; improved streets for public life; new public squares, promenades and parks; a revitalised network of lanes and arcades; several city-wide art programs; more places to sit and pause; more attractions; a 24-hour city; better cycle and public transport access; and integrated policy for paving and furniture; and a greener city. (Gehl 2018: 23)

The transformation of Melbourne from a 'doughnut city' that was dead in the middle to what it is now has taken decades of steadfast commitment and incremental change, orchestrated by a number of dedicated individuals and government structures that have encouraged collaboration between the state and city governments, with significant input from other major stakeholders.

The unique status of local government as a 'creature of the state' (Aulich 2005) within Australia's federal system of government helps to explain how the scene was set for new governance arrangements to be created. As elsewhere in Australia, local government in the State of Victoria is subject to the *ultra vires* principle, where it is restricted to those functions explicitly granted to it by higher levels of government. While the role of Australian local government has evolved over time (Dollery et al. 2006: 555–6), its limited authority is common to the 'Anglo' group—one of three broad models in Hesse and Sharpe's typology of local government systems found in Western industrialised countries (Cheyne 2008). The Minister for Local Government in each jurisdiction retains the authority to dismiss democratically elected local politicians if they consider a municipality is not well managed. Indeed, Melbourne's dysfunctional city government was sacked by the Liberal state government on Christmas Eve in 1980 (and again in 1993, as part of broader local government reforms) and replaced with commissioners (see Table 5.1). Melbourne illustrates the trend of Australian city governments that have 'been regularly dissolved, usually when state governments have pursued strong pro-development agendas' (Freestone 2010: 40).

An important part of this governance story is that, while the city government was democratically elected again in 1982, the new Labor state government removed its planning powers. The authority to approve all major planning applications within central Melbourne was delegated to planning minister (and former architect) Evan Walker, and the Victorian Government retains these planning powers. The government's effort to streamline planning approvals and make the city more attractive for developers resulted in wait times on development applications being slashed almost fivefold (Ministry of Planning and Environment 1984: 19). The same government also increased its infrastructure spending from 1982 onwards and drew on public–private partnerships, aiming to 'maintain the primacy of (and property values in) the CBD', in the context of a worsening economic recession (McLoughlin 1992: 232; Freestone 2010: 38). In 1984, it released its planning policy manifesto 'Framework for the Future', which was primarily designed as an economic strategy (Ministry of Planning and Environment 1984: 4). In 1985, planning power was further centralised in the state government when the Ministry of Planning and Environment subsumed the old MMBW's planning powers. In 1988, the government liberalised liquor licensing laws, enabling the establishment of many new restaurants and opening the streets for al fresco dining (Zajdow 2011).

In the meantime, the city government focused its efforts on management reforms and strategic planning processes. Building on the (never implemented) strategic plan from 1974, the City of Melbourne Strategy Plan 1985 was developed as an intervention to rehabilitate and stimulate the city following more than a decade of policy neglect (MCC 1992). As discussed in more detail in the next section, its development was guided by a steering committee, which led to a shared understanding and ownership of urban design strategies and the deliberate recruitment of consultants and experienced staff who shared their vision and values (Ord 2018: 39–40).

The 1985 strategy plan was strongly influenced by the community activists who had formed Melbourne Voters' Action (MVA), a coalition of inner-city residents' groups, in response to the conservative (Hamer) government's dismissal of the democratically elected city government (Ord 2018: 38). Led by social and environmental planners and activists, many of whom were members of the local Labor Party and who had contributed to the community consultation on the popular 1974 strategy plan, MVA monitored the commissioners appointed to run the city. They also lobbied the opposition Labor Party to reinstate the city government and institute fixed three-year terms if elected (Ord 2018: 37–8). When this happened and Melbourne's city government was reconstituted in 1982, many of the young activists from MVA were elected as local politicians (Neilson 2013; Ord 2018). Recognising economic and demographic changes in the city, the new city government extensively reworked the 1974 strategy plan to produce a comprehensive, detailed policy document that outlined goals and strategies for transforming Melbourne. The 1985 plan clearly articulated the different roles of state and local government in developing the city, which helped to resolve tensions between them, as both had been working to articulate different 'visions' for the city (Gardner and Clark 1998: 137–8).

Along with local activists-cum-politicians who spearheaded MVA, a key figure in the city's strategic planning process and wider liveability movement was—and still is—Rob Adams. Employed as part of the consultancy team designing the 1985 strategy plan, he was soon appointed to the City of Melbourne's executive and has remained there since, currently as the Director of City Design and Projects. He appears at multiple points in this story and his longevity and commitment to making Melbourne a place where people want to spend time constitute a crucial strand of the liveability focus that has been developed.

At the start of the 1990s, the city began comprehensive internal management reforms aimed at making decision-making processes within its executive more streamlined, consensual and efficient. Reflecting the broader New Public Management (NPM) reforms sweeping through Australian local government at the time (Aulich 2005), in Melbourne, this change was led by Elizabeth Proust, who became the council's CEO in early 1990, and whose lead was followed by her successor, Andy Friend. Central to this reform was an attempt to combat an entrenched 'vertical' management structure within the city council, which had siloed responsibility for different policy areas into different departments that rarely communicated effectively with one another. Under the new structure, three corporate managers who held multiple portfolios reported to the city's CEO, creating a 'team approach to management, which not only broke down barriers but also provided very clear leadership within the organisation' (Gardner and Clark 1998: 139). This new structure supported earlier efforts of elected members to create a more unified and productive organisation through targeted recruitment of executive officers and collaborative planning processes focused on urban design and social inclusion priorities (Ord 2018). The more consistent and efficient administrative practices were complemented and enabled by the state government reforms that reduced the frequency of local elections. These removed the destabilising previous arrangements whereby one-third of all councillors and the mayor were elected each year, which had resulted in decisions being regularly overturned and the newspapers dubbing the city 'Clown Hall' (Adams and Dovey 2018: 205; Ord 2018: 37).

The transformation of municipal management under the compulsory competitive tendering era, ushered in by Kennett's neoliberal government, saw services increasingly provided by external contractors (McKeown and Lindorff 2011). This resulted in consultants having a significant influence on urban design and local government policies throughout Australia (Stevenson 2000: 112). Insider accounts of Melbourne city planning highlight the important role (international) consultants played in the development of both the 1974 and the 1985 strategy plans (Ord 2018: 36, 39) and in demonstrating the significance of pedestrianisation and public seating to how people behave in the city (Gehl 2018: 22; see also Jones 2018: 103). The City of Melbourne's heightened appreciation of urban design reflects international trends in shifting from cities for cars to cities for people.

Around the world, city governments have turned to 'soft' policy domains such as arts and culture in their quest to improve quality of life and compete as 'creative cities', especially through urban regeneration (Blomkamp 2014). The 'Places for People' urban design framework adopted both in Melbourne city and at the national level in Australia (Gehl 2010; Department of Infrastructure and Transport 2011) represents a more human-centred and holistic approach to urban planning, influenced by transnational flows of consultants and the powerful 'creative city script' (Grodach and Silver 2013: 9–10; see also Landry 2000; Florida 2005). The 'creative city' concept was allegedly formulated in Melbourne in the 1980s, before anywhere else in the world (Yencken 2018: 73). Growing concerns about environmental sustainability and the ideas of urban activist Jane Jacobs (1961) have also been important international influences in Melbourne. They informed the 'grassroots approach to town planning' and the desire 'to create networks of walkable communities' that took root in the 1970s and spread through subsequent city plans and policies, such as the 1985 pedestrian strategy (Adams and Dovey 2018: 202–3; Jones 2018: 100; Ord 2018: 37). These trends have been reinforced by the global rankings that provide external validation of the city's focus on quality of life.

Unsurprisingly, the development of Melbourne as a city has been influenced by global trends and events. Along with those already discussed, immigration and related policies have significantly shaped Melbourne's vibrant culture. The traditional owners of the land, the people of the Kulin nation, were largely displaced by early settlers from England, Ireland and Scotland. Following the gold rushes of the 1850s, Melbourne became home to a diverse range of ethnicities during the land boom of the 1880s (and the rise of the Marvellous Melbourne label) and, later, through postwar migration in the mid-twentieth century (Damousi 2008). Although British immigrants continued to constitute a majority, 'non-English-speaking groups clustered in the inner city' from the beginning of the twentieth century (Damousi 2008).

National policymaking has also had an influence on the demographic make-up of Melbourne. Increased ethnic diversity—particularly in the form of refugees and migrants from Asia—followed the dismantling of the White Australia Policy and a turn to multiculturalism in all levels of politics. More recent influences on the transformation of central Melbourne that were outside the city's or state government's control include the deregulation of higher education and the subsequent increase of international fee-paying students, along with foreign investment from Hong Kong (in anticipation of unification with China), especially in residential towers in Southbank (Ord 2018: 41). The City of Melbourne has relished this increasing cultural diversity, epitomised in the resulting proliferation of festivals and restaurants with cuisine from many different cultural traditions. Thus, while the city and state governments can lay claim to enabling some impressive changes in central Melbourne, their policies have been shaped, constrained and complemented by a range of national and international factors.

Designing and delivering a liveable city

Despite—or perhaps even because of—its relatively limited role in planning following the changes described above, the city government proactively and constructively worked with the state government to improve 'liveability' in Melbourne. The new governance arrangements involved collaboration, negotiation and compromise between the state and city governments and significant and vocal non-governmental organisations. A sample of specific policy design processes is explored here to illustrate the different roles and approaches taken by these governmental actors.

The major strategic plans developed by the City of Melbourne between the mid-1970s and mid-1990s focused on making Melbourne a nicer place to live in and visit, especially by improving public amenities and promoting residential development. The City of Melbourne Strategy Plan 1985 sits at the heart of the relatively consistent approach to urban planning policy taken by the local government despite the wide array of challenges and changes it faced. The newly reinstated city government developed the 1985 strategy plan—based on the 1974 plan—over three years in the early 1980s. Their successors extended and updated this policy with 'Directions 1992–1995' (MCC 1992).

A guiding principle of the 1985 plan was 'full citizen engagement in the exercise such that at its conclusion there would be real citizen ownership of its recommendations' (Huggard, cited by Yencken 2018: 77). Building on the city's assets and 'local character', the plan aimed for incremental changes rather than 'grand schemes' (Adams and Dovey 2018: 204, 230). The plan explicitly sought to attract people 'to live, work, shop, and enjoy their leisure in the city' (MCC 1985: 15) and deliberately redefined the CBD as the 'CAD' (central *activities* district), emphasising the 'entertainment, government, civic and cultural activities' taking place alongside business in the city (Jones 2018: 128). Alexis Ord, a member of MVA who became Melbourne's first female mayor in 1987, emphasises the social dimensions of both the policy process and the content:

> There was a focus on opportunities for social interaction with the full spectrum of society, and self-expression in cultural and recreational activities. The city's programs and works over succeeding years were driven by the *Strategy Plan*'s aims that the city should emerge from the engagement of citizens in decisions that vitally affect their lives, and that it should symbolise the values and achievements of the larger Melbourne community. The extent to which Melbourne today is one of the world's most liveable cities is in no small way a result of informed and organised citizen engagement in its planning. (Ord 2018: 41)

The 1985 plan was distinctive at the time for taking a detailed, 'goal achievement' approach, aiming to counter the trends of population decline and economic productivity losses. It specified detailed objectives in each of the key areas on which it focused—the city's economy, commercial and industrial development, population and housing, community services, 'movement systems' (such as transport), tourism and leisure and the 'physical environment'—setting measurable goals for improvement in each area. Recognising the limited scope and resources of the city government, the goals were designed to be achievable over time and 'on very low budgets' (Adams and Dovey 2018: 204). The plan's development involved extensive research and consultation with the local community, taking into account data on traffic flows, pedestrian movement, space utilisation, analysis of previous policy and input from consultants (MCC 1985).

The incorporation of different forms of evidence and ideas and contributions from expert and community consultation contributed to building legitimacy, increasing the policy's chances of success. The city's own review of its 1985 plan concluded that two-thirds of the policies set out in the original plan 'have been completed or are ongoing' (MCC 1990: 10). The subsequent 'update' advocated slowing the pace of development and refining it, with the goal of making Melbourne an inclusive, artistic city, not just a busy, business-focused one (MCC 1992). New in the 1992 report was an outline of actions to be undertaken either by the Victorian Government or jointly by the state and city governments.

The City of Melbourne was thus ahead of its time, implementing strategic planning and reporting regimes that were to be applied to local government in Australian states from the late 1980s to the early 2000s. It followed the City of Sydney, whose 1971 strategic plan exemplified the 'new wave of progressive strategic city plans … experimenting with innovative methodologies and new-look emphases on urban design and environmental management' (Freestone 2010: 35). New provisions later set out in state legislation were accordingly designed to make local authorities more accountable and more responsive to community wishes, notably through mechanisms such as strategic planning and performance statements, as well as sometimes broadening the scope of local government activity (Aulich 2009).

Throughout the 1980s and beyond, the city government actively incorporated and promoted pedestrianisation as a key plank of liveability. As understood by the City of Melbourne and articulated in the 'Places for People' reports, 'liveability' is about how people experience the city, especially public space. In 1993, Adams, as the city's urban design manager, brought Gehl to Melbourne to conduct a large-scale planning and social study of the city. Gehl's subsequent 'Places for People' report studied the people of Melbourne and how they used their city, specifying for instance how long people spent walking between spaces and how long they stayed in each space. Explicitly focusing on making the city more 'liveable', the report suggested improving pedestrian links around the city and creating more functional and amenable 'gathering spaces' (City of Melbourne and Gehl 1994: 13–14).

The report ended by recommending two sets of goals: a series of numerical targets for pedestrian movement and space utilisation, as well as amenity development (for example, 'the number of outdoor café seats') to be met by 2001; and two pages of specific recommendations on how these goals might be achieved (City of Melbourne and Gehl 1994: 41–3). Its establishment of clear benchmarks for measuring the city's development was somewhat unusual in the context of local government planning in Australia at the time. Along with its emphasis on 'people-centric' design—resembling the language of the 1985 strategy plan—the report likely reflects the influence of Adams and his team over both documents. It also illustrates a more grounded approach to measurement that ultimately drives city planning, in contrast to the external validation offered by international indices of liveability.

The state government also emphasised good urban design as it developed and released its own plans for central Melbourne during this period, although it focused more on economic development. Appointed as head of the Ministry of Planning and Environment for the Cain Labor Government, David Yencken (2018: 73) defines 'high-quality urban design' as making the public realm 'as attractive to as many people as possible, to ensure that people find pleasure in public spaces and that the spaces in turn attract supportive activities'. Ten years later, the importance of 'good urban design'—defined as 'visual meaning, functional efficiency and broad access to change in cities and towns' (Freestone 2010: 39)—was also recognised and promoted by the national government's Urban Design Task Force. The planning policies released by the Cain Labor Government—'Central Melbourne: Framework for the future' (in 1984) and 'Shaping Melbourne's Future' (in 1987)—reflected this appreciation of urban design, but essentially as a way of harnessing central Melbourne as a tool to boost Victoria's economy. They focused on encouraging 'urban consolidation' and large-scale development. In contrast to the city's 'goal achievement' approach, 'Shaping Melbourne's Future' was arguably ineffective because it lacked clear implementation mechanisms and talked in vague terms; indeed, the 'implementation' section of the report is only two pages long (Ministry of Planning and Environment 1987: 56–7; Goodman et al. 2016: 29).

Nevertheless, elements of the state's plan were carried through to the 1990s and adopted by the Kennett (conservative) Government—in particular, through the first major policy document released jointly by the city and state governments. 'Creating Prosperity: Victoria's capital city policy' was designed principally to 'act as a guide to the private sector' (Government of Victoria and MCC 1994: 1). It aimed to make Melbourne a more internationally attractive city, focusing particularly on its strengths and opportunities as an appealing centre for big business, through initiatives such as building the Melbourne Exhibition Centre and a new Museum of Victoria and beginning the Docklands developments. Other commitments that reiterated the city's plans included promoting Melbourne as 'Australia's best place to live and visit' and 'Australia's premier retailing centre', by retaining the city's unrestricted (24-hour) trading hours, encouraging more activities in the main streets, upgrading and maintaining the city's lanes, arcades and footpaths and building new public space at Federation Square (Government of Victoria and MCC 1994: 5).

The city's 1985 strategy plan is the key local-level policy in this tale of urban revitalisation. Shaped by input from community activists and urban design professionals, it functioned as an important policy document to guide decisions and design in the administration. It also was used as a manifesto in city government election campaigns and as a vehicle for bringing together state and local government actors and other key stakeholders. Like the plans it immediately followed and preceded, the 1985 plan was shaped by community activists who had professional experience in planning and architecture, some of whom then became local government politicians (after lobbying the state's Labor Party to institute changes to local government) and who employed consultants and staff who shared their vision and values.

Gardner and Clark (1998: 138) suggest the 1985 strategy plan was successful where it outlined achievable policy and planning targets. Adams confirms the importance of targets—such as for 8,000 new residences—in keeping politicians and planners accountable (Adams and Dovey 2018: 206). He also suggests that strong alignment and collaboration between city and state planners were what enabled the policy changes that led to Melbourne becoming more liveable (Adams and Dovey 2018: 206). According to Freestone (2010: 38), the key factors that led to the successful implementation of the 1985 plan, specifically in terms of achieving increases in the city's residential population and conserving its local character, were 'political support, design-led delivery through area-partnerships, specific master plans, and public–private partnerships'.

After Melbourne was rated the world's equal most liveable city in one of the first global 'liveability' studies undertaken, in 1990, the state government began to focus on preserving and promoting this quality. 'Liveability' was a central and explicit focus of its 1994 'Melbourne Metropolitan Strategy Discussion Paper'. Identifying urban sprawl as a key threat to liveability and, noting that much of the region's growth was occurring on Melbourne's outer metropolitan edges, the state suggested a solution would be to further encourage housing development near and within the central city (Department of Planning et al. 1994: 23–5). Echoing and extending the city government's plans, it also suggested 'enhancing' the city's pedestrian environment, cultural and heritage features, universities, perceived level of safety and 'diversity'—in terms of demographics and the housing and jobs available for citizens (Department of Planning et al. 1994: 26–31).

The different policy documents developed by successive state and city governments demonstrate tensions between these two levels of government over the future of Melbourne, with each jockeying to instate their preferred plan for the city (McLoughlin 1992). Local community and stakeholder groups, in turn, fought for different visions of how and where the city would develop. As Freestone (2010: 37) puts it, describing the state government's approach to urban and suburban development in the 1990s, 'turmoil at the local level was often profound'. Each government proposed focusing on development in different parts of the city in their central policy documents.

In the 1980s, however, the tug of war between the state and city governments resulted in both parties giving much more attention to the central city than in preceding decades. Both parties had comprehensive, well-funded plans to redevelop the city and both agreed on key areas to be funded. The policy consensus was that *something* had to be done. Over time, the city appears to have taken on the role of managing smaller-scale urban design and infrastructure projects, focused on *how* people use the city, while the state government has retained responsibility for large-scale projects that define *what* people come to the city for. Despite local objections to urban consolidation, these policies helped to revitalise the inner city, leading to its 'liveable' qualities that are widely appreciated today. It can also be argued that increases in policing and improved perceptions of safety have contributed to the city's perceived 'liveability', by making it appear a safer place especially for wealthier people to live and work (Palmer and Warren 2013: 83–4).

Alongside these major battles centred on planning, 'Postcode 3000' was an important policy development aimed at encouraging and assisting residential development in the centre of the city. This policy was coordinated by the city government and supported by the state Department of Planning. Refusing to accept the state government's projected forecasts of a declining population, the city had set targets in its 1985 plan to increase housing types and add at least 8,000 new dwellings to accommodate a population increase of 16,000 residents (Jones 2018: 129). However, its initial mechanisms to implement this policy were unsuccessful and it was not until the property market crashed in the late 1980s that the subsequent empty commercial space provided an opportunity to realise this vision (Adams and Dovey 2018: 206–7).

Postcode 3000 provided financial incentives and technical and capital works support to developers proposing to build 30 or more residential units. These incentives were combined with a media strategy to promote the advantages of living in the city. At its heart was a demonstration building-conversion project, in which the city, working with industry partners, converted vacant floors of a historical building into apartments. Despite initial scepticism, the city recovered its investment as rents exceeded expectations and 'a long waiting list of prospective tenants' proved it had succeeded in persuading people to live in the CBD (Jones 2018: 129–30). The policy is credited with bringing redundant buildings back into use as apartments, helping the city meet its 15-year target for residential growth within 10 years, and with the creation of Birrarung Marr, a riverfront park reclaimed from underused rail sidings. An unanticipated side effect, however, was that, as rents increased and residential property investment became more attractive, low-income residents were forced out of the central city (Adams and Dovey 2018: 208).

A connected policy development was the transformation of Swanston Street, which similarly illustrates both tensions and collaboration between government actors, residents and other stakeholders. Swanston Street has been the site of prolonged debate and divergent policies between state and city governments over the past three decades. It has long been described as the 'civic spine' of Melbourne (Jones 2018: 106), despite in the 1980s being 'little more than a traffic artery; close to 90 per cent of the vehicles travelling along it had neither an origin nor a destination in the city' (Yencken 2018: 75). Early experimentation led to implementation that was later legitimated through external awards and changing attitudes and behaviours. Inspired by an international example shared by a young designer in the Ministry of Planning, the state government embarked on an experimental initiative in 1985 to show what was possible, while tensions between government departments and media criticism prevented more substantial change at the time. The 'greening of Swanston Street' closed part of the road to traffic for a street party over a weekend, when it was covered in grass sods. Although it was initially seen as a political stunt, about half a million people came to the central city to experience the event, which was reportedly 'loved to death' (Jones 2018: 102; Yencken 2018: 76).

After an international expert 'brought in to advise and reassure based on the European experience of pedestrianisation projects' failed to do more than preach to the converted, an economic study persuaded the state and city governments to reduce traffic in the area (Jones 2018: 103). A massive consultation then effectively identified practical implementation needs. Seven years after the 'stunt', Swanston Street was closed to vehicular traffic—an improvement that was considered 'the key to the City of Melbourne's receipt of the first Australia Award for Urban Design', in 1996 (Jones 2018: 104). The continued need for trams to use the street has thwarted full pedestrianisation, but the street now has the widest footpaths in Melbourne, is much safer for pedestrians and has more amenities—for instance, the number of cafes doubled between 1992 and 2003 (Jones 2018: 104–5). Its eventual (partial) pedestrianisation demonstrates Yencken's (2018: 74) argument that the best way to change perceptions of a city is by making physical changes to the environment and letting people experience them.

Enduring allure

Local and global legitimating factors have contributed to the enduring effects of the shared vision promoted by administrators, planners and activists in the 1980s. The localised focus of city government on tangible dimensions of people's experience in the city, genuine community input into planning processes and their recognition of existing assets can all be seen as success factors in this governance story. Over several decades, globally circulating ideas, indices and consultants have provided inspiration, information and external validation.

As key actors from this period point out, 'high-quality urban design is a long-term process' (Yencken 2018: 66), which needs to be considered far beyond electoral cycles and takes decades to achieve (Adams and Dovey 2018: 253; Jones 2018: 141). While state government legislation and planning guidelines introduced building height limitations in the 1980s, for instance, these were ignored and dismantled by subsequent governments, who 'bowed to developer pressure' (Yencken 2018: 69–71). It is remarkable that the city government, in spite of all the pressures and changes outlined above, managed a consistent approach to urban design and planning during this period. It was aided by the state's local government reforms that reduced the electoral changes in city government and the voting power of businesses (although property owners still have disproportionate electoral sway).

Local politicians' determination to include community voices and local data in planning processes and to establish organisational structures and internal capability also effectively ensured a relatively consistent implementation of strategic plans. The persistently 'people-centric' approach of the council administration, despite changing politics at the city and state levels and broader changes in the urban environment, may not have been possible if the key role of the Director of Urban Design had not been filled by the same person for more than three decades.

The 'political work' and 'craft work' of Rob Adams are an important factor in this governance success story. Ord (2018: 39) echoes others when she claims:

> The successful implementation of the 1985 *Strategy Plan* is in no small way due to the commitment of Rob Adams to see the principles embedded in all subsequent council decisions.

Adams's persistence and collaboration with a range of other important actors—notably, local politicians, state planners, international consultants and industry partners—have made a mark on the city. The cumulative effects of 30 years of incremental changes by state and city governments can be seen in Melbourne's streetscapes (Adams and Dovey 2018; Jones 2018: 93, 139).

Analysis and conclusions

The success on which we have focused in this chapter is a story about the changing governance arrangements that have reshaped central Melbourne. This story analyses the combination of state and city government policies and strategies over more than three decades. The increased capacities of state government reduced the formal capacity of the city government, but also gave it license to do things differently. The layered and emergent interactions between these two levels of government managed to combine economic and commercial interests with culture and liveability. NPM worked together with urban design principles and committed activists interested in citizens' rights; Melbourne rose from the ashes.

The state government changed numerous planning and strategy settings, making some unpopular decisions but using its legitimate power to shape the city at a macro level. Major building developments were pushed through in the face of opposition and determined efforts were made to attract people to Melbourne's centre as a place to live and play as well as work. Successive state governments redefined the scope of the municipality's powers and showed a determination to remove financially incompetent local politicians. Amalgamating what were then small municipalities with limited scope and abilities and changing the boundaries of the city so that it effectively straddled both sides of the Yarra River were also important, if unpopular, reforms.

Changes to the city government itself are also key to this governance success story. The changes that saw local politicians' roles move from an annually revolving door—even for the (then elected from within) mayor—to three-year terms and a directly elected mayor had significant effects. The city government's new focus on immediate and tangible things that matter a great deal to people as they move around the city was combined with a more visible, approachable and professional cadre of local politicians. The result was the removal of doubts about the legitimacy and competency of the municipal government, following years of perceived incompetence and financial mismanagement. Changes that modernised the city's administrative structures and procedures also bolstered its reputation. In what we would now easily recognise as NPM, many corporate management principles were imported to the city, followed by ideas about the importance of competition and the desirability of contracting out services. These moves added up to a clear signal that the city government had been transformed into a modern, responsible and professional organisation.

The social and environmental activists who first made an appearance in community consultations on the 1974 strategy plan, before becoming much more visible when the local politicians were sacked, and then numbered among the newly appointed politicians once elections were held again, were also an important part of this story of new governance arrangements. They can be credited with staunchly supporting the focus on good urban design that the state and city governments were beginning to embrace and that has since become so important to Melbourne's liveability. They are also likely to have had an enduring influence by promoting the incorporation of citizens' views into strategy documents.

This governance success story rests on the redefinition of the realms of responsibility of the state and city governments, which changed their capacities and their interactions. It also points to the symbolic importance of markers of success, which in this case helped to change residents' perceptions of their city and its standing in the world in the context of changing national and international trends. Landing towards the top of world liveability rankings was a very public marker of success that helped the state and city governments and Melburnians to continue to focus on the city's liveability as a core concern. All of these contributed to making Melbourne marvellous again.

References

Adams, R. and Dovey, K. 2018. 'The Marios talks.' In K. Dovey, R. Adams and R. Jones (eds), *Urban Choreography: Central Melbourne 1985–*. Melbourne: Melbourne University Publishing.

Aulich, C. 2005. 'Australia: Still a tale of Cinderella?' In B. Denters and L. E. Rose (eds), *Comparing Local Governance: Trends and developments*. New York: Palgrave Macmillan.

Aulich, C. 2009. 'From citizen participation to participatory governance.' *Commonwealth Journal of Local Governance* (2)(January).

Blomkamp, E. 2014. Meanings and measures of urban cultural policy: Local government, art and community wellbeing in Australia and New Zealand. PhD thesis, University of Auckland, Auckland, and University of Melbourne, Melbourne.

Campbell, A. H. 1987. *John Batman and the Aborigines*. Melbourne: Kibble Books.

Cheyne, C. 2008. 'Empowerment of local government in New Zealand: A new model for contemporary local–central relations?' *Commonwealth Journal of Local Governance* 1(1): 30–48.

City of Melbourne and Gehl, J. 1994. *Places for People: Melbourne city 1994*. Melbourne: City of Melbourne.

Damousi, J. 2008. 'Ethnic diversity.' In *eMelbourne: The encyclopedia of Melbourne online*. Melbourne: University of Melbourne. Available from: www.emelbourne.net.au/biogs/EM00533b.htm.

Department of Infrastructure and Transport 2011. *Creating Places for People: An urban design protocol for Australian cities*. Canberra: Commonwealth of Australia.

Department of Planning and Development, Department of Transport and Department of Conservation and Natural Resources 1994. *Melbourne Metropolitan Strategy: A discussion paper*. Melbourne: Department of Planning and Development.

Dollery, B., Wallis, J. and Allan, P. 2006. 'The debate that had to happen but never did: The changing role of Australian local government.' *Australian Journal of Political Science* 41(4): 553–67. doi.org/10.1080/10361140600959775.

Dovey, K. and Jones, R. 2018. 'Introduction.' In K. Dovey, R. Adams and R. Jones (eds), *Urban Choreography: Central Melbourne 1985–* . Melbourne: Melbourne University Publishing.

Economist Intelligence Unit (EIU) 2017. *The Global Liveability Report 2017*. London: The Economist Group. Available from: www.eiu.com/public/topical_report.aspx?campaignid=Liveability17.

Florida, R. L. 2005. *Cities and the Creative Class*. New York: Routledge.

Freestone, R. 2010. *Urban Nation: Australia's planning heritage*. Melbourne: CSIRO Publishing.

Gardner, L. and Clark, D. 1998. 'The City of Melbourne.' In B. Galligan (ed.), *Local Government Reform in Victoria*. Melbourne: State Library of Victoria.

Gehl, J. 2010. *Cities for People*. Washington, DC: Island Press.

Gehl, J. 2018. 'Move to Melbourne.' In K. Dovey, R. Adams and R. Jones (eds), *Urban Choreography: Central Melbourne 1985–* . Melbourne: Melbourne University Publishing.

Goodman, R., Buxton, M. and Moloney, S. 2016. *Planning Melbourne: Lessons for a sustainable city*. Melbourne: CSIRO Publishing.

Government of Victoria and Melbourne City Council (MCC) 1994. *Creating Prosperity: Victoria's capital city policy*. Melbourne: Government of Victoria.

Grodach, C. and Silver, D. 2013. Introduction: Urbanizing cultural policy.' In C. Grodach and D. Silver (eds), *The Politics of Urban Cultural Policy: Global perspectives*. London: Routledge.

Jacobs, J. 1961. *The Death and Life of Great American Cities*. New York: Vintage.

Jones, R. 2018. 'Melbourne, sung as it were a new song.' In K. Dovey, R. Adams and R. Jones (eds), *Urban Choreography: Central Melbourne 1985–*. Melbourne: Melbourne University Publishing.

Landry, C. 2000. *The Creative City: A toolkit for urban innovators*. London: Earthscan.

McKeown, T. and Lindorff, M. 2011. 'Temporary staff, contractors, and volunteers: The hidden workforce in Victorian local government.' *Australian Journal of Public Administration* 70(2): 185–201.

McLoughlin, J. B. 1992. *Shaping Melbourne's Future? Town planning, the state and civil society*. Cambridge: Cambridge University Press.

Manning, J. 2018. 'The Time Out city life index 2018.' *Time Out* [London], 30 January. Available from: www.timeout.com/london/citylifeindex.

Melbourne City Council (MCC) 1985. *City of Melbourne Strategy Plan 1985*. Melbourne: MCC.

Melbourne City Council (MCC) 1990. *City of Melbourne Strategy Plan: Issues for the 1990s*. Melbourne: City of Melbourne.

Melbourne City Council (MCC) 1992. *Directions 1992–1995: A Review of the City of Melbourne strategy plan 1985*. Melbourne: City of Melbourne.

Ministry of Planning and Environment 1984. *Central Melbourne: Framework for the future—Land use and development strategy*. Economic Strategy for Victoria 6. Melbourne: Government of Victoria.

Ministry of Planning and Environment 1987. *Shaping Melbourne's Future: The government's metropolitan policy*. Melbourne: Government of Victoria.

Museums Victoria 2018. 'Royal Exhibition Building.' In *Stories*. Melbourne: Museums Victoria. Available from: museumsvictoria.com.au/reb/stories/.

Museum Victoria n.d. *Marvellous Melbourne: A history of Melbourne*. Melbourne: Museum Victoria. Available from: museumsvictoria.com.au/marvellous/.

Neilson, L. 2013. City of Melbourne Strategy Plan 1985. Presented to Plans That Work: SGS Melbourne Seminar, June. Available from: www.sgsep.com.au/publications/plans-work-sgs-melbourne-seminar-june-2013.

Ord, L. 2018. 'Taking council.' In K. Dovey, R. Adams and R. Jones (eds), *Urban Choreography: Central Melbourne 1985–* . Melbourne: Melbourne University Publishing.

Palmer, D. and Warren, I. 2013. 'Zonal banning and public order in urban Australia.' In R. K. Lippert and K. Walby (eds), *Policing Cities: Urban securitization and regulation in a 21st century world*. London: Routledge.

Presland, G. 1994. *Aboriginal Melbourne: The lost land of the Kulin people*. Melbourne: McPhee Gribble.

Stevenson, D. 2000. *Art and Organisation: Making Australian cultural policy*. Brisbane: University of Queensland Press.

Yencken, D. 2018. 'The transformation of central Melbourne: 1982–88.' In K. Dovey, R. Adams and R. Jones (eds), *Urban Choreography: Central Melbourne 1985–* . Melbourne: Melbourne University Publishing.

Zajdow, G. 2011. 'Producing the market for alcohol: The Victorian example.' *Journal of Australian Studies* 35(1): 83–98. doi.org/10.1080/14443058.2010.541474.

6

The Child Support Scheme: What innovative collaboration can achieve

Meredith Edwards

The context and the problem

This chapter deals with the policy development process for Australia's Child Support Scheme (CSS), focusing particularly on the period 1986–88 but also briefly describing what happened in the subsequent implementation and evaluation phases until the present day.[1] Poverty among families with children—in particular, sole-parent families—was on the rise in the 1970s. One estimate of the poverty among female-headed sole-parent families suggested an increase from 38 per cent in 1972–73 to 50 per cent in 1981–82 (McClelland 2000: 23). By the time Labor came to power in 1983, it was clear that low-income families were in need

1 I am indebted to valuable comments on earlier drafts of this chapter from Kay Cook and the editors of this volume. I was both author of this paper and a participant in the development of the CSS from 1985 to 1988. My roles included: member of the Family Law Council (FLC) and co-author of the FLC paper referred to in the text; ministerial consultant and head of the Maintenance Secretariat in the Department of Social Security (DSS); and, later, head of the Social Policy Division in the DSS. While my unique position allows me to provide, hopefully, an accurate account of what occurred in the development of the CSS, I have attempted to minimise any bias that might colour my assessment of the scheme's performance by referring to sources that have independently assessed the impact and effectiveness of the scheme's operation and implementation.

of increased financial assistance and that some form of government action was required. However, the new Labor Government also realised it had to rein in government expenditure.

Apart from income support payments from the government to sole-parent families, additional payments came to some custodial parents from noncustodial parents in court orders for what were then called child maintenance payments. In 1983, relatively few noncustodial parents actually made payments to custodial parents and, where payments were made, they were at relatively low levels. It seemed as if the court system was deficient in collecting and enforcing maintenance payments.

In the mid-1980s, there was an attempt by the National Maintenance Inquiry to reform the court-based system of child payments (Attorney-General's Department 1984). That reform attempted, but failed, to address the way maintenance payments were assessed and hence left inadequate levels of payment. In addition, since no single government agency was prepared to take on the collection and enforcement functions, the inquiry was forced to recommend the setting up of a separate agency, the cost of which would take away most, if not all, of the savings the reform may otherwise have made. In any case, no benefits were to accrue to sole parents. Hence there was not much public support for this change. Yet the problem of few child support payments at relatively low levels remained.

Concern about sole-parent poverty as well as the growing government deficit led to a policy process around maintenance reform in the mid-1980s through several meetings of an interdepartmental committee (IDC) led by the Department of the Prime Minister and Cabinet (PM&C). However, the number of options put on the table for ministers to consider made it hard for them to agree on which option to pursue (see also Edwards et al. 2001: 67). Without a possible way forward, at this stage, it seemed that reform of the child maintenance system had reached a dead end.

What lay ahead was an opportunity to explore a more effective route to assess, collect and enforce payments from noncustodial parents—a proposal to use the tax system, which was put on the agenda by the Family Law Council (FLC). As it turned out, the FLC played a pivotal role in the eventual direction of child support reform. A paper presented by three of its members at the Family Law Conference in November 1984 canvassed the novel proposal of using the tax system to assess, collect and enforce payments from noncustodial parents based on a formula (Harrison et al. 1984). 'This is thought to be the first occasion upon which these proposals were publicly put forward' (CSEAG 1992: 45). The conference paper formed the basis of the FLC's discussions through 1985, including putting their proposal to the attorney-general in December 1985.

At that time, the proposal looked too radical to be feasible. There were multiple challenges for such a scheme to get off the ground, let alone be sustained, given how sensitive were the issues with which it dealt. First, there were no models anywhere in the world; no country had tried to integrate administrative and court-based systems for collecting payments, let alone using the tax system to administratively assess, collect and enforce payments. Second, there was strong bureaucratic resistance to the proposed scheme; no government agency wanted responsibility for it and scepticism about it even happening remained until the scheme was brought into legislation. Third, the proposal had ramifications across a number of government portfolios that made it harder to drive the reform, especially against such bureaucratic resistance. Finally, no lobby group was pushing for it, even though there was general recognition of the problem. Strong opposition came from lawyers but also social welfare groups, who saw the proposals as concerned mainly with raising revenue for the government.

Relevant in the policy context at this time were favourable institutional arrangements. A major review of social security policies was undertaken from the mid-1980s. One of the main concerns of this review was poverty among those on low incomes—in particular, sole-parent families. It recommended higher payments for low-income families, but the severe budget deficit at the time meant new revenue sources would be needed to support such a proposal. The ministers for social security and finance both had a stake, therefore, in a successful scheme that raised revenue as well as assisted in alleviating child poverty. Revenue from the proposed CSS was seen to provide that source (Edwards et al. 2001: 59). The CSS as a revenue source as well as a scheme to assist sole parents turned out to be the right policy at the right time.

Given the above, the existing system was ripe for reform if the policy design addressed the twin problems of lack of government revenue and child poverty. The eventually successful reforms began in a favourable political environment—Kingdon's (1984) window of opportunity had arrived. This was also an era in Australian public policy when big ideas did not scare off political action. What followed was a comprehensive and systematic policy process, including the use of evidence to inform key decisions at several stages.

The intention of the government to undertake major reform in this area was announced by the social security minister Brian Howe on 19 August 1986. The scheme was to be introduced in two stages. Three main elements of reform were introduced under stage one in June 1988: 1) a court assessment of the amount to be paid by the noncustodial parent; 2) the creation of the Child Support Agency (CSA) within the Australian Taxation Office (ATO) to collect payments from noncustodial parents covered by the scheme and, where appropriate, direct monthly payments (or automatic withholding) from wages and salaries;[2] and 3) distribution of the payments to custodial parents monthly by the Department of Social Security (DSS). Stage two began in October 1989 and replaced the stage one court assessment with administrative assessment by the tax system through the CSA as well as introducing a legislative formula related to the taxable income of the noncustodial parent.

The pay-as-you-earn system of collecting taxes would be used to collect child support payments. The CSA had the task of locating noncustodial parents, using the resources of the ATO if necessary (Daniels 1990: 5). The agency was also responsible for debt recovery. The DSS had as its main role to ensure that its pensioners and beneficiaries took reasonable action to obtain maintenance. In the initial scheme, all separated families were included but those not on a pension could, if they wanted, opt out.

A policy success?

In *programmatic* terms, the CSS can be considered a success in achieving its main aims: it increased the proportion of children of separated parents who received support and the amount paid and so assisted in reducing

2 The CSA was formed in 1988 as part of the ATO to administer the CSS. In 1998, the CSA was transferred to the Department of Family and Community Services before becoming part of the new Department of Human Services in 2004. The CSA operated largely as a separate agency until July 2008, when a departmental restructure brought its main enabling functions within the department (ANAO 2010: 27). The Department of Human Services has arrangements in place with the ATO to help facilitate accurate assessment as well as collection of parent income, including child support debts (ANAO 2017: 1.6).

poverty among sole-parent families; and it also increased the revenue for the government, leading to greater fairness for taxpayers (see, for example, MTCS 2005; Parkinson 2007; Smyth et al. 2015).

In August 1989, the Child Support Consultative Group (CSCG) reported favourably on the operation of stage one of the CSS, especially the substantial increase in coverage of sole-parent families receiving support and the amount they were paid. It was less favourable regarding the delays between court orders and payments being made to custodial parents by the CSA (CSCG 1989). An evaluation of the CSS published three years after the start of the scheme and once stage two had been introduced concluded:

> The direct successes of the reforms can be readily identified. The average court order has increased from $26 per child per week in 1988 to about $42 per child per week in 1991. The average stage two assessment is about $49 per child per week. The number of sole parent pensioners now receiving maintenance has increased from 26% to almost 40% and is greater for that proportion of the pensioner population who commenced a pension after the scheme started … The collection rate has increased from at most 34% in the years before the scheme to 65% at the present time … There is also a significant increase in child support payments outside the scheme by private arrangements between the parents.
>
> This result, achieved in such a short time, places Australia well ahead of the position in overseas countries. (CSEAG 1992: iv)

In contrast to most other countries (notably the United Kingdom), the Australian scheme was significant—as well as for the novel approach of using the tax system for assessing, collecting and enforcing payments—for improving on the adequacy of income levels for sole-parent families as well as limiting government expenditure (see, for example, McClelland 2000: 35). This contributed to both policy success and sustainability.

Fourteen years later, the aims of the CSS were still being achieved. According to the 2005 Ministerial Taskforce on Child Support (MTCS 2005: 2): 'To a considerable extent, the Child Support Scheme has achieved the objectives that successive governments have given for it.' Patrick Parkinson (2007: 181), who chaired the MTCS, subsequently said: 'The Fogarty Committee gave to Australia an excellent first generation child support scheme which has served the country well compared to the schemes of other countries.'[3]

3 The Fogarty committee is the Child Support Consultative Group (CSCG) chaired by Justice John Fogarty, which produced the 1988 report *Child Support: Formula for Australia*.

In terms of *political assessment*, the CSS rates highly. Both sides of politics considered action was required to improve the old child maintenance system, and the Opposition came in behind Labor to provide bipartisan support for the scheme. One journalist commented at the time that there was a

> bipartisan lull in the warfare between Government and Opposition since the Opposition has not had the nerve or the imagination to think of ways of opposing and criticizing a piece of legislation which is designed to benefit children. (Warden 1988: 13)

This was despite opposition from the usually influential Law Council of Australia as well as the lobby group representing noncustodial parents. Assisting the political acceptance was widespread public support for the CSS; a survey commissioned by the government suggested the CSS had the support of 92 per cent of those surveyed (Daniels 1990: 9). The 2005 MTCS report also saw the scheme as 'successful in promoting community acceptance of the idea of child support obligations' (2005: 2).

The policy *process* around the eventual birth of the CSS was comprehensive, from problem identification to evaluation (discussed in more detail below). It also had a couple of unusual features. One crucial factor in the policy process stands out: ensuring that the ministers as decision-makers discussed and decided on a set of values and other key issues before deciding on the principles to underpin the scheme and more detailed options. In this case, ministers moved systematically from their areas of agreement through to more difficult and contentious issues before getting into detailed options (Edwards et al. 2001: 71–2). For example, whether to use an administrative or a court-based system needed to be argued and decided before dealing with the issue of whether to use a formula. That issue was to be decided before the critical issue of which government agency to use to assess, collect and enforce payments (Edwards et al. 2001: 72).

The other factor was the use of unusual processes, such as the use of external expert lawyers, a problem-solving group of public servants (called 'contacts', from relevant departments) rather than an IDC, a closely involved set of ministers and the lead minister employing a ministerial consultant to drive the bureaucratic side of reform but with that consultant working out of the department rather than the minister's office.

Over the past 30 years, the CSS has managed to sustain its performance in terms of achieving its main goals in the face of changing circumstances (discussed further below) and has delivered valued social outcomes as well as earning a broad base of public and political support for its achievements. In addition, the innovative feature of using the ATO to assess and collect payments 'paved the way for other policy reforms'—notably, the Higher Education Contribution Scheme (ASSA 2017: 71).

In terms of assessing *endurance*, the CSS was not without its failings, especially in its administration. Throughout its 30 years of existence it has been plagued by problems with compliance and enforcement, if not fairness issues (see below). This has meant that some sole-parent families in need of support do not receive it (McClelland 2000: 35; Cook 2017). In addition, as early as 1990, in response to complaints from noncustodial parents about the unfairness of the scheme, the DSS reviewed the potential impact of the CSS on noncustodial parents with moderate incomes who had formed new relationships and parented more children (Daniels 1990: 18). Over time, a changed environment would require the scheme to be adapted to maintain its public support. A key political trade-off to manage over the years to ensure the continued legitimacy of the scheme was between the adequacy of payments for children and the perceived fairness of the treatment of nonresident parents.

Crafting the CSS

Agents of change

As indicated, parallel processes occurred in 1984–85 inside and outside government that reignited a focus on the child maintenance (support) issue and helped to shape the reform agenda, including a critical role played by the FLC. The chair of the FLC was Justice John Fogarty—a man who was passionate about child maintenance reform. Initially, he was sceptical about administrative assessment of child support but, fortunately for the CSS, he had changed his mind by 1986:

> I am now persuaded, contrary to my original reaction to this matter, that: (a) the present system is incapable of dealing with the problem and no amount of adaptation of it will meet the problem; (b) a largely administrative rather than legal response to this problem is now called for. (Fogarty 1986)

Fogarty was invaluable to the scheme's development from its inception well into its implementation. Such stewardship, from a well-recognised and respected judge, assisted in maintaining momentum and agreement across sectors.

Social security minister Howe became aware of the FLC proposal paper and was impressed by it. It was this paper that convinced him he needed to take a leadership role in policy development. The paper had largely adopted the novel proposal canvassed by Professor Irv Garfinkel from the Institute of Poverty Research at the University of Wisconsin in the United States. Professor Garfinkel was the architect of a pilot child support program based on a formula and using the assessment and collection functions of the tax office that was being tested at that time in the State of Wisconsin.

In 1985, I was able to take time out from the public service for a few months and went to The Australian National University (ANU), choosing to tease out further than the FLC paper had done the implications of a formula-based assessment of payments to be collected through the tax system. I delved deeply into key potentially controversial parts of a tax-based policy proposal. Professor Garfinkel was brought to The Australian National University to provide a keynote address at a conference there on child support and, while in Australia, he met the ministers who would form the subcommittee of Cabinet on child maintenance.

By far the most important individual in this story and the key driver of the reform was Howe. Towards the end of 1985, Howe was strategic in how he sold the idea of a Cabinet subcommittee on maintenance to prime minister Hawke. The subcommittee included treasurer Paul Keating, finance minister Peter Walsh, attorney-general Lionel Bowen, the Minister Assisting the Prime Minister on the Status of Women Susan Ryan and the community services minister Don Grimes. Howe also strategically involved others in the process from within and beyond government to support the reforms and contribute to the process—for example, one group he used as a sounding board was a subcommittee of caucus.

Within the DSS, a small group was set up, known as the Maintenance Secretariat, which included highly knowledgeable and committed lawyers brought into the department from outside specifically to work on the child support proposal, as well as an officer seconded from the Department of Finance. The unusual processes adopted by the secretariat turned out to be more appropriate for such a radical initiative than more traditional ways of working within the bureaucracy. This is an example of where a policy idea can assist—with the right combination of people and events, as occurred in this case—in moving a policy issue forward.

From problem framing to policy design

There is one critical stage in a good policy process: the policy problem needs to be clarified, well articulated and then owned by the policymaker(s) and, ultimately, the public. It is only once a policy issue is accepted as a problem that people can ask, 'What can we do about it?'

In the child support reforms, it was relatively easy to articulate the problem: why should kids suffer and taxpayers foot the bill just because parents decided not to live together? The ministerial subcommittee on maintenance, which had announced in August 1986 the principles underlying its proposed reforms, issued a discussion paper the following October called 'Child Support'. Under the section 'Why Reform', the paper said:

> There is widespread agreement that Australia's current system of child maintenance is in need of reform. The payment of maintenance is effectively a voluntary act, because those who do not want to pay need not do so, and the amounts that *are* paid are often low in relation to the non-custodial parent's capacity to pay. In the absence of adequate maintenance, an unfair burden is imposed on the taxpayer. (Cabinet Sub-Committee on Maintenance 1986: 6)

Because the policy initiatives were radical, complex, cross-departmental and involved politically sensitive issues, it was important that each of the policy stages was covered in the paper. The first necessary stage, considered above, involved identification and articulation of the problem. Also, as already indicated, before moving into policy analysis and deciding which options to put before ministers, it was important to attempt to understand the values that would frame the options.

The policy process—far from being a linear one—was like an improvised dance (cf. Althaus et al. 2018: 45). Stages in a policy process may need to be visited in a different order or revisited, and there can be backwards as well as forward movements across stages, or even overlapping stages. In this sense, the process can be seen as iterative. In some cases, it would have been inefficient to backtrack; in other cases, backtracking seemed to be the only way to reach a solution (Edwards 2004: 6).

An example of backtracking, as described more fully below, was, for political reasons, the phasing in of the scheme in two stages—as a result of successful lobbying and media attention about claimed unintentional consequences of the scheme. The first stage consisted of the more readily acceptable element of the collection of payments, leaving the more contentious formula issues until the second stage and after a review. Identifying the problem can overlap with a policy idea where the policy idea gives momentum to the reform agenda (Edwards 2004: 7). Thus, when Professor Garfinkel met with ministers, he was able to impress them with a policy solution as much as gaining acceptance of the problem. Thus, to generalise: 'The policy dance is sometimes seemingly random movements rather than choreographed order' (Althaus et al. 2018: 52). But, unless each stage is covered, major policy proposals will have less chance of turning into reality.

Few policy issues would have thrown up as many difficult and sensitive issues for analysis as did the child support reforms. As Smyth et al. (2015: 218) write:

> [C]hild support policy is an area fraught with high personal emotion. It is typically tempered by a litany of stakeholders, interest groups, anecdotes, and competing interpretations of what's going on … Value judgments about what constitutes 'fairness', highly technical legislation and policy rules, and complex interactions between child support and other policies … add additional layers of complexity. It is this mix of technical complexity, raw emotion, and disparate competing interests that makes child support one of the most contested areas of public policy.

Resolving in principle the key value issues helped this process, but nevertheless the policy analysis stage needed to be as rigorous and as comprehensive as possible. Gathering relevant data was an essential part of this process (see, for example, Edwards et al. 2001: 70ff.). There was a widespread and mistaken belief that insufficient revenue would be raised because most noncustodial parents had low incomes. Data from the Australian Bureau of Statistics (ABS) were sought and sophisticated modelling was undertaken of the revenue and distributional implications of the different options. Efficiency, equity and administrative simplicity criteria were used to assess possible formulas—especially: the impact on noncustodial parents (particularly those on low incomes), the possible disincentive effects on work, the extent of administrative simplicity and the financial implications (Edwards et al. 2001: 75–6).

In the consultation phase of policy development, the degree of participation by stakeholders and, more broadly, the public potentially affected by a possible decision will vary depending on the nature of the issue, its complexity and sensitivity. Processes can be formal or informal, continuous or episodic. Whom to consult, why, when in the policy process and how are a critical set of process issues (see Edwards et al. 2012), as is where good judgement is needed (Beauchamp 2016). A deliberate decision in the child support reform case was to use bilateral meetings with stakeholders but not open those meetings to the public (see Edwards et al. 2001: 77).

The Cabinet Subcommittee on Maintenance's October 1986 discussion paper on child support was the main public consultation document. This outlined the reasons for reform and the issues on which the views of the public would be sought. Importantly, the broad directions of reform—reflecting the key issues the subcommittee had been debating for the past few months—were stated as settled and not open for debate: the legislative formula, automatic withholding of noncustodial parents' payments at source, the use of the tax system to collect payments and the scheme's coverage of nonpensioners and nonbeneficiaries (Cabinet Sub-Committee on Maintenance 1986: 14–15). Discussion was sought on many other issues, such as: what type of formula to use, how to take into account the financial circumstances of custodial parents and paternity issues (Cabinet Sub-Committee on Maintenance 1986: 40).

The objectives of the proposed scheme, as set out in the discussion paper, were:

- NCPs [noncustodial parents] should share the cost of supporting their children according to their capacity to pay;
- Adequate support be available for all children of separated parents;
- Commonwealth expenditure be limited to what is necessary to ensure that those needs be met;
- The incentive to work be encouraged; and
- The overall arrangements should be simple, flexible, efficient and respect personal privacy. (Cabinet Sub-Committee on Maintenance 1986: 14)

There was considerable support for the reform proposals (see, for example, Daniels 1990: 1), but there were also some real concerns—for example, from custodial parents about whether this was just a revenue-raising scheme for the government and by how much children would benefit; and from noncustodial parents who wanted payments to be conditional on obtaining access to their children. And lawyers wanted a formula to provide some flexibility to determine payments on an individual basis. In response, the Cabinet subcommittee modified its position on several matters, although, importantly, not on the key principles of the scheme.

Ultimately, following refinement of the original proposals, the pivotal stage occurred and policy decisions emerged in what was a highly political context. This was when the political, policy and administrative impacts of the proposal were weighed.

Coming to decisions

It was not until the formal consultation process with the public had begun, late in 1986, that lobby groups and others realised the government was serious about pursuing reform. The radical policy proposal hit its biggest hurdle early in 1987 when media headlines gave attention to public criticisms from the Law Council of Australia and the likelihood that the government would back off from the reforms. One article in the *Australian Financial Review* highlighted the Law Council's concerns but also those of the Lone Fathers' Association about the 'unintended consequences' of the scheme—especially the use of a formula, but also whether the income of custodial parents would be taken into account in the formula, how self-employed people would be treated and whether unwed mothers would have to declare the name of the father of their children (*Australian Financial Review*, 13 January 1987, cited in Edwards et al. 2001). Further, an election was due later that year.

Minister Howe showed great skill at this stage in judging the need for the scheme to be modified and to suggest to his ministerial colleagues that the scheme could be broken up into two stages, as outlined above. Howe did not, however, lose sight of his longer-term vision. The government kept its resolve to have a formula to assess payments through the tax system and, in March 1987, it announced its firm policy (Daniels 1990: 1). To meet concerns, in May 1987, it appointed the CSCG to recommend what that formula would be as well as to monitor the introduction of stage one.

The CSCG fleshed out administrative aspects of the scheme alongside how the formula could be applied. It presented a unanimous report to the minister in May 1988, prior to the introduction of stage two the following year (Edwards et al. 2001: 79). Of strategic importance was not only the appointment of Justice Fogarty to chair the CSCG, but also appointing community representatives to the group, including a vocal noncustodial parent from the Lone Fathers' Association, Barry Williams. In this way, broad public support for the scheme was achieved and maintained.

Implementing the CSS and its legitimacy in a changing environment

Early implementation issues

One hard judgement for a policy advisor or policymaker to make is the ease with which potential policies can be implemented: those responsible for implementing will err on the side of caution; policy people will tend to underestimate the difficulties.

If the views of those charged with implementing the CSS were listened to at the beginning, it is highly likely the novel scheme would not have emerged, although many of the subsequent implementation issues may well have been easier to handle had they been more clearly anticipated as the scheme was being developed. As it transpired, despite sound policy design, implementation of the CSS left a lot to be desired.

Once it was clear from the 1986 budget announcements that the CSS would go ahead, collaboration across departments was required on the detailed policy and legislative issues yet to be resolved. Towards the end of 1986 and well into 1987, several implementation committees were set up to address issues such as property, constitutionality, costing and marketing issues, with different departments chairing different committees. Each committee reported to the whole-of-government 'contacts' group before their papers went into the Cabinet process.

Two key implementation issues emerged in this process. The ATO played the 'resources game' hard with what were considered by the Department of Finance and others to be excessive bids. The second issue was timing: a constant difficulty for the Maintenance Secretariat was getting departments to deliver to agreed but tight timelines.

It was generally agreed by senior ATO officials that the CSS was poorly implemented in the early days. Tax officers were expected to undergo a major cultural shift in dealing with face-to-face clients who were often distressed. They were largely untrained for the task. The ATO would claim that the original decisions and related resourcing did not take into account the need for more customer focus. Moreover, the system used by the CSA was designed more for tax processes than for a focus on activity at the counter. It was a profound reform that was appended to existing ATO functions rather than integrated into them and that was a large factor in leading to early implementation problems. One ATO officer involved in the development of the CSS remarked:

> The scheme had not won the hearts and minds of all the senior people in the Tax Office: the folklore was that 'we were told we had to have it'. I was the eighth person in my position in four or five years, including people just before retirement. It was a time of downsizing and hence there was a chance to transfer staff into the agency. So we could have put more investment into the different skills and attitudes and qualities that people in child support would need and we did not put enough investment into that sort of thing … We also didn't anticipate enough the cultural shift required. (David Butler, quoted in Edwards et al. 2001: 90)

Not surprisingly, the above factors were reflected in subsequent evaluations and, indeed, the persistence of implementation deficiencies appears to have been the main reason for the considerable scrutiny the CSS received in the 1990s.

Evaluations in the 1990s

Until the mid-1990s, there were five major evaluation reports over the fewer than seven years of the life of the CSS. This reflects continuing concern about the implementation of the scheme; until this point, most of the changes were administrative rather than major changes to the key policy settings.

Justice Fogarty, as chair of the Child Support Evaluation Advisory Group (CSEAG) in 1990, found:

> These reforms seem, even in the relatively short time they have been in operation, to have been largely successful. The legislation, with some minor exceptions, appears to be working satisfactorily. (CSEAG 1990: iv)

In 1990, the revenue clawback was not as high as expected but was sufficient to offset the administrative costs and stage two (introduced in October 1989) was expected to make a much larger contribution.

The CSEAG reported on the scheme as a whole at the end of 1991 and focused on its significant, if mainly administrative, problems (CSEAG 1992). It also believed it was important to monitor and refine the formula, noting the complaints from noncustodial parents who had second families:

> The debate now is not whether child support should be assessed by a formula but whether the formula in Australia is satisfactory or whether it can be improved. The debate now is not whether child support obligations should be enforced through the Taxation Office but whether its procedures need to be improved so as to become more efficient and effective. (CSEAG 1992: iv)

Many administrative refinements were made to the CSS after 1992, with almost continuous evaluation and/or client surveys. Of note was the first parliamentary inquiry into child support: in 1993–94, a joint select committee of parliament inquired into, among other things, 'the operation and effectiveness of the Child Support Scheme' (Parliament of Australia 1994). Although the committee's inquiry was wideranging and identified many problems in the design and operation of the CSS, it recommended the continuation of the scheme. In relation to early implementation issues, the committee noted:

> Two issues which were brought to light soon after the creation of the CSA also contributed to the early problems faced by the CSA and still remain unresolved. The first was the incorrect assumption that the CSA would only have minimal contact with its clients. The second issue was that the CSA was unable to handle the increased workload generated by the introduction of Stage 2 of the Scheme. (Parliament of Australia 1994: 92)

Among its 163 recommendations, the select committee called for work to be done to find out why a significant proportion of custodial parents received no child support or did not have child support arrangements. It also recommended a redrafting of the objective of the CSS to put more emphasis on both parents supporting their children according to their respective capacities to pay (taking out the childcare component of the custodial parents' disregarded income), that the child support formula be changed accordingly (Parliament of Australia 1994: xv–xvi) and that noncustodial parents be able to pay privately rather than through automatic withholding (p. xxii). It called for a review in 1996–97 of where the CSA should be administratively located, having expressed some concerns about its location within the ATO (Parliament of Australia 1994: xvi–xvii). Finally, it recommended that there be an independent study into the costs of raising children to evaluate the child support formula percentages (Parliament of Australia 1994: xxx). The government responded by accepting the recommendations that had no budgetary implications but putting off remaining ones until the 1996–97 Budget.

The Australian National Audit Office (ANAO) has undertaken efficiency audits of the CSS since its inception. In 1994, for example, it found unresolved administrative problems and 'serious deficiencies in the management and administration of the scheme, a major consequence of which is an unsatisfactory standard of service to clients', indicating that most of the 'administrative shortcomings' identified in the December 1991 CSEAG report remained (ANAO 1994: viii). Reporting four years later, it noted 'significant initiatives to improve on client service and staff development' as well as other improvements identified as lacking in the previous audit (ANAO 1998: xii). It did point out a continuing problem with debt collection and the need for agencies involved with the CSS to clarify their respective roles and responsibilities (ANAO 1998: xiii). In 2009, it noticed continuing problems in compliance with payments to noncustodial parents and, as late as 2017, while it assessed the efficiency of the collection arrangements and the administrative framework as 'sound', it recommended improvement, especially to ensure against fraud and tax evasion by noncustodial parents and the creation of a better compliance regime through improved data exchange between the ATO and the Department of Human Services (ANAO 2009).

The many evaluations of the CSS in the 1990s, not surprisingly, focused mainly on administrative deficiencies. But some issues were emerging that would lead to more major policy changes at the beginning of the next century to adapt the CSS to a changed environment in terms of family structures and social values—changes that would impact on the child support formula.

Policy adaptation to a changing environment

Despite the many reports and reviews into the operations of the CSS from its inception, it was not until 2003 that any substantial policy change began. The prime minister at this time, John Howard, pressured by noncustodial parents, established an inquiry to investigate '[w]hether the existing child support formula works fairly for both parents in relation to their care of, and contact with, their children' (Standing Committee on Family and Community Affairs 2003: xvii) and ways for parents to share the care of children post separation, as well as the fairness for parents of the child support formula.

In its report, *Every Picture Tells a Story* (2003), the Standing Committee on Family and Community Affairs recommended, among other actions, the setting up of the MTCS. The government adopted this as well as the majority of the child support recommendations in whole or in part. It considered proposed changes to the *Family Law Act 1975* to recognise

> the importance of children having the opportunity for both parents having a meaningful involvement in their lives and will include a new presumption of joint parental responsibility, except in cases involving child abuse or violence. (Commonwealth of Australia 2005: 2)

The taskforce recommended by the standing committee spearheaded a major process of policy change for the next five years. It justified the relatively major changes it recommended to the CSS on the basis of up-to-date evidence on the costs of raising children as well as changes in the circumstances of Australian families and in social security and income distribution policies since the start of the scheme. Moreover, it argued that there was now more emphasis on shared parental responsibility and on both parents remaining active in their children's lives and more mothers in the workforce (for more detail, see MTCS 2005: 2; Parkinson 2007: 180–2).

An independent 'expert' inquiry complemented the work of the MTCS 'to address a perceived "evidence gap"' (Regan 2017: 12–13). Importantly, while much evidence was gathered, especially on the costs of raising children, the evidence used was, as one of the participants in the process observed, 'within the boundaries of the moral imperative and other constraints such as what we knew would be politically acceptable and acceptable to stakeholders' (quoted in Regan 2017: 18). Thus, principles and values informed the evidence and the policy process, including that both parents were responsible for their children. This approach was considered necessary to fulfil the political function of bringing credibility and legitimacy to the findings of the taskforce (Regan 2017: 20).

The taskforce's report, *In the Best Interests of Children* (MTCS 2005), recommended major changes to the CSS (Parkinson 2007: 179), especially to the formula used to assess payment levels. It considered that, while the original CSS formula had served the country well, it could no longer be defended in the light of what was now known about the costs of raising children at the beginning of the twenty-first century (Parkinson 2007: 180). It proposed a new set of principles in which the balance was less on 'adequacy' (or sole-parent family poverty) and more on 'equity' between households (MTCS 2005: 117–20; Smyth and Henman 2010: 12).

Analysis by Cook and Natalier (2016: 163) reveals that many more fathers' than mothers' voices were included in the relevant chapter on the voices of parents. The economic modelling in 2008 of the impact of the revised formula and other reforms adopted by the government in response to the MTCS's recommendations showed that child support payments were lower and there was an increase in the proportion of custodial parents at an income disadvantage, although this was not quite as significant three years later (Smyth and Henman 2010; Smyth et al. 2015; Skinner et al. 2017: 89). An evaluation of the reforms concluded: 'Australia may not have made as much progress as it would have liked in this thorny area of social policy—especially in relation to compliance and perceptions of fairness' (Smyth et al. 2015: 217).

The latest review of the CSS, *From Conflict to Cooperation: Inquiry into the child support program* (Parliament of Australia 2015), occurred in 2014–15 through a parliamentary committee. As with previous reviews, this one concluded that the CSS 'is generally functioning as intended' (Parliament of Australia 2015: 2) and hence the committee's focus was on ways to improve the system for people with child support problems, 'while not disrupting the areas in which the [CSS] is working well' (p. 2).

An interesting suggestion the committee made was to explore the systems overseas that guaranteed child support payments to those parents whose children did not receive payments or received underpayments (Parliament of Australia 2015: 3; see also Cook 2017). This was proposed as part of the original scheme in the 1980s but fell by the wayside in the 1980s, partly as a casualty of an election that broke the CSS reform momentum. It is also interesting as an indication that placing the burden on custodial parents to obtain their payments had swung too far and there was a greater role the state could play in reducing sole-parent family poverty (for ways to increase the role of the state, see Cook and Natalier 2015).

The government accepted most of this report's recommendations, at least in principle, including agreeing to review parts of the child support formula and updating evidence on the costs of raising children. Significantly, it rejected the recommendation for a system of limited guaranteed payment of child support (Commonwealth of Australia 2016). Other than some technical changes, little change to the CSS has so far occurred.

Analysis and concluding reflections

What were the main factors that led to the introduction of such a radical scheme and its policy endurance? And to what extent might they be replicable to other policy issues? One of the main features of the child support case was the use of a comprehensive approach to developing its policy. Careful attention was paid to the economic and political contexts of the time in identifying and articulating the problem: the poverty of sole-parent families combined with the unfair burden on taxpayers at a time of government fiscal constraint. In this case, the problem was easy to articulate: why should children suffer financially just because their parents had decided to separate; and why should the taxpayer pick up the bill?

There was also constant use of relevant data and evidence to support arguments for reform and how that should progress. Where it was possible, confronting ministers early with key values-based issues helped them clarify their objectives and speed up the policy process. Further, consultation was quite inclusive for the times.

As with so many policies, this case illustrates a policy implementation gap: where the policy process fell down was in the implementation stage, as many subsequent evaluations identified. This reflects, in part, how hard it is to change the culture of an organisation such as the ATO, which was not used to dealing face to face with clients. Also, as this chapter has indicated, a constant theme throughout has been the failure of the CSS to deal satisfactorily with compliance and enforcement issues.

A comprehensive framework of the stages in developing policy is only part of the story if desired policy outcomes are to have a chance to succeed. A common thread in good policy processes (often not given due attention in the theory of policymaking) is giving careful consideration to organisational structures and processes within which policy work occurs.

A good example in this case is the critical decision taken to introduce the CSS in two stages when it appeared that public support for the proposal was waning (see Edwards et al. 2001).

In addition, there were strong relationships among key players; there was a cohesive network of players, each of whom knew each other across political, policy and non-governmental sectors. Highly knowledgeable and committed lawyers were hired and used effectively to come up with creative solutions. Above all, the policy was spearheaded by a determined and strategically insightful minister, with his ministerial colleagues closely involved, providing the necessary strong leadership.

In sum, the CSS—particularly its use of the ATO—was, and is, generally considered to be an innovative policy initiative in terms of being an effective mechanism for assessing, collecting and enforcing payments from noncustodial parents compared with the previous court-based system. It was the first scheme of its kind in the world. It illustrates how bold reform can happen when there is 'an alignment of political will, a clearly articulated policy problem and social science evidence for reform measures' (ASSA 2017: 70). As Justice Fogarty reflects:

> My belief is that social reforms of this sort rarely have a second opportunity. I think you catch one wave to the shore and, if you miss that, then you may wait a very long time before the next wave comes along. It was fortunate that [there was] the conjunction of committed people who were in the right place at the right time. There was a clear vision of what was to occur. It is unusual in a sense that the overall vision was clear … from 1985, but the detail of it remained relatively uncertain in some respects until very close to the end of the story. (Fogarty 1995)

Was there a unique set of factors in the CSS case that might not be applicable today or to other policy issues? Certainly, the economic, political and social contexts are very different today. Since the 1990s, there have been many significant changes in the policy environment that make achieving policy proposals that much harder: the great impingement of global forces, the advance of technology in unknown directions, a 24/7 media cycle that allows for ongoing debate over the 'right' policy problem and its solutions, tight budgets not helped by an ageing population, a more networked society, more dispersed power (including to ministerial advisors and non-governmental players), a blurring of boundaries across sectors, citizens less trusting but also more demanding of governments and minority governments becoming more common. Thus, policy outcomes are much more uncertain than in the past.

In addition, within public services it is now commonly argued that the capability to develop policy and to coordinate responses across government(s) has declined alongside a loss of institutional memory (e.g. Banks 2014a: 14). Also, it can be argued that there is a lack of political courage for a reform that is similar to the CSS in terms of its sensitivity and complexity. Indeed, there has been a lack of necessary courage to tackle reform within the CSS in recent years—witness the 2014–15 inquiry and the government's limited response.

The above factors affecting the policymaking process today are very different from those of the 1980s, but do they make achieving 'reform' so much more challenging? Policy reform may be harder to achieve today for the above reasons, but it is important to realise that most of the fundamental things about a good policy process remain the same and it remains as true today as before that 'good process makes not only for good policy, but ultimately for good politics too' (Banks 2013: 2). 'The fundamental principles of good policy processes should be timeless, even if the manner of their execution must adapt to the times' (Banks 2014b: 42). Now, as then, good policy development requires good analysis combined with an artful mix of process, people and politics.

Currently, despite the rhetoric to the contrary, there is much evidence of a risk-adverse public service environment, with middle management becoming less and not more empowered, so holding back innovative policy initiatives (e.g. Behm 2015: 135–6; Productivity Commission 2017: 198–200). In 2017, the head of PM&C, Martin Parkinson, implored public servants to break that mould: 'Think big. Aim high. Experiment. Be ruthless. Ask the simple questions if something is not working' (cited in Dennett 2017).

In describing a good policy development process, mention was made above of the importance of confronting ministers early, if possible, with values-based issues before detailed work on possible options occurs. Trade-offs are an inevitable part of making policy. The issue, for example, of the balance to be struck between adequate support for children, on the one hand, and fairness to parents on the other cannot be decided by an IDC or taskforce of officials (on this balance, see, for example, Smyth et al. 2015: 219). That balance has fluctuated over time, for example, with ministers in the 1980s taking a very different view of it than John Howard in his era. The result of his initiated reforms has been a rebalancing of the 'intractable policy problem' between payer, recipient and the needs of government for revenue (see Skinner et al. 2017: 92).

What will be required for the CSS to remain a success into the future? Community division is a real possibility unless there is courageous leadership. There is a need for a clear articulation by policymakers to the public of the merits of any changes to the CSS, given how contested the issues are between noncustodial parents and custodial parents. And, above all, policymakers will need to ensure any policy changes are implemented as intended.

References

Academy of the Social Sciences in Australia (ASSA) 2017. *The Social Sciences Shape the Nation*. Canberra: ASSA.

Althaus, C., Bridgman, P. and Davis, G. 2018. *The Australian Policy Handbook*. 6th edn. Sydney: Allen & Unwin.

Attorney-General's Department 1984. *A Maintenance Agency for Australia: The report of the National Maintenance Inquiry*. Canberra: AGPS.

Australian National Audit Office (ANAO) 1994. *Australian Taxation Office: Management of the Child Support Agency*. Audit Report No. 39 1993–94. Efficiency Audit. Canberra: ANAO.

Australian National Audit Office (ANAO) 1998. *Australian Tax Office: Management of selected functions of the Child Support Agency*. Performance Audit. Canberra: ANAO.

Australian National Audit Office (ANAO) 2009. *Child support reforms: Stage one of the child support reforms and improving compliance*. Performance Audit No. 19 2009–10. Canberra: ANAO.

Australian National Audit Office (ANAO) 2010. *Child support reforms: Building a better child support agency*. Performance Audit No. 46 2009–10. Canberra: ANAO.

Australian National Audit Office (ANAO) 2017. *Child support collection arrangements between the Australian Tax Office and the Department of Human Services*. Audit Report No. 50 of 2016–17, 15 May. Canberra: ANAO.

Banks, G. 2013. 'Good processes underpin strong, innovative policy.' *Australian Financial Review*, 22 March.

Banks, G. 2014a. 'Public inquiries, public policy and the public interest.' In G. Banks, *The Governance of Public Policy: Lectures in honour of eminent Australians*. Melbourne: ANZSOG.

Banks, G. 2014b. 'Return of the rent-seeking society.' In G. Banks, *The Governance of Public Policy: Lectures in honour of eminent Australians*. Melbourne: ANZSOG.

Barratt, G. 1999. *Sole parents, income support and family wellbeing*. Discussion Paper No. 411. Canberra: Centre for Economic Policy Research, The Australian National University.

Beauchamp, G. 2016. 'The role of government in innovation.' In Institute of Public Administration Australia (ed.), *Twelve Speeches 2016: A year of speeches from public service leaders*. Canberra: IPAA.

Behm, A. 2015. *No, Minister: So you want to be a chief of staff?* Melbourne: Melbourne University Publishing.

Cabinet Sub-Committee on Maintenance 1986. *Child support: A discussion paper on child maintenance*. Parliamentary Paper No. 292, October. Canberra: Parliament of Australia.

Child Support Consultative Group (CSCG) 1988. *Child support: Formula for Australia*. Report. Canberra: Department of Social Security.

Child Support Consultative Group (CSCG) 1989. *The Child Support Scheme: Progress of stage one*. August. Canberra: Department of Social Security.

Child Support Evaluation Advisory Group (CSEAG) 1990. *The Child Support Scheme: Adequacy of child support and coverage of the sole parent pensioner population*. August. Canberra: AGPS.

Child Support Evaluation Advisory Group (CSEAG) 1992. *Child Support in Australia: Final report of the evaluation. Volume 1: Main report of the Child Support Scheme*. Canberra: Commonwealth of Australia.

Commonwealth of Australia 2005. *A new family law system: Government response to Every Picture Tells a Story*. Response to the report of the House of Representatives Standing Committee on Family and Community Affairs Inquiry into Child-Custody Arrangements in the event of Family Separation, June. Canberra: Commonwealth of Australia.

Commonwealth of Australia 2016. *Australian government response to the House of Representatives Standing Committee on Social Policy and Legal Affairs report: From Conflict to Cooperation—Inquiry into the child support program*, August. Canberra: Commonwealth of Australia.

Cook, K. 2017. The gender of post-separation bureaucracies: A cross-national investigation. Paper presented to third International Conference on Public Policy, Singapore, 28–30 June. Available from: www.ippapublicpolicy.org//file/paper/5937a63a3b020.pdf.

Cook, K. and Natalier, K. 2016. 'Gender and evidence in family law reform: A case study of quantification and anecdote in framing and legitimising the "problems" with child support in Australia.' *Feminist Legal Studies* 24: 147–67. doi.org/10.1007/s10691-016-9317-9.

Daniels, D. 1990. *The child support scheme.* Parliamentary Research Service Background Paper, 11 October. Canberra: Department of the Parliamentary Library.

Dennett, H. 2017. 'Get ready for more disruption: Parkinson floats national citizen survey.' *The Mandarin*, 12 December.

Edwards, M. 2004. *Research, social science and public policy: From problem to practice.* Occasional Policy Paper No. 2. Canberra: Academy of the Social Sciences.

Edwards, M., Halligan, J., Horrigan, B. and Nicoll, G. 2012. Public Sector Governance in Australia. Canberra: ANU E Press.

Edwards, M., with Howard, C. and Miller, R. 2001. *Social Policy, Public Policy: From problem to practice.* Sydney: Allen & Unwin.

Fogarty, J. 1986. Commentary on the paper delivered by Edwards on the Family Law Council's proposals for maintenance reform, June. Unpublished.

Fogarty, J. 1995. Child Support Scheme Seminar. [Recording]. Centre for Public Policy, University of Melbourne, 4 September.

Harrison, M., Harper, P. and Edwards, M. 1984. 'Child support: Public or private?' In *Family Law in 84. Volume 2.* Canberra: Law Council of Australia.

Kingdon, J. 1984. *Agendas, Alternatives and Public Policies.* Boston: Little Brown.

McClelland, A. 2000. *'No child … ': Child poverty in Australia.* April. Melbourne: Brotherhood of St Laurence.

Ministerial Taskforce on Child Support (MTCS) 2005. *In the Best Interests of Children: Reforming the child support scheme.* May. Canberra: AGPS.

Parkinson, P. 2007. 'The future of child support.' *University of Western Australia Law Review* 33(2): 179–206.

Parliament of Australia 1994. *Child Support Scheme: An examination of the operation and effectiveness of the scheme*. Joint Select Committee on Certain Family Law Issues, November. Canberra: AGPS.

Parliament of Australia 2015. *From Conflict to Cooperation: Inquiry into the child support program*. House Standing Committee on Social Policy and Legal Affairs, July. Canberra: Commonwealth of Australia.

Productivity Commission 2017. *Shifting the dial: 5 year productivity review*. Report No. 84, August. Canberra: Productivity Commission.

Regan, S. 2017. Inquiring with evidence: How contemporary public inquiries bring evidence to policy. Paper presented to third International Conference on Public Policy, Singapore, 28–30 June. Available from: www.ippapublicpolicy.org//file/paper/593b61b1642ca.pdf.

Skinner, C., Cook, K. and Sinclair, S. 2017. 'The potential of child support to reduce lone mother poverty: Comparing population survey data in Australia and the UK.' *Journal of Poverty and Social Justice* 25(1): 79–94. doi.org/10.1332/175982717X14860543256937.

Smyth, B. and Henman, P. 2010. 'The distributional and financial impacts of the new child support system: A "before and day-after reform" comparison of assessed liability.' *Journal of Family Studies* 16(1)(April): 5–32. doi.org/10.5172/jfs.16.1.5.

Smyth, B., Rodgers, B., Son, V. and Vnuk, M. 2015. 'The Australian child support reforms: A critical evaluation.' *Australian Journal of Social Issues* 50(3): 217–32. doi.org/10.1002/j.1839-4655.2015.tb00347.x.

Standing Committee on Family and Community Affairs 2003. *Every Picture Tells a Story: Report on the inquiry into child custody arrangements in the event of family separation*. December. Canberra: Parliament of Australia.

Warden, I. 1988. 'Concern for our greatest resource provides a lull in partisan warfare.' *The Canberra Times*, 18 February.

7

The Australian water markets story: Incremental transformation

James Horne and R. Quentin Grafton

The lie of the land

The Australian water markets story is essentially a story of the Murray–Darling Basin (MDB), a major river basin in south-eastern Australia covering in excess of 1 million square kilometres. It is home to more than 2 million inhabitants, major irrigation industries, dryland farming and important environmental features.

Map 7.1 shows the key rivers and towns within the MDB. The Darling River is located in the northern MDB, which is characterised by 'flow of the river' extractions, which are permitted depending on the volume of water in the rivers. The Murray River is in the southern MDB, where many of the water extractions are made through irrigation systems and where the available volumes are highly dependent on water levels in large water storages.

Map 7.1 The Murray–Darling Basin

Source: MDBA (n.d.).

The water 'market' in the MDB is a cap-and-trade system whereby a specified volume of water can be extracted or diverted on an annual basis. A cap on surface water diversions was introduced in 1995 and, from July 2019, comprehensive caps on surface and groundwater use, called sustainable diversion limits (SDLs), will become operational as part of the MDB Basin Plan (Connell and Grafton 2011; Horne 2017b).

The water market involves two major types of trades: 1) water access entitlements, commonly known as water entitlements, which represent the consumptive share of the water resources within a catchment defined by a water resource plan; and 2) water allocations that are the physical volumes of water assigned to water entitlements in a given year. These vary depending on the volumes of water in storage and expected inflows. While trade in the MDB's two key water markets—for water access entitlements and water allocations—is mostly undertaken by irrigators, trades also include purchases and sales by the federal and state governments (principally for environmental purposes), by environmental non-governmental organisations (NGOs) and also by investors (Grafton and Williams 2018).

Understanding success

The MDB water markets are widely considered to be highly developed and well managed relative to other places in the world, including the United States (Grafton et al. 2011; Wheeler et al. 2014). In the southern MDB, water markets are accepted and trusted by water users and actively used by irrigators. They have contributed positively to both economic and environmental outcomes (Box 7.1). After a generation of water market development, most of the key technical design issues have been overcome and unforeseen technical and implementation issues addressed. Further, many of the state-based roadblocks and prohibitions on trade have been removed. Along with these developments has been a gradual accumulation of expertise by water users and significant improvements in water information availability and registry functions. But there was nothing straightforward or predestined about the generation-long policy development and implementation process that led to the water markets today.

Box 7.1 Impacts of water markets in the MDB

- The value of sales and the number of transactions in the water entitlement market and the water allocation market indicate strong user support and a mechanism to manage the extreme variability of streamflow within the MDB with both opportunistic cropping and perennial agriculture industries.
- The market facilitates the management of enterprise risk by increasing the flexibility of use of a key input as a result of:
  - Water users be able to determine the holding of a water asset on the balance sheet and water allocation use on the profit and loss account.
  - Water use and market participation can be adjusted to reflect water scarcity, mitigating the impact of drought on farm output.
- The market increases regional gross product by moving water to higher-value uses.
- It allows new entrants (for example, the almond industry) in new or established districts to satisfy their emerging water needs.
- Competitive and widely observed market prices support business planning and understanding of the marginal value of water in direct use.
- It allows government and private environmental waterholders to utilise environmental water on the same basis as other water users.
- It increases the transparency of how and where water is used.

Sources: Grafton and Horne (2014); Grafton et al. (2016); Horne (2017b).

In the early 1990s, trade in water in the MDB was limited, largely comprising intradistrict trade of allocated water. Interstate trade was non-existent. In 1994, against a background of national concern about how water was being used in rural Australia, including its environmental cost, a major reform program was embarked on under the auspices of the Council of Australian Governments (COAG). It was both ambitious and uncertain (COAG 1994) and progressed quickly into the work of the Murray–Darling Basin Ministerial Council (MDBMC) and the Murray–Darling Basin Commission (MDBC).

At this time, the states jealously guarded access to 'their' water. Indeed, while agreements on how to divide the resources of the Murray River existed and had been amended—and amended again in minor ways since Federation (Guest 2017)—they had, in essence, remained the same. Essentially, the upstream states—Queensland, New South Wales and Victoria—wished to ensure as many extractions as possible for the economic benefit of their irrigators. Despite support for cooperative actions from South Australia (Klunder 1993), there was considerable wariness among the upstream states about capping use because it would be perceived as constraining growth in irrigated agricultural production.

The two national water reform blueprints since 1994—the National Water Initiative (NWI) in 2004 and the *Water Act 2007* (Cwlth)—both emphasised a similar key role for water markets in addressing scarcity and efficiency, while recognising the needs of the environment and third parties. While agreement in principle for the development of water markets occurred in the 1990s, politics and state rivalries largely hampered its implementation. Indeed, it was the impact of the 'Millennium Drought', which affected most of the MDB during the decade to 2009, that ultimately catalysed water reform and water market development. Water markets were identified as a key means to redistribute water in a way that helped both buyers and sellers. Thus, in 2004, when the NWI was agreed to by the relevant governments and, in 2007, at the height of the drought, key decision-makers were much more supportive of removing barriers to water trading than they had been in 1994.

While the contemporary southern MDB water markets are now very large and comprehensive (Figure 7.1), the growth of the market has been a painstaking and precarious process. Trading in both water access entitlements and water allocations has grown significantly over the past two decades.

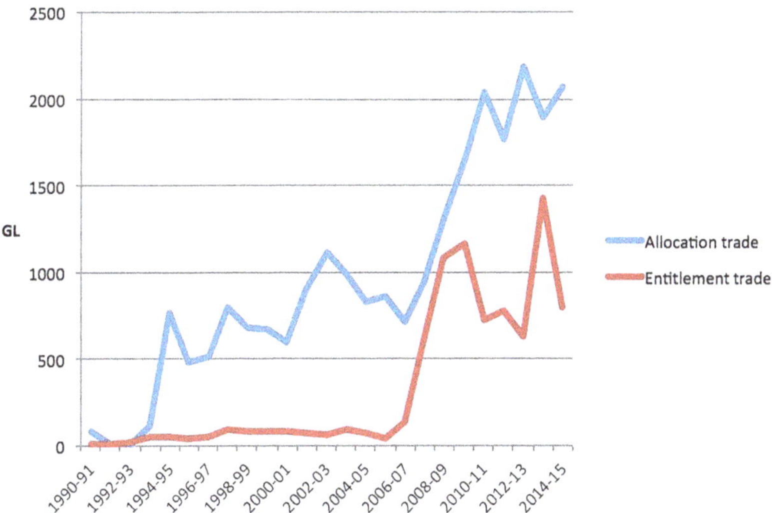

Figure 7.1 Southern MDB water allocation and entitlement trade

Source: ABARES (2016).

This market transformation has provided new agricultural opportunities and assisted with much needed structural adjustment, as the fortunes of specific agricultural products and the competitiveness of individual irrigation districts waxed and waned. The water markets have also been used by the federal and state governments to help achieve environmental objectives through their purchase and the use of water access entitlements for environmental and cultural purposes. Most economic models examining the likely impacts of expanding water markets and water trading in the MDB have also concluded that markets support an increase in the value of production and regional GDP, a reduction in vulnerability to drought and a reduced impact on regional communities from increased water scarcity (Kirby et al. 2014; Wheeler 2014).

A small number of observers blame water markets for causing poor business prospects and the ongoing depopulation of parts of rural and regional Australia (NSW Department of Trade and Investment, Regional Infrastructure and Services 2015; Peel et al. 2016), but the economic arguments proffered are far from persuasive. A more important critique has been of the provision of water entitlements almost entirely to irrigators who had preexisting water licences, but virtually no allocation to the First Peoples of Australia (Marshall 2017). A reallocation to First Peoples, as has occurred with water for the environment (Grafton and Wheeler 2018), is compatible with water markets should it occur through a voluntary buyback of water entitlements.

Contexts, challenges, agents

While water use has been the subject of intense political discussion since Federation (Guest 2017), this case study mirrors much of what has occurred in many other areas of the Australian economy and society over the past 25 years—namely, the increasing influence of the national government and markets in resource allocation. In particular, in the decade from the early 1990s there was a focus on reforming the infrastructure backbone of the Australian economy. This process included the road transport, electricity, gas and water sectors (NCC 1998, 1999).

In the MDB, water reform has involved reexamining and revising the water allocation process in each state. Not surprisingly, this was a complex and lengthy process and reflected the changing economy and society in rural and regional Australia, where markets in many areas of economic activity came to play an increasingly prominent role in daily life. The reform process responded, at least initially, to a collective national and state government judgement that broad-based water reform, including reforming the mechanism of water allocation, was required to support efficiency and to promote sustainable use across the nation.

The water reform component of the National Competition Policy (NCP) was called the 1994 National Framework for Water Reform (COAG 1994). Institutions and implementation processes were needed to undertake this unchartered task. The national and state governments, through the newly formed COAG, agreed to a reform process. Oversight of the implementation of the water reforms—originally conceived as a 10-year program—was entrusted to the independent National Competition Council (NCC), which was established as an advisory body to COAG. Most of the actions required state-by-state implementation, with the NCC playing an auditing role and national competition payments from the federal government to state governments providing a financial incentive for state actions (NCC 1999). This COAG framework identified the outcomes sought in each state's water management architecture and in cross-border arrangements relating to interstate trading of water within the MDB in particular. The reform program included the need for a comprehensive and clearly specified system of water entitlements, separation of property rights for land and water and trading of water and water entitlements (COAG 1994; NCC 1999).

The existing water policy framework—at that time largely determined and administered at a state level—was completely outdated. Water provision to both urban and rural users was heavily subsidised and water was not priced to reflect its scarcity value. There were also few opportunities to move water entitlements and their attached water allocations to service emerging high-value opportunities, as most water entitlements were still attached to land. Although most state governments had by this time halted issuing new entitlements, many entitlements already issued were not being fully utilised, leaving open the prospect of a future increase in water use.

A cap on water extractions was a necessary element to establish a market price for water and give greater visibility to scarcity issues. In 1994, there was no cap within the MDB as a whole or in specific valleys. Public servants administering water policy in individual states within the MDB were also ambivalent about water trading. It was said to be 'administratively difficult' to execute trades outside irrigation districts and virtually impossible to sell entitlements. Further, in the early 1990s, state-owned water infrastructure operators dominated licences and water rights were still, by and large, attached to land. Many local governments were also ambivalent about reform and shared a common concern that water trading might encourage the movement of water out of their region. Neither Indigenous water rights nor the environment as a water user were part of the public or high-level discourses on policy reforms (COAG 1993; COAG Working Group on Water Resource Policy 1994).

The policy process

Establishing allocation trading: A first step towards modern water markets

The initial reform period consisted of tweaking the existing administrative framework rather than contemplating a new water allocation framework or giving water users more control over their water assets. In 1994, the MDBMC and MDBC began discussing the substance of a new irrigation management strategy, the need for an annual cap on water extraction within the MDB and water market instruments to facilitate interstate trade (MDBC 1994, 1995b; MDBMC 1994). The work required to facilitate interstate trade was both basic and fundamental:

- defining water use, to assist in defining a cap on diversions
- identifying options to enable trade in water allocations
- defining what was to be traded
- defining where trade could occur (southern MDB and border rivers between New South Wales and Queensland)
- accounting for salinity and drainage credits
- developing institutional arrangements for trade and the changes required to the MDB agreement, which governed cooperative action between jurisdictions
- developing arrangements for trading within unregulated river systems (by June 1996)
- developing arrangements to facilitate water entitlement trade (known at the time as permanent water transfers), by June 1997 (MDBC 1995b).

A 1995 MDBC audit of water use in the MDB was undertaken as part of deliberations to set a cap on diversions (MDBC 1995a). It examined lowering annual allocations, restrictions on constructing off-river storages, reductions in entitlements by administrative decision or buyback, better monitoring, reporting and compliance and interstate trading arrangements. It did not propose a cap and gave little weight to the role of water markets or water trading, but it did suggest interstate trading was one approach that might help tackle the problem of the growing impact of diversions on the environment.

Trading in water allocations had been occurring intermittently within irrigation districts and within states for some years, but volumes were very small (NWC 2011). Limited interstate trading of water allocations was agreed for the 1995–96 water year, with rules for trading refined as experience deepened (MDBMC 1996). Volumes grew substantially over ensuing years, boosted by the onset of the Millennium Drought in the late 1990s. Trade in water allocations was a natural starting place for interstate trade, as it did not challenge the basic assumption that each state was in control of a defined parcel of statutory water rights. Moreover, it allowed unused water in particular years to be moved around (traded) and used interstate but did not change the ownership of the entitlement or right itself or where it was located.

Trading of entitlements: Challenging the basis of water allocation

An important first step towards the trading of water entitlements was to agree to a pilot project in the Mallee region in the southern MDB, which incorporated areas of three states (MDBMC 1996). A new schedule to the MDB agreement was needed and a plethora of technical matters had to be settled (MDBC 1997). In 1998, the MDBMC approved the pilot following much 'toing and froing', with extensive debate in project committees and the MDBC itself. The first trade under the pilot arrangements occurred in September 1998. During the next two water years, a minuscule quantity of water entitlements was traded, mainly comprising unused entitlements, which were sold for use in the viticulture, nut and citrus industries (MDBC 2000).

Notwithstanding the small volumes of trade and the restricted trade area, the pilot scheme provided a base from which to respond to various technical challenges with trade. This was very much a learning-by-doing process. A broad-based workshop involving the national and state governments, the irrigation sector, academics, water brokers and the MDBC, which examined the first two years of operation, concluded that 'permanent interstate water trade should ultimately be expanded beyond the Mallee region' (Tim Cummins & Associates 2000: 3). Potential barriers to market growth were also identified. Administrative systems governing interstate trade were characterised as fragile, with differences between states in the language used for identical assets proving problematic (Tim Cummins & Associates 2000).

Establishing interstate trading of water entitlements required states to improve their security and the processes needed to ensure trading could be completed efficiently and expeditiously. Many of these issues were raised in intergovernmental discussions and were the subject of discussion by academics and lobbying by peak interest groups. While the security around water entitlements gradually improved through legislative reform in each state, including water rights gradually being separated from land—although not until 2007 and 2008 in parts of Victoria (SRO 2017)—one of the most significant barriers to change came from within the irrigation sector itself. Key irrigation infrastructure operators (IIOs)—including Murray Irrigation Limited, Murrumbidgee Irrigation and Goulburn Murray Water—were concerned about the adverse impact of trading entitlements out of their district and the prospect of stranded assets (Hassall & Associates 2002). Transaction costs imposed by these entities by way of access, exit and termination fees had the potential to stifle trade, even if individual water owners within a district wished to trade with water users outside the district.

It was not until May 2003 that the MDBMC directed the MDBC to pursue opportunities to establish permanent interstate trade across the southern MDB (DAFF 2003; Interstate Water Trade Project Board 2004), although the press release from the chair of the ministerial council, the federal Minister for Agriculture, Fisheries and Forestry, did not mention the water trading outcome. What ensued were consultants' reports and dozens of meetings by numerous MDBC committees. The views of the Australian Competition and Consumer Commission (ACCC 2006) were commissioned in relation to access, exit and termination fees. The very limited progress was evidenced by the slow growth of trading in water entitlements and the very tentative political attempts to address increasing environmental degradation (Horne 2017b). While South Australia, Victoria and New South Wales had agreed to permanent interstate entitlement trading throughout the southern connected part of the MDB in late 2006, it was not until 2007 in the depths of the Millennium Drought that the MDBC consented to the key protocol that supported the reform of these fees and a lowering of transaction costs to trade (MDBC 2007).

The passage of time that ultimately resulted in interstate trading of water entitlements was an important part of the reform process. For example, revised state water legislation under the 1994 framework—for example, the *Water Act 2000* in New South Wales (WaterNSW 2018)—took considerable time to be implemented. The outcome was achieved in the context of national reform processes, with pressure kept on state bureaucracies through the NCP payment processes that provided financial incentives for states to achieve defined outcomes.

Increased national involvement in water markets

While the decision by COAG in June 2004 to support the NWI intergovernmental agreement was widely applauded, implementing the reform elements proved difficult. Indeed, in June 2005 and again in July 2006, governments felt the need in COAG meeting communiqués to reiterate their commitment to the NWI and to progressing unfinished elements of the water markets agenda. These unfinished elements included conversion of existing water rights into secure and tradable water access entitlements and establishing open and low-cost water trading arrangements. Notwithstanding the renewed commitment, the agreed timetable slipped (COAG 2005, 2006).

Partly as a response to these delays and increasing concerns about water scarcity in the MDB due to the Millennium Drought, in September 2006, prime minister Howard announced the formation of the Office of Water Resources in his own department, with a key focus on water trading (Howard 2006). This led to the new National Plan for Water Security, signalling a step up in national involvement in water issues, and the passage in late 2007 of the *Water Act 2007* (Cwlth).

The broader water reform elements of this story can be found elsewhere (Horne 2013, 2016, 2017b). They included greater national responsibility for overall water resource management in the MDB, including new institutional arrangements (including replacing the MDBC with the Murray–Darling Basin Authority, a national government body), introducing a role for the ACCC in water market operations within the MDB, a more prominent role in environmental water management with the establishment of the independent Commonwealth Environmental Water Holder and the provision of $3 billion to purchase water entitlements for environmental purposes. Further, specific Commonwealth Government programs focused on the future prospects of the irrigation sector and irrigation district efficiency and the provision of enhanced water information.

Some states were strongly opposed to increased national action on water reform more generally but, for the water markets, even after the change in national government in December 2007, attention turned to implementation. In particular, the ACCC's competition policy water agenda focused on strengthening the rights of irrigators to buy and sell their water assets more readily. At the time, irrigation districts were still imposing restraints on water trading (Commonwealth of Australia 2007; ACCC 2010, 2017). The development, and later introduction, of improved basin-wide water trading rules was also designed to improve the ease of trading and reduce risks. The new role for the Bureau of Meteorology (BOM) in water information—designed to increase the quality and availability of market information—would increase market transparency and reduce risk. State governments introduced new rules around the carryover of allocated water, improving the incentives to manage available water between water years.

By 2018, the southern MDB water markets had reached a level of maturity in terms of the annual volume of sales, but the water trading function (akin to the stock exchange function in shares) and water registries (akin to the land titles office for land) still have considerable room for improvement. The two traditional markets for water entitlements and water allocation continued to expand and dominate trading activity, but other fledgling markets (for example, trade in water delivery rights, forward allocation markets, water entitlement leases and carryover capacity) are expanding (ACCC 2017; ABARES 2018). Markets in the northern MDB are less developed and the attitudes of irrigators and administrators towards water as an asset (the water entitlement) remain immature.

A *Four Corners* investigation revealed systemic issues around water theft that were undermining confidence in the northern MDB (Horne 2017a). Anticorruption authorities are still investigating these matters, but they illustrate powerfully how well-functioning markets need strong, effective and ongoing regulatory governance. The exposure of possible corruption and water theft and a lack of adequate governance in New South Wales (Matthews 2017) also shows that states still have—through both action and inaction—the ability to derail water market reforms.

Slow and steady wins the race

Water market development in the MDB can be characterised as a 'success' from the vantage point of 2018, but certainly not an 'overnight' success. Within the southern MDB, the benefits of water trading envisaged over two decades ago have been substantially achieved but, as with most elements of policy, expectations change and the goal posts move.

Table 7.1 summarises key changes in the status of water markets, key policy actions, the changing roles at different levels of government and, in a general sense, the major benefits and costs directly associated with water markets. Taken as a whole, we view the development of the water markets over the period under discussion as transformational, and in large part extremely successful in terms of outcomes and the likelihood of enduring support. What we have outlined is, in essence, how the water allocation process in the MDB has been changed to better manage the risks around scarcity; this is the core achievement. As international experience profoundly illustrates, instances of successful reconfiguration of water allocation processes have been few and far between.

Table 7.1 Water markets in the MDB: Transformative, incremental development

Issue	1970–94	1995–2006	2007–18
Status of water markets	No water markets in contemporary sense Small volume of informal intradistrict water trading	Key foundation stones for intrastate and interstate water markets gradually established, including a cap on diversions in the southern MDB Allocation market gradually expands and pilot interstate trading entitlement trading commences Only lip-service paid to the environment	Water entitlement and water allocation markets mature and grow as restrictions are eliminated and transparency improves Enforcement of SDLs on surface and groundwater resources to be enforced from July 2019 New market for water delivery rights Ongoing acrimonious debate about the acceptability of water shares between agricultural and environmental interests
Key policy actions (what happened)	Widening role of joint MDB-wide science activities to assess and address declining environmental outcomes	Attributes required for water markets agreed, including: • Comprehensive system of water entitlements, including clear specification of rights • Separation of property rights for land and water • Trading rules for allocation of water and water entitlements • Introduction of consistent water sharing plans Cap on surface water extractions reflecting existing level of development agreed and implemented Stronger scientific role in understanding the impact of irrigation on the environment Pilot design architecture developed for interstate trading and significant expansion of allocation trading State water legislation modernised, strengthening water entitlements	Competition policy outcomes strengthened with new role for ACCC (e.g. through IIO charging and transformation) and MDB plan water trading rules New BOM function improves water information and availability Basin-wide water trading rules introduced New state policies on storage and carryover encourage more efficient water use Victoria's infamous 4 per cent rule restricting trade out of some districts eliminated New SDLs on surface and groundwater State registry processing times reduced Private digital trading platforms improve transparency

Issue	1970–94	1995–2006	2007–18
Roles of levels of government (a key element in how it happened)	Detailed state water policies and administration almost entirely within the domain of state governments National government involved in brokering overall agreements on the Murray River and on the formation of basin-wide institutions, the MDBMC and the MDBC	States remain firmly in control of water policy, particularly early in period Stronger national framework role: • 1994 National Framework for Water Reform agreed as part of national microeconomic reforms under the aegis of COAG, with strong flow through to MDB water market development • Independent NCP reviews backed by NCP payments to the states provide an incentive for state action • 2004 NWI and establishment of the National Water Commission strengthen national oversight of water markets	National oversight of MDB water markets increases significantly through new ACCC, BOM and Murray–Darling Basin Authority roles outlined in Water Act 2007 (Cwlth) New Commonwealth body, the Murray–Darling Basin Authority (MDBA), replaces MDBC, with basin-wide trading rules New Commonwealth Environmental Water Holder introduces basin-wide approach to use of environmental water, backed up by large water portfolio Key state roles of implementation and enforcement Shadow cast over NSW commitment to water market principles in northern MDB State restrictions inhibit Victorian rural–urban trade Increased role for community engagement
Benefits and costs	Little downside, but also very limited benefits	Significant benefits to many participants in annual allocation trading Restrictions on trading limit benefits and increase interyear and intrayear uncertainties Lack of carryover policies undermines potential benefits of trading	Water migrates to higher-value uses and to areas suited to strongly performing commodities Water use managed between years, depending on business and environmental needs Agricultural producers and environmental waterholders able to manage business more flexibly Trading allows businesses adversely affected by climate change and/or shifts in commodity markets to sell off valuable assets Trading allows environmental water allocations to be moved to service the environmental assets in greatest need

Explaining 'how' policy success was achieved, particularly success after 25 years, is fraught. Our thesis that it was achieved incrementally is hard to dispute, but it is much more difficult to pinpoint precisely why barriers were breached at any particular time.

Moreover, there was nothing inevitable about this progress. Persistence, resilience and alignment of some key factors resulted in gradual forward movement. What is clear from reviewing detailed historical documentation and from participation in those processes for over a decade is that each country, and indeed perhaps each river basin, will need to tackle its own specific circumstances (Grafton et al. 2017). At the process and political levels, the evolution of water market development has been very messy. Sometimes the political process has been pivotal to progress, while at other times it has hampered it.

Implementation time frames

The MDB water markets took an unexpectedly long period to develop and mature.

With the benefit of hindsight, the lengthy implementation phase is not so surprising. The world of rural water administration in the early 1990s was dominated by engineers and hydrologists and focused on states determining how water should be used and in what quantities on different types of land. Many agricultural commodities were centrally marketed. At that time, markets more generally, and what they represented, played only a limited role in the life of water users and water administrators.

Reconfiguring water resource management to respond to the needs of scarcity in a rules-based society requires concerted multidisciplinary actions that take time to develop (Grafton et al. 2016). The technical details of 'how to' had not been developed and individual governments proffered competing positions. Once administrators understood and agreed on how to move forward, political support was necessary to see this incorporated into the law of individual states or the national government. In the early 1990s, water was not perceived as a private good and, with use linked to land in the case of irrigation, it was not treated as a transferable asset as it is today. Further, the power of IIOs and bulk water providers tended to subjugate the interests of individual users. Upgrading the quality of the water property right was a central issue in developing confidence in the MDB water markets. It was the central issue in reshaping the water allocation system that had operated before the advent of extreme scarcity.

Role of leadership

There is a question of whether water market reform would have been made without concerted intervention from 'outside' forces promoting change. These were the central agencies at the state and federal levels—the departments of the prime minister and premiers and the state and federal treasuries—which were the champions of microeconomic reform more broadly and water market reform specifically. This also included the newly formed NCC, which oversaw financial incentives to state governments that met their commitments to put in place functioning markets. These were important forces, shepherding actions through the early stages of reform. These reform champions were aided by a period of severe drought (the Millennium Drought) and, later, by a national government prepared to step outside what had been seen as its traditional sphere of influence (Briese et al. 2009).

Whereas actions by state and federal water ministers often slowed market growth—sometimes aided and abetted by the unanimity decision-making rule of the MDBC—individuals did matter. The 2007 national intervention provided a major fillip to strengthening MDB water markets and the overall water reform process. It was a determined effort to break through logjams from existing institutional arrangements. Prime minister Howard and his water minister, Malcolm Turnbull, were prepared to act and take responsibility for difficult rural water issues thrown up by the Millennium Drought and address ongoing problems from existing institutional arrangements. This determination from the prime minister, backed up by financial resources, supercharged the reform process. Perceived constitutional issues were scrutinised but found not to be a hindrance to effective action (Briese et al. 2009).

While aspects of the reform have been heavily criticised (e.g. Grafton and Williams 2018), its focus on water markets is widely viewed as a success. For the MDB, the *Water Act 2007* (Cwlth) strengthened the water market framework sufficiently to underpin significant growth in transactions and in interstate trade and to facilitate greater resilience in the economy (Kirby et al. 2014).

Politics as a hindrance

Eventual 'success' in the MDB came notwithstanding the complex, lengthy and often acrimonious negotiations involving several levels of government and multiple interested parties from 2007 onwards. While the NSW premier's initial response was strongly supportive of the Commonwealth's proposals, the Victorian premier was antagonistic from the outset, arguing that he would cooperate providing certain conditions were met, but promptly proposing conditions he knew would be politically unacceptable to others. From a Commonwealth perspective, it appeared that protecting state interests compromised economic, social and environmental outcomes for the basin as a whole. One explanation of the acrimony is that the national government was proposing to become much more actively engaged in MDB water affairs in much the same way as it had in many other policy areas (for example, the closure of state-based stock exchanges and the national regulatory role in corporate affairs and electricity markets). This was regarded as a threat to established ways of doing business, rather than a positive step towards a more modern and efficient business model.

A microcosm of the post-2007 water policy implementation process was the attempt to upgrade state water registers to reduce transaction costs around interstate trade. The project sought to standardise water registers in New South Wales, Western Australia, South Australia, Tasmania, the Northern Territory and the Australian Capital Territory, and put in place a new register system, personal water accounting and tracking of water entitlement trade applications. The existing Victorian and Queensland water registers were not included in this project, but the aim was that all state registers would 'work together so that data can be transferred automatically between each register', facilitating efficient interstate trade, particularly in the MDB (Commonwealth of Australia 2007). Despite significant investment, the national government finally halted attempts to complete the national water market system and it remains a gap in MDB water market development today. Making information freely available at the basin-wide level would have required state actors to become more transparent in their actions.

At another level, community politics and buy-in are important factors in achieving success and resilience of policy actions. In the case of the water markets, strong support came from users—evidenced by their participation in market trading. It has grown slowly and organically, as users individually came to understand the benefits that can flow from them. This provides a contrast to the basin plan. The MDBA conducted 24 town hall meetings, 56 roundtable meetings with community leaders and key groups and 30 meetings with Indigenous communities. Nearly 12,000 submissions were received from the community, which led to 300 changes to the draft basin plan (Horne and Guest 2014). Yet there was still a level of discontent, with social media now an important channel to convey (mis)information.

Role of crises

At each of the key policy junctures (in 1994, 2004 and 2007), there were crises of sorts. In the early 1990s, broad-based microeconomic reform was needed and there was a clear consensus within central agencies and among heads of governments that many areas of the economy needed reforming. Water was one such area and markets were seen as potentially playing an important role. This was a challenge to agencies that traditionally handled water matters, as the operation of markets was outside their normal bounds of doing business. Heads of government directed action be taken, and within the MDB, responsible ministers were similarly directed. By the early 2000s, much had been achieved in water reform generally and within the MDB specifically, but with the Millennium Drought in progress, central agencies and heads of governments were again unhappy with progress, leading to a further intergovernmental process (the 2004 NWI) to renew pressure on reform. The year 2007 was materially different in that the central government agencies responded to the deepening drought in the MDB.

The adage of never wasting a crisis is apposite, but to do so it is critical to prepare well in advance. Prime minister Howard's 2007 Australia Day speech was not prepared 'on the back of an envelope', as one state water minister colourfully suggested, but came from months of detailed dialogue and critical analysis. The key point is that the shortcomings of a system are often well known among the active players; often, a real difficulty is finding leaders to address these shortcomings and the circumstances in which they can be resolved or mitigated.

There often are sharp differences in views about what can be done, particularly when incumbent interests are being challenged, and a real problem of 'industry capture' of public servants whereby the interests of key stakeholders, such as irrigators, are identified as the state or national interest. In part, this reflects elements of Australia's political system that seek to protect specific state interests, on the one hand, and sectoral interests (for example, prioritising rural over urban interests) on the other, with little regard to broader national or, in this case, basin-wide interests. One iconic example of this was the infamous 4 per cent trade-out rule restricting the sale of water entitlements in Victoria (ACCC 2009) outside irrigation districts, which was finally revoked in 2014.

Effective regulation critical to markets

The strength of the southern MDB water markets is their highly regulated structure and well-accepted fairness, buttressed by hydrology, even if there are minor ongoing concerns that IIOs might impose trade restrictions or levy fees that inhibit trading out of irrigation districts (ACCC 2017). The same is not true for the northern MDB, where the water markets are small in terms of the volume traded and the proportion of water available to trade. Thus, there still appears to be a much more cavalier attitude to water use by users and water theft appears to still be prevalent, even among some of the larger users.

Compliance in the NSW part of the northern MDB has been left to that state, which appears to have a major cultural problem in its public service towards compliance and enforcement of water plans and water licences, even in the otherwise generally well-managed MDB water markets (Horne 2017a; Matthews 2017; MDBA 2017). The difference illustrates how the overarching regulator of the MDB water markets, the MDBA, needs to play a more hands-on role. For example, it needs to ensure there is strong compliance of state water trading rules with the basin plan's trading rules, which became operational in 2014. Yet, as of 2018, no public audit had been undertaken of these rules.

Conclusions

The water story in the MDB shows that the path of developing the basin's water markets was neither linear nor optimal, but rather one of grasping opportunity at times of crisis, building coalitions of interests and actions by policy champions who were able to provide the intellectual framework and motivation for what has become transformational change. Success came after a long struggle, reflecting both policy initiatives and increased activity by water users. Effective and longstanding policy reform requires vision, diligence, persistence, vigilance and, sometimes, even luck. None of these should be taken for granted. Opportunities to strengthen the policy framework should be taken when they arise.

The lengthy time frames in water market development demonstrate not only the complexity of policy, but also the transitions in culture in the rural water sector, in public sector administration and among IIOs (both privatised and corporatised state-run organisations). The policy process that transformed the water markets is one in which many water users have been frustrated at the slow pace of change. It is also the case that, as participants in the market came to understand and trust its benefits, they warmed to the idea, underpinning its strong organic growth even as the Millennium Drought receded.

The process of water market development is ongoing, notwithstanding the transformation that has already occurred. There are, for example, opportunities to reduce transaction costs further by digitising the whole-of-market processes and providing greater transparency and real-time access to information for all market participants. Much greater attention must also be given to metering and compliance and also to inequities of water allocation to the First Peoples of Australia. Further, to ensure the long-term success of water markets, the central basin-wide regulatory authority, the MDBA, must account for the effects of water trade on return flows. These cultural and environmental considerations need to be part of the water markets story going forward.

References

Australian Bureau of Agricultural and Resource Economics and Sciences (ABARES) 2016. *Australian Water Markets Report 2014–15*. Canberra: Department of Agriculture and Water Resources. Available from: data.daff.gov.au/data/warehouse/9aaw/2016/awmr_d9aawr20161202/00_awmr2014-15_v1.0.0.pdf.

Australian Bureau of Agricultural and Resource Economics and Sciences (ABARES) 2018. *Australian Water Markets Report 2016–17*. Canberra: Department of Agriculture and Water Resources. Available from: www.agriculture.gov.au/abares/research-topics/water/aust-water-markets-reports.

Australian Competition and Consumer Commission (ACCC) 2006. *A Regime for the Calculation and Implementation of Exit, Access and Termination Fees Charged by Irrigation Water Delivery Businesses in the Southern Murray–Darling Basin*. 6 November. Canberra: Commonwealth of Australia.

Australian Competition and Consumer Commission (ACCC) 2009. *Water trading rules*. Position Paper, September. Canberra: ACCC.

Australian Competition and Consumer Commission (ACCC) 2010. *ACCC Water Monitoring Update 2009–10*. Canberra: ACCC.

Australian Competition and Consumer Commission (ACCC) 2017. *ACCC Water Monitoring Report 2015–16*. Canberra: ACCC.

Briese, R., Kingsland, A. and Orr, R. 2009. *Swimming in new waters: Recent reforms to Australian water law*. AGS Legal Briefing No. 90, 21 July. Canberra: Australian Government Solicitor. Available from: www.ags.gov.au/publications/legal-briefing/br90.htm.

Commonwealth of Australia 2007. *Water Act 2007*. Canberra: Commonwealth of Australia. Available from: www.comlaw.gov.au/Series/C2007A00137.

Connell, D. and Grafton, R. Q. 2011. 'Water reform in the Murray–Darling Basin.' *Water Resources Research* 47(12): W00G03. doi.org/10.1029/2010WR009820.

Council of Australian Governments (COAG) 1993. *Council of Australian Governments Communiqué*. 8–9 June. Canberra: COAG.

Council of Australian Governments (COAG) 1994. *Council of Australian Governments Communiqué: Attachment A—Water resource policy*. 25 February. Canberra: COAG.

Council of Australian Governments (COAG) 2005. *Communiqué*. Council of Australian Governments Meeting, 3 June. Canberra: COAG. Available from: webarchive.nla.gov.au/gov/20070829161939/http://coag.gov.au/meetings/030605/index.htm.

Council of Australian Governments (COAG) 2006. *Communiqué*. Council of Australian Governments Meeting, 14 July. Canberra: COAG. Available from: webarchive.nla.gov.au/gov/20070829162059/http://coag.gov.au/meetings/140706/index.htm.

Council of Australian Governments (COAG) Working Group on Water Resource Policy 1994. Report of the Working Group on Water Resource Policy to the Council of Australian Governments. Mimeo. Canberra.

Department of Agriculture, Fisheries and Forestry (DAFF) 2003. *The provision of future water supplies for Australia's rural industries and communities.* Supplementary Submission to the House of Representative Standing Committee on Agriculture, Fisheries and Forestry. October. Canberra: Parliament of Australia.

Grafton, Q., Garrick, D. and Horne, J. 2017. Water misallocation: Governance challenges and responses. Report prepared for the World Bank.

Grafton, R. Q. 2017. 'Editorial: Water reform and planning in the Murray–Darling Basin, Australia.' *Water Economics and Policy* 3(3): 1702001. doi.org/10.1142/S2382624X17020015.

Grafton, R. Q. and Horne, J. 2014. 'Water markets in the Murray–Darling Basin.' *Agricultural Water Management* 145(C): 61–71. doi.org/10.1016/j.agwat.2013.12.001.

Grafton, R. Q. and Wheeler, S. A. 2018. 'Economics of water recovery in the Murray–Darling Basin, Australia.' *Annual Review of Resource Economics* 10: 487–510.

Grafton, R. Q. and Williams, J. 2018. Failures to deliver on the key objectives of the Water Act 2007. Submission to the South Australian Royal Commission on the Murray–Darling Basin.

Grafton, R. Q., Horne, J. and Wheeler, S. A. 2016. 'On the marketisation of water: Evidence from the Murray–Darling Basin, Australia.' *Water Resources Management* 30(3): 913–26. doi.org/10.1007/s11269-015-1199-0.

Grafton, R. Q., Libecap, G., McGlennon, S., Landry, C. and O'Brien, B. 2011. 'An integrated assessment of water markets: A cross-country comparison.' *Review of Environmental Economics and Policy* 5(2): 219–39. doi.org/10.1093/reep/rer002.

Guest, C. R. 2017. *Sharing the Water: One hundred years of River Murray politics.* Canberra: Murray–Darling Basin Authority.

Hassall & Associates 2002. *Barriers to trade of irrigation entitlements in irrigation areas and districts in the Murray–Darling Basin.* Final Report, June. Sydney: Hassall & Associates Pty Ltd.

Horne, J. 2013. 'Economic approaches to water management in Australia.' *International Journal of Water Resources Development* 29(4): 526–43. doi.org/10.1080/07900627.2012.712336.

Horne, J. 2016. 'Water policy responses to drought in the MDB, Australia.' *Water Policy* 18: 28–51. doi.org/10.2166/wp.2016.012.

Horne, J. 2017a. 'A low-water mark for the Murray–Darling Basin: Political commitment to the basin plan is long overdue.' *Policy Forum*, [Online], 15 December. Available from: www.policyforum.net/low-water-mark-murray-darling-basin/.

Horne, J. 2017b. 'The politics of water reform and environmental sustainability in the Murray–Darling Basin.' *Water International* 42(8): 1000–21. doi.org/10.1080/02508060.2017.1412201.

Horne, J. and Guest, C. 2014. 'Australian water policy framework: A rejoinder to Daniel Connell "A time to regroup and reassess in the Murray–Darling Basin".' *Global Water Forum*, 7 April. Available from: www.globalwaterforum.org/2014/04/07/the-australian-water-policy-framework-a-rejoinder-to-daniel-connell-a-time-to-regroup-and-reassess-in-the-murray-darling-basin/.

Howard, J. 2006. Prime Minister the Hon. John Howard MP joint press conference with New South Wales Premier Morris Iemma, Victorian Premier Steve Bracks, South Australian Premier Mike Rann and Acting Queensland Premier Anna Bligh, Parliament House, Canberra, 7 November. Transcript, [Online]. Accessed from: pandora.nla.gov.au/pan/10052/200612210000/www.pm.gov.au/news/interviews/Interview2235.html (site discontinued).

Interstate Water Trade Project Board 2004. Barriers to trade out of irrigation districts. Agenda Item No. 3, Meeting 11, 17 February. Released under MDBA Freedom of Information 49 Doc #3.

Kirby, M., Park, R., Connor, J., Qureshi, M. E. and Keyworth, S. 2014. 'Sustainable irrigation: How did irrigated agriculture in Australia's Murray–Darling Basin adapt in the Millennium Drought?' *Agricultural Water Management* 145: 154–62. doi.org/10.1016/j.agwat.2014.02.013.

Klunder, J. 1993. The changing demands for surface water in the Murray–Darling Basin. Submission to Murray–Darling Basin Ministerial Council Meeting, No. 12, Melbourne, 25 June.

Marshall, V. 2017. *Overturning Aqua Nullius*. Canberra: Aboriginal Studies Press.

Matthews, K. 2017. *Independent investigation into NSW water management and compliance: Final report*. Sydney: NSW Department of Industry. Available from: www.industry.nsw.gov.au/__data/assets/pdf_file/0019/131905/Matthews-final-report-NSW-water-management-and-compliance.pdf.

Murray–Darling Basin Authority (MDBA) n.d. Murray–Darling Basin boundary. [Online]. Canberra: MDBA. Available from: www.mdba.gov.au/sites/default/files/pubs/Murray-Darling_Basin_Boundary.pdf.

Murray–Darling Basin Authority (MDBA) 2017. *The Murray–Darling Basin Water Compliance Review: Containing reports by the Murray–Darling Basin Authority and the Independent Review Panel.* Canberra: MDBA.

Murray–Darling Basin Commission (MDBC) 1994. *Irrigation management strategy pamphlet.* Agenda Item No. 11, Meeting No. 30, 16 September. Released under MDBA Freedom of Information 79/1/4, 2018.

Murray–Darling Basin Commission (MDBC) 1995a. An audit of water use in the Murray-Darling Basin: Water use and healthy rivers—Working towards striking a balance. Mimeo. Canberra: MDBA.

Murray–Darling Basin Commission (MDBC) 1995b. Irrigation management strategy progress report. Agenda Item No. 24, Meeting No. 32, 22 March. Released under MDBA Freedom of Information 79/1/7, 2018.

Murray–Darling Basin Commission (MDBC) 1997. Irrigation management strategy – water market reform – pilot water trading project. Agenda Item No. 5, Meeting No. 45, 11 November. Released under MDBA Freedom of Information 79/1/14, 2018.

Murray–Darling Basin Commission (MDBC) 2000. Interstate water trading: Permanent trade—Pilot project. Agenda Item No. 10.1, Meeting No. 56, 12 December. Released under MDBA Freedom of Information 79/1/18, 2018.

Murray–Darling Basin Commission (MDBC) 2007. Interstate water trade. Agenda Item No. 15, Meeting No. 92, 24 April. Released under MDBA Freedom of Information 49 Doc. #96.

Murray–Darling Basin Ministerial Council (MDBMC) 1994. The irrigation management strategy: Water market reform. Agenda Item No. 10.2, Meeting No. 13, 24 March. Released under Freedom of Information 79/1/3, 2018.

Murray–Darling Basin Ministerial Council (MDBMC) 1996. Water market reform. Agenda Item No. 8, Meeting No. 18, 28 June. Released under MDBA Freedom of Information 79/1/11, 2018.

National Competition Council (NCC) 1998. *Compendium of National Competition Policy Agreements.* 2nd edn. Canberra: AusInfo.

National Competition Council (NCC) 1999. *NCP Second Tranche Assessment. Volume 2. B10: Water reform.* Canberra: NCC.

National Water Commission (NWC) 2011. *Water markets in Australia: A short history.* Canberra: NWC. Available from: apo.org.au/system/files/27438/apo-nid27438-101806.pdf.

New South Wales Department of Trade and Investment, Regional Infrastructure and Services 2015. *Monitoring Economic and Social Changes in NSW Water Sharing Plan Areas: Irrigators' surveys 2009/2010 and 2013—A state wide comparison*. February. Sydney: NSW Department of Trade and Investment, Regional Infrastructure and Services. Available from: www.water.nsw.gov.au/__data/assets/pdf_file/0010/548362/irrigators_survey_report_2013.pdf.

Peel, D., Schirmer, J. and Mylek, M. 2016. *Farming challenges & farmer wellbeing.* 2015 Regional Wellbeing Survey: Farmer Report 1, October. Canberra: University of Canberra. Available from: www.canberra.edu.au/research/faculty-research-centres/ceraph/regional-wellbeing/survey-results/2015/Barriers-to-farm-development_26Oct2016.pdf.

State Revenue Office (SRO) 2017. *Water Entitlements After 1 July 2007.* [Online]. Melbourne: Government of Victoria. Available from: www.sro.vic.gov.au/water-entitlements-after-1-july-2007.

Tim Cummins & Associates 2000. *Workshop Report: Impediments to, and options for, expansion of permanent interstate water trading in the Murray–Darling Basin*. 15 December. Albury, NSW: Tim Cummins & Associates.

WaterNSW 2018. *Getting to Know the Water Management Act 2000.* [Online]. Sydney: WaterNSW. Available from: www.waternsw.com.au/customer-service/water-management-act-2000.

Wheeler, S. A. 2014. 'Insights, lessons and benefits from improved regional water security and integration in Australia.' *Water Resources and Economics* 8: 57–78. doi.org/10.1016/j.wre.2014.05.006.

Wheeler, S. A., Loch, A., Zuo, A. and Bjornlund, H. 2014. 'Reviewing the adoption and impact of water markets in the Murray–Darling Basin, Australia.' *Journal of Hydrology* 518: 28–41. doi.org/10.1016/j.jhydrol.2013.09.019.

8

National competition policy: Effective stewardship of markets

Alan Fenna

Introduction

In the mid-1990s, Australian Commonwealth and state and territory governments jointly developed, introduced and set about implementing a program of market liberalisation called the National Competition Policy (NCP). The NCP is widely considered a great success—'a landmark achievement in nationally coordinated economic reform' (PC 2005: viii). As well as being celebrated as a significant and successful suite of economic reforms, it is also hailed as an all-too-rare exercise in successful collaboration between the country's governments. Following the policy assessment framework proposed in the introduction to this volume, this chapter considers the extent to which, and the ways in which, the NCP was an instance of policy success in programmatic, process, political and durability terms. Unlike many other 'policies' evaluated in this volume and elsewhere, the NCP was explicitly named as such—formally articulated and documented, with clear definitions and boundaries—making its characterisation and study more straightforward than might otherwise be the case.

There were certainly ways in which the NCP was a triumph of policymaking, particularly in respect of its implementation. Like even the best policy, of course, the NCP had its difficulties as well as its critics.

Nonetheless, at the end of the decade of reform, key bodies were able to declare 'mission accomplished'. However, as far as the fundamental test about the degree to which the NCP achieved its stated goal of improving Australian economic performance, it is almost impossible to judge. With regards to the important ways in which the NCP clearly was a success, this chapter canvasses aspects of 'good process' that may have contributed; however, it also draws attention to the unusually favourable conditions that made success much more achievable and likely in this area than in many other policy situations. There are some lessons that can be gleaned from the NCP experience, but all too many of them are of the 'choose your target and your timing wisely' variety.

The policy's architecture

The NCP was a nationwide, multisectoral program of market liberalisation introduced in 1995 under the auspices of COAG, Australia's peak intergovernmental body. It ran through to 2005, when the last tranche of compensation payments was made to the states and territories and the program concluded. The NCP's main aim was to reduce the cost structure of the Australian economy by introducing competitive market forces to sectors protected by regulation or government ownership or some combination of the two. These, most importantly, were the major network utilities providing Australia's gas and electricity infrastructure as well as water and transport. However, the ambition extended well beyond those to encompass other market restrictions, whether in retailing, privately owned infrastructure or agricultural product marketing. It followed closely the recommendations of the committee of review of the application of the *Trade Practices Act 1974* (Cwlth) contained in its report, known as the 'Hilmer Report' (Hilmer et al. 1993).

The NCP was adopted with the signing of three intergovernmental agreements in April 1995. The 'Competition Principles Agreement' committed governments to the structural reform of public monopolies; application of the principle of competitive neutrality, requiring that 'government businesses do not enjoy competitive advantages over private companies as a result of their public ownership' (NCC 2005: 2.1); a regime for third-party access to private monopoly infrastructure; and review of legislation to determine whether continued protection of certain markets was warranted. The 'Conduct Code Agreement' committed governments to the extension to previously exempt businesses of competition surveillance under the Commonwealth's *Trade Practices Act*. The 'Agreement to Implement the National Competition Policy and Related Reforms' committed governments to the reform of energy, water and transport industries.

Implementation involved the creation of two new regulatory bodies under the *Competition Policy Reform Act 1995*. The merger of the Trade Practices Commission and the Prices Surveillance Authority created the Australian Competition and Consumer Commission (ACCC), with a broader mandate to identify and pursue anticompetitive behaviour. And a new body, the National Competition Council (NCC), was established to monitor the NCP's implementation and assess whether progress was sufficient to justify the scheduled reward payments promised to the states and territories by the Commonwealth.

It is important to note that the NCP was one element in a broad suite of reforms pursued by Australian governments at the state and federal levels through that period. Thus, there were a number of cognate liberalising reforms being undertaken or mooted by governments at the time that were not part of the NCP. Neither privatisation nor competitive tendering and contracting out, for example, were part of the NCP. Nor were there any macroeconomic aspects, although there were related developments in this area as well; the NCP was focused exclusively on microeconomic reform.

A policy success?

As noted above, the NCP has been celebrated—if not feted—as an instance of policy success on a grand scale. The NCC (2005: vii), whose task it was to assess progress of the reform, declared: 'Over the past decade, Australian governments have participated in the most extensive and successful economic reform program in the nation's history.' The OECD's (2005: 11) praise was almost as fulsome, referring to the way that, with the NCP and other reforms, 'Australia became a model for other OECD countries'. More careful evaluation leads, however, to conclusions that are slightly less clear cut and triumphal. Technical assessment is difficult and, while proponents such as the Business Council of Australia were happy with the policy (BCA 2014: 10), there were dissident voices from other sectors.

Process assessment

Much well-intentioned and perhaps even well-conceived policy notoriously comes unstuck in the process of implementation. The Ur-text of implementation studies details a quagmire of intergovernmental program failure in the United States in an initiative conceived and directed in Washington, DC, and rolled out in the city of Oakland, California (Pressman and Wildavsky 1973). Such was not the case with the NCP, which was a shining example of intergovernmental collaboration and coordination. In the NCC's (2005: xvii) assessment: 'Many reform objectives under the NCP have substantially been met.' The program was rolled out systematically, with clear objectives, formal assessment and adequate time. There were some derogations and there were some grievances; however, implementation was in general on schedule and comprehensive.

Programmatic assessment

The thornier question is whether the NCP and its constituent reforms delivered the promised benefits, translating policy *outputs* into the intended *outcomes*, without undue costs. Did the NCP achieve its goal of reduction in the cost structure of the Australian economy and a resultant improvement in Australia's competitiveness and economic performance? According to Australia's premier economic policy research and advisory body, the Productivity Commission, the answer is 'yes': the NCP 'has yielded benefits across the community' (PC 2005: viii). Central to this judgement is the commission's view that the NCP 'contributed to the productivity surge that has underpinned 13 years of continuous economic growth, and associated strong growth in household incomes'. Other benefits the commission identified included reducing the price of a number of consumer goods and helping to meet a major environmental goal through 'the more efficient use of water'.

If the NCP did contribute to a 'productivity surge'—and if that surge was the reason for at least the first 15 years of Australia's astonishing run of economic good fortune until the mining boom took over that job—it can certainly be judged a 'success'. However, determining what contribution the NCP made to overall economic performance is far from easy. It is quite possible that other liberalising reforms, such as tariff reduction, were far more important, or that the reforms in general were not the decisive variable. The Productivity Commission's elaboration was:

> While many factors can influence productivity growth, a number of analytical studies indicate that microeconomic reforms—including NCP—have been a major contributor to Australia's productivity surge in the 1990s, and to the economy's increased resilience in the face of economic disturbances. The reforms have achieved this by increasing the pressures on both private and government businesses to be more productive, through increased competition, while simultaneously enhancing their capacity to respond through more flexible work arrangements, the removal of unnecessary red tape and the like. (PC 2005: 17)

In summary, however, the commission acknowledged that 'it is not possible to draw an explicit link between specific reforms and the recent improvement in Australia's economic performance' and concluded simply that 'the timing of specific policy changes over the last two decades is strongly suggestive of a link' (PC 2005: 36). This, it barely needs saying, smacks of the fallacy of *post hoc ergo propter hoc* (Hancock 2005: 28). Such judgements are inevitably contaminated by prior position and ideology and the Productivity Commission's favourable assessment must be read in the context of its tireless advocacy of such reforms. Given this, the most that can be said on the available evidence is that the NCP *might* have achieved its main goal.

Questions have also been raised about the very idea that competition can be successfully introduced into some of the key industries addressed by the NCP. The 'distorted' markets in the network utilities sector may not be so much the consequence of ideology, interests, public ownership or anachronistic regulation as much as a reflection of the intrinsic challenges of managing natural monopolies and optimising 'imperfect markets' (Argy 2002). By their nature, the transmission and distribution of electricity, for instance, do not lend themselves to multiple providers and thus genuine competition. Given such economic realities, contrived competition may be the best that can be achieved. 'Structural separation' was intended to inject competitive market forces into the production and sale of electricity but has proven difficult. Similarly, King (2002) has asked what the public interest is in imposing 'competitive neutrality' provisions on government business enterprises and depriving them—and, through them, the consumers they supply—of access to investment capital at government rates.

Political assessment

Whether the NCP was a success in political terms is also difficult to judge. In one important regard it obviously was: governments on both sides of politics and at both levels of the federal system supported and persevered with the reforms. Cross-party support continued even through changes of government—a significant test and endorsement (Deighton-Smith 2001: 40–1). This continued commitment is particularly notable given the resistance the Labor Party faced from within its ranks and from significant parts of its constituency to further liberalising reforms at the outset (Harman 1996: 215–16).

Did the NCP burnish or did it tarnish the public reputation of policymakers? Did it 'align "good policy" with "good politics"' (Prasser 2006)? This is much less clear. There is little reason to think it was particularly 'good politics', in part because the NCP was seen in some quarters as yet more reform that put markets before people. Peak welfare body the Australian Council of Social Service (ACOSS) argued, for instance, that 'over the period since the introduction of NCP inequality has grown' and that

> a key criterion for NCP should be the extent to which it contributes to a reduction in disparities by raising the living standard of people living on low incomes or who are otherwise disadvantaged. (ACOSS 2005: 1)

Whatever contribution the NCP made to the substantial rise in general wealth and the move towards full employment that occurred over the period was too indeterminate to overcome contrary perceptions held by groups viewing the world somewhat differently.

In addition, the NCP became a lightning rod for discontent in parts of rural and regional Australia. From the very beginning, rural interests and their principal parliamentary representatives, the National Party, were deeply ambivalent about the NCP (Harman 1996: 216). This was not surprising given the Hilmer Report (Hilmer et al. 1993: 141) had described Australia's longstanding statutory marketing arrangements for agricultural products as 'often grossly inefficient'. In response to rural agitation, the matter was referred to the Productivity Commission for examination. That inquiry concluded that the NCP would deliver benefits to rural Australia, as it would to Australia as a whole, and the difficulties being experienced in rural and regional areas were largely the product of secular and cyclical market forces or of other (though perhaps related) policies (PC 1999).

The main direct threat to rural interests was the NCP's push to wind back those statutory marketing arrangements that operated across a range of rural industries from bananas to potatoes, milk and tomatoes to wheat. These were the dominant remaining 'form of assistance to agriculture' (PC 1999: 196). One particularly sticky matter was Australia's 'single-desk' wheat marketing agency, the Australian Wheat Board (AWB). A compromise reform resulted in a situation that was the worst of both worlds: a privatised AWB retaining its single-desk status, which paved the way for the Iraq oil-for-food scandal (Botterill 2012: 91–106). Such difficulties and perceptions may have helped fuel populist discontent as reflected in the rise of Pauline Hanson's One Nation Party.

Endurance assessment

A policy that is soon eroded or reversed cannot be regarded as successful. In the case of the NCP, however, momentum was maintained over the decade-long implementation period and, in the now more than a decade since mission accomplished was declared, there has been no retreat and no undoing of the policy. The NCP introduced 'general-interest' reforms that 'stuck' (Patashnik 2008). Complaints have since been made that more is not being done, that the reform momentum has been lost and 'complacency' has set in (e.g. Garnaut 2013; King 2015). The Productivity Commission (2005: xxiv–xxxix) immediately urged further reform the moment the NCP officially concluded and business regularly agitated likewise to meet perceived new competitiveness challenges (e.g. BCA 2014). However, there is little sense that existing reforms have been eroded and the slowing pace may well reflect not only the fact that with changing economic conditions (the mining boom, most importantly) the imperative has diminished, but also the fact that many of the most obvious reforms have now been implemented.

How did government get it right?

Insofar as the NCP was successful, what was the secret to that success? There is no doubt that in this case the government avoided some of the well-known pitfalls of policymaking—pitfalls that have contributed to policy failure in many instances. Contributing to the NCP's success may have been good process and design and an effective implementation framework.

Good design?

The NCP experience would seem to be consistent with one of the main lessons Grossman (2013: 179) drew from his review of a litany of 'economic policy disasters': 'reject policy proposals based primarily on ideology.' This seems reasonable; unfortunately, however, distinguishing between policies based primarily on ideology and those that are not is challenging. The idea that the NCP had the benefit of not being ideologically driven is, however, worth considering. To some, it will seem counterintuitive since the reform program of the 1980s and 1990s was criticised at the time for representing the *triumph* of ideology—variously known as 'economic rationalism' or 'neoliberalism'—over Australia's traditional model of widespread government regulation and public provision (e.g. Valentine 1999). However, in this case, the *criticism* may have been more ideological in nature than its target.

The primary indication that the NCP was not 'based primarily on ideology' is the fact it was driven by a Labor government at the national level and supported and implemented by Labor as well as Coalition governments at the state and territory level. The NCP was fundamentally bipartisan and reflected a long period of wrestling with the structural challenges of the Australian economy in a way that was informed by both economic theory and empirical observation (Fenna 2015). Labor was pursuing an agenda of economic liberalisation driven not by an ideological attachment to the underlying ideas of market individualism (to which it has never subscribed), but by reluctant conviction that these reforms were essential to the health and functioning of the Australian economy. The Liberal Party, meanwhile, demonstrated a much deeper affection for market liberalism that had been made painfully clear by its 'Fightback!' manifesto (Liberal Party of Australia 1991), which helped the Coalition lose 'the unlosable' 1993 federal election. The Liberals took a more ideological stand on the NCP, 'itemising the manner in which the Keating government was not pursuing a consistent line on competition on labour, the airlines, shipping and telecommunications infrastructure' (Harman 1996: 216). Winning the federal election only a year after the NCP was set in motion, the Coalition parties set about expanding the market liberalisation agenda with much more ideologically driven policy—most controversially in the industrial relations domain, culminating in the highly controversial 2005 'WorkChoices' legislation.

Good process?

It is common to point to good process as important in generating good policy (e.g. McConnell 2010; IPAA 2012). The chief lesson King and Crewe (2013) drew from the litany of governmental blunders they detailed in the United Kingdom is the importance of deliberative processes. Much bad policy would have been improved or rejected, they argue, in a more deliberative environment where ideas had to be tested at the conception stage before being found wanting in application. Australia's experience with the NCP would seem to be consistent with this emphasis on 'good process'. A researched basis for the policy was put forward by the Industry Commission (IC 1990). Rationale and framework were developed at length in the Hilmer Report (Hilmer et al. 1993). Most importantly, the NCP had to be negotiated through COAG and receive the endorsement and cooperation of the states and territories. Federalism was deeply implicated in the NCP and the policy was a key moment in Australian federalism (Painter 1998; Phillimore and Fenna 2017). One consequence of this was acceptance by the Commonwealth of the need to provide compensation payments to the states and territories (discussed below). The gestation period was five years.

Another consequence was that the implementation arrangements played to one of the strengths of federalism by leaving responsibility for the manner of reform to individual jurisdictions (Harman and Harman 1996). Accommodation could thereby be made for both the differing circumstances and preferences of the different jurisdictions and the fact that the different sides of politics were bound to have different notions of how far liberalisation and privatisation should go. This was particularly the case in respect of some of the largest questions, such as how to reform the state electricity systems. This is not to say the NCP entirely lived up to its promise and always accommodated legitimate or benign states' diversity of preferences (Churchman 1996; Charles 2001; Harwood and Phillimore 2015: 257).

Effective implementation?

What did government do that helped make the NCP an implementation success story? In the main, the answer would seem to be the way the task was delegated to the state and territory governments but overseen by a joint oversight body, the NCC, which was charged with assessing whether sufficient progress had been made for distribution of the promised financial sweeteners. The Commonwealth was not itself trying to reach across the country and manage policy with the associated risks that carries. At the same time, the assessment body was truly 'federal' in its constitution, rather than an arm of the Commonwealth, and thus was considered 'a fair and reasonable broker' by the states and territories (Harwood and Phillimore 2015: 253). And finally, the Commonwealth distributed approximately $5.7 billion in reward payments to the states and territories over the life of the policy (PC 2005: 29). These were widely 'regarded as being crucial to the successful implementation of the NCP' (Harwood and Phillimore 2015: 254; see also Deighton-Smith 2001: 37). Contributing to their efficacy was the fact that, rather than upfront funding, the reward payments were provided only after the fact, once the agreed reforms had been implemented.

Getting it right or having it easy?

Against the idea that the NCP was successful because government did the sorts of things that would make it successful must be weighed the not insignificant factors that were particularly conducive to policy success in this case. These factors substantially dilute the sense that government got it right by doing it right and thereby, unfortunately, diminish the utility of any lessons that might be learned.

A 'tame' problem

'The difficulty with policy often begins with the selection of unrealizable aims' (Ingram and Mann 1980: 19). This is indeed the case with many policy objectives and, as Ingram and Mann pointed out almost 40 years ago, the expectations of government propel policy in the direction of failure. If anything, the complexity and difficulty of these demands have increased since then and bedevil policymaking even more (Schuck 2014). Although Rittel and Webber (1973) argue that the problems addressed by public policy are in general 'inherently wicked', consensus holds that some of those problems are rather more wicked than others—indeed, perhaps considerably more wicked than others.

The NCP, it must be emphasised, was *not* addressing a particularly wicked problem. It was not dealing with a profound values dispute (few disagreed with the idea that making markets work better to deliver higher levels of economic growth was a good thing). It was not dealing with intractable social problems. It was not caught up in deep and often zero-sum conflicts such as that between industrialism and the environment. It did not involve the risky and controversial business of 'picking winners'. It did not involve the kind of ambitious investment and construction program that has often proven so challenging for governments. It did not involve the rolling out of administratively complex programs. And, it did not embroil the government in conflicts with powerful private-sector opponents—as, for instance, occurred in the more recent mining tax debacle (Marsh et al. 2014). On the contrary, it was strongly supported by business, particularly big business (Harman 1996). The current Chairman of the Productivity Commission has protested that the NCP 'was not the plucking of low-hanging fruit' (Harris 2014: 9). Perhaps it was not; however, it was the plucking of fruit that was within reasonable grasp. If you want successful policy, the obvious lesson is to tackle the eminently feasible. The NCP was well down the wickedness scale.

Prestructured deliberation

As acknowledged above, the NCP did benefit from a healthy amount of deliberation; however, this occurred largely as a consequence of Australia's federal system. Because the main targets of the NCP were state and territory government instrumentalities, the Commonwealth had to rely more on suasion and inducement than coercion. As a consequence, compromises were forced on the Commonwealth—compromises that certainly made the policy more viable. In particular, the Commonwealth was obliged to concede more collaborative institutions (the NCC), greater flexibility in implementation and reward payments. Insofar as the NCP was a triumph of cooperative federalism, that cooperative approach occurred as much out of necessity as out of prudent policymaking—and, even then, it did represent, in a soft power form, yet another expansion of the Commonwealth's influence over the states (Hollander 2006).

Preexisting momentum

Political and economic circumstances were particularly auspicious for the NCP. Politically, the path to the NCP had been well and truly smoothed by a decade of successful economic reform. The NCP was in many ways merely the logical and more systematic extension of what Australia's federal and state and territory governments had been doing for a decade. Pioneering reform of state electricity systems and movement towards the National Electricity Market were, for instance, well under way by the time the NCP was introduced (KPMG 2013; see also Wood and

Blowers 2018). Competition policy was part and parcel of the historic policy shift initiated by the Hawke Labor Government at the national level in 1983. Beginning with what was then seen as the radical decision to end fixed exchange rates for the Australian dollar, the program gathered speed through the 1980s, focusing on reduction of protective tariffs, privatisation of major government business enterprises and the cautious winding back of national wage-setting. This sea change came in response to a deep malaise in the Australian economy as the country's original growth model reached its limits (Fenna 2013).

Much less had occurred at the state level, which was not insignificant given the enormous role the states and territories play in regulation and infrastructure provision. 'Ironically, reform in the states was impeded by Commonwealth policies' (Painter 1998: 35). The large state-owned utilities paid substantial dividends into state treasuries; those would diminish if more competitive environments were introduced and would transmute altogether into Commonwealth Government tax revenue if the enterprises were privatised. In this context, the NCP was merely facilitating developments that were already under way or being held back.

Economically, the NCP benefited from two adventitious but very convenient economic factors. One was that, as a result of excess capacity in the electricity sector, prices came down over the period and thus reform seemed to be paying immediate dividends (Argy 2002: 38). The other was that the economy performed awfully well. After the 1990–92 recession, Australia enjoyed what Ross Garnaut (2013: 5) called, perhaps rather extravagantly, 'the longest unbroken period of economic expansion of any developed country ever'. This extraordinary run of good fortune over the entire period of the NCP and beyond contributed to the policy's 'success' in both subjective and objective terms. In subjective terms, it was bound to make a policy that was aimed at improving economic performance look like it was doing its job, even if—as discussed above—causality is extremely difficult to attribute. In objective terms, the policy also operated in a highly conducive environment as a consequence of a thriving economy. A significant risk in such policies is the potentially derailing effect of 'transitional costs': the problem that short-term adjustment pain will if not exceed, then possibly overshadow, short and medium-term general gain. Mitigation or minimisation of those costs becomes, then, an important contributor to success. In this case, liberalisation critic John Quiggin (1997: 256) insisted soon after the NCP was launched:

> [T]he dominant flow-on effects of microeconomic reform will be negative, arising from the fact that at least some of the workers directly displaced by reform will be permanently displaced from the employed labour force.

But this was scarcely the case; before long, continuing economic growth drove the labour market to as close to full employment as had existed since the postwar boom. Economic conditions thus worked to minimise one of the major risks associated with reformist policymaking of this nature.

Conclusion

No policy is without its blemishes and Australia's NCP is no exception. Rural reforms proved problematic in some sectors and a rural backlash occurred. Electricity reform remains challenging, with, among other things, state governments in Queensland and New South Wales expending considerable political capital pursuing privatisation. However, it certainly was not a policy failure, let alone that most scandalous but apparently not so rare event, a policy fiasco. The NCP was a well-considered policy linked to an effective implementation strategy that by and large achieved the policy's output aims without causing excessive collateral damage. Whether it achieved its intended *outcomes* is difficult if not impossible to judge authoritatively, but the evidence suggests it did contribute to Australia's ongoing economic success. Any realistic assessment of the NCP must acknowledge, however, that the success it enjoyed was due in no small part to the straightforward nature of its objectives compared with many of the nasty policy challenges governments face, the requirements for consultation and collaboration imposed by Australia's federal system, the broader reform momentum of which it was part and the extraordinarily good economic times in which it played out. Here *virtù* and *fortuna* seem to have nicely aligned, with auspicious conditions and good policymaking conspiring to produce policy success.

References

Argy, F. 2002. 'National competition policy: Some issues.' *Agenda* 9: 33–46.

Australian Council of Social Service (ACOSS) 2005. *National Competition Policy: ACOSS submission to the Productivity Commission*. Sydney: ACOSS.

Botterill, L. C. 2012. *Wheat Marketing in Transition: The transformation of the Australian Wheat Board*. New York: Springer. doi.org/10.1007/978-94-007-2804-2.

Business Council of Australia (BCA) 2014. *Submission to the Competition Policy Review*. Melbourne: BCA.

Charles, C. 2001. 'Reflections on national competition policy.' *Australian Journal of Public Administration* 60: 120–1. doi.org/10.1111/1467-8500.00233.

Churchman, S. 1996. 'National competition policy: Its evolution and implementation—A study in intergovernmental relations.' *Australian Journal of Public Administration* 55: 97–9. doi.org/10.1111/j.1467-8500.1996.tb01208.x.

Deighton-Smith, R. 2001. 'National competition policy: Key lessons for policy-making from its implementation.' *Australian Journal of Public Administration* 60: 29–41. doi.org/10.1111/1467-8500.00222.

Fenna, A. 2013. 'The economic policy agenda in Australia, 1962–2012.' *Australian Journal of Public Administration* 72: 89–102. doi.org/10.1111/1467-8500.12020.

Fenna, A. 2015. 'The economic context of policy analysis in Australia.' In B. Head and K. Crowley (eds), *Policy Analysis in Australia*. Bristol: Policy Press.

Garnaut, R. 2013. *Dog Days: Australia after the boom*. Melbourne: Redback.

Grossman, R. S. 2013. *Wrong: Nine economic policy disasters and what we can learn from them*. New York: Oxford University Press.

Hancock, K. 2005. 'Productivity growth in Australia 1964–1965 to 2003–04.' *Australian Bulletin of Labour* 31: 28–32.

Harman, E. 1996. 'The National Competition Policy: A study of the policy process and network.' *Australian Journal of Political Science* 31: 205–24. doi.org/10.1080/10361149651193.

Harman, E. J. and Harman, F. L. 1996. 'The potential for local diversity in implementation of the National Competition Policy.' *Australian Journal of Public Administration* 55: 12–25. doi.org/10.1111/j.1467-8500.1996.tb01196.x.

Harris, P. 2014. *Competition Policy and Deregulation: Challenges and choices*. Canberra: Crawford School of Public Policy, The Australian National University.

Harwood, J. and Phillimore, J. 2015. 'National competition policy and cooperative federalism.' In J. Wanna, E. A. Lindquist and P. Marshall (eds), *New Accountabilities, New Challenges*. Canberra: ANU Press.

Hilmer, F. G., Rayner, M. and Taperell, G. 1993. *National Competition Policy: Report by the Independent Committee of Inquiry*. Canberra: Commonwealth of Australia.

Hollander, R. 2006. 'National competition policy, regulatory reform and Australian federalism.' *Australian Journal of Public Administration* 65: 33–47. doi.org/10.1111/j.1467-8500.2006.00480.x.

Industry Commission (IC) 1990. *Annual Report 1989–90*. Melbourne: Industry Commission.

Ingram, H. M. and Mann, D. E. 1980. 'Policy failure: An issue deserving analysis.' In H. M. Ingram and D. E. Mann (eds), *Why Policies Succeed or Fail*. Beverly Hills, CA: Sage Publications.

Institute of Public Administration Australia (IPAA) 2012. *Public Policy Drift: Why governments must replace 'policy on the run' and 'policy by fiat' with a 'business case' approach to regain public confidence*. Canberra: IPAA.

King, A. and Crewe, I. 2013. *The Blunders of Our Governments*. London: Oneworld Publications.

King, S. 2015. 'Competition policy and the competition policy review.' *Australian Economic Review* 48: 402–9. doi.org/10.1111/1467-8462.12134.

King, S. P. 2002. 'The economics of national competition policy.' *Law in Context* 20: 6–33.

KPMG 2013. *National Electricity Market: A case study in successful microeconomic reform*. Sydney: Australian Energy Market Commission.

Liberal Party of Australia 1991. *Fightback! Taxation and expenditure reform for jobs and growth*. Canberra: Liberal Party of Australia.

McConnell, A. 2010. *Understanding Policy Success: Rethinking public policy*. Basingstoke, UK: Palgrave Macmillan.

Marsh, D., Lewis, C. and Chesters, J. 2014. 'The Australian mining tax and the political power of business.' *Australian Journal of Political Science* 49: 711–25. doi.org/10.1080/10361146.2014.954985.

National Competition Council (NCC) 2005. *Assessment of Governments' Progress in Implementing the National Competition Policy and Related Reforms: 2005*. Melbourne: NCC.

Organisation for Economic Co-operation and Development (OECD) 2005. *OECD Economic Surveys: Australia.* Paris: OECD Publishing.

Painter, M. 1998. *Collaborative Federalism: Economic reform in Australia in the 1990s.* Melbourne: Cambridge University Press. doi.org/10.1017/CBO9780511552236.

Patashnik, E. M. 2008. *Reforms at Risk: What happens after major policy changes are enacted.* Princeton, NJ: Princeton University Press.

Phillimore, J. and Fenna, A. 2017. 'Intergovernmental councils and centralization in Australian federalism.' *Regional and Federal Studies* 27: 597–621. doi.org/10.1080/13597566.2017.1389723.

Prasser, S. 2006. 'Aligning "good policy" with "good politics".' In H. K. Colebatch (ed.), *Beyond the Policy Cycle: The policy process in Australia.* Sydney: Allen & Unwin.

Pressman, J. L. and Wildavsky, A. 1973. *Implementation: How great expectations in Washington are dashed in Oakland; Or, why it's amazing that federal programs work at all; this being a saga of the Economic Development Administration as told by two sympathetic observers who seek to build morals on a foundation of ruined hopes.* Berkeley, CA: University of California Press.

Productivity Commission (PC) 1999. *Impact of Competition Policy Reforms on Rural and Regional Australia.* Melbourne: Productivity Commission.

Productivity Commission (PC) 2005. *Review of national competition policy arrangements.* Inquiry Report, 14 April. Melbourne: Productivity Commission.

Quiggin, J. 1997. 'Estimating the benefits of Hilmer and related reforms.' *Australian Economic Review* 30: 256–72. doi.org/10.1111/1467-8462.00025.

Rittel, H. W. J. and Webber, M. M. 1973. 'Dilemmas in a general theory of planning.' *Policy Sciences* 4: 155–69. doi.org/10.1007/BF01405730.

Schuck, P. H. 2014. *Why Government Fails So Often: And how it can do better.* Princeton, NJ: Princeton University Press.

Valentine, B. 1999. 'National competition policy: Legitimating economic rationalism.' *Australian Social Work* 52: 26–31. doi.org/10.1080/03124079908414106.

Wood, A. and Blowers, D. 2018. *Mostly Working: Australia's wholesale electricity market.* Melbourne: Grattan Institute.

9

The 'perfect storm' of gun control: From policy inertia to world leader

Philip Alpers and Zareh Ghazarian

A storm is brewing

Australian firearm policy had altered very little in 65 years prior to the 1990s. Events in April 1996, however, precipitated 12 days that dramatically changed national firearm legislation. Thirty-five people were killed when a gunman opened fire at the Port Arthur Historic Site in the State of Tasmania. This chapter explores how these events created a 'perfect storm' of outrage, law and leadership that forced policy reform. It considers the political and constitutional challenges the national government faced and details the swift legislative changes implemented following the massacre. Using more than 20 years of research and data, this chapter describes the attitude adjustments that enabled effective enforcement of firearm legislation and the notable improvements to public health and safety that followed. Although these changes are widely credited with establishing the nation as a world leader in the prevention of armed violence, unintended consequences of Australia's gun control laws may contain the seed of their own destruction.

In the 1980s and early 1990s, Australia suffered 14 mass shootings,[1] which claimed 117 lives. This spate of public killings culminated on 28 April 1996, when a single 'pathetic social misfit' (the judge's words at his trial) killed 20 innocents with his first 29 bullets in the space of 90 seconds at Port Arthur, Tasmania. The killer was empowered to achieve his final toll of 35 people dead and 18 seriously wounded by firing military-style semiautomatic rifles. Tasmania was one of the few remaining places in the Western world where an unlicensed individual could obtain such a weapon and had easily done so. The massacre elicited a swift policy response by the Australian Government that would have a long-term impact.

This chapter examines the uniform gun laws in Australia that were implemented following the Port Arthur tragedy. It explores the political context of the time and explains how the legislation is regarded as having achieved its policy aims, while also branding Australia as a global pathfinder in gun control. Before doing so, however, we examine the extent to which uniform gun laws in Australia have been a policy success.

A policy success?

Australia's reaction was immediate and strident: Port Arthur was the last straw. The earlier succession of mass shootings had made gun control a prominent public issue, but now widening coalitions for gun control ignited a wildfire campaign for law reform. The nation's newly elected prime minister was John Howard, its most conservative leader in decades (see Robinson 2007). If any constituency might be forgiven for assuming the legal status quo, it was the rural and gun-owning rump of the Liberal–National Coalition that had swept him to power. Yet, less than two weeks after Port Arthur, Howard's government delivered a nationwide bipartisan gun law reform. After decades of forcing politicians into repeated consultation, electoral weakness and delay, Australia's gun lobby was outpaced, outflanked and outwitted by a leader with both the mandate and the personal conviction to move decisively within 12 remarkable days.

1 The common definition of a 'mass shooting' in 1996 was five or more victims killed by gunshot in proximate events in a civilian setting, not including any perpetrator(s) killed by their own hand or otherwise. This excludes most of Australia's more common firearm-related spousal and family violence killings. In September 2014, a farmer in Lockhart, New South Wales, shot dead his family of four, then himself. In May 2018, at Osmington, Western Australia, another farmer shot dead six family members before taking his own life. In recent years, a lower threshold has been widely adopted, with 'mass shooting' coming to mean four or more victims shot dead, not including the perpetrator.

During the intense period in which the government sought to implement a national firearm policy, Australians heard numerous variations on Howard's interview mantra, repeated ever since: 'We do not want the American disease imported into Australia. Guns have become a blight on American society' (cited in O'Loughlin 2002). Public feeling—voiced through state-based coalitions for gun control—brought together hundreds of groups to support stronger, nationally uniform firearm legislation. From across the political spectrum, police unions, public health and suicide prevention practitioners, medical and law societies, women's groups, senior citizens' associations, rural counsellors, churches, the Country Women's Association, the War Widows' Guild—a total of 350 groups led by activist law student Rebecca Peters—all lent political support to tighter regulation of firearms (see Chapman 2013; Peters 2013). The beneficial social outcome of the policy, especially its potential to save lives, was clear as it aimed to decrease and prevent firearm-related death and injury. The policy focus was dictated by the Port Arthur tragedy: to reduce the availability of the semiautomatic long guns that had emerged as the mass killer's weapon of choice. By January 1997, all eight state and territory governments had commenced a national mandatory buyback of banned firearms. A total of 659,940 newly prohibited semiautomatic and pump-action rifles and shotguns were purchased from their civilian owners at market value and then destroyed (see Reuter and Mouzos 2003). The $500 million cost of the buyback was distributed equitably across society by means of a one-off levy on federal income tax, which cost the average taxpayer $15.

Ten months after it began, the main Australian firearms buyback campaign was over (Chapman 2013: 132). By 1 October 1997, criminal penalties including imprisonment and heavy fines applied to possession of any prohibited weapon in all states and territories (see Alpers et al. 2018a). During a second firearm buyback in 2003, 68,727 handguns—pistols and revolvers—were collected and destroyed (see Hudson 2004; Bricknell 2012). Tens of thousands of gun owners also voluntarily surrendered additional, nonprohibited firearms without compensation. In the 20 years from 1996 to 2015, at least 1 million privately owned firearms—one-third of the estimated national stockpile—are known to have been seized or surrendered and then melted down (see Alpers and Rossetti 2016).

In the 15 years preceding gun law reform, Australia saw 14 mass shootings in which a total of 117 people died. In the 20 years that followed, no mass public shootings occurred (see Alpers 2019). In the same two decades after gun law reform, the rate of fatal shootings that claimed fewer than five victims—that is, the majority of gun deaths—also showed a downward trend. But, as Figure 9.1 shows, that trend had been apparent for several years before the new firearm legislation was introduced.

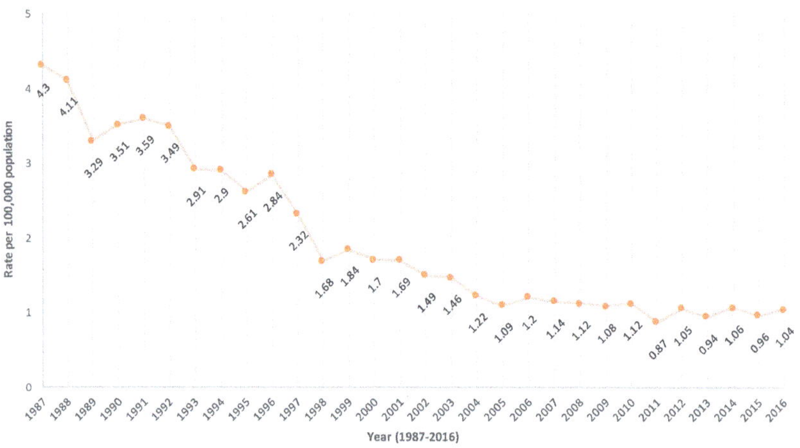

Figure 9.1 Rate of all gun deaths in Australia, 1987–2016 (per 100,000 people)

Source: Alpers et al. (2018b).

As seen in Figure 9.1, in the period immediately following the Port Arthur massacre, the risk of an Australian dying by gunshot fell by more than half. Twenty years later, that risk shows no sign of increasing and Australia's rate of gun homicide remains 25 times lower than that of the United States. Another sequel to gun law reform was the decline in firearm-related fatalities in categories few could have predicted. Of all gun deaths in Australia, more than 80 per cent have nothing to do with crime. Attention tends to focus on mediagenic gun homicides, which account for only 13–18 per cent of firearm-related deaths, while in 2016, gun suicides constituted 77 per cent of gun deaths. Unintentional shootings and shootings with undetermined causes make up the remainder. In the years after Port Arthur, suicide by firearm showed a significant decline. Here, law reform designed to reduce rare mass gun homicides was followed by a decreasing rate of much more common gun suicides. In addition, rates of non-gun homicide and suicide fell during the same period.

An analysis of these results must recognise an array of confounding factors. Researchers have used several methods to measure the effects of Australia's firearm legislation, with conflicting results. Leigh and Neill (2010: 1) found that 'the buyback led to a drop in the firearm suicide rates of almost 80%' for an estimated saving of 200 deaths by gunshot and A$695 million in costs each year. Chapman et al. (2006: 1) concluded that 'the rates per 100,000 of total firearm deaths, firearm homicides and firearm suicides all at least doubled their existing rates of decline after the revised gun laws'. In contrast, researchers for pro-gun lobby groups, Baker and McPhedran (2006: 9), interpreted essentially the same empirical findings to conclude the opposite—namely, that 'the gun buy-back and restrictive legislative changes had no influence on firearm homicide in Australia'. Lee and Suardi (2010: 2) found that Australia's new gun laws 'did not have any large effects on reducing firearm homicide or suicide rates'.

Shortly after the 20-year anniversary of the Port Arthur shooting, and with many more years of data, the most recent research by Chapman et al. (2016: 2) found:

> [T]here was a more rapid decline in firearm deaths between 1997 and 2013 compared with before 1997, but also a decline in total non-firearm suicide and homicide deaths of a greater magnitude. Because of this, it is not possible to determine whether the change in firearm deaths can be attributed to the gun law reforms.

This study also concluded that the 'implementation of a ban on rapid-fire firearms was associated with reductions in mass shootings and total firearm deaths'. No study has found evidence of substitution of other lethal means—for example, for suicide or for murderers moving to different methods.

In the 23 years since the introduction of the Howard Government's gun law changes, an international consensus has emerged that Australia did the right thing. A substantial reduction in the national availability of rapid-fire lethal weapons was followed by a reduction in overall gun deaths of more than 50 per cent, with no subsequent reversal. In the context of gun control and firearm injury prevention, the government is credited with achieving demonstrable and highly valued social outcomes. Two decades on, and with an increasing focus worldwide on mass shootings in the United States, public and political support for this policy has, if anything, been reinforced in Australia.

The introduction of uniform gun laws in Australia can be seen as an example of policy success. Based on a *programmatic* assessment, the policy had a very clearly defined public value proposition as it sought, and actually achieved, a substantial reduction in the national stockpile of the firearms shown to be at highest risk of misuse in mass shootings. This was followed by significant decreases in both firearm-related homicide and firearm-related suicide. As will be shown later in this chapter, the costs of this policy were borne primarily by Australians in rural and regional areas, which had a higher density of gun ownership relative to urban centres (see McPhedran 2014). While financial compensation was provided, many gun owners felt they were being penalised for the actions of a small number of criminals.

Based on *process* assessment, the newly uniform gun laws showed evidence of careful consideration of policy instruments. Various forms of the laws had been drafted and refined by police ministers and other stakeholders since the mid-1980s. This meant that, by the time the Howard Government made the announcement, the relevant resources and administrative capacity had already been developed and were ready for implementation. Mechanisms to deliver the policy, especially to identify high-risk firearms and to mount a buyback scheme, were also deployed, allowing the government to achieve the intended outcomes.

Uniform gun laws in Australia, based on an assessment of *political* performance, also achieved broad and deep community support. As discussed below, the Port Arthur shootings elicited a bipartisan approach, with opposition parties joining to support the government's policy proposals. The policy also enjoyed significant support among the community, although in some parts of Australia—especially in New South Wales, Tasmania and Queensland—this was not as strong as in metropolitan areas. Indeed, the Tasmanian and Queensland state governments had long rejected any attempts to join a national firearm agreement (see Smeaton 2013) or to ban the military-style semiautomatic firearms that gun dealers had been marketing for years as 'assault weapons'. Following a 1987 national 'gun summit' of state police ministers, then NSW premier Barrie Unsworth voiced his frustration at this impasse with tragic prescience: 'It will take a massacre in Tasmania before we get gun law reform in Australia' (cited in Byrne 1996).

The implementation of the policy also enhanced the political capital of John Howard, who had just begun his prime ministership. Once seen as a clumsy and ineffective opposition leader, Howard's swift and instinctive response to the Port Arthur massacre branded him as a strong and decisive prime minister. Later, these characteristics were on show in major policy discussions—for example, the GST and national security debates.

The following sections elaborate on and explain how the context, design and delivery of Australia's firearm policy contributed to its legitimacy and endurance since 1996.

Contexts, challenges, agents

Other liberal democracies had sought to act on gun control prior to Australia's response to the Port Arthur shootings. The UK Government implemented a ban on some rifles following a mass shooting in August 1987, while the administration of US president Bill Clinton moved to restrict the sale of newly manufactured or imported assault rifles in the United States in 1994 (see Chapman 2013: 99). In 1995, the Canadian Government introduced tighter controls on firearms by passing gun registration laws (since partially reversed) and, in March 1996, the UK Government banned handguns following the Dunblane school shooting (see Chapman 2013: 99–100).

The issue of national uniform gun laws had been mooted intermittently in Australia. The difficulty in mandating complementary legislation across jurisdictions was partly due to the way in which the Australian federation was framed. The Australian Constitution outlines the division of powers between the states and territories and the national government. State and territory governments hold constitutional authority over the provision of law and order, while the Commonwealth has authority to ban the importation of firearms under its customs regulations (see *Customs Act 1901*; Egger and Peters 1993). In this context, firearm legislation varied across the states. Depending on the jurisdiction, registration was not required for most firearms, semiautomatic weapons were allowed and there was no restriction on ammunition sales (see Norberry et al. 1996).

With such variation across states and territories, momentum was building for national uniform firearm legislation in the 1980s. Moves towards new laws were expedited as a spate of multiple killings occurred in Australia. Between 1987 and January 1996, at least 40 people were shot in nine separate incidents (see Norberry et al. 1996). In response to these events, uniform gun laws became the focus of meetings of the Australasian Police Ministers Council (APMC) and, by 1995, a working party was established to consider the harmonisation of state and territory gun laws (see Norberry et al. 1996). Before these proposals could be explored further in 1996, however, a federal election was called for March that year.

The 1996 election

The 1996 election marked a significant change in Australian politics. The ALP lost after 13 years in office. Bob Hawke had led Labor to victory in 1983, but was replaced with Paul Keating in 1991. Hawke was prime minister during several high-profile mass shootings in Australia in the late 1980s and early 1990s, including the Hoddle Street killings in Melbourne in August 1987, in which seven people were killed, and the Queen Street killings, also in Melbourne, in December of the same year, in which eight people were killed. While Hawke had called a special premiers' conference to discuss the issue of firearms in 1987, no agreement had been reached, as Queensland and Tasmania refused to participate in a national agreement—much to Hawke's chagrin (see Smeaton 2013).

Between August 1990 and August 1991, 11 more people were killed in mass shootings, in Sydney. Despite mounting public concern, the opposition to firearm law reform was ferocious. While Australia's gun lobby—long accustomed to stacking firearm consultative committees and holding sway in legislative bodies—lobbied hard against suggested public health measures, the Hawke Government appeared unable to respond to growing calls for a national policy. Although it established the National Committee on Violence (NCV 1990: L), which observed that 'as a community we have witnessed tragedies that were unthinkable a generation ago', its recommendations to establish uniform firearm laws across Australia were not implemented by government. This was despite the fact that some commentators described gun control as the 'hottest political issue in Australia' in 1991 (see Hawke 1991).

The issue haunted prime minister Hawke and began to overshadow his government's policy agenda. The media interest in the government's response to deaths from firearms was intense. This came to a head in a national television interview in August 1991 in which Hawke argued that the constitution limited the Commonwealth Government's capacity to introduce uniform gun laws:

> Interviewer: But where's the national law? Where's the national register?
>
> Hawke: … [U]nder the Constitution it requires the action and laws of the State governments and what I'm saying to you is that due to a lack of political will within the states the governments that have got the responsibility who must pass the laws won't do it. That's why I'm going to take the lead in November and say come on you've got to act. And it will

> probably be easier for the States to act under that national thrust. They'll be looking at one, will you do it, yes, yes, yes, if they'll all do it, and governments of different political persuasion we might get somewhere … I can't change the Constitution. I have not got the constitutional power to pass laws. (Hawke 1991)

This highlighted how successive national governments conceptualised the issue of uniform gun laws. As prime minister, Hawke reminded viewers that gun control was a power that could be exercised by the states rather than the Commonwealth Government, but his government demonstrated some appetite to bring about changes to the laws. Before he could do so, however, Hawke lost the leadership of the ALP and the prime ministership, to Paul Keating, in December 1991.

Keating continued the path set by Hawke when it came to national gun laws. While he signalled the Commonwealth Government's concern about deaths from gun injuries, as well as the number of mass shootings throughout the late 1980s and early 1990s, Keating was unable to bring about uniform laws. For example, at a heads of government meeting in May 1992, Keating facilitated an agreement that allowed goods that could be sold lawfully in one state to be sold freely in another. The legislation, however, would not apply to certain products including firearms and prohibited and offensive weapons (see Keating 1992).

Political pressure on the Keating Government intensified after August 1993, when three people were shot dead by a gunman in Sydney. While the government was still unable to implement national laws, Keating conflated gun control with broader community security matters. In 1995, he launched the government's 'Safer Australia' policy, which aimed to reduce crime. As Keating (1995) put it:

> Although the State and Territory governments have primary responsibility for law and order, the national government can play a role where it is appropriate to its functions in the task of providing a secure environment for Australians. We will continue working with the States and Territories on issues such as gun control. We will tighten Australia's already stringent gun importation restrictions and ban the importation of handguns that can be adapted to duplicate machine guns.

Despite the desire for uniform gun laws, successive national governments had failed to make any substantive changes in Australia. By late 1995 and early 1996, gun control dropped off the Keating Government's agenda as it shifted its focus to contesting a general election that opinion polls signalled would result in an electoral rout. The federal election was held in March 1996 and ended the ALP's 13 years in power. Labor lost 31 seats and its primary vote fell below 39 per cent—one of its worst performances in the postwar period. The Howard-led Coalition, comprising the Liberal Party and the rural and regional-oriented National Party, swept to power, winning 94 seats, while Labor held just 49 of the 148 seats in the House of Representatives.

The Coalition, however, did not win a majority in the Senate, where it had to rely on the support of the Australian Democrats, the Greens or an independent senator to pass legislation. Policies concerning leadership, the economy, employment and the environment were prominent issues during the 1996 election campaign (see Bean 1997). Gun control, however, was still not on the policy agenda. During his time as opposition leader, Howard said he wanted to stop Australia from replicating what he identified as American gun culture. In a prominent speech delivered in June 1995 on the role of government, Howard (1995) said:

> I am firmly on the side of those who believe that it would be a cardinal tragedy if Australia did not learn the bitter lessons of the United States regarding guns. I have no doubt that the horrific homicide level in the United States is directly related to the plentiful supply of guns … Whilst making proper allowances for legitimate sporting and recreational activities and the proper needs of our rural community, every effort should be made to limit the carrying of guns in Australia.

Despite airing such concerns, neither major party promised to implement uniform gun laws during the 1996 campaign (see Bean 1997). Instead, following its decisive victory, the Howard Government claimed a mandate from the electorate to implement its economic and social policy agenda (see Sugita 1997). The Port Arthur shootings in April 1996, however, derailed the government's legislative program and once again made gun control the 'hottest issue' in the political debate.

Design and choice

The shock and sadness of the community quickly transitioned to anger and it became apparent that public opinion was strongly in favour of changing existing gun laws (see Chapman 2013: 56). The day after the shootings, prime minister Howard announced his intention to pursue a range of gun control reforms, including the banning of self-loading weapons. He and his chief of staff, Grahame Morris, met with Daryl Smeaton, who had been senior private secretary to ministers for justice during the Hawke and Keating governments. Smeaton was an integral part of the APMC working party that had a hand in the recommendations of 11 previous national and state expert reviews, law reform commissions and parliamentary committees, along with research published by the National Coalition for Gun Control—all of which supported substantially similar measures (see Peters 2013). This had produced a blueprint for national gun laws gradually formulated in the 1980s and early 1990s, which Labor did not have the opportunity or determination to implement. Howard sought to utilise Smeaton's expertise, especially as he was now in the Attorney-General's Department. Upon meeting prime minister Howard, Smeaton recalled how strongly he wanted to bring about uniform gun laws. Moreover, the prime minister's office entrusted Smeaton with setting out the policy parameters. As Smeaton recalled: 'Grahame Morris said to John Howard, these guys know what they're doing … they can look after it.'[2]

Following their initial meeting, Smeaton and colleagues from the prime minister's office spent a day-and-a-half exploring options for new national laws. As Howard recalled in an interview, it

> was obvious what you could do … Once you're confronted with something it takes you all of five minutes to work out what the response is. The response was not intricate.[3]

The national laws decided on were drawn directly from the original APMC working party document.[4] The fact this document already existed greatly enhanced the government's capacity to respond to the policy crisis. Smeaton was regarded as the architect of the proposed laws that were presented to the Cabinet meeting held just over a week after the Port Arthur shooting.

Attending the Cabinet meeting to provide expert advice, Smeaton described the mood of ministers as being 'shocked and stunned' as they came to terms with the number of deaths and injuries following the shooting.[5] The prime minister led the discussion in Cabinet and, while

2 Daryl Smeaton, Interview with the authors, Canberra, 6 March 2018.
3 John Howard, Interview with the authors, Sydney, 18 April 2018.
4 See Smeaton, Interview with the authors.
5 ibid.

some ministers asked questions about the policy, there was no opposition to bringing about the new uniform firearm laws. As he had appropriated and centralised the expertise to draw up the reforms in his office, the prime minister was driving the policy, thus marginalising the attorney-general.[6] While deputy prime minister and leader of the Nationals Tim Fischer expressed some concern that the laws would affect his party's constituency, he assured the prime minister that he would smooth over any problems with rural voters and farmers affected by the changes.[7]

Delivery, legitimacy and endurance

In the leadup to the 1996 general election, Howard had stated he was in favour of reforming gun laws but did not believe that policy change on firearms was imminent. The Port Arthur shootings, however, provided the opportunity for action. As Howard explained:

> You never let a good crisis go to waste … you do have to recognise that sometimes a crisis forces people to focus on something … tragic though the event was, it gave us an opportunity to do something in the wake of it, so that those lives were not lost in vain. We would have wished it had not occurred, but it did occur so you have to look around and see what you can do. Well, if you couldn't do anything except shrug your shoulders and say it's a matter for the states, that seemed to be a bit of a cop-out. The federal system is not an excuse for doing nothing when the national interest requires you to do something.[8]

The government had to find solutions to the regulatory matters concerning firearm legislation. It did this by distilling a decade of public policy discussions on the topic of gun control into a single document—a set of resolutions for consideration at a meeting of the APMC scheduled for 10 May 1996. As Alpers (2017: 790) reminds us, although gun control had been on the agenda of 20 of 29 of these conferences since 1980 (see Daily Telegraph 1996; Millett 1996), no moment had emerged in which political conviction and a terrible massacre on home soil, followed by saturation media coverage and a national public outcry, could have so quickly coalesced into a single multipartisan declaration of intent.

6 See ibid.

7 See ibid.

8 Howard, Interview with the authors.

Buoyed by strident media support and 90–95 per cent public approval ratings, Howard made it known that, absent their consent to his plan, the recalcitrant state and territory governments would be threatened with a national referendum to strip them of legislative power over firearms. He was in no doubt that the 'referendum would have been carried'.[9] The resulting agreement became known as the National Firearms Agreement (NFA) (see APMC 1996).

The NFA

The wording of the NFA delivered no major surprises. Instead, the resolutions of that special firearms meeting of the APMC encapsulated a decade of recommendations to and from the NCV, established nearly 10 years earlier, and reinforced in whole or in part by each expert review, law reform commission and parliamentary committee report, along with the National Coalition for Gun Control and its member organisations. What was surprising was that the NFA had been agreed to by all parties. Every state and territory in Australia was now bound to reform its firearm legislation—some from the bottom up. In summary, the 1996 APMC resolutions required that all jurisdictions:

1. Ban the sale, transfer, possession, manufacture and importation of all automatic and most semiautomatic rifles, shotguns and their parts, including magazines. Only in exceptional circumstances may semiautomatic long guns be used by civilians in occupational categories licensed for a specified purpose, such as extermination of feral animals.
2. Ban competitive shooting involving the same firearms.
3. Immediately establish integrated licence and firearm registration systems to ensure nationwide compatibility, then link all databases through the National Exchange of Police Information to ensure effective nationwide registration of all firearms.
4. Exclude personal protection as a genuine reason for possessing or using a firearm.
5. Prohibit private gun sales, with all transfers to be processed by licensed firearm dealers.

9 ibid.

6. Require all applicants for a firearm licence to show one or more genuine reasons for owning, possessing or using each gun. Examples of a genuine reason include regular attendance at an approved gun club, practising mainstream shooting disciplines such as those seen at Commonwealth and Olympic games; proof of permission from a landowner for recreational shooting or hunting; proof of occupation as a primary producer, security employee or professional shooter; established bona fide collection of lawful firearms with historical interest; or limited authorised purposes such as using firearms in film production.
7. Over and above the genuine reason test, applicants for a licence to possess firearms in categories deemed to pose additional risk were also obliged to demonstrate a genuine need for that particular type of gun. For example, for a purpose not achievable by other means, a primary producer may be licensed to possess a single, limited-magazine–size semiautomatic rifle or a pump-action shotgun, possibly with restrictions on its place of use.
8. A person judged to be a bona fide collector may be licensed to keep inoperable nonprohibited post-WWII firearms without live ammunition and fireable guns manufactured before 1946.
9. The NFA also stipulated a minimum firearm licensing age of 18 and required: a 'fit and proper person' test decided by police; proof of identity; accredited, nationally uniform safety training; a photographic licence limiting its owner to certain firearm categories and ammunition; a minimum 28-day waiting period for licensing or firearm acquisition; and a maximum licence period of five years.
10. Each licence applicant has to comply with safe storage requirements by keeping firearms and ammunition in separate fixed, locked receptacles, must submit to the inspection of storage by authorities and is subject to immediate withdrawal of the licence and confiscation of firearms for failure to comply.
11. A firearm licence may also be refused or cancelled following a conviction involving violence; an apprehended violence, domestic violence or restraining order; reliable evidence of mental or physical unsuitability to possess a firearm; and for not notifying a change of address.

While the government appeared to have found a policy solution, it still had to find ways to assuage mounting anger from segments of its own electoral base. While the NFA resolutions had strong backing in metropolitan centres, support was much lower in many rural and regional areas (see Anderson 2017: 221). This had implications for the National Party as its constituency began to rebel against the policy. As John Anderson (2017: 221), the deputy leader of the Nationals, recalled, the policy cost him 'a number of friends and certainly added greatly to the National Party's challenges in the 1998 election'. In the joint party room meeting held a week after the shootings, Howard acknowledged that the uniform gun laws were a 'very tough proposal' and that care needed to be taken to deliver the message of the policy effectively (see Anderson 2017: 225). To raise and maintain support for the policy, the prime minister acknowledged the reforms would inconvenience the law-abiding citizens who owned firearms. In doing so, the government sought to 'reassure those people that they were not themselves criminal' (Anderson 2017: 224).

Another important strategy used to raise and maintain support for the policy was to foster bipartisanship and present a unified approach to the gun laws. An example of how Howard did this was by inviting the opposition leader and the leader of the Australian Democrats (which often held the balance of power in the Senate at the time) to join him on a visit to Port Arthur three days after the shootings. While the Prime Minister hoped it would be 'a gesture that gives some support and encouragement to those who have been so badly affected', the visit would also show that political support for banning semiautomatic weapons went beyond party lines (see Howard 1996). In fact, Howard was careful not to mention parties at all to avoid any prospect that the proposal to change gun laws would falter because of partisan divisions. Instead, he attended Port Arthur with his 'parliamentary colleagues' and said the

> event … has shaken the core of this country … in a way that no other individual crime has done in my lifetime, and the very least that the three of us can do is … identify ourselves with the difficulty and the pain and the anguish that … the people of Australia are experiencing at the present time. (Howard 1996)

While such events highlighted the wide support for uniform gun laws, both in parliament and in the electorate, some segments of Australian society felt disenfranchised and began to mobilise against the proposed policy.

This was seen most clearly in the State of Queensland, where successive governments had been obstructive on the issue of uniform firearm legislation. Opponents of uniform gun laws started to mobilise against the Coalition Government in that state and its premier, Rob Borbidge, who had led the Coalition to victory in the state election in February 1996. Premier Borbidge became a strong public supporter of the Howard Government plan for uniform gun laws, despite vocal concerns from rural and regional voters who had supported the Coalition about the impact of the reforms on their firearms. Furthermore, the government's policy began to polarise the broader electorate. While support was strongest in metropolitan centres, antigovernment sentiment was growing in rural and regional communities, especially as farmers feared they would have to give up the firearms they used to control stock and vermin. This was problematic, especially for the National Party. Nationals leader and deputy prime minister Tim Fischer was deeply concerned by the electoral response outside the capital cities. As he put it, surrendering firearms was 'giving away the family silver in the eyes of many a farming homestead, and to many an outer suburban recreational shooter, and we paid a price'.[10] This was a challenging period for his party and for the Coalition Government. Fischer recalled that, having been deputy prime minister for just several weeks:

> I had to face down bitter opposition on the matter of guns from places … where I was hung in effigy, complete with Akubra. To be able to turn the tide we had to go into the public square and explain, and explain, and explain [the policy]. It was very difficult.[11]

Maintaining support for the policy also appeared challenging for the government as the tension between metropolitan and rural-based parliamentarians appeared to divide the Coalition, especially in the media. Parliamentarians from Queensland were vocal in their opposition to the proposed laws. National Party MPs were also critical of the government's approach. According to Fischer, the MPs did not express their concerns

10 Tim Fischer, Interview with the authors, Melbourne, 7 April 2018.

11 ibid.

'in front of a microphone', but instead 'berated' the party's leadership privately. Bob Katter, from the National Party, and Pauline Hanson, who had been disendorsed by the Liberal Party prior to the 1996 election, were both attracting media attention for advancing views that countered the government's plans. As Fischer put it:

> There was an attempt to run it as the Nationals versus Liberal Party issue in the media. They [the media] were licking their lips that they [had] finally found a crack in the unity of the government … but we never stepped back on the issue … Harmonised registration between the states drains the suburbs of semiautomatic weapons.[12]

While the policy did not cause a division in the Coalition, opposing the government's gun policy was the focus of new political parties created in the aftermath of the Port Arthur shootings. Hanson launched the One Nation Party in 1997. One of the party's objectives was to provide Australians with 'reasonable access' to firearms to 'undertake various activities including the defence of themselves and their families in their own homes' (Pauline Hanson's One Nation 2003: 7). Reflecting on the contribution his government's gun policy played in precipitating the rise of One Nation, Howard (2016) noted that he had

> no doubt that discontent about gun laws played some role in the emergence of One Nation under Pauline Hanson. It wasn't the main reason, but it was a subsidiary and quite important reason.

The Howard Government's policy also had a role to play in the emergence of Katter's new party. While Katter did not leave the National Party immediately, he consolidated his reputation as a 'maverick' more concerned about advancing the interests of his constituency than toeing the party line when he vigorously opposed the Howard Government's gun policy. Katter left the National Party in 2001 and retained his seat in successive elections. In 2011, he created a new political party, the Katter Australia Party, with the abolition of gun registration as a core objective. The party won seats in the federal parliament as well as the Queensland state parliament in subsequent elections.

The political reaction in Queensland highlighted the difficulty of implementing uniform gun laws. In particular, it illustrated the strength of the social cleave in Australia between metropolitan and nonmetropolitan

12 ibid.

electorates (see Economou 2001). It also provided an opportunity for parliamentarians such as Hanson and Katter to stoke suspicions that the national government was dominated by metropolitan-based MPs who sought to impose socially progressive and cosmopolitan values across Australia. As Fischer explained, 'there was a difference in the acceptance of the policy between the southern states and Queensland. Queensland felt they had been run over' by a government beholden to metropolitan policy demands.[13] Similarly, Howard explained that some parliamentarians were able to mobilise support by accusing him of leading an 'insensitive, out-of-touch, particularly Sydney-centric, government taking away our weapons' (cited in Gordon 2018).

The NFA's defenders spent a couple of rough months crisscrossing the country, dampening angry opposition. At one rural meeting in a country town, Howard became the first Australian prime minister to be photographed wearing a bulletproof vest (see Chapman 2013: 57). In Melbourne, three weeks after the APMC decision, Australia saw its largest-ever pro-gun rally as rural voters brought their strong country protest to the streets of the city. Police estimated the crowd at 60,000 (see Sunday Telegraph 1996). But, by late July 1996, 10 weeks after the NFA was announced, Queensland, Western Australia and the Northern Territory had given up the fight and fallen into line (see Ansley 1996). The NFA was on its final journey to enactment in all jurisdictions.

Seeds of destruction

Although the Howard Government's policy push was a success, one unintended consequence of Australia's post-NFA firearm legislation may also contain the seed of its own destruction. Revised state gun laws now guarantee a multimillion-dollar annual income stream to the country's pro-gun lobby. Since 1996, each applicant for a firearm licence must prove a 'genuine reason' for gun ownership (see APMC 1996). This is no problem for some—primary production, for example, is a sufficient reason. But for many thousands of urban and other firearm owners, the only 'genuine reason' that fits is to join an approved gun club and shoot there regularly.

13 ibid.

Gun owners who fail to turn up for the mandated minimum number of club attendances each year risk losing their firearm licence, and shooting clubs have both a legal obligation and a financial incentive to report non-attenders to police. Gun club officials are expected to mentor members in firearm safety and the law, while keeping an eye on careless, troubled or suspicious gun owners. Pistol clubs have an added regulatory responsibility to approve or to block a new member's application for a licence to possess a handgun. Although such arrangements effectively outsource official responsibilities, they also reduce the involvement of specialised police in the vetting process.

Meanwhile, the hazards to governance and to the country's limits on the proliferation of firearms are more ideological and political. Gun clubs enshrine in society a core pledge of shooters, which is to introduce children to firearms as early as possible. Most shooters' appeals for political, financial or public support are made in the name of youth safety education. But perhaps more importantly, the majority of Australia's hundreds of shooting clubs are run by a single special interest group. In the 22 years since the NFA took effect, the Sporting Shooters' Association of Australia (SSAA) has benefited from a multimillion-dollar annual levy on tens of thousands of citizens who lack any other 'genuine reason' to own a gun. As a result, the SSAA is now one of the country's wealthiest hobby clubs—guaranteed an uncapped income in perpetuity from a government tax on shooters (see Alpers 2016).

From 50,000 members in 1996, the 400 SSAA shooting clubs now approach a combined national membership of 200,000 gun owners, many of whom are compelled by law to pay an annual fee and then shoot with politically committed enthusiasts several times each year. As the SSAA remains overtly determined to wind back the NFA—and, in concert with the Shooters, Fishers and Farmers Party, has already succeeded to some degree in every state and territory (see Alpers and Rossetti 2018)—gun clubs can still be effective agents for political mobilisation. Today, just seven top SSAA branches declare income of $20 million and net assets of $34 million, while the national branch alone collects $10 million in annual fees. This is more than double the assets of Swimming Australia and nine-tenths the income of Athletics Australia. In its most recent publicly available financial return, SSAA National in Adelaide reported accumulated capital of $6 million in cash.

The largest SSAA state branches have done even better. In 2015, SSAA Queensland collected income of $5 million and held assets of $15.7 million, of which $8.3 million was in cash. Adjusted for inflation, Queensland branch assets have increased by 2,675 per cent since compulsory gun club membership was written into legislation. As the law sets no limit on shooting club fees, the SSAA can levy this government-mandated tax on shooters in any amount it chooses. The net result is a multimillion-dollar war chest, ready to be used to lobby for the dismantling of gun laws agreed two decades ago by all major parties (see O'Malley and Nicholls 2017).

In recent years, however, Australian shooters' groups have been regularly discouraged from spending accumulated capital on large-scale attempts to roll back the country's firearm laws. The 2014 Lindt Café siege in Sydney, followed by high-profile family shootings at Lockhart in New South Wales, Margaret River in Western Australia and the Sydney suburb of Pennant Hills each resulted in renewed public clamour for restrictions on gun ownership. A concerted $500,000 campaign by shooters' groups and arms dealers to swing voters towards minority pro-gun parties in the 2017 Queensland election failed to noticeably influence even the country's most firearm-friendly large state (see McGowan 2018). In Tasmania, a Liberal Party election pledge to the local gun lobby to wind back several conditions of the NFA was abandoned following a public outcry (see Humphries and Dunlevie 2018).

In the public consciousness of Australia, stringent gun control is now firmly institutionalised. After decades of rejection by most states, uniform national gun owner licensing, firearm registration and the removal of guns from situations of domestic violence and self-harm are now seen as basic norms. Politicians, mass media and voters reliably voice alarm at attempts to weaken the regulation of firearms. Particularly in light of the mounting gun death epidemic in the United States, Australia's 1996 reforms and their effects—precipitous declines in mass shootings, gun homicides and gun suicides—are frequently cited as a source of national pride. Despite this, few observers doubt that, given the opportunity—perhaps a lull in high-profile shootings and electoral complacency—cashed-up shooters' groups and the gun industry will once again move to seize the day.

For Howard, there was also a politically unintended, or at least unforeseen, consequence of implementing uniform gun laws. Prior to winning the 1996 election, Howard had been characterised as an uninspiring, uncharismatic and gaffe-prone leader (see Coughlin 2007). Having led the Coalition to a heavy election loss in 1987 and toppled by colleagues in 1989, Howard likened the prospect of ever again being leader to 'Lazarus with a triple bypass' (see Hartcher 2010). This image, however, underwent a significant transition in the aftermath of the Port Arthur massacre, when media coverage presented Howard as a leader with empathy, determination and strong interpersonal skills (see Crosby 2006). Howard's talent for political leadership was also vaunted, especially for gaining the support of opposition parties. Moreover, the government's speed in implementing the NFA presented Howard as a decisive leader capable of making swift, difficult decisions. This had significant long-term implications for the Howard Government's policy agenda. As Howard joked, he often met people who said, 'I can't stand you, but I know what you stand for' (cited in Gordon 2018). This provided the Howard Government with the political capital and momentum it needed to advance other contentious policies, such as the GST, which would be at the core of the government's reelection campaign in 1998.

Analysis and conclusions

Despite the challenges it faced—both internally by way of rural and regional parliamentarians expressing concern and externally by way of firearm interest groups opposing the challenges (see Chapman 2013: 156)—the Howard Government persisted with its firearm reform policy and in 12 days reached an agreement with the states and territories to introduce national uniform gun laws. Several factors contributed to this swift and decisive achievement. First, it aligned with Howard's personal conviction—mirrored by both the public and the media—that Australia should not develop a gun culture like that of the United States. Second, the Howard Government presented itself as having a strong mandate to implement change. After all, it had just won power and enjoyed a 45-seat majority in the House of Representatives. As Howard put it:

> It fell into the category of responding to an unexpected crisis in an effective way … You had the combination; it was a terrible disaster, the country was reeling, I had just been elected and had a huge majority … and sensed if I don't use this authority to the ultimate, when are you ever going to do something about this?[14]

14 Howard, Interview with the authors.

Furthermore, the policy united political actors across party lines. This multipartisanship reflected high levels of public support that allowed the government to advance its national policy. The support, however, was strongest in metropolitan areas. Public support in rural and regional electorates was patchy as communities were concerned about how the policy would affect their use of firearms. While the National Party, led by Tim Fischer and John Anderson, continually met with affected communities, Howard also continued to make media appearances to explain the need for the reforms. This approach allowed the government to allay the concerns of rural and regional communities while continuing to build support for its policy.

The Port Arthur shootings broke the cycle of policy stasis. On day one, Howard seized the momentum and acted swiftly to implement uniform gun laws:

> Speed was absolutely essential. *Carpe diem*, you had to seize the day … I just felt it in my bones, that the weight of public opinion would work on the states.[15]

Part of the government's speed in tackling the issue was to ensure that pro-gun lobbies could not exert their customary delaying influence on the policy debate. As Smeaton reminds us, it was a strategy of the government to position the Port Arthur shootings as the 'last straw' and not an entrée to yet another round of discussions and debates about how to reduce gun violence in Australia.[16] But the government could only act with such speed because of the foundational work carried out by the APMC working party, whose cumulative briefing document gave the government a readymade policy framework to implement. This was the result of much policy work throughout the 1980s and 1990s and had been steadily influenced by submissions from the National Coalition for Gun Control and others on a range of public health topics such as suicide, homicide and domestic violence prevention (see Peters 2013). In effect, a decade of firearm injury prevention recommendations from a broad range of public interest groups stood ready for use by government to bring about a national firearms agreement across all states and territories.

15 ibid.

16 Smeaton, Interview with the authors.

As a result, Australia's gun control policy shift is assessed as being overwhelmingly successful. It had a clearly defined public value proposition that focused on delivering beneficial social outcomes. The cost of the policy, especially in terms of losing access to certain high-risk firearms, was borne by the many gun owners in rural and regional areas who were compensated for their firearms and were engaged by the National Party to keep them supporting the Coalition. Procedurally, the policy was the product of years of refinement thanks to the work done by the APMC meetings since the 1980s. It constituted an effective suite of policy instruments and delivery methods ready to be implemented so soon after the Port Arthur shootings. The national gun laws were also an example of successful politics. The Howard Government was able to unite different parties and stakeholders to present a deep and broad political coalition in favour of the new laws. In addition, the policy enhanced the political capital of prime minister Howard and would later be used as evidence of his skills as a strong and decisive leader. Ultimately, however, it was the alignment of the wide range of factors explored above that allowed the policy to be acted on and implemented so swiftly.

References

Alpers, P. 2016. 'Australian gun laws may seed their own destruction.' *University of Sydney News*, 4 December. Available from: sydney.edu.au/news-opinion/news/2016/12/04/australian-gun-laws-may-seed-their-own-destruction.html.

Alpers, P. 2017. 'Australian gun laws.' In A. Deckert and R. Sarre (eds), *The Palgrave Handbook of Australian and New Zealand Criminology, Crime and Justice*. Cham, Switzerland: Palgrave Macmillan.

Alpers, P. 2019. Mass gun killings in Australia, 1971–2018. [Online.] Sydney: GunPolicy.org, Sydney School of Public Health. Available from: www.gunpolicy.org/documents/5902-alpers-australia-mass-shootings-1971-2018.

Alpers, P. and Rossetti, A. 2016. 'Australian firearm amnesty buyback and destruction totals: Official tallies and media-reported numbers, 1987–2015.' *GunPolicy.org*, 3 May. Available from: www.gunpolicy.org/documents/5337-australia-firearm-amnesty-buyback-and-destruction-totals/file.

Alpers, P. and Rossetti, A. 2018. 'Firearm legislation in Australia 21 years after the National Firearms Agreement.' *Gunpolicy.org*, 2 April. Available from: www.gunpolicy.org/documents/6936-firearm-legislation-in-australia-21-years-after-the-national-firearms-agreement.

Alpers, P., Rossetti, A. and Picard, M. 2018a. *Australia: Gun facts, figures and the law*. Sydney School of Public Health, University of Sydney. GunPolicy.org, 3 October. Available from: www.gunpolicy.org/firearms/region/australia.

Alpers, P., Rossetti, A. and Picard, M. 2018b. Guns in Australia: Total *number of gun deaths*. Sydney School of Public Health, University of Sydney. GunPolicy.org, 3 October. Available from: www.gunpolicy.org/firearms/compareyears/10/total_number_of_gun_deaths.

Anderson, J. 2017. 'The challenge of reforming gun laws.' In T. Frame (ed.), *The Ascent to Power, 1996: The Howard Government. Volume 1*. Sydney: UNSW Press.

Ansley, G. 1996. 'Gun law rebels cave into Howard.' *New Zealand Herald*, 23 July.

Australasian Police Ministers' Council (APMC) 1996. *Nationwide Agreement on Firearms*. 10 May. Canberra: APMC. Available from: www.austlii.edu.au/au/other/apmc/.

Baker, J. and McPhedran, S. 2006. 'Gun laws and sudden death: Did the Australian firearms legislation of 1996 make a difference?' *British Journal of Criminology* 47(3): 455–69. doi.org/10.1093/bjc/azl084.

Bean, C. (ed.) 1997. *The Politics of Retribution: The 1996 Australian federal election*. Sydney: Allen & Unwin.

Bricknell, S. 2012. *Firearm Trafficking and Serious and Organised Crime Gangs*. Canberra: Australian Institute of Criminology.

Byrne, A. 1996. 'Unsworth gloomy on summit.' *Sydney Morning Herald*, 3 May.

Chapman, S. 2013. *Over Our Dead Bodies: Port Arthur and Australia's fight for gun control*. Sydney: Sydney University Press.

Chapman, S., Alpers, P., Agho, K. and Jones, M. 2006. 'Australia's 1996 gun law reforms: Faster falls in firearm deaths, firearm suicides, and a decade without mass shootings.' *Injury Prevention* 12(6): 365–72.

Chapman, S., Alpers, P. and Jones, M. 2016. 'Association between gun law reforms and intentional firearm deaths in Australia, 1979–2013.' *JAMA (Journal of the American Medical Association)* 316(3): 291–9.

Coughlin, C. 2007. 'Only a fool would bet against John Howard.' *The Telegraph*, 7 September. Available from: www.telegraph.co.uk/comment/personal-view/3642508/Only-a-fool-would-bet-against-John-Howard.html.

Crosby, L. 2006. 'John Howard implements unpopular policies and makes them popular. That's leadership.' *The Telegraph*, 6 August. Available from: www.telegraph.co.uk/comment/personal-view/3626929/John-Howard-implements-unpopular-policies-and-makes-them-popular.-Thats-leadership.html.

Daily Telegraph 1996. 'Success, or lethal shame.' *Daily Telegraph*, 10 May.

Economou, N. 2001. 'The regions in ferment? The politics of regional and rural disenchantment.' *Alternative Law Journal* 26(3): 69–73, 88.

Egger, S. and Peters, R. 1993. *Firearms law reform: The limitations of the national approach*. Australian Institute of Criminology Conference Proceedings No. 17. Canberra: Australian Institute of Criminology. Available from: aic.gov.au/sites/default/files/publications/proceedings/downloads/17-egger-peters.pdf.

Gordon, M. 2018. 'John Howard on leadership: "People would say I can't stand you but I know what you stand for".' *Sydney Morning Herald*, 23 January.

Hartcher, P. 2010. 'Howard unleashes: Elitist Costello blew his chance at power.' *Sydney Morning Herald*, 22 October.

Hawke, R. 1991. Interview with the Prime Minister and John Kerin. Transcript. *Ray Martin Midday Show*, [Sydney], 28 August.

Howard, J. 1995. The role of government. Transcript. The Menzies Research Centre: 1995 National Lecture Series. Available from: australianpolitics.com/1995/06/06/john-howard-headland-speech-role-of-govt.html.

Howard, J. 1996. Prime Minister's Doorstop Interview. Transcript. Port Arthur, Tasmania, 1 May.

Howard, J. 2016. 'Conversations with Richard Fidler.' *ABC Radio National*, 2 February.

Hudson, P. 2004. 'Victoria leads way in gun buyback.' *The Age*, [Melbourne], 8 August.

Humphries, A. and Dunlevie, J. 2018. 'Gun law changes dropped by Tasmanian Liberals following community backlash.' *ABC News*, 17 August. Available from: www.abc.net.au/news/2018-08-17/gun-law-review-in-tasmania-dropped-by-liberals/10132610.

Keating, P. 1992. *Communiqué: Heads of government meeting*. Canberra, 11 May.

Keating, P. 1995. Speech by the Prime Minister. [Transcript]. Brisbane, 18 May.

Lee, W. and Suardi, S. 2010. 'The Australian firearms buyback and its effect on gun deaths.' *Contemporary Economic Policy* 28(1): 65–79. doi.org/10.1111/j.1465-7287.2009.00165.x.

Leigh, A. and Neill, C. 2010. 'Do gun buybacks save lives? Evidence from panel data.' *American Law and Economics Review* 12(2): 509–57. doi.org/10.1093/aler/ahq013.

McGowan, M. 2018. 'Australian gun lobby invests in rightwing parties in push to weaken reforms.' *The Guardian*, 6 March. Available from: www.theguardian.com/australia-news/2018/mar/07/australian-gun-lobby-donations-right wing-minor-parties-weaken-reforms-control.

McPhedran, S. 2014. 'Does rural Australia have a gun problem?' *The Conversation*, 28 October. Available from: theconversation.com/does-rural-australia-have-a-gun-problem-33364.

Millett, M. 1996. 'Howard's gun gamble.' *Sydney Morning Herald*, 11 May.

National Committee on Violence (NCV) 1990. *Violence: Directions for Australia.* Canberra: Australian Institute of Criminology.

Norberry, J., Woolner, D. and Magarey, K. 1996. *After Port Arthur: Issues of gun control in Australia.* Current Issues Brief 16 1995-96. Canberra: Parliamentary Library. Available from: www.aph.gov.au/About_Parliament/Parliamentary_Departments/Parliamentary_Library/Publications_Archive/CIB/cib9596/96cib16.

O'Loughlin, T. 2002. 'Plan to fight American gun disease.' *Sydney Morning Herald*, 19 April.

O'Malley, N. and Nicholls, S. 2017. 'The killer quirk hiding in Australia's gun laws.' *Sydney Morning Herald*, 7 October. Available from: www.smh.com.au/politics/federal/the-killer-quirk-hiding-in-australias-gun-laws-20171006-gyvmho.html.

Pauline Hanson's One Nation 2003. *National Constitution 2003.* Brisbane: Pauline Hanson's One Nation.

Peters, R. 2013. 'Rational firearm regulation: Evidence-based gun laws in Australia.' In D. W. Webster and J. S. Vernick (eds), *Reducing Gun Violence in America: Informing policy with evidence and analysis.* Baltimore: Johns Hopkins University Press.

Reuter, P. and Mouzos, J. 2003. 'Australia: A massive buyback of low-risk guns.' In J. Ludwig and P. Cook (eds), *Evaluating Gun Policy: Effects on crime and violence.* Washington, DC: Brookings Institution.

Robinson, G. 2007. 'John Howard, Australian conservative.' *ABC News*, 17 December. Available from: www.abc.net.au/news/2007-11-25/john-howard-australian-conservative/968266.

Smeaton, D. 2013. Recording of an oral history conducted by E. Helgeby. Canberra: Oral Histories, Museum of Australian Democracy at Old Parliament House.

Sugita, H. 1997. 'Conflicting mandates: The Australian Democrats and the Howard Government.' *Policy, Organisation and Society* 13(1): 105–31. doi.org/10.1080/10349952.1997.11876661.

Sunday Telegraph 1996. 'Thousands march against gun laws.' *Sunday Telegraph*, 2 June.

10

The Goods and Services Tax (GST): The public value of a contested reform

Binh Tran-Nam

> We particularly had in mind whether the time had come to shift a greater burden of the revenue raising effort towards general consumption taxes, thus enabling reductions in personal income tax.
>
> — John Howard, Treasurer (1981: 758)

> Never ever. It's dead.
>
> — John Howard, Leader of the Opposition, 1995

Introduction

Modern governments require resources to provide essential goods and services, build infrastructure, make transfer payments (such as aged pensions and cash subsidies to businesses) and make interest payments on government debt. Governments can potentially derive their revenue from many different sources, such as tax collection, operating surpluses of government-owned enterprises, revenue from natural resources and investment returns from sovereign wealth funds. Taxation—as a process of transferring resources from the private sector to the public sector—represents by far the most important source of government revenue in most countries around the world. In the 2016–17 fiscal year, tax revenue constituted almost 94 per cent of total revenue of the general government sector in Australia (Commonwealth of Australia 2018: Table 1).

The tax system is not just a means of raising revenue to finance government spending; it also plays an important role in people's lives. It significantly influences the welfare of citizens and the development of society through its impact on the allocation of resources, stabilisation of the macroeconomy and redistribution of income and wealth.

Australia has undergone significant tax changes in the past 35 years. An example is the base-broadening income tax reform by the Hawke Labor Government, including the capital gains tax and fringe benefits tax, introduced in 1985 and 1986, respectively. Accompanying this base broadening was a reduction in income tax rates. In recent years, proposed tax reforms have held a priority position on Australia's political agenda.

However, no tax change has been as major and dramatic as the introduction of the goods and services tax (GST) by the Howard Coalition Government to replace the wholesale sales tax (WST) and a number of state taxes with effect from 1 July 2000. The GST, or value-added tax (VAT) as it is known in Europe and Japan, is an indirect tax (a sales tax levied on the purchase of goods and services). It is broad based as it is applied to most goods and services and imposed on all stages of the production and distribution processes. The GST is assessed incrementally on the value added (increase in value) of a good or service at each stage of the supply chain.[1] It is a tax imposed on domestic consumption, including imports but not exports.[2]

The Australian GST reform is more accurately described as a GST-based reform, although, for convenience, both GST reform and GST-based reform are employed interchangeably in this chapter. The reform involved four key elements: 1) the replacement of the federal WST

1 Thus, the GST is an *ad valorem* tax in the sense that it is calculated on the basis of the value of goods or services sold.

2 Further, a GST is normally taxed in the country where the private consumption ultimately takes place. This is known as the destination principle of taxation. The complexity of any GST system arises in the form of zero-rated and exempt supplies. The supplier of zero-rated (or GST-free) supplies (for example, exports or some food items) is not required to charge output GST but is entitled to claim back input GST paid. The supplier of an exempt supply (for example, financial services, educational services, residential accommodation) is not required to charge output GST but cannot claim back input GST paid. Another complication is that, in many countries but not Australia, there are many GST rates (one standard rate plus one or more reduced rates for essential goods).

and a range of state indirect taxes with the GST; 2) a comprehensive compensation package for the perceived 'losers' from the introduction of the GST; 3) a series of subsequent direct tax cuts, at both company and individual levels; and 4) reform of Commonwealth–state financial relations. This is why the federal Coalition Government described the GST-based reform not as a new tax, but as 'a new tax system' (Department of the Treasury 1998).

The GST model was first implemented in France in 1954. The modern model of the GST with a broad base and single rate (with which Australians are familiar) was introduced in New Zealand in 1984. In terms of the technical design and implementation of the GST, Australia was a slow follower, not a world leader. What distinguishes the Australian GST-based reform are the comprehensive compensation package and the innovative use of the GST to modernise the financial relations between the Commonwealth and state and territory governments.

The GST as a public policy success

The introduction of the GST can be regarded as a genuine tax reform that produced change for the better, albeit not with complete success. In *programmatic* terms, there is a well-developed and empirically feasible public value proposition that underpins the reform of the taxation system. The changes sought to stimulate economic growth and development by securing increased government revenue, enhancing business prosperity, stimulating greater investment and encouraging increased exporting (Department of the Treasury 1998: 14–15). The intent was to replace the outdated, inefficient and distorted system of state and federal indirect taxes with a new tax system that was fairer, simpler and more rewarding for individuals (Department of the Treasury 1998: 3–16). To achieve such ends, the means was a broad-based consumption tax (BBCT), preferably with a single rate. Among the menu of feasible alternatives, the Howard Government chose the GST as an appropriate policy instrument.

In terms of a theory of change, the GST is flexible enough to enable incremental adjustments to address changing conditions. For example, if Australian economic conditions require a greater amount of tax revenue to be raised from household consumption, it is possible to expand the GST base and/or raise the GST standard rate to more than the current rate of 10 per cent. Similarly, if the Australian macroeconomy calls for much less tax revenue to be raised from consumption, the GST rate can be reduced to less than 10 per cent. In practice, however, there are some legal and political constraints to such changes, thus reducing the flexibility of the GST as a tax policy instrument. This will be discussed further later in this chapter.

In *process* terms, the GST reform exhibited thoughtful and effective design and policymaking practices. The problem with Australia's indirect tax system, particularly the WST, lay in its narrow base and multiple tax rates. As a policy instrument, the GST followed the mantra from the previous Keating-era reforms of income tax: broaden the base and lower the rate. The choice of a broad-based, single-rate GST as the indirect tax reform measure in 1998 brought Australia into line with countries such as New Zealand. All tax reforms typically give rise to winners and losers and the GST proposal was accompanied by a comprehensive compensation package to smooth its passage (Department of the Treasury 1998: 16–19). Also, it was accompanied by substantial income tax cuts following its implementation. For example, the company income tax rate decreased from 34 per cent to 30 per cent in 2000–01. Similarly, the top individual income tax rate was reduced from 47 per cent in 1990–91 to 45 per cent in 2006–07, whereas personal income tax brackets have been enlarged (the tax-free threshold from $4,594 in 1985–86 to $6,000 in 2011–12, and then markedly to $18,200 in 2012–13); and taxable income thresholds for the top tax rate have been raised (from $50,000 in 1989–90 to $60,000 in 2000–01, $70,000 in 2004–05 and then markedly to $180,000 in 2008–09).

In rolling out the GST, the Howard Government had the advantage of inheriting the required administrative and technical details to implement the GST from John Hewson's revised 'Fightback!' package (Liberal Party of Australia 1991). The Australian Taxation Office (ATO) was given sufficient additional resources to cope with the administrative challenges of introducing the new system from 1998 to 2001 (D'Ascenzo 2005). The two-year gap between announcement and commencement allowed adequate time for the private sector to prepare for the implementation of the GST. The 'education first, enforcement later' approach adopted by the ATO resulted in a smooth implementation process with high levels of ongoing compliance. The timing of the GST was particularly helped by the strengthening of the Australian economy in the years leading up to 2001.

In *political* terms, the GST-based tax reform passes the test of public policy legitimacy. Howard and his government took a considerable risk in promoting a GST as the centrepiece of their reelection platform—a move described as a 'bold attempt to remedy long-acknowledged deficiencies in the system' (The Age 1998: 12). Howard's admittedly narrow 1998 electoral victory gave his government a historic mandate for indirect taxation reform. The broad public acceptance of the new tax system was quite remarkable considering the overwhelming public rejection a similar proposal had received just five years earlier. However, the legitimacy of the GST was somewhat diminished by the Treasury's attempt to portray the tax as a state tax in the early years after its introduction; but, as the GST revenue is distributed to the states under the previously mentioned intergovernmental agreement, the states have received stable and growing financial support from the Commonwealth and thus have been supportive of the measure once it was in place.[3]

Tax reform is an ongoing process. In terms of *endurance*, the GST has become a major part of Australia's tax system and appears likely to stay in place well into the future. Since its adoption, there have been only minor changes to the GST legislation. However, in terms of financial sustainability, the GST cannot be termed a 'great policy success'. Although the GST is a stable and growing source of revenue, its durability has often been questioned. This is because GST-exempt goods and services have increased more than the actual GST base. The GST base has shrunk over time as a percentage of household final consumption expenditure. To halt the erosion of indirect tax revenue, adjustments will need to be made to the base of the GST. There are, however, legal and political constraints to either changing the standard GST rate or expanding the GST tax base. These issues will be further discussed later in this chapter.

In sum, the GST is widely perceived as a policy success by various stakeholders, including tax academics and researchers, businesses and professional organisations and international organisations such as the OECD. Other countries have struggled to implement a GST as smoothly or successfully as Australia. For example, the introduction of the Canadian GST in 1991 was hampered by poor timing (the economy was in recession) and a lack of transparency and political legitimacy. Australia's

3 There are still Commonwealth–state disputes about the allocation of total GST revenue, as discussed later.

experience was much different. The core of Australia's GST success lies in the intended consequences that the Howard Government deliberately sought to achieve.

Distributional effects

These positive effects aside, the GST-based reform has not achieved or, more accurately, cannot achieve some of its specific objectives—namely, a simpler and fairer tax system. This is largely because it is a complex and regressive tax. The GST is a complex tax because: 1) its operation involves a very large number of registered businesses and tax administrators (compared with a revenue-equivalent WST); 2) registered businesses act as tax collectors on behalf of the government; 3) under the Australian method of calculation, the GST is a transaction-based method imposed on every sale; and 4) it is not legally simple. There is unambiguous evidence that the GST is by far the most burdensome tax with which small and medium businesses in Australia have to comply (Lignier et al. 2014: 239).

The distributional costs and benefits of the GST-based reform to Australians include a higher indirect tax burden and a lower income tax burden, respectively. Like most tax changes, the GST-based reform gave rise to winners and losers. Certain individuals, or groups of individuals, have been disproportionately affected by the changes. In the first group are low-income individuals who spend a high proportion of their income on consumption and pay little in income tax. The second group consists of older individuals who paid high income tax when they were young and are now facing higher indirect tax burdens. The second group appeared to be adequately compensated as there was a one-off 4 per cent increase in aged and service pensions under the new system (Department of the Treasury 1998: 18), whereas the one-off increase in the rate of inflation due to the GST was estimated to be about 2.8 per cent across Australia (Valadkhani and Layton 2004: 125).

Despite this compensation, a gap remains between people's absolute and relative levels of wellbeing. The distributional impact of the GST, as an indirect tax, is regressive in the sense that the GST burden relative to income declines as income becomes higher. Further, the distributional impact of income tax cuts is also regressive in the sense that income tax reduction relative to income tends to increase as income becomes higher. The combined distributional impacts of the GST and accompanying income tax cuts thus reduce the overall progressivity of the Australian tax system. This results in an increase in post-tax income inequality, which in turn implies that the GST-based reform cannot produce a fairer distribution of tax burdens.

Table 10.1 summarises several groups of winners and losers created through the introduction of the GST.

Table 10.1 Winners and losers as a result of the introduction of the GST

Winners		Losers	
Large businesses	Less distortionary taxation, lower company tax rate, promotes exports, cash flow benefits	Small businesses	GST compliance costs are higher than managerial benefits
High-income individuals	Overcompensated by income tax cuts	Very low-income individuals	Even if they are fully compensated, they are worse off relative to higher-income individuals
State and territory governments	Certain and growing financial support from the Commonwealth		

Context: A reform rooted in history

To comprehend the rise of the GST in Australia, we need to understand the historical basis and structure of the Australian tax system, especially during the 1990s. This section focuses on the two most relevant features leading to the introduction of the GST: Commonwealth–state financial relations and tax structure.

Commonwealth–state financial relations

As noted by many political scientists, the Australian Constitution is deliberately vague on the allocation of taxation powers between the Commonwealth and the states in view of the political sensitivity of this issue at the time of Federation (see, for example, Eccleston 2007: 68). Prior to Federation, several colonies had introduced general income taxes—for example, South Australia in 1884 and New South Wales in 1885. Comprehensive corporate and personal income taxation was introduced by the Commonwealth in 1915 to help fund Australia's effort in World War I. For almost three decades, income taxes were imposed by both the Commonwealth and the states.

In 1942, at the height of World War II, the federal Labor Government passed laws to raise the federal income tax rate and return some of the proceeds back to the states on the condition that all states abolished their income taxes. Four states—Queensland, South Australia, Victoria and Western Australia—challenged the legislation in the High Court but lost. This is known as the *Uniform Tax Case (1942)*. As a result of this significant centralisation of taxation power, an enduring situation of vertical fiscal imbalance developed in Australia; the states raised much less in revenue than the expenditures for which they were responsible, whereas the reverse situation existed for the Commonwealth.

Australia's vertical fiscal imbalance is the highest among all nations with federal systems of government (Garnaut and FitzGerald 2002: 291). As a result, Australian states have relied significantly on Commonwealth grants to fund their expenditure. There are two types of Commonwealth transfers to the states: general purpose payments and specific purpose payments (tied grants). These grants are provided to the states under the principle of horizontal fiscal equalisation, introduced in 1933, which distributes more funds to those states and territories that have a lower capacity to raise revenue or have a greater cost burden.

This structural feature has been a constant source of friction between the Commonwealth and the states. It forces the states to rely on narrow-based taxes (for example, stamp duties) for their own-source revenue. This has been exacerbated by the High Court's increasingly broad interpretation of the Australian Constitution in regard to customs, excise and bounties. Most relevantly, in *Ngo Ngo Ha and Anor vs State of NSW & Ors* (1997) HCA 34, the court ruled by a slim majority that state tobacco franchise fees were an excise—a tax constitutionally reserved for the Commonwealth. While the decision brought some clarity to a confusing area, it further exacerbated the impact of the vertical fiscal imbalance in Australia.

Tax structure

In terms of structure, the Australian tax system has become highly reliant on direct taxation, particularly personal income taxation. Towards the end of the twentieth century, about three-quarters of Commonwealth revenue was derived from direct taxation, with a little over half of it from individual income taxes (OECD 1997). Australia's personal income taxation in the early 1980s had a narrow base due to the many exemptions and deductions, but also as a result of judicial rulings and legislative inaction (Krever 1986: 349). This resulted in the application of high marginal income tax rates at relatively low levels of income and widespread tax avoidance and evasion (Freebairn 2005: 3). The legitimacy of the income tax system was increasingly called into question as wage earners faced rising tax burdens while growing numbers of professional and self-employed taxpayers were successfully evading or avoiding income tax (Eccleston 2007: 70).

During the same period, Australia's indirect tax system appeared to suffer the problems associated with having a narrow base. Australia's first general consumption tax, the WST, was introduced in 1930 to raise additional revenue, largely to counter the significant budget deficits arising from the onset of the Great Depression. It was a single-stage consumption tax levied on a wide range of nonessential goods, initially at the uniform rate of 2.5 per cent. The WST gradually grew into a cumbersome tax with a narrow base (the wholesale of goods), a multiple rate structure and a cascading effect on production. By 1995, the share of private consumption subject to the WST fell to 22 per cent and there were six different rates, not counting the zero rate that applied to excluded items (Reinhardt and Steel 2006: Table 2).

In summary, states' and territories' financial dependence on the Commonwealth, high marginal individual income tax rates at relatively low levels of income and the outdated and inadequate WST all served as the background for indirect tax reform in Australia.

Design and choice: Getting the GST across the line

Trials and failures

While the need to reform the WST was apparent, it took 25 years and many failed attempts for the WST (and several indirect state taxes) to be replaced with the GST. The first call for a BBCT was made in the Asprey Report more than two decades before reform occurred (Commonwealth Taxation Review Committee and Asprey 1975). However, the then newly elected Labor Government did not make any reference to a BBCT in its 1975 budget.

In February 1982, then treasurer John Howard made a submission to the Coalition Cabinet proposing a BBCT, with a number of options. While his proposal was rejected by the Cabinet, he persisted and later wrote:

> I have long believed that the single most important reform which is needed to the Australian taxation system is the broadening of the taxation base towards a greater reliance on general consumption taxes with a corresponding reduction in our current over-reliance on personal taxation as a source of revenue. (Howard 1984: 12)

In the closing chapter of a 1985 draft white paper (Department of the Treasury 1985), treasurer Paul Keating proposed a BBCT under 'Option C' (a 12.5 per cent broad-based retail sales tax[4] plus major personal income tax cuts) or 'Option B' (a 5 per cent broad-based retail sales tax plus modest personal income tax cuts). Both options B and C were rejected at the National Taxation Summit (1985), due mainly to the lack of support from the Australian Council of Trade Unions (ACTU) and welfare and business lobby groups.

The GST (with a broad base and a proposed standard rate of 15 per cent) then resurfaced, as the central element of John Hewson's 'Fightback!' package (Liberal Party of Australia 1991), which cost the Liberals the 1993 federal election. Immediately after the 1993 debacle, Howard ruled out a GST as part of the Coalition's policy for the next federal election, in 1996. In fact, he made a politically expedient commitment in 1995 'never ever to introduce a GST' (Megalogenis 1999: 99).

The GST returns

The Coalition under Howard's leadership enjoyed a landslide victory in the 1996 federal election. However, in the 12 months following the Coalition's return to office, Howard suffered a dramatic reversal in political fortune and his approval rating as preferred prime minister fell to 20 per cent (Aubin 1999: 216). Despite his own 1995 commitment, he was under pressure from many quarters, especially senior members of the business community, to proceed with an indirect tax reform (Eccleston 2007: 79).

---

4 A retail sales tax is imposed at the retail level (that is, from business to individual/household). A broad-based retail sales tax is roughly equivalent to a GST (with the same rate) in terms of revenue; however, a retail sales tax is simpler but more prone to evasion than a GST.

In the meantime, there were many signs of changing perceptions in the GST debate. First, Keating's political triumph at the 1993 election turned out to be short-lived. With tax revenue growth failing to meet expectations, the Keating Government could not deliver on its election promise of income tax cuts without raising indirect taxes. This government failure and the resulting increase in the WST and excises in the 1993–94 Budget cast a new and favourable light on the much-criticised GST.

Second, traditionally, the GST was favoured by business organisations and opposed by key welfare groups. A change in community attitudes towards the GST became apparent at a national tax summit hosted jointly by the Australian Chamber of Commerce and Industry and the Australian Council of Social Service (ACOSS) in 1996. At the meeting, both organisations broadly agreed on an indirect tax reform accompanied by compensating welfare benefits. There was also broad support for a GST from state premiers and a diverse range of bodies such as CPA Australia, the National Commission of Audit and the Productivity Commission (Harrison 1999). Third, there was the 1997 High Court decision that struck down state franchise taxes (or excises more generally) on constitutional grounds—paving the way for the GST, at least from the states' perspective.

This changing tide in the GST debate allowed Howard to seize the opportunity by taking steps to formulate a tax reform package that the majority of Australians could endorse (Eccleston 2007: 79). In designing a tax reform package that would determine the fate of his government, Howard was greatly assisted by his treasurer, Peter Costello. After a year of intense debate and speculation, the proposed new system was released in 1998.

This proposal foreshadowed the replacement of the WST with a comprehensive GST, with food in its base and a standard rate of 10 per cent. The proposed GST was projected to raise $27.2 billion in revenue in the first year (2000–01). The package also included social security and family assistance reforms (including a one-off 4 per cent increase across the board in social security payments) to compensate potential losers, substantial personal income tax cuts and changes to business taxation. Another essential element of the new system was the link between the GST and fiscal federalism. The package proposed to allocate all GST revenue to state governments as general-purpose grants (via the Commonwealth Grants Commission mechanism), provided they abolished certain indirect state taxes.

The comprehensive tax base of the proposed GST followed the New Zealand model. Its standard rate was kept low, at 10 per cent (compared with the standard rate of 15 per cent proposed in the 'Fightback!' package) to satisfy business demands while the increase in social security payments made the model acceptable to the welfare sector. The income tax cuts reflected Howard's personal view that his reelection depended heavily on middle-income earners who would favour such changes to the tax mix. Clearly, the novel and least anticipated feature of the new system was the restructuring of Commonwealth–state financial relations. As something of a master stroke, this ensured support from the states, which had been looking for a stable and growing source of unconditional transfers from the Commonwealth.

The reelection of the Howard Government in October 1998 on the platform of a new tax system—albeit with a swing against it[5]—was unprecedented in Australian federal history. No political party had ever been elected on a platform of a major new tax before. However, to achieve passage of the GST Bill through parliament, the government found it necessary to make several compromises with the Australian Democrats, who controlled the balance of power in the Senate.[6] These compromises narrowed the base of the GST that was initially proposed; the most notable change was the removal of fresh food, health services, medicines and education services from the GST base.

Even after the compromise had been struck, there was internal opposition against the modified GST within the Australian Democrats. This was evident when three Democrats senators crossed the floor and voted against the GST that their leader had successfully negotiated. (This would later lead to infighting and the eventual demise of the Australian Democrats as a political force). Thus, without the Australian Democrats' compromise, the GST would not have been passed by the Senate and another period of policy paralysis might have ensued.

The ALP opposed the GST when it was proposed by the Coalition at three federal elections, in 1993, 1998 and 2001. In 1993, using his political skills and experience as a former treasurer, prime minister

5 The Howard Government suffered a swing of 4.61 per cent against it and achieved a two-party preferred vote of only 49.02 per cent, compared with Labor's 50.98 per cent.

6 As a result of the GST negotiation between Australian Democrats leader Meg Lees and John Howard, the Australian Democrats split and were eventually annihilated following the 2007 federal election.

Keating defeated the Hewson-led Coalition and its 'Fightback!' agenda, despite the fact the Treasury under Keating's leadership had proposed a BBCT at the National Tax Summit eight years earlier. Subsequently, as opposition leader, ALP's Kim Beazley fought against the new tax system and narrowly lost the 1998 election. During the 2001 campaign, Beazley continued to oppose the GST, making a vague 'GST rollback' part of his election platform. The ALP's loss of the 2001 election[7] effectively ended any serious opposition to the GST in Australia.

The implementation experience

The amended GST was enacted on 28 June 1999 as *A New Tax System (Goods and Services Tax) Act 1999* (Cwlth). It gained assent on 8 July 1999 and became effective from 1 July 2000. The subsequent implementation of the GST reform was relatively smooth. Several factors combined to help ease the transition:

- The Australian economy was performing strongly in 2000.
- The reform was well designed and the Howard Government obtained all necessary planning and coordination details for implementing the GST from the 1992 'Fightback!' package (see, for example, the unpublished report of the GST Planning and Co-ordination Office).[8]
- The compensation package was appropriate and acceptable to the welfare sector.
- The lag time between the announcement of the new system and the commencement of the GST provided businesses with ample time to prepare for its operation.
- The ATO efficiently handled the administration of the introduction of the GST.

While most of the above factors are self-explanatory, it is worth elaborating on the ATO's contribution to the smooth implementation of the GST in Australia.

7 The 2001 federal election turned out to be dominated by the '*Tampa* incident' and border protection policy.

8 The unpublished report of the GST Planning and Co-ordination Office can be obtained from Michael Evans, who was the technical director in charge of the office in 1992–93.

The ATO steps up

The GST was associated with several new administrative issues, such as the Australian Business Number, GST registration, the replacement of all previous tax collection mechanisms with the pay-as-you-go (PAYG) system and the Business Activity Statement for reporting GST and other taxes. The ATO's strategy involved a broad and comprehensive education campaign and assistance program before, during and after the changes. A new division called GST was established within the ATO (later renamed Indirect Tax). The ATO targeted, in particular, businesses that would be brought into the tax system for the first time (for example, education and charitable sectors) and those with less sophisticated accounting systems (for example, small businesses).

The ATO conducted an extensive and intensive awareness, education and compliance campaign for GST implementation (Commonwealth of Australia 2003: 28). This two-year program included 5,200 seminars and workshops, the distribution of 170 million publications, telephone hotlines that received approximately 8.2 million GST-related phone calls and a tax reform website that recorded over 286 million hits. In addition, the ATO also made more than 440,000 free advisory field visits and actioned over 143,000 written requests for technical advice on the GST (Commonwealth of Australia 2003: 30).

The government allocated $500 million to assist small and medium enterprises, community organisations and education bodies to prepare for the GST (Commonwealth of Australia 2003: 33). This funding was administered by the GST Start-Up Assistance Office within the Treasury. As the major part of this assistance program, the Start-Up Assistance Office issued over 1.9 million $200 direct assistance certificates to assist eligible small and medium enterprises with the cost of purchasing GST-related products and services (Commonwealth of Australia 2003: 33).

The smooth implementation of the GST does not mean there were no adverse consequences. In fact, the introduction of the GST was associated with many negative outcomes. Here, we highlight two aspects—namely, economic growth and business compliance costs.

Transition and compliance costs

An examination of Australia's aggregate economic output reveals that the Australian economy experienced a sharp slowdown in the second half of 2000, which corresponded with the implementation period of the GST. Time-series data on GDP provided by the Australian Bureau of Statistics (ABS 2018) show the annual growth rate in Australia fell from 3.9 per cent in 1999–2000 to 2 per cent in 2000–01 (a relative decline of almost half). It is plausible that this slowdown was the result of a reduction in business profitability stemming from an inability to fully pass the GST on to consumers. However, this slowdown was only temporary, as the annual growth rate recovered to 3.9 per cent in 2001–02.

The compliance costs of implementing the GST refer to the resources expended by business taxpayers in their preparation to comply with the new requirements. A wide range of compliance cost estimates exist (for a summary of these, see Tran-Nam and Glover 2002: Table 1). The Australian Treasury offered a figure of $2.2 billion, which represented the lowest estimate. Other estimates varied considerably, ranging from $2.6 billion and $3.15 billion to $15 billion and $24 billion (Tran-Nam 2000: 338). The lower-end estimates are, however, perceived to be more credible. The author's own estimate of $2.8 billion indicates that implementation costs incurred by businesses represented more than 10 per cent of the initial estimate of GST revenue in 2000–01.

Endurance: An entrenched reform?

There have been many amendments to the GST legislation since its introduction. These changes have largely been incremental in nature given the significant legal obstacles that exist. Recently, there have been changes in response to the increasing importance of the digital economy, including the imposition of GST on digital products and services and on low-value imported goods.

In terms of endurance, the GST has had a mixed performance. It has become an established major tax and an integral part of the political landscape in Australia. However, from a temporal perspective, it cannot be regarded as a complete success. While there have been recent calls for its reform, there are legal and political obstacles that prevent such reforms taking place. Further, the allocation of GST revenue to the states is still problematic.

Financial sustainability

As discussed above, because some goods and services are GST exempt, the base of the implemented GST was smaller than that originally proposed. Furthermore, the GST-free goods and services have grown more rapidly than the GST base. As a result, the base has shrunk over time as a percentage of household final consumption expenditure. According to Australia's Future Tax System Review Panel (2009: 273), the GST base taxes only 57 per cent of consumption.

Additionally, household final consumption expenditure has grown more slowly than household income because people are saving more and consuming less. Combining these two effects, GST revenue has been falling as a proportion of GDP. For example, in 2003–04, the GST take was 3.85 per cent of GDP, while by 2012, that figure had fallen to 3.15 per cent (ABS 2012: Table 8). To make matters worse, from the perspective of the Australian states, while GST revenue is forecast to grow at a slower rate than GDP, the expenditure required to maintain current levels of health, education and other social programs is likely to increase at a rate faster than GDP. This implies structural budget problems for state governments in the long term.

In view of such issues, a natural response would be to expand the GST base, to raise the standard rate or a combination of both. Many tax experts and commentators support GST reform that would result in a more comprehensive tax base with minimal exemptions, along the lines of the original 1998 proposal or the New Zealand model (which also has a higher standard rate). There are, however, also tax scholars who argue that the GST-free status of certain goods and services is critical to taxpayers' perceptions of fairness, which in turn encourages tax compliance (Walpole 2017: 242). The very recent removal of the 'tampon tax' from the GST base serves to illustrate this point.

There are several problems associated with base broadening and rate increases. First, there are legal and political problems, which will be further discussed in the next subsection. Second, as with the introduction of the GST, to be politically palatable, any base broadening or rate hike would need to be part of a revenue-neutral package that also contains income tax cuts and a rise in social security payments so that the overall tax burden remains essentially unchanged.

Obstacles to base and rate changes

Any changes in the GST base or rate would require unanimous agreement from state and territory governments as per the authorising legislation, *A New Tax System (Commonwealth–State Financial Arrangements) Act 1999*. This requirement gives rise to both legal and political constraints in reforming the GST. Despite the GST being legally a federal tax, the Commonwealth Government cannot unilaterally expand its base or increase its rate without agreement from all state and territory governments. Politically, it would be very difficult for any state government to initiate GST revenue expansionary proposals without incurring severe public backlash. Under appropriate conditions and with sufficient political will, the Commonwealth Government could pass legislation that makes the GST a truly federal tax (that is, a tax whose base and rate can be unilaterally controlled and determined by the Commonwealth Government).

Allocation of GST revenue to states

As emphasised throughout this chapter, a revolutionary feature of the current Australian tax system is that the full amount of net GST revenue is made available to state and territory governments as unconditional grants via the Grants Commission. But this intergovernmental agreement has nothing to say about actual allocation of GST revenue to states. Not surprisingly, the distribution of GST revenue among the states and territories has been a source of friction between the Commonwealth and those states that receive less than 100 per cent of the GST collected from consumers in their states.

In August 2018, the leader of the ALP, Bill Shorten, made a commitment to enshrine the GST floor in law. Less than two months later, Prime Minister Scott Morrison responded by promising to legislate changes to GST distributions. The legislation is designed to guarantee that the GST share of any state will be no less than 75 per cent of GST revenue collected from that state. It is unclear whether the 75 per cent floor is acceptable to all states which receive less than 100 per cent due to horizontal fiscal equalisation. However, any deviation from the current distribution will see some states fare better than others. No legislation can change that.

Conclusion

Tax reform is typically a slow process, fraught with difficulties and uncertainties. There are many stakeholders with conflicting views, motives and approaches who can drive tax reform down a long and winding path. The introduction of a major tax such as the GST requires many factors, including a favourable economic climate, a well-designed tax reform plan, a relatively low initial tax rate, an acceptable compensation package and the ability of those politicians who are sponsoring it to respond effectively to the prevailing public mood and the concerns of stakeholders. In the Australian case, this was complicated by the federal system and the nature of intergovernmental financial relations. While John Howard can rightfully be regarded as the founder of GST reform in Australia, many other political leaders—such as Paul Keating, John Hewson and Peter Costello, in their different roles and capacities—contributed significantly to the eventual emergence of the GST.

The introduction of the GST can be viewed as a public policy success. A coherent and empirically feasible public value proposition and theory of change underpinned its introduction. It has achieved its principle aims—a stable and growing revenue source and less distortionary taxation—but it has not achieved some of its specific objectives (for instance, a simpler and fairer tax system). The GST-based reform improves economic efficiency but reduces social equity. This simply reflects the inherent and well-known trade-offs of tax policy objectives and the fundamental difficulties faced by tax policymakers in choosing an appropriate instrument.

The GST reform can also be considered a public policy success in terms of stakeholder support and public legitimacy for the policy. The electoral success of the new tax system, which gave the Howard Government its mandate to reform the indirect tax regime, significantly enhanced his personal reputation, as well as the political capital of his Coalition Government.

Further, the GST can be considered a public policy success in terms of process assessment due to its appropriateness as a policy instrument, the firm political commitment of the Howard Government, its well thought-out design, the adequate additional funding for the ATO, the realistic timeline for adjustment given to business taxpayers, the competent administrative capacity of the ATO and, importantly, the opportune timing of its introduction. As a result, the GST reform has achieved most of its intended outcomes with minimal costs and disruptions.

That said, the GST can reasonably be viewed as somewhat less successful in terms of its endurance over time. Of course, it remains in place and its permanence seems secure. However, in its current form, it cannot halt permanently the erosion of indirect tax revenue, which was articulated as a specific objective of Howard's new tax system and which lay the foundations for introducing the GST in the first place. Part of the initial attraction of Howard's proposal was the rigidity of the GST. Any changes to the GST base or rate require unanimous agreements from all state and territory governments. This imposes both legal and political constraints on adjusting the tax. Therefore, the ongoing endurance of the GST as a highly effective means of revenue generation will ultimately depend on the motivations and political will of leadership in Australia's Commonwealth Government and its state and territory governments.

References

Aubin, T. 1999. *Peter Costello: A biography—The full and unauthorised story of a man who wants to be PM*. Sydney: Harper Collins.

Australian Bureau of Statistics (ABS) 2012. *Australian National Accounts*. Canberra: ABS.

Australian Bureau of Statistics (ABS) 2018. 'Table 2: Expenditure of gross domestic product (GDP)—Chain volume measure.' In *Australian National Accounts: National income, expenditure and product*. Cat. No. 5206.0, June. Canberra: ABS. Available from: www.abs.gov.au/AUSSTATS/abs@.nsf/DetailsPage/5206.0Jun%202018?OpenDocument.

Australia's Future Tax System Review Panel 2009. *Australia's Future Tax System: Report to the Treasurer*. Canberra: Commonwealth of Australia.

Commonwealth of Australia 2003. 'Preliminary assessment of the impact of the new tax system.' *Economic Roundup Autumn 2003*. Canberra: Commonwealth of Australia.

Commonwealth of Australia 2018. 'Statement 5: Revenue.' In *Budget Paper No. 1. Budget 2018–19*. Canberra: Commonwealth of Australia.

Commonwealth Taxation Review Committee and Asprey, K. W. 1975. *Full Report.* 31 January. Canberra: AGPS.

D'Ascenzo, M. 2005. 'Administration and tax reform.' *Journal of the Australasian Tax Teachers Association* 1(2): 25–37.

Department of the Treasury 1985. *Reform of the Australian tax system.* Draft White Paper. Canberra: AGPS.

Department of the Treasury 1998. *Tax Reform: Not a new tax, a new tax system—The Howard Government's plan for a new tax system.* Canberra: AGPS.

Eccleston, R. G. 2007. *Taxing Reforms: The politics of the consumption tax in Japan, the United States, Canada and Australia.* Cheltenham, UK: Edward Elgar.

Freebairn, J. 2005. *A comparison of alternative tax bases.* Melbourne Institute Working Paper No. 11/05. Melbourne: Melbourne Institute of Applied Economic and Social Research.

Garnaut, R. and FitzGerald, V. 2002. 'Issues in Commonwealth-state funding.' *Australian Economic Review* 53(3): 290–300.

Harrison, J. 1999. *The GST Debate.* Canberra: Department of the Parliamentary Library.

Howard, J. W. 1981. House of Representatives, Debates, 12 March. Canberra: Parliament of Australia.

Howard, J. W. 1984. 'Taxation reform.' *Australian Tax Forum* 1(1): 8–15.

Krever, R. 1986. 'Tax reform in Australia: Base-broadening down under.' *Canadian Tax Journal* 34(2): 346–94.

Liberal Party of Australia 1991. *Fightback! Taxation and expenditure reform for jobs and growth.* Canberra: Liberal Party of Australia.

Lignier, P., Evans, C. and Tran-Nam, B. 2014. 'Tangled up in tape: The continuing plight of the small and medium enterprise sector.' *Australian Tax Forum* 29(2): 217–47.

Megalogenis, G. 1999. 'Tax triumph is a legacy lost.' In P. Kelly (ed.), *Future Tense: Australia beyond the 1998 election.* Sydney: Allen & Unwin.

National Taxation Summit 1985. *Record of Proceedings.* Canberra: AGPS.

Organisation for Economic Co-operation and Development (OECD) 1997. *Revenue Statistics 1965–1996.* Paris: OECD Publishing.

Reinhardt, S. and Steel, L. 2006. 'A brief history of Australia's tax system.' *Economic Roundup Winter 2016*. Canberra: Commonwealth of Australia.

The Age 1998. 'A tax revolution worthy of the name.' *The Age*, [Melbourne], 14 August.

Tran-Nam, B. 2000. 'The implementation costs of the GST in Australia: Concepts, preliminary estimates and implications.' *Journal of Australian Taxation* 3: 331–43.

Tran-Nam, B. and Glover, J. 2002. 'Estimating the transitional compliance costs of the GST in Australia: A case study approach.' *Australian Tax Forum* 17(4): 499–536.

Valadkhani, A. and Layton, A. P. 2004. 'Quantifying the effect of GST on inflation in Australia's capital cities: An intervention analysis.' *Australian Economic Review* 37(2): 125–38.

Walpole, M. 2017. 'Exclusions from a GST: The arguments in favour of their preservation.' In *The Australian Taxation System: The 2017 great debate*. Sydney: Australian Tax Research Foundation.

11

Medicare: The making and consolidation of an Australian institution

Anne-marie Boxall

A popular and entrenched institution

Medicare, the foundation of Australia's universal healthcare system, has been in place for nearly 35 years. It has hardly changed during that time. Medicare's main objective was to ensure all citizens had access to affordable basic health care. Its core features came on line fairly quickly. Universal entitlement to subsidies for medical services came into effect from 1 February 1984 after the Hawke Government passed legislation to establish a medical benefits scheme. Free treatment in public hospitals was also guaranteed because the Commonwealth had already successfully negotiated funding agreements with the states and territories.

While public support for Medicare was fragile in the leadup to its introduction, its popularity has grown over time. Medicare is now widely considered to be one of the country's greatest policy achievements—or, in the words of a 2014 opinion piece: '[I]f a popularity contest was staged for Australian government programs Medicare would walk into the final' (Wade 2014).

Data to substantiate this claim came from a 2011 Essential Poll, in which respondents were asked their views on some of the most significant Commonwealth Government policy decisions over several decades. Medicare received overwhelming support, with almost 80 per cent of people saying it was good or very good. Approval of Medicare rated far higher than either the floating of the Australian dollar or free-trade agreements (Wade 2014). In the most recent iteration of this poll, published in 2016, the proportion of people who agreed that Medicare was good for the country had fallen to 56 per cent, but it was still ranked as the second most popular government initiative (compulsory superannuation was ranked first) (Essential Research 2016).

Medicare's popularity does have a downside. The public is now so fond of Medicare that it is difficult for governments to make any changes to it at all. The Coalition Government discovered this when it proposed a $7 co-payment for a visit to a general practitioner (GP) in the 2014–15 Budget (Department of the Treasury 2014). The government said the change was needed to ensure the growing costs of health services were sustainable and argued that the move demonstrated its commitment to Medicare long into the future (Department of the Treasury 2014). The public did not buy it and the controversial proposal was eventually dropped.

In 2016, the Coalition was reminded how much the public loved Medicare when it suggested that the back-end payment systems might need modernising (Glance 2016a). The government proposed a taskforce to investigate the options, but one of them was to have private companies run the Medicare payment system (Glance 2016b). The Labor opposition seized on the idea, characterising it as the 'privatisation of the Medicare system', 'the thin end of the wedge' and the beginning of the Coalition's attempt to savage 'bulk billing and eliminate universal healthcare in this country' (Shorten 2016).

Despite widespread criticism of Labor's tactics, the 'Mediscare' campaign, as it became known, was effective. It gave Labor a significant boost in the polls and forced the Coalition to spend the rest of the campaign publicly defending its commitment to Medicare (Muller 2017). The Coalition eventually won the election, but by only one seat (AEC 2016). It now seems that even the most peripheral, behind-the-scenes changes to Medicare carry substantial political risks for governments.

Context: Medicare's tumultuous trajectory

Because support for Medicare is now so strong, it is hard to imagine it was ever a contentious policy, but it was. The ALP first proposed a universal health insurance scheme in July 1968. In the following years, public opinion on the relative merits of universal health insurance and private health insurance fluctuated widely (Grant 2000: 261). When the Whitlam Labor Government eventually implemented universal health care in 1975—in a scheme called Medibank—public support for it was fragile. The majority of people polled said they preferred Medibank over private insurance, but a large proportion of people were undecided (Grant 2000: 261).

The medical profession was far from undecided. Large sections of the medical community vehemently opposed Medibank. The peak medical body, the Australian Medical Association (AMA), mounted a massive campaign designed to stop the introduction of Medibank. It led to a legislative stalemate that was resolved only after a double-dissolution election and the first (and only) joint sitting of parliament, in 1974. After Medibank eventually became law, it was another year before the Whitlam Government could convince all the states and territories to sign up to Medibank (their cooperation was needed to implement the hospital side of Medibank). Medibank was finally up and running across the country by October 1975. Just weeks later, the Whitlam Government was dismissed (Boxall and Gillespie 2013).

When the Fraser-led Coalition Government was elected in December 1975, it promised to maintain Medibank, despite years of opposing the scheme in public and in parliament. Fraser (1976) explained away his policy backflip by stating:

> Look, time marches on. Circumstances change and you deal with circumstances as they are. Medibank was introduced. Amongst many people it was plainly popular. It would have been destructive and unreasonable to attempt to break Medibank.

Fraser did not keep his promise once in government. Within six months of coming to power, the government began modifying Medibank. After a series of major changes designed to find a way of balancing Medibank with private health insurance, in 1981, the Fraser Government decided to abolish Medibank. Australia was left with a system of voluntary private insurance and the shame of being the only advanced economy to have dismantled a universal healthcare system (Boxall and Gillespie 2013).

Fortunately, Australia's health reform journey did not end there. When the Hawke Labor Government came to power in 1983, it began making plans to implement Medicare—a virtual carbon-copy of Medibank.

Public support for universal health care waxed and waned during the Fraser years, but polls taken in 1983 and 1984 showed the majority of people were in favour of Medicare. As time went on, the number of people undecided about the merits of Medicare fell and support for it continued to grow (Grant 2000: 264). Some powerful segments of the medical profession (medical specialists in particular) were still strongly opposed to Medicare, but they were in the minority. The Coalition, however, was still dead against it. In 1983, when Labor was preparing to implement Medicare, opposition health spokesman Jim Carlton threatened to abandon it as soon as the Coalition was reelected (Blewett 1983: 410). The Coalition was still threatening to dismantle Medicare almost a decade after it was fully implemented. In opposition in 1987, John Howard reportedly said Medicare had 'raped the poor of this country' and he would stab Medicare in the stomach if the Liberals regained office (O'Connor 2003; Elliott 2006).

The Coalition did not fully accept Medicare until 1995. Like Fraser before him, Howard (1995) explained that his party had changed its mind on Medicare because Australians wanted to keep it. It had become clear to the Coalition that there would be serious electoral consequences for opposing Medicare. Data from the Australian Electoral Study over time highlight the point. In five of the six election surveys conducted after 1990, respondents ranked Labor higher than the Coalition on health issues. According to analyst Richard Grant, this can be explained in part by perceptions that Labor would spend more on health, but the results also reflected the public's strong preference for retaining Medicare. Grant argues that the margin between the parties was greatest in 1993 when voters were still uncertain about the Coalition's commitment to Medicare (Boxall and Gillespie 2013: 156–7).

Since 1995, both sides of politics have been competing to demonstrate their commitment to Medicare, with both claiming to be its principal advocate and protector (Boxall and Gillespie 2013).

Agenda-setting: Getting Medicare (back up)

The Hawke Labor Government was elected on 6 March 1983 when Australia was in the midst of the worst economic recession for 50 years. Inflation was high, at about 11 per cent, and unemployment had skyrocketed from 5.5 to 9.9 per cent between March 1982 and March 1983 (ABS n.d., 1983). Despite this, the Hawke Government managed to implement Medicare on 1 February 1984, less than a year after coming to power. This was possible only because Medicare had been an integral part of Hawke's key election pitch to introduce the Prices and Incomes Accord.

The accord was an agreement on economic reform, negotiated in 1982 between the ALP, while in opposition, and the powerful Australian Council of Trade Unions (ACTU). The accord's main aim was reviving the economy, creating new jobs and establishing the conditions for strong economic growth into the future. To succeed, however, the accord had to find a way of preventing an explosion in wage growth once the economy began to recover. Labor's plan was to get the unions to cooperate and agree to accept a return to centralised wage fixing and refrain from making any additional wage claims (except in extraordinary circumstances) (Kelly 1992: 61–2).

As a former ACTU leader, Hawke knew the unions would demand something in return for their cooperation on wage restraint—for example, better social welfare. He also knew the impact social welfare reforms would have on the Budget; Medibank, Whitlam's universal health insurance scheme, cost $1.6 billion in its first year of operation (1975–76) (Biggs 2004). The brilliance of Hawke's accord was that it managed to find a way of offsetting the costs of social welfare reforms without losing union support for its key elements.

Hawke promoted the concept of the 'social wage' as a means of securing union support for the accord, explaining that it would deliver benefits in lieu of wage rises until the economy began to recover (Kelty and Howe 2003). The social wage included Medicare and other promised improvements in areas such as industry and education and training for the unemployed.

Medicare was the most important element of the social wage. Neal Blewett, Hawke's first health minister, explained that because the concept of the social wage was vague, the unions wanted to be able to say to their members: 'We're asking for wage restraint, but we are giving you Medicare.'[1] Bill Kelty, then secretary of the ACTU, agreed with Blewett that Medicare was a critical element of the accord.[2] He explained that Medicare was a strategically important issue for the ACTU because all unions supported it.

Restoring universal health care had become important to the unions during the turbulent Fraser years. While in power, between 1976 and 1983, the Fraser Government made a series of major changes to Australia's health insurance system. The first came in 1978, when the government made health insurance optional, effectively ending universal health care. In 1981, the government abandoned the public insurance scheme (Medibank), which pushed people into private insurance or no insurance at all (Boxall and Gillespie 2013). After the Fraser Government abolished Medibank, the unions became the chief advocates for restoring universal health care. They could see that their members—many of whom were low and middle-income earners—had the most to gain from making health care more affordable (Blewett 1983: 410; Boxall and Gillespie 2013).

Blewett (1983) made the integral links between Medicare and economic recovery plain when he introduced the Medicare legislation into parliament in 1983. He explained that the Bills (the Health Legislation Amendment Bill 1983 and related levy Bills)

> are an essential part of the Government's economic strategy. Not only do they embody a health insurance system that is simple, fair and affordable, but they represent an advance in the social wage and our accord with the trade union movement, and in moderating the impact of inflation. Medicare will play its part in economic recovery. (Blewett 1983: 410)

He went on to highlight that Medicare was estimated to reduce the consumer price index by 2.6 per cent in the first half of 1984, making it a key part of the government's anti-inflation strategy (Blewett 1983: 410).

1 Neil Blewett, Interview with the author, Blackheath, NSW, 4 December 2006.

2 Bill Kelty, Interview with the author, Melbourne, 15 March 2007.

Design and choice: Medicare's value proposition

The Hawke Government's central promise during the 1983 election campaign was to fight inflation and unemployment simultaneously (Kelly 1992: 60). However, the problems the government faced in health policy also required urgent attention.

Access to affordable health care had become a major problem in Australia, particularly after Medibank was abolished in 1981. In 1982, a survey by the Australian Bureau of Statistics (ABS 1984) found that 2 million Australians were without health insurance cover (from a total population of approximately 15 million). Just a few years earlier, all Australians had been covered under Medibank.

One of the main benefits of the Medicare scheme was that it was simple, particularly compared with the complex private insurance arrangements that existed under the Fraser Government. Under Medicare, there would be one national insurer and all Australians would be automatically covered for basic hospital and medical services. Medicare would entitle people to treatment in a public hospital, as an inpatient or outpatient, without charge. It would also cover part or all of the cost of treatments provided by GPs, medical specialists and surgeons and diagnostic services (such as radiology and pathology). Benefits for a limited range of nonmedical services, including optometry and selected dental surgical procedures, would also be available (Blewett 1983: 401).

After 1978, when health insurance became optional, people had to decide whether or not to purchase health insurance. This meant making an assessment of the risk of ill health (yours and your family's), and then deciding whether to purchase private health insurance or to self-insure (by paying the cost of any health expenses out of your own pocket). Various factors had to be considered when making this decision because government benefits for medical services varied according to income level and insurance status and some benefits were payable only after a substantial copayment was made (Boxall and Gillespie 2013: 79).

In stark contrast with the complicated arrangements under the private insurance scheme, Medicare would pay a single medical benefit rate for all patients. In his second reading speech on the Medicare Bills, Blewett (1983: 400) explained that, under the current arrangements, the Commonwealth Government paid 85 per cent of the scheduled medical fee for pensioners, 30 per cent for people with private insurance and nothing for people without health insurance. He went on to outline the problems that arose because there were different income limits for different entitlement cards. These arrangements meant that pensioners could earn more than a low-income earner but still retain their health concession card. He then illustrated the complicated decision-making process required of individuals:

> [A]n itinerate labourer on varying weekly incomes is asked to average his income from the last four weeks, check to see if it is less than $193 a week for a married couple, and notify the Department of Social Security if his income exceeds that average by more than 25 per cent in any one week. (Blewett 1983: 400)

As well as being simpler, Medicare was also promoted as being far more efficient than the private health insurance scheme. Eligibility checks would not be required under Medicare and doctors and hospitals would no longer have to chase bad debts, which would reduce the administrative burden on them (Blewett 1983). One of the key features of Medicare was that it allowed doctors to direct bill, or 'bulk-bill' as it is now known. If they opted to bulk-bill, doctors would be paid directly by the government on the condition that they accept the Medicare benefit rate as full settlement of the account for that service.

The government also estimated that it would cost about $40 million a year less to administer medical benefits through a single national insurer than it would through existing private insurers (there were about 80 in operation at the time). Blewett (1983: 408) explained that the Health Insurance Commission (which administered the government-run private health insurance fund, Medibank Private) would be administering Medicare and it had lower overheads than comparable private insurers.

One of the strongest public arguments the government made for Medicare, however, was that it was more equitable than the existing private health insurance scheme. Blewett explained that the cost of health care had become a strain for many people. If they chose to self-insure and then became ill, people who were ineligible for government support faced high medical and/or hospital expenses. The alternative—taking out private health insurance—was also becoming increasingly unaffordable for many low and middle-income earners. As premiums rose, it was far more difficult for those on low and middle incomes to afford insurance.

In contrast with private insurance, Medicare would be financed through a levy on taxable income. This meant all Australians would 'contribute towards the nation's health costs according to his or her ability to pay', but people would have the same entitlements to care regardless of their income (Blewett 1983: 400).

Medicare was undoubtedly simpler and more equitable and efficient than the private health insurance scheme; however, there were alternative policy proposals canvassed at the time that also had merit. The two main options were: expanding the Community Health Program or establishing health maintenance organisations.

The Community Health Program was implemented by the Whitlam Government in 1973. It established community health centres across Australia and aimed to support alternative methods of delivering health care (De Voe 2003). These centres had a strong focus on preventive health and early intervention, providing support and education to reduce the risk of disease and the consequences of it and to deliver care to the local community (Sax 1984: 104–6). The proposal to expand community health centres was controversial because many centres required medical practitioners to become salaried employees.

Health maintenance organisations (HMOs) were also considered as an alternative to Medicare. This policy idea was first floated in 1973 as an alternative to Medibank and was revived in 1979 by Labor's shadow minister for health Richard Klugman. It was rejected once again, largely because it meant moving away from the longstanding fee-for-service funding model for doctors (Scotton and Macdonald 1993). The main reason Medicare was chosen over these alternatives was because it would be relatively quick to implement. Because Medibank had operated between 1974 and 1981, the government already had the infrastructure it needed to process health insurance claims across the country.

The cash-strapped states and territories signed up to the Medicare hospital agreements within weeks of the Commonwealth's offer. Once Medicare began, free access to public hospitals was restored. The government also did not have to do much to explain Medicare to the public. Because Medicare was identical to the original Medibank scheme (which operated until 1978), the public and healthcare providers already knew how Medicare would work and what it would mean for them.

The case for implementing Medicare was also clear. Blewett (1983: 411) pointed out that Labor had outlined its plans for Medicare, including detailed costings, more than a year before the 1983 election. It had also produced a booklet entitled *Labor's Health Plan: Summary of arguments* and circulated it widely among journalists and the public. In his second reading speech, Blewett (1983: 399) also acknowledged that the 'principles of the Medicare plan [were] similar to those of Medibank as it was originally introduced in 1975'. Although associating itself with the Whitlam Government carried some political risk for Labor, in the case of Medicare, it was worth it because Whitlam had begun advocating for an equitable, efficient and simple health insurance scheme in 1968 (Boxall and Gillespie 2013).

Implementation: Making Medicare a reality

On the first anniversary of Labor's election, on 5 March 1984, Bob Hawke gave a speech to the Health and Research Employees' Association celebrating the government's achievements in transforming Medicare from 'nothing more than a policy document' into a 'simple, equitable, efficient and universal health scheme' (Hawke 1984). The celebration, while justified eventually, was premature.

Hawke's rhetoric was an attempt to hose down a major dispute with the medical profession that had erupted over Medicare. The key point of contention was doctors' rights to practice privately in public hospitals. The bulk of Hawke's speech was dedicated to defending the government's position on the issue and outlining the compromises it had already made in an attempt to resolve the dispute. Despite Hawke's efforts, the dispute intensified and dragged on for another year.

The dispute with the medical profession began even before the details of Medicare's implementation were finalised. Early in his tenure as health minister, Blewett was putting pressure on the medical profession to accept lower increases in the scheduled fee for medical services as part of the government's pursuit of wage restraint (Legge and Metherell 1984). When the government subsequently proposed changes to employment contracts for doctors working in public hospitals as part of Medicare, relations with the medical profession—and medical specialists in particular—deteriorated further.

The problem, according to medical specialists, was that the proposed changes to the Commonwealth's *Health Insurance Act* would give the Minister for Health a role in determining employment contracts for doctors in public hospitals (previously a state matter) and put limits on medical specialists' salaries and fees. The dispute had national implications even though it was most intense in New South Wales (doctors there had different contract arrangements with public hospitals than their colleagues in other states) (AMA 2012).

In January 1984, just a month before Medicare was due to start, the government tried to deescalate the dispute by announcing an inquiry into medical specialists' rights to private practice in public hospitals. The move led to a fragile truce between the government and the peak medical group, the AMA, but it did not last long (Haley 1984). A month after Medicare began, in March 1983, medical specialists were threatening week-long rolling strikes and the AMA was still demanding the Commonwealth withdraw its legislative changes on hospital contracts (Milliner 1984a, 1984b).

The government soon made a series of concessions that made the hospital contracts more acceptable to medical specialists in all states except New South Wales (the main concessions made were agreeing to formal consultations with the profession on the proposed legislative changes and appropriate arbitration and appeal procedures in the event of ongoing disagreement) (Cook 1984). In New South Wales, industrial action continued, and specialists began resigning their posts in numbers large enough to frighten the state and Commonwealth health ministers. In May 1984, more than 100 orthopaedic surgeons had resigned from public hospitals in New South Wales. Other specialists soon followed, and the number of resignations grew to more than 1,000. The number of surgeries in public hospitals was cut by half and waiting times for some elective procedures grew by 18 months (AMA 2012).

In April 1985, more than a year after Medicare began, the government made further concessions and withdrew its proposed amendments to the relevant section of the *Health Insurance Act* (Section 17). The following month, medical specialists returned to work in public hospitals and the Commonwealth's legislation was passed (Adams 1986; AMA 2012). The dispute was the most significant implementation challenge the government faced over Medicare.

While the dispute did have a major impact at the time, particularly on access to public hospital care for patients in New South Wales, the Hawke Government had a much easier time introducing Medicare than the Whitlam Government had with Medibank. While the AMA fought vigorously to change the legislation concerning doctors' hospital contracts, it did not object to Medicare on principle. In contrast, the AMA strongly opposed Medibank and invested enormous organisational and financial resources into stopping it being introduced. After several years of sustained, vigorous campaigning against it, the AMA eventually lost the battle over Medibank and the organisation was substantially diminished as a result. Its loss over Medibank affected its ability and willingness to oppose the introduction of Medicare.

Several leading medical advocates have attributed the AMA's declining influence over government policy decisions to the battle over Medibank. One of the main reasons was a proliferation of medical interest groups during that period, which meant the profession was fragmented and unable to promote a unified position (Boxall 2008: 198–200). One former AMA president admitted that, by the time Medicare came along, Blewett was able to 'divide and conquer'.[3] Even at the time, Blewett acknowledged the political battle over Medicare was far more rational and reasoned than the debate over Medibank had been. In his second reading speech, Blewett (1983: 399) said:

> I am pleased to say that while there has still been considerable opposition to our health insurance proposals, on this occasion the debate has been more reasoned and rational in its tone. Our opponents for the most part restricted themselves to differences of opinion, rather than the litany of distortions and alarums of 1973 and 1974.

Many years later, Blewett confirmed this, recalling that negotiations with the AMA over Medicare were quite reasonable. He explained that the AMA leadership wanted to find a compromise because it did not want another stand-up fight like the one it had with Bill Hayden over Medibank.[4]

3 L. Thompson, Interview with the author, Sydney, 21 November 2006.
4 Blewett, Interview with the author.

Medicare's endurance (and limitations)

Using policy endurance as a measure, Medicare is a remarkable success. It continues to guarantee all citizens access to public hospitals without charge and provides benefits for a wide range of medical services inside and outside hospitals. Its scope has expanded a little over the period, with benefits for allied health services and dental services for children now available, but only in limited circumstances.

Measured against its original programmatic objectives—simplicity, efficiency and equity—Medicare still performs relatively well. It is still funded through taxation, ensuring that access to care is determined by clinical need rather than ability to pay. Rules on eligibility and entitlement to benefits are still simple, clear and consistently applied.

Australia also achieves good health outcomes relatively efficiently, according to a recent OECD report on the performance of Australia's health system (OECD 2015). Government expenditure on health as a proportion of total expenditure remains relatively stable. Between 2005–06 and 2015–16, government health expenditure hovered between 66.9 per cent (2014–15) and 69.9 per cent (2011–12) (AIHW 2017). While total health expenditure has outpaced economic growth over the past 25 years, it has not grown any faster than government revenue or the wealth of individuals (AIHW 2016a).

In recent years, bulk-billing rates have become the litmus tests of a government's commitment to Medicare and its inherent fairness (Boxall and Gillespie 2013: 176). Bulk-billing preserves equity in the health system because patients do not incur any charges for the services provided. Politicians from both sides proudly claim the highest bulk-billing rates on record whenever they are in government (Norman and Gillespie 2013; Hunt 2018). However, as a measure of success, bulk-billing rates are a curious choice. Politicians generally only highlight bulk-billing rates for GP services, which are high compared with other types of care. National data from the December 2017 quarter show that 84 per cent of GP visits were bulk-billed. For the same quarter a decade earlier, in 2007, the bulk-billing rate was 78 per cent (Department of Health 2017).

In contrast, bulk-billing rates for some other services are very low and vary considerably across geographic regions. Nationally, only 31 per cent of medical specialist services were bulk-billed in the December 2017 quarter.

In Western Australia, only 20 per cent of specialist services were bulk-billed in the December 2017 quarter, compared with 38 per cent in the Northern Territory. Only 28 per cent of allied health services funded under Medicare were bulk-billed in the Australian Capital Territory during that same period, while in South Australia the figure was 75 per cent.

What these low bulk-billing rates in some areas reveal is that Medicare's ability to deliver on its promise of equitable, affordable access to care depends in part on the type of care you need and where you live. While this was true to some extent at the time of Medicare's inception, the problem has become more significant over time as people's health needs have changed.

When Medicare was designed in the 1960s, the main causes of ill health or premature death were childbirth, poor nutrition and communicable diseases, such as influenza and tuberculosis. Today, chronic diseases such as diabetes, cancer and heart disease are the main causes of ill health and premature death (Lozano et al. 2012). The growing burden of chronic and complex diseases means that people need health care over long periods, from many different types of health professionals, not just medical doctors. As technology has advanced, much of the care people need can now be provided in the community instead of hospitals. And in some areas—surgery, rehabilitation and mental health, for example—most activity occurs in private, not public, hospitals (AIHW 2016b).

The gradual shift in service delivery away from medical and public hospital–based care is revealing Medicare's limitations as a means of ensuring affordable access to care. This has significant implications for Medicare and its legitimacy and endurance, now and into the future. For many people with chronic and complex conditions, nursing, dental and allied health services (for example, from physiotherapists and dieticians) are essential. Often, they are provided outside public hospitals and attract limited or no Medicare benefits. As a result, many patients have to pay for these services out of their own pockets.

The ABS survey on patients' experiences of health care found that some people were reporting they delayed access to care because of the high cost. In the 2016–17 survey, for example, nearly one in five people (18 per cent) who needed to see a dental professional said they delayed treatment or did not seek it due to cost. The figures were higher among people living in areas of most socioeconomic disadvantage (26 per cent) compared with those living in areas of least disadvantage (11 per cent) (ABS 2017). There is also evidence that some people are finding it difficult to access services even when they are covered by Medicare. Data from the 2016–17 ABS survey on patient experiences show that one in 14 people (7 per cent) surveyed who needed to see a medical specialist said they delayed or did not seek treatment due to cost (ABS 2017).

Almost half of all Australians purchase private health insurance, which provides coverage and benefits over and above Medicare. There is also evidence, however, that affordable access to care is even a problem for some people who have purchased private health insurance. The extent of the problem was outlined in a 2017 Senate committee inquiry into the value and affordability of private health insurance and out-of-pocket medical costs (Senate Community Affairs References Committee 2017). The committee's report noted that the number of private insurance policies that excluded cover for certain types of care had dramatically increased in recent years. It highlighted numerous cases where people faced large, unexpected healthcare costs. In one case, a consumer complained that they had held top-level cover with a major private insurer for over 15 years, but when they needed to make a claim on it (for their daughter's braces and an operation), they found they were not covered and had to pay $16,000 out of pocket (Senate Community Affairs References Committee 2017: 8).

The committee's report also highlighted the impact of high out-of-pocket costs on access to care for people with chronic conditions. A submission from Allied Health Professions Australia, for example, argued that high out-of-pocket costs for people with chronic diseases were making health services less accessible and people were 'avoiding treatment and increasing their risk of avoidable health issues' (Senate Community Affairs References Committee 2017: 17). In another submission, Parkinson's Australia explained that it was aware that some of its members had mortgaged their houses or dipped into their superannuation to pay for treatment that was considered to be appropriate and cost-effective (Senate Community Affairs References Committee 2017: 18).

The equitable nature of Medicare is one of its core objectives and achievements, but it is being undermined as the cost becomes a barrier to accessing essential health care. While public and political support for Medicare remains strong, it is difficult to imagine that this will continue if problems with affordable access to care persist.

As discussed earlier, alternatives to Medibank and Medicare were considered at crucial decision points. In the late 1960s, the Whitlam-led Labor opposition gave cursory consideration to expanding the Community Health Program as the means of delivering on its promise to ensure universal health care. In the late 1970s, when Medibank was being dismantled, Labor considered introducing HMOs (Boxall and Gillespie 2013). Both policy alternatives had some advantages over Medicare in terms of ensuring affordable access to health care, particularly for chronic conditions.

The vision for an expanded Community Health Program was for salaried doctors working in the community to coordinate a range of health services, including preventive health care (Sax 1984: 102). The costs of care could be controlled if doctors were paid a salary instead of a fee for each service delivered. A key advantage of the HMO model was that the organisation would take responsibility for delivering all healthcare services to members, inside and outside hospitals. Members would pay a fixed fee, which would limit the risk of unexpectedly high out-of-pocket costs (Sax 1984: 202).

Neither option was taken up at the time, but the existence of viable alternatives does raise the question of whether or not it might be time to consider an alternative to Medicare—one that is better able to address the health policy challenges of the twenty-first century.

Some analysts argue strongly that Medicare is so structurally flawed that fundamental reforms to the health system are needed. Jeremy Sammut (2016: 4) from the Centre for Independent Studies, for example, explains:

> Medicare does not in all cases provide access to the full range of medical, pharmaceutical and allied healthcare that might ensure chronic conditions are properly managed to stop patients ending up in hospital

He criticises government inertia on major health system reform, arguing that

> the political reality is that neither level of government has been willing to address the real chronic condition in the Australian health system: the structural problems that mean that Medicare is not a 'health system' per se, but primarily functions as a series of provider-oriented payment mechanisms for separate sets of non-hospital and hospital-based services.

> Medicare does not operate as a comprehensive health insurance system that offers patients all necessary and beneficial care, no matter the setting or provider. (Sammut 2016: 5)

Other analysts agree that Medicare has flaws but suggest a less radical approach to reforming the health system. Stephen Duckett, former secretary of the Commonwealth Department of Health and currently Health Program Director at the Grattan Institute, argues that Medicare has been a great success in terms of what it set out to achieve. He goes on to highlight the major problems that need to be addressed through reform:

- removing the financial barriers to care
- reducing waiting times for surgery and emergency department care
- improving the safety, quality and efficiency of care
- making care more seamless
- developing a stronger emphasis on preventing ill health.

However, in contrast with Sammut, Duckett (2014) argues that the next generation of health reformers needs to recognise that our current health system has many strengths and they must find a way to build on them and fill the gaps left by Medicare.

Conclusion

As this chapter has shown, on all dimensions of policy success—programmatic, process and political—Medicare is now an outstanding success. However, the most valuable lessons from the Medicare case study come from examining it in the context of time. As far as notions of success go, Medicare's history and its future are the most interesting dimensions.

Because Medicare has endured for so long, it gives policy analysts the opportunity to examine how dimensions of policy success might change over time. This chapter shows that tensions between the political and programmatic dimensions of success can emerge over time, creating challenges for policymakers. Medicare was initially more successful in programmatic and process terms. Over time, Medicare has become a major political success, but weaknesses in the program have begun to emerge.

Medicare now has iconic status in Australian health policy and politics. It is the high-water mark against which bold new policy proposals are compared, in health and other social policy portfolios. When the landmark National Disability Insurance Scheme was proposed, prime minister Julia Gillard (2010) claimed that it rivalled 'Medicare as a nation-changer'. The degree to which Medicare has become a political success is now undermining the prospects of long overdue reform to elements of the program.

Medicare's history is also a critical dimension of its success. Medicare was introduced in Australia in the mid-1980s—a time when governments around the world were scaling back state welfare expenditure, particularly universal programs such as health care. The Hawke Government made Medicare affordable by introducing it as part of a larger program of economic reform. However, the most critical dimension of the successful introduction of Medicare was that it had been implemented before. It is very unlikely the Hawke Government would have proposed introducing Medicare if Medibank had not preceded it.

Medibank softened the ground for Medicare. The value proposition for Medicare had already been made, the details of how the program would work were well known, the public and providers had experienced it in practice, the infrastructure was in place and most of the medical profession was no longer willing to fight against it. Many years after the event, Neal Blewett, the health minister responsible for implementing Medicare, commented that he was aware the government had little time to waste if it wanted to implement Medicare. He explained: '[M]y theory has always been the later you did this, the tougher the battle would be.' He went on to say:

> [B]y international comparisons we did it [implemented Medicare] just in time … if we had tried to do it in 1984 without, I think, the preliminary of Medibank, it would have been very, very much harder and may not have been possible. Medibank, for all its short-term survival, did a lot to make the task ten years later a much easier.[5]

5 ibid.

Instead of distancing itself from the Medibank scheme and the negative associations it had with the controversial Whitlam Government, the Hawke Government embraced it. Perhaps Medicare's greatest claim to success is that it looked to the past—in particular, past failures—as a means of securing the opportunity for reform.

References

Adams, A. I. 1986. 'The 1984–85 Australian doctors' dispute.' *Journal of Public Health Policy* 7(1): 93–102. doi.org/10.2307/3342127.

Australian Bureau of Statistics (ABS) n.d. *The Labour Force Australia: March 1983*. Catalogue No. 6202.0. Canberra: ABS.

Australian Bureau of Statistics (ABS) 1983. *Consumer Price Index: March quarter 1983*. Catalogue No. 6401.0, 28 April. Canberra: ABS. Available from: www.ausstats.abs.gov.au/ausstats/free.nsf/0/C42EBF2ACD5B659ECA25753C001108C1/$File/64010_Mar1983.pdf.

Australian Bureau of Statistics (ABS) 1984. 'Health.' In *Year Book Australia, 1984*, Catalogue No. 1301.0. Canberra: ABS. Available from: www.abs.gov.au/AUSSTATS/abs@.nsf/DetailsPage/1301.01984?OpenDocument.

Australian Bureau of Statistics (ABS) 2017. *Patient Experiences in Australia: Summary of findings, 2016–17*. Catalogue No. 4839.0, 13 November. Canberra: ABS. Available from: www.abs.gov.au/ausstats/abs@.nsf/mf/4839.0.

Australian Electoral Commission (AEC) 2016. *2016 Federal Election: House of Representatives—Final results*. Canberra: AEC. Available from: results.aec.gov.au/20499/Website/HouseDefault-20499.htm.

Australian Institute of Health and Welfare (AIHW) 2016a. *25 Years of Health Expenditure in Australia: 1989–90 to 2013–14*. 5 February. Canberra: AIHW.

Australian Institute of Health and Welfare (AIHW) 2016b. *Australia's Hospitals 2016–17: At a glance*. Health Services Series No. 85, Cat. No. HSE 204, 27 June. Canberra: AIHW. Available from: www.aihw.gov.au/getmedia/d5f4d211-ace3-48b9-9860-c4489ddf2c35/aihw-hse-204.pdf.aspx?inline=true.

Australian Institute of Health and Welfare (AIHW) 2017. *Health Expenditure Australia 2015–16*. 6 October. Canberra: AIHW. Available from: www.aihw.gov.au/reports/health-welfare-expenditure/health-expenditure-australia-2015-16/contents/data-visualisations.

Australian Medical Association (AMA) 2012. *More Than Just a Union: A history of the AMA*. Sydney: AMA. Available from: ama.com.au/article/more-just-union-history-ama.

Biggs, A. 2004. *Medicare*. Background Brief, 29 October. Canberra: Parliament of Australia. Available from: www.aph.gov.au/About_Parliament/Parliamentary_Departments/Parliamentary_Library/Publications_Archive/archive/medicare.

Blewett, N. 1983. Second reading speech, House of Representatives. *Hansard*, 6 September. Canberra: Parliament of Australia.

Boxall, A. 2008. Resolving tensions: The development of Australia's health insurance system. PhD thesis, University of Sydney, Sydney.

Boxall, A., and Gillespie J. A. 2013. *'Making Medicare: The politics of universal health care in Australia.* Sydney: NewSouth Publishing.

Cook, S. 1984. 'Doctors in all states but NSW halt strike.' *The Australian*, 7 April.

De Voe, J. 2003. 'A policy transformed by politics: The case of the 1973 Australian Community Health Program.' *Journal of Health Politics, Policy and Law* 28(1): 77–108. doi.org/10.1215/03616878-28-1-77.

Department of Health 2017. *Annual Medicare Statistics*. Canberra: Department of Health. Available from: www.health.gov.au/internet/main/publishing.nsf/content/annual-medicare-statistics.

Department of the Treasury 2014. *Budget 2014–15: Health*. Canberra: Commonwealth of Australia. Available from: www.budget.gov.au/2014-15/content/glossy/health/download/Health.pdf.

Duckett, S. 2014. 'Happy birthday, Medicare. Now, how can we make you better?' *The Australian*, 31 January.

Elliott, A. 2006. 'The best friend Medicare ever had? Policy narratives and changes in Coalition health policy.' *Health Sociology Review* 15(2): 132–43. doi.org/10.5172/hesr.2006.15.2.132.

Essential Research 2016. *Essential Report: Privatising Medicare*. [Online]. 28 June. Available from: essentialvision.com.au/?s=medicare&searchbutton=Search.

Fraser, M. 1976. Transcript of interview with George Negus. *This Day Tonight*, 28 May.

Gillard, J. 2010. National Press Club Address, 26 May. Canberra.

Glance, D. 2016a. 'Modernising Medicare is a great idea but needs a radical approach.' *The Conversation*, [Online], 11 February. Available from: theconversation.com/modernising-medicare-is-a-great-idea-but-needs-a-radical-approach-54477.

Glance, D. 2016b. 'Simple processing and clever apps? Don't hold your breath for a user-friendly Medicare IT system.' *The Conversation* [Online], 21 June. Available from: theconversation.com/simple-processing-and-clever-apps-dont-hold-your-breath-for-a-user-friendly-medicare-it-system-61368.

Grant, R. 2000. Parties, press and polls: Institutional influences on public attitudes to social security and health policy in Australia, 1945–99. PhD thesis, The Australian National University, Canberra.

Haley, K. 1984. 'Concessions to the AMA achieve a fragile truce.' *The Age*, [Melbourne], 17 February.

Hawke, R. 1984. Speech by Prime Minister to Health and Research Employees' Association. [Transcript]. Sydney, 5 March. Available from: pmtranscripts.pmc.gov.au/release/transcript-6332.

Howard, J. 1995. Headland speech 1: The role of government—A modern Liberal approach. Menzies Research Centre 1995 National Lecture Series, Liberal Party of Australia.

Hunt, G. 2018. 'Highest bulk-billing rate on record.' Media release, 6 March. Canberra: Commonwealth of Australia.

Kelly, P. 1992. *The End of Certainty: The story of the 1980s*. Sydney: Allen & Unwin.

Kelty, B. and Howe, B. 2003. 'The accord, industrial relations and the trade union movement.' In S. Ryan and T. Bramston (eds), *The Hawke Government: A critical retrospective*. Melbourne: Pluto Press.

Legge, K. and Metherell, M. 1984. 'The AMA drops call for 7pc rise.' *The Age*, [Melbourne], 5 January.

Lozano, R., Naghavi, M., Foreman, K., Lim, S., Shibuya, K., Aboyans, V., Abraham, J., et al. 2012. 'Global and regional mortality from 235 causes of death for 20 age groups in 1990 and 2010: A systematic analysis for the Global Burden of Disease Study 2010.' *The Lancet* 380(9859): 2095–128. doi.org/10.1016/S0140-6736(12)61728-0.

Milliner, K. 1984a. 'AMA refusing to see Blewett for talks.' *The Canberra Times*, 23 March.

Milliner, K. 1984b. 'Talks between Dr Blewett and AMA try to find solution.' *The Canberra Times*, 3 April.

Muller, D. 2017. *Double, double toil and trouble: The 2016 federal election*. Research Paper Series 2016–17, 30 June. Canberra: Parliament of Australia.

Norman, R. and Gillespie, J. 2013. 'FactCheck: Were just 67% of GP visits bulk-billed when Tony Abbott was health minister?' *The Conversation*, [Online], 4 September. Available from: theconversation.com/factcheck-were-just-67-of-gp-visits-bulk-billed-when-tony-abbott-was-health-minister-17652.

O'Connor, G. 2003. Second reading speech, House of Representatives. *Hansard*, 16 June. Canberra: Parliament of Australia.

Organisation for Economic Co-operation and Development (OECD) 2015. *Reviews of Health Care Quality: Australia 2015—Raising standards*. Paris: OECD Publishing. Available from: read.oecd-ilibrary.org/social-issues-migration-health/oecd-reviews-of-health-care-quality-australia-2015_9789264233836-en#page20. doi.org/10.1787/9789264233836-en.

Sammut, J. 2016. *Medi-value: Health insurance and service innovation in Australia—Implications for the future of Medicare*. Research Report No. 14, April. Sydney: Centre for Independent Studies. Available from: www.cis.org.au/publications/research-reports/medi-value-health-insurance-and-service-innovation-in-australia-implications-for-the-future-of-medicare/.

Sax, S. 1984. *A Strife of Interests: Politics and policies in Australian health services*. Sydney: Allen & Unwin.

Scotton, R. B. and Macdonald, C. R. 1993. *The Making of Medibank*. Australian Studies in Health Service Administration No. 76. Sydney: School of Health Services Management, University of New South Wales.

Senate Community Affairs References Committee 2017. *Value and Affordability of Private Health Insurance and Out-of-Pocket Medical Costs*. Canberra: Parliament of Australia. Available from: www.aph.gov.au/Parliamentary_Business/Committees/Senate/Community_Affairs/Privatehealthinsurance.

Shorten, B. 2016. 'Bill Shorten's budget reply in full.' *Sydney Morning Herald*, 5 May.

Wade, M. 2014. 'Medicare ahead by a mile in popularity stakes.' *Sydney Morning Herald*, 10 May.

12

Avoiding the Global Financial Crisis in Australia: A policy success?

Stephen Bell and Andrew Hindmoor[1]

> The puzzle that hasn't really been addressed is why, if we all operated within that same set of global rules, were countries like Canada largely untouched by the global financial crisis and Australia as well? Why, within countries that have been badly scarred, do some banks continue to do well, and why even in our own case where the financial system has coped better than most other countries, did some of our institutions still dip their toes into the more complex instruments?
>
> — John Laker, former chairman, Australian Prudential Regulation Authority (ASIC 2009: 48)

Staying out of harm's way

The depth and spread of the international financial crisis that erupted in 2007–08 were not primarily due to the bursting of the credit-fuelled asset price bubble in the US housing market (Dodd and Mills 2008; Gorton 2008). Many countries suffered bigger real estate collapses than the United States without experiencing a financial crisis (Reinhart and Rogoff

1 This chapter, while written for the purposes of this volume, draws on interview material and analysis published in Bell and Hindmoor (2015: particularly Ch. 8).

2009: 245). Instead, in the United States, the United Kingdom and parts of Europe, the crisis was largely driven by the scale of the exposure of banks and financial institutions to highly leveraged investments in US residential and commercial mortgage-backed securities.[2] Such exposures reflected a historical reorientation of banking towards high-risk, high-return banking and business models (Erturk and Solari 2007; Crotty 2009). The subsequent panic in financial markets and huge uncertainties regarding counterparty risks saw short-term credit markets become illiquid, placing further severe funding pressure on banks and other financial institutions, leading many to collapse.

Many accounts of the crisis have focused on general factors such as international financial imbalances, voluminous global liquidity flows, the growth of asset bubbles and the impact of the Basel regulations in encouraging off-balance-sheet banking activities (Acharya and Richardson 2009; Davies 2010). Other accounts have focused on national market conditions featuring high levels of bank competition and takeover threats that placed a premium on the pursuit of short-term profits, on 'light touch' national regulatory conditions (Turner 2009: 86–8) and on implicit bailout guarantees provided by governments and central banks (Ritholtz 2009). For his part, former governor of the Bank of England Mervyn King (2009: 10) has argued that 'unsustainable capital flows provided the fuel and an inadequately designed regulatory framework ignited the fuel' that blew up financial systems.

Missing in such generalised 'checklist' accounts is a focus on the highly variable comparative nature of bank performance prior to the crisis, as noted in the opening quote of this chapter by John Laker from the Australian Prudential Regulation Authority (APRA). Australia and Canada, for example, did not experience a major banking crisis, while the United States, the United Kingdom and many countries in Europe did. In these countries, banks' risk-assessment standards were relaxed, leverage and dependence on short-term funding grew and speculative trading in risky financial instruments was encouraged—eventually with disastrous results.

2 Mortgages were packaged into saleable financial assets (securities), with residential mortgage securities often referred to as residential mortgage-backed securities.

There is an important causal logic at work here. If banks operating within 'the same set of global rules', to quote Laker, can behave so differently in a comparative sense, this means global conditions can only have operated as a permissive rather than a substantive cause of the crisis. The decision to trade in securitised assets (or not) was taken by individual banks and the bankers within them, in part reflecting banks' motives and in part reflecting variable national conditions in markets and regulation. We therefore need to focus on bankers as key agents, particularly the way in which prevailing ideas and institutional and governance arrangements shaped banking behaviour.

This chapter focuses on one facet of this wider comparative institutional puzzle: the performance of the four major Australian banks—Westpac, the Commonwealth Bank, the Australia and New Zealand Bank (ANZ) and the National Australia Bank (NAB). Because they depended in part on overseas wholesale funding to supplement their domestic deposits base, the Australian banks were not immune to the effects of the GFC and they suffered from the global credit squeeze following the collapse of Lehman Brothers in late 2008. Some smaller institutions could not obtain wholesale funding and failed, while the big four banks had their credit guaranteed by the government. Nevertheless, not one of the four banks had its credit rating downgraded and, by late 2009, four of the nine global banks with an AA credit rating from Standard & Poor's were Australian (RBA 2009: 25). Moreover, aggregate pre-tax profit at these four banks fell only marginally, from \$6.3 billion in 2007 to \$5.1 billion in 2008 and \$5.4 billion in 2009.

The big Australian banks did well because they remained focused largely on traditional banking practices and had limited exposure to the kinds of leveraged securities trading that challenged or devastated so many overseas banks. ANZ and NAB did accumulate some exposure in the years before the crisis, which resulted in losses. Although NAB lost about \$1 billion, such losses were relatively minor when compared with its overall balance sheet and the experiences of many overseas banks. True, the government stepped in and guaranteed the debts of the big banks in offshore funding markets, but no panic occurred in local financial markets, although bank share prices suffered for a period. Banks kept lending and money kept flowing through the economy. There were no mass foreclosures of homes the mortgages of which could no longer be paid.

In this volume, a policy is assessed as successful when it: 1) demonstrably achieves highly valued social outcomes and a broad base of public and political support for these achievements; and 2) manages to sustain this performance for a considerable period even in the face of changing circumstances. These were achieved in Australia in this case, yet 'success' lay mainly in the achievement of a series of 'non-events'. Australia was one of a handful of OECD economies that did not experience a major breakdown in its financial institutions and avoided an economic recession during and after the crisis. Dodging the danger, the economy managed to maintain its remarkable run of continuous economic growth (at the time of writing, this has extended to a record-breaking 108 quarters and shows no signs of abating).

A key question is why the Australian banks did not succumb to the crisis and why they did not 'reinvent' (Erturk and Solari 2007) themselves in the decade before the crisis in the way that many banks in the United Kingdom and the United States did? This chapter outlines the performance of Australia's major banks and shows that they pursued a traditional 'boring but safe' business model based largely on commercial and mortgage lending. It is argued that in an era of 'global' finance, interactions by banks with national market and regulatory conditions were a key driver of Australian outcomes.

Yet, there was a considerable element of luck involved. In particular, a key reason the big Australian banks did not become much involved in the highly leveraged financial trading that was at the centre of the crisis overseas was that the local banks were making strong profits in traditional mortgage markets and because regulation had reduced banking competition—a key driver of the bank behaviour and risk-taking in the crisis-hit banks' overseas markets. The luck involved was due to the fact that the regulation that helped limit banking competition—especially the ban on takeovers within the banking sector (the so-called four pillars policy)—was in fact designed to strengthen banking competition by preventing bank takeovers. The four pillars policy insisted that the big banks could not be taken over, thus eliminating a key competitive pressure on the large banks—namely, the threat of a hostile takeover in the context of possible equity market displeasure if a given bank was assessed to be performing below par.

The events and outcomes recounted in this chapter do amount to a 'policy success', but this was largely inadvertent—an unintended consequence. This chapter is thus unlike many in this volume. In the case analysed here, an explicit policy was not designed and implemented to tackle a known problem. The financial crisis that overwhelmed the core financial markets in the United States and the United Kingdom and which rippled around the world was not anticipated, and certainly in Australia, the key four pillars policy in question was not aimed at saving the banks from the GFC; it had been initiated years earlier. Yet, by limiting a certain type of banking competition (notably, takeovers of the major banks), it helped limit competition and save the Australian banks during the GFC.

The chapter proceeds by first outlining Australian banking performance during the crisis. It then argues that a banking crisis in the early 1990s followed by the collapse of the insurance giant HIH in 2001 had a salutary impact on the banks and helped tighten their prudential regulation. However, by far the most significant factors in shaping bank behaviour were strong markets and profits in traditional banking activity, combined with the four pillars policy. We analyse these sources of banking resilience in terms of programmatic, process and political assessments, showing how key policies can sometimes inadvertently achieve 'policy success'.

Australia's banking performance

The big four banks which had come to dominate the Australian deposit base and mortgage sector experienced a booming market in the 1990s and 2000s, with strong economic growth and rising house prices fuelling strong bank asset growth and very high rates of return on equity by world standards (Hawtrey 2009: 108). The big Australian banks also remained heavily dependent on traditional banking, with residential mortgages as a key source of income. Gross loans (mortgages and commercial loans) constituted, on average, 72 per cent of the assets of the four largest banks in 1999 and 70 per cent of assets by 2006. In the United Kingdom, by contrast, at the five largest banks, gross loans fell from 59 per cent of total assets in 2000 to just 48 per cent in 2007. Australian banks also largely eschewed the subprime mortgage market. The obvious contrast here is with the United States, where the banks were increasingly drawn into the subprime market (FCIC 2011: 67–82). Australia's bank regulator, APRA, estimates that the

> non-conforming housing loan market in Australia (the closest equivalent to the sub-prime market in the United States) accounted for only around 1 per cent of the mortgage market in mid-2007, compared to around 13 per cent in the United States. (quoted in RBA 2009: 18)

Australian banks' impaired loan ratio was the lowest in the world in the runup to the GFC, at just 0.2 per cent of total loans outstanding in 2006, compared with 1.8 per cent in the United Kingdom and 2.3 per cent in the United States.

In addition, and most importantly, Australian banks were not heavily exposed to 'toxic' securities. Although traded securities rose to $20.2 billion in 2007 among the four largest banks (based largely on sound local securities), traded securities still only constituted an average of 4.6 per cent of assets in 2007 (down from 4.8 per cent of total assets in 1999). By contrast, in the five largest UK banks, securities trading was so central it accounted for 56 per cent of pre-tax profits in 2006. Similarly, in the United States, banks such as Merrill Lynch were earning 55 per cent of their revenue from securities trading, while Lehman was earning 80 per cent of revenues from trading (McGee 2010: 128–9; FCIC 2011: 66). International banks were trying to sell US-originated residential mortgage-backed securities products in Australia but, compared with what was happening overseas, there was not much interest in such exotica from the big Australian banks. As the Reserve Bank of Australia (RBA 2010: 18) argued in its 2010 *Financial Stability Review*:

> One of the reasons why the Australian banks' earnings have remained comparatively stable is that their business models were focused on domestic lending. As a result, they had relatively little exposure to the kinds of securities that were a significant source of losses in the North Atlantic countries worst affected by the crisis.

A former RBA board member, John Edwards (2008), has similarly argued that 'Australian banks do not engage in trading activities to the same extent as the major global banks. They are closer to the model of the traditional balance sheet.'

Previous banking crises and lesson learning

Despite avoiding the GFC in 2008, Australia did have previous 'form' when it came to financial crises and major economic downturns. The global recession of 1929 hit Australia hard, all but destroying the newly elected Scullin Labor Government. Policy paralysis resulted, and the depth and duration of the ensuing Great Depression left deep scars. The crisis of stagflation (high inflation plus recession) in the 1970s also received an initially muddled macroeconomic policy response, which saw a pattern of stop/go economic growth and two recessions—one in the mid-1970s and another in the early 1980s (Bell and Keating 2018). The post-1983 Labor Government introduced a new and more successful approach built around a wage accord with the unions. However, financial deregulation during the 1980s and the entry of foreign banks encouraged Australian banks to defend their market share through aggressive credit practices that led to a credit-fuelled asset price boom, especially in commercial property (Kelly 1992: 487–508; Bell and Keating 2018). Hence, financial deregulation and inept handling by the government and the RBA saw a credit explosion and a commercial property boom that eventually ended with high interest rates as a control mechanism and an inadvertent policy-induced recession in the early 1990s. Financial deregulation had been aimed at letting markets play a greater role in the governance and operations of the financial and banking system. But this market perspective tended to limit or eschew concerns about 'systemic risk' in the system—marked by the buildup of doubtful debt and speculative activity in asset markets, especially, as it turned out, in commercial property markets.

This lack of oversight was a big policy mistake, as was the policy-induced recession. Senior journalist Max Suich (1991: 16) offered the following observations:

> The Reserve Bank of Australia must be judged to have been asleep at the tiller … The RBA, which during regulation had firm control of the banks, changed from nanny to couch potato, issuing instructions but taking little intelligent interest in how they were being observed—not least where the quality of bank lending was concerned.

The policy-induced recession that quelled the financial boom was deep and the recovery was weakened by slowness in reducing interest rates and a tardy fiscal policy response (Bell 2004a). Economic policymakers were convinced that the automatic stabilisers—government expenditures that increase automatically in a recession—would cut in, but this judgement turned out to be wrong and a 'hard landing' and a deep and costly recession in the early 1990s resulted. The upside was that lessons were learned and policymakers and central bankers became more determined to do whatever it took to try to ward off future recessions (Bell and Quiggin 2006). The outcome has been that, since the early 1990s, Australia has avoided the worst fallout from both the Asian Financial Crisis and the GFC, sustaining the longest expansion in the history of any capitalist economy.

In policy process terms, monetary policy and regulatory lessons were also learnt. The RBA finally found a workable monetary policy approach based on flexible inflation targeting. It was also determined to try to avoid any further policy-induced recessions and handled the Asian Financial Crisis of the late 1990s adroitly by not raising interest rates and defying pressure on the currency by financial markets (Bell 2005).

For their part, the banks were hit hard by the recession of the early 1990s but were able to learn from such experiences. The boom and bust resulted in the failure of some smaller institutions and the near-implosion of one of the majors, Westpac (Carew 1997). ANZ also had some trouble. That crisis spurred institutional learning in the sector, which took the form of bankers developing a keener institutional memory of what had led to the crisis and what had gone wrong. It also took the form of feeding off this memory to develop a banking culture that had greater insight into potential risks and a greater degree of risk aversion. A former Westpac chief executive argues that 'one of the reasons things went so right' during the 2007–08 international meltdown 'is that they went so wrong in the 1980s and early 1990s' (quoted in Cornell 2009). Former bank chief economist John Edwards (2008) agrees: 'Sixteen years later the salutary lessons of Australia's last deep recession still influence the conduct of the major banks.' Edwards (personal communication) continues: '[A]n entire cohort of bankers was emptied out after [the] early 1990s and replaced with more cautious bankers.' Ian Harper, a member of the 1998 Wallis inquiry into Australia's financial system, comments that, during the 1990s:

> inside the banks there was a titanic struggle between the investment bankers and the credit risk managers. It was a culture war. But throughout the period, the chief executives were old-style bankers; the tyre-kicking cautious bankers in the end swept aside those who were hungry for yield. (quoted in Colebatch 2009)

In an interview with the authors, Saul Eslake, a former chief economist at ANZ, said the trauma of the late 1980s and early 1990s crisis was important: '[T]here were plenty of people within ANZ who retained a very strong corporate memory of the fact that they almost went out the door in the early 1990s.'

Westpac's Bob Joss (quoted in ASIC 2009: 52) argues that 'Australian banks were ahead of the curve compared to other major banks around the world, and were early adopters of better risk management systems and practices'. David Morgan, who became Westpac's CEO in the late 1990s, pushed further reforms, institutionalising the 'risk/reward' committee, bringing together all the major risk managers and senior managers at the bank and enforcing a conservative culture. As Morgan (quoted in Cornell 2009) recalls: 'Westpac had a near death experience in 1992 … We didn't forget it.' Similarly, APRA's John Laker (2009: 52) argues that there were 'enough reminders that good times come to an end for boards to stay focussed … There was a whole generation of bankers who'd been burnt. That corporate memory was very important'.

As John Laker explained to the authors in an interview, this led 'to greater visibility and much greater punching power for risk management functions within the banks'. This conservative culture is reflected in Westpac's attitude to the sorts of structured investment products that were regularly offered to the bank by overseas investment banks. As one insider commented:

> [O]n one occasion a note went around. Do we understand this product? Does it make sense to rely on the credit ratings agency? Do we know the underlying exposures? Do we have an appetite for the volatility we have seen in these things before? (quoted in Cornell 2009)

Clearly, the Australian banks were chastened, and lessons were learned from the late 1980s and early 1990s. But while a general lesson may have been learned among Australian bankers about risk and the potential for boom to turn to rapid bust, the specific lessons learned stemmed from the fragility of commercial property markets. These lessons were less relevant in dealing with the leveraged trading at the core of the 2008 crisis. As a senior Australian banker explained to us:

> [O]bviously, for ANZ and Westpac, they were near-death experiences back in the early '90s, and so that certainly set the risk at the time for banks in Australia. That said, a lot of the core earnings coming out of the early '90s was around concentration risk, driven very much by an overexposure to commercial property. The Global Financial Crisis was not so much about such concentration risk.

In an interview with the authors, the NAB's Chief Economist, Alan Oster, said: '[A] good chunk of the people dealing these things [securities] would have not remembered the 1990s or wouldn't have been employed in the bank in the 1990s.' Charles Goode, former chairman of the ANZ, agrees: 'I don't think there were many in the banks that had been through 1991 in 2007 … also, [unlike the early 1990s] it was an imported crisis, like a disease from overseas' (cited in Bell and Hindmoor 2015: 263).

Explanations based essentially on interpretative agents and lesson-learning also beg questions about why UK and US bankers did not learn from their own earlier failures in the runup to 2007–09—for example, the failure of the Bank of Credit and Commerce International (in 1991), Barings Bank (in 1995) and the Equitable Life Assurance Society (in 2000) in the United Kingdom or, in the United States, the savings and loans debacle of the 1980s and the 1998 implosion of Long-Term Capital Management. A potential problem with invoking arguments about agency-based lesson-learning is that they fail to tell us enough about key agents and the circumstances and institutional conditions in which lessons are learned (or not). A key issue here is not just the way in which bankers were shaped by their immediate institutional history or context, but also by how they were shaped by wider institutional contexts. In the Australian context, we need to examine the impact of national regulatory conditions and how these shaped national market structures and conditions.

The ramping up of banking prudential regulation

There were important regulatory shifts. The RBA's lacklustre performance in bank regulation in the 1980s and early 1990s saw it stripped of responsibility for prudential regulation of the banks and financial institutions, in 1998, as part of recommendations from the Wallis inquiry (Bakir 2003). The task was instead given to the new Australian Prudential Regulation Authority (APRA). A further critical event was the 2001 collapse of the insurance giant HIH, with losses of about $5 billion. In the wake of this collapse, APRA took a 'public lashing', according to Laker. Charles Littrell, an executive general manager at APRA, told the authors in an interview it was a 'huge jolt' to the organisation. The episode revealed a lack of regulatory alertness on the part of APRA. APRA's former chief executive Graeme Thompson observes that the regulator was initially established under a broad approach designed to be non-intrusive and nonprescriptive (quoted in Clark 2009). A subsequent royal commission in 2003 encouraged APRA to adopt a 'more skeptical, questioning and, where necessary, aggressive' regulatory stance (quoted in Bell and Hindmoor 2015: 278). APRA subsequently adopted this approach and remained confident it had a robust prudential regulatory framework covering the banks, nonbanking institutions and superannuation funds.

On the whole, APRA has established a close but authoritative relationship with the banks. It relies far less on black letter law enforcement of the kind found in jurisdictions such as the United States and more on supervision and suasion, trying to inculcate sound risk management principles among the banks. As APRA's Littrell puts it: 'We look more like a shepherd, if you will, not a traffic cop.' APRA's David Lewis (2008: 6) notes: 'It is a relationship that recognises that regulation works best when its goals and principles are internalised within the culture of the institutions being regulated.'

In the years after the HIH crisis and before the 2007–08 crisis, APRA intervened to reduce systemic risks in a number of ways. In 2002, it introduced a new risk assessment system designed to assess the unique risk profile of each regulated institution. Individual onsite and offsite reviews of the banks have been complemented since 2002 with a series of system-wide stress tests that have assessed banks' resilience to exogenous shock scenarios. APRA has also sought to minimise risk exposure through capital adequacy controls. First, APRA has, in its chairman's words, 'taken a pretty strong approach' to the question of what banks are allowed to count as tier-one capital (ASIC 2010: 14). Second, APRA (2004) has required banks making 'low documentation' housing loans to set aside additional capital. Third, APRA adopted a stringent approach in the runup to Basel II implementation in 2008 and to the new Basel III capital controls in the wake of the GFC.[3] Fourth, APRA (2006) has required banks to hold additional capital against riskier aspects of banking practices, such as trading in financial assets. APRA has also insisted that banks using third-party loan originators must ensure that the credit assessment standards used by the originators match the standards of the host bank. APRA also communicates with the entire bank board, not just with senior management. It also has the power to vet and recommend against board candidates.

Successive federal governments have supported APRA's approach. Ian Harper argues that, in Australia, 'we are allowed to get on with regulation. We can distinguish between the role of the executive government and the public service. Regulators are allowed to get on with the job' (quoted in Cornell 2009).

3 The Basel capital controls require banks to hold adequate levels of capital (such as retained earnings and equity capital) on their balance sheets to help absorb losses in a downturn and help make them more resilient in a crisis.

Littrell (2011: 5) underlines the importance of political support for the bank regulator:

> Effective intervention over the necessary years and decades is impossible without broad public-sector support, most of all from politicians across the political spectrum. If you show me a country where politicians listen to the banks more than they listen to regulators, I will show you a country which is guaranteed to have a banking crisis.

But did bank regulation save the Australian banks from the GFC?

In explaining Australia's bank performance before and during the GFC, former federal treasurer Peter Costello (2009) has emphasised the strong 'regulatory and prudential arrangements that kept capital requirements strong, subprime lending low and toxic derivatives out of systemically important institutions'. It is not at all clear, however, that prudential regulation did keep 'toxic derivatives out of systemically important institutions', given the exposure (albeit limited) of two of the major banks—NAB and ANZ—to such securities. Nevertheless, APRA regulated in a way that supported prudent mainstream banking and, certainly, APRA's approach was a far cry from the 'light touch' or permissive regulatory approach in the United Kingdom (Turner 2009: 86–8) and the United States (FCIC 2011: 52–66) in the runup to the GFC.

Yet effective regulation is not an explanatory panacea in this case. APRA's regulatory and supervisory effort was focused mainly on risks associated with mainstream or traditional balance sheet banking in mortgage markets and commercial lending (that is, 'normal' banking). Yet the fact that NAB and ANZ engaged in what turned out to be risky securities trading before the GFC underlines the fact that APRA did not directly seek to limit nontraditional banking through, for example, limits on proprietary trading or fixed limits on the value of derivatives banks could hold as a proportion of their total assets. Indeed, APRA was not particularly focused on US mortgage-backed securities as a source of risk. As Littrell explained in his interview, as far as exotic securities were concerned:

> There wasn't a lot of analysis going into it. No-one was doing that analysis. Because everyone had essentially bought in, and I think to some extent APRA was in that camp. You know, it's AAA rated, it's well secured. All these people were saying there's absolutely no problem with it.

The Commonwealth Bank and Westpac were more circumspect and did not buy these securities, as explained more fully below. As Littrell says: 'Some banks naturally were a bit more cautious than others.' But the fact remains that two of the major banks, supervised by APRA, did trade in these securities. As noted, NAB got into trouble and, as NAB's Alan Oster explained in his interview:

> I'm sure most people didn't understand what they were doing. They just trusted the ratings agencies. So, I actually think it's a combination of a lot of things. APRA, sure, but the honest answer to me is that it had a lot more to do with the way banks operated in their environment.

Overall, then, while APRA's role as a regulator and supervisor may have helped discipline and shepherd the banks in the arena of traditional lending risk, APRA did not act as a significant and direct restraint on the kind of securities trading that compromised ANZ and NAB and that was at the centre of the GFC in overseas markets, especially in the United States and the United Kingdom. As a NAB group executive explained to us in an interview in relation to APRA's oversight of that bank's US mortgage-backed securities trading: '[W]e wouldn't have been doing it if APRA had concerns about it, okay? Now, whether they understood it any more than the banks, I don't think so.'

As explained in the next section, and echoing Oster, national market structures and conditions played a much more prominent role than APRA in shaping bank behaviour in Australia, especially in relation to exposure to US mortgage-backed securities trading.

National market regulation and market conditions

Market regulation and conditions in banking and mortgage markets played a central role in keeping the Australian banks relatively safe. First, the Australian banks benefited greatly from the strong economy and a growing but largely stable mortgage market in the 1990s and 2000s. This was partly due to stabilising actions by the RBA. Second, regulation of the banks through the ban on corporate takeovers was also important.

By far the most important sources of profit for Australia's commercial banks have been traditional commercial and mortgage lending markets. These markets have been fuelled by high levels of immigration, a China-driven resources boom and high rates of domestic economic growth (Debelle 2009; Jordan and Jain 2009). As the RBA's Ric Battellino (ASIC 2009: 48) has argued: 'The banks chasing profitable lending opportunities in Australia could grow their balance sheet by 15 per cent a year … without having to take on new additional risks.' Similarly, in his interview, Saul Eslake said:

> [T]he Australian banks didn't feel under any need to enhance their income or profit-generating performance by acquiring risky and, as it turned out, toxic securities in the way that US and European banks did.

Moreover, unlike in many other countries, the Australian property market, although highly inflated, did not collapse, bubble-like, and thus did not expose the banks. One factor in the stability here was a combination of sound macroeconomic management and regulation. As noted above, in the wake of the crisis and recession in the early 1990s, macroeconomic policy and the stance of the RBA were to promote growth and avoid recessions (Bell and Quiggin 2006). But the RBA was also focused on avoiding a blowout in the property market, especially after its humiliating experience in the early 1990s. This is a major example of policy learning and programmatic reassessment. The RBA had formed the view that credit and property markets were a key source of systemic risk in the financial system. During the 2000s, the RBA ran a higher interest rate policy than was the case in many other countries, especially in the United States, where interest rates were kept low after the tech stock crash and September 2001 terrorist attacks (Roubini and Mihm 2010: 73). The RBA also raised interest rates to deliberately help cool and stabilise the property market in 2003 and 2004, when a degree of overheating was apparent. In preemptively raising interest rates, the RBA was one of the few Western central banks prescient enough (and perhaps bold enough) to tackle this form of asset price inflation (Bell 2004a). The result of such actions, together with strong housing demand, helped stabilise the property market, underpin economic growth and expand the balance sheets of the banks—all of which supported strong bank profit performance in a sustainable manner.

In terms of programmatic and process assessment, the RBA's approach was largely experimental. Monetary policy is a blunt instrument and it was not clear what effects higher rates would have on credit and property markets. In terms of political assessment, the policy was risky. Although the RBA enjoyed policy independence from government, it was not clear whether credit and housing market interventions of this type were part of the RBA's mandate (although broader goals of financial stability were). Certainly, the Howard Government was not impressed with policy adventurism of this type and made its views known (Bell 2004a: 195). In such a context, the RBA's actions on this front were not made explicit and instead were presented as part of its normal inflation targeting (Bell 2004b; Macfarlane 2006: 112).

Other regulations were also useful in moderating mortgage credit and property markets in Australia. Unlike the United States, Australia had full-recourse mortgages, meaning banks could pursue a loan defaulter's assets, encouraging the latter to be prudent. Nor could Australian households deduct mortgage interest payments against their tax liability, thus discouraging borrowers from maintaining a higher mortgage balance for tax reasons. Australia also has a system of uniform credit codes that impose clear legal obligations on lenders to properly assess the creditworthiness of borrowers.

Arguably, however, the most important factor in shaping bank behaviour was not traditional prudential regulation of the banks, but regulation of a different type, centred on competition policy in the banking sector. In terms of programmatic and process assessments, a particular type of competition policy in the banking sector was developed. In the early 1990s, in the face of attempted takeover activity among large financial institutions that threatened to limit competition, the federal Labor Government formulated the 'six pillars' policy, which prevented the four largest banks and the two largest insurance firms from merging. The subsequent Liberal Government removed the insurance companies from the policy, creating the 'four pillars' policy among the banks (Bakir 2005). The four pillars policy is designed to ensure market competition. By giving the four largest banks a stronger incentive to take over or merge with smaller, regionally based banks—such as BankWest (bought by the Commonwealth Bank in October 2008) and St George (bought by Westpac in November 2008)—the policy has, however, created an oligopoly among the large banks. This oligopoly has also been preserved by restrictions on the entry of foreign banks into the Australian market or the takeover of Australian banks by overseas-based operations (Barth et al. 2010: 449).

In this context, the four pillars policy was aimed at regulating the market for corporate control in the banking sector. In so doing, it preserved competition between the big four banks, but also curtailed the banking takeover market. Ian Macfarlane (2009: 42) argues that, by reducing the threat of corporate takeovers, the four pillars policy reduced the pressure on the largest banks to protect their share price and short-term profits by engaging in 'excessive lending and risk taking'. The policy reduced competition 'to a sustainable level and thus prevented our banks from moving too far in the risky direction … that saved us from the worst excesses that characterised banking systems overseas'. In an interview with the authors, the Commonwealth Bank's chief risk officer agreed:

> [I]n a market dominated by the four major banks, none of us had compelling incentives to go down the risk curve and grow our books as much more contested markets have.

Charles Goode, former chairman of the ANZ, told us in an interview:

> If you look at the countries that came through this crisis well, in a banking sense, you think of Australia, Canada, Singapore, Hong Kong and Israel. They're all countries where in domestic banking there were three or four major banks—and really stable. So, you'll find an oligarchic structure without much international presence in domestic banking in the countries that survived.

Bell and Hindmoor (2015) show that the success of the Canadian banks in similarly avoiding the GFC stems from the same kind of regulation that structures the Australian national banking market to prevent big bank takeovers and hence moderate competition. They also show that the more intense competitive pressures and active takeover markets in banking were a key source of pressure that pushed the banks in the United States and the United Kingdom to take on extra leverage and risk in the runup to the GFC. The Australian national market structure in banking is thus very different to that found in the United States and the United Kingdom. In these two countries, successive governments have aimed to reduce barriers to competition (Claessens 2009). In the leadup to the GFC, competitive pressures shaved bank margins and profits and had the unintended effect of encouraging the banks to expand leverage and risky trading operations to sustain or boost profits.

In Australia, however, competitive pressures were far from absent. Even within the four pillars framework, the four major banks competed for market share and profits. As Westpac's head of risk reward put it in an interview with the authors, just because four pillars 'preserves you from takeover, it doesn't stop you from competing with one another'. Hence, the local banks were interested in financial innovation and new profit opportunities. As a senior Australian banker put it in an interview with the authors: 'At the end of the day, if there are opportunities to add shareholder value at the margin, we will look at those opportunities.' Indeed, since the late 1990s and early 2000s, the local banks have invested in structured credit products, securitised domestic mortgages and used structured investment vehicles to remove mortgages from their balance sheets to economise on capital. In the runup to the GFC, the banks looked at and, in some cases, dipped into the US mortgage-backed securities market, as we have seen. In surveying the banks' attitudes to such investment, Laker recalls in his interview:

> I know that at least one of the big four quite explicitly looked at this as an option and rejected it. Two of the banks looked at some involvement and had modest involvement. The fourth was not interested at all.

The two banks that rejected such investments were the Commonwealth and Westpac. The risk team at the Commonwealth Bank conveyed serious concerns about US mortgage-backed securities to senior management and to the bank's board. They concluded in an interview with us:

> We really did feel that there were serious risk concerns attached to these kinds of portfolios … We had a good look at what the true risks were and we just didn't like them … There was a whole heap of reputational and other risks that we thought outweighed any financial benefits that might come from a little bit of extra business we might be able to book.

Edward Bosworth argues that Westpac had negative experiences with the US corporate debt market in the early 2000s amid the collapse of Enron, Worldcom and other companies. Bosworth told us in an interview that later, when US mortgage-backed securities started coming on the market, 'we applied a subjective overlay' based on the earlier experience:

> We elected, by conscious decision, that it was not an appropriate strategy … [Instead, we sought] to derive growth from our domestic market, where both subjectively and quantitatively we felt we had a better handle on the risks … The judgement call was whether we believed we had learned sufficiently from prior experience to step back into those waters.

The lack of or limited interest displayed by the big Australian banks reflected the fact that none had large investment banking operations. As Eslake explained in his interview: '[T]he Australian banks are commercial as distinct from investment banks and perhaps, more importantly, are run by commercial bankers as opposed to investment bankers.' This is important because, according to Ian Harper in an interview with us:

> There may have been a different outcome had any of the major banks been run at the chief executive level by an investment banker rather than a traditional balance sheet banker.

In his interview, Laker argued that the Australian banks 'weren't building huge trading desks, they weren't setting up large offshore operations … and their Treasury functions weren't doing large amounts of proprietary trading'. The banks, as Laker explained,

> were really focused on growing their retail books in Australia, because that's where the opportunities were … we have an inward-looking banking system. Our major banks are focused on growing the domestic markets … 2005, 2006, and 2007—these were golden years for the Australian banking system doing domestic business.

Charles Goode agrees. In his interview, he told us: the 'big thing was that our economy was strong and our balance sheet didn't have problems'. Moreover, the profit returns on overseas structured credit products were small, particularly the AAA-rated and AA-rated products, which, with safe ratings, generated limited returns.

It is also the case that, unlike many overseas markets, especially in Europe, the big Australian banks were not sitting on surplus funds looking for investment opportunities. As Goode puts it: 'We had a lot of demand for lending from our normal clients within the country; you didn't have to look anywhere else.' Market structures and conditions thus provided strong incentives for banks to pursue traditional banking practices and not become heavily involved in proprietary trading or other risky behaviour in securities markets. The limited profit margins on highly rated securities, together with the costs of funding and insuring such securities, meant they were not all that attractive to the Australian banks.

Finally, in terms of political assessment, there is no doubt that in Australia the regulatory controls and market structuring that saved the Australian banks were politically popular. The public has long had a distrust of the banks and their high profits and sometimes questionable lending behaviour. Banking regulation has long been a feature of the Australian policy landscape, except for the 1980s, when it was (wrongfully) assumed that markets could successfully govern the system. Indeed, voters see controls over the banks as legitimate and they are thus politically sustainable in Australia. The four pillars policy is disliked by the banks, which have lobbied to retrench it, arguing they need to merge to grow in scale to become more internationally competitive. This argument has been rejected by successive governments in a political culture that also distrusts the big banks (Bakir 2005). Financial and banking regulation thus has high legitimacy in Australia. If the public had a better understanding of how the policy and market regulation and structuring of the banking sector helped steer and save the banks, the policy approach would be even more popular. Given recent banking scandals over rate fixing, assistance to money-launderers and poor customer service, more regulation is likely to be on its way.

Conclusion

This chapter has explained how bankers as interpretative, institutionalised agents operated within banks, regulatory arrangements and markets—all of which shaped banking behaviour. Overall, the behaviour of Australia's bankers produced a relatively traditional banking model that largely (although not wholly) eschewed leveraged investment strategies in the kinds of structured credit products that devastated many overseas banks. The lessons drawn from proximate institutional histories within the banks, together with the role played by APRA, may have supported a certain degree of restraint within the banks but, as argued, the regulatory structuring of markets around issues of competition and the broader dynamics of banking and mortgage markets were the most decisive influences in shaping bank behaviour in Australia. It is also the case that regulation and market dynamics broadly worked in Australia in a complementary fashion, helping to propel the banks in a mainly conservative direction.

A further lesson—especially if we compare Australia with, say, the United States—is that banking is likely to be more stable and secure if it is not exposed to major asset price bubbles in key markets. Here, an activist central bank willing to 'lean against the wind' in the face of asset price inflation can provide an important source of stability (Bell 2004b).

Australia has thus developed a national style of banking regulation and market structuring. Prudential regulation has been strengthened but, as argued, the main form of regulation—the four pillars policy—which helped steer the banks away from excessive risk-taking, was designed not for this task, but instead to sustain banking competition by retaining the big four banks as an oligopoly. The approach limited certain forms of competition—especially in the market for corporate control—which turned out to be very beneficial. The policy outcomes in question were thus an accident—there by dent of good luck. In other words, the design of the four pillars policy was aimed not at limiting competition or stabilising risk in the banking sector. This underlines the fact that policies can sometimes have beneficial, if unintended, consequences. Luck and happenstance can matter in shaping policy success.

References

Acharya, V. and Richardson, M. 2009. 'Causes of the financial crisis.' *Critical Review* 21(2): 195–210. doi.org/10.1080/08913810902952903.

Australian Prudential Regulation Authority (APRA) 2004. APRA releases changes to home loan risk-weighting. Press release, 16 September. Sydney: APRA. Accessed from: www.apra.gov.au/MediaReleases/Pages/04_33.aspx (site discontinued).

Australian Prudential Regulation Authority (APRA) 2006. *Implementation of the Basel II Capital Framework 6: Securitisation and the standardised approach to credit derivatives in the banking book*. Discussion Paper, 13 November. Sydney: APRA.

Australian Securities and Investments Commission (ASIC) 2009. Global Crisis: The big issues for our financial markets. ASIC Summer School 2009, Sydney, 2–3 March. Available from: download.asic.gov.au/media/1311565/ASIC-summer-school-report-may-2009.pdf.

Australian Securities and Investments Commission (ASIC) 2010. *Securities and investment regulation: Beyond the crisis*. Report, ASIC Summer School, Melbourne, 1–3 March. Available from: download.asic.gov.au/media/2125947/summer-school-2010.pdf.

Bakir, C. 2003. 'Who needs a review of the financial system? The case of the Wallis inquiry.' *Australian Journal of Political Science* 38(3): 511–34. doi.org/10.1080/1036114032000134029.

Bakir, C. 2005. 'The exoteric politics of bank mergers in Australia.' Australian Journal of Politics and History 51(2): 235–56. doi.org/10.1111/j.1467-8497.2005.00372.x.

Barth, J., Marchetti, J. and Nolle, D. 2010. 'World Trade Organization commitments versus reported practices on foreign bank entry and regulation: A cross-country analysis.' In A. Berger, P. Molynexu and J. Wilson (eds), *The Oxford Handbook of Banking*. Oxford: Oxford University Press.

Bell, S. 2004a. *Australia's Money Mandarins: The Reserve Bank and the politics of money*. Cambridge: Cambridge University Press. doi.org/10.1017/CBO9780511550737.

Bell, S. 2004b. 'Inflation-*plus* targeting at the Reserve Bank of Australia.' *Australian Economic Review* 37(4): 391–401. doi.org/10.1111/j.1467-8462.2004.00340.x.

Bell, S. 2005. 'How tight are the policy constraints? The policy convergence thesis, institutionally situated actors and expansionary monetary policy in Australia.' *New Political Economy* 10(1): 67–92. doi.org/10.1080/13563460500031263.

Bell, S. and Hindmoor, A. 2015. *Masters of the Universe, Slaves of the Market*. Cambridge, MA: Harvard University Press. doi.org/10.4159/9780674425590.

Bell, S. and Keating, M. 2018. *Fair Share: Competing claims and Australia's economic future*. Melbourne: Melbourne University Publishing.

Bell, S. and Quiggin, J. 2006. 'Asset price instability and policy responses: The legacy of liberalisation.' *Journal of Economic Issues* XL: 629–50.

Carew, E. 1997. *Westpac: The bank that broke the bank*. Sydney: Transworld Publishers.

Claessens, S. 2009. *Competition in the financial sector: Overview of competition policies*. IMF Working Paper WP/09/45. Washington, DC: International Monetary Fund. Available from: www.imf.org/-/media/Websites/IMF/imported-full-text-pdf/external/pubs/ft/wp/2009/_wp0945.ashx.

Clark, A. 2009. 'Why we are different but not necessarily safe.' *Australian Financial Review*, 4 December.

Colebatch, T. 2009. 'How Australia avoided the global financial meltdown (touch wood).' *The Age*, [Melbourne], 6 June.

Cornell, A. 2009. 'How Australia's banks dodged the crisis.' *Australian Financial Review*, 21 December.

Costello, M. 2009. 'Parting thoughts of a political party's proud and fortunate son.' *Sydney Morning Herald*, 8 October.

Crotty, J. 2009. 'Structural causes of the Global Financial Crisis: A critical assessment of the "new financial architecture".' *Cambridge Journal of Economics* 33(4): 563–80. doi.org/10.1093/cje/bep023.

Davies, H. 2010. *The Financial Crisis: Who is to blame?* Cambridge: Polity.

Debelle, G. 2009. A comparison of the US and Australian housing markets. Address to the Sub-Prime Mortgage Meltdown Symposium, Adelaide, 16 May. Available from: www.rba.gov.au/publications/bulletin/2008/jun/pdf/bu-0608-5.pdf.

Dodd, R. and Mills, P. 2008. 'Outbreak: US subprime contagion.' *Finance and Development* 45(2): 14–18.

Edwards, J. 2008. The sub-prime mortgage meltdown: Origins, trajectories and regional implications—Australia's experience in the sub-prime crisis. Address to the Flinders University International Expert Symposium, Adelaide, 16 May. Available from: treasury.gov.au/speech/the-sub-prime-mortgage-meltdown-origins-trajectories-and-regional-implications-australias-experience-in-the-sub-prime-crisis/.

Erturk, I. and Solari, S. 2007. 'Banks as continuous revolution.' *New Political Economy* 12(3): 369–88. doi.org/10.1080/13563460701485599.

Financial Crisis Inquiry Commission (FCIC) 2011. *The Financial Crisis Inquiry Report*. New York: US Government Publishing Office.

Gorton, G. 2008. Slapped in the face by the invisible hand: Banking and the panic of 2007. Prepared for the Federal Reserve of Atlanta's Financial Market Conference, Atlanta, 11–13 May. Available from: www.frbatlanta.org/news/Conferen/09fmc/gorton.pdf.

Hawtrey, K. 2009. 'The global credit crisis: Why have Australian banks been so remarkably resilient?' *Agenda: A Journal of Policy Analysis and Reform* 16(3): 95–114.

Jordan, C. and Jain, A. 2009. 'Diversity and resilience: Lessons from the financial crisis.' *University of New South Wales Law Journal* 32: 1–32.

Kelly, P. 1992. *The End of Certainty: Power, politics and business in Australia*. Sydney: Allen & Unwin.

King, M. 2009. Speech to Scottish Business Organisations. Bank of England, Edinburgh, 20 October.

Laker, J. 2006. Basel II: Observations from down under. Speech to Second Annual Conference on the Future of Financial Regulation, London School of Economics, London, 6 April.

Laker, J. 2009. The regulatory landscape 2009–2010. Speech to FINSIA Financial Services Conference, Financial Services Institute of Australasia, Sydney, 28 October.

Laker, J. 2010. The Australian banking system under stress? Speech to Australian Business Economists, Sydney, 9 June.

Lewis, D. 2008. Weathering the storm: APRA's role in financial crisis management. Speech to Business Continuity Expo, Melbourne, 27 November.

Littrell, C. 2011. Responses to the Global Financial Crisis: The Australian prudential perspective. Speech to APEC Regional Symposium, Melbourne, 8 March.

Macfarlane, I. 2006. *The Search for Stability*. ABC Boyer Lectures. Sydney: Australian Broadcasting Corporation.

Macfarlane, I. 2009. The crisis: Causes, consequences and lessons for the future. ASIC Summer School, Sydney, 2–3 March. Available from: download.asic.gov.au/media/1311565/ASIC-summer-school-report-may-2009.pdf.

McGee, S. 2010. *Chasing Goldman Sachs*. New York: Crown Business.

Reinhart, C. M. and Rogoff, K. S. 2009. *This Time is Different: Eight centuries of financial folly*. Princeton, NJ: Princeton University Press.

Reserve Bank of Australia (RBA) 2009. *Financial Stability Review*. March. Sydney: RBA.

Reserve Bank of Australia (RBA) 2010. *Financial Stability Review*. March. Sydney: RBA.

Ritholtz, B. 2009. *Bailout Nation: How greed and easy money corrupted Wall Street and shook the world economy*. New York: Wiley.

Roubini, N. and Mihm, S. 2010. *Crisis Economics: A crash course in the future of finance*. New York: Penguin.

Suich, M. 1991. 'Bankrupted.' *The Independent Monthly*, 15–17 May.

Turner, A. 2009. *The Turner Review: A regulatory response to the global banking crisis*. London: Financial Services Authority.

13

Thinking outside the box: Tobacco plain packaging and the demise of smoking

Becky Freeman[1]

Plain packaging and the fight against smoking

In 2010, Australia was the first nation to announce it would adopt tobacco plain packaging laws. Before this, Australian cigarette packs were required only to include a graphic health warning that covered 30 per cent of the front and 90 per cent of the back of the pack. The remaining 70 per cent of the front of the pack was fully utilised by the tobacco industry to entice new smokers, reassure continuing smokers and promote its brands. Under the new laws, cigarette packs would no longer be permitted to carry any branding or company logos (see Plate 13.1); all tobacco packaging must be a drab dark brown and the cigarette box must be constructed of rigid cardboard with no shiny finishes or any other embellishments. Plain packaging also requires that all packs display a large pictorial health warning on both the front (75 per cent of the surface) and the back (90 per cent of

1 The author does not receive funding from the tobacco industry, the electronic cigarette industry or any affiliated bodies. She has been awarded research grants from the National Health and Medical Research Council of Australia and has undertaken paid consulting work for non-governmental organisations, the World Health Organization and Australian national and state government health departments and has written extensively on the plain packaging policy experience in Australia. Portions of this chapter draw on her previous writing on the subject, including Freeman et al. (2008); Freeman (2011, 2017); Chapman and Freeman (2014); Scollo et al. (2016); and Crosbie et al. (2018).

the surface) and that the product brand and variant name be written in a standard font, size and shade of grey. No company logos, trademarks or brand colours are permitted (Department of Health and Ageing 2012b).

Plate 13.1 The WHO designed this promotional poster, based on Australian plain packaging requirements, for use around the world during the 2016 World No Tobacco Day, on 31 May

Source: WHO (2016).

Despite attempts from the tobacco industry to thwart this policy by undertaking political lobbying, conducting high-profile media campaigns, hiding behind small retailers and pursuing multiple legal challenges, it is a public health policy success story. Australia has a long history of implementing effective tobacco control policies that have worked together to reduce smoking rates. Plain packaging laws represent the next step in a series of ever tightening regulations that prevent the tobacco industry from promoting its deadly products (Freeman 2017).

Cigarettes, when used exactly as the manufacturers intend, will kill two out of three smokers (Banks et al. 2015). There is simply no other legal product sold openly on the market today that has this same devastating human toll. Policies that can reach whole populations and prevent future smokers from starting, assist those who smoke to quit and not restart and protect people from secondhand smoke are enshrined in the World Health Organization Framework Convention on Tobacco Control (WHO FCTC). Australia, along with 181 other parties, has ratified the WHO FCTC to halt the global tobacco epidemic (WHO 2017a). Plain packaging is just one of a comprehensive suite of policy recommendations contained within that international policy framework and, in the Australian context, it came on the wings of decades of ever-deepening policy interventions designed to arrest smoking (see Table 13.1).

Table 13.1 Tobacco control timeline: Australian policy highlights

Year	Policy
1973	Health warnings first mandated on all cigarette packs in Australia.
1976	Bans on all cigarette advertising on radio and television in Australia.
1986–2006	Phasing in of bans on smoking in workplaces and public places.
1990	Bans on advertising of tobacco products in newspapers and magazines published in Australia.
1992	Increase in the tobacco excise.
1993	*Tobacco Advertising Prohibition Act 1992* (Cwlth) prohibits broadcasting and publication of tobacco advertisements.
1994–2003	Bans on smoking in restaurants.
1995	Nationally consistent text-only health warnings required on packaging.
1998–2006	Bans on point-of-sale tobacco advertising across Australia.
2006	Graphic health warnings required on packaging of most tobacco products.
2010	25 per cent increase in the tobacco excise.

Year	Policy
2011	First complete state or territory ban on point-of-sale tobacco product displays.
2012	Publishing tobacco advertising on the internet or other electronic media made an offence.
2012	Introduction of tobacco plain packaging and updated and expanded graphic health warnings.

Source: Department of Health and Ageing (2018).

A policy success

The adoption of plain packaging laws in Australia is a public health success story. The use of innovative policy measures to reduce the prevalence of smoking and the subsequent health burden is a cornerstone of tobacco control. Plain packaging joins a long list of other successful policy measures, such as bans on tobacco advertising and sponsorship, emotive mass media campaigns urging smokers to quit, high tobacco taxes and smoke-free public places (WHO 2017b). Together, these policies have seen Australia's adult regular smoking rate cut almost in half in less than 20 years—from 27 per cent in 1998 to 14 per cent in 2016 (Greenhalgh and Bayly 2018). Plain packaging stands out as a unique case study on the Australian tobacco control landscape as no other policy was as openly and vociferously attacked by the tobacco industry (Daube et al. 2012). Despite this, it became a policy success.

Programmatic assessment

The plain packaging measure builds on existing tobacco control policy success that has an overall focus on reducing the demand for tobacco products (Gravely et al. 2017). Reducing the appeal of smoking and tobacco products leads to a reduction in consumer demand and decreased smoking rates. Key demand reduction measures include high tobacco taxes, smoke-free public places, emotive mass media campaigns that warn of the harms of smoking and urge smokers to quit and comprehensive bans on all tobacco advertising, promotion and sponsorship. Additionally, plain packaging increases the size, and refreshes the content, of on-pack graphic health warnings—a policy already proven to be effective.

One year after the implementation of plain packaging, increased numbers of Australian adult smokers disliked their cigarette pack and perceived it to have lower appeal, lower cigarette quality, lower satisfaction and lower value (Wakefield et al. 2015). Increased numbers of smokers also no longer believed that brands differed in terms of prestige. More adult smokers also noticed the new and larger graphic health warnings, attributed motivation to quit to the warnings, avoided specific warnings when purchasing a pack and covered up their packs. Similarly, among Australian adolescents who had seen a cigarette pack in the previous six months, the appeal of cigarette packs and brands had decreased and there was a large increase in the proportion disagreeing that some brands had better-looking packs than others (White et al. 2015).

There is also evidence that the larger health warnings and plain packaging reforms had an impact on adult smokers' quitting behaviours (Young et al. 2014; Durkin et al. 2015). There was a 78 per cent increase in the number of calls to the Quitline (a toll-free, telephone-based smoking cessation counselling service) with the introduction of plain packaging, which peaked four weeks after plain packs initially appeared for sale at retail outlets (Young et al. 2014). This increased call rate was sustained for 43 weeks. In a study comparing a series of smoker cohorts who were surveyed about quitting behaviours before, during the transition period of plain packs coming on to the market and one year after implementation, there were significantly greater increases in rates of attempts to quit in the transition period and one year after compared with the period before plain packaging (Durkin et al. 2015).

The incidence of smoking is significantly higher among lower socioeconomic groups, and even more so in groups facing multiple personal and social disadvantages. Smoking is one of the major factors driving poorer health status in economically disadvantaged areas and groups (Greenhalgh and Scollo 2018). Policies that reduce smoking have significant potential to reduce inequalities, provided the positive effects are experienced across the population. Overall, the absolute gap in smoking prevalence between the most and least disadvantaged Australians has stayed fairly constant for the decade 2004–13, at about 14 per cent, before narrowing to about 12 per cent in 2016. Encouragingly, smoking rates have reduced among Australian school students across all socioeconomic groups, and generally there is very little difference in smoking status among socioeconomic groups during childhood (Greenhalgh and Scollo 2018).

The costs of the policy are borne almost entirely by the tobacco industry itself. While the Australian Government has had to contribute significant funds to defending the policy from three separate cases of legal action by the tobacco industry, these costs have been offset, as the industry was required to pay some of these costs (Gartrell 2017).

Process assessment

The recommendation that tobacco products be sold in standardised packaging, without any branding, had a firm evidence base. It was presented as part of a comprehensive set of public health policy recommendations made by an independent expert body. This body, the Preventative Health Taskforce, was established in 2008 by then health minister Nicola Roxon. The taskforce released a draft report for public consultation and comment in October 2008 (Moodie et al. 2008), with more than 400 submissions received. A final report was issued to government in June 2009 and, two months later, released publicly (National Preventative Health Taskforce 2009). The report describes plain packaging as a policy that

> would prohibit brand imagery, colours, corporate logos and trademarks, permitting manufacturers only to print the brand name in a mandated size, font and place, in addition to required health warnings and other legally mandated product information such as toxic constituents, tax-paid seals or package contents. A standard cardboard texture would be mandatory, and the size and shape of the package and cellophane wrapper would also be prescribed. A detailed analysis of current marketing practices suggests that plain packaging would also need to encompass pack interiors and the cigarette itself, given the potential for manufacturers to use colours, bandings and markings, and different length and gauges to make cigarettes more 'interesting' and appealing. Any use of perfuming, incorporation of audio chips or affixing of 'onserts' would also need to be banned. (National Preventative Health Taskforce 2009: 181)

Political assessment

Unlike some other areas of public health reform, tobacco control has greatly benefited by attracting support from across the major political parties in Australia. While the plain packaging legislation was led by Labor, the Liberal Party (the official opposition at the time, led by Tony Abbott)—after some initial 'dithering' (Grattan 2011)—did not oppose the legislation and eventually came to enthusiastically support it, ensuring it was easily passed through parliament.

Civil society engagement and advocacy for plain packaging were exceptionally high. High-profile health groups—such as the Cancer Council Australia, the Heart Foundation, VicHealth, the Public Health Association, Action on Smoking and Health, the Australian Council on Smoking and Health and the Australian Medical Association (AMA)—and high-profile public health, medical and legal academics contributed to the advocacy efforts. These public agencies and figures were positioned as being credible and trustworthy opponents of an industry riddled with reputational issues.

The Liberal Party feared that if it decided to not support the plain packaging reforms, this could damage its reputation—especially given the high profile and influence of the health groups that had thrown their support behind the reforms (Chapman and Freeman 2014). Siding with the tobacco industry—the most visible and vocal opponent of the reforms—would be likened to siding with the merchants of death. Few politicians want to be seen as being in partnership with an industry that is known for overtly lying about the addictiveness and harmfulness of its products (Chapman and Freeman 2008). A 2011 opinion poll showed the majority of Australians also supported the policy (Cancer Council Australia 2011), which served to reassure policymakers that adopting the reforms would enhance their political capital.

The genesis of plain packaging

Globally, tobacco use is one of the leading preventable causes of early death and disease. Prevention of tobacco uptake and addiction is a cornerstone of tobacco control. Most people start smoking when they are teenagers or very young adults. The key influences on young people taking up smoking are the advertising and promotion of tobacco products. This is despite the fact the tobacco industry has always claimed that it has no interest whatsoever in attracting new, non-smoking youth customers but is interested only in stimulating brand-switching and maintaining brand loyalty among current adult smokers. While Australia long ago banned most overt forms of tobacco promotion, arguably the most effective and personal form of promotion, the tobacco package itself, had been left largely untouched.

Packaging design is a major way of differentiating and promoting brands and is particularly important in homogeneous consumer products such as cigarettes, for which—like bottled water, for example—few objective differences exist between brands. Marketing literature routinely highlights the critical role played by package design in the overall marketing mix, emphasising that the 'product package is the communication life-blood of the firm', the 'silent salesman' that reaches out to customers and that packaging acts 'as a promotional tool in its own right' (Freeman et al. 2008). The other important goal of packaging design that is unique to tobacco products is the use of the package to obscure, downplay and minimise government-mandated health warnings that compel smokers to quit.

Australian context

Australia has long been a leader in advocating and implementing tobacco control legislation (Chapman and Wakefield 2001; Scollo 2012). Prior to the implementation of plain packaging laws, tobacco packages sold in Australia featured graphic health warnings and could not be visible at retail outlets where they were sold. Tobacco products could not be advertised or promoted to the public, including through event sponsorship. Tobacco products were highly taxed and emotive campaigns compelled smokers to quit. Communities and politicians of all stripes welcomed laws that banned smoking inside all public places, workplaces, licensed premises and many outdoors areas. This set the scene for both political and public acceptance of the seemingly radical policy to completely remove all branding imagery from tobacco packages. Plain packaging was the next step in implementing a comprehensive approach to tobacco control and Australia was ideally suited to be the first nation to implement the innovative policy (Freeman 2017).

At the time plain packaging was announced, Australia's regular smoking rate ('regular' is defined as smoking at least weekly) among adults aged over 18 years was 18 per cent. This was about half the rate of 1980, when it was about 35 per cent. The latest available national survey data (at the time of writing), from 2016, put this regular smoking prevalence at a low of 13 per cent (Greenhalgh et al. 2018). This is a rate comparable with other high-income countries with a history of implementing tobacco control measures, such as Sweden, Canada, Iceland and Norway. Australia's low smoking rate is attributable to 'concerted, sustained, and comprehensive public policy efforts from all levels of government and action from public health organisations' (Department of Health and Ageing 2018).

Plain packaging: A brief history

While plain packaging laws were first implemented in Australia in 2012, initial discussions about this policy reform among health and medical professionals and tobacco control researchers can be traced back to Canada in the mid-1980s. In 1995, a Canadian parliamentary committee endorsed plain packaging as a government policy, but legal challenges to existing Canadian tobacco control laws, changes in health ministers and intense tobacco industry lobbying meant the issue lost momentum in that country (Freeman 2017). In 2000, Canada did pave the way for governments to acquire significant control of the appearance of tobacco packaging, by becoming the first country to require large, full-colour, graphic health warnings on all tobacco packages. While other countries, including Australia, moved to follow Canada's lead on requiring large graphic warnings on packs, plain packaging reforms were largely left aside, and no significant policy progress was made to remove branding elements from packaging (Chapman and Freeman 2014). Following Australia's success, Canada is now poised to adopt even more advanced plain packaging requirements, with the release of draft regulations in June 2018. The proposed regulations extend to standardising the size and appearance of cigarettes themselves and mandating that the graphic health warnings take up more surface area on the pack than in any other country in the world (Canadian Cancer Society 2018a).

In 1992 in Australia, the Australian Ministerial Council on Drug Strategy proposed large new warnings for all tobacco packages and requested a report on plain packaging. In 1995, however, the Australian Senate's Community Affairs Reference Committee (Parliament of Australia 1995) released a lengthy report that concluded that, 'on the basis of the evidence received, there is not sufficient evidence to recommend that tobacco products be sold in generic packaging'. Belatedly, in 1997, the Australian Government replied to the committee's report:

> In response to the mounting interest in generic packaging, the Commonwealth obtained advice from the Attorney-General's Department on the legal and constitutional barriers to generic packaging. This advice indicates that the Commonwealth does possess powers under the Constitution to introduce such packaging but that any attempt to use these powers to introduce further tobacco control legislation needs to be considered in the context of the increasingly critical attention being focussed on the necessity, appropriateness, justification and basis for

> regulation by such bodies as the Office of Regulatory Review, the High Court, and Senate Standing Committees. In addition, further regulation needs to be considered in the context of Australia's international obligations regarding free trade under the General Agreement on Tariff[s] and Trade (GATT), and our obligations under international covenants such as the Paris Convention for the Protection of Industrial Property, and the Agreement on Trade-Related Aspects of Intellectual Property Rights (TRIPS). (Department of Health 1997: 30)

More than 13 years later, and these same arguments—that plain packaging was both a free-trade violation and counter to the protection of intellectual property rights—would once again be espoused by the tobacco industry and its lobby groups. However, this time, under the leadership of Roxon, a health minister trained as a lawyer, who knew these arguments did not hold water, the Australian Government was not so easily intimidated by the legal sabre rattling.

Drivers and stewards

As mentioned, in April 2008, the recently elected Labor Government established the National Preventative Health Taskforce to develop policy and program recommendations with a focus on three priority areas: tobacco, alcohol and obesity. A group of experts was convened for each priority area and prepared a discussion paper and final report to help inform government policy action.

The discussion paper on tobacco included a wide range of policy initiatives, including plain packaging. Following the release of the paper, there was an extensive period—until April 2009—for consultation and public submissions. The taskforce's final report, delivered to the health minister on 30 June 2009 and subsequently released on 1 September 2009, recommended plain packaging as part of a comprehensive approach:

> Mandate standard plain packaging of all tobacco products to ensure that design features of the pack in no way reduce the prominence or impact or prescribed government warnings the pack. (Tobacco Working Group 2009: VII)

Nearly eight months passed until 29 April 2010, when prime minister Kevin Rudd and Roxon announced that Australia would mandate plain packaging from July 2012. The policy was finally fully enacted in December 2012. Table 13.2 outlines the major policy milestones that occurred between the April announcement and the Bill being passed into law.

Table 13.2 Timeline of major milestones in the development of the tobacco plain packaging legislation

Date	Milestone
9 April 2008	Health minister Nicola Roxon announces establishment of the National Preventative Health Taskforce.
10 October 2008	Release for consultation of the draft report of the Preventative Health Taskforce, entitled Australia: The healthiest country by 2020, which contained a large number of recommendations, including one concerning plain packaging of tobacco products.
15 April 2009	National Preventative Health Taskforce announces it has considered more than 400 submissions received on its draft report released in October 2008.
30 June 2009	National Preventative Health Taskforce provides final report, entitled *National Preventative Health Strategy: The roadmap for action*, to the government for consideration.
1 September 2009	Minister Roxon releases the final report of the Preventative Health Taskforce, which recommends plain packaging as part of a comprehensive suite of measures to make Australia the healthiest country in the world by 2020.
29 April 2010	The Australian Government announces its decision to implement plain packaging for tobacco products and to mandate updated and expanded graphic health warnings.
7 April 2011	The Australian Government releases an exposure draft of the legislation alongside a consultation paper, with comments to be received within the following 60 days.
31 May 2011	The Opposition announces it will not oppose plain packaging.
6 June 2011	The government receives over 250 submissions on the draft plain packaging legislation.
6 July 2011	Plain packaging Bill introduced into the House of Representatives, first and second reading moved.
7 July 2011	House of Representatives refers Bill to Standing Committee on Health and Aged Care.
22 August 2011	House of Representatives Standing Committee on Health and Aged Care tables the report on its inquiry into tobacco plain packaging.
24 August 2011	Second reading debate; third reading agreed to passage of legislation through House of Representatives.
25 August 2011	Bill introduced and read a first time in Senate; second reading moved.
11 October 2011	Second reading debate in Senate commences.
2 November 2011	Minister Roxon announces the implementation of plain packaging will be delayed until 1 December 2012 as a result of delays in the Senate's review of the Bill.

Date	Milestone
9–10 November 2011	Bill returns to Senate, including revised timelines. Second reading debate continues; second reading agreed to; third reading agreed to.
21 November 2011	Final passage of amended Tobacco Plain Packaging Bill through House of Representatives. Vote on Tobacco Plain Packaging Bill as amended by the Senate. The Bill passes the Australian Parliament, including amendments to extend the time frame for implementation (Parliament of Australia 2011).
1 December 2011	Governor-General signs Tobacco Plain Packaging Act 2011 into law.
October 2012	Some packs with plain packaging start to appear in retail outlets.
1 December 2012	From this date, all tobacco packages in Australia must appear in plain packaging, as specified in the Tobacco Plain Packaging Act 2011.

The pushback from the tobacco industry and its allies was strong and immediate (Kelly et al. 2011). The tobacco industry has a long and consistent history of fighting the adoption of policies that reduce both the demand for tobacco products and the social acceptability of smoking (Chapman and Carter 2003). On the surface, plain packaging could be seen as just the next in a very long line of measures the tobacco industry has railed against in an effort to maintain tobacco use and sales. However, in the years preceding the plain packaging announcement, the Australian tobacco industry had largely stepped back from directly commenting on and campaigning publicly against changes to Australian tobacco control policy (Cadzow 2008; McLeod et al. 2009). The planned plain packaging laws marked a dramatic change in the tobacco industry's tactics and saw it not only actively appearing in news articles and programs, but also launching its own paid media campaigns.

For example, in August 2010, the Alliance of Australian Retailers (AAR) launched national advertisements online, in newspapers and on television and radio featuring actors portraying concerned retailers who said plain packaging would not work and would damage their businesses.[2] Following this high-profile media campaign, an Australian investigative news program revealed the extent of tobacco industry involvement in the formation and funding of the AAR. On the day the AAR was formed, it received funds from the three main tobacco companies operating in

2 The AAR ads can be viewed here: www.youtube.com/user/analogcreative/videos?view=0.

Australia, Imperial Tobacco Australia ($1 million), British American Tobacco Australia ($2.2 million) and Philip Morris ($2.1 million) (Scollo et al. 2016).

The AAR campaign appeared to backfire. A survey of 2,101 Victorians found it failed to persuade people that plain packaging would not be effective, with 86.2 per cent saying it made no difference to their views about plain packaging and 8.4 per cent of respondents claiming the advertisement actually increased their support for plain packaging reforms (Quit Victoria 2011).

The degree to which the tobacco industry protested against plain packaging suggests the public health community was on to a policy that would really impact its profitability. A key counter-lobbying strategy was addressing the 'plain packaging won't work' argument through research evidence gathered, synthesised and then disseminated through countless news articles and interviews, opinion pieces, blog posts and social media posts. The Cancer Council Victoria and Quit Victoria—Australian non-governmental agencies—prepared a comprehensive electronic evidence review of plain packaging. The review summarised all of the 25 published experimental studies that examined the likely impact of plain packaging on young people and current smokers. The primary finding of these studies was that adults and adolescents perceived cigarettes in plain packages to be less appealing, less palatable, less satisfying and of lower quality compared with cigarettes in existing packaging. Plain packaging would also affect young people's perceptions of the characteristics and status of the people who smoked particular brands.

Policy design and choice

In a demonstration of unwavering political commitment to the Preventative Health Taskforce process, on 29 April 2010, Roxon and Rudd announced that Australia would be the first country to adopt plain packaging laws, with an anticipated implementation date of July 2012 (implementation was subsequently delayed until December 2012). Funding was committed for both the expected tobacco industry legal challenges and an extensive evaluation of the policy. The effort and deduction of the public servants tasked with progressing tobacco plain packaging into law were recognised at the 2012 World Conference on

Tobacco or Health, in Singapore, when the Australian health department was awarded the American Cancer Society's Luther L. Terry Award for outstanding leadership by a government ministry.

Tobacco plain packaging was primarily framed as a protective measure aimed at preventing young people from taking up tobacco use. Preventing young people from ever starting smoking is an investment that reaps rewards in the future in terms of reduced disease burden and mortality from tobacco use. The highly addictive nature of tobacco products means that youth experimentation with smoking can lead to a lifelong addiction that some smokers find incredibly difficult to break. Very few people start smoking beyond adolescence and early adulthood and there is near universal regret among established smokers about ever having started.

The final agreed design of plain packaging was a result of extensive consumer testing and consultation. The dark brown colour was chosen as consumers found

> this colour to be less appealing, to contain cigarettes that were perceived to be more harmful to health, of lower quality, and to make it harder to quit smoking. Additionally, this colour was not at all similar to any existing cigarette brand and failed to generate any positive associations for consumers. (GfK Blue Moon 2011)

The goals of the plain packaging law were clearly and purposefully developed to ensure they could be readily and transparently evaluated. Specifically, plain packaging was designed to:

- reduce the appeal of tobacco products to consumers
- increase the effectiveness of health warnings
- reduce the ability of the retail packaging of tobacco products to mislead consumers about the harmful effects of smoking or using tobacco products (Department of Health and Ageing 2012a).

The costs associated with the plain packaging policy are largely borne by the tobacco industry. Apart from the initial costs of preparing the legislation and defending it in legal proceedings, there are limited ongoing costs for the government. Additionally, in terms of unintended consequences, many of the negative arguments raised against the implementation of plain packaging never came to fruition. Indeed, one unintended immediate positive outcome appeared to be that smokers perceived their plainly packaged cigarettes as tasting terrible and went so far as accusing the government of reformulating cigarettes alongside the packaging (Siegel 2013).

An essential public health policy message is that plain packaging is just one part of Australia's successful approach to tobacco control. Plain packaging laws are likely to be most effective when accompanied by large graphic health warnings and implemented as part of a comprehensive smoking prevention and cessation strategy. Plain packaging was not implemented in isolation. The same day the reforms were announced, an immediate tobacco tax increase of 25 per cent was also adopted—the first real tobacco tax increase beyond the consumer price index since 1999. Tobacco taxes are the most effective and necessary policy tool for reducing smoking rates, but are further enhanced by support services, social marketing campaigns and policy changes that reduce the appeal of smoking. It is estimated a 10 per cent increase in tobacco prices will be followed by a decrease in tobacco consumption of about 4.8 per cent (Gallet and List 2003).

So far in the history of tobacco control, there is no single magic policy approach to make smoking rates plummet overnight; reductions are incremental and occur slowly as a result of prolonged investment in public health measures and increasingly strict regulation.

Delivery, legitimacy and endurance

It was fully expected that the tobacco industry would issue legal challenges to plain packaging laws and initial arguments opposed to plain packaging questioned whether the Australian Government could enact such a law. Fortunately, the government was well prepared for and resourced to take on these legal challenges. The industry launched three separate legal challenges: first, to the Australian domestic courts (Liberman 2013); second, through an investment treaty with Hong Kong; and third, by supporting four countries—Cuba, Honduras, Indonesia and the Dominican Republic—to file disputes through the World Trade Organization (Voon and Mitchell 2011). All three challenges were resolved in Australia's favour and, in the case of the first two disputes, the industry was ordered to pay the government's legal costs.

There are no 'win–win' solutions in tobacco control that see both public health and the tobacco industry benefit. A common barometer known as the 'scream test' measures how likely it is a tobacco control policy will succeed by how loudly the tobacco industry opposes it (McKee 2017). When public health measures are adopted, the tobacco industry must fail. The WHO FCTC embodies this principle in Article 5.3, which states:

> In setting and implementing their public health policies with respect to tobacco control, Parties shall act to protect these policies from commercial and other vested interests of the tobacco industry in accordance with national law. (WHO 2005)

Extensive independent research and evaluation have shown plain packaging was, and remains, successful as measured against its stated objectives. In December 2014, the Department of Health commenced a post-implementation review of plain packaging. The body of studies included in the review demonstrated the tobacco plain packaging measures had an impact by reducing the appeal of tobacco products, increasing the effectiveness of health warnings and reducing the ability of the packaging to mislead smokers. The studies also provided early evidence of positive changes to smoking and quitting behaviours (Department of Health 2018).

The primary beneficiaries of the plain packaging policy are those who quit smoking and the children who are prevented from ever taking up smoking. It is estimated that the packaging changes resulted in a 0.55 per cent decline in Australia's smoking prevalence—equivalent to 108,228 fewer smokers—between December 2012 and September 2015. The policymakers and stakeholders who supported and drove the implementation of plain packaging have also benefited. International accolades and awards have been bestowed on Nicola Roxon and the Australian health department alike. Additionally, and perhaps most substantially, Australia has paved the way for other nations to adopt similar measures.

Since Australia first implemented plain packaging, there has been an international movement to make this policy a global standard in the fight against tobacco-related deaths. Plain packaging has been adopted in nine countries and is under consideration in at least 16 other jurisdictions (Canadian Cancer Society 2018b). Plain packaging has been implemented in France (in 2016), the United Kingdom (2016), Norway (2017), Ireland (2017), New Zealand (2018) and Hungary (2018); it will be implemented in Uruguay (in 2019) and Slovenia (2020) and is in process or under consideration in Canada, Belgium, Thailand, Georgia, Singapore, Nepal, Sri Lanka, South Africa, Romania, Jersey, Guernsey, Taiwan, Chile, Finland and Saudi Arabia. The governments of Mauritius, Kenya, Gambia, Botswana and Burkina Faso have also expressed support for implementation of plain packaging. As has happened with other successful tobacco control policies, momentum appears to be continuing to build and this list will grow longer each year.

The primary 'loser' in the plain packaging saga is the tobacco industry itself. In Australia, tobacco is no longer grown or manufactured so there is no 'homegrown' industry that requires transition assistance as smoking rates decline. All three major tobacco companies that operate in Australia are wholly owned subsidiaries of overseas parent companies. Despite launching the three separate legal challenges to the policy, the industry has not been successful in overturning the law nor has it been compensated for any financial or intellectual property losses as a result of the legislation. The industry suffered further loss to its already slim credibility when it was revealed that a media campaign against plain packaging—which was supposedly being led by small Australian retailers—was in fact fully funded by three international tobacco companies, as previously discussed.

Analysis and conclusions

The single biggest hurdle to the success of plain packaging was essentially a question of timing. While tobacco control advocates and the tobacco industry itself long recognised that the packages were powerful advertisements and inducements to smoke, it took decades from when the idea was first mooted until the right conditions converged to allow such a 'radical' idea to become law. The election of a government that recognised that taking on the tobacco industry was both legally possible and politically desirable created an opportunity to push through a policy that was previously considered too extreme. A short six years later and plain packaging is no longer on the fringes of acceptable public health actions but is a standard that has been set for other nations equally concerned about tobacco use.

Nicola Roxon has emphasised several factors as key drivers of the tobacco plain packaging success, including: the strong evidence base, the reputation and coherence of the tobacco control community and the high level of expertise in the public service, legal profession and public health sphere (Chapman and Freeman 2014). In turn, Roxon's role as political champion is cited as being critical to moving plain packaging from a recommendation in yet another government report to a concrete action enshrined in law. The public acceptance of plain packaging laws is reflective of decades of work that have seen smoking, and the tobacco industry, move from socially desirable and acceptable to a behaviour and an industry that conjure images of death, disease and deceit. There are no negative consequences to taking on an industry that lacks genuine allies; many of its best customers are feeling hooked rather than enthused. Tobacco control advocates have been highly successful in developing the dominant frame that equates the tobacco industry with corporate malfeasance. There is no government reputational loss or genuine threat to policy success when the only opposition is best known for preying on vulnerable children and addicting them to deadly products.

Unlike some other areas of public health, where policy goals are perhaps more complex and nuanced, tobacco control goals have long been clear and consistent: reduce the number of people who take up smoking, help those who already smoke to quit and protect non-smokers from harmful secondhand smoke. Equally, the unequivocal exclusion of the tobacco industry as a partner in developing policies that achieve these goals is unique. In other areas of public health reform—such as alcohol, gambling and food—there is a struggle to disentangle the powerful commercial influences from the policymaking process. As a result, policies that are meant to improve public health are often ineffective as they do little to impede the marketing and sales success of the products and companies that harm public health. These industries have observed how the exclusion of the tobacco industry from the policymaking table has made it easier to advance public health and have taken steps to safeguard their interests (Kickbusch et al. 2016).

There is little concern that plain packaging legislation—having survived legal challenges and undergone extensive evaluation—will be overturned. Other jurisdictions have taken steps to strengthen their plain packaging laws, including increasing the size of the health warning and applying more stringent measures to the size and shape of the cigarettes themselves (Canadian Cancer Society 2018b). A possible future threat to the success of the policy—and tobacco control in general—is a well-funded and determined tobacco industry that is attempting to rebrand itself as a good corporate citizen with new 'harm reduction' products. Launched in 2017, the Philip Morris International Foundation for a Smokefree World, headed by former WHO senior executive Derek Yach, is part of a portfolio of public relations initiatives to supposedly rehabilitate the industry (Foundation for a Smoke-Free World 2018). It is also naive to assume that plain packaging will bring an end to tobacco marketing. Tobacco companies still rely heavily on their relationships with retailers to ensure their brands are readily available to consumers, are positioned as market leaders and are sold alongside other everyday items. Tobacco marketing remains largely unregulated and allows the tobacco industry to offer retailers incentives and discounts to push its brands to consumers (Freeman 2017).

When reflecting on what additional potential lessons for policy design, political management and policy leadership might be drawn from this case that could aid in this success being replicated, the importance of structural factors becomes clear. A strong and united tobacco control workforce that is truly multidisciplinary proved crucial. This workforce took decades to build, mirroring the time it took for plain packaging to be adopted. While earlier tobacco efforts involved only a small number of outspoken advocates, tobacco control is now an established field that draws expertise from the legal profession, economists, the public service, politicians and political advisors, academia, civil society, human rights movements, social service organisations and even high-profile philanthropists such as Bill and Melinda Gates and Michael Bloomberg.

The commitment of resources—both human and financial—globally, nationally and locally has given not only stability within the Australian tobacco control workforce, but also tacit approval of its principles and ideas. This 'mainstreaming' of public health activism served to legitimise tobacco control and, in turn, plain packaging. The professionalisation of tobacco control through research, training and expansion beyond public health programs positions its policy reforms and goals as valid priorities for action.

References

Banks, E., Joshy, G., Weber, M. F., Liu, B., Grenfell, R., Egger, S., Paige, E., Lopez, A. D., Sitas, F. and Beral, V. 2015. 'Tobacco smoking and all-cause mortality in a large Australian cohort study: Findings from a mature epidemic with current low smoking prevalence.' *BMC Medicine* 13: 38. doi.org/10.1186/s12916-015-0281-z.

Cadzow, J. 2008. 'Hi ho hi ho it's off to work we go.' [*Good Weekend*], *Sydney Morning Herald*, 27 September.

Canadian Cancer Society 2018a. Canada to have the world's best tobacco plain packaging requirements. Press release. Ottawa: Canadian Cancer Society. Available from: www.cancer.ca/en/about-us/for-media/media-releases/national/2018/canadian-plain-packaging-requirements/?region=on.

Canadian Cancer Society 2018b. *Cigarette Package Health Warnings: International status report*. 6th edn. Ottawa: Canadian Cancer Society. Available from: www.cancer.ca/~/media/cancer.ca/CW/for%20media/Media%20releases/2018/CCS-international-warnings-report-2018---English---2-MB.pdf?la=fr-CA.

Cancer Council Australia 2011. Plain tobacco packaging a winner with Australians: New poll. Media release, 29 May. Sydney: Cancer Council Australia. Available from: www.cancer.org.au/news/media-releases/media-releases-2011/plain-tobacco-packaging-a-winner-with-australians-new-poll.html.

Chapman, S. and Carter, S. 2003. '"Avoid health warnings on all tobacco products for just as long as we can": A history of Australian tobacco industry efforts to avoid, delay and dilute health warnings on cigarettes.' *Tobacco Control* 12: S13–S22. doi.org/10.1136/tc.12.suppl_3.iii13.

Chapman, S. and Freeman, B. 2008. 'Markers of the denormalisation of smoking and the tobacco industry.' *Tobacco Control* 17: 25–31. doi.org/10.1136/tc.2007.021386.

Chapman, S. and Freeman, B. 2014. *Removing the Emperor's Clothes: Australia and tobacco plain packaging*. Sydney: Sydney University Press.

Chapman, S. and Wakefield, M. 2001. 'Tobacco control advocacy in Australia: Reflections on 30 years of progress.' *Health Education & Behavior* 28: 274–89. doi.org/10.1177/109019810102800303.

Crosbie, E., Thomson, G., Freeman, B. and Bialous, S. 2018. 'Advancing progressive health policy to reduce NCDs amidst international commercial opposition: Tobacco standardised packaging in Australia.' *Global Public Health* 13(12)(December): 1753–66. doi.org/10.1080/17441692.2018.1443485.

Daube, M., Moodie, A. R. and Chapman, S. 2012. 'Plain packaging of tobacco products: Plainly a success.' *Medical Journal of Australia* 197: 537–8. doi.org/10.5694/mja12.11612.

Department of Health 1997. *Government Response to the Report of the Senate Community Affairs Reference Committee: The tobacco industry and the costs of tobacco-related illness*. September. Canberra: Commonwealth of Australia.

Department of Health 2018. *Evaluation of Tobacco Plain Packaging in Australia.* Canberra: Commonwealth of Australia. Available from: www.health.gov.au/internet/main/publishing.nsf/content/tobacco-plain-packaging-evaluation.

Department of Health and Ageing 2012a. *Introduction of Tobacco Plain Packaging in Australia.* Canberra: Commonwealth of Australia. Available from: www.health.gov.au/internet/main/publishing.nsf/content/tobacco-plain.

Department of Health and Ageing 2012b. *Tobacco Plain Packaging: Your guide.* Canberra: Commonwealth of Australia. Available from: health.gov.au/internet/main/publishing.nsf/Content/tppbook.

Department of Health and Ageing 2018. 'Tobacco control timeline.' In *Tobacco Control Key Facts and Figures*. Canberra: Commonwealth of Australia. Available from: www.health.gov.au/internet/publications/publishing.nsf/Content/tobacco-control-toc~timeline.

Durkin, S., Brennan, E., Coomber, K., Zacher, M., Scollo, M. and Wakefield, M. 2015. 'Short-term changes in quitting-related cognitions and behaviours after the implementation of plain packaging with larger health warnings: Findings from a national cohort study with Australian adult smokers.' *Tobacco Control* 24: ii26–ii32. doi.org/10.1136/tobaccocontrol-2014-052058.

Foundation for a Smoke-Free World 2018. Website. Available from: www.smokefreeworld.org/.

Freeman, B. 2011. 'Tobacco plain packaging legislation: A content analysis of commentary posted on Australian online news.' *Tobacco Control* 20(5): 361–6.

Freeman, B. 2017. 'Making the case for Canada to join the tobacco plain packaging revolution.' *QUT Law Review* 17: 83–101. doi.org/10.5204/qutlr.v17i2.703.

Freeman, B., Chapman, S. and Rimmer, M. 2008. 'The case for the plain packaging of tobacco products.' *Addiction* 103: 580–90. doi.org/10.1111/j.1360-0443.2008.02145.x.

Gallet, C. A. and List, J. A. 2003. 'Cigarette demand: A meta-analysis of elasticities.' *Health Economics* 12: 821–35. doi.org/10.1002/hec.765.

Gartrell, A. 2017. 'Philip Morris ordered to pay Australia millions in costs for plain packaging case.' *Sydney Morning Herald*, 9 July. Available from: www.smh.com.au/politics/federal/philip-morris-ordered-to-pay-australia-millions-in-costs-for-plain-packaging-case-20170709-gx7mv5.html.

GfK Blue Moon 2011. Market research to determine effective plain packaging of tobacco products. Media release. Sydney: GfK Blue Moon. Accessed from: www.yourhealth.gov.au/internet/yourhealth/publishing.nsf/content/8B0333A18648BCF3CA25796E0023D826/$File/Market%20Research%20-%20Plain%20Packaging%20of%20Tobacco%20Products.pdf (site discontinued).

Grattan, M. 2011. 'Leadership lacking as Libs squabble over smoking.' *Sydney Morning Herald*, 27 May. Available from: www.smh.com.au/politics/federal/leadership-lacking-as-libs-squabble-over-smoking-20110526-1f693.html.

Gravely, S., Giovino, G. A., Craig, L., Commar, A., D'espaignet, E. T., Schotte, K. and Fong, G. T. 2017. 'Implementation of key demand-reduction measures of the WHO Framework Convention on Tobacco Control and change in smoking prevalence in 126 countries: An association study.' *The Lancet Public Health* 2: e166–e174. doi.org/10.1016/S2468-2667(17)30045-2.

Greenhalgh, E. and Bayly, M. 2018. 'Prevalence of smoking: Adults.' In M. Scollo and M. Winstanley (eds), *Tobacco in Australia: Facts and issues.* Melbourne: Cancer Council Victoria.

Greenhalgh, E. and Scollo, M. 2018. 'Smoking and social disadvantage.' In M. Scollo and M. Winstanley (eds), *Tobacco in Australia: Facts and issues.* Melbourne: Cancer Council Victoria.

Greenhalgh, E., Bayly, M. and Winstanley, M. 2018. 'Prevalence of smoking: Adults.' In M. Scollo and M. Winstanley (eds), *Tobacco in Australia: Facts and issues.* Melbourne: Cancer Council Victoria.

Kelly, J., Maher, S. and Australian Associated Press 2011. 'Big tobacco to fight Rudd's cigarette plain packaging plan.' *The Australian*, 29 April. Available from: www.theaustralian.com.au/archive/politics/big-tobacco-to-fight-rudds-cigarette-plain-packaging-plan/news-story/edcb84582d8b4bb5d90074cce37b5a6d.

Kickbusch, I., Allen, L. and Franz, C. 2016. 'The commercial determinants of health.' *The Lancet: Global Health* 4: e895–e896. doi.org/10.1016/S2214-109X(16)30217-0.

Liberman, J. 2013. 'Plainly constitutional: The upholding of plain tobacco packaging by the High Court of Australia.' *American Journal of Law & Medicine* 39: 361–81. doi.org/10.1177/009885881303900209.

Lloyd, P. 2010. 'The tobacco files.' *Lateline*, 10 September. Available from: www.abc.net.au/lateline/the-tobacco-files/2256476.

McKee, M. 2017. 'The tobacco industry: The pioneer of fake news.' *Journal of Public Health Research* 6(1). doi.org/10.4081/jphr.2017.878.

McLeod, K., Wakefield, M., Chapman, S., Smith, K. C. and Durkin, S. 2009. 'Changes in the news representation of smokers and tobacco-related media advocacy from 1995 to 2005 in Australia.' *Journal of Epidemiology and Community Health* 63: 215–20. doi.org/10.1136/jech.2007.072587.

Moodie, A. R., Carnell, K., Connors, C. and Larkin, S. 2008. 'Australia: The healthiest country by 2020.' *Medical Journal of Australia* 189: 588–90.

National Preventative Health Taskforce 2009. *Australia: The healthiest country by 2020—National preventative health strategy: The roadmap for action*. Canberra: Commonwealth of Australia.

Parliament of Australia 1995. *Report of the Senate Community Affairs Reference Committee: The tobacco industry and the costs of tobacco-related illness*. Canberra: Parliament of Australia.

Parliament of Australia 2011. House of Representatives, *Hansard*, No. 18, 21 November: 12913. Canberra: Parliament of Australia.

Quit Victoria 2011. Tobacco industry persuades people to support plain packaging of cigarettes. Media release, [Online], 3 March. Melbourne: Quit Victoria. Accessed from: www.quit.org.au/media/article.aspx?ContentID=27_mar_201103 (site discontinued).

Scollo, M. 2012. 'Introduction.' In M. Scollo and M. Winstanley (eds), *Tobacco in Australia: Facts and issues.* Melbourne: Cancer Council Victoria. Available from: www.tobaccoinaustralia.org.au/introduction.

Scollo, M., Freeman, B. and Greenhalgh, E. 2016. 'Packaging as promotion.' In M. Scollo and M. Winstanley (eds), *Tobacco in Australia: Facts and issues.* Melbourne: Cancer Council Victoria.

Siegel, M. 2013. 'Law spoils tobacco's taste, Australians say.' [Online]. *The New York Times*, 10 July. Available from: www.nytimes.com/2013/07/11/business/global/law-spoils-tobaccos-taste-australians-say.html?_r=0.

Tobacco Working Group 2009. *Tobacco in Australia: Making smoking history.* Technical Report No. 2. Canberra: National Preventative Health Taskforce. Available from: content.webarchive.nla.gov.au/gov/wayback/20160923060300/http://www.preventativehealth.org.au/internet/preventativehealth/publishing.nsf/Content/tech-tobacco.

Voon, T. and Mitchell, A. 2011. 'Face off: Assessing WTO challenges to Australia's scheme for plain tobacco packaging.' *Public Law Review* 22: 218–36.

Wakefield, M., Coomber, K., Zacher, M., Durkin, S., Brennan, E. and Scollo, M. 2015. 'Australian adult smokers' responses to plain packaging with larger graphic health warnings 1 year after implementation: Results from a national cross-sectional tracking survey.' *Tobacco Control* 24: ii17–ii25. doi.org/10.1136/tobaccocontrol-2014-052050.

White, V., Williams, T. and Wakefield, M. 2015. 'Has the introduction of plain packaging with larger graphic health warnings changed adolescents' perceptions of cigarette packs and brands?' *Tobacco Control* 24: ii42–ii49. doi.org/10.1136/tobaccocontrol-2014-052084.

World Health Organization (WHO) 2005. *WHO Framework Convention on Tobacco Control.* [Online]. Geneva: WHO. Available from: apps.who.int/iris/bitstream/10665/42811/1/9241591013.pdf?ua=1.

World Health Organization (WHO) 2016. 'Posters: Get ready for plain packaging.' In *World No Tobacco Day*, 31 May. Geneva: WHO. Available from: www.who.int/campaigns/no-tobacco-day/2016/posters/en/.

World Health Organization (WHO) 2017a. *Parties to the WHO Framework Convention on Tobacco Control.* [Online]. 23 November. Geneva: WHO. Available from: www.who.int/fctc/signatories_parties/en/.

World Health Organization (WHO) 2017b. *Tobacco Free Initiative.* [Online]. Geneva: WHO. Available from: www.who.int/tobacco/mpower/publications/en/.

Young, J. M., Stacey, I., Dobbins, T. A., Dunlop, S., Dessaix, A. L. and Currow, D. C. 2014. 'Association between tobacco plain packaging and Quitline calls: A population-based, interrupted time-series analysis.' *Medical Journal of Australia* 200: 29–32. doi.org/10.5694/mja13.11070.

Part II: Policy successes in New Zealand

14

New Zealand's universal no-fault accident compensation scheme: Embedding community responsibility

Grant Duncan

In November 2016, I was careless enough to fall, head first, and suffered mild concussion. Still on my feet, I made two visits to a private accident and emergency clinic. There was no charge. On the second visit, I was advised to go to the emergency room at the local public hospital, where I stayed for three nights. I received three CT scans and was seen by a neurosurgeon, who decided on conservative management—meaning no surgery. On discharge, there was no bill. A few days later, I was called by a case manager from the Accident Compensation Corporation (ACC), who informed me that my claim (lodged already on my behalf by the accident and emergency clinic) had been accepted, asked how I was doing and advised that I could apply for weekly compensation if I was unable to work. She arranged home visits by an occupational therapist and a physiotherapist, at no charge. There was also a visit to a head injury specialist, at no charge, taxi fares included. I recovered and was back at work in time for the new semester. The accident did not happen at work; nor was it covered by private health insurance. But the whole incident cost me almost nothing, other than some serious headaches and inconvenience. Or, more to the point, I had already contributed, through a compulsory payroll levy, to the state monopoly fund for personal injury caused off-the-job. The flipside is that I am barred from suing anyone for damages in any New Zealand court.

Visitors to New Zealand are often surprised to learn that, on arrival, they are automatically covered by the same universal personal injury insurance scheme and, in return, they too are barred from suing for compensation. It is in part because of this that the visitor can enjoy risky activities such as bungy-jumping and whitewater rafting. Insuring against negligence claims would be a significant, possibly prohibitive, business cost for adventure tourism—a field in which New Zealand excels. Nonetheless, visitors from Australia and the United States often wonder why New Zealanders deprived themselves of the right to hold a negligent party to account for one's pain and suffering and incapacity for work, even though one can still sue for defamation. The removal of this basic element of common law rights is particularly incomprehensible to civil litigators who specialise in personal injury. Moreover, the state monopoly deprives the insurance industry of a lucrative market—albeit one with long-tail risk.

Some often cited principles of public policy suggest the ACC, as a state monopoly with compulsory levies, is not an ideal institutional arrangement, as it lacks contestability and reduces the effect of general deterrence. Public choice theory holds that state monopolies are inherently inefficient. Law and economics logics suggest the threat of damages awarded in court poses an incentive to act with greater regard for others' safety. The costs arising from personal injury and from damages awards may all be insured against and mitigated in a free market, but variable insurance premiums send price signals that inform choices between activities with differing risks, while internalising and spreading the costs. Moreover, in a competitive market, insurers and rehabilitation providers must innovate and adopt best practice in achieving efficiencies and assuring good outcomes for injured persons.

This gives a first impression of how the ACC works, but also raises doubts about whether it represents the best institutional model. My aim, then, is to explain why this state monopoly has endured and why it is a success in political, economic and wellbeing terms. In so doing, we will nonetheless observe that its founding principles have often been compromised and that there remain some outstanding problems. This success story is not an unqualified one.

A brief history will show how New Zealand acquired its unique universal accident insurance system, based on compulsory contributions into a state monopoly with no right to sue. The 1967 report of a royal commission of inquiry (the 'Woodhouse Report') laid out the blueprint for the scheme, based on five founding principles, summarised below. To this day, any national debate about ACC law and policy inevitably refers back to the Woodhouse principles, and this sustained influence in itself represents a notable success. So, what made the Woodhouse Report so effective? There is no 'secret sauce' and policymakers everywhere could benefit from emulating Woodhouse's example: elegant, jargon-free prose; an unwavering focus on the wellbeing of the affected population, coupled with a concern for efficiency; and clear and bold principles that address well-defined problems. Although the royal commission was to inquire into workers' compensation, its report exceeded the terms of reference and made more wideranging recommendations for personal injury *outside of work* and for an end to the application of common law. These bold recommendations came 'out of the blue', as they were not addressing a critical policy failure or public controversy at that time. Nonetheless, the clarity and coherence of the analysis and the guiding principles set the agenda, leading to legislative reform and a new public institution. That institution, the ACC, remains in operation to this day.

While New Zealanders are often dissatisfied with particular aspects of accident compensation law and administration, and although the Woodhouse principles have been 'watered down', the basic 'public value proposition' embodied in the ACC scheme is clear and has stood the test of time. That proposition is: affordable universal no-fault personal injury insurance and rehabilitation in return for the relinquishment of the right to sue. This covers all personal injuries caused by accident, at work or not, occupational diseases and medical misadventure. The enduring political legitimacy and practical application of this proposition constitute a significant *programmatic* success.

The Woodhouse Report was, however, only the beginning of a longer policymaking process. After summarising the report itself, I also outline some key policy steps that considered its merits, resulting in legislation in 1972 supported on both sides of the House of Representatives. All the same, it took a change of government to give the scheme its *universal* coverage. A rigorous bipartisan policy *process*, with strong support from officials across departments, was a necessary element in the successful implementation of the ACC.

There have since been legislative overhauls, institutional changes and political controversies around the ACC. The endurance of the state monopoly model has been contentious, given the preference for competition in New Public Management and public choice theories, plus real-world pressures from employers and insurers for 'freedom to choose', especially during the 1990s, when 'the New Zealand model' was internationally regarded as a leading example of public management reform (Boston et al. 1996). At the time of writing, however, there is no longer any serious political pressure for either competition or the right to sue. So, there is a noticeable *political* success, in that the no-fault state monopoly insurer persists, by cross-party consensus, for the foreseeable future. The Woodhouse Report is still influential, even after 50 years, and the ACC scheme has been in operation for well over 40 years. For sheer *endurance*, this is a significant success.

Box 14.1 Sir Owen Woodhouse (1916–2014)

Sir Owen Woodhouse is the 'architect' of the Accident Compensation Corporation scheme. He received a law degree in 1940 and served in the Royal New Zealand Navy during World War II. In 1961, he was appointed judge of the New Zealand Supreme Court. He was commissioned as chair of the Royal Commission to Inquire into Compensation for Personal Injury in 1966. His report was published in December 1967. In 1974, he was commissioned by the Australian Government to conduct a similar inquiry. In 1981, he became president of the Court of Appeal—at that time the highest office in New Zealand's judiciary. He retired as a judge in 1986 and then served as president of the New Zealand Law Commission until 1991. He contributed to seminars on accident compensation well into his 90s.

The Woodhouse principles

Summarising Woodhouse's five principles is made easy thanks to the clarity of his original report. But first, what was the problem?

The royal commission took stock of the whole system that addressed incapacity for work. At the time, victims of accidents had three main sources of support or remedy. They could sue for damages on grounds of negligence under common law. This was historically the oldest approach, but, in by far the majority of cases, it 'had proved to be no remedy at all' (New Zealand 1967: 32). When remedies were awarded, they could range from full indemnity to virtually nothing, depending on the attribution of fault between the parties. The second approach dated back to 1900, when New Zealand followed the examples of Germany and Britain in adopting a workers' compensation system to replace the old employer liability laws. At the time of the Woodhouse Report, the *Workers' Compensation Act 1956* was in force, providing no-fault cover, with loss-related income replacement, funded by employers. The third source of support was the social security system, which, since 1938, provided flat-rate benefits for sickness and long-term disability, alongside free public hospitals.

The problem was there were three mutually inconsistent systems with different entitlements, even for people with effectively the same injuries, disabilities and needs. It meant that a person injured at work (and covered by workers' compensation) received a much better income-related entitlement than the flat-rate social security benefit that may have applied if the same person received the same injury immediately after stepping outside the factory gate. And a dependent spouse injured at home would receive nothing, due to means testing of social security. Sometimes an injured person could 'double-dip', such as by receiving statutory compensation plus common law remedies. In all of the above three systems, however, the costs were, in the end, borne by the whole community. Employers' liability insurance and workers' compensation levies—as costs of doing business—were passed on to consumers. And social security was funded by all taxpayers. Surely, the royal commission reasoned, it would be far better for the community to have 'uniformly generous treatment of all injuries regardless of cause [and] to deal with the whole problem on a basis both comprehensive and consistent' (New Zealand 1967: 35)?

It is not possible to eliminate all accidents and injuries. Every accident is preventable, but a certain rate of accidents is statistically inevitable. The aim should be an optimal balance between the benefits of freedom of action and the costs of prevention, law enforcement, penalties and compensation. General deterrence theory rejects banning or penalising risky activities and/or paying for accident costs through taxes that people cannot avoid. It recommends that accident costs be internalised in the prices of activities, thus

> giving people freedom to choose whether they would rather engage in the activity and pay the costs of doing so, including accident costs, or, given the accident costs, engage in safer activities that might otherwise have seemed less desirable. (Calabresi 1970: 69)

Woodhouse did *not* support this general deterrence or market approach. Instead, he favoured the principle of *community responsibility*. He asserted that, as the whole of society benefits from the productive work and voluntary activities of citizens, and as predictable risks of injuries and incapacity are inherent therein, so society should accept responsibility for supporting and rehabilitating those who fall victim. This would lead to a strong version of socialised risk-sharing.

The second principle—*comprehensive entitlement*—addressed the problem of the fragmentation and inconsistency in the legal and institutional status quo ante. Equal losses should be treated equally by society, regardless of the particular place or time of the accident.

Third, 'the consideration of overriding importance must be to encourage every injured worker to recover the maximum degree of bodily health and vocational utility in a minimum of time' (New Zealand 1967: 40). This encapsulates the principle of *complete rehabilitation*.

By *real compensation*, Woodhouse intended that the actual losses experienced, both physical and economic, should be recompensed, rather than, as in the social security system, only covering basic needs; this should recognise permanent impairments.

Woodhouse also addressed *administrative efficiency*. The collection of funds and distribution of benefits 'should be handled speedily, consistently, economically, and without contention' (New Zealand 1967: 41). In a 'comprehensive, universal, and compulsory system of social insurance … there could be no point in retaining *any form* of adversary system in regard to the assessment of compensation' (New Zealand 1967: 125; emphasis added). Thus, Woodhouse proposed the extinguishment of common law rights regarding personal injury *and* the implementation of an administrative appeals system based on 'inquiry and investigation' rather than adversarial techniques (New Zealand 1967: 127).

The Woodhouse principles are clear and bold, and they produced a blueprint for a comprehensive universal scheme with no right to sue. But, as the proverb goes, there's many a slip 'twixt the cup and the lip. Table 14.1 presents a timeline of the policymaking and legislative steps that established and developed the ACC.

Table 14.1 Timeline of key events, reports and legislation

1967	Report of the Royal Commission of Inquiry into Compensation for Personal Injury in New Zealand.
1969	'Commentary' by officials on the report of the royal commission is tabled in the House of Representatives and referred to an ad hoc select committee (the 'Gair committee').
1970	The Gair committee report is tabled. National Party members divided; Labour Party members support Woodhouse principles. National government approves the committee's recommendations 'in principle'.
1971	Accident Compensation Bill introduced and referred to select committee.
1972	Bill passes unanimously, covering work-related and motor vehicle accidents.
1972	Election leads to change to Labour Government.
1973	*Amendment Act* universalises the scheme to include students, people not in paid employment and visitors to New Zealand.
1974	Accident Compensation Commission opens.
1982	ACC changes from Commission to Corporation, with a governing board appointed by the responsible minister.
1992	National Party Government passes new legislation to make scheme 'insurance-based' and remove 'hidden unemployment'.
1998	*Accident Insurance Act* introduces competitive private sector provision for workers' compensation.
1999	Six insurance companies enter the market.
2000	New Labour–Alliance coalition government repeals 1998 Act, terminates accident insurance contracts and renationalises workers' compensation.
2001	New legislation reestablishes the ACC as a compulsory state monopoly.

Legislation to implement a new scheme was introduced by the National Party Government in 1972, but only covering those in paid employment and motor vehicle accidents, thus falling short of Woodhouse's recommendation for universality or comprehensive entitlement. The change to a Labour Government in the 1972 election led to a legislative amendment to universalise the scheme, covering students, people not in paid employment and visitors to New Zealand (Palmer 1979). Even then, as recounted below, not all of Woodhouse's recommendations were adopted. (Some commentators attribute recent problems in the scheme to these departures from the original plan—for example, Wilson 2008; Palmer 2013.)

The ACC was opened for business in 1974, after which common law actions were completely barred. A plaintiff's suit would be struck out unless the ACC cover had been lawfully denied, (in very rare cases) if exemplary or punitive damages were warranted or if the claim was for mental injury to a bystander who received no physical injury (Miller 2003). There is some lack of clarity around what exactly is not covered by the ACC—and thus is potentially actionable—such as a pregnancy following a failed sterilisation (Tobin 2008). But, at the time of writing, no political party or vocal interest group is calling for reinstatement of the right to sue for personal injury compensation, although some authors have put the case forward (Duffy 2003; Wilkinson 2003). The universal cover is still in place, providing medical treatment, social and vocational rehabilitation and weekly income-related compensation. It is funded by compulsory levies on employers, wage-earners, motor vehicle registrations and fuel consumption taxes, as well as a government contribution for non-wage-earners.

Sir Geoffrey Palmer (2013: 209), a prominent lawyer and former politician who was closely involved in these policy processes, regards 'the removal of the common law action for damages' as the scheme's greatest accomplishment and 'biggest policy point'. He argues that, organisationally, the corporation has, however, not been such a success. Originally formed as a commission under three appointed commissioners, the ACC was converted in 1982 into a Crown entity with a governing board, appointed by the responsible minister, and a chief executive. Policy advice was the responsibility of the former Department of Labour. Along with its largely separate levy revenue, this made the ACC 'an outlier within the government system', and Palmer (2013: 211) argues instead that it should be administered as 'a department of state operating on the conventional principles of ministerial responsibility'.

Risk-related or flat-rate funding?

One key recommendation of the Woodhouse Report that was *not* adopted was for a flat-rate employers' levy across all industries. It is common practice in accident insurance systems to vary premiums according to the accident risks of different industries or activities. The royal commission noted there were 137 industrial classifications determining the contributions from employers to the workers' compensation scheme. The commission also addressed 'merit rating' (or 'experience rating') in which an individual firm's industry-based contributions may retrospectively receive a penalty or rebate, depending on the numbers and costs of claims attributed to its activities. The commission rejected both industrial classification and experience rating of firms. Instead, it recommended 'a uniform levy based upon salary or wages paid' set at 1 per cent (New Zealand 1967: 172).

The basic point against industry classification was that 'all industrial activity is interdependent' (New Zealand 1967: 130). The high-risk industry of coalmining supplied fuel to power generators, which in turn kept the lights going for staff in universities. The last benefited from the work of those facing greater risks. Even so, it proves politically difficult to persuade the employers of university professors and librarians that their payroll-based levy should be the same percentage as that for employers of coalminers. With a flat rate, employers complain about cross-subsidisation.

As for experience rating, Woodhouse (New Zealand 1967: 134) rejected the theory that 'premiums should be made to fit the accident record [of the firm] and so act as a spur to safety'. This theory assumes that managers have more control over the incidence and severity of accidents than they genuinely have. Moreover, employers are liable, regardless of their degree of actual culpability. One-off errors, accidents due to failure to follow safety rules and training and incidents arising from another operator or a neighbouring site can result in penalties to the employer of the injured worker. Employers who dispute the attribution of individual claims against their accounts will look through the lens of fault.

Woodhouse also argued that the financial incentives of experience rating correlate with only an 'insignificant' portion of the costs of accidents, taking into account losses of production and property damage. Moreover, there was no conclusive evidence that experience rating actually improved safety. 'There has [instead] been a tendency to withhold reports of accidents or to contest claims in order to produce a low accident ratio' (New Zealand 1967: 135). Indeed, there is still no conclusive evidence to support claims that experience rating boosts investment in safety, reduces accidents and improves return-to-work rates (Mansfield et al. 2012).

Woodhouse's argument for a flat rate was succinct and persuasive—but unsuccessful. The 1972 Act provided for risk rating of industries and experience rating of firms. Experience rating has been used most rigorously since the 1992 overhaul of the legislation. The idea that 'good' employers should not subsidise 'bad' ones was easily swallowed and the National Party Government of the day wanted to make the scheme look more insurance based. Nowadays, the ACC itself resorts to justice-based arguments in favour of experience rating, rather than claiming it has efficiency advantages. As there is little hard evidence for a positive impact of experience rating on injury rates, it argues that it is 'fair' that employers with higher than average claim rates and costs should pay more. Experience rating, however, produces disputes over work-relatedness and rehabilitation plans; it encourages suppression of claims rather than prevention of injuries.

So, the Woodhouse vision of flat-rate levies was not realised. Industry classifications and experience rating may not lead to genuine efficiency gains, but the business community supports the reduction of cross-subsidisation on the grounds it is 'fairer' and managers see value in performance feedback about injury frequencies and costs. To give some larger employers increased control, those with adequate inhouse systems may also administer their own claims, in accordance with statute.

How did the ACC avoid deregulation?

In the 1990s, 'the New Zealand model' of public management and privatisation was held up as a leading and radical example (Boston et al. 1996; Pollitt and Bouckaert 2004). And, as a state monopoly performing an insurance function, the ACC looked ripe for disaggregation and competition. To begin with, the employers' account could be carved off and converted back into a standard workers' compensation scheme, underwritten by competing private insurers.

There were strong cases in favour of a private insurance model from interest groups including the New Zealand Business Roundtable (NZBRT), the Employers' Federation and the Insurance Council. The NZBRT took the most radical approach. It recommended dismantling the ACC, terminating all state provision and deregulating the accident insurance market. Insurance cover itself and its particular benefits would be voluntary and not state-mandated. Contracting parties would be free to accept higher wages, lower prices or warranties of compensation in return for limiting or waiving rights to sue.

Most employers and the insurance industry, however, were content with the idea of competitive provision on a state-mandated model. The *Accident Insurance Act 1998* gave employers the 'freedom to choose' an insurer, including a new state-owned enterprise as default provider. In practice, this meant *compulsion* to choose, as a firm's refusal or failure to negotiate an insurance contract would lead to prosecution. The insurance contracts commenced in mid-1999, with no regulation of pricing, but with a prudential regulator overseeing the market. Otherwise, the ACC continued in operation, covering the non–work-related and motor vehicle accidents—more or less as before—and the ban on the right to sue remained.

Before the 1998 Act was passed, however, the Labour Party (then in opposition) warned the insurance industry that, if successful in gaining office after the 1999 election, it would repeal the Act, the insurance contracts would be terminated and all work-injury cover would be returned to the state monopoly. The insurance industry was 'in the business of risk' and could adjust their pricing accordingly.

Indeed, Labour formed a coalition government with the Alliance after the 1999 election and soon carried out the promise to renationalise workers' compensation—much to the annoyance of many employers. So, the state monopoly model was restored. Private insurance contracts were terminated (by force of law) after only 12 months in operation (Duncan 2002).

In the midst of these dramatic political events and legislative about-turns, a thorough debate about the relative merits of the two delivery models occurred, focused especially on the question of efficiency. Efficiency can mean many things, depending on the goals for which one aims, but the debate around the 1998 Act tended to interpret efficiency as meaning 'lower premiums for employers', associated with the incentives to prevent accidents and injuries and to return injured employees to work. Economic theory supported competition, but there was no robust international comparative evidence that state monopoly schemes were more costly for employers than competitive multi-insurer schemes, or vice versa. The Department of Labour, however, advised the government that employers' premiums could rise due to competitive delivery. Some jurisdictions with competitive schemes, such as California, had employers complaining about rapidly rising premiums (Duncan 2002). The critical factor behind costs appeared to be the statutory entitlements, not the institutional model of provision, so calling for lower premiums meant calling for lower benefits—or cost-shifting from employers to injured employees and their families (McCluskey 1998). With New Zealand's comprehensive legislation, it could also mean cost-shifting from the employer's account to the wage-earner's account by making work injuries out to be not work-related. If benefits became too restrictive, injured workers and trade unions could start to demand a reinstatement of the right to sue.

The competition policy story did not end in 2000, however. A National-led government came into office in 2008 and began a 'stocktake' of the ACC. The National Party's 2011 election manifesto promised: 'We will introduce choice to the ACC Work Account [for employers] while retaining ACC in the market, and investigate introducing choice in the Motor Vehicle and Earners' accounts' (New Zealand National Party 2011).

The ACC earners' account covers off-the-job injuries that are not motor vehicle related. It is funded by a flat-rate percentage levy on all liable wages and salaries, paid via the taxation system. At the time of writing, the rate was 1.21 per cent. A steering group set up to advise the government in 2010 recommended competitive private delivery of the wage-earners' account along with the work account. The employee's default insurer would be the same as the employer's or the employee could bundle off-the-job injury insurance with other insurance contracts. Insurers, it was argued, could risk rate premiums deducted from every employee's wage based on information about their age, leisure activities, and so on. This aimed to reduce cross-subsidisation between groups of individuals. After all, why should spectators (or any risk-averse, able-bodied individual) subsidise the frequent injuries experienced by rugby players?

It was never clear whether the insurance industry was prepared to risk rate every employee in the country, nor whether there exists a fair and cost-effective methodology for doing so. Problems of the interrelatedness of activities and the difficulty of locating individual liability (as identified originally by Woodhouse) were never fully explored. Indeed, the recommendation was not implemented. But, from time to time, debates have erupted in New Zealand about whether, for instance, sports clubs should pay an ACC levy or whether individuals with no claims should receive a rebate. If the government had followed its steering group's recommendation, and if the insurers had applied differential levies based on age, leisure activities and so on, there would have been no end to the public debates over the 'unfairness' of levy variations. Moreover, each insurer would presumably have applied its own methods.

Another debate addressed medical practitioners. The ACC covers 'treatment injury' or personal injury due to treatment by a registered medical practitioner that is not a necessary part or ordinary consequence of the treatment, given the person's underlying health condition and the state of clinical knowledge at the time. This means medical practitioners cannot be sued for malpractice and need only general public liability cover. The ACC's Treatment Injury Account is funded by contributions from general taxation and the levy-funded earners' account, not directly by medical practitioners. The National Party Government's steering group recommended this also be subject to private delivery so that medical practitioners and healthcare organisations would purchase malpractice cover as part of general professional indemnity insurance. On the face of it, this seems eminently fair. But medical professionals—not unlike Woodhouse—pointed out that any new insurance premiums would be passed on through user charges anyway, and that put an end to the public debate.

The National Party was returned to office after the 2011 election (and again in 2014), but the policy 'to introduce choice' was never implemented. The ACC's chief executive stated publicly in August 2013 that ministers had advised him that competitive provision was no longer the government's policy. No explanation was offered and there was no public complaint from employers or insurers. A clue as to why the National Government changed its mind, however, is found in a regulatory impact statement provided by the former Department of Labour (the main advisory agency on ACC policy at that time). The minister had recommended that the Cabinet agree in principle to introduce competition to the delivery of the ACC work account, but officials advised that the option of allowing employers a choice of private insurer (with or without the ACC remaining in the market as a competitor) 'would require claims cost savings in the order of 20% to 26% to offset the higher expenses of private insurers' (Department of Labour n.d.: 17–18). The alternative to such dramatic claims costs savings would have been off-setting rises in employers' premiums.

So, the simplest explanation for National's abandonment of the policy to reintroduce competition was that it did not want to choose between either cutting claim costs or imposing higher employer premiums to such a degree, as the advice implied that a 'competitive' insurance market was comparatively *un*competitive. Employers were satisfied that the existing provisions gave them a degree of performance-related cost control (or the appearance thereof) and, for many larger employers, inhouse administration of claims. Moreover, the ACC was on the way to being fully funded. This growing publicly owned fund was deriving investment incomes that, in turn, helped to reduce the ACC's levies. Privatisation would have transferred these premium and investment incomes to foreign-owned funds and their shareholders.

The National Government did introduce four differential levies for motor vehicles, based on a classification of risk derived from police-reported crash data. Given the size of the levies (at most, $80 per annum) in relation to the prices of vehicles, however, the differentials are too small to constitute a real economic incentive to purchase a newer vehicle with superior safety design. There are other motives (status, comfort, reliability, and so on) for buying a late-model car anyway, so the relatively small reductions are a negligible reward for people who are wealthy enough to own one—or a regressive tax on those who are not—with no efficiency in accident prevention.

Full funding

The next significant controversy concerns the scheme's overall funding model. The view of the royal commission was that financial contributions to the scheme 'may be regarded as a form of taxation' and, for economy of administration, should be collected by the Inland Revenue Department. The commission did not recommend the *fully funded* model required of commercial insurance companies that accumulate reserves sufficient to meet the present *and all future costs* of current claims. It reasoned that 'a formal system of funding cannot be regarded as essential to the stability of the whole system' because the scheme 'must in the final resort receive the backing of the State' (New Zealand 1967: 175). As the ACC was a state monopoly, pay-as-you-go funding sufficed, although any surpluses could be invested.

As it turned out, ACC funding was unstable. In the first decade, reserves were slightly in excess of one year's expenditure. But the 1982 Act allowed for pay-as-you-go, levies were cut, income declined below expenditure and reserves plummeted towards zero. The fourth Labour Government had to dramatically increase employers' levies to avert bankruptcy of the scheme. But they also permitted an open-ended entitlement to weekly compensation, which, along with rising unemployment, led to rapid increases in expenditure. Reserves were restored for a while, but then declined again during the 1990s, as levies failed to keep up with the higher costs. The position of the employers' account was especially perilous. Although total expenditure on work-related injuries was declining due to the 1992 Act, the employers' levies, in total, fell short for five consecutive years (1991–95). The employers' account end-of-year reserves balance was then *negative* for three consecutive years (1994–96). This posed a significant problem for the 1998 policy of introducing competitive provision. Employers had to choose a new insurer, but they also had shared liabilities remaining in the ACC scheme from previous unfunded work injuries. Hence, they had to pay a 'residual levy' to the ACC on top of the insurance premium (Duncan 2002).

It became clear that 'the introduction of choice' is best done only *after* fully funding the state monopoly scheme. Actuarial valuation and full funding of the ACC began in 1998, and continued under consecutive governments, both National and Labour, up to the present. As the ACC reported in 2017:

> Our broad financial sustainability objective is to ensure each levied account is in a fully funded solvency position. Full funding means that, at any point in time, the value of our investment portfolio is enough to pay for the future costs of every claim we have received to date. (ACC 2017a: 34)

Levied accounts in total were 121.7 per cent funded. This valuation and funding policy is consistent with the adoption of generally accepted accounting practices in public finance—an integral part of 'the New Zealand model' of public management reform. Any unfunded contingent liability in the ACC now weighs against the Crown's consolidated balance sheet. And, in the 2017 annual report, investment revenue was roughly half the total amount of levy revenue, showing how much the reserve fund contributes to keeping premiums low, while acknowledging the investment risk that accompanies this. The full-funding model has had its critics, however. One may ask why a state monopoly with compulsory contributions needs to be valued and funded as if it were a commercial insurer. Or, if it really must be, why does the New Zealand Government not actuarially value and fully fund all of its social entitlements (Littlewood 2009; Palmer 2013)?

Success does not mean 'problem-free'

While the long-term success of the ACC must be traced back to the Woodhouse Report, implementation has often departed from its recommendations. There are numerous other problems in the present scheme—of the very kinds that Woodhouse wished to avoid.

Concerning the principle of complete rehabilitation, Woodhouse gave a clear description of what that should mean:

> [The rehabilitation process] begins with the earliest treatment of the injury or disease. It does not end until everything has been done to achieve maximum social and economic independence. The aim is that this should be achieved in a minimum of time. (New Zealand 1967: 141)

The present statutory provisions for vocational rehabilitation do encourage early treatment, and rehabilitation planning must be initiated within 13 weeks post injury. But they do *not* meet Woodhouse's requirement that rehabilitation should continue 'until everything has been done to achieve maximum social and economic independence'. Indeed, the status of what is now termed 'vocational independence' frequently falls short of that. A two-stage work capacity assessment is performed, beginning with an occupational assessment of the claimant's qualifications, skills and experience for various kinds of work. A medical assessor then provides an opinion as to which of the occupations identified as 'suitable' are viable and safe after taking account of the effects of the personal injury. This work capacity assessment is not, however, necessarily carried out with direct observations of the actual performance of work tasks. Its technical validity is further compromised by the fact that it is conflated with the assessment of eligibility for weekly compensation.

The criteria for vocational independence may range from readiness for the same job as at the time of injury to readiness for any similar job or for any job for which the claimant is suited through education, training or experience. This often means that skilled tradespeople who, due to permanent impairment or risk of reinjury, cannot return to a hazardous occupation are occupationally and economically down-skilled to any jobs they may have done in the past, having regard to the personal injury. Termination of weekly compensation does not require that there be any current job vacancy for the claimant to apply for, nor that there be such employment within commuting distance of the claimant's home. The ACC law no longer provides for a permanent partial disability pension that could compensate for a long-term drop in income and it does not require full retraining into a comparably skilled trade. Many of those found to be 'vocationally independent', and whose compensation is subsequently terminated, transition to lower-paid occupations or even to means-tested social security benefits—or sometimes to no income at all. This means many former claimants suffer long-term economic loss, but with no right to sue for compensation in respect of those permanent losses (Crichton et al. 2011).

Advocates for claimants have pointed out other problems with the ACC. Disputes over what is or is not covered by the statute are common and are often experienced negatively by claimants—for instance, when ageing is found to be a factor. 'Personal injury caused wholly or substantially by the ageing process' is excluded by the 2001 Act, but the phrase 'wholly or substantially' leaves a wide interpretative scope for medical evidence and opinion, and for official determination. Bones that have become brittle due to ageing may break more easily in a fall, and hence this kind of injury could be denied cover. The Act does not follow the so-called 'egg-shell skull principle' that the compensation authority should accept claimants as it finds them. What looks like an accident, in commonsense terms, to the victim may not be assessed by the administrator as covered by the Act.

While the ACC model means that workers injured outside work receive the same treatment and entitlements as those injured at work, there are still relative disadvantages to people whose disability is caused by sickness, degeneration or congenital disorders that are not covered by the ACC. The last groups may receive public health subsidies and social security benefits, but these are much less generous. For those with severe long-term incapacity, the discrepancy between accident and illness makes a significant difference. People with equal needs are not being treated equally. Woodhouse foresaw this problem. In line with his principle of comprehensive entitlement, and with the aim of reducing disputes, he recommended eliminating any discrimination between work and non-work accidents. In this, he was successful. But he also realised that there was an equally persuasive argument to cover all forms of incapacity for work, whether caused by sickness or by personal injury. He stopped short of recommending such a fully comprehensive scheme, but he did argue that, in time, this should be given serious consideration. The extension of the comprehensive ACC model to cover sickness has indeed been investigated several times, not least by the Royal Commission on Social Policy and the Law Commission (the latter chaired by Woodhouse) in 1988. The then Labour Government, in 1989, announced legislation to cover all forms of incapacity, saying 'there was a failure of social equity in the gulf between accident compensation and assistance for disability and sickness' (Palmer 2013: 215). But the Bill was dropped by the incoming National Government after the 1990 election.

More recently, a woman with severe disability due to multiple sclerosis argued before the Human Rights Review Tribunal that the less generous benefits under health and welfare subsidies, compared with those under the ACC, amounted to unlawful discrimination on grounds of disability (Duncan 2008). The case went to the Court of Appeal, which accepted that there is prima facie discrimination, but this is 'justified' under the *New Zealand Bill of Rights Act 1990*, as the ACC law was created on reasonable grounds for recognised public policy aims. The relative disadvantage to people with disabilities that happen not to be covered by the ACC remains a source of grievance for the disability community, and there is no sign at the time of writing that it will be resolved. Cost has always been the sticking point, even though significant costs of sickness are already being paid for through healthcare subsidies and welfare benefits, and in spite of evidence that the ACC rehabilitation model may return to work people with functionally equivalent incapacity more promptly than the social security system (McAllister et al. 2013; Paul et al. 2013).

What makes the ACC a success?

Having outlined so many anomalies and compromises in the ACC scheme, one may ask: 'What makes it a success?' And, if it is a success: 'Why has no other jurisdiction adopted the model?'

I address the latter question first. Woodhouse also conducted an inquiry in Australia, under Labor prime minister Gough Whitlam. The Australian Government was persuaded to extend the terms of reference to include sickness, which delayed the final report. The inclusion of sickness became an obstacle, however, and a redrafted Bill—this time covering only injury—was ready to be introduced in November 1975, just when the Whitlam Government was dismissed (Luntz 2003). So, there is a simple historical explanation for the policy not being implemented in Australia.

Furthermore, the interest groups who opposed the reform (lawyers, insurers and some trade unions) were stronger in Australia than in New Zealand. The royal commission in New Zealand also encountered objections from lawyers and insurers, as both groups stood to lose significant income. But many lawyers supported the proposal and the insurers were loath to take their opposition into the public arena. Australia's federal constitution made such a law change more complicated, as both workers' compensation and torts are governed by state laws. New Zealand is a unitary state with no upper house and no written constitution, so there were few constitutional barriers to such an extinguishment of civil legal rights.

In the United States, constitutional barriers and vested economic interests are even more formidable and are backed by academics in the fields of torts and welfare economics. Even during the 1970s, when there was political debate about no-fault compensation, 'Americans never closely inspected the Woodhouse strategy' (Gaskins 2003: 223); they largely preferred to test and develop rights through judicial activism. Meanwhile, economic theory held that optimal investment in safety is best determined in the courts, by assigning home the costs of compensation directly to the party that was 'at fault' and was therefore in a position to prevent future injuries (Gaskins 2003). The tort system, however, has unacceptably high transaction costs, delivering less than 50 cents in benefits to injured persons for every dollar spent. It is 'a colossal waste of money for no good reason' (Palmer 1995: 1167).

There is an element of luck, then, in New Zealand's ACC history. The commission contained 'the right people in the right place at the right time' to produce bold policy proposals that would eventually be adopted in law. While the scheme has matured over four decades, it looks increasingly unlikely to be taken up as a model elsewhere. But, within New Zealand, it looks increasingly unlikely to be dismantled, too. The most powerful interest groups that have rallied against the ACC in the past are those representing the business community, especially the insurance industry. The ACC is now on a sustainable financial footing, levies are relatively low and there is no longer any serious challenge to the comprehensive monopoly model. In terms of sheer longevity, then, the Woodhouse principles and the ACC make a success story—qualified by the challenges and compromises described above.

There are also substantial outcome-related reasons for regarding the ACC as a relatively successful model. In terms of rehabilitation and efficiency, it compares favourably with workers' compensation schemes in Australian states, most of which have multi-insurer or hybrid public/private arrangements, including self-insurers and third-party providers. In 2014–15, the incidence rate of long-term work-related claims (those needing income-related compensation for 12 weeks or more) was lower in New Zealand (2.3 claims per 1,000 workers) than in Australia (2.8 claims per 1,000 workers). And employers' levies are lower in New Zealand—partly because the ACC does not directly cover mental health conditions such as stress. In 2014–15, the Australian standardised average premium was $1.39 per $100 payroll, ranging from $1.19 in Queensland to $2.42 in South Australia, compared with $0.60 in New Zealand (Safe Work Australia 2017: viii, 3). A state monopoly has the advantages of economies of scale, not paying tax or shareholders' dividends and not having to invest in competitive marketing and sales.

Moreover, the ACC has a relatively good record for returning injured employees to work. In a cross-Tasman survey (in 2013–14) of injured workers who had 10 or more days off work and whose claims were submitted seven to nine months earlier, 77 per cent had returned to work following their injury and were still working when interviewed. The rate in New Zealand was closely comparable with the average in the Australian states (Social Research Centre 2016).

Even though a fundamental aim of the ACC was to eliminate causes of litigation, there are still disputes over cover, entitlements and 'vocational independence'. Nonetheless, the rate of reviews and appeals is relatively low. In the Australian workers' compensation schemes, formal appeals (including reviews or mediation, but *excluding* common law actions) arise in over 6 per cent of active claims per annum. In New Zealand, the comparable rate declined to 0.6 per cent in 2014–15 (Safe Work Australia 2017: 31).[1]

1 A claimant may apply to the ACC for a review of any of its decisions on their claim. The ACC contracts an independent agency to conduct the dispute-resolution service, and the Corporation's decisions are upheld 84 per cent of the time. There is a right of appeal to the District Court.

The lack of general deterrence under compulsory monopoly schemes is thought by some, however, to reduce the incentives to act safely and prevent accidents, and hence necessitates stricter penalties and/or greater investment in law enforcement (Calabresi 1970); while others have argued that there is no evidence that the elimination of torts diminishes safety standards (Campbell 1996). Rates of personal injury are determined by complex social, legal, economic and environmental factors. A jurisdiction's means for insuring against and compensating personal injury are only one set of factors among many, and we cannot attribute differing rates of injuries to those factors any more than others. New Zealand's economy depends on hazardous industries such as fisheries and forestry, it has long, windy rural roads and contact sports are very popular—all of which may contribute to higher injury rates.

The numbers of work-related and compensated fatalities in New Zealand (73 in 2013–14 and 80 in 2014–15) compare poorly with numbers of work-related traumatic fatalities in New South Wales (36 in 2013–14 and 42 in 2014–15) (Safe Work Australia 2017: 6), even though the latter's population is 1.6 times greater.[2] And road accident fatality rates (per million inhabitants) are relatively high in New Zealand: 69.9, compared with 53.7 in Australia—but 109.4 in the United States, despite its relatively litigious environment (OECD 2018). To investigate whether these countries' differing legal and administrative systems predict these differences, we would have to take account of the severity of penalties, the effectiveness of law enforcement, the quality of safety education and training as well as accident compensation and control for numerous extraneous variables. In the absence of comparative research with such sophisticated controls, one can only *hypothesise* that New Zealand's universal no-fault system may have reduced incentives to prevent accidents at work and on the roads, leading to higher injury rates. If so, stricter law enforcement to counteract a 'failure' of general deterrence could be one remedy.

Similarly, physicians and surgeons in New Zealand cannot be sued by patients for negligence. (They must, of course, follow ethical codes and there are disciplinary actions for misconduct.) Nonetheless, 'the type and number of treatment injuries in New Zealand hospitals is comparable to other countries' (ACC 2017b: 9). The advantage of having a state monopoly insurer along with a public health system is that coordinated

2 Due to differing criteria and methods of data collection, these statistics may not be closely comparable.

monitoring and prevention strategies are much easier to carry out. And the absence of torts makes open and transparent reporting of errors easier for practitioners and healthcare organisations, as they are less constrained by defensive legal advice.

Despite an absence of torts in New Zealand, it possibly benefits from an 'umbrella' provided by larger countries that permit product liability claims. New Zealand imports manufactured goods such as automobiles, machine tools, pharmaceuticals and surgical equipment. Arguably, the discipline placed on manufacturers in countries that retain torts, especially the United States, raises the standards of product safety, leading to fewer accidents—or fewer and less severe injuries—thanks to the improved crashworthiness of motor vehicles. New Zealand is perhaps freeriding on the 'imported value' of safety investments made by foreign manufacturers who face product liability suits.

For the time being, however, market theory has not prevailed. The National Government's efforts to rekindle enthusiasm for 'choice' in the period 2010–13 was initially energetic (judging by the number of reports) but came to nothing. There was no outcry of complaint when the plans for competition were shelved and the business community appears satisfied with the deal it is now getting.

Trade unions are probably the ACC's staunchest supporters, but many of the most articulate advocates for the Woodhouse principles are lawyers. There may be occasions when one sympathises with an accident victim's wish to sue on grounds of negligence, but the legal profession largely accepts the scheme's overall principles and benefits. Hardly anyone bemoans their inability to sue fellow citizens.

Measured by the costs of accident insurance to individuals and firms, New Zealanders get a good deal. And, except at the margins, claims are processed and accepted expeditiously. Nonetheless, when return to a pre-injury occupation has been ruled out on medical grounds, some long-term claimants are left worse off, due to the lack of entitlement to either pensions for permanent partial disability or retraining for a low-risk occupation of equal status and income.

New Zealanders receive a good standard of medical treatment, rehabilitation and income support from the ACC. There are relatively few disputes, and hence less of the anxiety that goes with them. Negligence action remains a 'lottery'—and a slow motion one, at that—and New

Zealanders are better off without it (Palmer 1995, 2008; Luntz 2008). In spite of the lack of emulation abroad and the domestic squabbles about particular provisions, the ACC model has basically been a success for New Zealanders, whether we judge it in terms of longevity, political legitimacy, economic efficiency or individual and social wellbeing.

Conclusion

In drawing lessons from this case study, it makes no sense to recommend that other countries adopt the Woodhouse principles. In spite of well-known problems with the common law as a remedial system, it would require unusually strong public and political support for any other country to follow New Zealand's example. Economic interests and constitutional hurdles stand in the way. Looking at the reasons Woodhouse's vision became a long-term success story, however, does point to some general lessons.

We can begin at the policy blueprint stage. Clearly expressed principles that address both wellbeing and efficiency, written in succinct and jargon-free prose, were critical success factors. Woodhouse presented a bold and compelling case that captured attention and drew support from a range of stakeholders and lawmakers. The ACC's implementation and long-term success have been aided by strong advocacy from vocal supporters—mainly trade unionists, academics and lawyers. Naturally, there was opposition from interest groups and political support has not been universal. The National Party was less enthusiastic than Labour about the Woodhouse principles (especially 'community responsibility') and they have preferred commercial insurance principles and competitive provision. But both political parties have repeatedly acknowledged the relevance of Woodhouse's principles by claiming that their various reforms have upheld them—even if those claims are not always convincing. Both parties have passed legislation that does not fully represent the initial blueprint. But the important point is that there is a clear, consistent and robust blueprint that cannot be ignored.

The royal commission's recommendations were unexpected, as its authors exceeded the terms of reference of their commission, making a bold proposal to terminate key civil legal rights, even though there had been no critical policy failure or public outcry that appeared to necessitate radical reform. It succeeded due to the intelligence and foresight of the chair of the commission (Woodhouse) and to the particular constitutional environment of New Zealand. As a senior judge, Woodhouse must have been aware that terminating civil legal rights was achievable for New Zealand's unicameral parliament, as it lacks a written overarching constitution with entrenched rights and it does not require the consent or cooperation of states or provinces. But the relinquishment of rights could be acceptable (politically and legally) only with a 'social contract' that guaranteed automatic entitlement to a reasonable alternative. In the 1970s, 'community responsibility' (in contrast to the methodological individualism of neoclassical economics) was a more readily accepted ideal. So, the lesson here is that success can depend on the 'fitness' of policy proposals to their social, historical and constitutional contexts.

Whereas other case studies in this volume present enduring successes of New Public Management reforms, the ACC story represents an exception. And yet the scheme performs well, in terms of efficiency and effectiveness. Costs did get out of control in the late 1980s as unemployment rose, so it seemed reasonable then to propose that the private sector might do a better job. Tighter controls over rehabilitation and claim termination after 1992, however, levelled out expenditure. Full funding has produced investment incomes and helped to stabilise premiums—and businesses want premiums to be both low and stable. Now that the ACC is financially more sustainable, the case for competitive private sector provision looks weaker, especially given the advice that competition could lead to *greater* costs unless benefits were to be radically curtailed. The 'deal' that underpins the ACC—a ban on all negligence actions, in return for state-guaranteed compensation—means that, if benefits were significantly reduced, there would be demands to bring back the right to sue. If the deal collapsed, insuring against the risk of damages awards would load new costs on to firms and medical practitioners. So, accident compensation policy in New Zealand appears to have reached an 'equilibrium', wherein the public is satisfied to forgo the right to sue, everyone pays relatively low premiums and (with some exceptions) cover is promptly assessed and granted. After my accident, my first thought was neither 'Will my insurer cover this?' nor 'Whom can I sue?' My sole concerns were treatment and recovery.

References

Accident Compensation Corporation (ACC) 2017a. *Investing in New Zealanders: Annual report 2017*. Wellington: ACC. Available from: www.acc.co.nz/assets/corporate-documents/a62a168a11/acc7811-annual-report-2017.pdf.

Accident Compensation Corporation (ACC) 2017b. *Supporting Patient Safety: Treatment injury information*. Wellington: ACC.

Boston, J., Martin, J., Pallot, J. and Walsh, P. 1996. *Public Management: The New Zealand model*. Auckland: Oxford University Press.

Calabresi, G. 1970. *The Costs of Accidents: A legal and economic analysis*. New Haven, CT: Yale University Press.

Campbell, I. 1996. *Compensation for Personal Injury in New Zealand: Its rise and fall*. Auckland: Auckland University Press.

Crichton, S., Stillman, S. and Hyslop, D. 2011. 'Returning to work from injury: Longitudinal evidence on employment and earnings.' *ILR Review* 64(4): 765–85. doi.org/10.1177/001979391106400407.

Department of Labour n.d. *Response to the recommendations of the ACC stocktake*. Regulatory Impact Statement. Wellington: New Zealand Government. Available from: treasury.govt.nz/sites/default/files/2010-12/ris-dol-raccs-dec10.pdf.

Duffy, A. 2003. 'The common-law response to the Accident Compensation Scheme.' *Victoria University of Wellington Law Review* 34(2): 367–85. Available from: www.victoria.ac.nz/law/research/publications/vuwlr/prev-issues/vol-34-2.

Duncan, G. 2002. 'Workers' compensation.' In M. Lloyd (ed.), *Occupational Health and Safety in New Zealand: Contemporary social research*. Palmerston North, NZ: Dunmore.

Duncan, G. 2008. 'Boundary disputes in the ACC scheme and the no-fault principle.' *New Zealand Law Review* (1): 27–36. Available from: heinonline.org/HOL/LandingPage?handle=hein.journals/newzlndlr2008&div=10&id=&page=.

Gaskins, R. 2003. 'The fate of "no-fault" in America.' *Victoria University of Wellington Law Review* 34(2): 213–37. Available from: www.victoria.ac.nz/law/research/publications/vuwlr/prev-issues/vol-34-2.

Littlewood, M. 2009. *Why does the Accident Compensation Corporation have a fund?* Pension Commentary 2009-1, 12 October. Auckland: Retirement Policy and Research Centre, University of Auckland. Available from: docs.business.auckland.ac.nz/Doc/PensionCommentary-PC-2009-1-Why-does-the-Accident-Compensation-Corporation-have-a-fund.pdf.

Luntz, H. 2003. 'Looking back at accident compensation: An Australian perspective.' *Victoria University of Wellington Law Review* 34(2): 279–92. Available from: www.victoria.ac.nz/law/research/publications/vuwlr/prev-issues/vol-34-2.

Luntz, H. 2008. 'A view from abroad.' *New Zealand Law Review* (1): 97–128. Available from: heinonline.org/HOL/LandingPage?handle=hein.journals/newzlndlr2008&div=14&id=&page=.

McAllister, S., Derrett, S., Audasa, R., Herbison, P. and Paul, C. 2013. 'Do different types of financial support after illness or injury affect socio-economic outcomes? A natural experiment in New Zealand.' *Social Science and Medicine* 85(May): 93–102. doi.org/10.1016/j.socscimed.2013.02.041.

McCluskey, M. 1998. 'The illusion of efficiency in workers' compensation "reform".' *Rutgers Law Review* 50(3): 657–941. Available from: heinonline.org/HOL/LandingPage?handle=hein.journals/rutlr50&div=24&id=&page=.

Mansfield, L., MacEachen, E., Tompa, E., Christina, K., Endicott, M. and Yeung, N. 2012. 'A critical review of literature on experience rating in workers' compensation systems.' *Policy and Practice in Health and Safety* 10(1): 3–25. doi.org/10.1080/14774003.2012.11667766.

Miller, J. 2003. 'Trends in personal injury litigation: The 1990s.' *Victoria University of Wellington Law Review* 34(2): 407–21. Available from: www.victoria.ac.nz/law/research/publications/vuwlr/prev-issues/vol-34-2.

New Zealand National Party 2011. Committed to a fair, affordable & sustainable ACC. Press release, 21 November. Wellington: New Zealand National Party. Available from: community.scoop.co.nz/2011/11/committed-to-a-fair-affordable-sustainable-acc/.

New Zealand Royal Commission to Inquire into and Report upon Workers Compensation 1967. *Compensation for Personal Injury in New Zealand: Report of the Royal Commission of Inquiry.* Wellington: R. E. Owen, Government Printer. Available from: digitool.auckland.ac.nz/R/-?func=dbin-jump-full&object_id-33050&silo_library=GEN01.

Organisation for Economic Co-operation and Development (OECD) 2018. Road accidents indicators. [Online]. Paris: OECD eLibrary. doi.org/10.1787/2fe1b899-en.

Palmer, G. 1979. *Compensation for Incapacity: A study of law and social change in New Zealand and Australia*. Wellington: Oxford University Press.

Palmer, G. 1995. 'The design of compensation systems: Tort principles rule, O.K.?' *Valparaiso University Law Review* 29(3): 1115–69.

Palmer, G. 2003. 'The Nineteen-Seventies: Summary for presentation to the Accident compensation symposium.' *Victoria University of Wellington Law Review* 34(2): 239–47. Available from: www.victoria.ac.nz/law/research/publications/vuwlr/prev-issues/vol-34-2.

Palmer, G. 2008. 'Accident compensation in New Zealand: Looking back and looking forward.' *New Zealand Law Review* (1): 81–95. Available from: heinonline.org/HOL/LandingPage?handle=hein.journals/newzlndlr2008&div=13&id=&page=.

Palmer, G. 2013. *Reform: A memoir.* Wellington: Victoria University Press.

Paul, C., Derrett, S. M. S., Herbison, P. and Beaver, C. S. M. 2013. 'Socioeconomic outcomes following spinal cord injury and the role of no-fault compensation: Longitudinal study.' *Spinal Cord* 51(12): 919–25. doi.org/10.1038/sc.2013.110.

Pollitt, C. and Bouckaert, G. 2004. *Public Management Reform: A comparative analysis.* Oxford: Oxford University Press.

Safe Work Australia 2017. *Comparative Performance Monitoring Report: Comparison of work health and safety and workers' compensation schemes in Australia and New Zealand.* 18th edn rev. Canberra: Safe Work Australia. Available from: www.safeworkaustralia.gov.au/collection/comparative-performance-monitoring-report-18th-edition.

Social Research Centre 2016. *Return to Work Survey 2016: Summary research report (Australia and New Zealand).* Canberra: Safe Work Australia.

Tobin, R. 2008. 'Common law actions on the margin.' *New Zealand Law Review* (1): 37–53. Available from: heinonline.org/HOL/LandingPage?handle=hein.journals/newzlndlr2008&div=11&id=&page=.

Wilkinson, B. 2003. 'The accident compensation scheme: A case study in public policy failure.' *Victoria University of Wellington Law Review* 34(2): 313–27. Available from: www.victoria.ac.nz/law/research/publications/vuwlr/prev-issues/vol-34-2.

Wilson, R. 2008. 'The Woodhouse vision: 40 years in practice.' *New Zealand Law Review* (1): 3–10. Available from: heinonline.org/HOL/LandingPage?handle=hein.journals/newzlndlr2008&div=7&id=&page=.

15

New Zealand's economic turnaround: How public policy innovation catalysed economic growth

Michael Mintrom and Madeline Thomas

On 14 June 1984, New Zealand prime minister Sir Robert Muldoon announced a snap general election, to be held the following month. Muldoon, then in his 60s, had served continuously as both prime minister and finance minister since 1975. As prime minister, Muldoon wielded significant power in his Cabinet and in the conservative National Party. His election announcement was calculated to catch the Labour Party opposition off guard. But Muldoon's snap election announcement saw hubris triumph over astute political judgement. On 14 July 1984, David Lange, a charismatic politician in his early 40s, a lawyer by profession with a quick and cutting wit, led the Labour Party to victory in an electoral landslide.

Following the 1984 general election, there was a broadly shared sense that the country faced new possibilities. Those new possibilities were seized, but in ways that many people did not expect. Significant public policy innovations were introduced. In the process, considerable economic and political disruption ensued. Disputes concerning economic management and social policy within the Labour Party saw the National Party win the 1990 general election. The newly elected National Government broadly accepted the inherited policy settings. Policy development continued across the spectrum of government activities under the direction of various Labour and National governments over the subsequent decades. Nonetheless, the key public policies adopted between 1984 and 1990 remain in place and have been the foundation for later policy development.

A policy success?

Starting in 1984, Lange and a very capable group of Cabinet colleagues introduced a comprehensive and intellectually coherent range of public policy innovations. They had major impacts on the functioning of both the New Zealand economy and the New Zealand public sector. Here we discuss four areas of innovation: 1) reduction of market interventions; 2) simplification of the tax system and the introduction of a goods and services tax (GST); 3) creation of state-owned enterprises (SOEs) and subsequent privatisation efforts; and 4) introduction of independence for the Reserve Bank in driving monetary policy. The success of public policies can be assessed from a number of perspectives. These policy innovations have now remained in place for decades. Thus, judged by endurance, they have been highly successful. We also consider their success from programmatic, process and political perspectives.

From a *programmatic* perspective, the changes in economic policy were intended to reduce government interventions in the economy and, in the process, improve the government's fiscal position. A highly coherent theory of change guided the development of these policy innovations. After a relatively short time, it was clear the changes were producing beneficial outcomes. However, there were adjustment costs, which were manifest most starkly in unemployment figures, which rose during the 1980s and took many years to decline.

From a *process* perspective, the policy innovations were well designed and generally well managed. Changes to market interventions and taxes were implemented swiftly. In the case of the introduction of the GST, implementation was delayed to ensure it would work effectively. Creation of SOEs took much more planning. The subsequent privatisation process did not always go smoothly. The change to monetary policy was carefully planned and implemented. Reform of market interventions and the sale of SOEs contributed to unemployment. Other than this, there were limited negative consequences of these policy innovations.

From a *political* perspective, the story is more complicated. These policy innovations generated losses for certain sectors of the economy, and those who bore the brunt voiced their opposition. The government elected in 1984 was returned to power in 1987 after a strong electoral win. However, shortly afterwards, the governing coalition began to fragment. The epicentre of this fragmentation was the relationship between prime minister Lange and finance minister Roger Douglas. That relationship deteriorated as Douglas pushed to extend the logic of the limited state through extensive sales of government assets and changes in social policy. Lange pushed back, voicing his concern over the social costs of the reforms that had already been adopted.

The story we tell has been told before in different ways. Economists have tended to view the innovations positively. Using a set of key indicators, they have shown that the policy changes were both dramatic in how they halted specific past practices and significant in the positive impacts they delivered (Bollard 1994; Brash 1996; Evans et al. 1996). In contrast, various assessments have viewed these policy reforms negatively. In such interpretations, the changes have been considered unnecessarily radical, given the prevailing economic conditions when they began (Goldfinch and Malpass 2007). The policy innovations have also been construed as following too slavishly the predominant international fashion in economic thinking at that time (Larner 1997; Goldfinch 1998). Others have pointed to both the economic and the social costs of adjustment and have suggested the changes did more harm than good (Kelsey 1997; Dalziel 2002). Still others have noted how the policy innovations served to reduce the reach of the state and have suggested the end result was a significant redistribution of power into the hands of globalised financial elites (Easton 1997; Jesson 1999).

Our contribution involves analysing the economic turnaround as a public policy success. We take as our starting point the comprehensive assessments provided by well-placed economic observers of this period (Bollard 1994; Evans et al. 1996). We acknowledge the critiques. The reforms contributed to significant short-term stress in the New Zealand economy in the form of increased unemployment. This had highly damaging effects on vulnerable individuals, families and communities. In addition, aspects of the privatisation process were poorly handled. Where we depart from the critics is in our view of plausible alternative reform paths. No critical assessment has posited a set of counterfactual reforms that would have been achievable and more desirable than the path chosen. Paul Dalziel (2002) comes closest to offering such an assessment—but that assessment discounts the seriousness of the imbalances in the New Zealand economy in mid-1984.

We next contextualise New Zealand's economic situation prior to 1984 and outline the four key policy innovations implemented between 1984 and 1990. In the decades since that period, these reforms have acquired strong political legitimacy. They have been accepted by successive governments embracing a range of different philosophical perspectives concerning good political and economic management.

Context, challenges and agents

Many commentators have described the New Zealand economy in 1984 as dysfunctional due to excessive government interventions. Lange quipped that, under the Muldoon Government: 'We ended up being run very similarly to a Polish shipyard' (Lange, quoted in New Zealand Herald 2005). That was an exaggeration (Goldfinch and Malpass 2007). Nonetheless, it has now been clearly documented that the economy at that time was subject to many unsustainable policies (Bollard 1994; Evans et al. 1996). They emerged from a specific historical period—from the end of World War II through to the mid-1970s. During that period, New Zealanders enjoyed high living standards relative to citizens of other countries (Easton 1997; Greasley and Oxley 2000). Policy approaches taken during those years of prosperity—which seemed beneficial to the country at the time—proved damaging when applied by Muldoon during his time as prime minister and finance minister. His approach to economic management fell out of step with the new orthodoxy in economic thinking that had been emerging internationally since the early 1960s. (Overviews of that new orthodoxy have been produced by, among others, Friedman 1962, 1977; Yergin and Stanislaw 2002; Greenspan 2008.)

It is useful to review the contextual factors and policy choices that created the economic and governmental management challenges the incoming fourth Labour Government faced in 1984. New Zealand became wealthy during the twentieth century through the export of meat, wool and dairy products (Hawke 1985). Most of those products were supplied to the United Kingdom. As early as the Great Depression, political leaders in New Zealand recognised the risks in this economic model. Whenever the economy of the United Kingdom weakened, the New Zealand economy weakened, too. In response, governments acted to safeguard the New Zealand economy. One such action involved promoting the development of a significant manufacturing sector. By placing high tariffs on imported items, the government provided protection to fledging industries. The strategy was quite successful. Nonetheless, high tariffs made many imported goods expensive to consumers. The grumbling this caused was delayed largely because the economy was doing well overall. Those people who desired imported goods over domestic substitutes were prosperous enough to pay the higher prices the tariffs created. The result was bearable so long as average incomes were relatively high.

New Zealand developed a comprehensive welfare state during the twentieth century, built on systems established earlier (Mintrom and Boston forthcoming; Oliver 1988). Compulsory public education was introduced in the late nineteenth century, followed by the creation of systems to support public health. Rudimentary measures to provide income support to the most needy also dated back to the nineteenth century. Following the Great Depression, these forms of social security were expanded to include an unemployment benefit. During the years of growing prosperity after World War II, elements of the welfare state were expanded. In the 1970s, two expensive additions were made. The first was the introduction of the Domestic Purposes Benefit to support sole parents who could not participate in the workforce. Introduced in 1973, this was primarily a benefit for unmarried mothers, and it resulted in far fewer adoptions of children born out of wedlock. The second addition was the creation of national superannuation in 1977, under Muldoon's National Government. This was a generous pension payable from general taxes to all people over a designated age of retirement; it was not means tested. As the welfare state expanded over several decades, the government bureaucracy needed to maintain it also grew incrementally. Consequently, many systems of service provision were built around approaches established long before the middle of the twentieth century. Inefficiencies were noted (Polaschek 1958); however, there was no political appetite for reform.

Beginning in the mid-1970s, New Zealand started to experience levels of unemployment that were unusual, given it had enjoyed decades of full employment. This unemployment was driven by several factors. With the United Kingdom joining the European Community in 1973, the long-guaranteed market for New Zealand's agricultural exports shrank. Reduced export earnings dampened demand for locally manufactured products. Unemployment rose among unskilled agricultural workers and unskilled factory workers.

The international oil shocks of 1973–74 and 1978–79 further adversely affected the New Zealand economy. Being highly dependent on foreign oil supplies, New Zealand was susceptible to the sharp price increases instigated by the Organisation of Petroleum Exporting Countries oil cartel. In response, Muldoon's National Government took various actions, the most significant of which was the introduction of a major infrastructure building program. Announced in 1977 under the label 'Think Big', the program was intended to deliver two positive effects for New Zealand. First, it was expected to further insulate the New Zealand economy from international market changes. The logic was that if the country produced more domestic energy and switched to the use of energy sources it had in abundance—such as natural gas and hydroelectricity—susceptibility to the adverse effects of international shocks would decline. The second intended effect was to create more work, in the same way that infrastructural projects in the 1930s had made use of surplus labour and kept many households afloat during the Great Depression. However, the extra employment generated by these projects was modest, due to significant advances in construction technology over previous decades.

New Zealand Government revenues throughout the twentieth century were based primarily on company and income taxes. Over years of economic prosperity, incremental increases in marginal income tax rates were judged broadly acceptable. By the late 1970s, high-income earners were subject to a marginal tax rate of 66 cents in the dollar. As economic conditions worsened in the late 1970s and early 1980s, the Muldoon Government began imposing new, highly targeted forms of taxation as revenue-raising initiatives. These produced various economic distortions. The National Government used other regulatory actions to address growing inflation, including the imposition in 1982 of a general freeze on wages and prices. Efforts were also made to fix interest rates.

By 1984, the New Zealand economy was subject to extensive government intervention. There was a popular but expensive welfare state. The government ran many businesses associated with the delivery of infrastructure. In addition, the government was continuing to administer an elaborate system of tariffs on imported goods and various forms of financial subsidies to the manufacturing and agricultural sectors. Individuals and households were feeling the effects of high taxes and various regulations intended to moderate the effects of New Zealand's long-term decline in economic prosperity. Despite it all, the economy was performing poorly. Policy actions that might have worked during a time of economic prosperity were no longer having positive effects. Sentiment grew that the government was exercising too much control over economic activity.

In describing this background, it is useful to note two other matters. First, during the early 1980s, the attention of many New Zealanders and their politicians was absorbed not by issues of economic performance and management, but by two other public issues: New Zealand's sporting contacts with South Africa and the country's stance on nuclear warfare. A tour of New Zealand by the South African Springboks rugby team in 1981 had generated high levels of political unrest. Sporting contact with South Africa was viewed as lending support to that country's apartheid regime. By allowing that tour to continue, Muldoon had gained many detractors (Fougere 1989). While the National Party subsequently won the election of 1981, it returned to power with a slim majority in parliament. With respect to nuclear issues, many New Zealanders were concerned that defence alignments with the United States were forcing the country to support a repellent form of weaponry. The Labour Party made clear in the early 1980s that, should it win government, it would declare New Zealand nuclear-free (Clements 2015).

The second matter to note concerns the development of alternative conceptions of economic management. Significantly, economic management was not at all central to the political campaign rhetoric or the party leader debates that took place in the month leading up to election day in 1984. Lange (2005: 163), who was about to lead the Labour Party to electoral victory, has been clear on this: 'The fact of it is that Labour went into the election without an agreed economic policy.' He has elaborated:

> Our [Labour Party] differences over economic policy were not played out in public in the way we had argued about the nuclear-free policy. Towards the end of 1983 [Roger] Douglas [who was the party's finance spokesperson and would become the Minister of Finance after the July 1984 election] produced an economic policy package … It was by any test a radical document … I remember being surprised but not in the least perturbed. I expected him to think outside the square. The package was a long way from becoming policy. It would go to caucus and policy council and it would be thrashed about at the party conference in the second half of 1984. (Lange 2005: 162–3)

The anticipated debate never happened. The Douglas proposals received mixed responses in the party. A rival view was put forward that acknowledged the need for economic adjustment but assumed the government would continue to play a leading role in economic activity. Geoffrey Palmer, who was deputy leader of the Labour Party and who would become deputy prime minister after the 1984 election, wrote a short paper to reconcile different viewpoints. When the snap election was called, Palmer's paper became the party's default policy.

How the Labour Party struck upon its economic policy tells us something about the lack of agreement within the party and the parliamentary caucus from the outset. There are other details worth noting. Most importantly, the economic policy package presented by Douglas was informed by advice he had received from the Treasury. When Lange assumed leadership of the Labour Party in February 1983, he appointed Douglas as his shadow Minister of Finance. Lange 'expected him to prepare for the day when the Muldoon government would be gone' (Lange 2005: 154). As shadow Minister of Finance, Douglas had a direct line of communication with the Treasury and its senior staff from February 1983. At this time, the Treasury had established a group of analysts in a division called Economics II. This division was led by Roger Kerr and comprised between 10 and 15 economists. Many of them had postgraduate degrees in economics and broadly supported the Chicago School view that limited government and reliance on market processes were key to economic efficiency. Kerr established a culture within Economics II whereby efforts to address challenging policy questions would begin with careful reading of relevant analysis in current economics journals. Through a long-established process of 'rotation' of economic analysts every few years across divisions of Treasury, the culture of the organisation was such that analysts well beyond Economics II were informed by this approach. Kerr was key to creating a think tank atmosphere in Treasury and emphasising the importance of clear expression in the presentation of policy advice. (Kerr left the Treasury in 1986 to lead the New Zealand Business Roundtable, a think tank that would have considerable influence on economic policy for the next two decades.)

New Zealand's economic problems were connected to a highly interventionist form of economic management. The changing global economic context and the rise of free-market economic orthodoxy suggested such policy mechanisms were outdated. People in and around the New Zealand Government, including Douglas and Treasury officials, recognised this.

Policy design and choice

When Lange and his fellow Cabinet members were sworn into office, all were aware that drastic change was needed in the role played by government in the New Zealand economy. In those days, the New Zealand dollar was fixed at a constant level against the US dollar, with that level determined by the government of the day. During the brief election campaign, talk arose that the New Zealand dollar was overvalued and that a Labour Party electoral victory would be followed by a significant devaluation. Speculators began to sell New Zealand dollars and buy foreign currency, with the intention of selling that foreign currency at a profit once devaluation had occurred. The selling off of the New Zealand dollar forced the government to draw down on its foreign capital reserves. Following the Labour Party victory, senior officials from the Reserve Bank and Treasury advised that currency trading should be curtailed until a devaluation had taken place. Muldoon reluctantly agreed to demands from the incoming government to immediately devalue the New Zealand dollar by 20 per cent. This action stemmed the losses from the government's foreign capital reserves, but the crisis made clear that the old ways of doing things were not sustainable. Douglas (1993: 17)—who was about to assume the role of Minister of Finance in the new government—later grouped the fixed exchange rate and the run on the dollar with a range of other government interventions in the economy that 'brought us to our knees in 1984'.

The Labour Party, delivering on an election promise, held the Economic Summit Conference at Wellington's parliament buildings over three days in September 1984. It was attended by representatives from government departments, the trade union movement, the business community, the primary production sector and social, community and other groups. David Lange chaired the event. The summit produced a communiqué unanimously endorsed by all delegates, stating:

> The conference agrees that sound economic management must have five basic policy objectives—sustainable economic growth, full employment, price stability, external balance and an equitable distribution of income—while fully respecting social and cultural values and avoiding undue environmental costs. (ESC Secretariat 1984: 302–3)

At the same time, the participants exhibited distinct differences in what they cared most about (Dalziel 1986). This was an early indication of the dilemmas Lange would confront as prime minister.

A significant program of public policy innovation was about to occur. Here, we discuss: 1) market interventions; 2) taxation; 3) SOEs and privatisation; and 4) monetary policy. An unusual degree of intellectual effort went into policy design at this time. Throughout the period 1984–90, the New Zealand Treasury was the most influential source of policy advice to the government. All of these initiatives had their origin in deliberations between Douglas, as finance minister, and Treasury officials. Of the relationship between Douglas and the Treasury, Lange (2005: 192) observed: 'Theirs was a perfect marriage.' Treasury analysts showed a great desire to engage with relevant literature and to seek insight from colleagues in other departments and from external experts as they pursued their planning work. Further, many policy proposals were developed in ways that allowed for high levels of public consultation. Debate within Cabinet and associated Cabinet committees was vigorous. Evidence of the careful policy design work is most readily found in the Treasury's post-election briefing papers produced in 1984 and 1987.

The papers of 1984 were subsequently made public as *Economic Management* (The Treasury 1984)—a book that provided an intellectually coherent blueprint for how the incoming government could go about implementing economic reforms. Most importantly, the message of the briefing papers was that market mechanisms tended to be superior to administrative systems for efficiently allocating resources in society. The papers proposed that efforts be made to promote greater efficiency in many areas of government activity. It was suggested that this could be done by reform of taxation and by having government entities operate consistently with the practices of private sector firms.

The Treasury produced another highly influential set of briefing papers for the incoming government in 1987. Titled *Government Management* (The Treasury 1987), this document discussed the role and limits of government and desirable ways to restructure the public sector. In addition, it provided a thorough discussion of appropriate directions for reform of social policy and reiterated many points made in 1984's *Economic Management* concerning the appropriate management of the macroeconomy. Christopher Hood, in his classic 1991 article on the New Public Management (NPM), said of *Government Management* that it 'comes closest to a coherent NPM "manifesto", given that much of the academic literature on the subject either lacks full-scale elaboration or enthusiastic commitment to NPM' (Hood 1991: 6).

Market interventions

While Lange was chairing the economic summit and engaging in various prime ministerial activities outside the economic domain, Douglas was working with the Treasury on the government's first budget, delivered in November 1984. This budget made provision for the phased reduction of tariff protections for import-substituting industries and removal of a range of tax concessions and subsidies for the farming sector. The wage and price freeze introduced in 1982 was to end. By announcing these policy changes, Douglas revealed a preference for having markets and prices direct the allocation of resources in the economy, rather than arbitrary systems of government intervention. Consistent with this theme, Douglas announced that a comprehensive review of the tax system would be undertaken in 1985, paving the way for widening the tax base. He said that greater efficiency would improve New Zealand's economic performance but would not necessarily ensure that the benefits would be shared fairly. Therefore, he announced that the government would carry out a longer-term review of social policies to protect vulnerable groups and guaranteed adequate access to resources. (Subsequently, the Royal Commission on Social Policy was established in 1986.) The Budget included a package to provide substantial immediate relief to low-income families with dependent children. It also increased most other benefits and allocated more funds to education and health care. The Budget introduced a surcharge on the additional income earned by superannuants, which was unpopular with the elderly. However, it confirmed that the government was willing to remove pockets of privilege.

Taxation

The fourth Labour Government recognised that the taxation system it had inherited encouraged misallocation of resources. Too much weight was placed on the direct taxation of personal incomes. Because the overall tax base was narrow, average and marginal income tax rates were high. There was a view that this regime was encouraging tax avoidance and evasion. The government's long-term objective was to simplify the tax system, broaden the tax base and flatten the tax scale. Significant tax design work ensued, drawing on expertise both within and outside government.

In 1986, all wholesale sales taxes were abolished and replaced with a broad-based value-added tax (the GST) with a single rate of 10 per cent (raised in 1989 to 12.5 per cent). The GST included everything except financial services in the tax net. This was done recognising that only by taking this approach would economic distortions be avoided and the compliance costs involved in collecting the tax minimised. At the same time, cuts were made in the rate of income tax: an earlier five-rate scale was cut to three rates, with the highest 48 cents in the dollar—down from 66 cents. This scale was simplified further in 1988, with a two-rate scale of 24 per cent and 33 per cent. The company tax rate was reduced from 48 per cent to 33 per cent in recognition of the desirability of having the company tax rate equal to the top personal rate. The overall effect of these measures was to reduce the proportion of tax revenue derived from income taxes. Consequently, New Zealand's tax structure came to be viewed internationally as one of the least distortionary.

State-owned enterprises and privatisation

When the fourth Labour Government assumed office, the government owned and operated many services that could potentially operate in private hands or at least in a business-like fashion. These services included the Bank of New Zealand, Air New Zealand, an international shipping line and all electricity generation and distribution facilities. During its time in power, the fourth Labour Government established such activities as SOEs. In its 1984 briefing to the incoming government, *Economic Management*, the Treasury had given initial advice regarding the merits of placing some government activities on a more commercial footing. At this time, other governments around the world had begun to step back from the control and ownership of many previously state-owned and operated assets. For example, under Margaret Thatcher's leadership, the Conservative Government in the United Kingdom was implementing a major program of commercialisation and privatisation of government activities (Abromeit 1988; Jenkinson and Mayer 1988). Douglas (1993: 178) recalled:

> My first attempt to obtain agreement on a comprehensive approach to State-owned enterprise reform was in May 1985. I wanted to transform them into competitive State-owned businesses by removing their monopoly status wherever possible, and transferring any of their non-commercial obligations to other government agencies. Managers could then become personally accountable for SOE performance.

The view was that many government activities that could and should operate on a commercial basis and face competition were actually a drain on public resources. Further, those presiding over them lacked accountability for their decisions.

In December 1985, the government announced the principles it would apply to SOEs in the future, which were subsequently incorporated into legislation. The attorney-general and deputy prime minister Geoffrey Palmer developed an umbrella statute to streamline the reform process. This became the *State-Owned Enterprises Act*, adopted in December 1986, which came into effect in April 1987. At that time, nine government entities became SOEs. In December 1987, Douglas announced the government's intention to significantly reduce its debt position through a program of asset sales. During the next two years, major privatisations included the Bank of New Zealand, Petrocorp, New Zealand Steel, the New Zealand Shipping Corporation, State Insurance and Telecom.

The changing status of these operations certainly resulted in greater efficiency, which was manifest in both lower production costs and improvements in customer services. There were two downsides. First, the privatisation process did not run smoothly in several instances. Second, the promotion of more efficient operations in several large industries contributed in the short term to increased levels of unemployment. These two matters tended to obscure many of the benefits that resulted for New Zealand from the SOE and privatisation agenda (Brash 1996).

Monetary policy

Following the exchange rate crisis of July 1984, the fourth Labour Government was keen to develop policy approaches that would, as Douglas put it, 'Muldoon-proof' key aspects of monetary policy (quoted in Brash 1996: 14). Two actions were taken towards this goal, both of which removed much of the potential for any government to capriciously intervene in the workings of the broader monetary system.

In March 1985, Douglas announced the floating of the New Zealand dollar. This was a significant move and followed discussions between the Reserve Bank and the Prime Minister and Cabinet (Lange 2005: 207). If the New Zealand dollar had been floating in 1984, the exchange rate crisis of July 1984 would never have happened. Under the change, the Reserve Bank would no longer announce official buy and sell rates for the New Zealand dollar, but it was not required to withdraw completely from the market and would still be instructed to meet the government's requirements for foreign exchange. This was important for debt servicing. The bank could also monitor market trends and developments through minor market dealings and retained the option of entering the market during episodes of undue volatility to smooth exchange rate fluctuations (Reserve Bank of New Zealand 1986: 14).

In May 1989, the government introduced the Reserve Bank of New Zealand Bill into parliament, where it was passed unanimously. This legislation was world-leading with respect to the level of independence that it accorded to the Reserve Bank. In subsequent years, many governments developed legislative frameworks for their central banks that were closely informed by the New Zealand model (Bernanke and Mishkin 1997). The legislation was based on several key principles. It was acknowledged that monetary policy can affect the rate of inflation; however, monetary policy should not be manipulated to promote faster rates of growth or to sustain higher levels of inflation. The *Reserve Bank Act* explicitly stated that monetary policy must be used for the sole task of 'achieving and maintaining stability in the general level of prices'. In practice, written policy target agreements are signed between the Minister of Finance and the bank's governor. This target was generally kept in the range of 0 to 2 per cent per annum. The framework has proven very successful and, since its enactment, inflation in New Zealand has been kept under tight control—a major improvement over the situation in the period from the mid-1970s to the mid-1980s.

Delivery, legitimacy and endurance

The public policy innovations introduced by the fourth Labour Government have stood the test of time. While unemployment continued to rise during the government's term in office, inflation was slowly brought into check. Likewise, the government's debt situation slowly came under control, although little debt reduction happened before 1990. Here, we discuss the delivery, legitimacy and endurance of the innovations.

All the innovations endured—including the privatisation of government assets, which was the most controversial. With the exception of the privatisation program, they were accorded a high degree of legitimacy from the outset. It was well understood that market interventions had become burdensome and frequently ineffectual during the Muldoon years. While the removal of subsidies to the farming sector brought a share of pain, it was relieved by removal of many import protections. The move to a more independent Reserve Bank came after several years of a floating New Zealand dollar, which was also viewed as a key element of market liberalisation; it was therefore uncontroversial.

With respect to changes in the taxation system, the flattening of the income tax scale was generally viewed favourably. Some members of the Labour Party expressed concern that this was benefiting the wealthy and middle class over the lower classes, but this was a minority view. Likewise, there were inevitable complaints about the introduction of the GST. However, the comprehensive nature of the tax, and the efforts made to compensate the worst-affected consumers via incremental adjustments in welfare benefits, ensured the grumbling rapidly dissipated. The creation of SOEs also acquired rapid legitimacy. While it added to unemployment levels, the move to achieve greater efficiency in these organisations also resulted in improved service provision for citizen consumers.

The privatisation program was much more problematic because asset sales can be complicated; implementation challenges were greater in this element of the reforms than in any other discussed above. Considerable privatisation was initiated before 1990, and the National Government elected in 1990 continued the program. This suggests that, overall, privatisation was a policy success. But it created major debate within the Labour Government and the Labour Party. Further, while this initiative was under way, Douglas was strongly advocating in Cabinet for major changes to social policy. In this, he was spurred on by advice from the Treasury, as illustrated in *Government Management* (1987). Lange's serious misgivings regarding the merits of privatisation and radical proposals for changes to social policy created a rift between him and Douglas.

Problems with privatisation

During his budget speech in parliament in June 1987, Douglas announced a program of asset sales to reduce government debt. Earlier in the year, an experiment with partial privatisation had occurred, when the government allowed the Bank of New Zealand to raise capital through selling shares to the public. Reflecting concerns within the broader Labour Party, Lange was uneasy with this new development that Douglas was introducing. Following the Labour Government's reelection in August 1987, Lange made changes in his Cabinet that were designed to reduce Douglas's influence. While Douglas remained the Minister of Finance, those who had supported him as associate finance ministers were moved to other portfolios. One of those was Richard Prebble, who became the Minister for State-Owned Enterprises. Other elements of the Cabinet changes were designed to protect the social policy portfolios from major reform efforts.

As the SOEs minister, Prebble received his advice from the Treasury and he remained close in his engagements with Douglas. Given Douglas's prior announcement to privatise assets, it now fell to Prebble to preside over the process of getting various SOEs ready for sale.

Concerned by how asset sales might be perceived by the Labour Party and the broader public, in November 1988, Lange moved to establish a review of the privatisation process. His view was that ministers needed to be distanced from the process, to avoid perceptions of undue influence and corruption. When Prebble refused to consult the Labour Party over the sale of the Shipping Corporation, Lange removed him from his role as SOEs minister. In a subsequent television interview, Prebble said Lange was acting like a dictator. The inevitable happened: Lange sacked Prebble from the Cabinet. The privatisation process continued. Views on how it faired are mixed. Jarrod Kerr and colleagues (2007) provide a positive assessment, noting that the asset sales greatly increased the size and value of the New Zealand share market and those who bought shares in privatised companies tended to receive better returns than the market average. Others have been more critical. For example, Brian Gaynor (2000) has suggested the government could have received more revenue from its various partial and full asset sales had it managed the sales process more carefully. A common view is that several wealthy New Zealanders and their companies benefited greatly from the privatisation process at the expense of the government and taxpayers (Jesson 1999). Certainly, there was a degree of exuberance and naivety about early aspects of the process. A fair assessment would be that some sales were poorly managed. The government needed to rely on third parties to coordinate sales, and this did not always go well. But there was also a lot of learning during the implementation process, which stretched over more than a decade.

Things fall apart

Although few significant changes were made to social policy during the period 1984–90, discussion of social policy became a site of significant contestation within the fourth Labour Government. Douglas and Treasury advisors went to great lengths to dominate social policy discussions. When Douglas launched the privatisation program in December 1987, he also announced plans to reduce the income tax to a flat rate and to introduce a Guaranteed Minimum Family Income. This announcement was viewed as cutting across more consultative efforts regarding the direction of social policy—most notably, the work of the Royal Commission on Social Policy. In January 1988, Lange curtailed the flat tax and Guaranteed Minimum Family Income changes. From then on, tensions between Lange and Douglas precipitated the demise of the fourth Labour Government.

A month after sacking Prebble from Cabinet in November 1988, Lange accepted Douglas's reluctant resignation. In August 1989, when his Labour caucus colleagues voted for Douglas to return to Cabinet, Lange resigned as prime minister. The reform agenda of the fourth Labour Government ended. Former deputy prime minister Geoffrey Palmer became prime minister, lasting in the role for little over a year. He was succeeded by Mike Moore in September 1990. The next month, Moore led the Labour Party into the general election, which the Labour Party lost in a landslide to the National Party. Once acrimony between Lange and Douglas boiled over into Cabinet, the fourth Labour Government lost confidence in itself and, inevitably, the confidence of the electorate.

The 1990 election was not a referendum on the appropriateness of the fourth Labour Government's public policy innovations. Rather, it was a referendum on which politicians could now most effectively lead the government into the future. Even though a new government came to power in 1990, it did nothing to overturn the policies Labour had introduced. Indeed, the new National Government took those policies as foundations and built on them.

Analysis and conclusions

In the early 1980s, global events and the New Zealand Government's responses to them drove the country towards economic collapse. Debt, inflation and unemployment grew. To address the crisis, the fourth Labour Government introduced public policy innovations in the style of what came to be called New Public Management. The innovations set New Zealand on a path towards much improved economic conditions. Since then, governments displaying a variety of ideological commitments have had opportunities to abandon the innovations. While there has certainly been evolution and adjustment, the policies introduced in those years remain in place. That said, as a small trading nation, New Zealand will always be vulnerable to changing global market conditions. The policy innovations clarified what actions might be taken to maintain broadly positive economic conditions in the face of continuous challenges.

Given the unique nature of New Zealand democracy, its location and its economic foundations, care must be taken in drawing lessons for other countries from this policy success. In closing, we suggest several lessons for policy designers. Periods can arise when those in power are unwilling to make policy changes, even when evidence suggests change is necessary. When this happened in New Zealand in the early 1980s, key advisors kept working at developing their arguments for why change was needed and what changes would be most appropriate. They prepared for a change of government. The relationship between the Treasury and Roger Douglas was fundamental.

The case also seems to support the view that policy innovation occurs when political actors take advantage of windows of opportunity (Kingdon 1995). In 1984, it was clear the old ways of managing the economy were no longer working. There was no hope that economic circumstances would improve by doing more of what had been done in the past. What makes this case particularly interesting is that, when we stand back from the cut and thrust of politics of the period, we see a major battle of ideas was in play. New ideas about how to govern an economy were rapidly implemented. The short-term benefits that came from the policy innovations were sufficient to sustain their political legitimacy. That legitimacy ensured the innovations remained in place and could subsequently deliver longer-term benefits.

This case also underscores that sound policy innovation takes time. Time is required to determine appropriate directions forward and to consult about design issues. Through listening and working with others—even those who might have strong objections to a proposal—it is possible for advocates of change to improve policy design and build a strong coalition to support change. The converse is also true: trying to win debates without listening closely to others can derail change efforts and generate mistrust.

Lost trust can be difficult to regain. The policy innovations discussed here certainly exhibited intellectual coherence; however, intellectual coherence is not a substitute for building and maintaining a powerful supportive coalition.

Given the pressures that central figures in the fourth Labour Government confronted, and others they created by pursuing a fast-paced reform program, perhaps it was inevitable that various forms of interpersonal acrimony would develop. Further, given that the Labour Party had many members who continued to believe in the power of government to do good things in society, in retrospect, it is hardly surprising that big clashes occurred in Cabinet. It is fruitful to reflect on this. What approaches to policy discussion, the implementation of the privatisation program and overall political management might have allowed this government to serve for longer? Looking back, Douglas took the view that moving rapidly on multiple policy fronts was the only way to secure fundamental changes. However, subsequent New Zealand governments have achieved important reforms while moving more slowly and working to ensure implementation is well managed. For example, the National Party–led coalition of 2009–17 established a new program of privatisation of government assets. Important work was done that drew on lessons from the past and that met considerable success. This suggests moving rapidly is not the only game in town; careful implementation planning is just as important as careful policy design.

The policy innovations introduced from 1984 to 1990 also demonstrate that achieving success in one area of policy innovation can sometimes lay strong foundations for achieving success in others. The reformers in New Zealand learned a lot about how the operations of the core public service could be improved through placing state trading activities on a commercial footing. They desired to transfer those lessons to social policy design. However, that pursuit of intellectual coherence was undercut by a lack of sophistication in the assessment of the political feasibility of such an agenda.

In sum, we judge New Zealand's economic turnaround to have been a major public policy success. Innovative public policy changes catalysed economic growth. In the process, much was learned about the role of government in the economy, how government might be effectively managed and how advisory systems might be structured to attend both to present challenges and to stewardship for the future. While problems certainly arose, the principles of policy design pursued during this reform period continue to be of relevance in many areas of public policy, well beyond those we have discussed.

References

Abromeit, H. 1988. 'British privatisation policy.' *Parliamentary Affairs* 41(1): 68–85.

Bernanke, B. S. and Mishkin, F. S. 1997. 'Inflation targeting: A new framework for monetary policy?' *Journal of Economic Perspectives* 11(2): 97–116. doi.org/10.1257/jep.11.2.97.

Bollard, A. 1994. 'New Zealand.' In J. Williamson (ed.), *The Political Economy of Policy Reform*. Washington, DC: Institute for International Economics.

Brash, D. 1996. New Zealand's remarkable reforms. Address to the Fifth Annual Hayek Memorial Lecture, London, 4 June. Available from: www.rbnz.govt.nz/research-and-publications/speeches/1996/speech1996-06-04.

Clements, K. 2015. *Back from the Brink: The creation of a nuclear-free New Zealand.* Wellington: Bridget Williams Books.

Dalziel, P. 2002. 'New Zealand's economic reforms: An assessment.' *Review of Political Economy* 14(1): 31–46. doi.org/10.1080/09538250120102750.

Dalziel, P. C. 1986. 'The 1984 economic summit conference: A search for policy objectives.' *New Zealand Economic Papers* 20(1): 41–51.

Douglas, R. 1993. *Unfinished Business*. Auckland: Random House.

Easton, B. H. 1997. *The Commercialisation of New Zealand.* Auckland: Auckland University Press.

Economic Summit Conference (ESC) Secretariat 1984. *Economic Summit Conference: Proceedings and conference papers.* Wellington: Government Printer.

Evans, L., Grimes, A., Wilkinson, B. and Teece, D. 1996. 'Economic reform in New Zealand 1984–95: The pursuit of efficiency.' *Journal of Economic Literature* 34(4): 1856–902.

Fougere, G. 1989. 'Sport, culture and identity: The case of rugby football.' In D. Novitz and B. Wilmott (eds), *Culture and Identity in New Zealand.* Wellington: P. D. Hasselberg, Government Printer.

Friedman, M. 1962. *Capitalism and Freedom*. Chicago: University of Chicago Press.

Friedman, M. 1977. 'Nobel lecture: Inflation and unemployment.' *Journal of Political Economy* 85(3): 451–72. doi.org/10.1086/260579.

Gaynor, B. 2000. 'How asset sales went wrong.' *New Zealand Herald*, 30 June.

Goldfinch, S. 1998. 'Remaking New Zealand's economic policy: Institutional elites as radical innovators 1984–1993.' *Governance* 11(2): 177–207. doi.org/10.1111/0952-1895.00065.

Goldfinch, S. and Malpass, D. 2007. 'The Polish shipyard: Myth, economic history and economic policy reform in New Zealand.' *Australian Journal of Politics & History* 53(1): 118–37. doi.org/10.1111/j.1467-8497.2007.00446.x.

Greasley, D. and Oxley, L. 2000. 'Outside the club: New Zealand's economic growth, 1870–1993.' *International Review of Applied Economics* 14(2): 173–92. doi.org/10.1080/02692170050024732.

Greenspan, A. 2008. *The Age of Turbulence: Adventures in a new world*. New York: Penguin.

Hawke, G. R. 1985. *The Making of New Zealand: An economic history*. Cambridge: Cambridge University Press.

Hood, C. 1991. 'A public management for all seasons?' *Public Administration* 69(1): 3–19.

Jenkinson, T. and Mayer, C. 1988. 'The privatisation process in France and the UK.' *European Economic Review* 32(2–3): 482–90. doi.org/10.1016/0014-2921(88)90194-8.

Jesson, B. 1999. *Only Their Purpose is Mad: The money men take over New Zealand.* Palmerston North, NZ: The Dunmore Press.

Kelsey, J. 1997. *The New Zealand Experiment: A world model for structural adjustment?* Wellington: Bridget Williams Books.

Kerr, J., Qiu, M. and Rose, L. C. 2007. 'Privatisation in New Zealand and Australia: An empirical analysis.' *Managerial Finance* 34(1): 41–52. doi.org/10.1108/03074350810838217.

Kingdon, J. W. 1995. *Agendas, Alternatives and Publics Policies*. 2nd edn. New York: Harper Collins.

Lange, D. 2005. *My Life*. Auckland: Viking/Penguin.

Larner, W. 1997. '"A means to an end": Neoliberalism and state processes in New Zealand.' *Studies in Political Economy* 52(1): 7–38. doi.org/10.1080/19187033.1997.11675320.

Mintrom, M. and Boston, J. forthcoming. 'From social protection to social investment in Australia and New Zealand.' In K. Baehler and J. Straussman (eds), *The Oxford International Handbook of Public Administration for Social Policy: Promising practices and emerging challenges*. Oxford: Oxford University Press.

New Zealand Government 1984. *View from the Summit: A look at the '84 economic summit conference*. Wellington: Government Printer.

New Zealand Herald 2005. 'David Lange, in his own words.' *New Zealand Herald*, 15 August.

Oliver, W. H. 1988. 'Social policy in New Zealand: An historical overview.' In New Zealand. Royal Commission on Social Policy (ed.), *The April Report. Volume 1*. Wellington: Government Printer.

Polaschek, R. J. 1958. *Government Administration in New Zealand*. Wellington: New Zealand Institute of Public Administration.

Reserve Bank of New Zealand (various years). 'New Zealand economic chronology.' In *Reserve Bank Bulletin*. Wellington: Reserve Bank of New Zealand.

The Treasury 1984. *Economic Management*. Wellington: Government Printer.

The Treasury 1987. *Government Management*. Wellington: Government Printer.

Yergin, D. and Stanislaw, J. 2002. *The Commanding Heights: The battle for the world economy*. New York: Basic Books.

16

Nuclear-free New Zealand: Contingency, contestation and consensus in public policymaking

David Capie

Introduction

On 4 June 1987, the New Zealand Parliament passed the *New Zealand Nuclear Free Zone, Disarmament and Arms Control Act* by 39 votes to 29. The legislation marked the culmination of a decades-long effort by a disparate group of peace and environmental activists to prevent nuclear weapons from entering New Zealand's territory. More than 30 years later, the law remains in force, it has bipartisan support and it is frequently touted as a key symbol of New Zealand's national identity.

In some ways, it should be puzzling that New Zealand has come to be so closely associated with staunch opposition to nuclear arms. The country is far removed from key strategic territory and even at the height of the Cold War was one of the least likely countries anywhere to suffer a nuclear attack. The fact the adoption of the antinuclear policy led to the end of New Zealand's alliance relationship with the United States under the Australia, New Zealand, United States Security (ANZUS) Treaty—an agreement once described as the 'richest prize' in New Zealand diplomacy—only adds to the puzzle (Catalinac 2010). How, then, did a group of activists and politicians propel an issue into the public consciousness and, despite the staunch opposition of the most powerful country in the world, work to see it enshrined in legislation?

This chapter explores nuclear-free New Zealand as an example of a policy success. It does so in four parts. First, it examines the social and political contexts in which the policy emerged. Unlike some cases in this book, there was no single moment of 'design' when the nuclear-free policy was created in response to a clearly defined problem. Rather, opposition to nuclear weapons and nuclear power evolved over decades and advocates pressed for a number of different policy initiatives. In the 1970s and 1980s, the idea that New Zealand should be nuclear-free found a new political class willing to embrace it and take it to the heart of electoral politics. Even then, it took some contingent events to generate widespread public support and become law.

Second, the chapter considers the decision to embed the nuclear-free policy in legislation. Why was this path taken when previous governments had been happy to issue statements of declaratory policy? What made a legislative commitment—something strongly opposed by New Zealand's allies—the preferred option? I argue that the nuclear-free case reminds us that even chaotic policymaking processes can produce powerful policy. Third, the chapter explores the nuclear-free policy's durability and legitimacy. How has a policy that was opposed by all of New Zealand's closest security partners and one of the country's two major political parties come to have deep bipartisan support? And how have New Zealand's antinuclear 'credentials' been used by successive governments as a way of branding the country and giving it a special voice in international affairs?

Before exploring the origins of New Zealand's nuclear-free movement, it is necessary to clarify precisely what policy success is under consideration here. Different parts of what is sometimes assumed to be a monolithic 'antinuclear movement' had quite distinct goals as they agitated for action from successive governments in the decades before 1987 (Leadbeater 2013). Some sought to prevent nuclear-armed vessels from entering New Zealand territory. Others were equally concerned about the perceived risks of nuclear energy, especially the nuclear propulsion systems used on ships and submarines. Some advocates argued nuclear-free was a policy designed only for New Zealand and 'not for export', while others felt New Zealand should also advocate internationally for complete nuclear disarmament—a goal that clearly remains elusive.

For the purposes of this chapter, I will focus on the substance of the policy embedded in the 1987 legislation—namely, a legal prohibition on nuclear weapons and nuclear-powered vessels entering New Zealand. Where did this policy come from? How did it become law? And what has made it popular, durable and legitimate? I argue that, if policy successes can be measured by reference to programmatic, process, political and endurance aspects, the nuclear-free policy was far from successful in programmatic or process terms. However, it has been astonishingly successful in political terms and has proved remarkably durable.

Identifying the problem, demanding a response

New Zealanders' antipathy to nuclear weapons can be traced back to the early Cold War. While the use of atomic bombs against Hiroshima and Nagasaki to end World War II was generally welcomed by a war-weary public, testing of nuclear weapons—especially more powerful thermonuclear weapons—in the Pacific Ocean gradually began to provoke opposition from across New Zealand society. High-yield American atmospheric tests in Micronesia created effects visible even thousands of kilometres away. David Lange (1990: 10) remembered that, when he was young, one test turned the sky over Auckland blood red and caused it to pulse with red and white beams of light, leaving him with 'a chill sense of dread'.

The 15-megaton American 'Castle Bravo' test, which destroyed Bikini Atoll and contaminated the Japanese fishing vessel *Lucky Dragon* in March 1954, sparked a new public consciousness about the effects of radioactive fallout. It provided 'the key impetus for the emergence of [an] anti-nuclear weapons movement in many countries', including New Zealand (Rudig 1990: 54–5). As Malcolm Templeton notes, from April 1954 onwards, 'there was a dramatic increase … in the correspondence [about this issue] received by the Prime Minister from organisations and private citizens in New Zealand'. The opposition came from a broad swathe of society: '[C]hurches, trade unions, Labour Party branches and individuals wrote letters or signed petitions calling for a ban on testing and on the H-bomb itself' (Templeton 2006: 66).

If there was modest but steadily growing opposition to American and British nuclear testing, antipathy intensified in 1962 when France indicated it would relocate its nuclear testing program from the Sahara Desert to French Polynesia. The New Zealand embassy in Paris was told to inform the French Government that testing in the Pacific 'would arouse greater concern' than US and UK testing at Christmas and Johnston islands

> because there is less obvious need for such tests in the interests of Western security and because there could be greater risk of fallout drifting to New Zealand territory and Western Samoa. (Templeton 2006: 108)

In August 1963, more than 80,000 New Zealanders signed a petition asking the government to take the necessary steps to 'ban the bomb south of the line' and keep the southern hemisphere free of nuclear arms (McKinnon 1999: 148). The Federation of Labour together with the Methodist Church began to organise a boycott of French goods (Templeton 2006: 117).

A central driver of the early antinuclear protest movement was fear of the health and environmental consequences of testing. While the New Zealand Government provided naval assistance to British 'Grapple' tests in the Gilbert and Ellice Islands (now Kiribati), it also sought assurances that fallout from the tests posed no threat to New Zealand (Maclellan 2018: 205–19). Concerns about pollution from French atmospheric testing at Moruroa led to public anger when higher than normal levels of strontium-90 were found in milk in Samoa and New Zealand in the late 1960s (Williams 2016). By the 1970s, a thriving environmental movement, including groups such as Greenpeace and Friends of the Earth, had adopted the issue. In 1971, the National Party Government told the United States it would not accept visits by nuclear-powered ships until Washington agreed to accept liability in the event of a nuclear accident. Congressional legislation accepting such liability was passed in 1974, but Labour was in power by then and the government decided not to invite any warships into New Zealand waters. A further symbol of the growing concern about the risk posed by nuclear power came in 1976, when a petition presented under the banner of the 'Coalition for Non-Nuclear Futures' and signed by 333,000 people was presented to parliament.

If concerns about the health and environmental risks posed by nuclear testing and energy dominated the early years of New Zealand's antinuclear movement, fears of nuclear war between the major powers began to play a greater role as the Cold War went on. In the late 1950s, the first

New Zealand branches of the Campaign for Nuclear Disarmament (CND) were formed, inspired by the British peace movement's Easter March to the nuclear weapons facility at Aldermaston (Locke 1992: 170). Kevin Clements (2015: 101) says the New Zealand branches of the CND were 'initially very imitative' and their appeal to younger people benefited from the radical reputation of the British movement. The New Zealand CND grew dramatically from 1961 to 1963 and began to focus its advocacy on one policy goal: the creation of a nuclear-free zone in the southern hemisphere. New Zealand towns and cities began to declare themselves 'nuclear-free' following similar moves overseas. The Holyoake Government remained unenthusiastic, but the 1963 Partial Test Ban Treaty banned most atmospheric tests and took some of the energy out of the protests. (It was quickly revived by the resumption of French testing in Polynesia in 1966.)

Concerns about the threat of nuclear war reached a peak in the early 1980s. After the détente of the 1970s, the Soviet invasion of Afghanistan and the election of Ronald Reagan as US president launched a renewed phase of strategic confrontation between the United States and the Soviet Union, with a concomitant fear of catastrophic war. Reagan's use of the rhetoric of the 'Evil Empire' and jokes such as the infamous 'we begin bombing in five minutes' served only to increase tensions.

The 'new Cold War' of the early 1980s included the development of counterforce strategies to fight a limited nuclear war and the deployment of new weapons such as the MX missile. Washington had plans to test fire the MX with a splashdown in the Tasman Sea in 1983 but, after a backlash from parts of the Australian Labor Party and peace groups, eventually withdrew the plans. The US decision to deploy short-range Pershing II and cruise missiles in West Germany similarly prompted huge public protests organised by the CND. There can be little doubt about the role of the European peace movement in inspiring its New Zealand counterparts. Peace groups began to argue that the transit of nuclear weapons through New Zealand on US vessels made the country complicit in the doctrine of 'mutually assured destruction' and even made New Zealand a nuclear target. The theory of 'nuclear winter' also found followers, raising the possibility that New Zealand's remote location would not spare it from the destruction from a limited nuclear war in the northern hemisphere (Mydans 1988).

This convergence of health, environmental and strategic concerns prompted what Kennedy Graham (1987: 223) has called a 'metamorphosis' in New Zealanders' threat perceptions. A country that for most of its history had sought protection from a great and powerful state increasingly asked itself whether its alliance with the United States brought greater risks than rewards. A 1986 defence committee of inquiry established by the government carried out a survey asking people what they regarded as the 'greatest present worry'. Nuclear war was identified by 48 per cent of respondents as the greatest threat to New Zealand (55 per cent of younger people) compared with just 11 per cent who feared an armed invasion of the country (Clements 2015: 158).

The social and political contexts

If there was a growing sense of public opposition to nuclear weapons, New Zealand governments were still cautious about protesting too vigorously or enacting measures that might upset relations with important international powers. This began to change in the early 1970s with the emergence of a group of activists and politicians who came of political age during the second half of the 1960s. This group included some influential figures in the fourth Labour Government, including Helen Clark, Jim Anderton, Richard Northey and Phil Goff.

The most important issue uniting these groups was opposition to the Vietnam War, which 'raised important questions about New Zealand's role in the world and about the relationship with the United States that lay at the heart of its post-war foreign policy' (Rabel 1991: 96). Again, Clements (2015) notes that many of the New Zealand protests were derivative, including the antiwar 'teach-ins' inspired by US groups such as Students for a Democratic Society. But, alongside Vietnam, a broader range of social issues also mobilised young people and caused them to demand the country move in a new political direction. These included environmentalism (such as the campaign to prevent the use of Lake Manapouri for a massive hydroelectricity project), demands for women's equality and greater rights for Māori and new Pacific migrants. As Rabel (1991: 99) puts it: '[T]hese issues and the groups that now promoted them could not be easily accommodated by the old political order.'

Jock Phillips similarly identifies the emergence of an influential minority who were increasingly important in shaping New Zealand opinion:

> Over half of the 1987 Labour MPs had previously been teachers, lecturers, researchers, scientists or broadcasters—people who were concerned with transmitting ideas ... These people came to political power in 1984 with the youngest and best-educated cabinet in New Zealand's history; they replaced an administration that in its early years had contained seven people who fought in World War II. (Phillips 1991: 195)

This group embodied a new nationalism based on New Zealand's South Pacific identity. This, Phillips says:

> [C]hanged our perception of the threats to New Zealand. Communist China, Soviet Russia, and Communism in Southeast Asia do not seem like credible dangers. They are seen as inhabiting a very distant and different world. Instead, when we look out to the South Pacific we see the looming shadow of France exploding atomic bombs and suppressing the Kanak movement; we look upon American ships and bombs as dangerous and unnecessary interlopers in this part of the world. (Phillips 1991: 197)

Gerald Hensley (2013: 207), who served as a senior official to prime ministers Lange and Sir Robert Muldoon and was an avowed opponent of the nuclear-free policy, comes to a similar conclusion, saying, 'there is no doubt the ANZUS quarrel marked a revolution in New Zealand's outlook on the world'. This was part of a broader political shift. It included the sense of shock brought about by the United Kingdom's entry into the European Common Market in 1973, as well as public opposition towards the war in Vietnam.

> [T]he changes in foreign policy were the manifestations and not the drivers of a deeper shift in national attitudes. Over the previous decade a comfortable national consensus had splintered into warring fragments, in angry arguments over economic policy, the environment, women's rights, the meaning of the Treaty of Waitangi and even that patriotic icon, rugby football. New Zealand's old image of itself had gone for good; something new and equally compelling was needed to take its place. An uneasy nationalism floated in the air, like gas in a mine, and ANZUS was the spark that touched it off. Foreign policy became the battleground in the war for a new national identity. (Hensley 2013: 305)

Contingency

The salience of a problem also owes much to contingency, and several events in the late 1970s and 1980s had a dramatic effect on the way New Zealanders saw the nuclear issue, giving the issue much greater public prominence and also widening the group of people opposed to nuclear power and weapons testing.

One such factor was a series of highly publicised accidents that released radioactive pollution into the atmosphere and called into question the safety of civilian reactors. These included the Three Mile Island leak in Pennsylvania in March 1979, which led to the creation of a 32-kilometre evacuation zone and eventually cost more than US$1 billion to clean up. Much worse was to come in April 1986, when an explosion at the Chernobyl nuclear power plant in Ukraine killed between 30 and 50 people, forced more than 100,000 to flee and led to the release of a radioactive cloud across Western Europe. It was the first accident to be rated a level seven (the highest possible) incident on the International Atomic Energy Agency's Nuclear Event Scale.[1]

A second pivotal event was the bombing of the Greenpeace vessel *Rainbow Warrior* in Auckland harbour on 10 July 1985, which killed a Portuguese photographer on board. This was quickly exposed as an act of state terrorism carried out by agents of the French Directorate-General for External Security. The New Zealand public—already angry about French nuclear testing—was outraged. The failure of the United States or the United Kingdom to condemn the French actions (the *Wall Street Journal* published an editorial sympathising with the French) further rankled and fed a sense that New Zealand was being picked on by the big powers (Capie 2009: 593). As Kevin Clements (2015: 116) put it, the bombing

> generated considerable public antagonism towards France, boosted support for the independence movement in New Caledonia/Kanaky, and reminded people of the contemptuous way in which French authorities had handled regional opposition towards the French Pacific nuclear programme for over twenty years.

1 A senior figure close to prime minister Jim Bolger was once asked why National had changed its position just weeks before the 1990 election and decided to support the nuclear-free policy. His one-word reply was: 'Chernobyl' (Author's conversation with former New Zealand official, 27 September 2018).

Design and choice

The election of the fourth Labour Government brought together this issue and a new generation of highly motivated politicians willing to question many longstanding orthodoxies in New Zealand's foreign and defence policy. It also coincided with a range of extraordinary events that generated greater public support for a nuclear-free stance as a manifestation of a new nationalism. But this convergence does not, on its own, explain the decision to enshrine the nuclear-free policy in law.

There were various efforts to express a nuclear-free policy over several decades before the passage of the New Zealand nuclear-free zone legislation in 1987. In 1957, responding to a comment by the British defence minister that it might be necessary to deploy nuclear weapons to defend members of the Southeast Asia Treaty Organization, then deputy prime minister Keith Holyoake said New Zealand would not be a base for the storage of nuclear weapons. Six years later, this time as prime minister, Holyoake repeated the commitment that the country would not acquire, use or store nuclear weapons. New Zealand's early ratification of the 1968 Nuclear Non-Proliferation Treaty turned those commitments into a formal legal obligation (Templeton 2006: 147).

However, these statements notwithstanding, New Zealand's opposition to nuclear weapons remained partial and waxed and waned depending in part on which party was in power. In 1963, the National Government voted against a UN resolution calling for the prohibition of nuclear weapons. Throughout the 1960s, 1970s and 1980s, US naval vessels capable of carrying nuclear weapons visited New Zealand ports. Indeed, it is widely believed, although has never been officially confirmed, US ships carrying nuclear weapons made port calls during this period. Governments from both major parties issued annual 'blanket approvals' for US ship visits, apart from those that were nuclear powered. In 1976, prime minister Muldoon said in response to a question about nuclear-propelled vessels that

> the warships that will visit New Zealand ports *may well carry nuclear weapons of the tactical or short-range variety* but so do conventionally powered warships. They do not carry long-range ballistic missiles. Such missiles are carried only by strategically armed submarines which will not come to New Zealand. (White 1997: 8; emphasis added)

As Robert White (1997: 8) notes, these remarks 'got him [Muldoon] into trouble with the Americans … concerned in case he was saying that no American submarines would be allowed to visit, a confusion he hastily corrected'. A note from the prime minister's department in October 1983 concerning the planned visit of the nuclear-powered submarine USS *Phoenix* said: '[I]t is almost certainly equipped with anti-submarine missiles, some of which probably have nuclear warheads on them' (cited in White 1997: 11).

There were several attempts to enact a nuclear-free policy in legislation prior to 1987, although none was successful. In August 1983, the leader of the small Social Credit Party, Bruce Beetham, introduced a Bill with such an aim, which was referred to a parliamentary select committee. Labour MP Richard Prebble then introduced his own Nuclear Free New Zealand Bill. The vote in parliament saw two government MPs cross the floor to support the opposition and, although the Bill was defeated by one vote, it prompted then prime minister Muldoon to call the snap election in which the Lange Labour Government was elected.

There were at least two distinct reasons peace activists and some in the Labour Party wanted the nuclear-free policy enshrined in legislation. First, the National Party pledged that if it were reelected it would ensure New Zealand rejoined ANZUS. It claimed it would be doing so while upholding the antinuclear position, although precisely how it would achieve this was never persuasively explained, other than by saying National would trust the United States and United Kingdom to respect New Zealand Government policy. Unsurprisingly, the nuclear-free movement was not willing to go along on this basis. Setting the policy down in law would obviously make it harder for it to be overturned in the future.

Second, those in the peace movement and on the left of the Labour Party were also suspicious about the commitment to the policy of some in the Lange Government (Clements 2015: 132–4). This was particularly the case between the election in July 1984 and early 1985, when there were exploratory efforts to see whether a compromise might be found that would allow US ships to visit, without requiring Washington to breach its policy of neither confirm nor deny. Lange certainly gave US officials the impression he was open to a compromise that would allow US vessels to visit New Zealand if the government could conclude they were not nuclear armed (Lange was also well known to be less concerned about nuclear propulsion). As part of these efforts, by late 1984, the United

States had agreed to send a vessel to test the legislation. The USS *Buchanan*, a Charles F. Adams–class frigate, was not nuclear powered and almost certainly not nuclear armed. However, Lange did not share information about the vessel or the proposed visit with his Cabinet colleagues and instead disappeared for a visit to Tokelau, where he was incommunicado.

Some in the party worried Lange was going to water down the nuclear-free policy. On 24 January 1985, Margaret Wilson, president of the Labour Party, met with backbench MPs Clark, Wilde and Anderton, and they agreed with a formulation that would leave no room for ambiguity about whether a ship was nuclear armed. The next day, the Labour Party National Executive endorsed the definition, which demanded that any ship would be banned from New Zealand waters if it were 'capable of carrying nuclear weapons' (Wilson 1989: 65). In her memoir, Wilson recalls: '[I]t seemed important to us [the National Executive of the Labour Party] to remain firm that there was no compromise, there was no ability to negotiate policy.' Helen Clark had the same aim. Interviewed by Michael Bassett (2002), Clark said the plan was 'to lock the Government into its policy'.

Lange returned to New Zealand from Tokelau on 28 January and went immediately into a Cabinet meeting where he discovered his colleagues were now interpreting the nuclear-free policy as a ban on any vessels capable of carrying nuclear weapons. The USS *Buchanan*'s antisubmarine rockets meant it was capable of carrying weapons, even if the official advice from the defence department and the External Intelligence Bureau was that it was unlikely to be doing so. This notwithstanding, the strict interpretation pressed by Wilson and her colleagues prevailed. Lange lamented later that he found himself 'in a minority of one' (Hensley 2013: 109). Opposed by the broader caucus and the Labour Party leadership, Lange dropped his plans for compromise. The *Buchanan* was denied entry. When the US refused to nominate another vessel, the die was cast. In February, a relatively junior US state department official, Bill Brown, was sent to meet the New Zealand prime minister while he was in Los Angeles to inform him the United States was ending most forms of intelligence and military cooperation with New Zealand.

Legitimacy and endurance

The *Nuclear Free New Zealand Act* passed its third reading in parliament on 4 June 1987 and became law. On 15 August, Labour was returned to power in a landslide, winning 57 of the 97 seats. The nuclear issue was a major issue dividing the parties during the campaign, with National Party leader Jim Bolger calling the law 'an exercise in futility' and saying it did nothing to advance arms control or protect New Zealand from nuclear weapons (Evans 1987). National retained its opposition to the law until a few weeks before the 1990 election, when, worried by tightening polls, it reversed its policy, leading its defence spokesperson Don McKinnon to resign in protest.

Although National won the 1990 election, the prohibition against nuclear weapons remained uncontested. This was helped by the decision of the US administration of George H. W. Bush in 1991 to remove nuclear weapons from all US surface vessels. The challenge posed by the policy of 'neither confirm nor deny' was no longer relevant; the only obstacle to a resumption of visits was the ban on nuclear propulsion. Clearly of a mind to change this, the Bolger Government appointed a Special Committee on Nuclear Propulsion, which concluded that British and American nuclear-powered vessels were safe. But public opinion was still in favour of the ban and, as Kate Dewes (2012: 117) concludes: '[T]he report was so aggressively pro-nuclear the government did not risk using it and instead quietly buried it.'

The next major challenge to the policy did not come until the 2005 election, when newly elected National Party leader Don Brash raised the possibility of holding a referendum on the nuclear-free stance. National commissioned another review, which recommended that the law be repealed and replaced with a ban as a matter of policy only. In August 2005, Brash said National might change the law without a referendum if it had a 'clear mandate' to do so. And, during the 2005 election campaign, it emerged that, in January 2004, Brash had apparently told a visiting US congressional delegation that if he were elected, the nuclear-free policy would be 'gone by lunchtime'. After 15 years of relative peace, the nuclear issue was squarely back in the heart of electoral politics.

On the campaign trail, Labour prime minister Helen Clark used the difference over antinuclear policy as a stick to beat Brash. Launching Labour's foreign policy, Clark described the nuclear stance as

> an important symbol of New Zealand's values in the twenty-first century … New Zealand has built a reputation as a country which makes a strong contribution to international affairs and which is prepared to think and speak for itself. (New Zealand Labour Party 2005)

Her foreign minister, Phil Goff, said the antinuclear position was

> part of the way we see ourselves, part of the way we promote ourselves to the world—and for many New Zealanders it is also symbolic of New Zealand's right to make its own decisions. (quoted in Capie 2006: 322)

After National was narrowly defeated on election day, party strategist Murray McCully conceded foreign policy issues 'played a big part' in the outcome (Capie 2006: 326).

Brash was replaced as party leader with John Key, who quickly stated that if National were elected to government he had no plans to change the nuclear-free policy. McCully told US officials in February 2006 that the shift sought to 'clarify existing policy by removing any reference to a possible referendum on whether to repeal the legislation' (Wikileaks 2006). As a US embassy cable noted, however:

> While at first glance the potential change seems significant, in reality it was always unlikely National could meet the current policy's pre-condition of public support for a vote. It was even less likely the result would be a majority vote in favor of removing what many see as an iconic piece of legislation. (Wikileaks 2006)

In 2007, on the twentieth anniversary of the law, McCully conceded that the National Party did not easily embrace the nuclear-free legislation, but 'the retention of this legislation that is called iconic, and that is symbolic of our independence of thought and judgment in international affairs, is not in question' (New Zealand Parliament 2007).

On 8 June 2017, the New Zealand Parliament passed a motion to commemorate the thirtieth anniversary of the antinuclear legislation. It reflected the high degree of support for the policy among parties across the political spectrum. National Party foreign affairs minister Gerry Brownlee called the nuclear-free legislation 'a defining aspect of this country's international reputation' (Brownlee et al. 2017: 18671). Kennedy Graham (2017), a Green MP, called it 'something we all take pride in'. This convergence also underlined the remarkable shift that had taken place in New Zealand politics around the policy.

Analysis and conclusions

At one level, evaluating the programmatic success of New Zealand's nuclear-free policy is a fairly simple endeavour. Since the legislation was passed, no nuclear weapons or nuclear-powered vessels have entered New Zealand's territory. Since 1990, successive New Zealand governments from across the political spectrum have proclaimed their support for the law. Even as New Zealand and the United States moved to normalise their defence relations after 2006, there was no serious prospect that the legislation would be revoked or amended.

If New Zealand's position has remained consistent, the United States has, arguably, 'blinked'. Secretary of state Hillary Clinton visited New Zealand in 2010 and signed the 'Wellington Declaration', which set out a new program of joint security initiatives, mostly focused on nontraditional security issues in the South Pacific. In 2012, the Washington Declaration relaunched more traditional defence activities, including cooperating on 'deployable capabilities, in support of peace and security in the Asia-Pacific' (USNZ Council 2012). In 2012, the Royal New Zealand Navy was welcomed back to the largest US-led military exercise, the Rim of the Pacific (RIMPAC), in Hawai'i. A US Navy vessel, USS *Sampson*, berthed in New Zealand in 2016—the first in more than 30 years—and polls indicated 75 per cent of New Zealanders approved of the visit. Remarkably, in 2017, a Royal New Zealand Navy frigate, *Te Kaha*, was embedded with the nuclear-powered USS *Nimitz* aircraft carrier for operations in the Sea of Japan. New Zealand is not a formal US ally but now has closer defence relations with the United States than it has had for more than four decades. All of this has happened while New Zealand's nuclear-free policy remains in place.

Whether the policy has achieved 'valuable impacts' is more debatable. US surface vessels have not carried nuclear weapons since 1994. Given nuclear-powered, ballistic missile–carrying submarines rarely visit foreign ports, it is extremely unlikely nuclear weapons would have entered New Zealand territory after that date anyway—law or no law. If the policy was supposed to function as a symbol of opposition to nuclear weapons and deterrence more generally, arguably, it has had little to no impact. The number of de facto nuclear weapon states in the world has increased by three since 1987 (India, Pakistan and North Korea). Nuclear alliances continue to be salient for many states, including New Zealand's closest partner, Australia. Attitudes to nuclear power remain mixed, although concerns about climate change and carbon emissions have certainly improved the image of the industry in recent years.

Assessing the nuclear-free policy's success from a *process* perspective is less complicated. If opposition to nuclear weapons had emerged as a widely held position among New Zealanders by the 1970s, formal development of government policy after Labour won the 1984 election was chaotic and confused. Much of the blame here seems to belong to David Lange. The Cabinet meeting that led the government to turn away the USS *Buchanan* and commit to the 'nuclear-capable' formulation is one of the clearest examples. Lange shared almost no information about the ship visit he had encouraged and was away, incommunicado, for the week before one of the most consequential decisions in the country's history was taken. At the Cabinet meeting itself:

> no Ministers had been briefed and no Ministers had any papers on the [ship visit] request … In this case the methodical Cabinet process—circulation of papers, Cabinet committee consideration and decision in Cabinet itself were bypassed in the panic over party unity. (Hensley 2013: 106–7)

Amid the confusion, one group of backbenchers seized their moment and showed that clear policy formulation backed with strong arguments could make the difference in winning support for policy change.

Opinion polls showed New Zealanders wanted to have their cake and eat it, too: to ban 'nuclear ships' but to stay in ANZUS. If such a compromise were possible (and some in the fourth Labour Government believed it was) then such an aim was not well served by the policy process that led to the refusal of the USS *Buchanan*.

All this notwithstanding, it is hard to conclude that the policy has been anything other than an astonishing *political* success. One clear indicator is the way that even parties which originally opposed the nuclear-free position have recalibrated their stance to be more accommodating towards it. Indeed, rather than simply just tolerating the antinuclear position, there are striking examples of National Party governments going out of their way to play up the importance of New Zealand's antinuclear credentials. Jim Bolger, for example, who had vowed to reverse the policy until just a few weeks before the 1990 general election, told US president George H. W. Bush in a September 1991 meeting that 'New Zealand as an identified, high-profile, non-nuclear nation could play a constructive role in promoting the non-proliferation agenda which both New Zealand and the US pursued' (Bolger 1998: 149). In 1995, Bolger's government further embraced the antinuclear identity and took France to the International Court of Justice to try to end nuclear testing in Polynesia.

Arguably, this brand became even more valuable after 11 September 2001, as the United States became more anxious about nuclear proliferation and terrorists accessing weapons of mass destruction. In 2010, New Zealand was one of a group of nations invited to attend the first Nuclear Security Summit in Washington, DC. Ironically, as prime minister Key recalled: 'The first time President Obama rang me, the first thing he raised was New Zealand's anti-nuclear stance and the important role that that played in the world' (Young 2010). In 2017, the Key–English Government supported the development of the Nuclear Weapons Convention—a treaty to ban all nuclear arms—and supported it despite the opposition of the United States and Australia. In February 2018, Prime Minister Jacinda Ardern pledged that

> disarmament is as vital today as it was when Norman Kirk and David Lange proclaimed New Zealand's opposition to nuclear weapons and nuclear testing in the Pacific. In a modern context, the greatest challenge comes from North Korea, situated right here in our region. (Ardern 2018)

This case also shows that a test of a policy's durability can also emerge in surprising ways. The election of Brash as National Party leader in 2003—and his leaked comment that were he to become prime minister the policy would be 'gone by lunchtime'—thrust the nuclear issue back to the heart of electoral politics. It raised real questions about the extent of public support for the policy, especially given changes in world politics since 1987. But the fact the issue cost National votes and played an important role in its narrow defeat in the 2005 election left party leaders determined to take away what they saw as one of Labour's 'strongest weapons' (Wikileaks 2006). The result was the unconditional support for the status quo offered by new leader John Key in November 2006. The policy had become untouchable.

New Zealand's nuclear-free legislation emerged from a highly contested, confusing, even chaotic political and policymaking process and was helped in important ways by some remarkable, unanticipated events. Despite this, it has overcome political challenges, built a broad coalition of supporters and achieved something remarkable: it has come to be seen as something more than a policy—an untouchable symbol of independence and nationhood. There are perhaps few replicable lessons for other areas of public policy in New Zealand's nuclear-free experience, but, if nothing else, this case does illustrate that it is possible to bring about and sustain dramatic change, even when powerful international actors and entrenched bureaucratic interests favour the status quo.

References

Ardern, J. 2018. Speech to New Zealand Institute of International Affairs. 27 February. Wellington: New Zealand Government. Available from: www.beehive.govt.nz/speech/speech-new-zealand-institute-international-affairs-2.

Baker, R. W. (ed.) 1991. *Australia, New Zealand and the United States: Internal change and alliance relations in the ANZUS states.* New York: Praeger.

Bassett, M. 2002. The collapse of New Zealand's military ties with the United States. Fulbright Lecture, Georgetown University, Washington, DC, 2 December. Available from: www.michaelbassett.co.nz/articles.php?a=fulbright.

Bolger, J. 1998. *A View from the Top: My seven years as prime minister.* Auckland: Viking Press.

Brownlee, G., Graham, K. and Flavell, T. U. 2017. *New Zealand Parliamentary Debates: Motions—New Zealand Nuclear Free Zone, Disarmament, and Arms Control Act 1987. 30th anniversary* (8 June) 723, 18671. Available from: www.parliament.nz/en/pb/hansard-debates/rhr/document/HansS_20170608_050550000/brownlee-gerry-graham-kennedy-flavell-te-ururoa.

Capie, D. 2006. 'Gone by lunchtime: New Zealand's foreign policy consensus and the 2005 election.' In S. Levine and J. Johansson (eds), *The Baubles of Office: The New Zealand general election of 2005.* Wellington: Victoria University Press.

Capie, D. 2009. 'New Zealand and the world: Imperial, international and global relations.' In G. Byrnes (ed.), *The New Oxford History of New Zealand.* Oxford: Oxford University Press.

Catalinac, A. 2010. 'Why New Zealand took itself out of ANZUS: Observing "opposition for autonomy" in asymmetric alliances.' *Foreign Policy Analysis* 6: 317–38. doi.org/10.1111/j.1743-8594.2010.00115.x.

Clements, K. 2015. *Back from the Brink: The creation of a nuclear free New Zealand.* Wellington: Bridget Williams Books.

Dewes, K. 2012. 'Peace and disarmament activism.' In J. Headley, A. Reitzig and J. Burton (eds), *Public Participation in Foreign Policy*. London: Palgrave Macmillan.

Evans, C. 1987. 'New Zealand nuclear aversion.' *The New York Times*, 14 June.

Graham, K. 1987. 'New Zealand's non-nuclear policy: Towards global security.' *Alternatives* 12(2): 217–42.

Graham, K. 2017. 'NZ zone a precursor to a total nuclear weapon ban.' *Green Blog*, 14 June. Wellington: The Green Party of Aotearoa New Zealand. Available from: blog.greens.org.nz/2017/06/14/nz-total-ban-nuclear-weapons/.

Hager, N. 2011. *Other People's Wars: New Zealand in Afghanistan, Iraq and the war on terror*. Auckland: Craig Potton.

Hensley, G. 2013. *Friendly Fire: Nuclear politics and the collapse of ANZUS, 1984–1987*. Auckland: Auckland University Press.

International Atomic Energy Agency (IAEA) 2011. 'Updates of 12 April 2011.' In *Fukushima Nuclear Accident Update Log*. Vienna: IAEA.

Lange, D. 1990. *Nuclear Free: The New Zealand way*. Auckland: Penguin.

Leadbeater, M. 2013. *Peace, Power and Politics: How New Zealand became nuclear free*. Dunedin: Otago University Press.

Locke, E. 1992. *Peace People: A history of peace activities in New Zealand*. Christchurch: Hazard Press.

McKinnon, M. 1999. 'Realignment: New Zealand and its ANZUS allies.' In B. Brown (ed.), *New Zealand in World Affairs. Volume 3 1972–1990*. Wellington: Victoria University Press.

Maclellan, N. 2018. *Grappling with the Bomb: Britain's Pacific H-bomb tests*. Canberra: ANU Press. doi.org/10.22459/GB.09.2017.

Mydans, S. 1988. 'New Zealand ponders a nuclear survival kit.' *The New York Times*, 17 February.

New Zealand Labour Party 2005. Nuclear free policy reflects New Zealand's values. Press release, 13 September. Wellington: New Zealand Labour Party. Available from: www.scoop.co.nz/stories/PA0509/S00328.htm.

New Zealand Parliament 2007. *New Zealand Parliamentary Debates: Motions—Nuclear-free legislation. 20th anniversary* (12 June) 639, 9759.

Phillips, J. 1991. 'New Zealand and the ANZUS alliance: Changing national perceptions, 1945–88.' In R. W. Baker (ed.), *Australia, New Zealand and the United States: Internal change and alliance relations in the ANZUS states*. New York: Praeger.

Rabel, R. 1991. 'The world turned upside down: Change and continuity in New Zealand politics in the postwar era.' In R. W. Baker (ed.), *Australia, New Zealand and the United States: Internal change and alliance relations in the ANZUS states*. New York: Praeger.

Rudig, W. 1990. *Anti-Nuclear Movements: A world survey of opposition to nuclear energy*. Harlow, UK: Longman.

Templeton, M. 2006. *Standing Upright Here: New Zealand in the nuclear age, 1945–1990*. Wellington: Victoria University Press.

United States New Zealand (USNZ) Council 2012. *The Washington Declaration on Defense Cooperation between The Department of Defense of the United States of America and The Ministry of Defense of New Zealand and the New Zealand Defense Force*. 19 June. Washington, DC: USNZ Council. Available from: usnzcouncil.org/us-nz-issues/washington-declaration/.

White, R. E. 1997. *Nuclear free New Zealand: 1984—New Zealand becomes nuclear free*. Working Paper No. 7, July. Auckland: Centre for Peace Studies, University of Auckland.

Wikileaks 2006. National contemplates end of nuke ban in 2006. Cable from Wellington to Washington (Confidential), 17 February. Available from: multimedia.stuff.co.nz/sstimes/cables.pdf.

Williams, M. 2016. 'Nuclear free legacy a source of pride.' *Hawke's Bay Today*, 30 July.

Wilson, M. A. 1989. *Labour in Government, 1984–1987*. Wellington: Allen & Unwin/Port Nicholson Press.

Young, A. 2010. 'Why Obama wants John Key at the summit.' *New Zealand Herald*, 13 April.

17

Treaty of Waitangi settlements: Successful symbolic reparation

Janine Hayward

Treaty settlements as policy success

New Zealand's ambitious Treaty of Waitangi settlements policy aims to achieve the 'full and final' settlement of the historical injustices Māori suffered through Crown[1] action and inaction that breached the 1840 treaty. In the broadest sense, treaty settlement policy can be judged a success. The process of addressing treaty grievances began tentatively in the 1970s under considerable, sustained pressure from Māori. It gathered momentum in the 1990s with bipartisan political support (despite public ambivalence) and is now nearing completion. The Waitangi Tribunal is the independent commission tasked with inquiring into Māori claims and making recommendations to the government for redress. To date, it has issued more than 100 reports relating to almost 80 per cent of New Zealand's landmass. The government department negotiating treaty settlements, the Office of Treaty Settlements (OTS), aims to complete historical settlements with all 'willing and able groups' by 2020. By March 2018, the OTS had completed more than 60 settlements.

1 'The Crown' is used when discussing treaty settlement policy to refer to the non-Māori treaty partner. At different times in New Zealand history, 'the Crown' could refer to the Queen, colonial government, representative settler government or contemporary government.

The Crown's purpose in developing the settlement policy has been, in its own words, to 'devise an approach to financial and commercial redress' through negotiated settlement that resolves Māori grievance, contributes to Māori economic and social development and is fair between different Māori claimant groups. This approach also 'takes account of New Zealand's ability to pay, considering all the other demands on public spending such as health, education, social welfare, transport and defence' (OTS 2002: 87).

The significance of treaty settlements broadly speaking cannot be underestimated. Settlements have altered New Zealand's political, economic and social landscapes. The process has, arguably, laid bare New Zealand's colonial history, established new relationships between the Crown and *iwi* (tribes) and reestablished an economic and cultural base for future local and regional Māori development. The New Zealand public has not been directly engaged in this policy process; it is kept at arm's length from settlements, which are a political negotiation between the treaty partners, Māori and the Crown. Private land cannot be used in settlements. This has also relieved the public of 'guilt by association'; New Zealanders today are not held accountable for the sins of their colonial past. Public support for settlements policy has waxed and waned over the years; despite this, governments of the left and the right have stayed the course.

Using Marsh and McConnell's (2010) framework for assessing policy success, the following discussion of the treaty settlement policy reveals that, in *programmatic* terms (which relate to the implementation and outcomes of the policy), the value underpinning the policy from the perspective of Māori was always clear. Māori have argued tirelessly since 1840 for the Crown to honour the treaty. By the 1970s, their protests could no longer be ignored and the government saw value in acting pragmatically to take the heat out of Māori demands. As time went on, governments came to see treaty settlements as 'the right thing to do'. The treaty settlement process has evolved as events and incidents have encouraged—and, in some cases, forced—the government and Māori to act. Crocker (2016: i) describes the policy as responding to 'a combination of factors, such as the broad context of the "Māori Renaissance", social shifts in understanding the past, legal cases and political pressure from iwi'. The success of the settlements policy in terms of outcomes is also clear, to an extent. Māori grievances have been heard and acknowledged for the public record; the Crown has atoned and made some reparations for its historical actions and inactions that caused extensive grievances for Māori. The policy has also been enduring and enjoyed bipartisan support. But, as McConnell (2010: 351) notes: '[S]uccess is in the eye of the beholder, depending on the factors such as a protagonist's values, beliefs and extent to which they are affected by the policy.' From the perspective of Māori, who are most affected by the policy, the policy's success is qualified: only a fraction of Māori loss has been repaired and the material and political outcomes for Māori are limited.

In terms of *process* (relating to the legitimacy and sustainability of the policy), both Māori and the Crown have done considerable learning over time as the extent of treaty grievances and the scale of the project became clear. Māori have adapted as the Crown's policy process unfolded—at times pushing back against limitations imposed by the government relating to the redress paid to Māori and the time frame for the process. The Crown has also shown, as discussed below, some willingness to adapt and develop the policy over time in response to Māori demands and changing circumstances.

Settlements policy is also significant in *political* terms, particularly in relation to the way various governments have managed to sustain the policy through time, despite the public's ambivalence (and sometimes hostility) towards it. The policy itself has never been legislated; it is a political conversation sustained over several decades between the treaty partners. This relationship has endured and developed despite a general lack of public support for the policy over time. Both treaty partners have evolved and been shaped by the necessary political manoeuvring, negotiation, tension and compromise. But perhaps the most striking thing about the policy process is its *endurance* through time—surviving for over 40 years and five changes of government since its earliest inception in 1975.

Contexts, challenges, agents

Māori had lived in Aotearoa New Zealand for many centuries prior to the arrival of Europeans (Anderson et al. 2014). By 1840, Māori had been engaging productively with traders from around the world for many decades. However, amid increasing Māori concerns that their authority in their own lands was under threat, they signed a treaty in 1840 with the British at Waitangi in the Bay of Islands. Drafted by the British and translated into te reo Māori (the Māori language), the Treaty of Waitangi succinctly describes an exchange of rights and obligations between two sovereign nations. But the two versions of the treaty describe these rights in significantly different ways; the Māori-language version of the treaty was debated and signed by the majority of Māori *rangatira* (chiefs).

In the first article of the English-language treaty, Māori 'cede to Her Majesty the Queen of England absolutely and without reservation all the rights and powers of Sovereignty'. In the Māori-language treaty (translated back into English), however, the chiefs 'give absolutely to the Queen of England forever the complete government over their land'. In the second article in English, Her Majesty guarantees to Māori

> the full exclusive undisturbed possession of their Lands and Estates Forests Fisheries and other properties … so long as it is their wish and desire to retain the same in their possession. (Orange 1987: 31)

The Māori translation, however, says:

> The Queen of England agrees to protect the chiefs, the subtribes and all the people of New Zealand in the unqualified exercise of their chieftainship over their lands, villages and all their treasures. (Orange 1987: 326)

The third article of the treaty, in both languages, extends to Māori all the 'Rights and Privileges of British Subjects' (Orange 1987).

Despite the treaty's guarantees to Māori for 'unqualified chieftainship over their lands', protected by the Queen's governance, Māori rapidly lost control of their land after 1840 through Crown actions and inactions, including land confiscations, dubious land sales, the individualisation of land title (which Māori had traditionally held communally) and other mechanisms. By the early twentieth century, Māori had lost possession of most of their lands and resources (Ward 1999). The socioeconomic cost of this loss was soon apparent. Māori migrated in large numbers into cities and became overrepresented in statistics relating to poor health, low educational achievement, substandard housing and unemployment. Throughout this time, Māori tirelessly maintained calls on the Crown to honour its treaty obligations (Walker 2004).

In the late 1960s and early 1970s, circumstances converged to finally draw the nation's attention to the guarantees the Crown had made to Māori in the treaty and to confront questions about race relations in New Zealand (Hamer 2004: 3). Māori protests, marches and occupations heaped pressure on the government to address the loss of Māori land and to honour the treaty's guarantees. It was one particular protest, however, that captured the nation's attention at a crucial time. A *hikoi* (march) in 1975 from the top of the North Island to the parliament buildings in Wellington confronted the New Zealand public with images of large numbers of Māori men, women and children marching beneath banners proclaiming, 'Not one more acre!'. Within an international environment charged with American civil rights and South African anti-apartheid protests, the whole of New Zealand, and beyond, looked on as New Zealand's own 'race relations' were put under the spotlight. Māori protesters erected a tent assembly in the parliament grounds and refused to leave until the government took action.

Inside parliament, Māori MP Matiu Rata proposed a Bill to establish a commission of inquiry to address Māori demands. Rata was pioneering a uniquely New Zealand response to confronting its colonial past. The government—unaware of the full extent of Māori grievance and anxious to take the heat out of Māori protest and avoid international embarrassment (Hamer 2004: 5–6)—passed the Treaty of Waitangi Bill into law in October 1975.

The *Treaty of Waitangi Act* established a commission, the Waitangi Tribunal, to inquire into Māori allegations of Crown treaty breaches that occurred after 1975. The legislation was introduced by a Labour government and passed into law by the National Government that came to office in 1975. Despite its bipartisan support, the tribunal's contemporary jurisdiction did not appease Māori demands for long. In 1985, as Māori pressure began to mount again, the government—still unaware of the extent of Māori historical grievance—granted the tribunal a retrospective jurisdiction to inquire into the Crown's actions and inactions dating back to 1840. This irrevocably changed the landscape of Crown–Māori relations and set the stage for an ambitious and significant policy to address and redress New Zealand's colonial past. The tribunal itself could not negotiate or settle treaty grievances, but it could hold hearings, produce reports and make recommendations to the government in relation to treaty breaches. Over the next 15 years as the tribunal diligently went about this task, successive governments—particularly the National Party Government of the 1990s—would come to appreciate the scale of the project ahead. From 1990 to 1999, the government established an institutional framework and policy process to negotiate, settle and redress the large numbers of historical grievances Māori were bringing to the Waitangi Tribunal.

Box 17.1 The Waitangi Tribunal

The Waitangi Tribunal was established in 1975 under the *Treaty of Waitangi Act*. It is a permanent, independent commission of inquiry with authority to inquire into Māori claims of Crown actions and inactions that breached the principles of the 1840 Treaty of Waitangi. For the most part, the tribunal makes recommendations to the Crown to redress treaty breaches.

The 1980s were a time of dramatic economic, social and cultural change for New Zealand. The Labour Government (1984–90) implemented a radical program of economic and social reform and supported significant social policy developments that advocated for biculturalism in social policy (New Zealand 1988). Changes were also occurring beyond government: Pākehā (non-Māori) historian Claudia Orange published *The Treaty of Waitangi* (1987), which began to shape a new national narrative about New Zealand's founding document and colonial past. Court rulings also changed the landscape of treaty relations between Māori and the Crown. In 1987, the Court of Appeal had cause for the first time to define the 'principles of the Treaty of Waitangi' (a phrase first used in the *Treaty of Waitangi Act*). In brief, the Court of Appeal held that the Crown was not acting according to its own legislative requirement (under the *State-Owned Enterprises Act 1986*) to take into account the principles of the Treaty of Waitangi. It defined those principles as—among other things—the Crown's duty to act reasonably and in good faith and to actively protect Māori interests.[2] The court instructed the Crown to negotiate with Māori to address these concerns, which the Crown proceeded to do.

In 1988, the Waitangi Tribunal was given the power to make binding recommendations on the Crown in very specific circumstances. The tribunal has used this binding authority only once, but it has been described as the 'sword of Damocles' hanging over the government and encouraging progress on claims (Graham 1997: 50–1). In 1989, a second court case, over forest rentals, led to the establishment of a key institution in the treaty settlement process, the Crown Forestry Rental Trust. The trust was paid rents from leased Crown forest lands and this money was used for research to support treaty claims. The funding was significant and, over time, the rental trust became a more substantial contributor to treaty claims research than even the Waitangi Tribunal itself (Wheen and Hayward 2012: 18).

2 *New Zealand Maori Council v Attorney-General*, 1987, New Zealand Law Reports 1: 642–3.

Within this charged political environment in the late 1980s, the Waitangi Tribunal began to report on the first of its claims. In response, the Labour Government established the Treaty of Waitangi Policy Unit in 1988 within the Department of Justice to coordinate the Crown's response to the tribunal's recommendations. In 1989, the government announced a set of principles that would apply to all settlements that it hoped to negotiate with Māori on a pantribal basis (Jones 2016: 89). These included the principles of government (by the Crown), self-management (by Māori), equality, reasonable cooperation and redress (Department of Justice 1989). The courts' interventions in treaty issues were not welcomed by the government, and it took the opportunity to assert that treaty settlements would be political—not legal—negotiations including only Māori and the Crown. As Durie notes (1998: 188):

> By 1989 when the government published its Treaty of Waitangi principles, it was obvious that the Crown was planning a deliberate strategy to return Treaty issues to the political arena, rather than relying on the [Waitangi] Tribunal or a court of law … Sir Robin Cooke [Court of Appeal judge] had concluded that it was ultimately for the courts to decide whether the government met its obligations under the principles of the Treaty of Waitangi. [Prime minister Geoffrey] Palmer responded, 'It must be made clear that … the government will make the final decisions on Treaty issues.'

When the National Government came to office in 1990, it maintained the Labour Government's aspiration to get treaty issues out of the courts and return them to the political arena. For the next 10 years, as discussed below, the National Government—and, in particular, its Minister of Treaty Negotiations, Douglas Graham—developed the treaty settlement institutions and processes that would manage the volume of reports and recommendations emerging from Waitangi Tribunal hearings. Although the Labour Government's support of treaty claims is explained by Māori voters' traditional support for Labour MPs, the National Government's engagement with treaty settlements after 1990 is less immediately self-evident, particularly against a backdrop of public disquiet about the cost to taxpayers of settling treaty grievances.

Policy design and evolution

After 1990, the National Government began in earnest to develop the institutions required for treaty settlements. It was treading a fine and difficult line between Māori expectations and poor public understanding of and tolerance for the treaty. In the National Government's first term (1990–93), it was also presented with broader challenges as it continued to pursue the economic and social policy agenda established by the previous Labour Government. Its policies relating to treaty settlements have been described as 'more reactionary than deliberate' and progress on settlements was hard fought and won. But the number of claims registered with the Waitangi Tribunal was increasing: by 1990, 90 claims were registered and, by 1993, that had increased to 423 (Crocker 2016: 111).

In September 1992, Cabinet agreed on the concept of a fund to pay settlement compensation for historical claims. At the same time, private land was excluded from settlements in response to public outcry that landowners should not feel the impact of the Crown's redress to Māori. 'Land banks' were established to set aside surplus Crown land available for settlements. Also in 1992, the government concluded a complex pan-Māori negotiation relating to fisheries. Through the *Treaty of Waitangi (Fisheries Claims) Settlement Act 1992*, the government compensated Māori losses of fisheries with $170 million worth of fishing quotas and part-ownership of the Sealord fishing company. The settlement became known as the 'Sealord deal'.

Perhaps bolstered by its success in fisheries, the National Government devised its own principles to guide the emerging settlement process without significant consultation with Māori (Crocker 2016: 120). The government was aware that it needed to offer reassurance to the New Zealand public that settlements were justified, in the public interest and would not be detrimental to non-Māori New Zealand. A 1994 opinion poll of 1,000 adults found that over 70 per cent thought Māori 'get a fair go' in New Zealand and there was no need to embark on settlements (Crocker 2016: 103). The government's principles—paraphrased and as amended by the Labour Government in 2000—are (OTS 2002: 30):

- **Good faith:** The negotiating process will be conducted in good faith based on mutual trust and cooperation towards a common goal.
- **Restoration of relationship:** The restoration of Crown–Māori relations is integral and will be reflected in any settlement.

- **Just redress:** Redress should relate to the nature and extent of the breaches suffered, with existing settlements benchmarking future settlements where appropriate.
- **Fairness between claims:** Claimant groups must be treated consistently in terms of the levels of financial and commercial redress to ensure the durability of claims.
- **Transparency:** Claimants must have sufficient information and the general public must be encouraged to understand the settlement process.
- **Government-negotiated:** Negotiations are between the government and claimants as the only two parties who can, *by agreement*, achieve durable, fair and final settlements.

In 1993, the National Government created the portfolio of Minister in Charge of Treaty Negotiations to bring leadership to the negotiations process. The appointment of Douglas Graham as the first treaty settlements minister was crucial to the progress made over the following years. Graham accepted that wrongdoing had occurred on the part of the Crown and was aware of the weight of Māori demands. He brought his often-reluctant colleagues in the National Government with him as the settlement process began to take shape. His investment in treaty settlements, supported by then prime minister James Bolger, was essential to establishing the bipartisanship that has characterised treaty settlement policy since the 1990s. As Māori scholar Mason Durie (1998: 194) notes:

> Doug Graham, as Minister in Charge of Treaty Negotiations, carried out much of the burden and in so far as the outcomes have been successful, much of the credit must rest with him.

In 1994, the government released the details for its comprehensive proposals 'to settle all claims without utilising natural resources or the conservation estate, and to limit the total value of all claims to a billion dollars' within a 10-year time frame (Durie 1998: 191). As Crocker (2016) notes, the idea of a fund for settlements had been discussed among officials since 1992, although the figure of $1 billion including the fisheries settlement was a political decision, made by Graham and the Cabinet. There was also debate within the Cabinet about whether that fund should be legislated for; again, under Graham's guidance, the decision was made that the settlement fund would be policy, not law (Crocker 2016: 108–9). The government's policy also distinguished between historical and contemporary treaty claims; grievances relating to matters prior to

21 September 1992 (the date of the Cabinet committee meeting) would be historical claims subject to the limits of the fund, while those after 1992 would be contemporary claims.

As previously noted, the government's policy was developed with 'negligible Māori input' (Durie 1998: 190) and was soundly rejected by Māori, who objected to both the lack of consultation and to the low level of compensation available for historical settlements (Palmer 2008: 264). In January 1995, Māori across the country gathered together and unanimously rejected the proposals. Of all the aspects of this policy, the billion-dollar limit on redress—dubbed 'the fiscal envelope'—was the most controversial. Durie notes:

> The amount was non-negotiable … [and] neither the methodology used to calculate the amount, nor the basis for deciding affordability was disclosed. The cap was simply stated as a given, even though most claims had not yet received due consideration, while others had yet to be filed. (1998: 192)

By April 1995, the future of the fiscal envelope was in doubt, although it appeared in the government's budget in 1995 and again in 1996. Despite these setbacks, the government pushed ahead with the institutional structures required to negotiate settlements with Māori. In 1995, the OTS replaced the Treaty of Waitangi Policy Unit with a mandate to negotiate and settle Māori claims on behalf of the government. Also in 1995, the Crown achieved its first historical settlement, with Waikato-Tainui Māori. The passage of the *Waikato Raupatu Settlement Act 1995*, which gave effect to the settlement, was historic: for the first time, the Queen gave her royal assent to New Zealand legislation in person during a royal visit to the country (Durie 1998: 195).

Box 17.2 The Office of Treaty Settlements

The Office of Treaty Settlements is a government department within the Ministry of Justice. It was established in 1995 to negotiate the settlement of historical Treaty of Waitangi claims.

Following the general election in 1996, the government was forced to formally abandon the fiscal envelope as a result of coalition negotiations between National and the minor political party New Zealand First. By that time, however, three settlements had been negotiated using the fiscal restraint set out in the policy: the fisheries settlement, Waikato-Tainui and the Ngāi Tahu settlement, which covered most of the South Island of New Zealand (Durie 1998: 193). The Waikato-Tainui and Ngāi Tahu settlements included 'relativity clauses' in their legislation to safeguard those claimants against future increases in the overall quantum. At about $170 million each, those settlements constituted about 17 per cent of the overall quantum the government had set aside for settlements. If more was spent than the anticipated $1 billion in settlements, those *iwi* would receive additional redress to maintain their relative share of the overall amount.

In 1997, the Waitangi Tribunal published its 'National Overview' reports to encourage the government to appreciate that settlements would ultimately cover most of New Zealand's landmass and involve all *iwi*. The tribunal also began to develop new ways of hearing claims and reporting more quickly to government in response to the growing number of claims. For example, it made improvements in the way it organised the vast amounts of evidence it managed for major historical inquiries and the way it conducted its hearings, thereby reducing the number of years typically required for large-district inquiries (Waitangi Tribunal 1997).

Despite the tribunal's innovations, government concern was mounting about how long it was taking for large claims to proceed through the inquiry process. When Labour came to power in 1999, it encouraged Māori claimants to consider direct negotiations with the Crown, rather than pursuing their claims through the Waitangi Tribunal hearings process. As Māori scholar Carwyn Jones (2016: 89) notes, from that time, the Waitangi Tribunal, 'while still important to Māori, became slightly peripheral to the settlement process'. In 2002, the tribunal registered its 1,000th claim and the pace of new claims showed no sign of abating. Amid mounting public pressure for the government to signal an end to the treaty settlement process, the Labour Government passed a significant and controversial amendment to the *Treaty of Waitangi Act* (Section 6AA), in 2006, to once again limit the tribunal's jurisdiction. After 1 September 2008, no Māori would be able to submit a historical claim to the tribunal (defined as acts or omissions by the Crown before 21 September 1992). An unprecedented 1,800 historical claims were lodged with the tribunal in the few years prior to the 2008 deadline; this was more than the number of claims the tribunal had previously received in its history. This influx of claims brought new challenges for the tribunal to develop processes to determine which of those claims would be accepted and how to reach finality with all historical claims. Many Māori could see some merit in proposals to advance claims. As Durie (1998: 193) notes: 'The idea of putting to rest long-standing grievances as soon as possible made sense; and the advantages of avoiding costly litigation had considerable appeal.' Overall, however, from 2000 to 2006, the Labour Government found it hard to make settlements with Māori despite their historical relationship through the Māori electorates (which Labour MPs had traditionally won). Instead, this period was characterised by a rift that opened between Māori and Labour after the government legislated to remove legal avenues for Māori to pursue treaty claims to the foreshore and seabed (Boast 2005).

When National came back into office in 2008, it increased the pace of treaty settlements and further developed the infrastructure around the policy. The appointment of Christopher Finlayson as the Minister in Charge of Treaty Negotiations created a momentum in settlements last seen when Graham held the position in the 1990s (Dreaver 2017: 116–17). Finlayson spearheaded further innovations in treaty negotiations, establishing a more senior Crown negotiating team and placing a greater emphasis on comprehensive settlements encompassing a single region at the same time (Dreaver 2017: 116–17). In 2013, National also established the Post Settlement Commitments Unit, which had responsibility for auditing Crown compliance with settlement agreements. New positions relating to treaty settlements were also established in key government departments not traditionally aligned with treaty settlements, such as the Ministry for Business, Innovation and Employment. These roles were looking to the future and 'tasked with responding to the enhanced expectations and capacity of iwi and hapū [subtribes] following settlement' (Dreaver 2017: 120).

In 2015, the Waitangi Tribunal announced its ambition to complete historical (pre-1992) claims by 2020 and to then transition into the completion of all other outstanding claims by 2025. The National Government maintained its own policy (albeit with a shifting deadline) to settle all historical grievances. By October 2017, when Labour again took office, 85 deeds of settlement had been signed by the Crown, reflecting approximately 61 per cent of the expected settlements. As the OTS (2017) noted in its brief to the incoming government, approximately 53 claims remained unsettled, although the Crown was actively engaged in negotiations with 47 of these groups, some of which were close to settlement.

Delivery, legitimacy and endurance

The negotiation and settlement of Treaty claims have generally followed a four-step process, established by the National Government in the 1990s and modified by the Labour-led Government after 2000: 1) preparing for negotiations, 2) pre-negotiations, 3) negotiations, and 4) ratification and implementation. It is important to reiterate that these processes are not governed by law, but rather are political negotiations between Māori and the Crown.

In preparing for negotiations, Māori register a claim with the Waitangi Tribunal. Under Section 6 of the *Treaty of Waitangi Act 1975*, the tribunal has the authority to consider claims by any individual or group of Māori claiming they are, or are likely to be, prejudicially affected by (among other things) ordinances, regulations, policies, actions and inaction by or on behalf of the Crown. For the purposes of the Act, 'Māori' is defined as 'a person of the Māori race of New Zealand; and includes all descendants of such a person'.

Once a claim is accepted and registered, claimants proceed to negotiations through Waitangi Tribunal hearings and report writing or they seek direct negotiations with the Crown. The latter is the Crown's preference, but to date, claims relating to only 9 per cent of New Zealand's landmass have been directly negotiated with the Crown; the remaining 91 per cent have been involved in claims heard through Waitangi Tribunal hearings. In preparing for negotiations, claimants are required to give a mandate to representatives of their claimant group to advance their claim. This mandating process can create tensions and conflict within claimant communities (Jones 2016: 90) and has been a controversial aspect of the settlement process.

In the pre-negotiation stage—the second stage of the settlement process—the Crown and claimants agree to the terms of negotiations and establish which issues are on and off the table. Claimant funding is also determined. The Crown makes a contribution to claimant costs, which is separate from the redress received; claimants do not bear the cost of negotiations (OTS 2002: 54–60).

The negotiations stage is led by OTS officials and claimant negotiators, but may also include officials from other government departments relevant to the negotiations. The negotiations are private and confidential to the parties involved. For the most part, negotiations escape media scrutiny and the public is unaware that negotiations are proceeding (unless a significant controversy arises) until they hear of the legislation reaching parliament. The objective of the negotiations phase is to reach an agreement in principle (also known as a heads of agreement) and then a deed of settlement (OTS 2002: 61–8).

Finally, ratification is a crucial step in the fourth stage of negotiations to test that the claimant community supports the outcomes. This is not simply a formality; there have been examples of claimant communities demonstrating their opposition to settlement packages, although only one claimant group, Whakatōhea, took the step, in 1996, of entirely rejecting the settlement at this point (Durie 1998: 198–9). To this day, Whakatōhea claims remain unsettled.

The implementation phase requires the claimant community to establish a post-settlement governance entity (PSGE)—a legal entity that can receive the settlement funds and assets. These entities have also been controversial for some Māori claimants. As Jones (2016: 99) notes, PSGEs are not entities based in Māori *tikanga* (culture), but rather are based on

> models of corporate governance primarily concerned with financial propriety, commercial accountability, and economic sustainability … Quite simply, PSGEs can be constituted in a way that leads decision-makers to act in a way that is at odds with the principles of tikanga.

With negotiations completed and settlements ratified by claimant groups, nearly all deeds of settlement need to be implemented by settlement legislation. Settlement acts ensure the settlement is 'full and final' by removing the ability of the courts and the Waitangi Tribunal to reopen historical claims or deeds of settlement. The legislation also provides the statutory instruments required to implement the settlement, removes statutory memorials from land titles in the claim area and vests any land in the claimants' governance group. A settlement Bill ratifying negotiation follows the standard parliamentary process. The Bill is read three times and is subject to a select committee process that provides an opportunity for dissenting claimant groups to engage in further debate on the settlement package. The select committee stage is not, however, used to renegotiate the substance of the deed of settlement. As the OTS (2002: 78) explains, this 'reflects the long-established Parliamentary practice that Parliament should not use its sovereignty … to change legal agreements between the Crown and a third party, unless this is necessary in the national interest'.

Since the first settlements in the 1990s, settlement acts have comprised a historical account and apology from the Crown, financial redress and cultural redress. In terms of restoring the relationship between claimants and the Crown, the historical account and Crown apology are arguably the most important aspect of the settlement. The historical account is a statement at the start of the legislation agreed to by the Crown and the claimants. It sets out the key facts of the historical relationship between the claimant group and the Crown and lays bare the treaty breaches the settlement addresses. The Crown then proceeds to express its regret and unreserved apology for those breaches and losses and for the resentment and grief suffered by Māori. These statements can be expressed in both English and in te reo Māori and may include *karakia* (prayers) and *waiata* (songs) significant to the claimants (OTS 2002: 85).

Crocker (2016: 173–4) notes that the Labour Government (1984–90) was not prepared to offer Māori an apology as part of a settlement, but the National Government took advice from officials during the Waikato-Tainui negotiations to acknowledge the wrongs done and to apologise. The resulting Crown apology to Tainui in 1995 (delivered in person by the Queen during her royal visit) was 'ground-breaking' (Crocker 2016: 173). As Hickey (2012) argues, by the late 1990s, the government came to accept that reconciliation between Māori and the Crown required more than financial redress and restored cultural recognition. Minister Graham was responsible for the Crown's decision to formally acknowledge and apologise for the historical injustices the Crown had inflicted on Māori. This would, in Graham's words, put those events in their 'proper place—not forgotten, but accepted' (Hickey 2012: 82). With few exceptions, apologies have become 'a valued part of the settlement process' (Hickey 2012: 90), which can 'help to recognise the validity of the grievances, reconcile the past and reset the Treaty relationship. It may also provide a sense of closure' (p. 91). Given the significance of the settlement apology, it is worth considering a Crown apology more closely as an example of an agreed account of New Zealand's colonial history now on the public record. The following is the Crown apology in the *Ngāi Tuhoe (Claims) Settlements Act 2014* (Section 9):

> The Crown acknowledges that its conduct during its attacks on Te Urewera and its surrounds between 1865 and 1871 included—
>
> (a) the failure to properly monitor and control the actions of the armed forces, resulting in—(i) the execution of unarmed Tūhoe prisoners at Mangarua (near Waikaremoana) in 1866 and at Ngātapa in 1869; and (ii) the execution of Tūhoe prisoners at Ruatāhuna in 1869; and (iii) the killing of non-combatants, including men, women, and children, and the desecration of bodies, human remains, and urupā [burial grounds] at Te Whata-a-pona, Ōpūtao, Tahora, and in the Ruatāhuna district; and
>
> (b) the use of the scorched earth policy that resulted in the widespread destruction of kāinga [settlements], pā [fortified settlements], cultivations, food stores, animals, wāhi tapu [sacred places], and taonga [treasures].
>
> The Crown acknowledges that the impacts of these actions on Tūhoe included widespread starvation and extensive loss of life. The Crown's actions had an enduring and devastating effect on the mana [authority/prestige], social structure, and well-being of the iwi. The Crown acknowledges that its conduct showed reckless disregard for Tūhoe, went far beyond what was necessary or appropriate in the circumstances, and was in breach of the Treaty of Waitangi and its principles.

A second component of settlements is financial redress—the part of the settlement that is economic or commercial and given monetary value. The Crown has acknowledged that 'the losses to Māori amount to tens of billions of dollars' (OTS 2002: 89), but it has never offered complete compensation. Māori have compromised and settled for a fraction of the value of what was taken from them; the redress paid to Māori has been estimated at less than 1 per cent of the loss suffered (Stone 2012: 145). Financial redress includes cash and commercial redress in the form of Crown assets such as property (mostly held in land banks established in the 1990s). In determining financial redress, the Crown is guided by the principle that 'the quantum of redress should relate fundamentally to the nature and extent of the Crown's breaches of the Treaty and its principles' (OTS 2002: 87). The quantum offered is 'negotiated' by the Crown and claimants, although, as Stone (2012: 145) notes:

> [S]ettling groups are faced with a difficult decision: they can either accept what most would consider a relatively minute settlement offer; take their chances in litigation against the Crown; or wait and see if Crown policy may change significantly in the future, resulting in more valuable settlements.

While it is true the Crown has the upper hand in negotiations, Jones (2016: 91) notes that even the Crown is constrained by broader fiscal limits on the government's budget and the precedents set by earlier settlements. As noted above, the billion-dollar fiscal envelope was formally abandoned in 1996 and the billion-dollar cap was surpassed in 2012; however, the constraints of the relativity clauses are still in place.

The third component of a settlement package is cultural redress, encompassing, for example, the loss of Māori *kaitiakitanga* (guardianship) of significant sites, the loss of access to traditional *mahinga kai* (food-gathering places) and the exclusion of Māori from environmental decision-making (OTS 2002: 96). In considering cultural redress, the Crown makes it clear that it is required to balance the interests of Māori with the interests of the general public. Therefore, although the Crown usually does not return ownership of a resource to Māori, through cultural redress it can try to meet the underlying interests Māori have in that resource and establish a future relationship with the resource for Māori. Cultural redress aspects of the settlement package do not have a direct monetary value, so do not count against the financial redress negotiated between Māori and the Crown (OTS 2002: 98). A wide variety of cultural redress has been realised through treaty settlements since the very early Ngāi Tahu settlement included new ownership and management regimes for the *taonga* of *pounamu* (greenstone) and *tītī* (muttonbird) (Stevens 2012: 124).

Although the components described above are consistently applied to all settlements, two recent examples—the Ngai Tūhoe settlement in 2014 and the Whanganui River settlement in 2017—demonstrate that the Crown will innovate beyond the established norms of treaty settlements and legislate new arrangements. Despite the Crown's policy that the conservation estate would not be available as settlement redress, the Ngai Tūhoe settlement vested title to Te Urewera National Park in a new legal entity with representation from Ngai Tūhoe and the Crown in equal measure. In this way, the Crown stopped short of actually transferring title of the national park to Tūhoe, while achieving an outcome that reflected the significance of the land for the claimants. In the case of the Whanganui River, the *Te Awa Tupua (Whanganui River Claims Settlement) Act 2017* gives legal personality to the river itself and establishes a board (Te Pou Tupua) with Crown and *iwi* appointees as the human face of the river to promote and protect the river's health and wellbeing. Jones acknowledges the significance of these settlement innovations, but also notes their limitations, saying: 'These settlements make significant advances in terms of establishing a framework that reflects a Māori perspective on human relationships with the natural environment and specific landscape features', although they stop short of establishing a 'just' relationship between Māori and the government and of recognising Māori legal traditions (2016: 98).

The final phase of historical treaty settlements will bring additional challenges to the policy process. It is possible that not all Māori will settle with the Crown. The Post Settlement Commitments Unit, established in 2013 in the Ministry of Justice, will play an important role to ensure the durability of treaty settlements. The Waitangi Tribunal and the OTS will continue to evolve as their function and focus shift from historical to contemporary claims.

Beyond treaty settlements, there is other policy work to be done in relation to the treaty. After its election in 2017, the Labour-led Government signalled a new direction beyond settlements with the creation of a portfolio for Crown–Māori relations. This policy unit has also been located in the Department of Justice, and the newly appointed minister, Māori MP Kelvin Davis, is currently engaging with Māori through a series of *hui* (meetings) across New Zealand to consult on the roles and expectations of that policy in future.

Conclusion

Through the Treaty of Waitangi settlement process, New Zealand has made important, substantive progress in addressing its colonial past. By 2015, when the Waitangi Tribunal celebrated its fortieth anniversary, it had registered about 2,500 claims, partly or fully reported on over 1,000 claims, published more than 100 final reports and issued district reports covering almost 80 per cent of New Zealand's landmass (Waitangi Tribunal 2015). The tribunal's work has laid the basis for most settlements negotiated between Māori and the Crown that acknowledge the Crown's breaches of the Treaty of Waitangi. The Crown has apologised unreservedly to Māori for treaty breaches and taken steps to establish new relationships with Māori. Māori have finally had their grievances acknowledged on the public record, have heard the Crown atone for its past actions, have been provided an economic base on which to build and, in many cases, have had important cultural connections with land and resources formally restored. As Cowie (2012: 64) notes:

> [T]he settlement process is not just about spending money and reaching settlements. Loftier nation-building outcomes are being realised. The process restores the honour, or moral legitimacy, of the Crown to govern on behalf of *all* New Zealanders. It also affords to Māori the opportunity to take real ownership of a future that is different from their past. These intangible benefits of reaching settlements—international respect, a truly post-colonial government, tribes with economic power and sound governance that instil pride and confidence in their people—could yet prove to be the most significant legacies of the Treaty settlement process.
>
> Despite its controversial place in New Zealand society, the ambitious programme of negotiating historical claims comprehensively, finally and quickly has seen significant success. (p. 62)

As noted in this chapter, the policy has gained cross-party support. 'It appears that everyone, including most Māori and politicians, want the job completed, fast' (Cowie 2012: 62). And, as the OTS noted in its briefing to the incoming minister in 2017:

> While not all elements of the Treaty settlement process are universally supported, settlements have been signed with 61% of all expected groups and have traditionally enjoyed broad cross-party support. Treaty settlements have also gained greater public understanding and support over the last two decades. (OTS 2017: 3)

The treaty settlement process has also endured through time as both Māori and the Crown have evolved in response to changing circumstances. Despite the Crown's extensive control over the treaty settlement policy, it has been moulded and shaped by the settlement process over the years (Dreaver 2017: 114). In the 1990s, the government backtracked on its ambition to negotiate pan-Māori settlements and also formally abandoned the fiscal envelope in the face of fierce Māori opposition. More recently, it has found innovative ways to navigate around the principles that national parks will not be transferred to Māori through settlements (Dreaver 2017: 120). *Iwi* have also 'changed considerably, and … have an increased capacity now to take responsibility for their own destinies' (Dreaver 2017: 128). Moreover, *iwi* leaders now have a profile in public discourse that did not exist when the first settlements were made over 20 years ago. Pan-Māori organisations and leaders who dominated the political landscape prior to settlements—as Māori demanded the Crown's attention—have diminished in profile. Settlements have also created new levels of resilience and capacity among *iwi*. As Dreaver (2017: 124) notes, the negotiating process has provided mandated *iwi* groups and negotiators 'with resources to establish and maintain a level of operational capability, which, in a modern setting, had never existed'.

The public has also been changed by settlements policy. '[F]or the public, the settlements process has arguably been highly transformative, in a way that has at times been subtle and slow, but seems also constant and immutable' (Dreaver 2017: 126). As Durie notes, after the tribunal's establishment in 1975:

> [it] began to sketch an historical backdrop which had been largely hidden from the eyes of ordinary New Zealanders. Case by case there was examination of injustices that had never been resolved in the past, nor openly admitted, and again and again it was found that the Crown had failed to meet its obligations under the Treaty. Most New Zealanders were surprised to know that the Crown did have Treaty obligations. (Durie 1998: 175)

Generally, public concern has diminished over time; where treaty settlements used to be in the top five concerns of voters at election time, now they rarely feature (Dreaver 2017: 125).

McConnell (2010: 351) defines a policy as successful if 'it achieves the goals that proponents set out to achieve and attracts no criticisms of any significance and/or support is virtually universal'. By this definition, the treaty settlements policy is a success, but the numerous criticisms of the policy are important to consider and tend to focus on its limited objectives with regard to outcomes for Māori. Dreaver (2017: 116) notes that settlements 'are not about restoring the status quo of Māori groups as they existed in 1840'. And Sharp (1997: 285) argues: 'Justice for the Māori … can never be done. It will never be done.' But, he acknowledges, 'there is enough political community' between Māori and the Crown 'for justice to be negotiated' (Sharp 1997: 285, 287). There are differences in the benefits that have accrued to *iwi* who settled early compared with those who have had to wait significantly longer to settle (Dreaver 2017: 124–5). Some Māori are still waiting, and a small proportion may never settle. As Sharp (1997: 299) warned when the process was in its infancy in the 1990s:

> [S]ettlements will be seen to have borne little relationship to questions of need or any other conceptions of distributive justice. Reparation has been made and will be made to the best organised teams, not to the most needy.

Finally, as Jones (2016: 107) concludes, settlements are 'symbolic reparation' that acknowledge the grievances suffered by Māori across New Zealand, restore relationships between Māori and the Crown for the future (Dreaver 2017: 120) and restore the Crown's honour.

So what policy lessons can be learned by other nations from New Zealand's treaty settlements? Sharp (1997: 283) argues that, in relation to other nations dealing with reparations for Indigenous peoples:

> precisely *what* should be repaired and *how* is arbitrary and unpredictable by the use of reason. It is a matter rather of long history, of the conventions of particular societies constructed only semi-consciously over long tracts of time … The metaphors of reparation, remedy and restitution, and so on … [vary] from society to society.

Treaty settlement policy has succeeded to the extent that it has for a number of important reasons that may be unique to the New Zealand experience. But those circumstances are worth consideration all the same. Māori have maintained pressure on the government to honour the treaty since it was signed in 1840. From the 1970s, when their voice could no longer be ignored, National and Labour governments alike demonstrated a commitment to addressing and redressing treaty grievances; that commitment has been maintained through time despite strong ongoing public ambivalence about the policy. Settlements have been a political process, not a legal one, and governments have set limits and expectations on what treaty settlements can and will achieve as symbolic reparative justice.

References

Anderson, A., Binney, J. and Harris, A. 2014. *Tangata Whenua: An illustrated history*. Wellington: Bridget Williams Books.

Boast, R. 2005. *Foreshore and Seabed*. Wellington: LexisNexis.

Cowie, D. 2012. 'The treaty settlement process.' In N. Wheen and J. Hayward (eds), *Treaty of Waitangi Settlements*. Wellington: Bridget Williams Books. doi.org/10.7810/9781927131381_3.

Crocker, T. 2016. Settling treaty claims: The formation of policy on Treaty of Waitangi claims in the pioneering years, 1988–1998. PhD thesis, Victoria University of Wellington, Wellington.

Department of Justice 1989. *Principles of Crown Action on the Treaty of Waitangi*. Wellington: Government of New Zealand.

Dreaver, M. 2017. 'Coming of age: Transformation and the treaty settlement process.' In R. Bell, M. Kawharu, K. Taylor, M. Belgrave and P. Meihana (eds), *The Treaty on the Ground: Where we are headed and why it matters*. Auckland: Massey University Press.

Durie, M. 1998. *Te Mana Te Kawanatanga: The politics of self-determination*. Auckland: Oxford University Press.

Graham, D. 1997. *Trick or Treaty*. Wellington: Institute of Policy Studies.

Hamer, P. 2004. 'A quarter century of the Waitangi Tribunal.' In J. Hayward and N. Wheen (eds), *The Waitangi Tribunal: He roopu whakamana i Te Tiriti o Waitangi*. Wellington: Bridget Williams Books. doi.org/10.7810/9781877242328_1.

Hickey, M. 2012. 'Apologies in treaty settlements.' In N. Wheen and J. Hayward (eds), *Treaty of Waitangi Settlements*. Wellington: Bridget Williams Books. doi.org/10.7810/9781927131381_5.

Jones, C. 2016. *New Treaty, New Tradition: Reconciling New Zealand and Māori law*. Wellington: Victoria University Press.

McConnell, A. 2010. 'Policy success, policy failure and grey areas in-between.' *Journal of Public Policy* 30(3): 345–62. doi.org/10.1017/S0143814X10000152.

Marsh, A. and McConnell, A. 2010. 'Towards a framework for establishing policy success.' *Public Administration* 88(2): 564–83. doi.org/10.1111/j.1467-9299.2009.01803.x.

New Zealand. Royal Commission on Social Policy 1988. *The April Report*. Vols 1–5. Wellington: Government of New Zealand.

Office of Treaty Settlements (OTS) 1994. *Crown Proposals for the Settlement of Treaty of Waitangi Claims*. Wellington: Department of Justice.

Office of Treaty Settlements (OTS) 2002. *Ka Tika ā Muri, Ka Tika a Mua: Healing the past, building a future—A guide to Treaty of Waitangi claims and negotiations with the Crown*. Wellington: Department of Justice.

Office of Treaty Settlements (OTS) 2017. *Vote treaty negotiations*. Briefing for the incoming minister. Wellington: Department of Justice.

Orange, C. 1987. *The Treaty of Waitangi*. Wellington: Allen & Unwin and Port Nicholson Press.

Palmer, M. 2008. *The Treaty of Waitangi in New Zealand's Law and Constitution*. Wellington: Victoria University Press.

Sharp, A. 1997. *Justice and the Māori: The philosophy and practice of Māori claims in New Zealand since the 1970s*. 2nd edn. Auckland: Oxford University Press.

Stevens, M. 2012. 'Settlements and taonga: A Ngāi Tahu commentary.' In N. Wheen and J. Hayward (eds), *Treaty of Waitangi Settlements*. Wellington: Bridget Williams Books. doi.org/10.7810/9781927131381_9.

Stone, D. 2012. 'Financial and commercial dimensions of settlements.' In N. Wheen and J. Hayward (eds), *Treaty of Waitangi Settlements*. Wellington: Bridget Williams Books. doi.org/10.7810/9781927131381_10.

Waitangi Tribunal 1997. *Te Manutukutuku*, No. 41. Wellington: Waitangi Tribunal.

Waitangi Tribunal 2015. *Te Manutukutuku*. No. 68. Wellington: Waitangi Tribunal.

Walker, R. 2004. *Ka Whawhai Tonu Matou: Struggle without end*. Auckland: Penguin.

Ward, A. 1999. *An Unsettled History: Treaty claims in New Zealand today*. Wellington: Bridget Williams Books.

Wheen, N. and Hayward, N. (eds) 2012. *Treaty of Waitangi Settlements*. Wellington: Bridget Williams Books.

18

The *Fiscal Responsibility Act 1994*: How a nonbinding policy instrument proved highly powerful

Derek Gill[1]

Introducing the *Fiscal Responsibility Act*

Sir Robert Muldoon, New Zealand's prime minister from 1975 to 1984, was recorded as observing that 'most people wouldn't recognise a Budget deficit if they fell over it in the street' (Kerr 2008: 3). While that statement might have applied to New Zealand at the time, it would not be made about contemporary New Zealand, where the major parties compete for the fiscal responsibility label. The fiscal responsibility provisions in the *New Zealand Public Finance Act 1989* (introduced as the *Fiscal Responsibility Act* or *FRA*) have become an enduring part of New Zealand's public management regime since coming into force in 1994. Fiscal responsibility provides the foundation for the Treasury's budgeting process, is embedded in the wider political discourse and is now part of New Zealand's constitutional arrangements. The *FRA* is one of the significant factors that help explain the success of successive administrations in running

1 The author would like to acknowledge the key people involved in the *FRA* who made themselves available for interview. Any errors or omissions remain the responsibility of the author. The author was working for the Treasury at the time of the development of the *FRA* and was a senior official at the State Services Commission at the time of the 2004 *Public Finance Act* amendments but was not directly involved in either process.

sustained structural fiscal surpluses and reducing net public debt from a peak in 1992 of just less than 50 per cent of GDP to close to zero by 2006 (Figure 18.1).

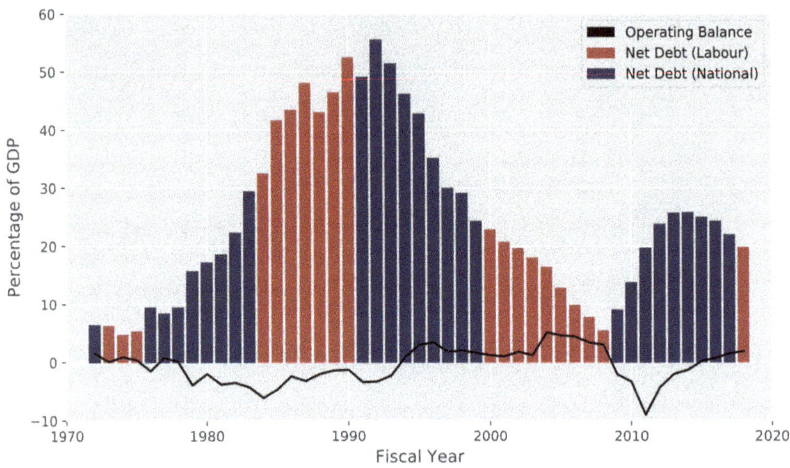

Figure 18.1 New Zealand Government net debt and fiscal balance, 1970–2018

Source: NZIER (n.d.).

While the *FRA* was not the catalyst—as the improvement in New Zealand's fiscal position pre-dates its enactment—the Act was an effective commitment device (Boston 2016) that helped cement fiscal discipline in New Zealand. In addition, the *FRA* was flexible enough to accommodate the recession of 2008–10 and the fiscal impact of the Canterbury earthquake sequence, while ensuring New Zealand returned to a fiscally sustainable track (see Figure 18.2). Arguably, the GFC, Canterbury earthquakes and the Kaikoura earthquake have also helped cement the cross-party political commitment to fiscal discipline—in other words, regular 'external' shocks continue to remind policymakers of New Zealand's economic vulnerability.

In preparation for the 2017 general election, the opposition Labour and Green parties publicly committed themselves to Budget responsibility rules. These were subsequently included largely word-for-word in the 2018 Budget Policy Statement (BPS) and in the first Budget of the new Labour–Green–New Zealand First Coalition Government. These rules included a commitment to keeping spending below 30 per cent of GDP, running an operating surplus over the cycle and reducing net debt to below 20 per cent of GDP by 2022.

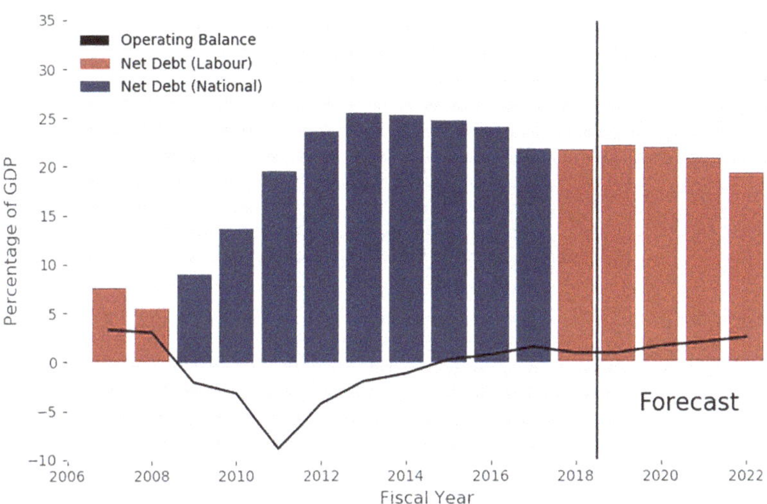

Figure 18.2 The recent track and outlook for the operating balance and net public debt, 2006–22

Source: The Treasury (2018).

New Zealand was a pathfinder on fiscal responsibility and the success of the *FRA* in making fiscal responsibility an active part of everyday political discourse is striking given the mixed record of most countries' experiences with legislated targets for Budget balances, spending and debt of various sorts. It is even more striking given the relatively arcane and technical nature of the *FRA* provisions (discussed in Box 18.1) and the lack of overt legal penalties for breaching the rules. The surprising success of a weak, nonbinding policy instrument is because it has political force even if it is not legally enforceable. In essence, the *FRA*:

1. Makes the government of the day responsible for articulating how it proposes to operationalise the principles of fiscal responsibility when developing its Budget (the principles are detailed in Box 18.1 and include targets for net debt levels and a balanced Budget over the business cycle).
2. Requires the Treasury to provide twice-yearly independent economic and fiscal updates, including specified ex-ante information on the fiscal strategy, the current economic conditions and fiscal outlook and risks to that outlook, a preelection update, the outlook over 10 years and every four years over a 40-year term.

3. Gives the Secretary of the Treasury an independent statutory role in ex-ante and ex-post financial reporting based on generally accepted accounting principles (GAAP). These principles are set by an independent accounting standards body, as the accounting framework for all ex-ante and ex-post fiscal reporting minimises the scope for 'creative accounting'.

Box 18.1 The principles of responsible fiscal management

The principles of responsible fiscal management, incorporated since 2004 in the *Public Finance Act* of 1989, require governments to:

- Ensure the achievement and subsequent maintenance of 'prudent levels' of public debt, by running operating balances that, on average over time, are non-negative and consistent with the desired trajectory of the debt.
- Achieve and maintain levels of the Crown's net worth that provide an adequate buffer against potential future events adversely impacting the Crown's balance sheet.
- Manage prudently the fiscal risks facing the government.
- Pursue policies consistent with reasonable stability and predictability of tax rates.

In 2013, the principles were amended to incorporate considerations relating to:

- the interaction between fiscal and monetary policies
- the likely impact of any fiscal strategy on present and future generations
- the efficiency and fairness of the tax system
- the effectiveness and efficiency in management of the Crown's resources.

The emphasis on greater openness and transparency increases the focus on more strategic and long-term fiscal issues, relative to short-term and political factors. In addition, the *FRA* offers escape clauses ('safety valves') for cyclical fluctuations or systemic events such as natural disasters. This ensures the government of the day has discretion about how it applies the principles in the face of changing circumstances.

A tripartite success?

Budgeting is simultaneously an inherently political process and a technocratic exercise. The *FRA* has succeeded at both levels. At the technocratic level, the *FRA* has been a *programmatic* success as New Zealand's fiscal aggregates have been turned around since the early 1990s, with large structural operating fiscal surpluses, as shown in Figure 18.1, until the period of the GFC. Figure 18.1 also shows how, until 2008, net government debt as a percentage of GDP plummeted. As a result, government net worth has increased dramatically. This fiscal consolidation was part of a package of economic reforms initiated since 1984, which, along with improvement in the external trading environment (including the rise of the Asian economies), caused the 'faster growth (steeper upward trend) from the early 1990s to 2010' in New Zealand's GDP per capita (Lattimore and Eaqub 2011: 7). This renewed economic growth is in marked contrast with the period of poor economic performance and relative economic decline from the mid-1970s to the early 1990s.

The exception to the pattern of fiscal consolidation was the period after the GFC and the Canterbury earthquake sequence, shown in Figure 18.2. Undoubtedly, this period was part of the success of the *FRA*. At the technical level, the buffer created by low public debt meant the government had the fiscal space to achieve broader stabilisation objectives in more difficult times. At the political level, the GFC, the Canterbury earthquakes and the 2016 Kaikoura earthquake have also helped cement the cross-party political commitment to fiscal discipline. A series of major external shocks, along with more minor shocks, such as severe droughts and biosecurity scares, helped to remind policymakers of New Zealand's economic vulnerability.

The sustained commitment since the early 1990s to prudent fiscal management by successive National Party governments (shown in blue in Figures 18.1 and 18.2) and Labour-led administrations (shown in red) means New Zealand now has one of the lowest public debt to GDP ratios in the OECD. While other factors, discussed in more detail below, underpinned the cross-party political commitment to fiscal responsibility, the transparency of fiscal forecasts required by the *FRA* had an important role to play in cementing in prudent fiscal management. The *FRA* provided the foundations for the fiscal management regime. This helped keep fiscal strategy issues on the political agenda, buttressed the Treasury's fiscal management approach and provided an independent scoring mechanism, which increased the credibility of political commitments to fiscal responsibility.

At the *process* level, the *FRA* was a success, as the policy design process resulted in an innovative approach to the fiscal constitution based on principles of fiscal responsibility rather than legislatively fixed fiscal targets. Buckle (forthcoming) describes how 'New Zealand was a pioneer in the development of governance arrangements to improve fiscal transparency in order to strengthen fiscal accountability' and was followed by other countries including Australia, with its *Charter of Budget Responsibility Act 1998* (Cwlth), and the United Kingdom, with its Charter for Budget Responsibility (2011).

Two principles stand out for the attention they receive in New Zealand—net debt reduction and maintaining an operating surplus—while the other principles have not achieved the same traction. This approach generally proved easy to implement as the *FRA* was largely codifying the Treasury's budgetary practice of the time and successive ministers of finance have found it a useful device for managing the Cabinet through the Budget process. After 25 years, the principles still provide the framework the Treasury uses to guide the development of the fiscal strategy and the 'rules of the game' under the fiscal management approach (Lomax et al. 2016). By contrast, the 40-year fiscal and economic outlooks introduced into the *FRA* in the 2004 legislative reforms have had little direct impact on political discourse.

At the *political* level, the concept of fiscal responsibility—in particular, the focus on net debt and operating surpluses—has been adopted by the main political parties across the spectrum. This was epitomised during the 2017 election campaign when the opposition Labour and Green parties signed an electoral pact that included Budget responsibility rules that were aligned with the provisions of the *FRA*. Fiscal responsibility is now deeply embedded in the everyday political discourse. When the *FRA* was introduced, there was limited opposition but widespread scepticism about whether it would have much impact. Support for the *FRA* is much stronger and more widespread now than at the time of its introduction. Thus, it has proved to be an enduring policy success.

This political success is striking given the *FRA* was developed by the then National Government through a very top-down policy process within the executive branch, with no public or cross-party engagement before consideration by the select committee. Just how fiscal responsibility has become an integral part of everyday political discourse backed by a multiparty consensus will be explored in the next section of this chapter.

New Zealand has no single constitutional document, so its constitutional arrangements can be found in a range of places. While it has no prescriptive legal status, the *Cabinet Manual* itself is regarded as an authoritative description of New Zealand's constitutional conventions and statutes. In the introduction to the *Cabinet Manual*, Sir Kenneth Keith (2017), one of New Zealand's leading jurists, explicitly mentions the *Public Finance Act* as one of the statutory sources of the New Zealand constitution. Then finance minister Sir William English, when introducing the 2013 *FRA* amendment said: '[G]iven the constitutional significance of the fiscal responsibility provisions, it was important that we discussed the changes with other parliamentary parties before introducing them to Parliament' (quoted in Lipski 2015: 8). As such, the fiscal responsibility provisions in the *Public Finance Act* now form an integral part of New Zealand's Constitution.

Box 18.2 and Figure 18.2 show how the *FRA* has endured through three long-running administrations, one major recession (2006–09) and the major fiscal shock of the Canterbury earthquake sequence (9–10 per cent of GDP). The imprimatur of fiscal responsibility is very important for all the major and minor parties on both the left and the right, as evidenced by the 2017 Labour–Green agreement on Budget responsibility rules. The absence of a large and strong populist party with no concern for long-term fiscal prudence has helped, as has the absence of a 'Tea Party' type conservative party committed to low taxes but not necessarily lower expenditure.

Box 18.2 *Fiscal Responsibility Act* timeline

January 1993: Finance minister Ruth Richardson summons the outgoing Treasury secretary and Treasury officials to a retreat.

Early 1993: The Treasury provides a stream of advice to the Minister of Finance to develop a regime based on fiscal responsibility principles rather than legislated fiscal targets, leading to a Cabinet paper.

Mid-1993: Cabinet approves the policy and subsequently the draft legislation.

September 1993: Fiscal Responsibility Bill introduced to parliament.

October 1993: First preelection economic and fiscal update published.

November 1993: General election, with the National Party returned with a significantly reduced majority; the majority in the referendum favours a new mixed-member proportional (MMP) system over the traditional first-past-the-post (FPP) system. Ruth Richardson is replaced as finance minister, does not take up another Cabinet position but is appointed chair of the Finance and Expenditure Select Committee (FEC).

Early 1994: The FEC considers the Fiscal Responsibility Bill. There is limited opposition but only lukewarm support, as there is widespread scepticism about whether it will have much impact (Scott 1995).

April 1994: Select committee report reflects bipartisan support for the general thrust of the Bill but a split over whether fiscal responsibility principles should be legislated (favoured by the government majority) or left to the government of the day (favoured by Labour).

May 1994: The Budget includes a dry run of the operation of the *FRA*, including a fiscal strategy report.

1 July 1994: The *FRA* assent comes into force.

May 1995: First Budget under the *FRA*.

October 1999: Election of the fifth Labour-led government, headed by Helen Clark.

2004: An omnibus public management reform Bill is introduced that makes three major amendments to the *FRA*, as well as some minor technical changes:

- the *FRA* is folded into the *Public Finance Act*
- the Treasury is required to provide economic and fiscal projections with a 40-year horizon every four years
- clarification is made that the focus of the Budget policy statement will be the broad fiscal parameters and priorities, to more clearly differentiate the contents of the statement from the more detailed discussion in the fiscal strategy report.

November 2008: Election of the fifth National Party–led administration, under the leadership of John Key.

2013: Amendments to the *Public Finance Act* fiscal responsibility provisions change the tax policy principle and include additional principles:

- the interaction between fiscal and monetary policies
- the likely impact of any fiscal strategy on present and future generations
- the effectiveness and efficiency in management of the Crown's resources.

February 2017: The opposition Labour and Green parties commit to Budget responsibility rules.

September 2017: The sixth Labour-led administration elected, headed by Jacinda Ardern.

In this chapter, the story of the design, rollout and increased acceptance of the *FRA* is explored by drawing on the available literature as well as through the words of its designers and implementers. A qualitative methodology was adopted, based on a literature scan and semistructured interviews with the key decision-makers who were directly engaged in the *FRA*. The interviews included two former Treasury secretaries, a former finance minister, a former budget director and the current chief accounting advisor.

The remainder of the chapter will explore how fiscal responsibility has become an integral part of New Zealand's constitutional arrangements and is now a part of everyday political discourse. It will discuss how the success reflects a combination of careful policy work by the Treasury for the initial political champion, sustained support from successive ministers of finance and some fortuitous circumstances that helped cement the regime.

The contextual imperative

In early 1993, when the *FRA* first emerged as a fiscal policy initiative, New Zealand was into the eighth year of the most wrenching and wideranging reform program undertaken by any OECD country. Only the countries of Eastern Europe—emerging from four decades of communist rule—had been through more extensive change (see Chapter 15, this volume). This reform program was a reaction to the excesses of the Muldoon National Government (1975–84), which had introduced an increasingly unorthodox style of economic management following a period of sustained poor economic performance and economic stagnation. The policies of the Muldoon Government had culminated in an 18-month wage and price freeze underpinned by a reported fiscal deficit that grew to 9 per cent of GDP (7 per cent of GDP on a basis comparable with other statistics in this chapter). Sustained structural fiscal deficits had resulted in public debt growing from about 5 per cent of GDP in the early 1970s to about 45 per cent of GDP by 1984 (shown in Figure 18.1).

Reformist governments—first under Labour (1984–90) and then under National (1990–99)—set about addressing the structural imbalances that had developed over the previous decades, including turning around the fiscal balance and reducing public indebtedness. The incoming National Government in 1990 faced the unpleasant surprise of a deteriorating fiscal outlook, which was accentuated by the need to bail out the failing Bank of New Zealand. In opposition, it had based its election commitments on the Budget forecasts, which were much more benign. In response, in the December 1990 statement and the 1991 Budget, the National Government had to abandon most of its preelection manifesto and instead introduced 'the mother of all Budgets'. This announced wideranging spending cuts and social policy reforms, including reductions in social welfare benefit payments. Public disquiet with the reform programs of both major parties was growing and political polls showed people favoured a new mixed-member proportional (MMP) representation system over the traditional first-past-the-post (FPP) system. An indicative referendum in 1992 signalled a change to the electoral voting system, which a binding referendum combined with the 1993 election was expected to confirm.

Political champion

The political champion for the *FRA* was the finance minister Ruth Richardson, who tasked the Treasury with developing a fiscal analogue to the *Reserve Bank Act*. Whereas monetary policy is essentially technical, fiscal policy is inherently political, as the Budget is an overt expression of the government's priorities.

The immediate political driver for the minister's request was the fiscal position National inherited on taking office in 1990, together with the threat of a change to the MMP system in 1993 and the view that minority and coalition governments were prone to weak fiscal control and deficit spending. The other driver was New Zealand's recent experience of fiscal deficits and the political costs of deficit reduction. The minister wanted to leave a legacy so that no Minister of Finance would go through what she (and previous Labour finance ministers) had been through. In this, she was supported by the prime minister, who was concerned to ensure that future governments should not expect the unpleasant fiscal surprise that their administration had inherited.

Box 18.2 includes a chronology of events leading up to the enactment of the *FRA* and beyond. It shows that, while National was returned to office after the 1993 election, it was with a significantly reduced majority. Richardson, when replaced as the Minister of Finance, did not take up another Cabinet position but was appointed as chair of the Finance and Expenditure Select Committee (FEC). As the chair of the committee considering the Fiscal Responsibility Bill, she could drive it through the parliamentary process to enactment. Shortly thereafter, Richardson resigned from parliament and left politics.

Bureaucratic steward

If Richardson was the political champion for the introduction of the *FRA*, the Treasury was the bureaucratic steward. While the Minister of Finance was initially attracted by the US style of legislated fiscal rules setting targets for spending, deficits and debt, Treasury officials were very sceptical about legislated targets in fiscal constitutions. This scepticism was based on an understanding of a range of countries' experiences and the US experience particularly with the *Gramm–Rudman–Hollings Balanced*

Budget Act. (The Treaty on European Union—or Maastricht Treaty—which introduced statutory deficit and debt limits, and which came into force in 1993 as the *FRA* was being developed, did not significantly influence official thinking in New Zealand as there was no experience on which to draw.) Treasury officials, however, had positive experiences with increased fiscal transparency over the period of the reforms, which suggested that transparency could be a very effective fiscal tool. In 1992, the Treasury had been able to release a set of unqualified consolidated Crown accrual accounts that covered the wider state sector using GAAP. The resulting information was influential in avoiding a double downgrade by the international credit rating agencies.

The *FRA*, based on transparency about fiscal responsibility principles and a medium-term focus, offered a number of technical opportunities to:

- lock in good budgetary practices moving from one-year Budgets to disclosure of three-year fiscal forecasts—practices that emerged during the reform era but were not always observed
- clarify roles to ensure the independence of the Treasury in preparing economic and fiscal forecasts
- enable the Budget to be driven by generally accepted accounting practices based on independently set accounting standards and to move away from the previous cash accounts (so-called Table 2), which were riddled with inconsistencies in treatment and had lost credibility
- strengthen the public sector management reform agenda through cementing the use of GAAP
- provide a commitment device to redress the time inconsistency problem by highlighting the future consequences of current policy settings
- increase the credibility of fiscal policy, using transparency to help shape expectations and hence reduce the risk premiums on public debt
- introduce a stronger top-down discipline on fiscal policy, giving up control of the little numbers to get control of the big numbers (to paraphrase the words of the Secretary of the Treasury).

Richardson, a powerful politician championing the *FRA*—first as the Minister of Finance and then as chair of the FEC—with active backing from the prime minister, put the *FRA* on the political agenda and kept the Bill moving through the legislative process with the Treasury's support.

There was no overt program to build support for the *FRA*. When it was introduced, the *FRA* received limited opposition but only lukewarm support. Early on, opposition politicians thought the legislation would be ineffectual because of its unenforceability. Lipski (2015: 8) quotes Winston Peters's speech to the House, in which he said: '[L]egislation of this type in this country is meaningless unless this Parliament means to keep faith with the public.' In a similar vein, Michael Cullen—who would become finance minister in the Clark administration—called the *FRA* 'constitutional nonsense' and suggested the 'notion that this Parliament will somehow bind future Governments on fiscal policy by stating such matters as it must "maintain a fiscal surplus in any year", is constitutional stupidity' (New Zealand Parliament 1994a: 225). Paul Swain—later a senior minister in the Clark Government—suggested 'it is neither possible nor desirable for this Government to try legislatively to "strait-jacket in" policy directions in the area of fiscal policy for future Governments' (New Zealand Parliament 1994b: 610.

However, leaving aside point-scoring in parliamentary debates and quibbles over the legislation binding subsequent parliaments, the *FRA* could build on a bipartisan political consensus that supported fiscal prudence. With a strong political champion, the Bill became law.

The new regime initially attracted favourable international attention. As Lipski (2015: 7) observed:

> When introduced in 1994, the provisions were seen as world-leading and influential institutional reform. They have been cited as best practice by international agencies such as the Organisation for Economic Cooperation and Development and the International Monetary Fund. (see also, for example, IMF 2007)

The continued external support is reflected in the 2013 'National Integrity System Assessment' conducted by Transparency International.

Policy design from the top down

The policy design process was remarkably quick by contemporary policy standards—from conception to enactment in less than 18 months. Consistent with the modus operandi at the time, it was a top-down process driven by the finance minister, with the full backing of the prime minister and supported by the Treasury. The policy design encountered few challenges within the government and limited interest and little sustained opposition when introduced into the House. The rollout was similarly uncontroversial, as the approach was technically easy to implement. The *FRA* was essentially codifying the approach already adopted in the 1994 Budget. The chain of events from conception in January 1993 through to application in the May 2018 Budget is shown in Box 18.2.

Looking at the sequence of events between conception of the idea in 1993 and enactment of the Bill in June 1994, a number of things deserve comment:

- **Speed of design:** New Zealand politicians have a reputation for being 'the fastest law-makers in the West' (Palmer 1979: 77). In this case, the elapsed time from conception to enactment was less than 18 months, and that included a general election after introduction but before select committee consideration of the Fiscal Responsibility Bill. While rapid, the time required was not unprecedented, as the style of the government of the day was to execute priorities quickly.
- **Top down and executive driven:** The initiative for the *FRA* came from the Minister of Finance, who requested the Treasury in January 1993 design the fiscal policy equivalent to the *Reserve Bank Act* for monetary policy independence. A small Treasury team, working closely with the Minister of Finance, then presented a stream of advice that culminated in the Fiscal Responsibility Bill, introduced to the House in September 1993.
- **The lack of challenge:** While within the executive there were critical voices (the Ministry of Justice had concerns about parliament legislating the executive's Budget process), there were no significant challenges. Similarly, once in the House, there was little sustained comment or opposition (unlike, say, the challenge raised to the proposals for the Regulatory Responsibility Bill in 2010).
- **Bipartisan consensus on fiscal responsibility as a concept:** The opposition supported the broad thrust of the *FRA* on introduction but thought it would be ineffective in practice.

The rules of the game

Under New Zealand's political rules of the time, political power was extremely centralised. With a single House, an FPP electoral system, the Westminster system of Cabinet collective responsibility and two well-established and strongly disciplined dominant parties, New Zealand's system was described not unfairly as 'an elected dictatorship' (Palmer 1979: 10). With a forceful finance minister, backed by the most powerful government department and with the prime minister's active support, legislative change was reasonably easy to achieve.

The institutional feature that constrained that 'unbridled power' was the fact that New Zealand's Treasury had a strong tradition of having a view independent of its minister. The initiative for the *FRA* came from the Minister of Finance, who had in mind a regime of legislated fiscal targets and rules similar to those used at the state and federal levels in the United States. The Treasury assembled a small, focused team to respond to the minister's request. The advice it provided concluded that legislated fiscal targets and rules had proved singularly ineffective in a wide range of jurisdictions. To quote from recent work by the Cato Institute:

> [T]argets will be missed or abandoned, creative accounting and overoptimistic forecasts will be used to hit targets, exceptional needs for spending will be declared, and transition periods to hit targets will be lengthened. (Bourne 2018: 6)

Instead, the Treasury proposed an innovative approach based on transparency about the principles of fiscal responsibility and independent forecasts and accounts. As one official observed:

> Essentially debt and surplus targets are required to be committed to by the government of the day, and that's a harder target to miss or abandon than one that has been set for you by others.

This approach was accepted by the government and continues to set the framework for fiscal policy in New Zealand today.

What is meant by fiscal rules is there are set numerical targets or limits on the Budget balance, debt, spending and tax revenue. These rules operate within a framework of a more general fiscal constitution set out in the *Public Finance Act*, Standing Orders and the *Cabinet Manual* and related documents. Examples of such rules include:

- Those that make the decisions of the Executive government are subservient to those of Parliament in a unicameral system, and/or of a second chamber in the case of a bicameral government
- The principle that Parliament will not delegate the power to tax
- The rule that government money cannot be spent except in accordance with parliamentary appropriations
- Rules relating to voting arrangements on fiscal matters. (Wilkinson and Acharya 2014: 53–4)

These general Budget rules also form an important constitutional context for the operation of the *FRA*.

Implementation by the executive

The *FRA*, once enacted, proved relatively easy to implement as it was largely codifying the Treasury's budgetary and accounting practices of the time. The accounting infrastructure introduced by the 1989 *Public Finance Act* could be applied to fiscal decision-making and accountability. The 1994 Budget was used as a dry run, so when the *FRA* came into force for the 1995 Budget, it was business as usual. Piloting was not essential to the success of the policy, but it did reinforce the case for enacting the *FRA*. The Treasury did, however, have to introduce a new information technology (IT) system as the old Budget management system lacked the required functionality to support the monthly fiscal reporting of progress against Budgets and forecasts required by the *FRA*.

Budgeting is a technical process that serves a political purpose. Successive ministers of finance under Labour and National-led administrations found the transparency and disclosure requirements of the *FRA* a useful discipline to tame the spending aspirations of their Cabinet and caucus colleagues.

It is instructive to compare the traction the principles for the operating balance and net debt have achieved with the lack of any direct impact of the long-term fiscal statement. The latter was introduced in the 2004 amendments to the *FRA* and required the Treasury to produce 40-year economic and fiscal outlooks every four years. There was no dry run prior to the introduction of the long-term fiscal statement, no requirement for the government to formally respond and limited direct political use for the projections. Unlike the four-year fiscal strategy, for which the government sets formal targets and the Treasury reports against those goals, the 40-year fiscal projections stand in splendid isolation. As one former Treasury official observed: 'We legislated before we knew what it was' and 'we still don't know what a good 40-year fiscal forecast looks like.' The Office of the Auditor-General was similarly polite but scathing in its recent performance audit of the 2016 statement on New Zealand's long-term fiscal position (OAG 2017).

There are three parts to New Zealand's Budget system:

1. the *FRA* principles, which provide the foundation
2. the annual BPS and fiscal strategy of the government of the day, along with supporting material prepared by the Treasury on the fiscal and economic outlooks, which provide the structure
3. the fiscal management approach of the Treasury, which operationalises these fiscal principles and strategies.

The *FRA* principles have been discussed above and are outlined in Box 18.1. While these provide a foundation, it is up to the government of the day to articulate how it proposes to operationalise the principles. Box 18.3 compares the Budget responsibility rules used by the Labour-led administration in the 2018 BPS with the corresponding statement of the previous National-led administration in 2017.

Box 18.3 Comparison of Budget responsibility rules

Reducing net debt to 20 per cent of GDP within five years of taking office and maintaining at prudent levels thereafter *(later than in the 2017 Budget policy statement)*.

Running sustainable operating surpluses across the economic cycle *(no change from 2017)*.

Maintaining expenditure within the recent historical range of spending to GDP ratio *(2017: over time, core Crown expenses are reduced to below 30 per cent of GDP)*.

Ensure a progressive taxation system that is fair, balanced and promotes the long-term sustainability and productivity of the economy *(2017: pursue policies consistent with reasonable stability and predictability of tax rates)*.

The government will strengthen net worth consistent with the debt and operating balance objectives *(2017: ensure net worth remains at a level sufficient to act as a buffer to economic shocks)*.

Prioritise investments to address the long-term financial and sustainability challenges facing New Zealand (no direct counterpart in the 2017 BPS, which did include: *manage prudently the fiscal risks facing the government*).

One of the key features of the 2018 BPS is that only two of the fiscal aggregates are expressed as measurable targets: the operating balance and net debt. Successive administrations have committed themselves to running fiscal surpluses (operating surpluses across the economic cycle). There is a longstanding cross-party consensus on the need to reduce public debt. Both major parties are currently committed to reducing net debt to below 20 per cent of GDP; the only point of difference is the timing.

There has been much less traction with the principles relating to tax, risk and net worth. Although there have been fewer surprise announcements of tax changes, there is no evidence that the *FRA* tax principles have had any practical effect, and the lack of commentary on the changes to the tax principles (shown in Box 18.3) reinforces this. Ministers of finance are answerable for the operating balance of taxes and spending (before accounting gains and losses) but there has been much less focus on change in net worth. The government's investment statement, introduced by the 2013 amendments to the *Public Finance Act*, has attempted to increase the focus on the Crown's management of its balance sheet but so far with limited success. The risk principle is operationalised in the Budget economic and fiscal update, with a detailed discussion of the key risks facing the economy (including two alternative scenarios) as well as disclosure of specific fiscal risks (both quantified and unquantified). As the Treasury secretary has statutory independence on the preparation of this material, the effect is to reinforce the integrity of the fiscal forecasts. Arguably, the increased transparency also encourages governments to address the risks that may hit them in the near future by taking action earlier.

To give effect to the government's fiscal strategy, the Treasury has developed a fiscal management approach. The key features of this approach were developed in the 1990s; it was fully formed in the early 2000s and is still applicable today. The approach includes:

- fixed nominal baselines with no allowance for inflation
- operating allowance for new initiatives (on a net basis) with limited exclusions such as debt servicing and major accounting gains or losses
- capital allowances for new financial or major physical investments
- technical forecasting changes including the operation of automatic stabilisers through welfare benefits and tax revenue changes, as well as New Zealand Superannuation

- fiscally neutral changes, which can be agreed within the financial year
- Contingencies for between-Budget baseline changes.

As one of the *FRA*'s architects commented, 'the Act codified and embedded an emergent culture'. This culture in turn reflected a wider cross-party consensus on the imperative for greater transparency and fiscal responsibility. The *FRA* likely also represented a return to the culture of fiscal conservativism in New Zealand that had existed until the 1970s.

In a regulatory impact statement in support of the 2013 *Public Finance Act* amendments, the Treasury said:

> There is no legal sanction for breaching the provisions, and it would also be possible for a government to comply with the form of the provisions but not their substance. The success or otherwise of the fiscal responsibility provisions therefore *depends on the level of acceptance and support they receive across government*. (The Treasury 2012: 1; emphasis added)

Put another way, the *FRA* has political force even if it is not legally enforceable.

Parliament largely absent

The discussion to date has focused on how the executive has implemented the *FRA*. We turn now to the legislature, as a key part of the design was increased scrutiny by parliament. The *FRA* provides for a BPS for parliament to scrutinise how the government proposes to operationalise the fiscal responsibility principles. The BPS is generally provided in February—well in advance of the Budget (in May).

In practice, the select committee's reviews of the BPS have rarely been very enlightening or insightful. The size of the New Zealand Parliament, unlike its British parent, is too small for politicians to make a career leading the work of select committees. As one interviewee observed:

> The role of a unicameral parliament in our version of the Westminster system is to focus on lawmaking not scrutiny. To the extent it is involved in scrutiny, it has been down in the weeds (the standard estimates questionnaire of inputs and individuals' expenses) rather than in the sky focusing on the big picture of fiscal strategy.

This is consistent with Mark Prebble's 'iron rule of political contest', which can be defined as 'the opposition in parliament does not criticise the government to improve it; they criticise it to lawfully overthrow it' (Prebble 2010: 35–8). Unless the BPS provided an opportunity for the opposition to attack the government, the standard and level of scrutiny would not be high.

The transparency, quality and multiyear focus of the fiscal information have been useful to the Controller and Auditor-General in providing the context for parliamentary briefings and for the opposition in helping them shape their policy platform. The *FRA* has been successful in ensuring that no incoming government has experienced the unpleasant fiscal surprise that faced the 1990 National Party administration.

Monitoring by commentators and capital markets

Parliamentary monitoring, by analogy with policing, was based less on regular patrols than on waiting for alarms to go off. The Treasury, in its role as the independent and credible scorekeeper, was an important source of information to trigger the alarms. Economic commentators and financial market analysts are both active users of that financial information who can then sound the alarm.

As one of the architects of the *FRA* told the author:

> One clear consequence of financial market reforms was the speed at which markets would respond to poor policy and, in particular, to poor fiscal policy. The aggregate fiscal policies of governments were closely assessed by financial analysts and could be quickly reflected in interest rates. The discipline being imposed by financial markets has played quite a significant role in supporting much better fiscal policy and transparency.

Political commentators and economic analysts (such as bank economists) were also actively scrutinising the fiscal information for inconsistencies with the 'Wellington consensus' on the importance of prudent fiscal management.

Gaining broad acceptance

Fiscal policy has become part of the wider political discourse as parties compete for the 'fiscal responsibility' mandate. Parties across the political spectrum put considerable effort into costing their preelection policies.

As discussed above, the electoral agreement between the opposition Labour and Green parties on Budget responsibility rules has flowed directly into the 2018 BPS and Budget documents. Following the release of the 2018 Budget, the *National Business Review*, New Zealand's leading business journal, featured a lead article with the headline: 'Well-being budget will put pressure on budget responsibility rules' (Edwards 2018). There are dissenting voices suggesting the *FRA* provisions are a 'false idol' (Nana 2017) or a 'straitjacket' (Eaqub 2018). The more widespread view is that it is a useful addition to the public management system and provides a framework that can be used to assess other target-setting regimes such as the Child Poverty Reduction Bill (Easton 2018).

Durability in the face of fluctuations

One of the key dimensions of policy success is how well the policy regime endures over time following political changes in administrations and in the face of economic expansions and contractions. Figure 18.1 shows how successive National and Labour-led administrations before the GFC ran sustained structural surpluses, driving down the net public debt to GDP ratio accordingly. For example, New Zealand ran sustained structural surpluses in the range of 1.5–6 per cent of GDP from 1994 to 2006. Net public debt over the same period fell from just over 60 per cent of GDP to just under 5 per cent. Indeed, the ratio fell below zero if the New Zealand Superannuation fund is also included.

While it is tempting to attribute that reduction in public indebtedness to the *FRA*, in fact, the start of the improvement in New Zealand's fiscal position pre-dates its enactment. While the transparency required by the *FRA* had an important role to play, other factors were more important:

- The legacy of the Muldoon years with a bipartisan political commitment to fiscal responsibility.
- The establishment of the New Zealand Superannuation Fund (the so-called Cullen Fund) to partially prefund the increased future cost of the New Zealand Superannuation pension, due to population ageing.
- The increasing recognition of the importance for a small trading nation of fiscal resilience and sustainability.

The *FRA*, while not the catalyst, helped cement fiscal discipline into the political discourse and budgeting practice in New Zealand. As one interviewee observed: 'It is less about whether the *FRA* helped achieve a better fiscal performance, and more about whether it helped sustain it.'

Fiscal strategy needs to focus on short-term macroeconomic stability as well as medium-term fiscal sustainability. One of the criticisms of the Fiscal Responsibility Bill in the select committee was that the medium-term focus would constrain the government from undertaking an anticyclical fiscal policy, beyond the operation of automatic stabilisers. These fears have proved unjustified. If anything, the opposite has occurred, as New Zealand has experienced some of the biggest swings in the OECD in its structural fiscal balance.

The Treasury's analysis suggests the *FRA* framework, while focusing on medium-term fiscal sustainability, places little attention on shorter-term macroeconomic stability, such as the impact of procyclical increases in government spending. Brook (2013: 71) suggests:

> New Zealand's current fiscal policy framework—with its emphasis on a debt target—gives insufficient emphasis to macro stabilisation during upturns in the business cycle, especially once the debt target has been met. In a small open economy such as New Zealand, with a floating exchange rate, pro-cyclical fiscal stimulus is unlikely to have much impact on aggregate demand (because of leakage into imports and the offsetting impact of tighter monetary policy), but it does have a significant impact on the mix of macro-economic conditions. Higher real interest rates, and associated exchange rate appreciation, is [sic] unhelpful to an economy already experiencing macroeconomic imbalances.

Figure 18.3 compares the cyclically adjusted (or structural) fiscal balance with the output gap. It covers the second and third terms of the Clark Labour-led Government and the first term of the Key National-led Government.[2]

2 For an independent account of New Zealand fiscal policy before the GFC, see Norman and Gill (2010); for an official summary of fiscal policy since the GFC, see Bose et al. (2016); and for a detailed account of the history and evolution of the *FRA*, including a more technical assessment using the sustainability, stability and structural roles of fiscal policy, see Buckle (forthcoming).

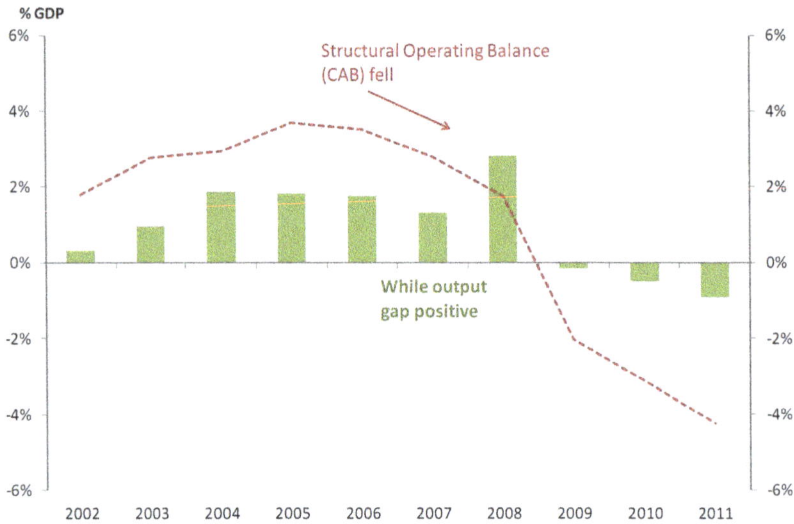

Figure 18.3 Destabilising fiscal stance: The operating balance and the output gap, 2002–11
Source: The Treasury (2012).

In 2008—an election year in New Zealand—there was a marked easing in the stance of fiscal policy despite the output gap still being significantly positive. This reflects windfall gains in taxation revenue, which were used to fund permanent increases in operating spending such as enhancements to the 'Working for Families' policy. The tax revenue increases proved temporary and their reversal coincided with the onset of the GFC and, subsequently, the impact of the Canterbury earthquake sequence (about 10 per cent of GDP over three years). As a result, New Zealand faced a record fiscal deficit of about 9 per cent of GDP in 2011. The framework provided by the *FRA* meant that, when the National-led administration committed itself to return to fiscal surplus, this was seen as credible and the impact on financial markets was minimised. The government successfully delivered a small fiscal surplus in 2014 (shown in Figure 18.2).

The experience of fiscal management in the face of sustained economic growth led the Treasury to recommend an additional fiscal anchor based on medium-term expenditure or revenue constraints to augment the anchor provided by debt (The Treasury 2008), and subsequently to develop the case for additional fiscal responsibility principles, which were introduced in 2013 (included in Box 18.1). Figure 18.3 is drawn from the Treasury's regulatory impact statement for the 2013 amendments to the fiscal responsibility provisions in the *Public Finance Act*. It is difficult to discern any impact from the 2013 amendments. For example, it is not clear whether the three new principles informed the 2018 BPS and the fiscal strategy report, and the lack of explicit mention has not attracted unfavourable comment.

The endurance of fiscal transparency and responsibility

New Zealand's generally positive experience with the *FRA* contributing to sustained surpluses and debt reduction is consistent with the old saying about 'good things taking time'. When the *FRA* was introduced, there was limited opposition but widespread scepticism about whether it would have much impact. Support for the *FRA* is now much stronger than at the time of its introduction.

Since its enactment in 1994, the *FRA* has set the framework within which fiscal policy has been formulated in New Zealand. Its emphasis on the transparency of forecasts has been key to ensuring fiscal responsibility and resilience. The durability of the regime lies in the fact the *FRA* does not specify, for example, what constitutes a 'prudent level of public debt'. It is left to the government of the day to operationalise what is meant and to disclose this in the annual fiscal strategy report. Similarly, with the notable exceptions of the operating balance rule, net worth and net debt, the other fiscal aggregate principles are qualitative and not readily measurable, leaving the interpretation to the government of the time.

The flexibility of this approach allows the framework to adapt to changing circumstances (the Canterbury earthquake sequence and cyclical fluctuations such as the GFC provide examples from recent history). Arguably, recent shocks have also helped cement the cross-party political commitment to fiscal discipline. This suggests the *FRA* can remain a success in the future as long as the cross-party commitment to fiscal responsibility is sustained.

New Zealand's experience with a regime based on transparency also speaks to the ongoing debate about fiscal targets and fiscal constitutions. Looking at a range of countries' experiences with entrenching fiscal targets, the Cato Institute concluded:

> The academic evidence and historical record show that formal fiscal rules are neither necessary nor sufficient to obtain sound public finances … The key is to design rules that are simple enough to be well understood and monitored, but flexible enough to be durable against unforeseen economic shocks that temporarily derail that goal. Doing so requires well thought-through procedural details and means of enforcement. (Bourne 2018: 6)

The enduring and increasing success of the *FRA* has several unexpected features:

- An apparently weak instrument proved politically powerful when backed by an independent and credible scorekeeper and monitoring by financial markets and commentators.
- Policy success is very path dependent: that the *FRA* has been increasingly influential and adopted by political parties across the spectrum is a result of both careful design and good luck.
- Budgeting is inherently a political statement (as well as a technocratic process), which means that technocratic Budget rules can influence details of how the game is played but do not change the fundamental nature of the political game.
- Ownership of goals matters: the *FRA* required the government of the day to articulate the fiscal goals. This reduces the amount of cheating and gaming as the government owns the goals rather than having targets set in legislation.
- Widespread consultation and buy-in to the design of a policy regime are not preconditions for success: the *FRA* was developed by the National Government through a short, very top-down policy process, with almost no public or cross-party engagement before select committee consideration.
- The unexpected and indeed astonishing success of the *FRA* arose from a technical policy solution providing a valuable political management tool for ministers of finance.
- Transparency about fiscal responsibility is not enough on its own.

The success of the approach, as Teresa Ter-Minassian, former director of the IMF's fiscal affairs department observed, is down to the

> quality, comprehensiveness, reliability and timeliness of the budget documentation, to facilitate adequate scrutiny by the Parliament, and by society at large, of the consistency of the Government's fiscal strategy with

> the above-listed principles. Accordingly, New Zealand has pioneered, and refined over the years, comprehensive fiscal reporting requirements, intended to ensure transparency, and to promote time consistency and a broad debate of the fiscal policy choices of successive Governments. (2014: 14)

Equally important is that the ex post financial information is of the same quality as the ex-ante budget information. The *FRA* is underpinned by a consolidated set of government financial statements that are consistent with GAAP set by an independent accounting standards body. The accounts are prepared by the Treasury. Treasury, as the most powerful government department, is an influential institution in New Zealand in its own right. In the case of the *FRA*, it has been given statutory independence in the preparation of the fiscal forecasts and financial statements. This means, as one interviewee observed, 'that New Zealand has the cleanest set of financial accounts in the west', which are not subject to the accounting fiddles and off-balance-sheet shenanigans seen in other jurisdictions and in New Zealand in the past.

Merely supplying information does not mean it will be used. While the intended demand for financial information from parliament did not eventuate, economic commentators and financial market analysts have been active users of that information. This active monitoring served to reinforce the Minister of Finance's position within Cabinet on the importance of fiscal responsibility.

Unfinished business

Nonetheless, the framework provided by the *FRA* is not without potential risks and problems.

The first is that the future durability of the *FRA* is dependent on popular support for the importance of fiscal responsibility and that cross-party commitment to fiscal responsibility is sustained. To date, New Zealand politics has been notable for the absence of a large and strong populist party with no concern for long-term fiscal prudence or a 'Tea Party' type conservative party committed to low taxes but not necessarily lower expenditure.

Second, the ongoing integrity of the *FRA* framework is heavily reliant on the Treasury continuing to actively pursue its stewardship role, including as an independent scorekeeper.

Third, while the *FRA* provides a useful framework for executive government, the fiscal regime is largely silent on where the other political parties fit. New Zealand is one of the few OECD countries without an independent budget office. While New Zealand's size may mean building an independent economic and fiscal forecasting capability is not realistic, there remains the role of assisting other political parties with costing policy proposals (Wilson 2017). The 2018 Budget announced the government was developing a proposal for an independent budget office, so the gap in the current fiscal framework may be addressed by this initiative.

Fourth, the framework has had limited effectiveness in taking into account the effect of the business cycle. Figure 18.3 shows the changes in the structural fiscal balance, with New Zealand experiencing some of the biggest swings in the OECD. While net debt provides a powerful fiscal anchor for medium-term sustainability, it is less robust for dealing with macroeconomic stability.

Conclusions

These caveats aside, there are unique factors that could limit how broadly the lessons from this case can be applied. There were both political and technical preconditions that were required to underpin the operation of the *FRA*. The *FRA* principles need to be supported at the political level by the commitment of the government of the day to a prudent fiscal strategy and at a technical level by a fiscal management approach to operationalise the government's fiscal strategy.

At the technical level, the *FRA* was backed by a powerful treasury with a suite of tools and techniques to make the fiscal strategy stick. The *FRA* gave fiscal policy a top-down discipline for sustaining a long-term regime of fixed nominal baselines, while the financial management reforms delivered the required bottom-up flexibility. As one source commented: 'Introducing the *FRA* in 1984 simply wouldn't have worked.'

Without political will, however, the techniques of fiscal management will not deliver fiscal discipline. As the *FRA* is not legally enforceable, it needs to have political force. Political will is not something that exists in isolation. The ongoing legacy of the Muldoon years is an enduring consensus across the major political parties on the importance of prudent fiscal policy. Financial market and other nonpolitical monitoring processes have helped sustain that political will. The *FRA* helped to codify and embed into political discourse and budgeting practices a commitment to fiscal prudence and lent credibility to the Budget process. But, without that political commitment, fiscal responsibility principles would have remained just principles, with government statements complying with the form of the provisions but not their substance.

In summary, the *FRA* was a commitment device that helped cement fiscal discipline into New Zealand's budgeting system and policy discourse rather than the catalyst that started it. In the process, the *FRA* provides the foundations for the Treasury's budgeting process, is embedded in the wider everyday political discourse and is now part of New Zealand's constitutional framework.

References

Bose, D., Philip, R. and Sullivan, R. 2016. *Returning to surplus: New Zealand's recent fiscal consolidation experience*. Treasury Working Paper 16-05, 3 February. Wellington: New Zealand Government. Available from: treasury.govt.nz/publications/wp/returning-surplus-new-zealands-post-gfc-fiscal-consolidation-experience-wp-16-05.

Boston, J. 2016. 'Committing to a better future: The nature, design, and limits of commitment devices.' In J. Boston (ed.), *Governing for the Future: Designing democratic institutions for a better tomorrow. (Public Policy and Governance, Volume 25)*. Bingley, UK: Emerald Group Publishing. doi.org/10.1108/S2053-769720160000025009.

Bourne, R. 2018. *Budget restraints that work: Lessons from Chile, Switzerland, the United Kingdom, and the United States*. Tax & Budget Bulletin No. 81, February. Washington, DC: Cato Institute. Available from: object.cato.org/sites/cato.org/files/pubs/pdf/tbb-81.pdf.

Brook, A. 2013. 'Making fiscal policy more stabilising in the next upturn: Challenges and policy options.' *New Zealand Economic Papers* 47(1): 71–94. Available from: ideas.repec.org/a/taf/nzecpp/vv47y2013i1p71-94.html.

Buckle, B. forthcoming. 'Fiscal policy governance and institutional developments in New Zealand: 1994 to 2018.' In G. Karacaoglu and E. Berman (eds), *Public Policy and Governance Frontiers in New Zealand*. Bingley, UK: Emerald Group Publishing.

Eaqub, S. 2018. 'The Budget: A delicate dance on a fiscal tightrope.' *Stuff.co.nz*, 20 May. Available from: www.stuff.co.nz/business/opinion-analysis/104012769/the-budget--a-delicate-dance-within-a-straightjacket.

Easton, B. 2018. 'Improving the Child Poverty Reduction Bill.' *Pundit*, 3 May. Available from: www.pundit.co.nz/content/improving-the-child-poverty-reduction-bill.

Edwards, B. 2018. 'Well-being budget will put pressure on budget responsibility rules.' *National Business Review*, 21 May.

International Monetary Fund (IMF) 2007. *Manual on Fiscal Transparency*. Washington, DC: IMF. Available from: www.imf.org/external/np/fad/trans/manual/sec02b.htm.

Keith, K. 2017. 'On the Constitution of New Zealand: An introduction to the foundations of the current form of government.' In *Cabinet Manual*. Wellington: Department of the Prime Minister and Cabinet. Available from: www.dpmc.govt.nz/our-business-units/cabinet-office/supporting-work-cabinet/cabinet-manual/introduction.

Kerr, R. 2008. 'Do economists agree on anything?' *NZ Business Roundtable*, 1 April. Wellington: New Zealand Initiative. Available from: nzinitiative.org.nz/reports-and-media/reports/do-economists-agree-on-anything/.

Lattimore, R. and Eaqub, S. 2011. *The New Zealand Economy: An introduction*. Auckland: Auckland University Press. Available from: www.press.auckland.ac.nz/en/browse-books/all-books/books-2011/The-New-Zealand-Economy-An-Introduction.html.

Lipski, J. 2015. Accountability and the fiscal responsibility provisions of the New Zealand Public Finance Act 1989. LLB (Hons) paper, Victoria University of Wellington, Wellington. Available from: researcharchive.vuw.ac.nz/xmlui/bitstream/handle/10063/5025/paper.pdf?sequence=1.

Lomax, N., McLoughlin, S. and Udy, B. 2016. The New Zealand fiscal management approach. Conference Paper. Wellington: The Treasury. Available from: www.nzae.org.nz/wp-content/uploads/2016/10/3228152_FINAL-Conference-Paper-Guide-to-NZs-FMA.pdf.

Nana, G. 2017. 'Has fiscal responsibility become a false idol?' *Pundit*, 26 April. Available from: www.pundit.co.nz/content/has-fiscal-responsibility-become-a-false-idol.

New Zealand Government 2018. *He Puna Hao Pātiki: 2018 investment statement*. Wellington: The Treasury. Available from: treasury.govt.nz/publications/investment-statement/2018-investment-statement.

New Zealand Institute of Economic Research (NZIER) n.d. Data1850. [Online]. Wellington: NZIER. Available from: data1850.nz.

New Zealand Parliament 1994a. *New Zealand Parliamentary Debates* (26 May), 540, 225.

New Zealand Parliament 1994b. *New Zealand Parliamentary Debates* (7 June), 540, 610.

Norman, R. and Gill, D. 2010. 'Budgeting in New Zealand after the reforms: From radical revolutionary to cautious consolidator.' In J. Wanna, L. Jensen and J. de Vries (eds), *The Reality of Budgetary Reform in OECD Nations: Trajectories and consequences*. Cheltenham, UK: Edward Elgar. doi.org/10.4337/9781849805636.00012.

Office of the Auditor-General (OAG) 2017. *Commentary on He Tirohanga Mokopuna: 2016 statement on the long-term fiscal position*. Wellington: OAG. Available from: www.oag.govt.nz/2017/long-term-fiscal-position/docs/long-term-fiscal-position.pdf/view.

Palmer, G. 1979. *Unbridled Power? An interpretation of New Zealand's constitution and government*. Wellington: Oxford University Press.

Prebble, M. 2010. *With Respect: Parliamentarians, officials, and judges too*. Wellington: Institute of Policy Studies.

Scott, G. 1995. 'New Zealand's Fiscal Responsibility Act.' *Agenda* 2(1): 1–13.

Ter-Minassian, T. 2014. *External Review of the Treasury's Fiscal Policy Advice: New Zealand*. Wellington: The Treasury. Available from: treasury.govt.nz/sites/default/files/2014-10/tfpa-2908566.pdf.

Transparency International 2013. *New Zealand national integrity system assessment 2013*. Integrity Plus 2013. Berlin: Transparency International. Available from: www.transparency.org/whatwedo/publication/new_zealand_national_integrity_system_assessment_2013.

The Treasury 2008. *Briefing to the Incoming Minister of Finance: Economic and fiscal strategy—Responding to your priorities*. Wellington: New Zealand Government. Available from: www.beehive.govt.nz/sites/default/files/Treasury2_BIM_0.pdf.

The Treasury 2012. *Amendment to part 2 of the Public Finance Act 1989 (the fiscal responsibility provisions)*. Regulatory Impact Statement. Wellington: The Treasury. Available from: treasury.govt.nz/sites/default/files/2012-08/ris-tsy-pfafrp-aug12.pdf.

The Treasury 2018. *Budget 2018*. Wellington: The Treasury. Available from: treasury.govt.nz/publications/budgets/budget-2018.

Wilkinson, B. and Acharya, K. 2014. *Guarding the public purse: Faster growth, greater fiscal discipline*. Report. Wellington: New Zealand Initiative. Available from: nzinitiative.org.nz/reports-and-media/reports/guarding-the-public-purse/.

Wilson, P. 2017. *Keeping the bastards honest*. NZIER Insight 72. Wellington: New Zealand Institute of Economic Research. Available from: nzier.org.nz/media/keeping-the-bastards-honest-nzier-insight-72.

19

Early childhood education policy pathways: A learning story

Sandy Farquhar and Andrew Gibbons[1]

Introduction

Aotearoa New Zealand's twenty-first-century policy directions for early childhood education and care were set out in *Pathways to the Future* (MoE 2002). *Pathways* is regarded as a significant policy development within New Zealand and internationally (Wells 2015; May 2017). Developed by a centre-left, Labour-led coalition government, it ushered in a period of radical, far-reaching, progressive changes within the early childhood education sector. While not fully achieving its goals within its targeted 10-year period, it was and still is a reference point for the long-term governance of early childhood education (ECE). In 2002, the government's restructuring of the economy posed major challenges to social policy development in New Zealand, including that for ECE. Despite the reforms, *Pathways* looked like a runaway success until it was curtailed following the election of the National Government in 2008. Political commentator Colin James suggested it was 'arguably Labour's most important initiative, its biggest idea' (cited in May 2015). This big idea—a comprehensive vision and framework for the sector—was internationally recognised as an innovation in education policy.

1 The authors report no known conflict of interest.

As a policy innovation, *Pathways* recognised and promoted ECE as being worthy of significant investment and development. It articulated a vision of all children participating in ECE and identified the strategies required to develop and maintain high-quality education. Providing a coherent, far-reaching direction for a fast-growing sector, *Pathways* offered a blueprint for funding and regulation and served as a mechanism for supporting community-based ECE development. It suggested stronger government engagement with ECE provision and promoting teacher qualifications and professionalisation as hallmarks of quality. It set out three goals—to 'increase participation in quality ECE services', improve the quality of ECE services and 'promote collaborative relationships'—the last of which includes strategies for the 'building of an ECE sector responsive to the needs of Māori and Pasifika peoples' (MoE 2002: 3).

Strategies for implementing *Pathways* were summarised by the Ministry of Education (MoE 2002) as involving a complex mix of approaches: funding, regulation, information and support. Effectively, *Pathways* laid the foundation for a raft of changes to support the development of ECE. In terms of education spending, funding rates increased for all teacher-led services, equity funding grants were introduced, study grants provided incentives for staff to increase their qualifications and extra funding was available for teachers' professional development. *Pathways* included a revision of ECE regulations and a review of the early childhood curriculum, *Te Whāriki* (MoE 1996), particularly its support for curriculum development in early childhood care and education centres. In terms of informing and supporting the sector, the Ministry of Education established a collaborative research initiative called Centres of Innovation, showcasing exemplars of inquiry into curriculum practices in ECE. The ministry followed this plan, rationalising, regulating, integrating and supporting ECE providers and developing a series of ongoing evaluations of policy developments. Throughout this period, rapid change occurred in the sector, including a move towards increasing the qualifications of teachers (an anticipated 100 per cent qualified by 2012) and registration of all early childhood teachers. These shifts were accompanied by the introduction of pay parity with schoolteachers for kindergarten teachers and the development of professional standards for kindergarten teachers (MoE 2004). Curriculum delivery was supported with the development of the assessment guidelines, *Kei Tua o te Pae: Assessment for learning—Early childhood exemplars* (MoE 2005, 2007, 2009a) and the implementation of teacher self-review guidelines (MoE 2006). To support increased participation, '20 Hours Free ECE' was introduced (for further analysis, see Farquhar and Gibbons 2010; Gibbons and Farquhar 2014).

Successful pathways

The success of *Pathways* as government policy is most evident in its innovative management of the diverse and complex issues that influence ECE. A successful ECE policy program and process in Aotearoa New Zealand has to navigate significant political tensions and challenges, both philosophically and pragmatically. These tensions and challenges include resistance to shifts from normalised childrearing traditions towards institutionalised care and education; disagreement over the relationships between care and education for children before school associated with a history of confusion as to where the sector's portfolio should lie; and the ongoing emergence of sometimes contradictory research evidence regarding child development, pedagogy and outcomes. As a noncompulsory sector, ECE has many different provider organisations. There is competition between for-profit ECE providers and not-for-profit community services, which introduces tension to the sector. Broader challenges for ECE policy development include political agendas that contemplate the use of the sector as leverage for social, political and economic goals, at both the national and the global levels.

Pathways was (and continues to be, to some extent) successful because it acknowledged these political issues and regarded inclusive and robust debate as vital to its strategic vision. In this sense, *Pathways* had broad social and political appeal. It responded to well-documented statistics and research on the needs of the labour market, on the changing dynamics of (mainly dual-income) families and on the benefits of ECE as a social good. It mobilised a series of networks and programs to keep policy attuned to the changing social and political climate, embracing the strength of the whole sector as critical to success, rather than targeting and isolating the sector's various elements.

Historically, the contest for provision of ECE has been fraught at a number of levels that broadly reflect differing social and political values around the role of women and children and differing philosophies about how rights are conferred on particular groups in society. Conservative and neoliberal governments in Aotearoa have construed education as a *private* good accruing to individuals, as a form of self-investment. Social-democratic governments in Aotearoa tend to recognise ECE as a *public* good, although they continue to support private investment and have stopped short of free universal provision. Hence, *Pathways* has successfully walked a political tightrope, steadfastly promoting its core goals for more than a decade and maintaining general acceptance across the political spectrum.

Esteemed internationally as one of the first strategic plans for ECE, *Pathways* has been celebrated by leading scholars and international organisations for its role in the development of an integrated and bicultural approach to both curriculum and policy. Peter Moss (2007, cited in May 2015: 147) argues that New Zealand's early childhood policy direction has led the way in confronting 'wicked issues', providing 'integrated approaches to funding, regulation, curriculum and qualifications'. The OECD's *Starting Strong II* report (2006) also lauds New Zealand for its commitment to an integrated system of funding and regulation. Despite recent backsliding by government and a generally unfavourable political climate, *Pathways* has maintained social and political currency within the sector, with its central tenets of quality, participation and collaboration supported by an active global policy push and a localised demand for affordable quality care to respond to the expectations of working families.

Pathways has been the most far-reaching early childhood policy strategy in Aotearoa in recent times and is clearly a policy success for a number of reasons. It had structural implications for the entire sector, addressing the needs of families, government and society. It featured inclusive consultation and collaboration and has been kept alive by recognised and credible leaders within the sector. It did the hard social and political work needed for later policy initiatives to flourish. Its implementation mechanisms provided evidence of ongoing success and, furthermore, it has sustained engagement with key stakeholders over a long period. Its effectiveness lay in the power of its policies and its emphasis on collaboration within the sector, providing optimal conditions for a thriving ECE sector and for future policy development. Mintrom and Norman (2009: 649) suggest that 'small teams can do much to draw attention to policy problems, present innovative policy solutions, build coalitions of supporters, and secure legislative action'. *Pathways* is an ideal example of such movement; it is an innovative policy solution that has garnered strong sectoral, social and political support. As Wells argues, its success stems from its focus on children and families, its deliberateness and its collaborative process:

> Ngā Huaraki Arataki [*Pathways to the Future*] was not a random event or simply a good idea at the time. It was evidence based, and built on the experiences and knowledge of the sector. It sat within a world view that what happens for our youngest citizens matters. It was at a time

> when significant research around brain development was emerging, children's first years being critical in shaping their future. The focus was unequivocally on children and their families and whānau [family]. (Wells 2015: 7)

Pathways provided a cohesive platform for diverse curriculum and policy developments to support a dynamic and rapidly evolving sector, focusing strongly on building social cohesion through the promotion of collaborative relationships. The advocacy and scholarship of a number of key individuals played a vital role in policy development, providing a strong thread of continuity of care and stewardship.

The GFC in 2008, along with the election of a right-leaning government, signalled strong headwinds for a number of the plan's goals, although the program and its intentions continued to be valued and supported by many in the sector. At the time of writing (2018), a newly elected, left-leaning coalition government had reinvigorated many of the unrealised intentions of *Pathways*, announcing a consultative process for developing a new strategic plan for early childhood.

Social, political and institutional contexts and challenges

This section addresses the social and political contexts in which *Pathways* developed, sets out the challenges faced by the stewards of this policy in achieving its aims and traces the complex dynamics that influenced its development. *Pathways* emerged as part of a 'third way' approach to social policy in the early 2000s. It had its roots in the early advocacy work of women in the 1970s and 1980s, in wider public concerns about social justice and Māori empowerment (concerns acknowledged in establishing the Ministry for Women and the Department of Māori Affairs) and in a growing interest in child development research (May 2017). *Pathways* was, then, a clear and successful manifestation of three decades of advocacy by many key individuals and groups around the country. From the mid-1980s, a radical-right restructuring of political, economic and social policy moved Aotearoa from a liberal welfare state to a neoliberal state. Thus, *Pathways* is embedded in a number of narratives about economic rationalism, labour markets and gender over a period of intense economic and political change. While these narratives have shifted over the years in response to a range of social, economic and political directions, what remains constant is the need for ECE policy to gain social acceptance and political traction.

The first part of this section briefly sets out the early policy advocacy work of the 1980s and 1990s that was designed to secure government support for education and care as a way to improve the lives of children and women. It then explores the impact of a period of neoliberal reforms from 1984 to 1999 focused on economic productivity and efficiency as part of the global economy, which had harmful and long-lasting effects on individual and social wellbeing at the local level. The prevailing narrative focused on labour market needs, the expansion of care for children in institutions outside the home and an increasingly economic thrust of ECE policy under the influence of international institutions such as the OECD. This is the context from which *Pathways* emerged in the early 2000s. The third part of this section addresses a set of goals, broadly established some years earlier (Meade 1988) and developed in the plan as a response to what may be seen as an ongoing failure of the New Zealand Government's social policy. The goals addressed three perceived concerns: young children's lack of participation in ECE—particularly Māori and Pasifika children; inconsistent quality of provision and implementation of the curriculum; and the deleterious effects of marketisation on communities. Table 19.1 outlines key policy and curriculum developments since 1980.

Table 19.1 Key policy and curriculum developments, 1980–2018

State Services Commission's *Report on Early Childhood Care and Education*	1980
Education to be More	1988
Before Five	1988
Te Whāriki: He Whāriki Mātauranga mō ngā Mokopuna o Aotearoa—Early childhood curriculum	1996
Pathways to the Future: Ngā Huarahi Arataki—A ten-year plan for early childhood education	2002
Kei Tua o te Pae: Assessment for learning—Early childhood exemplars	2005, 2007, 2009
Ngā Arohaehae Whai Hua: Self-review guidelines for early childhood education	2006
Te Whatu Pōkeka: Kaupapa Māori assessment for learning—Early childhood exemplars	2009
An Agenda for Amazing Children: Final report of the ECE Taskforce	2011
Te Whāriki: Early childhood curriculum.	2017

Prior to 1980, as a legacy of more than 140 years of British colonisation, the normalised model of ECE involved families (that is, mothers) raising their children at home (Ritchie and Ritchie 1970). The New Zealand Free Kindergarten Association provided free, public, sessional education for three- and four-year-olds, although the morning or afternoon sessions did not generally release a parent or caregiver to seek employment. Long-day childcare arrangements were marginally acceptable in exceptional circumstances, such as when normal family life had broken down. Aside from kindergartens, ECE was largely unregulated, fragmented, staffed by an unqualified workforce and, for the most part, ignored by politicians and the general public (see Ritchie and Ritchie 1970).

Throughout the 1980s, various reports emerged in response to a growing demand for child care—for example, the State Services Commission's *Report on Early Childhood Care and Education* (1980). The Early Childhood Workers Union and the New Zealand Childcare Association voiced concerns about poverty, the plight of women and children and workers' conditions in early childhood centres. When the Labour Party came to power in 1984, it was the first time its policy manifesto mentioned early childhood services—in particular, 'the support of child care with an affirmative action for women' (May 1990: 102). With progressive and supportive intentions, the government made small steps towards developing policy for ECE, shifting the responsibility for all early childhood services to the Department of Education and introducing funding provisions, training initiatives and support services. Although many in early childhood saw these as steps in the right direction, they were limited and none of the promised support was felt by parents in terms of affordability and access or by childcare workers, who still received 'the lowest wages in New Zealand' (May 1990: 102).

Despite minimal shifts in both policy and associated conditions for early childhood services, the Labour Government was generally seen as empathetic—a background against which a working group led by Anne Meade was established to identify key issues and directions for the nation's youngest learners and its diverse education sector. The resulting report, *Education to be More* (Meade 1988; generally referred to as the Meade Report), was followed soon after by the Government policy *Before Five* (Department of Education 1988). These two documents marked the recognition of ECE as a legitimate and important sector in education. The Meade Report set out a blueprint for the organisation and structuring of the entire sector, including a level of funding that, if delivered, would have supported all early childhood services. The Meade Report and *Before Five* ensured a strong foothold for ECE within education, recommending a comprehensive system of funding and an organisational framework for the entire sector predicated on equity for women and children and a belief in state provision. The scene was set for the later development and implementation of the curriculum, *Te Whāriki* (MoE 1996)—the world's first fully recognised national and bicultural curriculum dedicated to ECE.

However, the intentions of the Meade Report were never fully realised. The report was stymied by reforms within the wider education sector, which was inextricably caught up in neoliberal political and economic discourses, which championed decentralisation, deregulation and devolution of services that had traditionally been provided by the state (Kelsey 1995; May 2017). Changes ensued across all areas of social policy, including education and ECE. This neoliberal turn undermined some of what was intended in the first iteration of *Before Five*. Hastily rewritten to ensure acceptance by Treasury, *Before Five* still managed to provide a strong policy platform for ECE, despite many of its intentions being effectively thwarted by budget cuts and legislation that promoted a decentralised and entrepreneurial culture. When prime minister David Lange introduced *Before Five*, he told early childhood representatives that gaining funding was like 'snatching raw meat out of the jaws of a Rottweiler' (Mitchell 1994: 97). The New Zealand Business Roundtable and other key proponents of the New Right's economic discourse were spelling out the political and economic advantages of decreasing government expenditure. The Treasury wrote a paper for the Cabinet, advising minimal increases for nonkindergarten services and a funding decrease for kindergartens—all in the name of equity. Treasury also said any extra money needed could come from a decrease in university expenditure (Meade 1990).

Education was increasingly treated as a marketplace in which to invest, and early childhood education and care emerged in the eyes of policymakers in New Zealand and worldwide as a promising economic resource (OECD 2006). It would prepare the learner for the knowledge economy, release family members to serve the labour market and provide a competitive and rapidly growing educational market for ECE services. Without a history of public education and with very few collective safeguards in place, ECE was easily picked off for early marketisation and commercialisation—directions that accorded well with the neoliberal government. In its new devolutionary mode, the government reconceptualised the market as a modern form of democracy. ECE became a service to be delivered as part of an enterprise culture, organised according to market principles with concurrent elements of competition, profit-making and entrepreneurialism.

For the next decade, enterprise culture prevailed in ECE, with attendant budget cuts and growth in market-provided services. In 1990, the government released its *Economic and Social Initiative* (Bolger et al. 1990), a neoliberal economic and social agenda that wreaked havoc on social and health policy, including education. This agenda appropriated ideas of fairness, self-reliance, efficiency and personal choice (Wells 2015) in neoconservative ways as social welfare benefits were cut and new laws effectively undermined working conditions. The *Employment Contracts Act 1991* favoured employers and weakened the collective bargaining powers of unions. Within the ECE sector, a range of measures impeded sectoral development, including deregistration of kindergarten teachers and their removal from the *State Sector Act*, the introduction of bulk-funding childcare centres and a new regime of contestable funding for advisory support services. These initiatives painted a gloomy picture for early childhood teachers and the social sector overall:

> Kindergarten teachers are the lowest paid teachers in the state sector. Childcare workers' pay rates vary, but may be as low as the minimum wage. And the rights of the workers to fair employment arrangements have been eroded since the passing of the Employment Contracts Act. (Mitchell 1995: 78)

There was a widespread and growing malaise about the failure of the neoliberal reforms. Social and economic prosperity was promised through the sale of state assets, the corporatisation of welfare services and an ethos of competitive individualism and consumer choice. The failure of the project was well documented at the time, particularly in education (see, for example, Haworth 1994; Kelsey 1995; Wilkinson 1995; Peters and Marshall 1996; Marginson 1997; Jesson 1999; Peters and Roberts 1999). Also well documented are the social and economic consequences of a decade of market-based reforms characterised by a shift in economic benefits from the public to the private sphere and an associated deterioration in social and economic conditions, particularly for historically marginalised communities (Kelsey 2002).

Linda Mitchell (2015) sees policy agendas during this time reflecting two distinctly different views of the role of the state in ECE: a supportive state and a minimal state. These views mark out, respectively, a Labour-led collaborative approach of support and community and a National-led 'responsibilising' of families to meet social obligations, although neither of these approaches is pure. What emerged around the turn of the century is what became known in some Western economies as 'the third way' (Blair 1998)—a centrist political path that tries to reconcile right-wing neoliberal politics and left-wing social-democratic politics by advocating a varying synthesis of centre-right economics and centre-left social policies. As in the New Zealand experiment during the 1980s (Kelsey 2002), this middle ground involved a minimisation of the role of government and a rise in managerialism and performance cultures across all traditionally public service sectors (Giddens 2002).

The third way was not without its critics, having been depicted as a 'political project whose objective is short-term political management, not transformation … a more deeply embedded form of neoliberalism that perpetuates the tensions which the Government was elected to relieve' (Kelsey 2002: 50). Nevertheless, New Zealand followed suit, with the then social development and employment minister Steve Maharey preferring to call this approach 'the new social democracy'. He saw it as a bringing together of values and politics, with some common themes emerging from consideration of economic management in relation to the role of the welfare state. The new social democracy, he claimed, was about:

> An active role for the state in a mixed economy. A new alignment between economic and social policy. Partnership, citizen engagement, and democratic governance. A refurbishing of the institutions of the state and the institutions of civil society … [and] much more besides. (Maharey 2001)

Third-way values promoted an inclusive approach to politics, so the social and political climate was right for the emergence of *Pathways*. In 2002, the new Labour-led Government espoused values such as equality, community and social justice, with the education minister Trevor Mallard emphasising a commitment to ECE funding—specifically, more support for community-based provision and funding for the development of an early childhood strategic plan. The minister worked closely with Linda Mitchell, in particular—a collaboration regarded as critical to the development of the plan and its grounding in a language of rights and participation (May 2017). From 1999, there was a stronger policy emphasis on ECE. An early childhood education strategic plan working group was set up in 2000, led by Anne Meade, who had developed *Education to Be More* a decade earlier. The group engaged in nationwide consultation, reflecting Aotearoa New Zealand's 'long tradition of community involvement and provision' (Meade and Podmore 2002: 29), and maintained a focus on key issues identified decades earlier in *Before Five*—funding, quality, access and participation—albeit with quite different purposes.

Pathways to the Future: Ngā Huarahi Arataki (MoE 2002) was Aotearoa's first 10-year strategic plan for the sector. As with *Education to be More*, quality, access and funding remained pivotal and critical issues were identified around adult–child ratios, teacher qualifications, sectoral regulation and teacher registration. However, some of the policy drivers had changed. ECE was now integral to the nation's economic and social planning. *Pathways* reflected the government's view of how ECE would contribute to the future economic health of the nation, arguing that the early years were critical to a child's later academic and vocational success. The plan focused on fostering stronger links with family, community, social services, health services and schools, as part of a seamless educational paradigm. It set out goals for increasing participation rates, particularly for Māori and Pasifika children. Unlike pre-1980s, there was widespread support for ECE outside the home to support parental employment.

Political decision-making process: Motivations and contextual factors

The design process of *Pathways* is interesting, due to the sector's political history, its engaged advocacy over a sustained period and its variable connectedness as a sector. Capitalising on the government's turn towards a socially progressive direction, *Pathways* drew on the sector's collective history and advocacy, artfully addressing political and social concerns. It effectively supported the diversity of the sector, rather than approaching issues of quality and participation through increased regulation or technocratic policy design. Other factors impacting on design were the cohesiveness of curriculum and assessment developments, the emerging international narrative of children's rights and growing support for systematic provision of education.

The 1990s was a difficult period for the realisation of quality goals in ECE, in terms of funding, qualifications and research. Nevertheless, the sector was strongly positioned by the development of the curriculum, *Te Whāriki*—a national curriculum for ECE. As sectoral advocates and internationally recognised academics, Helen May and Margaret Carr were well positioned and successful in their bid to develop this curriculum and led a highly consultative and collaborative process of curriculum design and development for more than four years. Working alongside Tilly and Tamati Reedy and Rose Pere (leaders in Māori education and Kōhanga Reo),[2] they developed both a bicultural and a Māori immersion curriculum for ECE. The draft document of *Te Whāriki* was released for consultation in 1993, followed by the final version in 1996, which received international accolades. Curriculum is a highly contestable area of engagement, requiring political savvy, technical knowhow and a socially nuanced response to competing demands. May and Carr, between them, had a history of political advocacy and the right leadership experience to gain the acceptance and trust of a very diverse sector in driving through the radical changes. As leaders, they had an intimate knowledge of the sector at all levels and had been politically active for decades in mapping the landscape.

Unions also influenced the design process. In 1996, *Future Directions: Early childhood education in New Zealand* (NZEI 1996), a report from a group of community-based ECE organisations, provided a blueprint for the future of the sector. The report argued for equity funding (including pay equity with primary schoolteachers), sessional funding, accessibility for all children, accountability tied to quality, an increase in funding for discretional grants, initiatives to encourage Māori and Pasifika into ECE teaching, the Diploma of Teaching ECE to be set as a benchmark for the person responsible in a childcare centre and funding for the development of an early childhood strategic plan. Wells argues:

> While never attributed to the report or as a result of the sector and public pressure during the campaign, a number of policy changes were subsequently made … increases to funding, and the introduction of a framework and tools to improve quality—the 'Quality Journey', a new category of 'quality' funding, the development of equity criteria, and funding for pathway programmes to upgrade qualifications. (Wells 2015: 6)

2 Te Kōhanga Reo National Trust for Māori language immersion early childhood education.

Although the focus to that point had been on a national early childhood context, what arose during this period was an increasingly active global political agenda supporting the development of ECE in Aotearoa. The United Nations and the OECD strongly influenced policy and curriculum direction. The United Nation's *Convention on the Rights of the Child* (UN 1989) impacted on curriculum and social policy development and was influential in bringing attention to equity issues for children—specifically, children's poverty and their lack of a voice in determining their own futures. The OECD's emphasis was different—focused more on strengthening global economies through economic and social wellbeing. Its reports on the significance of human and social capital in a nation's economic advancement argued that ECE had a significant, instrumental role in supporting labour markets, promoting social cohesion and furthering the economic success of a country (OECD 2001, 2006). Early childhood education and care, it argued, were important to the economic and social realms of member countries, so member countries should maintain strong ECE systems that integrated both policy and curriculum. The OECD's Starting Strong series of publications has provided education policymakers with data on member nations' ECE sectors and analysis of ECE policy—the purpose being to provide ongoing policy guidance in such a way as to leave no doubt about the critical role of government in attending to the contribution of ECE to a nation's wellbeing and economic competitiveness.

It is within this context—of national curriculum and policy emerging in response to international economic reports—that the new Labour-led Government came to power in 1999 and the effects of a seemingly kinder, gentler third-way approach began to be felt. Kindergarten teachers who had been removed from the *State Sector Act* were reinstated and the 2000 Budget boded well for ECE development. In an address to the New Zealand Educational Institute (NZEI) conference, Mallard (2000) emphasised the government's commitment to ECE, outlining as key areas of development increasing participation, quality and qualification, and a new strategic plan to develop a coherent strategy for ECE, building on *Before Five*. The strategy was to address issues of support for Māori and Pasifika children; it also promised to increase participation, reduce costs to parents, address teacher supply shortages, increase support for professional development, expand grants to support the provision of new services and introduce structural support for a qualified workforce (Farquhar 2000).

Before its election in 1999, the Labour Party pledged to convene a working group to develop a strategic plan for ECE policy (Meade and Podmore 2002). This was the first strategic plan for early childhood or for any education sector in New Zealand. The working group members represented key stakeholder organisations and, despite not always agreeing, they 'managed through democratic processes and some common values to shape a final report' (Mitchell 2011: 219).

The working group argued that ad hoc changes in policy over the previous 10 years had caused a number of significant difficulties and put forward 20 strategies for Cabinet consideration. Their report to the Minister of Education (in October 2001) set out four directions. They argued for increased access, participation and engagement, strengthening collaborative relationships and improving quality and sustainability. Three major themes characterised the proposals: enhancing policies and settings to facilitate the full implementation of *Te Whāriki*, better coordination of services and transformation of the role of government so ECE would be provided in partnership with government.

The final version of *Pathways* was developed over 15 months, with a working group of 31 members, chaired by Anne Meade. It involved open consultation with the wider ECE sector, including several *hui* (meetings) with Māori and *fono* (meetings) with Pasifika peoples, attracting more than 1,300 submissions. It set out ways for increasing participation, quality and collaboration through review of regulations and funding systems, through investment in ongoing research to inform future policy and monitor progress and through involving the sector in ongoing policy development and implementation. *Pathways* clearly signalled a change from 'business as usual'; regulations and funding were to be revised, but the biggest shift in direction was the call for

> better support of community-based ECE services, including licence-exempt groups … professional registration requirements for all teachers in teacher-led ECE services … better co-operation and collaboration between ECE services, parent support and development programmes and education, health and social services … [and] greater involvement by the Government in ECE, focussing particularly on communities where participation in quality ECE is low. (MoE 2002: 2)

As a comprehensive, stepped plan, *Pathways* is arguably the most important piece of ECE policy in recent times. It articulated the political and social vision for later policy initiatives. It laid out targets and monitoring mechanisms for the next 10 years and it successfully synthesised previous decades of advocacy and piecemeal policy responses into one coherent and widely accepted plan. It provided clearer and more visible goals for the Ministry of Education and provided greater impetus and support for the implementation of *Te Whāriki*. It focused on the development of a strong, community-based sector, supported through government provision, particularly in areas of need—specifically, Māori and Pasifika children and families. It was comprehensive in its prescription for developing the sector: equity grants for establishing childcare centres in areas not well served by ECE, discretionary grants to support teacher qualifications to reach a 100 per cent qualified workforce by 2012, professional learning provisions for teachers and a sector that was informed by research. This last initiative was realised through the highly acclaimed teacher–research partnership Centres of Innovation, reflecting the policy focus on support and information. The published version of the strategic plan did not include all the working group's recommendations, although it was considered aspirational for the government and the sector:

> [T]he government had shifted from a minimal role, providing only low-regulated staffing standards, limited funding and a competitive market framework in teacher education and advisory support services during the early 1990s to a much more supportive role in these aspects especially during the years 2000 to 2009 (the three terms of a Labour-led government). (Mitchell 2011: 219)

The influence of the OECD on ECE was felt both nationally and internationally through reports steeped in human capital theory, such as *Babies and Bosses* (OECD 2002) and the beginning of a series of reports entitled *Starting Strong* (OECD 2001, 2006). The OECD's influence continued with their later report *Starting Strong III* (OECD 2012), dedicated to policy design through the development of a policy toolbox—a metaphor identifying key policy 'levers': goals and regulations; curriculum and standards; qualifications, training and working conditions; engaging families and communities; and data, research and monitoring. Each of these levers can be seen as having a role to play in the design of the strategic plan, giving *Pathways* a perceived seal of international approval.

In terms of its third-way policy aims, the design process for *Pathways* can be seen as an attempt to balance tensions inherent in the role of government regulating a very new education market. While the working group developed a comprehensive plan for government management of ECE to further social and community goals, private sector lobby groups such as the Early Childhood Council (formed in 1991) favoured decentralisation and marketisation of services. For them, the effectiveness of *Pathways* would be measured in terms of reduced policy intervention and increased participation.

Implementation, legitimacy and enduring change

Specific actions to support implementation of the strategic plan were decided in 2002 and developed in subsequent years. The collaborative, sector-driven approach of *Pathways* was supported by the Ministry of Education, which engaged in intensive consultation with the ECE sector on all regulatory proposals regarding standards. Ministry consultation extended from 2003 up to the implementation of the new regulatory framework in late 2008. In this way, the country achieved strong acceptance of proposals for regulatory change and workable mechanisms for implementation. The framework provided a clear and transparent statement of regulated requirements. It set out the legislative and regulatory criteria to be used in assessing compliance and standards (OECD 2012). During this period, a new funding system was established incentivising teacher-led services to employ registered teachers: 'ECE was given new financial priority during the implementation of the strategic plan and government expenditure on ECE increased almost fourfold' (Mitchell 2011: 291).

Significant progress was made towards achieving the 100 per cent qualified teacher target and improving teachers' professional learning and support. Improvements included teacher professional development, publication of assessment for learning exemplars *Kei Tua o Te Pae* (MoE 2005, 2007, 2009a), self-review guidelines for teachers (MoE 2006) and the establishment of the Centres of Innovation—a government-funded research initiative that linked childcare centres with research associates to research their own innovative practices. Progress was made on salary equity between kindergarten teachers and schoolteachers. Additional funding in the form of '20 Hours Free ECE' (later renamed '20 Hours ECE') reflected the plan's focus on increasing participation by making ECE more affordable.

A further critical element in the success of *Pathways* was the way it set out a framework in which curriculum and assessment developments within the sector were implicit. Curriculum and assessment became the objects of intense scholarship and the development of new ECE curriculum and assessment discourses contributed to the formation of the sector's character and contribution. At this time, gains were being made in the ECE research community, with growing teams of academics working in the new faculties of education (formed by mergers of teacher education institutions with universities)—raising awareness of the significant role Aotearoa New Zealand was playing in ECE. The plan for a qualified sector had generated significant growth in the provision of ECE teacher education and in undergraduate student numbers, providing growth for the tertiary sector. This resulted in more academic pathways for ECE teachers to work in tertiary education. Hence, the period 2002–08 was recognisably fertile in terms of the development of ECE, including an openness to critical debate about issues impacting the sector. It was acceptable to question the drivers of the sector and how early childhood care and education centre communities understood and provided quality education and care. Watchdog organisations such as the Child Forum emerged with a focus on issues of quality.

Concerns about the growth and direction of the sector were amplified when a new centre-right government was formed in 2008, which held power for three terms (nine years). A number of economic and political factors effectively curbed the improvements that *Pathways* might otherwise have provided for the sector, effectively cutting short comprehensive, systemic reform. Compounding the effect of a more conservative government, a global economic downturn halted and reversed the aims of *Pathways*. According to Mitchell (2015), within weeks of the new conservative government being elected, *Pathways* was removed from the Ministry of Education's website, foreshadowing changes that were to come. The first half of 2009 saw a raft of funding halts, including severe cuts to teachers' professional development, axing of Centres of Innovation research, dropping the 100 per cent qualified teacher target, eliminating the top funding bands for qualified staff and removing the word 'free' from '20 Hours Free ECE'. Effectively, there was a strong move towards market-based ECE, an equalisation of funding for community-based and market-based provision and a shift from universal to targeted provision (Mitchell 2015).

Although another strategic plan did not emerge until 2018, there was a range of policy and curriculum actions in the interim, including a taskforce to review ECE policy and a working group to review the implementation of *Te Whāriki*. In 2010, the ECE Taskforce, led by Michael Mintrom, was established to review and reform ECE policy and to propose a new funding model that did not increase expenditure. The taskforce was operating within limited terms of reference, which were to focus on efficiency, effectiveness and cost-saving. Its report the following year, *An Agenda for Amazing Children*, stressed that the taskforce was 'concerned to show that universal access to high quality ECE for every young person is our best bet for placing New Zealand on an upward trajectory in terms of both social and economic outcomes' (MoE 2011: 4). Among its recommendations was a review of the implementation of the curriculum, amid unease about the quality of care and education for infants and toddlers and home-based services. May (2015) argues that this report was a repositioning of the strategic plan away from government support for universal provision and a reprioritising of spending towards 'priority children'. The report received mixed reviews:

> While a number of aspects of the report were well received, others were of concern. The report stopped short of recommending a return to [the] 100% qualified teacher target … parents pay more for ECE … Some traction [was] gained, but by and large the recommendations remain just that. (Wells 2015: 10)

It is useful to view this period of policy development in light of the government's social policy direction. The Better Public Services Advisory Group was established to provide advice on state sector reform, with the goal to produce 'a public service and state sector that is achieving value-for-money, is innovative, provides high-quality services and manages change effectively' (New Zealand Government 2011: 3). The group identified two critical areas for improvement: 'services for children aged 0–6 from families with multiple issues' (New Zealand Government 2011: 29) and 'educational outcomes for a sizeable cohort of young Māori and Pasifika' (p. 31). The advice focused on increasing accountability and communication across services, citing the global economic downturn as the reason for needing to contain costs and realign services. In full business-speak, it suggested gearing up state services to enable system-wide change to produce 'measurable results' and 'action plans' (New Zealand Government 2011: 10) that enhance 'flexibility', suggesting that agencies 'drive continuous business process improvement through the use of "lean" methodologies, and drive innovation by benchmarking activity, identifying and implementing best practice from across the system' (p. 11). Public services were to have stronger coordination to capitalise on economies of scale and 'more interaction with citizens, including via new technologies' (New Zealand Government 2011: 20). The reforms were to achieve 'better results', 'better services', 'value-for-money', 'stronger leadership' and 'the right culture and capability' (New Zealand Government 2011: 22).

This climate of business-style efficiency and improvement underpinned the models for targeting priority areas for the next six years. In 2010, the ECE Participation Programme was launched, targeting areas of society with low ECE participation rates—namely, Māori, Pasifika and low socioeconomic communities. Initiatives were set up to encourage participation, including discretionary funding to providers to establish services, family caseworkers in schools and supported playgroups. It is within this context that the 2011 discussion paper on vulnerable children was launched, with a highly controversial amendment to the *Social Security Act*. One of the key reforms was that any social security beneficiary with a preschool-aged child was required to enrol their child in ECE, under the sanction of benefit cuts for noncompliance. The new direction caused strong commentary and concern about the stigmatising of children as vulnerable and the coercive nature of the new government requirement. May (2015) suggests the debate about universal and targeted approaches to funding is illustrative of deeper, conflicting political agendas. On the one hand, ECE is seen as part of an interventionist strategy to 'redress the "risks" created by "vulnerable families and communities"'; on the other, ECE is viewed 'as a right for the young child citizen' (May 2015: 166). This tension between universal rights and targeted interventions has been a major challenge for ECE policy in New Zealand since the mid-1980s. *Pathways* has successfully catered to both interventionists and rights advocates by taking a flexible approach that ensured the plan would endure.

Analysis and conclusion

Although *Pathways* may not have achieved all of its original intentions, it has provided scope for political resistance, the testing of agendas and consistent advocacy for stronger government support for the sector. It constitutes a coherent platform for systematic development of national curriculum initiatives that attenuate the worst impacts of global economic imperatives. Addressing the Early Childhood Convention in 2015, chief executive of New Zealand Kindergartens Clare Wells (2015: 13) observed that, over the past decade or so, it feels like New Zealand has taken two steps forward and one step back, although, she claims, 'we are still moving forward':

> We are seen as a world-leader in early childhood education for our diversity, our integrated approach, and our curriculum Te Whāriki. Our belief that every child has a right to high quality early childhood education is unequivocal. The past few decades have seen remarkable change in the world of early childhood education in Aotearoa New Zealand: the early childhood education landscape has shifted in response to drivers and influencers of change—in whose interests? (Wells 2015: 1)

The positioning of New Zealand as a world leader is debatable, given the OECD's data and rankings on early childhood policies, practices and conditions and, in particular, New Zealand's lowest ranking for teacher pay (OECD 2012). Nevertheless, the development of policies, including *Pathways*, is world leading. *Pathways* can be considered a success for the way it—along with associated policies since *Before Five*—contributed to a comprehensive (albeit hotly debated) early childhood agenda and to the very idea of becoming world-leading. However, New Zealand still has a long way to go in dealing with educational and health inequities for children.

From 2002 to 2008, *Pathways* provided a blueprint for strong early childhood policy at the same time as allowing for ongoing dialogue and debate. During this time, the sector experienced significant growth, which translated into associated growth in higher education and in research and scholarship. The strength in research and scholarship provided further support for enduring leadership and advocacy for children and for ECE. This strength will, no doubt, be called on again, as the coalition government elected in 2017 has recently announced the development of a new strategic plan. As before, the success of the new strategic plan will be assessed in terms of its capacity to increase national awareness of the complexity of the sector through ongoing political debate. It will also be important to reconcile (or at least balance) competing politics and philosophies. And it will be vital to realise quality care and education for children, families and communities.

References

Blair, T. 1998. *The Third Way: New politics for the new century*. London: The Fabian Society.

Bolger, J., Richardson, R. and Birch, W. 1990. *Economic and Social Initiative: December 1990. Statements to the House of Representatives*. Wellington: Government Printer.

Department of Education 1988. *Before Five: Early childhood care and education in New Zealand*. Wellington: Government Printer.

Farquhar, S. 2000. A narrative analysis of policies and reforms in early childhood education (Aotearoa/New Zealand). Unpublished Masters thesis, University of Auckland, Auckland.

Farquhar, S. and Gibbons, A. 2010. 'Early childhood education.' In M. Thrupp and R. Irwin (eds), *Another Decade of New Zealand Education Policy: Where to now?* Hamilton, NZ: Wilf Malcolm Institute of Educational Research, University of Waikato.

Gibbons, A. and Farquhar, S. 2014. 'Mapping policies and pathways in early childhood education: A note from Aotearoa New Zealand.' *New Zealand Research in Early Childhood Education Journal* 17(1): 1–10.

Giddens, A. 2002. *Where Now for New Labour?* Cambridge: Polity Press.

Haworth, N. 1994. *Neo-liberalism, Economic Internationalism and the Contemporary State in New Zealand*. Auckland: Auckland University Press.

Jesson, B. 1999. *Only their Purpose is Mad*. Palmerston North, NZ: Dunmore Press.

Kelsey, J. 1995. *The New Zealand Experiment: A world model for structural adjustment?* Auckland: Auckland University Press.

Kelsey, J. 2002. *At the Crossroads*. Wellington: Bridget Williams Books.

Maharey, S. 2001. Values and politics: Some reflections on the new social democracy in a New Zealand context. Comments to a seminar hosted by the Foundation for Policy Initiatives, Auckland, 26 March. Available from: www.beehive.govt.nz/speech/values-and-politics-some-reflections-new-social-democracy-new-zealand-context.

Mallard, T. 2000. 'Speech notes.' In New Zealand Educational Institute, *Policy, Practice and Politics: NZEI Te Riu Roa Early Childhood Millennium Conference Proceedings*. Wellington: NZEI Te Riu Roa.

Marginson, S. 1997. 'Is economics sufficient for the government of education?' *New Zealand Journal of Educational Studies* 32(1): 3–12.

May, H. 1990. 'Growth and change in the early childhood services.' In S. Middleton, J. Codd and A. Jones (eds), *New Zealand Education Policy Today*. Wellington: Allen & Unwin.

May, H. 2015. 'New Zealand: A narrative of shifting policy directions for early childhood education and care.' In K. Stewart (ed.), *An Equal Start? Providing early childhood quality and care for disadvantaged children*. Bristol: Policy Press.

May, H. 2017. 'Documenting early childhood policy in Aotearoa New Zealand: Political and personal stories.' In L. Miller, C. Cameron, C. Dalli and N. Barbour (eds), *Sage Handbook of Early Childhood Policy*. London: Sage.

Meade, A. 1988. *Education to be More: Report of the Early Childhood Care and Education Working Group*. Wellington: Government Printer.

Meade, A. 1990. 'Women and young children gain a foot in the door.' *Women's Studies Journal* 6(1): 96–110.

Meade. A. and Podmore, V. 2002. *Early Childhood Education Policy Co-ordination under the Auspices of the Department/Ministry of Education: A case study of New Zealand*. Paris: UNESCO.

Ministry of Education (MoE) 1996. *Te Whāriki: He Whāriki Mātauranga mō ngā Mokopuna o Aotearoa—Early childhood curriculum*. Wellington: Ministry of Education.

Ministry of Education (MoE) 2002. *Pathways to the future: Ngā huarahi arataki—A ten year plan for early childhood education*. Wellington: Ministry of Education.

Ministry of Education (MoE) 2004. *Professional Standards for Kindergarten Teachers and How to Integrate These into Kindergarten Performance Management Systems: A practical resource for kindergarten associations, kindergarten teachers, head teachers and senior teachers*. Wellington: Ministry of Education.

Ministry of Education (MoE) 2005. *Kei Tua o te Pae: Assessment for learning—Early childhood exemplars*. Books 1–10. Wellington: Learning Media.

Ministry of Education (MoE) 2006. *Ngā Arohaehae Whai Hua: Self-review guidelines for early childhood education*. Wellington: Learning Media.

Ministry of Education (MoE) 2007. *Kei Tua o te Pae: Assessment for learning—Early childhood exemplars*. Books 11–15. Wellington: Learning Media.

Ministry of Education (MoE) 2009a. *Kei Tua o te Pae: Assessment for learning—Early childhood exemplars*. Books 16–20. Wellington: Learning Media.

Ministry of Education (MoE) 2009b. *Te Whatu Pōkeka: Kaupapa Māori assessment for learning—Early childhood exemplars*. Wellington: Ministry of Education.

Ministry of Education (MoE) 2011. *An Agenda for Amazing Children: Final report of the ECE Taskforce*. Wellington: Ministry of Education.

Mintrom, M. and Norman, P. 2009. 'Policy entrepreneurship and policy change.' *The Policy Studies Journal* 37(4): 649–67. doi.org/10.1111/j.1541-0072.2009.00329.x.

Mitchell, L. 1994. 'Current policy issues for women: What has happened to early childhood education.' *Women's Studies Journal* 10(2).

Mitchell, L. 1995. 'Crossroads: Early childhood education in the mid-1990s.' *New Zealand Annual Review of Education* 5: 75–92.

Mitchell, L. 2011. 'Enquiring teachers and democratic politics: Transformations in New Zealand's early childhood education landscape.' *Early Years* 31(3): 217–28. doi.org/10.1080/09575146.2011.588787.

Mitchell, L. 2015. 'Shifting directions in ECEC policy in New Zealand: From a child rights to an interventionist approach.' *International Journal of Early Years Education* 23(3): 288–302. doi.org/10.1080/09669760.2015.1074557.

New Zealand Educational Institute (NZEI) 1996. *Future Directions: Early childhood education in New Zealand*. Wellington: NZEI Te Rui Roa.

New Zealand Government 2011. *Better Public Services Advisory Group Report*. Wellington: New Zealand Government.

Organisation for Economic Co-operation and Development (OECD) (n.d.). *International Early Learning and Child Well-being Study*. Paris: OECD Publishing. Available from: www.oecd.org/edu/school/international-early-learning-and-child-well-being-study.htm.

Organisation for Economic Co-operation and Development (OECD) 2001. *Starting Strong: Early childhood education and care*. Paris: OECD Publishing.

Organisation for Economic Co-operation and Development (OECD) 2002. *Babies and Bosses*. Paris: OECD Publishing.

Organisation for Economic Co-operation and Development (OECD) 2006. *Starting Strong II: Early childhood education and care*. Paris: OECD Publishing.

Organisation for Economic Co-operation and Development (OECD) 2012. *Starting Strong III: A quality toolbox for early childhood education and care*. Paris: OECD Publishing.

Peters, M. and Marshall, J. 1996. *Individualism and Community: Education and social policy in the postmodern condition*. London: The Falmer Press.

Peters, M. and Roberts, P. 1999. *University Futures and the Politics of Reform in New Zealand*. Palmerston North, NZ: Dunmore Press.

Ritchie, J. and Ritchie, J. 1970. *Child Rearing Patterns in New Zealand*. Wellington: A. H. & A. W. Reed.

State Services Commission 1980. *Report on Early Childhood Care and Education*. Wellington: State Services Commission.

United Nations (UN) 1989. *Convention on the Rights of the Child*. New York: United Nations.

Wells, C. 2015. In whose interests: Looking back—Thinking forward. Keynote address to Early Childhood Convention: He Wai Whakariporipo—Making Waves in Early Childhood—Surviving the Storm, Rotorua, New Zealand, 4 October.

Wilkinson, M. 1995. 'Rationality, efficiency and the market.' In J. Boston (ed.), *The State Under Contract*. Wellington: Bridget Williams Books.

20

KiwiSaver: A jewel in the crown of New Zealand's retirement income framework?

Kirsten MacDonald and Ross Guest

Retirement income policy design

New Zealand is a relative newcomer to the world of national superannuation vehicles to support private saving. In 2007, just before the GFC, New Zealand implemented KiwiSaver—a voluntary superannuation system to sit alongside the government pension, New Zealand Superannuation (NZS). Being a small nation in the South Pacific has never stopped New Zealand from standing out from the crowd. Whether in rugby union, the America's Cup or economic reform, the world has watched with interest because New Zealand is seen to be doing things differently and often winning. Retirement income policy is no exception, with the innovation of automatic enrolment in KiwiSaver among other distinctive features of its design. The examination of retirement income policy in the current context of ageing populations, pressure on government budgets in terms of social support, the need to increase self-funding for retirement and the shift of risk and decision-making to individual investors enables us to learn from successful policy design and implementation in the face of challenges and the need for adjustment over time in response to changing environmental conditions.

Based on the World Bank's (1994) three-pillars approach, New Zealand's retirement income policy is primarily based on a tax and transfer 'pay-as-you-go' (PAYG) system, including a unique near-universal flat-rate pillar-one pension. Since 2007, NZS has been complemented by KiwiSaver—a hybrid, Pillar 2/3 scheme. KiwiSaver is funded by a mix of individual and employer contributions plus a government subsidy known as member tax credit. KiwiSaver members are automatically enrolled on starting new employment, although they can opt out or take contribution holidays. Membership is not limited to those in employment, so even children can join. Savers also have the option to make additional voluntary contributions and to hold other forms of voluntary private savings outside KiwiSaver. Table 20.1 summarises the design features of the New Zealand retirement income system as of April 2018.

Table 20.1 Summary of design features of the New Zealand retirement income system in 2018

The pillars	
Pillar 1	NZS, a universal pension, funded from PAYG. The New Zealand Superannuation Fund was established in 2001 to commence partial funding of NZS from 2020.
Pillar 2	KiwiSaver is a hybrid of Pillar 2 and Pillar 3 schemes. Minimum employer contributions is a Pillar 2 feature, and the employee opt-out, along with optional higher contribution rates, is a Pillar 3 feature.
Pillar 3	Voluntary private superannuation separate from KiwiSaver. Taxation is the same as for KiwiSaver. No private saving tax incentives.
Public pension	
Eligibility	Age 65, subject to residence test[a]
Amount[b]	*Singles* 42% of 2016 median weekly wage/salary Approximately 40% of average national income (male and female) per beneficiary *Couples* 32% each of 2016 median weekly wage/salary
Means testing	None
Taxation	Taxable at marginal rate

Private pension (superannuation)	
Minimum contribution rates	*Employer contribution* Minimum 3% of gross earnings *Employee contribution* Minimum and default rate 3% (optional rates 4% or 8%) of gross earnings Applies to employees aged 18–65 but employers may choose to continue to contribute for employees aged 65+ A contribution holiday cannot be taken in the first year of membership without evidence of financial hardship. Beyond the first year, can apply for between three months and five years without providing a reason, renewing the holiday at any time or taking an unlimited number of future contribution holidays. Employer contributions also cease during this period.[c]
Taxation[d]	*Employer contribution* Employer superannuation contribution tax is charged at rates from 10.5% to 33% depending on marginal tax rates applicable to prior years' earnings *Employee contribution* Employee contributions made from after-tax income (i.e. already taxed at marginal rate), thus no cap on contributions *Superannuation fund earnings* Widely held superannuation funds: 28% Portfolio investment entities: applicable prescribed investor rate, ranging from 10.5% to 28% *Withdrawals* Available at age 65, tax-free
Withdrawals	*Homeownership*[e] Funds including employee, employer, member tax credits and associated returns are accessible for owner-occupied housing purchases subject to eligibility requirements and minimum balance of $1,000 after withdrawal *Decumulation phase* KiwiSaver members able to continue to invest or withdraw beyond age 65 with little restriction, including lump-sum or regular withdrawals with low or no minimum withdrawal per transaction depending on a particular fund's rules. No default annuity products but can be purchased in the market. Less-developed market for annuities and home equity release products.

[a] For New Zealand residence requirements, see Ministry of Social Development (n.d.).

[b] These figures are calculated from the 2016 median New Zealand weekly earnings of NZ$924 (A$883) and maximum after-tax weekly 2016 pension payments of NZ$384.76 (A$367.66) (Statistics NZ 2018).

[c] As of June 2017, approximately 5 per cent of the membership base is on contribution holidays, the majority of which are over 60 months in length (IRD 2017).

[d] For taxation of superannuation in New Zealand, see IRD (2019a).

[e] See IRD (2019b).

Source: Adapted from Guest (2013).

A policy success?

The addition of KiwiSaver to New Zealand's retirement income framework in 2007 can be considered both a *process* and a *political* success. KiwiSaver has been remarkably successful in signing up New Zealanders for retirement saving, despite its voluntary nature. Although there were political challenges at the outset and through periods of political upheaval, multiparty support has enabled the hard yards to be achieved in terms of streamlining reporting and transparency for investors and providing strong governance in the KiwiSaver market. Nonetheless, from a *programmatic* standpoint, the results are mixed. New Zealand has shown the world how to implement an administratively cost-effective system through the existing tax platform. But, according to a seven-year multiagency KiwiSaver evaluation steering group—incorporating members from the Ministry of Business, Innovation and Employment, the Treasury, the Commission for Financial Capability, the Financial Markets Authority, the Ministry of Social Development, Victoria University of Wellington, Statistics New Zealand, the Inland Revenue Department and research companies and contractors—KiwiSaver has been marginally successful at best in achieving its policy goals in the short term, with limited evidence to support wealth accumulation (IRD 2015).

KiwiSaver was launched with a set of highly criticised government incentives. Those who stood to benefit the most were likely to be those already saving elsewhere rather than KiwiSaver's target cohort, who might struggle to save despite the incentives. The seven-year evaluation and reporting process had the purposes of providing evidence of the effectiveness of KiwiSaver when considered against the objectives of the policy: to encourage a long-term savings habit and asset accumulation by individuals who are not in a position to enjoy standards of retirement similar to those in preretirement, to increase individuals' wellbeing and financial independence, particularly in retirement, and to provide retirement benefits. While the scheme was successful in exceeding membership targets, only one-third of KiwiSaver members are from the target group (IRD 2015). Political change has led to fiscal restraint being applied over time to unwind the inbuilt benefits. However, the conclusion of the evaluation program echoes the initial political and financial services concerns over KiwiSaver in terms of social inclusion and the participation of low-income earners. Those who have benefited the least from KiwiSaver to date are typically young, low-income and low net worth, less educated singles and renters (Colmar Brunton 2010; IRD 2015).

The following sections unpack the programmatic, procedural and political perspectives of the addition of KiwiSaver to New Zealand's retirement income framework. An analysis of how different design features impact on success and to what extent policy objectives are achieved is followed by consideration of political perspectives on KiwiSaver and its policy journey through time.

Programmatic assessment

The design features of both the public and the private components of the New Zealand retirement income system have public policy implications for retirement outcomes and the fiscal cost of the system. The Commission for Financial Capability (CFFC 2010) identified eight policy objectives that influence how public policy on retirement income systems is designed.[1] This section assesses the programmatic success of the KiwiSaver program against the policy objectives of income support, citizenship dividends, fiscal restraint, voluntary saving, cohort self-funding, wellbeing, longevity risk-pooling and lifetime consumption smoothing, with the common economic success factors in the evaluation of retirement income policy being equity, stability, sustainability, adequacy and economic efficiency.

Equity

Equity can be measured both between and within generations and is impacted by both KiwiSaver and NZS. Intergenerational equity can be thought of in terms of the burden on the current workforce to contribute towards the cost of government pensions for the retired population. The fiscal implications of NZS—essentially an intergenerational social contract and an unfunded pension liability due to the PAYG nature of the scheme—are volatile costs due to changes in the age structure of the population (CFFC 2010). The ratio of the working-age (15–64 years) to retired (65 years and over) population is expected to halve in New Zealand between 2013 and 2060 (Coleman 2015), creating a high

1 The Commission for Financial Capability was formerly known as the Commission for Financial Literacy and Retirement Income and, before that, the Retirement Commission.

rate of cost-shifting between generations due to population ageing and a universal rather than means-tested age pension. However, an increasing degree of cost-shifting to future generations does not always lead to intergenerational inequity.

Numerous factors, both monetary and nonmonetary, impact intergenerational equity and offset the negative economic consequences of the increasing cost of government pensions. From the suffragette movement to war efforts and the general innovation and investment of prior generations, current and future generations benefit not only in standards of living, but also in higher incomes (Gemmell 2017). At a reasonable projected long-run labour productivity growth of 1.5 per cent per annum and accounting for an increase in tax to cover increasing government pensions, average disposable incomes can be expected to be 70 per cent higher in 30–40 years (Guest 2013), improving the opportunities for cohort self-funding via KiwiSaver to reduce future intergenerational equity concerns. Moreover, Gemmell (2017) identifies that baby boomers have little effect on New Zealand's long-term dependency ratios, with the persistent ageing problem more strongly related to health care and other advances impacting on longevity. While current workers may pay more collectively to support the baby boomers, they are likely to live longer themselves and receive government pensions for longer, even if they retire somewhat after age 65. Gen X and Gen Y are also more likely to inherit wealth from their families, but some within a generation may fare better than others.

Intragenerational equity considers the welfare of those within a generation. Prior to and beyond the introduction of KiwiSaver, NZS has been successful in achieving a lower rate of poverty in the over-65 population in New Zealand than in most of the world (OECD 2016). Guest (2013) suggests this is evidence of a stronger correction in the New Zealand retirement income system for income inequality experienced at a younger age. NZS provides income support for almost all of the over-65 population. Those with lower working-life incomes seem relatively better off in retirement, but NZS provides a poor level of income replacement for middle to high-income earners. The provision of NZS to those who are financially well off may be viewed as less equitable than in other countries, but equity is coloured by philosophical views of NZS, which may even impact attitudes towards KiwiSaver.

NZS can be thought of as a citizenship dividend that treats the productive efforts and contributions made by citizens from all walks of life equally, providing the same recognition and entitlement from the age of eligibility and removing any stigma associated with applying for targeted welfare (CFFC 2010). In this regard, the universal nature of NZS provides a positive impact on social cohesion compared with means-tested age pensions that may have a more divisive impact on the eligible community. On the other hand, those who view government support as an entitlement rather than a safety net are more likely to view personal savings through voluntary savings vehicles such as KiwiSaver as additional to requirements and have different spending priorities. They are also more likely to game the system where there is the opportunity to do so in a means-tested regime (Stephen 2016). NZS gets the balance about right, with a payment sufficient to cover the essentials, large enough neither to incentivise early retirement or large spending to collect it nor to lead the public to believe it is enough to live on. As incomes rise and NZS does, too, the indexation rate may need to be reconsidered for both behavioural reasons and sustainability.

Sustainability

The New Zealand retirement income system is vulnerable in terms of sustainability despite the addition of KiwiSaver and even after the removal of many of KiwiSaver's inbuilt incentives. The sustainability of current settings in relation to NZS in the face of demographic change and the impact on fiscal costs has been questioned. Although they are difficult to predict in the long run, the fiscal costs of the government pension are expected to grow as the number of retirees grows and this is compounded by the universal nature of NZS. From an administrative cost perspective, New Zealand performs among the best in the OECD (OECD 2011). KiwiSaver achieves operational efficiencies through the use of the income tax platform, lower tax concessions and no access to tax-free withdrawals until age 65, resulting in a percentage of GDP cost of only 0.35 for KiwiSaver (Guest 2013). However, the sustainability of policy choices also concerns the cost of borrowing. All else being equal, net debt in New Zealand is projected to rise to 69 per cent of GDP by 2045 (The Treasury 2016). Strategies are in place to manage unfunded public pension liabilities related to NZS after 2020, which will ease the need for future borrowing, although it is unlikely the New Zealand Superannuation Fund will be accessed so soon.

Stability

KiwiSaver has experienced frequent change over one decade in contrast with the relative stability of NZS since 1990—although changes are expected in a young system over time to get things right and NZS has previously experienced periods of high instability (see, for example, Littlewood 2008). However, both possible and actual policy changes to retirement income systems impact on stability. There has been ongoing debate regarding an increase in the age of eligibility for NZS, a return to means testing for NZS and whether or not KiwiSaver ought to be compulsory, among other issues. For example, evidence shows that individuals and employees consider the possibility of KiwiSaver changing or being discontinued as a major barrier to joining (IRD 2015). The downside of cumulative change and perceptions of future change impact on attitudes and behaviours in relation to retirement saving and spending, with flow-on effects to the achievement of policy objectives and other success factors such as adequacy.

Adequacy

KiwiSaver strengthens an individual's ability to derive an adequate income from the New Zealand retirement income system, but there is still much room for improvement. Adequacy concerns how well the combined total of income from government pensions and private accumulated wealth cover meets retirement needs. NZS ensures low poverty rates in the over-65 population in New Zealand, but poverty (financial deprivation) is a very low level of support, particularly for medium to high-income earners (OECD 2017). Superannuation and other assets can be used to bring overall retirement income up to a desired level of income replacement—often in the range of 65–95 per cent, but typically 70 per cent of preretirement earnings. Survey evidence from New Zealand reveals that individuals are generally aware of their needs in retirement, but actual savings fall well short of target savings (ASB Bank 2012). Half of those surveyed expect to fall short of a comfortable retirement and one-third are concerned they will not even meet basic needs (Law et al. 2011). Although NZS is universal, differences in the design of private savings vehicles such as KiwiSaver are what have greater impact on the adequacy of retirement income.

Cohort self-funding

In New Zealand, the KiwiSaver coverage rate of 58 per cent of the total population is a relative success given the voluntary nature of the scheme (IRD 2017; Statistics NZ 2018). KiwiSaver opt-out statistics remain high, at approximately 30 per cent of automatically enrolled members—equivalent to about 12 per cent of the gross membership base. One-third of opt outs are due to affordability issues, with slightly less related to the belief there are better financial alternatives (IRD 2015). The distinguishing characteristic of KiwiSaver members who opt out is their level of income, with the majority earning less than $30,000—well below the mean and median gross earnings for KiwiSaver members and a number that generally reflects the New Zealand wage and salary population. Opt-outs are spread relatively evenly across age groups and most report being in full-time work with low net worth (Colmar Brunton 2010; IRD 2015). Adequacy is less of a concern for the majority of opt-outs, with NZS providing the strongest replacement rate for low-income workers. For those remaining in the scheme, contribution rates and asset allocation are the key to accumulating wealth to support retirement adequacy.

KiwiSaver offers a range of 3 per cent, 4 per cent or 8 per cent contribution rates for employees. Yet, the majority of KiwiSaver members have a joint employer–employee contribution rate of 6 per cent of gross earnings—the default contribution rate (IRD 2016). Taking no action or choosing the lowest contribution rate can be expected to significantly impact superannuation balances, especially given the very conservative asset allocations under KiwiSaver, including legislative restrictions to have no more than 25 per cent growth assets in default funds. The average superannuation balance in 2013–14 was NZ$8,000 (A$7,600) in KiwiSaver (IRD 2017). Given KiwiSaver is a young scheme that includes children and those not in the workforce, it makes more sense to consider a representative individual on average earnings throughout their working life and the combined retirement income from KiwiSaver and the age pension. The representative individual is expected to achieve a level of preretirement income replacement rates of approximately 60 per cent (MacDonald et al. 2012); however, income distributions are skewed to the right and not all assets to fund retirement are held as financial assets.

An analysis of asset holding in New Zealand reveals a preference for investment in real assets including businesses and farms. This is not surprising due to the voluntary nature of KiwiSaver and the short time frame over which it has been running. The flexibility of KiwiSaver allows members to go on a contribution holiday and redirect funds to consumption or alternative investments. This has been seen as a negative feature in terms of the impact on future superannuation balances. However, in compulsory systems, individuals often borrow for current consumption and thus adjust the amount of their savings or adjust the mix of their assets—for example, by purchasing property, with the intention to repay later from superannuation balances (Guest 2013). The potential impact may be more significant in New Zealand with the opportunity to borrow without necessarily having continuing superannuation contributions locked in as an asset for offset. It is clear, however, that governments have more control over the form of saving than over the amount of saving, calling into question the net welfare benefit added by mandatory superannuation given the associated costs.

Retirement adequacy is also impacted by demographic differences, which impact salaries and wages and patterns of work, which in turn impact on the size and continuity of superannuation contributions. KiwiSaver data show a direct correlation between income and contributions, with males contributing more than females and Māori contributing the least of all members identifying as being from a non-European background (IRD 2015). Females fare better in New Zealand than other nations in terms of the gender superannuation gap as a result of a smaller gender pay gap (Guest 2013), but the strength of this finding is limited due to the New Zealand balances excluding other saving sources of retirement saving. Also, wealth accumulation in KiwiSaver was for a five-year period—a time frame unlikely to provide insights into patterns of periods off work, for example, due to parent and carer roles often undertaken by women. Other asset holdings may also favour males due to small business ownership and workplace superannuation schemes in effect many decades prior to the introduction of KiwiSaver. Across the Tasman, Bianchi et al. (2016) identified significant retirement gaps for Indigenous Australian males (27 per cent lower) and females (39 per cent lower) compared with a median non-Indigenous male worker. Such studies point to the broader policy framework on education and employment to strengthen New Zealand working life incomes to improve adequacy.

The ability to examine the assets available for retirement alone and consider their potential to create income is limited given the choices individuals exercise in investing and borrowing outside superannuation and their approach to drawdown and consumption in retirement. Home equity may be accessed through reverse mortgages or downsizing and some assets are not yet accounted for, such as transfers of intergenerational equity. The design features of KiwiSaver that provide an element of choice—such as withdrawal for homeownership, opt-outs for those automatically enrolled and contribution holidays—score highly in terms of nonmonetary aspects of wellbeing. However, when combined with a low default contribution rate and more conservative asset allocation, New Zealanders need to carefully consider their choices to strengthen their retirement adequacy. Future cohort analysis may reveal more detailed insights, and further investigation needs to be done to support those who stand to benefit the least from national superannuation programs.

Longevity risk-pooling

Even if individuals accumulate sufficient wealth with the potential to improve retirement outcomes, they may deplete their superannuation balances too soon for many reasons, including underestimation of their own longevity, increasing debt to repay in ageing households, healthcare shocks, costs of aged care, market conditions and, in means-tested systems such as Australia's, spending fuelled by moral hazard. NZS acts like a lifetime annuity and provides similar degrees of longevity risk-pooling. Government pensions are effective in longevity risk-pooling because they are inflation-protected annuities from the age of eligibility until the end of life (Commission for Financial Literacy and Retirement Income 2012). But the problem remains the lack of longevity protection for private superannuation.

The New Zealand Government has realised the problem created by the relative lack of attention to and control over the decumulation phase of private superannuation versus the accumulation phase. In countries such as New Zealand, where annuitisation is voluntary, annuities have not been popular—hampered by the unfavourable nature of the tax system. New Zealand has a poorly developed market in which supply-side problems further restrict choices due to private sector unwillingness to assume longevity and inflation risks without effective hedging opportunities (Berthold 2013). Economists and market commentators have called for the development of a generic government-managed annuity decumulation product to exploit the best attributes of KiwiSaver and the potential to include long-term care provisions (St John 2014). Nevertheless, even with government support for the decumulation of private superannuation, government pensions will continue to play a central role in individuals' portfolios.

Empirical evidence highlights the role of government pensions in providing flexibility in portfolio management and protection against changing market conditions. Not only is compulsory annuitisation likely to be highly unpopular, but also Pfau (2013) shows that the combination of financial assets with annuities is more successful to support individuals' trade-offs for minimum spending needs, lifestyle goals and unexpected contingencies. To the extent that there is likely to be a long implementation phase should any changes occur to NZS, a guaranteed income source such as NZS provides KiwiSaver members with some volatility protection to enable them to take a less conservative investment position and adjust their rate of withdrawal from superannuation as required (Finke et al. 2011). Although New Zealand has been shown to have one of the highest safe withdrawal rates in the world (Drew and Walk 2014; Pfau and Dokken 2015; Blanchett et al. 2016)—that is, the rate of drawdown from the portfolio while avoiding portfolio ruin—investors with low accumulated balances (less than $200,000), particularly those in conservative investments, face a 'no frills' retirement even when combining regular KiwiSaver withdrawals with NZS. Long-run lower future market return expectations mean that NZS is important even for those with larger KiwiSaver balances ($350,000 to $500,000) who would also face significant adjustments to standards of living should they have reduced access to or funding from NZS through future changes, particularly in the face of increased retirement horizons (MacDonald 2016).

Economic efficiency

Economic efficiency considers the wider social and economic effects of retirement income policy such as labour participation and employment, labour productivity, saving incentives, lifetime consumption smoothing and wellbeing.

Labour participation and productivity

Increasing labour participation and productivity is an effective approach to reducing the fiscal costs associated with ageing populations. KiwiSaver and NZS provide strong incentives to work. New Zealand reports high labour participation rates across all age groups, including the over-65 population (ILO 2011). The addition of KiwiSaver has impacted the cost of employment, but at a lower level than in other countries with higher employer contribution rates. Not being able to access either NZS or KiwiSaver until age 65 means only those with additional private savings are likely to retire early, with those who leave the workforce prior to age 65 due to health or unemployment reasons able to access welfare support. Labour productivity has a more complex relationship with retirement income policy. It is difficult to determine the impact of factors from the retirement income system or even the overall direction of the impact (for full analysis, see Guest 2013).

Savings

Although economic indicators show that New Zealand household and national savings are low against international standards, evidence that suggests New Zealanders are saving enough highlights the problems with different approaches to measuring saving (Orr and Purdue 2001; Le et al. 2009). It is difficult to determine the net effect on saving in New Zealand, with both positive and negative effects from NZS and KiwiSaver, but overall it is likely to be positive. KiwiSaver's opt-out provision is limited to a small set of members—those over the age of 18 who were automatically enrolled on commencing new employment. This has a negative effect on household savings, along with contribution holidays, which have no limits on time or the number of holidays taken. Despite the choice of higher contribution rates (4 or 8 per cent), the majority of members who do not opt out invest at the minimum and default rate (IRD 2015). Possible reasons include a lack of cash flow, the universal nature of NZS or investor inertia or myopia, with only half of KiwiSaver members rating themselves somewhere between neutral and highly engaged (Colmar Brunton 2010). On the positive side, KiwiSaver does not require a member to be in employment so even children can be encouraged to participate with a view to impacting saving behaviour in the long term across the whole population. But those with small balances or on a contribution holiday risk the erosion of their savings from fees while small or no contributions are made. A further negative effect is moral hazard—the unintended consequence of relatively generous government pensions such as NZS that reduce the need to save for retirement.

Lifetime consumption smoothing

The elements of choice regarding when and how to save can assist with proper balancing of spending and saving during the different phases of one's life. KiwiSaver members are also provided with welfare advantages, to the extent that their choices are 'rational' and based on their financial circumstances. However, the favourable tax environment for housing—with no capital gains tax or stamp duty—means the incentives for saving are stronger for investment in housing, particularly with either the opt-out or withdrawal for homeownership provisions available in KiwiSaver or even a contribution holiday while paying down student loan debt or borrowing for housing. The choice to spend on housing—a less liquid asset—is not necessarily problematic in terms of retirement outcomes. Poverty rates in New Zealand are much higher for those renting, so homeownership impacts positively on wellbeing during working life and retirement (IRD 2015; OECD 2016).

A summative assessment

Table 20.2 summarises the programmatic assessment of the addition of KiwiSaver to the New Zealand retirement income system. Together, NZS and KiwiSaver strengthen the system, which stands out for its intragenerational equity, choice, flexibility, incentives to work and administrative simplicity. Importantly, where one component is negative, the two components of the system have an offsetting effect. Table 20.2 identifies weaknesses in the system as cohort self-funding and fiscal costs. The evaluation is simplistic, with the assumption of equal weighting of economic success factors and policy objectives and inclusion of subjective measures, equity and wellbeing. For the long-term success of the system, more attention needs to be paid to the design of KiwiSaver and NZS to support adequacy and sustainability.

Table 20.2 Programmatic evaluation: Performance against success factors and policy objectives

Success factor/policy objective	Australia		New Zealand		Which system is better?
	Age pension	SG[a]	NZS	KiwiSaver	
Intergenerational equity	✓	n		n	Australia
Intragenerational equity					NZ
Income support	✓	n	✓✓	n	
Citizenship dividend	✓	n	✓✓	n	
Stability	✓	x	✓✓	x	NZ
Sustainability					Australia
Fiscal restraint[b]	✓	x	x	n	
Adequacy					Australia
Cohort self-funding	x	✓✓✓	x	✓✓	
Longevity risk-pooling	✓✓✓	n	✓✓✓	n	

Success factor/policy objective	Australia		New Zealand		Which system is better?
	Age pension	SG[a]	NZS	KiwiSaver	
Economic efficiency	x	✓		✓	NZ
Voluntary saving	x	✓	x	✓✓	
Wellbeing	✓	✓✓	✓✓	✓✓	
Lifetime consumption smoothing	x			✓	

✓✓✓ strong

✓✓ moderate

✓ limited or weak

x negative

n neutral

[a] Superannuation Guarantee

[b] In contrast to the approach of the Commission for Financial Capability (CFFC 2010), labour market effects are included under the wellbeing objective.

Note: This table summarises the strengths and weaknesses of components of the retirement income systems in New Zealand and Australia relative to each success criterion and policy objective based on the discussion.

Source: Adapted from Guest (2013).

Process and political assessment

New Zealand governments as early as 1898 established government pensions and explored ways to encourage private retirement savings (Preston 2001). However, it was not until 1975—in what looked like an early version of KiwiSaver—that any significant progress was made. The Labour Party established a short-lived (37 weeks) compulsory superannuation scheme with a combined employee–employer contribution rate to be phased in at up to 8 per cent of earnings (Preston 2001). But—in what is now considered one of the largest election bribes of all time and a major shift in public spending that some might describe as 'intergenerational theft'—the National Party promised a very generous government pension (equivalent to 80 per cent of the average ordinary wage for couples from age 60 from 1978), won the election and ended the compulsory superannuation scheme (George 2010). Tinkering with retirement income policy to adjust fiscal costs to economic conditions continued through successive governments, yet it would be almost 30 years until another Labour government would introduce a major policy change to seek to address private retirement savings.

The original design of KiwiSaver, as per the 2005 Budget announcement, implemented automatic enrolment for new employees aged 18–65, with the ability to opt out, employee contributions at either 4 per cent (the default level) or 8 per cent of gross earnings, boosted by government payments of a one-off tax-free $1,000, an annual $40 fee subsidy and any voluntary additional employee contributions (IRD 2008). Employers were eligible for an exemption from the employer superannuation contribution tax for employer contributions up to a maximum of 4 per cent of an employee's gross pay (IRD 2016). In introducing the KiwiSaver Bill to parliament, the policy's political champion, Labour finance minister Michael Cullen, announced there had been extensive consultation and already some changes, but six main features remained: automatic enrolment to tilt the playing field towards long-term savings; savings locked in until retirement; choice for members in how their funds are managed; minimum compliance costs for employees, employers and providers; prudential oversight; and the ability for existing schemes to join in and encouraging homeownership (New Zealand Parliament 2006a).

At the first reading of the Bill, there was a mixture of support and concern. Opposition parties raised issues such as: 1) no scheme being able to solve the problems underlying New Zealand's savings deficit; 2) concerns about the mixed purpose of KiwiSaver incorporating home deposit savings; 3) the likelihood that the $1,000 kickstart payment would 'lose its glow' over time; and 4) a strong desire to focus on taxation reform and freedom of choice so people could access money when they needed it—particularly those with shorter lifespans (New Zealand Parliament 2006a). National Party leader John Key felt it was unconscionable to require households to compromise on their needs when KiwiSaver would not help those with an inability to save due to low incomes. Rather than a savings problem, it was a problem with productivity, social welfare, overtaxation and infrastructure bureaucracy that could not be solved by KiwiSaver (New Zealand Parliament 2006a). The political concerns that KiwiSaver could not resolve undersaving and the unclear purpose of and inconsistencies within the scheme (housing versus retirement) were echoed from the business and financial services communities. The Retirement Policy and Research Centre proposed economic growth as the only practical approach to managing the impact of an ageing population (New Zealand Parliament 2006c).

It was argued that KiwiSaver was a high-cost solution to a savings problem for which there was insufficient evidence (Gibson and Le 2008; Yong and Cox 2008). There was significant scrutiny of incentives, including the cost of government and employer contributions, and design features, such as the opportunity to withdraw funds for first-home purchases and questions about whether these incentives would be effective in creating new savings (Toder and Khitatrakun 2006; St John 2007; Yong and Cox 2008; Le et al. 2009; St John et al. 2014). There were further concerns about the potential effects of KiwiSaver in relation to NZS and equity. In 2007, Treasury and the Retirement Commissioner warned that the cost and inequity of KiwiSaver would have implications for the sustainability of NZS. The substitution of existing savings for KiwiSaver was expected to undo some of the equity created by NZS (St John 2007; Le et al. 2009). A 40-year-old KiwiSaver member on a high income could end up with $100,000 to $150,000, or 33 per cent of their accumulated wealth, at age 65, funded by taxpayers (St John 2008). Taxpayers and employers would carry the cost burden and employees and fund providers would enjoy the benefits (Yong and Cox 2008).

A last-minute change to KiwiSaver—against select committee recommendations—was the addition of a mortgage diversion facility, allowing up to 50 per cent of employee contributions to be paid into a mortgage after one year of membership (St John 2007). The facility was described as 'policy on the hoof', squeezed in just four hours before the second reading of the Bill, and was criticised for being rejected previously due to insufficient time to conduct analysis. The opposition parties did not support turning a savings account into a costly cheque account. Their focus remained on low-income earners trying to save, which led to lobbying for a 2 per cent contribution entry point. Labour argued that 2 per cent was not enough to save for retirement and it would be too hard to administer small accounts. However, the mortgage diversion itself would leave only a 2 per cent contribution in KiwiSaver (New Zealand Parliament 2006b). A transitional arrangement to compulsory employer contributions would now also be allowed—for example, so employers and employees could split equally the minimum 4 per cent contribution of gross earnings (Mercer 2007). Concerns then turned to the issue of employers finding out this news so late in the debate. The unexpected impact of co-contributions in future wage round negotiations might lead to employees effectively paying for their own contributions (New Zealand Parliament 2006b).

By the third reading, only the National Party voted against the Bill (71 to 48). Low income and affordability were still major concerns, with nearly 2 million people on incomes of less than $25,000 a year. National saw this as a problem if the assumption underlying system design and lack of savings was assumed to be inertia. Initially, National had not supported KiwiSaver due to the lack of incentives; now it was due to the design of the incentives. Cullen was criticised for having a longstanding position that savings incentives would not work in any form, realising at the last minute they were required and then rushing poorly designed incentives through (New Zealand Parliament 2006c).

Further changes to KiwiSaver included pushing back the implementation date, from 1 April to 1 July 2007, the introduction of a member tax credit (a dollar-for-dollar match up to $20 a week or $1,042.86 per annum), compulsory employer contributions to be phased in evenly over four years (increasing from 1 per cent on 1 April 2008 to 4 per cent on 1 April 2011) and an employer tax credit ($20 per week up to $1,042.86 per annum per employee in KiwiSaver) to partially offset the costs of compulsory employer contributions (Toder and Khitatrakun 2006; Gibson and Le 2008). National, the major opposition party, did not agree that KiwiSaver would be effective in its current form, while a minor party, United Futures, looked forward to when, 'in 10 years' time private savings by New Zealanders may be, let us say, $100 billion' (New Zealand Parliament 2006c: 4994).

Ten years on, KiwiSaver is almost halfway there, with $40 billion in funds under management (Parker 2017a). Unfortunately, National's points of debate—that only 25 per cent of New Zealanders would have a 'serious' KiwiSaver account in five years and that New Zealand would be like Ireland with 92 per cent of accounts dormant or Singapore with empty accounts due to mortgage diversion (New Zealand Parliament 2006a, 2006b)—are reflected somewhat in the current state of KiwiSaver. The average balance is now just under $15,000, the number of noncontributing members stands at 38 per cent, the number of members taking long contribution holidays is increasing and $601 million has been withdrawn for housing (IRD 2015, 2017). In contrast, the factor that far exceeded expectations is participation in KiwiSaver—at 58 per cent of New Zealand's working population and 75 per cent of the total population (IRD 2017; Parker 2017b). However, there is criticism of the make-up of this membership.

Through its incentives, KiwiSaver has attracted a large group of members who already held non-KiwiSaver superannuation—dominated by high-income earners. The target investor group KiwiSaver sought to increase represents only about one-third of members who reported being unlikely or very unlikely to have saved via a vehicle other than KiwiSaver. The members of this target group are predominantly younger, have lower incomes and lower net worth and are less educated, single and renters (Colmar Brunton 2010). Very low-income earners (less than $30,000 per annum) dominate those who opt out. Opting out can, however, be positive for the wellbeing of low-income earners and prevents poverty during their working lives compared with their post-retirement income from NZS (Gibson et al. 2008). Labour has gone on to drop its campaign for compulsory membership, recognising the challenge of disposable income (Parker 2017b).

Endurance assessment

Many changes have been made to KiwiSaver over the past 10 years to correct what could be argued to have been poor initial design or rushed policy or both. The ill-fated mortgage diversion was closed in 2009 due to complexity, lack of use and unnecessary compliance costs, among other issues (IRD 2009). Other changes were made to address high fiscal costs, equity issues and market inefficiencies. The National Party removed the $1,000 kickstart in 2015 to save $125 million over four years after $2.5 billion had been spent over the previous eight years (NZ Herald 2015). Another notable change related to market reforms and governance of KiwiSaver, made possible by broad support from all parties for the review of fees and the introduction of standardised reporting legislation (New Zealand Parliament 2011, 2013). While operational and cost efficiencies are important, two key areas that have received less attention—despite having the most impact on retirement outcomes—are contribution rates and asset allocation.

The way in which contributions are split between stakeholders (employees, employers and the government) has undergone a number of changes since KiwiSaver's inception on 1 July 2007. Early evaluation examined the drivers of and barriers to KiwiSaver membership and found the primary barrier to enrolment was the minimum 4 per cent contribution and default rate (IRD 2008: 26), reflecting the previous debate in parliament about the affordability of participation. In 2009, National introduced the 2 per cent contribution rate previously lobbied for by the Green Party under the Labour Government. Concerned by statistics that 3 per cent of employees had increased their contribution rates since joining but three times as many had reduced their contribution rate (Colmar Brunton 2010), the Savings Working Group (SWG 2011) submitted a proposal to the government to maintain the 2 per cent minimum contribution level, but return the default setting to 4 per cent. The National Government's 2011 Budget answered the call of the Savings Working Group for a return to a 6 per cent default rate but with equal 3 per cent shares between employers and employees—with the rationale of increasing the employee contribution to offset tax changes and halving the member tax credit to avoid debt and to support national savings.

In 2013, default fund asset allocation was considered as part of the scheduled default provider review. The National Government confirmed the continuation of the very conservative investment approach, imposing a maximum of 25 per cent equity in default funds. The decision was made on the basis that it was most appropriate while the government was making decisions about other people's money (New Zealand Government 2013). While KiwiSaver has been a political success in the longer term (unlike NZS), this decision highlights a weakness in the retirement income framework, reflecting rational behaviour for the government, but not necessarily the best interests of KiwiSaver members in the long run—a sentiment also echoed by Littlewood (2008). However, the decision to stick to the status quo was a case of damned if they do, damned if they don't.

Concluding reflections

The final-year evaluation report concluded that KiwiSaver had not only a limited effect on the accumulation of net wealth, but also potentially a negative impact due to the conservative nature of default schemes (IRD 2015). These results were during a period of reasonable market performance. Had New Zealand been affected more by the GFC, the findings might have been different. Default funds are often viewed as a government endorsement of the investment. A loss relating to an increase in investment risk would impact not only members' saving behaviour—and therefore the likelihood of achieving the goals of KiwiSaver—but also investors' attitudes towards the government. With the majority of submissions and earlier government-initiated reviews conducted by the Capital Market Development Taskforce (2009) and the Savings Working Group (SWG 2011) calling for change, the decision to forgo the opportunity to adjust the strongest lever available to address adequacy was disappointing, particularly in light of the difficulties found in other markets relying on financial education strategies and investor engagement to shift investors from default funds to funds more appropriate for their circumstances.

Considering the findings from the procedural, political and programmatic perspectives together, it is clear that a stronger focus is needed on the most important aspect of retirement savings for KiwiSaver members: retirement outcomes. Important questions arise from the evaluation of the addition of KiwiSaver to the New Zealand retirement framework:

1. Is the weak evidence of programmatic success due to the approach taken in the evaluation? How does the seven-year time frame impact the analysis? Are there alternative approaches available?

The seven-year evaluation by the multiagency KiwiSaver evaluation steering group included a survey of members of the evaluation team. The survey results indicated a 'very good' result in terms of effectiveness and satisfaction. Importantly, the respondents felt the seven-year time frame for the evaluation was not long enough. The evaluation team members supported regular reviews of KiwiSaver moving forward to consider new challenges such as the decumulation phase. They also note that the current evaluation cannot be extrapolated to consider the success of KiwiSaver in five to 10 years (IRD 2015). The methodological approaches to pension finance applied in other markets (e.g. Blake et al. 2007; Basu and Drew 2010) offer insights into the future of KiwiSaver. Modelling retirement savings over a KiwiSaver member's working life highlights both the weaknesses and the opportunities in KiwiSaver's design (MacDonald et al. 2012; MacDonald 2016).

2. Is the weak evidence of programmatic success due to the design of KiwiSaver? Is KiwiSaver capable of increasing the ability for cohort self-funding and delivering retirement adequacy in conjunction with NZS as it is? What design changes or investor behaviour changes can improve retirement outcomes?

Table 20.2 reveals the importance of exploring improved adequacy in KiwiSaver to counterbalance the sustainability challenge of NZS in the future. Changes to contribution rates in KiwiSaver over time have not seen a shift from large numbers of KiwiSaver members contributing at the default contribution rate. Examining the passage of KiwiSaver through parliament reveals a strong theme of reform of the broader taxation and economic policy framework to facilitate the ability to live on and save from working-life incomes to improve the number of KiwiSaver members from the target cohort and increase contribution rates into the future, as seen in international markets as their retirement vehicles have matured. However, even if contribution rates increase, when modelling KiwiSaver investment over a 40-year savings horizon, making higher contributions to conservative KiwiSaver asset allocations may still lead to unattainable retirement goals (MacDonald et al. 2012).

While default funds have lower equity risk, they place investors at a much higher risk of shortfall in achieving their retirement target (Basu and Drew 2010; MacDonald 2016). KiwiSaver investors moving out of default and conservative investments into even a moderate fund can increase their retirement adequacy without substantially increasing their downside risk. Moderate and high-growth KiwiSaver funds offer the opportunity for New Zealanders to accumulate levels of wealth that, in conjunction with NZS, are expected to provide adequate retirement outcomes (MacDonald 2016). More growth-oriented portfolio choices are made by those given financial advice (Zhang 2014), but the number of New Zealanders seeking such advice is low, at about 20 per cent (Matthews 2013; Risk Info 2017). New Zealand needs to address investor engagement—specifically, issues such as myopia, procrastination and excessive risk-aversion in investment, often due to young people sitting in default funds with an asset allocation that may not be appropriate for their individual circumstances.

The relatively modest success of KiwiSaver towards its goals in the short term does not prevent the realisation of a programmatic success in the future. For KiwiSaver to be seen as an enduring procedural and political success, the most pressing concerns are consideration of further evaluation points and a political champion(s) to address adequacy. Issues of particular concern relating directly to retirement outcomes are default fund design and consideration of the decumulation phase to support the use of accumulated KiwiSaver wealth in conjunction with NZS to replace income in retirement.

References

ASB Bank 2012. 'KiwiSaver contributions short of retirement savings goals.' *Scoop*, 13 June. Available from: www.scoop.co.nz/stories/BU1206/S00354/kiwisaver-contributions-short-of-retirement-savings-goals.htm.

Basu, A. K. and Drew, M. E. 2010. 'The appropriateness of default investment options in defined contribution plans: Australian evidence.' *Pacific-Basin Finance Journal* 18: 290–305.

Berthold, T. 2013. *Assuring retirement income.* Working Paper 01/13. Wellington: Ministry of Social Development.

Bianchi, R. J., Drew, M. E., Walk, A. N. and Wiafe, O. 2016. 'Retirement adequacy of Indigenous Australians: A baseline study.' *Economic Papers* 35(4): 359–74. doi.org/10.1111/1759-3441.12154.

Blake, D., Cairns, A. J. G. and Dowd, K. 2007. 'The impact of occupation and gender on pensions and defined contribution plans.' *The Geneva Papers* 32: 458–82.

Blanchett, D., Serhan, A. and Gee, P. 2016. 'Safe withdrawal rates for Australian retirees.' *Morning Star*. Accessed from: www.morningstar.com.au/smsf/article/withdrawal-rates/7529/2?q=printme (site discontinued).

Capital Market Development Taskforce 2009. *Capital Markets Matter: Summary report of the Capital Market Development Taskforce.* Wellington: Ministry of Business, Innovation and Employment. Available from: www.med.govt.nz/business/economic-development/pdf-docs-library/cmd-capital-markets-matter-exec-summary.pdf.

Coleman, A. 2015. 'Pension payments and receipts by New Zealand birth cohorts, 1916–1986.' *New Zealand Economic Papers* 50: 51–70. doi.org/10.1080/00779954.2015.1095787.

Colmar Brunton 2010. *KiwiSaver evaluation: Survey of individuals—Final report prepared for Inland Revenue.* Wellington: Inland Revenue Department. Accessed from: www.ird.govt.nz/resources/0/3/03e46600437177c5a25eb24e9c145ab7/ks-evaluation-individuals.pdf (site discontinued).

Commission for Financial Capability (CFFC) 2010. *2010 Review of Retirement Income Policy.* Wellington: CFFC. Available from: www.cffc.org.nz/assets/Documents/RI-Review-2010-Full-Report.pdf.

Commission for Financial Literacy and Retirement Income 2012. *Longevity Risk Pooling*. Wellington: Commission for Financial Literacy and Retirement Income. Available from: www.cffc.org.nz/assets/Documents/Retirement-Income-Position-Paper-4-Longevity-Risk-Pooling-2012.pdf.

Drew, M. E. and Walk, A. N. 2014. *How safe are safe withdrawal rates in retirement? An Australian perspective*. Research Report. Sydney: Financial Services Institute of Australasia. Available from: www.finsia.com/docs/default-source/Retirement-Risk-Zone/how-safe-are-safe-withdrawal-rates-in-retirement-an-australian-perspective.pdf?sfvrsn=2.

Finke, M., Pfau, W. D. and Williams, D. 2011. *Spending flexibility and safe withdrawal rates*. Online paper, 8 November. doi.org/10.2139/ssrn.1956727.

Gemmell, N. 2017. *Reforms to New Zealand Superannuation eligibility: Are they a good idea?* Working Papers in Public Finance No. 08/2017, June. Wellington: Victoria Business School. Available from: www.victoria.ac.nz/__data/assets/pdf_file/0003/909507/WP_08_2017_Reforms_to-_New_Zealand_Superannuation.pdf.

George, G. 2010. 'Laughable super comments.' *Otago Daily Times*, 24 December. Available from: www.odt.co.nz/opinion/laughable-super-comments.

Gibson, J. and Le, T. 2008. *How much new saving will KiwiSaver produce?* Working Paper in Economics No. 03/08. Hamilton, NZ: University of Waikato.

Gibson, J., Hector, C. and Le, T. 2008. *The distributional impact of KiwiSaver incentives*. Working Paper in Economics No. 02/08. Hamilton, NZ: University of Waikato.

Guest, R. 2013. *Comparison of the New Zealand and Australian retirement income systems*. Background Paper prepared for the 2013 review of retirement income policy by the Commission for Financial Literacy and Retirement Income. Auckland: Commission for Financial Capability. Available from: www.cffc.org.nz/assets/Documents/RI-Review-2013-Comparison-NZ-Aus-Retirement-Income-Systems.pdf.

Inland Revenue Department (IRD) 2008. *KiwiSaver Evaluation: Annual report 1, 1 July 2007 – 30 June 2008*. Wellington: IRD. Accessed from: www.ird.govt.nz/resources/0/4/04c0c6804bec321183fdab1877c64b2b/ks-evaluation1.pdf (site discontinued).

Inland Revenue Department (IRD) 2009. *Taxation (Budget Tax Measures) Act 2009: Closing the KiwiSaver mortgage diversion facility*. Wellington: IRD. Available from: www.ird.govt.nz/technical-tax/legislation/2009/2009-14/leg-2009-14-closing-ks-diversion.html.

Inland Revenue Department (IRD) 2015. *KiwiSaver Evaluation: Final summary report—A joint agency evaluation 2007–2014*. February. Wellington: National Research and Evaluation Unit, IRD. Available from: www.ird.govt.nz/resources/3/8/38e71a99-51cd-4971-abb7-87ee68497b23/ks-evaluation-final-summary-report.pdf.

Inland Revenue Department (IRD) 2016. KiwiSaver contributions. [Online]. Wellington: IRD. Available from: www.kiwisaver.govt.nz/already/contributions/.

Inland Revenue Department (IRD) 2017. KiwiSaver statistics by year. [Online]. Wellington: IRD. Available from: www.kiwisaver.govt.nz/statistics/annual/.

Inland Revenue Department (IRD) 2019a. KiwiSaver and tax. [Online]. Wellington: IRD. Available from: www.kiwisaver.govt.nz/already/contributions/tax/.

Inland Revenue Department (IRD) 2019b. KiwiSaver benefits: Savings withdrawal to purchase your first home. [Online]. Wellington: IRD Department. Available from: www.kiwisaver.govt.nz/new/benefits/home-withdrawl/.

International Labour Organization (ILO) 2011. *Key Indicators of the Labour Market (KILM)*. Geneva: Department of Economic and Labour Market Analysis, ILO.

Law, D., Meehan, L. and Scobie, G. 2011. *KiwiSaver: An evaluation of the impact on retirement saving*. New Zealand Treasury Working Paper. Wellington: The Treasury.

Le, T., Scobie, G. and Gibson, J. 2009. 'Are Kiwis saving enough for retirement? Evidence from SOFIE.' *New Zealand Economic Papers* 43(1): 3–19. doi.org/10.1080/00779950902803951.

Littlewood, M. 2008. *A condensed history of public and private provision for retirement income in New Zealand: 1975–2008*. In Pension Briefing: A briefing paper from the Retirement Policy and Research Centre. Auckland: University of Auckland Business School.

MacDonald, K. L. 2016. KiwiSaver and retirement adequacy. PhD thesis, Griffith University, Brisbane.

MacDonald, K. L., Bianchi, R. J. and Drew, M. E. 2012. 'KiwiSaver and retirement adequacy.' *Australasian Accounting Business and Finance Journal* 6(4): 61–78. Available from: ro.uow.edu.au/aabfj/vol6/iss4/5.

Matthews, C. 2013. *KiwiSaver and retirement savings in 2012*. Report. Sydney: Financial Services Institute of Australasia. Available from: www.finsia.com/docs/default-source/industry-reports-retirement-risk-zone/kiwisaver-and-retirement-savings-in-2011.pdf?sfvrsn=9b41de93_4.

Mercer 2007. *Recent KiwiSaver and Taxation Changes: Impact on employers and trustees*. Auckland: Mercer New Zealand. Accessed from: www.superfacts.com/files/MercerWealthSolutionNZ/document/20071219135044sjdierk7116.pdf (site discontinued).

Ministry of Social Development n.d. Residency requirements for New Zealand benefits and pensions: A guide to the residency requirements for New Zealand benefits and pensions. [Online]. Wellington: Ministry of Social Development. Available from: www.workandincome.govt.nz/pensions/travelling-or-moving/moving-to-nz/residency-requirements-for-new-zealand-benefits-and-pensions.html#null.

New Zealand Government 2013. KiwiSaver default provider review completed. Media release, 17 October. Wellington: New Zealand Government. Available from: www.beehive.govt.nz/release/kiwisaver-default-provider-review-completed.

NZ Herald 2015. 'Budget 2015: New KiwiSavers lose $1000 "kick-start".' *NZ Herald*, 21 May Available from: www.nzherald.co.nz/personal-finance/news/article.cfm?c_id=12&objectid=11452492.

New Zealand Parliament 2006a. *New Zealand Parliamentary Debates* (2 March) 629, 1673.

New Zealand Parliament 2006b. *New Zealand Parliamentary Debates* (24 August) 633, 4845.

New Zealand Parliament 2006c. *New Zealand Parliamentary Debates* (30 August) 633, 4994.

New Zealand Parliament 2011. *New Zealand Parliamentary Debates* (7 April) 671, 17846.

New Zealand Parliament 2013. *New Zealand Parliamentary Debates* (27 August) 693, 12999.

Organisation for Economic Co-operation and Development (OECD) 2011. *Pensions at a Glance 2011: Retirement income systems in OECD and G20 countries*. Paris: OECD Publishing. doi.org/10.1787/pension_glance-2011-en.

Organisation for Economic Co-operation and Development (OECD) 2016. OECD Data: Poverty rate. [Online]. Paris: OECD. Available from: data.oecd.org/inequality/poverty-rate.htm#indicator-chart.

Organisation for Economic Co-operation and Development (OECD) 2017. *Pensions at a Glance 2017: OECD and G20 indicators*. Paris: OECD Publishing. doi.org/10.1787/pension_glance-2017-en.

Orr, A. and Purdue, D. 2001. *Saving and investment in New Zealand, and the super fund*. Westpac Institutional Bank Occasional Paper. Wellington: Westpac Institutional Bank.

Parker, T. 2017a. 'KiwiSaver hits $40b, but balances stay low.' *NZ Herald*, 15 May. Available from: www.nzherald.co.nz/personal-finance/news/article.cfm?c_id=12&objectid=11856222.

Parker, T. 2017b. 'Sir Michael Cullen: KiwiSaver should be mandatory.' *NZ Herald*, 30 December. Available from: www.nzherald.co.nz/personal-finance/news/article.cfm?c_id=12&objectid=11884009.

Pfau, W. D. 2013. 'A broader framework for determining an efficient frontier for retirement income.' *Journal of Financial Planning* 26(2): 44–51.

Pfau, W. D. and Dokken, W. 2015. *Rethinking retirement: Sustainable withdrawal rates for new retirees in 2015*. White Paper. Bozeman, MT: WealthVest. Available from: www.fa-mag.com/userfiles/stories/whitepapers/2015/WealthVest_Sept_2015_Whitepaper/12040-Pfau-Sustainable-Withdrawal-Rates-Whitepaper-.pdf.

Preston, D. A. 2001. *Retirement Income in New Zealand: The historical context*. Wellington: Office of the Retirement Commissioner.

Risk Info 2017. 'Client numbers fall despite increased demand for advice.' *Risk Info*, 1 November. Available from: riskinfo.com.au/news/2017/11/01/client-numbers-fall-despite-higher-demand-for-advice/.

St John, S. 2007. 'KiwiSaver and the tax treatment of retirement saving in NZ.' *NZ Economic Papers* 41(2): 251–68. Accessed from: www.symposium.ac.nz/08/filelibrary/KiwiSaver_tax_treatment_of_saving.pdf (site discontinued).

St John, S. 2008. 'Labour and National must agree to review KiwiSaver after the election.' *NZ Herald*, 13 October. Available from: www.nzherald.co.nz/retirement/news/article.cfm?c_id=305&objectid=10537308.

St John, S. 2014. 'What has New Zealand's retirement policy framework got to offer the international debate?' *Policy Quarterly* 10(3): 29–34. Accessed from: apo.org.au/files/Resource/policyquarterly_nz-retirement-policy_2014.pdf (site discontinued).

St John, S., Littlewood, M. and Dale, M. C. 2014. *Now we are six: Lessons from New Zealand's KiwiSaver*. Retirement Policy and Research Centre Working Paper 2014-1. Auckland: University of Auckland Business School Retirement Policy and Research Centre.

Savings Working Group (SWG) 2011. *Saving New Zealand: Reducing vulnerabilities and barriers to growth and prosperity—Savings Working Group final report to the Minister of Finance.* Wellington: The Treasury. Available from: treasury.govt.nz/sites/default/files/2011-02/swg-report-jan11.pdf.

Statistics NZ 2018. NZ.Stat. [Online]. Wellington: Statistics NZ. Available from: nzdotstat.stats.govt.nz/wbos/index.aspx.

Stephen, E. 2016. *Old age wealth decumulation in New Zealand.* LLM Seminar Paper Laws 543: Elder Law. Wellington: Faculty of Law, Victoria University of Wellington. Available from: researcharchive.vuw.ac.nz/xmlui/bitstream/handle/10063/5235/paper.pdf?sequence=1.

Toder, E. and Khitatrakun, S. 2006. *Final Report to the Inland Revenue: KiwiSaver evaluation literature review.* Washington, DC: Tax Policy Center. Available from: www.taxpolicycenter.org.

The Treasury 2016. *He Tirohanga Mokopuna: 2016 statement on New Zealand's long-term fiscal position.* November. Wellington: New Zealand Government. Available from: treasury.govt.nz/sites/default/files/2016-11/ltfs-16-htm.pdf.

World Bank 1994. *Averting the Old Age Crisis: Policies to protect the old and promote growth.* New York: Oxford University Press.

Yong, S. and Cox, N. 2008. The compliance costs of the KiwiSaver scheme. Presented to the Accounting and Finance Association of Australia and New Zealand Conference, Sydney, 6–8 July.

Zhang, A. C. 2014. 'Financial advice and asset allocation of individual investors.' *Pacific Accounting Review* 26(3): 226–47.

21

Whānau Ora: An Indigenous policy success story

Verna Smith, Charlotte Moore, Jacqueline Cumming and Amohia Boulton

A policy success?

Whānau Ora (which can be translated as 'family wellbeing')[1] is an innovative approach to Indigenous health and social services policy in Aotearoa New Zealand. The initiative empowers *whānau* (family) as a whole and devolves to *whānau* members self-determining processes to improve their cultural, social and economic wellbeing. The initiative's designers aimed for 'the potential of whānau to do for themselves' (Humpage 2017: 480) by minimising their dependence on state-delivered benefits and interventions. Building *whānau* resilience, and the skills and resources of members to manage their own affairs without interference from others, is critical. Intrinsic to this approach is the concept of a 'strengths' perspective.[2]

1 The term '*whānau ora*' can be translated in many ways. For the purposes of this research and consistent with usage in the report of the Taskforce on Whānau-Centred Initiatives (2010: 12), it means 'family wellbeing', where 'family' is defined as Māori who share 'familial ties that extend over two or three generations' and have 'collective interests that generate reciprocal ties and aspirations'.

2 Increasingly common also in mainstream service delivery, according to Rapp et al. (2005), strengths-based social work has six hallmarks: it is goal oriented; it requires a systematic assessment of strengths; it sees the environment as rich in resources; it has explicit methods for using these strengths for goal attainment; it is hope-inducing; and the practice of meaningful choice is central and clients have the authority to choose.

The failings of mainstream social services to meet the needs of Māori were outlined in 1988 in the landmark report *Puao-te-Ata-tu* (*Day Break*) (Ministerial Advisory Committee on a Māori Perspective for the Department of Social Welfare 1988). In particular, the report stated that mainstream services were monocultural and the impact of institutional racism within government agencies was a significant barrier to Māori wellbeing. However, in spite of numerous efforts on the part of government to improve outcomes for Māori over the following decades, Māori have continued to experience health inequities, lower life expectancy and disproportionate representation within both the care and protection and the criminal justice systems (Boulton et al. 2013). As a result, it became clear to Māori leaders and policymakers that solutions that better reflected Māori aspirations, cultural practices and world views were needed.

Launched in April 2010 following extensive consultation with Māori communities across Aotearoa New Zealand, the Whānau Ora initiative ultimately seeks to address endemic issues of the overrepresentation of Māori *whānau* in poor social and health outcomes. This is the first time in New Zealand's history such an approach to social service delivery has been funded and implemented nationally, although there have been many localised initiatives resembling Whānau Ora that paved the way. Whānau Ora itself has evolved significantly since its inception and there are a number of grounds on which its success can be demonstrated.

In the first instance, the successful *programmatic* features of Whānau Ora include: its clear public value proposition that significant outcomes in *whānau ora* can be achieved 'through eliminating poverty, advocating for social justice and advancing Māori social, cultural, economic and community development in the best interests of the nation' (Māori Party 2008); a plausible underpinning theory of change based on both mainstream and Māori scholarship (Durie 1999; Rapp et al. 2005; Boulton et al. 2013); evidence of considerable progress towards achieving its intended outcomes; and equitably offering access to the program to all New Zealanders. Whānau Ora has achieved early gains for its intended beneficiaries and has succeeded in engaging *whānau* who were not connected to mainstream social services, or for whom the fragmentation of existing services had led to poor outcomes. Connecting Māori service providers and wrapping support around *whānau* have helped to overcome this fragmentation, while Whānau Ora 'navigators' have proved successful in building trusting relationships with *whānau*.

The designers also achieved success in the *process* of design (described below). The initiative was designed with high fidelity to Indigenous concepts of *whānau ora*—appropriately, as *whānau* were intended to be its primary beneficiaries. To a great extent, it was coproduced with these potential beneficiaries and crafted from extensive consultative dialogue with Māori communities throughout New Zealand in its formative phase. Although it did not attract the funding levels and administrative structures identified as desirable by its designers, a new ministerial portfolio has ensured representation at the highest levels within the executive, increasing funding with each successive year of its operation and, over time, increasing administrative independence from central government controls. Despite criticism by the Controller and Auditor-General at a key point in its development—which referred to unclear purpose, implementation delays and excessive administrative spending—Whānau Ora evolved and has been embedded as a unique policy innovation, improving Māori governance over services for Māori.

In *political* terms, Whānau Ora should also be seen as a story of strikingly successful policy entrepreneurship, in which a committed politician, Dame Tariana Turia, and her colleagues seized a window of opportunity to devise and implement an approach capable of delivering major social-value impacts for Māori *whānau*. The fact a policy approach explicitly designed around Indigenous concepts, practices and values was established within a political environment that had proved itself to be indifferent to Māori initiatives at best, and outright hostile at worst, is remarkable. The creation of a dedicated ministerial portfolio and budget appropriation signalled to the public that Whānau Ora represented a significant shift away from previous approaches, which often amounted to little more than the cooption of Māori language and concepts into mainstream policies.

With regard to Whānau Ora's potential for *endurance*, Patashnik (2008) articulates a framework for assessing whether general interest reforms (by which he means non-incremental change of existing policy) are at risk of unravelling over time. He suggests that factors critical to a reform's survival over time include: the extent to which it has created a new policy network to sustain it; whether it threatens existing competitors in its marketplace; and whether it generates, through policy feedback effects, a new and supportive mindset among preexisting agencies. We argue that Whānau Ora has initiated a new and complementary approach to social development that does not conflict with existing agencies. Patashnik's model of post-reform dynamics envisages a situation in which interest groups remain stable, have common policy preferences and make investments based on the expectation that the reform will continue. Whānau Ora has presented an approach for social service agencies to better serve their Māori clients, and we argue that they are showing signs of embracing this approach and incorporating it into their way of working. However, the reactions and coalitional patterns that political actors have towards Whānau Ora do risk the future of this approach. If the new Labour-led Government can embrace this approach to working with Māori *whānau*, the designers will have created a social development program for Māori with enhanced levels of decision-making and self-determination, which is their legacy.

In this chapter, the story of the design and implementation of Whānau Ora is told through the words of its designers, implementers and evaluators. A qualitative methodology was adopted, utilising documentary analysis and seeking semistructured interviews with decision-makers, leaders and participants who were directly engaged in the design of Whānau Ora.

In the next section, we present the key concepts embodied in Whānau Ora and the context in which it arose. The policy problem of the continued failure of mainstream social services to meet Māori needs is discussed. In the section 'Design and choice', we describe the development of initiatives to address that problem and show the policy window in which Whānau Ora was created, setting out the resulting timeline of activity and the details of programs and structures established under Whānau Ora. Finally, we analyse the extent to which Whānau Ora can be considered a policy success and present our conclusions.

Contexts, challenges and agents

Indigenous concepts lie at the centre of the Whānau Ora policy success story. In New Zealand, the terms '*whānau*' and 'family' are often used interchangeably in social policy documents. However, this serves to oversimplify what is a far more expansive, fluid and complex social structure while at the same time reinforcing Western cultural assumptions that centre on nuclear family constructions (Lawson-Te Aho 2010). Traditionally, *whānau* were multigenerational groupings connected by genealogical links traced through both male and female lines. This meant individuals may have links and obligations to more than one *whānau* (Taiapa 1994). *Whānau* were a key site for the development of

Māori identity, a place where the teaching of things Māori occurred and an environment where particular responsibilities and obligations were maintained (Moeke-Pickering 1996). *Whānau* was also understood as the smallest unit of Māori society, followed by the *hapū* (subtribe) and *iwi* (tribe). The interests of individuals or the nuclear family were intimately connected to (and often secondary to) the interests of the wider *whānau* (Metge 1990). This understanding is critical to unpicking the major departure of *whānau*-centred approaches from mainstream social service delivery, which is structured around providing services to individuals who may or may not reside within (nuclear) families.

'*Ora*' is another term used widely within New Zealand's health and social sectors, which is often translated simply as 'wellbeing'. According to Walker (2004: 30), 'the concept of ora means a lot more than wellbeing because it is spiritual, emotional and profound'. In the health sector, *ora* has been connected with a number of initiatives and the term is often used in compounds such as *hauora* ('spirit or breath of life'), *rapuora* ('seeking health'), *waiora* ('healthy environments') and *tipuora* ('growing/developing health') (Durie 1994, cited in Metge 1995: 86). At a broad level, we can therefore summarise the philosophy of *whānau ora* as the holistic wellbeing of a multigenerational family group. The wellbeing of the individuals within *whānau* is inextricably linked to the wellbeing of the collective, and vice versa. How this *philosophy* of *whānau ora* was transformed into, and implemented as, a *social policy approach* has created a unique series of challenges and opportunities for policymakers, practitioners and communities.

A number of policy developments have contributed to the evolution of the Whānau Ora approach. These include reforms of New Zealand's health sector, the adoption of whole-of-government approaches to social policy issues and an increasing focus on families and children in policy initiatives. However, while these policy developments arguably created a space in which an integrated approach to social services based on Māori values could evolve, it was a series of political developments that enabled a more comprehensive and innovative Whānau Ora approach to become established.

A significant factor in the evolution of the Whānau Ora approach is the transformation that occurred in New Zealand's public sector in the 1980s and 1990s. As part of a broader political project of structural adjustment (Kelsey 1995), reforms in the health sector saw a shift from a state-run bureaucracy to a system of devolved authorities (Boulton et al. 2004). The subsequent separation of the funding and provision aspects of health services in 1993 saw contracting become a central part of the health system, which in turn created a space for Māori organisations that were keen to bid for government contracts. Whereas the state saw the development of Māori health providers as an opportunity for Māori to develop an economic base through partnerships in the health and disability sector (Chant 2013), Māori saw an opportunity for self-determination and an ability to deliver services to their people that were better aligned with their own customs and world views. The number of *kaupapa Māori* ('by Māori, for Māori') organisations offering services underpinned by *tikanga Māori* (Māori values and practices) and Māori models of holistic wellbeing expanded rapidly, from about 25 in 1993 to somewhere in the region of 300 such organisations currently (Boulton et al. 2013; Chant 2013).

The participation of Māori within the health sector was strengthened with further reforms introduced by the Labour-led Government in 2001. The *New Zealand Public Health and Disability Act* (2000) was particularly important; for the first time, reference to the Treaty of Waitangi was incorporated in such a way as to make provisions for Māori to participate not only in the provision of services, but also in decision-making processes (Boulton et al. 2013). Newly created district health boards were not only required to include Māori representation in proportion to their population (with a minimum of two Māori members), but the Act also compelled them to reduce disparities and improve Māori health outcomes (Boulton et al. 2004). These developments led to a separate Māori health strategy, He Korowai Oranga (lit., 'the cloak of wellness'), which was launched by associate health minister Tariana Turia in 2002. The overall aim of the strategy was for 'whānau ora: Māori families supported to achieve their maximum health and wellbeing' (Ministry of Health 2002: 1). The strategy also acknowledged Māori desire for self-determination:

> He Korowai Oranga seeks to support Māori-led initiatives to improve the health of whānau, hapū and iwi. The strategy recognises that the desire of Māori to have control over their future direction is a strong motivation for Māori to seek their own solutions and to manage their own services. (Ministry of Health 2002: 1)

However, although '*whānau ora*' was the stated goal of He Korowai Oranga, there was no operational definition of the concept in the document. As Boulton et al. (2004) argue, this was problematic, for while

Māori may understand the philosophy of *whānau ora*, this understanding may not be shared by non-Māori or other stakeholders within the health sector. Furthermore, it was also clear that the effectiveness of the strategy was likely to be limited given that many of the variables impacting on Māori health outcomes lay outside the health sector, in areas such as housing, employment and education.

Placing *whānau* at the centre of social initiatives and social policy is not a new phenomenon, and *whānau*-centred approaches can be traced back to programs initiated by the Māori Women's Welfare League in the 1950s and the *Tu Tangata* programs of the 1970s (Moore 2014). Durie argues that, although the Waitangi Treaty settlement process that emerged during the 1980s and 1990s saw an increasing emphasis on *iwi* as a focus for Māori development, building capacity at the *whānau* level was critical in achieving tangible outcomes for Māori:

> [A]lthough iwi development will likely continue as an important pathway for Māori advancement, it is also likely that there will be an increasing emphasis on building whānau. Expectations that iwi gains might trickle down to whānau are probably unrealistic, given contemporary Māori affiliations and different priorities between small groups such as whānau and large groups such as iwi. Iwi may well contribute to whānau aspirations but for the most part the tools necessary for building iwi capacities will not be the same tools required for developing whānau capacities, including the capacities for caring, for creating whānau wealth, for whānau planning, for the intergenerational transfer of knowledge and skills within whānau, and for the wise management of whānau estates. (2005: 10)

An evolving focus on *whānau* within Māori social services also runs parallel with a shift towards policies that focus on families and children and attempts to introduce whole-of-government approaches to complex social issues that have taken shape within the mainstream policy environment over recent decades. One example of this is the Strengthening Families initiative piloted in the mid-1990s in Waitakere City and extended nationally in 1999. The program's aim was to 'deliver core services in the welfare, health and education sectors more effectively to that group of families experiencing the most serious disadvantage' (Department of Social Welfare 2001: 13).

The opportunity to expand the scope and reach of Whānau Ora beyond the health sector arose with the establishment of the Māori Party and the relationship that formed between it and the New Zealand National Party following the 2008 election. In 1996, changes in New Zealand's electoral system created enhanced opportunities for Māori to wield political influence. The number of dedicated Māori seats was, for the first time, made proportional to the Māori electoral population, which saw an increase in the number of seats from four to seven by 2002. At the same time, a shift from a first-past-the-post to a mixed-member proportional representation system enabled voters to cast both an electoral and a party vote, which created greater opportunities for smaller parties to enter parliament.

The Māori Party was founded by Tariana Turia and Pita Sharples in 2004, following Turia's resignation from the Labour Party. Turia's resignation was in response to the government's introduction of the *Foreshore and Seabed Act* (2004), which removed the ability of Māori to test their claims to areas of the foreshore and seabed by vesting ownership in the Crown. Many Māori viewed this move as yet another instance of land confiscation by the Crown and as a betrayal by the Labour Party, which had historically held many of the dedicated Māori seats. By 2008, the Māori Party held five of the seven Māori seats. As a minority government, the National Party's need for support from minor parties saw it enter into a relationship accord and confidence and supply agreement with the Māori Party as part of a National-led government. This enabled key policy concessions for Māori including a review (and eventual replacement) of the foreshore and seabed legislation and a review of New Zealand's constitutional arrangements. However, the most significant policy win was arguably a commitment on the part of National to support the '*whānau* first' approach outlined in the Māori Party's political manifesto.

The manifesto had acknowledged *whānau* as the 'unheralded model for achieving economic security, creating social cohesion and stability and strengthening cultural identity' (Māori Party 2004: 21). This reflected the passionate championing of this concept by Turia over the previous decade, initially expressed through He Korowai Oranga (Moore 2014: 51). The accord of 2008 explicitly sought 'significant outcomes in whānau ora' and, once appointed the Minister for the Community and Voluntary Sector under the new government, Turia convened the Taskforce on Whānau-

Centred Initiatives to develop a policy framework for 'a new method of government interaction with Māori service providers to meet the needs of whānau' (Moore 2014: 53–4).

The taskforce was led by Sir Mason Durie, a prominent Māori academic. It defined *whānau* as a 'multi-generational collective made up of many households that are supported and strengthened by a wider network of relatives' (Taskforce on Whānau-Centred Initiatives 2010: 13). The concept of Whānau Ora was seen as a philosophy, a model of practice for providers, an outcome goal, a funding mechanism and a foundation for future generations. Fundamental to the Whānau Ora vision set out by the taskforce is that providers should work with *whānau* instead of only one or two people within a *whānau*. Also fundamental was the concept of strengths-based rather than deficit-based approaches to *whānau* needs. Finally, funders, providers and *whānau* would need to work together and focus on results, not inputs, of service. Taken together, this set of concepts had the potential to drive transformational change in the delivery of government support for *whānau*.

Design and choice

There have been two distinct phases in the implementation of Whānau Ora, marked by a change in the structure of delivery. We discuss them here as phase one and phase two.

Phase one consisted of three key initiatives: *whānau* innovation, integration and engagement (WIIE), which involved funding *whānau* to make plans to improve their lives and assistance to carry these out; provider capacity-building, to enable groups of providers to establish a combined ability to deliver coordinated and *whānau*-centred services; and integrated contracting and government support for the initiatives, involving the cooperation of Te Puni Kōkiri (the Ministry of Māori Development), the health and social development ministries and district health boards to develop integrated contracts.

The WIIE Fund was launched to fund *whānau* to develop their own outcome plans. Up to $5,000 was available to develop a plan and up to $20,000 to implement it. *Whānau* had to apply for the funding through a legal entity rather than be funded directly, reflecting perceived concerns about the political and financial risks of directly funding *whānau*. During the four years in which this fund was available, 2,595 *whānau* were funded to prepare a plan and, of these, 564 were funded to carry out some or all of their plan (OAG 2015: 28).

Box 21.1 *Whānau* innovation, integration and engagement (WIIE) grants

In March 2010, the Cabinet agreed that Te Puni Kōkiri would administer the WIIE Fund to invest in a range of activities to build *whānau* capability, strengthen *whānau* connections, support the development of *whānau* leadership and enhance best outcomes for *whānau*. Below are examples of how the WIIE Fund has been used, drawn from *Kōrero Mai e te Whānau* ('family stories') (TPK 2013: 20–2).

- A *whānau* with seven members, the majority of whom are deaf, has had a long-term relationship with a local disability support trust—an NGO service provider—and a Māori sign language interpreter who offered them an opportunity to engage with the WIIE Fund. This process has enabled them to progress a *whānau* vision that began 10 years earlier. Their goal is to be able to bridge the gap and reduce the barriers between the deaf and Māori cultures, and they want to support other *whānau turi Māori* ('families with hearing disabilities') to do this, too. They provide many goals and solutions that may be useful to increase *whānau turi Māori* participation in the WIIE Fund, in *te ao Māori* ('the Māori world') and in society.
- A *whānau* engaged with the WIIE Fund through an NGO service provider after seeking support to gain custody of their *mokopuna* ('grandchildren'). The grandparents have a long history of gang affiliation and they openly share their story, identifying activators of change and reflecting on what has supported them to dispel the stereotypes they faced. Their WIIE Fund plan has a primary focus on the safety and wellbeing of their grandchildren, and *whānau* members have achieved many outcomes so far. In particular, it has been meaningful for them to work through barriers to accessing services as well as actively increasing their engagement in wider society to support their *mokopuna*. This has included *kōhanga reo* ('Māori language revival'), Grandparents Raising Grandchildren, the local community board and other services.
- A *whānau* has been working on a plan for their *whenua* ('land') to create future opportunities for the *whānau* as well as to provide benefits to their small, isolated community as a whole. There are 30 participating *whānau* members and they were able to access the WIIE Fund through their existing *whānau* trust. The resource has enabled them to actively advance the planning of activities to fulfil their collective *moemoeā* ('vision') of employment, economic development and utilisation of the *whenua*. They discuss the *whānau* outcomes already achieved, including the strengthening of *whānau* connections to each other and to the *whenua*. In addition, approximately 200 individuals attended a *whānau* WIIE Fund event that was open to members of the local community.

The service delivery capability fund was available to collectives of providers who held contracts with district health boards or the ministries of health or social development, and who were willing to enter into a formal, collaborative relationship to deliver services for *whānau*—services that were both easier for *whānau* to access and delivered in a *whānau*-centred way. To complement this work, a team within the Ministry of Social Development designed and implemented an integrated contract, subsuming multiple contracts, for 28 providers within the collectives. Initially, services were dispersed through a network of locally based collectives, guided by 10 regional leadership groups comprising community representatives and regional officials of the joint agencies. Collectives were funded to prepare a program of action and some were then funded to carry out these programs. Such plans included the creation and employment of Whānau Ora navigators to work intensively with *whānau* to prepare *whānau* plans and access services and to assist providers to improve their delivery practices for *whānau*.

Box 21.2 Whānau Ora navigators

Navigators were a new workforce employed to work intensively with *whānau* and were funded mostly through the WIIE and provider program of action funding. The Controller and Auditor-General found there were three main roles:

- working with *whānau* to help them get more control over their lives, such as by helping *whānau* to identify their needs and prepare a whānau plan and helping them use services effectively
- if needed, helping *whānau* to access services that meet their needs
- helping the provider collective to change their mindset and practices to deliver *whānau*-centred services, which might include proposing new services.

A case study in the Auditor-General's report exemplifies this:

> A navigator worked with a man and his children (and their partners and grandchildren) to get him prosthetic legs and other aids, which involved advocating for him with the hospital, writing support letters, and applying for grants; get funding—from three sources—for vehicle modification, bathroom alterations and house modifications; resolve delays in getting financial help he was entitled to, which resulted in an improved financial situation … and refer him to the rural nurse for help in managing his diabetes … the approach the navigator took enabled family relationships to be strengthened in a range of ways, and the family achieved a greater level of self-management. (OAG 2015: 42)

Phase two of implementation saw the focus of activity shift from regionalised management of devolved funding through Te Puni Kōkiri to the development of funding streams more distanced from *whānau* control and management but also more independent of government processes.

In 2014, funding was devolved to three independent non-governmental commissioning agencies: Te Pou Matakana (North Island), Te Pūtahitanga o Te Waipounamu (South Island) and Pasifika Futures (Pacific peoples). Strategic leadership was provided by the Whānau Ora Partnership Group of six ministers of the Crown and six *iwi* members nominated by the *iwi* chairs forum. The commissioning agencies provided funding support for building the capability of *whānau* and acted as 'brokers in matching the needs and aspirations of whānau with initiatives that assist them to increase their capability (TPK 2016: 8).

Delivery, legitimacy and endurance

Since their inception, the three commissioning agencies have diverged somewhat in their focus and approach to implementing Whānau Ora. In part, this is due to significantly different levels of funding, which is allocated on the basis of population, geography, level of deprivation and income (TPK 2016). As a result of this funding model, Te Pūtahitanga o Te Waipounamu and Pasifika Futures receive substantially less than Te Pou Matakana—appropriate to reduced levels of need. Another key factor in the differences between agencies is that both Te Pou Matakana and Pasifika Futures emerged out of existing service provider contexts. In particular, Te Pou Matakana was able to leverage significant experience and expertise from Māori social services provider Te Whānau o Waipareira, while Pasifika Futures built on Pasifika Medical Association health services. In contrast, Te Pūtahitanga o te Waipounamu was a newly formed organisation representing a partnership between the nine *iwi* of the South Island. This newness enabled the South Island commissioning agency to move away from traditional approaches to service delivery and towards investment in *whānau* innovation and enterprise. As one of our interview participants explained:

> What has been helpful about our commissioning approach has been that we were very clear from the onset that we are not there to threaten or to replicate contracts that service delivery [providers] have had up until now. So, we are not going to compete for existing services. I know that Te Pou Matakana will try to, they will compete for existing services. So, their approach … there are advantages and disadvantages. I mean, we don't have a 20-year back history of working together as mainstream service providers. The approach that Te Pou Matakana took is because they had the benefit of establishing an infrastructure and they have a proven track record of large multi-million-dollar social service contracts. (Participant 2)

Given the constraints on funding, it was critical that the agency's investment strategy required recipients to build sustainability plans with the expectation that enterprises would become financially independent. An evaluation of the establishment and early delivery phases of Te Pūtahitanga o te Waipounamu found that where *whānau* held the funding and therefore the balance of power in any partnership, successful capability-building was more likely. The key to building *whānau* capability was found to be 'a commissioning model which provided a purpose for capability to be built and that whānau led their own capability building in the pursuit of their aspirations' (Savage et al. 2016: 124–5). This was a process of disruptive innovation—unsettling at first and succeeding when strong and strategic leadership was established.

In a case study of the economic impact of one of the agency's phase one initiatives, describing a scheme to support skills development in young Māori to deliver lifetime benefits, the net present value of potential economic benefits was estimated to be $5.5 million for an investment of $780,000—or seven times its cost in economic benefits (Dalziel et al. 2017: 3).

With regards to the *programmatic* outcomes of Whānau Ora, there are a number of key features that have proved successful. These include the flexibility and enhanced responsiveness of the approach in addressing the needs of *whānau*, as well as the way in which Whānau Ora has enabled connection with services for *whānau* who have previously been less engaged with mainstream providers.

The policy development process that led to Whānau Ora was intended to resolve concerns that

> health and social services often intervene after matters went wrong for the individual rather than restoring full whānau functioning or extending whānau capabilities … [and] that government contracting practices had led to many Māori providers competing for contracts which fostered a piecemeal approach and inhibited collaboration and coordination. (OAG 2015: 9)

Whānau Ora has enabled organisations working alongside *whānau* to be more flexible and responsive in terms of the range of supports they are able to offer:

> When Dame Tariana sent the taskforce out, she knew that Māori service providers, when they went into a house, they could have been quit-smoking coaches or health educators, but the *whānau* wouldn't want to deal with all that until the other needs in their household had been met … she recognised that unless you deal with whatever is important to the family then you are not going to get the focus on the health-related conditions that you require. And similar to Maslow, who says that

> everybody has needs that … need to be met at particular times … unless you deal with those essential items to live then you can't self-actualise. So Whānau Ora is really consistent with that. You deal with whatever is immediate then we can focus on your potential. (Participant 1)

Participants in this research were clear that the flexibility and responsiveness of the approach were key to meeting the needs of Māori for whom mainstream services had failed:

> You can look at the majority of social and health policy in this country and it is just there for the transaction … Care and protection up until the Oranga Tamariki [Ministry for Children] changes [meant] we will just come in and take the child out, they are safe, job is done. Whānau Ora would say we have to follow where the *tamaiti* [child] or *tamariki* [young] go; we have to stay here with mum and dad because how do we make sure [that] at some stage they are strengthened [and] they are safe for that child to return? What [the child protection system] didn't do was do any of that healing. They didn't heal the situation; they just removed the ability to be in an unsafe environment … Whānau Ora stays and says, 'Come on, what are we going to do?' Follow the *tamariki, tamaiti* to make sure they stay connected. (Participant 1)

Another participant suggests the approach is about a deeply shared experience:

> Relationships. It is almost as blunt as Māori can work with Māori because they know and feel the things that affect them. Māori can work with non-Māori as well but, despite the good hearts and the empathy that nurses, doctors have for the general public in social terms and health terms, they cannot make the connection. Despite their own empathy, love, *aroha* and all that, they just can't make the connection. (Participant 3)

Another significant indicator of programmatic success is the recognition of the critical role navigators have played in Whānau Ora, as described below:

> There are two strands: a focus on what better can we do collectively and what better can we do within that *whānau*? Navigation was always the key to working better in that *whānau*. Working in a *whānau*-centred way was always key to Whānau Ora and 'navigators' was the label that was given to them. That is offputting for some, as it seems to mean pointing in the right direction, but really, effective navigators get under the guts of what is occurring in that *whānau* and … work with them to develop their goals and aspirations. (Participant 1)

Whānau Ora navigators have played a critical role in building trusting relationships with *whānau*. One participant describes being with the prime minister and the finance minster at meetings with *whānau* who were beneficiaries of the approach:

> On every occasion, tears were shed on the back of what Whānau Ora navigators had done for families … 'That person saved my life' … they still talked to her as 'Aunty'. This was hugely compelling for me. (Participant 3)

The navigator role has been recognised in analytical work by the New Zealand Productivity Commission as a key innovation arising from Whānau Ora to support seamless access to social services (New Zealand Productivity Commission 2015). It has also been evaluated and assessed as having a significant positive impact, particularly for *whānau* with complex needs, at an individual and a collective level, in a survey of 50 case studies of services delivered through Whānau Ora navigators in the South Island in 2016 (Savage et al. 2016).

However, extending the gains made by Whānau Ora to the social sector more broadly has also been challenging, with some social sector policies and priorities at times conflicting with *whānau*-centred approaches. Despite the investment in developing ways of working differently with *whānau*, the Auditor-General found in her review of Whānau Ora's first four years that the Ministry of Social Development and the Ministry of Health had no plans to change to a funding model that would take advantage of this shift in focus and practice (OAG 2015: 53). Also problematic is the focus on children in government social policy, which has been further expanded through the recent government's social investment strategy.

How to capture and measure collective outcomes rather than individual outcomes also presents a number of challenges. The set of outcomes initially designed for the program by Te Puni Kōkiri reflected those presented by the taskforce, but also conveyed a greater emphasis on explicit goals for achievement of individual self-management, health, educational, cultural and economic outcomes as well as *whānau* cohesion and stewardship of the environment (OAG 2015). However, the Auditor-General concluded that the measures and the systems implemented to report on them were confusing for all parties. For instance, the measures of Whānau Ora provider collective performance for 2011–12 on which Te Puni Kōkiri chose to report were infant immunisation and early childhood education. It has taken several years for the building of knowledge and experience to result in the program delivering its expected benefits. One participant commented that while the principles and outcomes listed in the taskforce's report formed the basis of their model of implementation, principles such as coherent service delivery were less important than supporting innovation and *whānau* integrity:

> In terms of implementation, our focus has been on the Whānau Ora outcomes as being the model … If I look back at those principles, they are certainly the reason for being—for why we are doing the things we are doing. So, you know, *kaupapa tuku iho* ['traditional ideas'], best *whānau* outcomes, all of those form the rationale for the different work streams that we have. We probably underplay the one on coherent service delivery whereas we overplay the *whānau* integrity one. So, for our implementation of Whānau Ora, we have put a lot more focus on *whānau* innovation, the responsibilities and the obligations of *whānau* to do for themselves, rather than, say, traditional services and providers. (Participant 2)

In an evaluation of Whānau Ora initiatives conducted in 2017, 54 *whānau* participating in 38 initiatives were interviewed to construct a meaningful framework of outcome indicators and to document *whānau* perceptions of impacts against these outcomes. Outcomes of *whānau* cohesion, healthy lifestyle and participation in *te ao Māori* ('the Māori world') dominated the social value impacts achieved, with self-management, full participation in society, economic security and environmental stewardship achieving lesser impact (Savage et al. 2016: 11).

Whether Whānau Ora can be judged a success in terms of *process* is less clear. On the one hand, centring the approach on Indigenous values and practices, coupled with the commitment to community consultation during the design phase, meant that Māori *whānau*, organisations and communities were enthusiastic about the potential of Whānau Ora. However, it can be argued that the implementation of the approach has been impacted by the lack of a clear communication strategy, the institutional realities of New Zealand's New Public Management–intensive approach to state services delivery and limited resourcing.

The transition from design to delivery was characterised by questions about the nature and definition of Whānau Ora. A participant describes the designers' dilemma when seeking to build support for the Whānau Ora initiative:

> A lot of people who are not Māori fail to understand the concept because of the words. Rather than unpicking it and understanding the phraseology, I think the response is that it is some kind of crazy Māori idea. Do you then turn it around and give it a Pākehā [European] term? And we have thought about that. And, to date, my inclination is no—and the reason is that Pākehā are not as well-endowed to do *whānau ora*. So, if you did that [gave Whānau Ora a Pākehā name], you would give the impression that they are endowed in a way that they are not. Nevertheless, I think that the language difficulty in this case is a barrier to understanding. (Participant 4)

Another participant noted the difficulties in attempting to implement a program that was still being developed:

> Definitely, where we have the ability to implement something new and innovative, we have to give it time to develop the foundation, which includes communication. So, if I take on board some of the big ministries, like [the] Ministry of Social Development, they had good understanding at the top, but you start to dig down lower and they didn't understand. And even back down to the service desk of the Work and Income New Zealand [WINZ] office, they never got the messaging around Whānau Ora. So *whānau* became empowered but they still had to take the Whānau Ora worker with them because the WINZ worker was being really difficult. You give the system the ability to develop properly the foundations required to implement it, then you communicate what it is broadly across the system so you have that understanding before implementation starts. And then as you go you have to have quality improvement. (Participant 1)

Subtle changes in the processes of decision-making and choice blunted the intent of the taskforce's recommendations to establish a collective-oriented, strengths-based, *whānau*-led approach to achieving improved outcomes. Actors in the political coalition supporting the policy were adaptive in the face of this pressure. As one participant commented: 'You learn to adapt. You have to go with what the government determines. If they are going to make those investment decisions, you have to adapt' (Participant 1).

Adaptation has been a defining feature of the implementation of Whānau Ora. Following the release of the taskforce's report in 2010, decision-makers chose to defer the recommendation to establish a Māori-led independent trust to govern Whānau Ora. Instead, Te Puni Kōkiri was made the lead agency, with the Ministry of Health and the Ministry of Social Development in support ('the joint agencies'). A national-level governance group of community representatives and chief executives of the joint agencies was established. This step reflected the desire of Turia, as the Minister for the Community and Voluntary Sector, to retain close personal and departmental oversight of the development of Whānau Ora (OAG 2015: 13). This was wise given the novelty of the initiative and the new partnership established through the relationship accord—both of which created a heightened climate of political risk. However, commentators saw the Whānau Ora funding arrangements that were implemented as 'a discrete and finite series of contracts between the state and some selected providers', creating a context in which the processes of implementation were said to have been coopted into mainstream and bureaucratised frameworks (Moore 2014: 64). The changes made to institutional arrangements in phase two of Whānau Ora were intended to address this risk.

The Whānau Ora philosophy came into immediate conflict with the institutional realities of New Zealand's NPM-intensive approach to state services delivery. The decision to initially manage Whānau Ora through a Crown department, Te Puni Kōkiri, meant conventional funding and accountability structures rather than the innovative arrangements recommended by the taskforce were chosen, driving it towards a framework of state-determined and individualised outputs delivered within an essentially competitive provider sector (Moore 2014: 63). Accountability for funding was expressed in terms of outputs rather than outcomes, and the goal of establishing high-trust, integrated 'single, simple, results-focused contracts' was ultimately delivered only for a very small number of providers.

Tensions around accountability within the program were exacerbated by inconsistent and confusing descriptions of the aims and the expected results of the first set of initiatives. Consequently, difficulties among providers in interpreting expectations of Whānau Ora, and among evaluators establishing its achievements, occurred in the first four years.

Finally, the reach of Whānau Ora has been limited as a result of the levels of funding allocated by government. In the wake of the 2008 GFC, a climate of fiscal rigour and a determination to return to budget surplus while reducing government debt resulted in severe cuts to public expenditure. The decision was made to reduce the proposed $1 billion appropriation for Whānau Ora to $130 million of repurposed existing funding. According to one participant:

> It would have had … more substantive resources to start with and it would have been independent. We were still working on whether it would be a trust or whether it would be some form of Crown entity. All of these things were still being worked through and then, all of a sudden, it's within TPK [Te Puni Kōkiri], it has a much smaller budget and it has completely changed character from what it was. (Participant 4)

In the first four years of implementation, much of the reduced funding appropriation for Whānau Ora was diverted to administration. During that time, $20 million was utilised to meet the costs of direct services to *whānau*. More than one-third was utilised for administration (including research and evaluation) (OAG 2015: 5), giving rise to claims that the program had become more 'provider ora than Whānau ora' (Moore 2014: 63). Despite this, the Auditor-General (OAG 2015: 5) found that 'Whānau Ora has been a success for many families who have a plan to improve their lives' and that 'bringing whānau members together to prepare plans seems to have had benefits that are wider than the plans themselves'.

Whānau Ora owes its existence to the changed political situation in New Zealand in 2008, which enabled a relationship accord to be negotiated between the Māori Party and the National Party. Clearly, Whānau Ora represented a political success for both parties, ensuring the survival of the coalition government. Furthermore, having an independent Māori Party in parliament in 2008 was critical in gaining the leverage required to progress what remains a controversial policy. As a participant observes:

> Having a political manifesto commitment to a policy is absolutely fundamental. If we hadn't … put Whānau Ora into not just the 2008 relationship accord, but the 2011 and 2014 relationship accords, if it hadn't been written in black ink in those documents, that would have been a big risk. (Participant 2)

Also crucial to the success of the program have been the drive and commitment of political leaders to champion Whānau Ora. In particular, the role played by Dame Tariana Turia in maintaining her commitment to *whānau*-centred approaches—first, in her role as associate health minister in the Labour-led Government during the early 2000s, and then through leading the Māori Party into a relationship with the National Party in 2008. Turia conforms to Kingdon's (2010) classic model of the policy entrepreneur enabled to 'sell' their policy during an open window of opportunity, combining her own agency with an opportunity for structural change to achieve major and non-incremental policy innovation. This entrepreneurship was identified by several participants as being critical to progressing Whānau Ora:

> Tariana herself and later Te Ururoa [Flavell, co-leader of the Māori Party following the resignation of Pita Sharples]—they really modelled Whānau Ora by always taking it seriously. You know, they would refer to their *mokopuna* [grandchildren], or the love of their *mokopuna*; they would have photos of their beautiful families; there would always be an emphasis on returning home to Whanganui, or Rotorua, and so there was that consistent messaging that meant that this was not just a policy that was meant for Wellington. This was a policy for life. It was about a passionate leader, but also it aligned with their own personal philosophy and approach. (Participant 2)

> You can definitely put that down to the leadership of the time and the ability of Dame Tariana to convince her political colleagues that there is a different way of doing things and statistically Māori are not doing better … so let us try something different … That kind of leadership she displayed is critical to social change because she could have those conversations: 'Change the economics of my people and we will see better outcomes for communities.' (Participant 1)

However, regardless of this leadership, Whānau Ora is likely to remain vulnerable to challenge in a political climate that is not always receptive to policies that are explicitly shaped around Indigenous needs, practices and values. Policy initiatives that are perceived to be responding to Māori needs or interests are often subject to intense levels of public and political scrutiny (Moore 2014).

Analysis and conclusions

Although Whānau Ora was developed as a Māori response to Māori needs, the scope of the program was widened from its initial focus on Māori *whānau* to encompass all New Zealanders in need. Again, this reflected the need to manage political risk in an environment unsympathetic to policies proposing special arrangements to redress disadvantage in Māori communities (Moore 2014). Also challenging was the idea that, through the formation of *whānau* plans, *whānau* took a leading role in identifying their own priorities for change, rather than simply being passive recipients of established social services. Leader of the New Zealand First Party, Winston Peters, was a vocal critic of the WIIE Fund, arguing that it used taxpayer money to fund 'family reunions' (New Zealand First 2012). As a result of enhanced levels of scrutiny, Whānau Ora has been subject to a number of government-initiated reviews, with yet another review announced at the time of writing. This scrutiny places increased pressure and costs on those involved in the approach to demonstrate its value. As one interview participant involved in the Whānau Ora commissioning process commented:

> We have been in a climate of, I guess, resistance or conservatism about whether Whānau Ora works. And we have always known that we have to be vigilant in proving the impact. That's really why I've insisted that every aspect of our work we get evaluated. We commission our own evaluation so that we can have something available once the criticisms come out. (Participant 2)

Given that Whānau Ora was a signature policy for the Māori Party, the party's failure to reach the required threshold to return to parliament following the 2017 general election means the future of Whānau Ora is now in the hands of a coalition government that may not have the same sense of ownership and commitment to the policy. This is particularly the case given the coalition government currently includes New Zealand First, whose leader has been a persistent and vocal critic of Whānau Ora. In 2018, the new Minister for Whānau Ora, Peeni Henare, announced that a review of Whānau Ora had been commissioned. A review had been planned at this stage of the policy implementation process by previous ministers. The new minister said he wished to see that the Whānau Ora service delivery model was accountable and transparent in the achievement of outcomes for *whānau* but also asked for ideas to see how the program could be expanded and improved. The review panel, chaired by the independent Centre for Social Impact associate Caren Rangi, has been asked to:

- assess the ability of the Whānau Ora commissioning approach to effect sustainable change in the wellbeing and development potential of *whānau*
- scope the applicability of a *whānau*-centred approach as a useful exemplar for improving outcomes for *whānau* across the government, with an emphasis on the social sector
- explore the extent to which the Whānau Ora service delivery model and commissioning approach are accountable and transparent in the achievement of outcomes for *whānau* (TPK 2018: n.p.).

The terms of reference reflect preelection statements from the Labour Party about the need for further investment in the approach (New Zealand Labour Party 2017) and indicate that the new government continues to view Whānau Ora as an important inclusion within the social policy mix, not least because their supporters in the Māori electorates demand this of them.

Although underpinned by clear principles, Whānau Ora has arguably been a policy approach that was developed and implemented 'on the go'. The structures, accountabilities and funding arrangements supporting Whānau Ora have evolved since its launch in 2010, and the approach is likely to continue to evolve in line with the new government's priorities and vision. It is also important to understand that, irrespective of whether or not a Whānau Ora policy approach is continued in its current form (or, indeed, in any form) by government, the philosophy of *whānau ora* and *whānau*-centred approaches will remain a central aspect of Māori organisations and communities, as it was before the advent of 'Whānau Ora' as the state-led social policy approach. Furthermore, the capacity of Māori organisations to respond to the needs of their communities, which grew in response to the reforms of the public health system in the 1990s, has been further expanded through the investment, commissioning structures and leadership that have resulted from the approach.

References

Boulton, A., Simonsen, K., Walker, T., Cumming, J. and Cunningham, C. 2004. 'Indigenous participation in the "new" New Zealand health structure.' *Journal of Health Services Research & Policy* 9(2): 35–40. doi.org/10.1258/1355819042349853.

Boulton, A., Tamehana, J. and Brannelly, T. 2013. 'Whānau-centred health and social service delivery in New Zealand: The challenges to, and opportunities for, innovation.' *Mai Journal* 2(1): 18–32.

Chant, L. 2013. Hauora Kotahitanga: Māori health experiences as models for co-operative co-existence between indigenous and non-indigenous peoples. Doctor of Philosophy in Community Health thesis, University of Auckland, Auckland.

Dalziel, P., Saunders, C. and Guenther, M. 2017. *Measuring the Impact of Whānau Ora Programmes: He Toki ki te Mahi case study*. Christchurch: Lincoln University.

Department of Social Welfare 2001. *Welfare to Wellbeing.* Wellington: Department of Social Welfare.

Durie, M. 1999. 'Te Pae Mahutonga: A model for Maori health promotion.' *Health Promotion Forum of New Zealand Newsletter* 49(2–5 December).

Durie, M. 2005. *Te Tai Tini transformations 2025.* CIGAD Working Paper Series 5/2005. Palmerston North, NZ: Massey University.

Families Commission 2010. *Whānau Strategic Framework 2009–2012.* Wellington: Families Commission.

Families Commission 2011. *Whānau Yesterday, Today, Tomorrow.* Wellington: Families Commission.

Families Commission 2013. *What Works with Māori: What the people said.* Wellington: Families Commission.

Humpage, L. 2017. 'Does having an indigenous political party in government make a difference to social policy? The Māori Party in New Zealand.' *Journal of Social Policy* 46(3): 475–94. doi.org/10.1017/s0047279417000022.

Kelsey, J. 1995. *The New Zealand Experiment: A world model for structural adjustment?* Auckland: Auckland University Press with Bridget Williams Books. doi.org/10.7810/9781869401306.

Kingdon, J. W. 2010. *Agendas, Alternatives, and Public Policies.* 2nd edn. London: Longmans.

Lawson-Te Aho, K. 2010. *Definitions of Whānau: A review of selected literature.* Wellington: Families Commission.

Māori Party 2004. *Tiriti o Waitangi.* Policy statement. Rotorua: Māori Party. Accessed from: d3n8a8pro7vhmx.cloudfront.net/maoriparty/pages/39/attachments/original/1455484702/Māori-Party-Policy-2004.pdf?1455484702 (site discontinued).

Māori Party 2008. *Relationship and Confidence and Supply Agreement between the National Party and the Maori Party.* 16 November. Rotorua: Māori Party. Available from: d3n8a8pro7vhmx.cloudfront.net/maoriparty/pages/47/attachments/original/1443172230/Maori-Party-Confidence-Supply-Agreement-2008.pdf?1443172230.

Metge, J. 1990. 'Te rito o te harakeke: Conceptions of the whaanau.' *Journal of the Polynesian Society* 99(1): 55–92.

Metge, J. 1995. *New Growth from Old: The whānau in the modern world.* Wellington: Victoria University Press.

Ministerial Advisory Committee on a Māori Perspective for the Department of Social Welfare 1988. *Pūao-te-ata-tū: The report of the Ministerial Advisory Committee on a Māori Perspective for the Department of Social Welfare.* Wellington: Department of Social Welfare.

Ministry of Health 2002. *He Korowai Oranga: Māori health strategy*. Wellington: Ministry of Health.

Moeke-Pickering, T. 1996. *Māori Identity Within Whānau: A review of literature.* Hamilton, NZ: University of Waikato.

Moore, C. 2014. A whakapapa of Whānau Ora. Master of Arts thesis, University of Auckland, Auckland.

New Zealand First Party 2012. Peters questions Whānau Ora funding. Press release, 7 February. Available from: www.scoop.co.nz/stories/PA1202/S00059/peters-questions-whanau-ora-funding.htm.

New Zealand Labour Party 2017. Labour pledges more for Whānau Ora. Press release, 11 September. Available from: www.scoop.co.nz/stories/PO1709/S00171/labour-pledges-more-for-whanau-ora.htm.

New Zealand Parliament 2010. *New Zealand Parliamentary Debates* (17 February) 660, 34.

New Zealand Productivity Commission 2015. *More Effective Social Services.* Wellington: New Zealand Productivity Commission.

Office of the Auditor-General (OAG) 2015. *Whānau Ora: The first four years.* Wellington: OAG.

Patashnik, E. 2008. *Reforms at Risk.* Princeton, NJ: Princeton University Press.

Rapp, C. A., Saleebey, D. and Sullivan, W. P. 2005. 'The future of strengths-based social work.' *Advances in Social Work: Special Issue on the Futures of Social Work* 6(1):79–90.

Rochford, T. 2004. 'Whare Tapa Wha: A Māori model of a unified theory of health.' *Journal of Primary Prevention* 25(1): 41–57. doi.org/10.1023/B:JOPP.0000039938.39574.9e.

Savage, C., Leonard, J., Grootveld, C., Edwards, S. and Dallas-Katoa, W. 2016. *The Evaluation of Wave One Initiatives: Te Putahitanga o te Waipounamu.* Wellington: Ihi Consultancy.

Smith, V. 2018. *Bargaining Power: Health policymaking in England and New Zealand.* Singapore: Palgrave Macmillan. doi.org/10.1007/978-981-10-7602-2_7.

Taiapa, J. 1994. *The Economics of the Whānau: The Māori component—Tā Te Whānau Ohangā*. Palmerston North, NZ: Department of Māori Studies, Massey University.

Taskforce on Whānau-Centred Initiatives 2010. *Report of the Taskforce on Whānau-Centred Initiatives.* Wellington: Office for the Community and Voluntary Sector.

Te Puni Kōkiri (TPK) 2009. *Pānui Whāinga 2009–2012: Statement of intent 2009–2012*. Wellington: TPK.

Te Puni Kōkiri (TPK) 2013. *Kōrero Mai e te Whānau: Whānau stories of integration, innovation and engagement*. Wellington: TPK.

Te Puni Kōkiri (TPK) 2016. *Formative Evaluation of the Whānau Ora Commissioning Agency Model.* Wellington: TPK.

Te Puni Kōkiri (TPK) 2018. *Whānau Ora Review*. Wellington: TPK. Accessed from: www.tpk.govt.nz/en/whakamahia/whānau-ora/whānau-ora-review (site discontinued).

Walker, R. 2004. *Ka Whawhai Tonu Matou: Struggle without end*. 2nd edn. Auckland: Penguin.

www.ingramcontent.com/pod-product-compliance
Lightning Source LLC
Chambersburg PA
CBHW052008030426
42334CB00029BA/3138